FROM REVIEWS OF THE 1ST EDITION

This book is a testament to the invaluable and distinctive contribution that Macrory has made to environmental law scholarship over the years. This book is an excellent reference work on environmental law. The material that Macrory has selected for inclusion covers a diverse range of issues, from the scope of environmental law to the role of the ECJ in furthering environmental objectives. By including publications that span four decades, it charts the evolution of contemporary thinking in environmental law and governance, thus providing a useful insight into not only how environmental law has developed in the past, but also how it might look in the future. All in all, it is an extremely important and valuable addition to the environmental lawyer's bookshelf.

Carolyn Abbot *Journal of Environmental Law*

This is an excellent and stimulating collection of works from a noted leader in environmental law. Among his many achievements, Professor Richard Macrory is Director of the Centre for Law and the Environment at University College London and an Honorary Queen's Counsel, and in the United Kingdom he is known for his landmark 2006 Cabinet Office study, 'Regulatory Justice—Making Sanctions Effective'.

Most of the material included in this collection (twenty-six chapters comprising over 700 pages) has been published before, but the key appeal and contribution of this work is that it pulls together different types of publication, all of which are important to environmental law . . . In all these different forms, Macrory shines as an excellent communicator with a strong command of the subject and a deep desire to convey its importance. For those of us in academic institutions, it is also a reminder of what our research 'impact' could look like! . . . In summary, this collection is many good things: a readable and full introduction to the issues which can and should be part of the environmental law conversation; deep analysis of interest to scholars; pieces of immediate use to practitioners and policymakers; and, from a practical perspective, it comes with a good index.

Dr Abbe E L Brown, *Climate Law*

The latest scholarly book by Professor Richard Macrory, a leading authority in the field, chronicles the development of environmental law and policy in the UK. It is a dense volume of work, but a valuable one . . . a useful tool for students and professionals alike seeking to better equip themselves for the future challenges – and opportunities – of environmental law.

Jacqueline Goodrum *Environmental Law Foundation Line*

This compilation of Richard Macrory's engaging work comprises a selection of public lectures, academic articles, book chapters, a Cabinet Office report and policy briefings. Spanning his notable thirty year career, the book provides extensive evidence of Macrory's intellect, energy and sense of humour. Macrory is one of the few pioneers of environmental law who are still active in that area. Now Director of the Centre for Law and the Environment at University College, London and a member of Brick Court Chambers, Macrory was the first Professor of Environmental Law in the UK. A founding member and first chairman of the UK Environmental Law Association, specialist advisor to Parliamentary Select Committees in both the Lords and Commons, a long standing member of the

Royal Commission on Environmental Pollution, a board member of the Environmental Agency, England and Wales, and most recently, honorary Queen's Counsel for his work on the development of environmental law, it is fair to say that Macrory knows a thing or two about the subject. One can find no better guide to the winding road along which the subject has travelled than this treasure chest. Neither a textbook nor a monologue, it offers a fascinating overview of the rapid development of the subject, through the lens of Macrory's own work . . . I read this book in one sitting. It is rare to find a volume which consumes one's attention for 765 pages – and rarer still that such a blockbuster be a law book. In his foreword, Sir Robert Carnwath suggests that this book should be essential reading for anyone concerned with the development of environmental law and policy. I suggest that this mandate be broadened: the real strength of this book lies in the overarching insights it provides into law and governance. Macrory does this by means of an environmental lens but this book is not solely for environmental enthusiasts – it should be essential reading for anyone concerned with the institutional reform, transparency and accountability in the UK and EU.

Catherine MacKenzie, *Cambridge Law Journal*

In selecting the material, Macrory tried to avoid, as he put it in an introduction, 'any analysis of detailed black letter law, but focused on material dealing with major themes concerning the nature of regulation, institutional arrangements, and enforcement which underlie the substantive detail of the law'. He has largely succeeded in this effort, and the articles are throughout easily readable, well argued and mostly convincing in their conclusions. There are two topics which pass through these articles almost like a leitmotif: on the one hand, the influence which the European Union and its environmental law had on British administrative practice, policy and legislation. And on the other hand the practical application of environmental law in the United Kingdom and in the European Union. Educated in the tradition of the UK common law system, Macrory is well qualified to follow the evolution of the first. And as, in my opinion, the practical application of environmental legislation is the biggest legal challenge which environmental lawyers face, it is no wonder that Macrory all the time returns to this problem, searching and offering analyses, criticism and solutions . . . The 'Macrory system of sanctions' is by now well known in the United Kingdom and will, without doubt, strongly influence the evolution of UK administrative law in the coming years. The content of this reform is not to be described here; suffice it to indicate that Macrory invested in this reform project his experience of thirty years as academic teacher, practising lawyer at the Bar, and adviser to several public bodies and agencies.

Anyone interested in the evolution of environmental law in Western Europe during the last four decades will read this collection with profit . . . Younger lawyers, Internet-oriented and less inclined to consider the evolution of law, might well learn from this inter-generational reflection on environmental law at the turn of the 20 to the 21 century, where we come from, where we are going and, what is most important, where we should and could go in order to keep this planet in an environmental state that is not worse than that of the 1960s or 1970s.

Ludwig Krämer *Common Market Law Review*

Anyone interested in environmental law is likely to be familiar with the name Richard Macrory. Appointed as the first Professor of Environmental Law in the United Kingdom, Macrory continues at the forefront of the academic development of the subject. Further, Macrory's career as a practising barrister has allowed him to fuse academic rigour with an awareness of the practical realties of environmental law.

At first sight, this book seems to resemble a 'text, cases and materials' on environmental law. However, while the scope is undoubtedly broad, the coverage of environmental law is by no means comprehensive. Perhaps an appropriate description would be: environmental law seen through the prism of the scholarship of Macrory. For those seeking a black letter account of environmental law, this book is to be avoided. However, this in no way should be construed as a criticism; unsurprisingly given Macrory's standing as one of the pre-eminent environmental lawyers of his generation, the extracted materials are academically rigorous and demonstrate a profound analytical understanding of the shape of environmental law as a whole. For established scholars of environmental law, many of the materials reproduced will already be familiar; nevertheless, the book represents an invaluable point of reference. Even those already familiar with Macrory's work will benefit from the introductory section of each of the book's six parts, where the catalyst and background to the arguments advanced in the proceeding extracts are clearly highlighted. This book is surely destined to become a 'must read' for anyone (academic, practitioner or student) interested in the development of regulation, enforcement and environmental governance.

Patrick Bishop *IUCN Academy of Law Newsletter*

This 765 page volume, authored by barrister Richard Macrory, is clearly destined to become the classic reference work on regulation and enforcement of environmental law . . . The author combines serious scholarship with extensive practical experience in the world of environmental policy and regulation . . . The work under review is indeed monumental. But it is also formidable in its length, complexity and format.

Ayesha Dias, *Oil and Gas Law Intelligence*

REGULATION, ENFORCEMENT AND GOVERNANCE IN ENVIRONMENTAL LAW

Regulation, Enforcement and Governance in Environmental Law is an updated edition of Richard Macrory's most influential writings. Spanning his entire career, these are all works which have helped shape contemporary environmental law and policy. The book includes the full text of his 2006 Cabinet Office Review on Regulatory Sanctions, new chapters on the Climate Change Act 2008, the Environment Tribunal, and analysis of recent leading cases.

The book is divided into five thematic sections: Regulatory reform, Institutional Reform and Change, Dynamics of Environmental Law, Courts and the Environment, Europe and the Environment.

Regulation, Enforcement and Governance in Environmental Law

Second Edition

Richard Macrory

·HART·
PUBLISHING

OXFORD AND PORTLAND, OREGON
2014

Published in the United Kingdom by Hart Publishing Ltd
16C Worcester Place, Oxford, OX1 2JW
Telephone: +44 (0)1865 517530
Fax: +44 (0)1865 510710
E-mail: mail@hartpub.co.uk
Website: http://www.hartpub.co.uk

Published in North America (US and Canada) by
Hart Publishing
c/o International Specialized Book Services
920 NE 58th Avenue, Suite 300
Portland, OR 97213-3786
USA
Tel: +1 503 287 3093 or toll-free: (1) 800 944 6190
Fax: +1 503 280 8832
E-mail: orders@isbs.com
Website: http://www.isbs.com

British Library Cataloguing in Publication Data

Data Available

ISBN: 978-1-84946-450-5

Typeset by Forewords, Oxon
Printed and bound in Great Britain by
CPI Group (UK) Ltd, Croydon CR0 4YY

To Sarah, Sam and Robbie

Foreword to the Second Edition

It is less than five years since I was privileged to write a foreword to the first edition of Richard Macrory's valuable collection of writings on this important topic. I will not repeat what I said then of his long and distinguished contribution to the development of environmental law in this country and abroad. From such an energetic and prolific source, it is no surprise that the intervening years have seen so many important additions to his academic writings on a variety of fascinating topics.

As a judge with a special interest in the practical application of environmental law through the courts, I am particularly interested in his discussion of what he rightly calls 'the long and winding road' to the development of a specialist environmental jurisdiction in the courts or tribunals of this country, a journey which has proved frustrating at time and is far from completed. He is also able to bring an expert and objective viewpoint to his discussion of the contribution of the courts at European and domestic level, and of the problems of effective and consistent interpretation of European environmental law.

As I said of the first edition, this book should be essential reading for anyone concerned with the development of environmental law and policy. It is designed for a wide readership, not limited to seasoned specialists. As Dr Ludwig Kramer in a review of the first edition:

> Younger lawyers, Internet-oriented and less inclined to consider the evolution of law, might well learn from this inter-generational reflection on environmental law at the turn of the 20 to the 21 century, where we come from, where we are going and, what is most important, where we should and could go in order to keep this planet in an environmental state that is not worse than that of the 1960s or 1970s.

Robert Carnwath

Foreword to the First Edition

I am delighted to be able to contribute a Foreword to this important collection. I have been lucky to have known and worked with Richard for many years, and have admired his intellect, his energy, and his fun (including his conjuring skills). He has had a distinguished and distinctive career, and has made a unique contribution to the development of environmental law in this country and abroad. He was the first editor of the Journal of Environmental Law, now recognized as one of the foremost scholarly Journals of its kind in the world. He has been specialist adviser to Parliamentary Select Committees in both the Lords and Commons, a long standing member of the Royal Commission on Environmental Pollution, and a board member of the Environment Agency, England and Wales. He was a founding member and first chairman of the UK Environmental Law Association which continues to thrive, and of which I am privileged to be the President. All this has been combined with practice at the Bar, and a brilliant academic career. He was the first Professor of Environmental Law in this country, and is now Director of the Centre for Law and the Environment at University College, London.

Regulation, Enforcement and Governance of Environmental Law is a selection of some of his most important writings and is focused on major themes concerning the nature of regulation, institutional arrangements, and enforcement. Richard's combination of serious scholarship and extensive experience in the world of environmental policy and regulation make this a particularly significant collection. It starts from his first article published in the New Journal some thirty years ago (a characteristic reflection on the law concerning bicycles –still relevant today), and brings the story right up to date, with the full text of his 2006 Cabinet Office Review on Regulatory Sanctions. His analysis and recommendations in this Review laid the basis for the core provisions in the Regulatory Enforcement and Sanctions Act 2008. They should have a profound effect on the way we think about regulatory sanctions in this country, far beyond the field of environmental law. The value of his work in this area is already being recognized in other countries.

This book should be essential reading for anyone concerned with the development of environmental law and policy. I hope also that it will be read by the next generation of environmental lawyers. They will be facing profound environmental challenges, which will undoubtedly require fresh legal solutions. The material in this collection will stand not only as a record of remarkable achievement, but as an inspiration for innovative thinking in the future.

Robert Carnwath

Introduction to the Second Edition

Laws concerning environmental protection have a long history in the United Kingdom, but the last 30 years have seen an unprecedented development not just in the substantive body of environmental legislation, but also in thinking about underlying principles and institutional arrangements. To the current generation of environmental lawyers it is almost unimaginable how rapid the change in profile of the subject has been in such a comparatively short time. My own exposure to environmental law began as a newly qualified barrister working for Friends of the Earth in London in the mid-1970s, then the only UK environmental group which employed a lawyer. Legal actions before the courts at that time seemed a largely fruitless and costly activity, and most of the legal effort was focused on pressuring the government for legislative reform and using public inquiries in the planning field as a forum for exposing the inadequacies and short-sightedness of government policy in addressing longer term environmental issues. Shortly afterwards I began my first academic appointment at Imperial College, London, consciously working with environmental scientists, who then appeared to offer a more sympathetic intellectual environment than traditional law schools, where the discipline of environmental law was scarcely acknowledged. I well remember meeting at this time a fairly intimidating Law Lord of the old school (and now long deceased) who asked me my field of specialism. I naturally replied 'environmental law', only to be faced with silence and an expression that somehow combined utter incomprehension and slight distaste.

The materials in this book should at least demonstrate what a long way we have come in less than a generation. In making a selection of my publications, I have largely avoided any analyses of detailed black letter law, but focused on material dealing with major themes concerning the nature of regulation, institutional arrangements and enforcement which underlie the substantive detail of the law. A number of pieces, though, including the chapters on the Climate Change Act and the environmental integration principle in the EU Treaty, deliberately consider the relevant provisions through a fairly detailed legal lens, trying to explore what might be their real legal effect, if any. Since the first edition was published an Environment Tribunal has been set up in England and Wales, the country's first such specialist judicial body, and the Environment Agency and Natural England now have powers to serve civil sanctions under Part III of the Regulatory Enforcement and Sanctions 2008. I have therefore been able to include pieces which reflect on these developments. The courts both at European and national level continue to play a key role in developing principles and interpreting environmental legislation, and the case analysis chapters deal with some of the most important recent decisions.

Many contemporary environmental issues are global in nature and can in the long run probably only be tackled at global level. International environmental treaties have grown in number and complexity over the last 30 years, and international public law is one of the core elements of the subject. A number of international treaties, such as the Aarhus Convention, find their way into this book, and I would have liked to have included more on international law generally. But fairly early on my academic career I decided it simply was not possible to be a specialist at all levels of environmental law. I was already well versed in national environmental law, but it was Nigel Haigh's pioneering 1984 book, *EEC Environmental Policy and Britain*, that really first made me fully aware of the significance of the European Economic Community, as it then was, to the development of environmental law. Nigel's work was largely concerned with the impact of the EEC's environmental legislation on British law and policy. I became especially interested in the influence of the European Court of Justice and, following a short secondment to the Legal Unity of DG Environment in the European Commission, the significance of the Commission's enforcement mechanisms against Member States. Much of the material included in this collection was therefore initially stimulated by UK or European Union legal and policy developments, but many of the themes considered should have more universal resonance.

Part I is concerned with major issues concerning regulatory reform, and in particular the debates on whether traditional British approaches towards constructing regulatory sanctions are best suited to contemporary needs. Part II considers challenges to current institutional arrangements, including the need for a specialised environmental court and tribunal, and the environmental implications of the major constitutional changes that have taken place in the United Kingdom in the last decade. Part III contains material that reflects on the shifting dynamics of environmental law as it copes with changing expectations of how we handle the development of new environmental standards, the opportunities of new technologies to assist enforcement and the need to develop new notions of responsibility. Part IV is a selection of reports of leading environmental cases over the last decade, illustrating how both the Court of Justice of the European Union and the higher courts in the United Kingdom have grappled with the interpretation of environmental legislation and the development of legal principle. Part V focuses on European dimensions. It starts with material relating to key principles of European Union law, such as environmental integration, free trade, consistent interpretation and subsidiarity, and how these influence and interact with the development of environmental law. It then considers the enforcement of European Union's environmental law and the unique, though by no means perfect, mechanisms that have been developed under the Treaties to ensure that Member States comply with their obligations.

The scale and scope of environmental issues which face both this country and the world are becoming ever more apparent. Law and legislation on their own cannot possibly resolve all these challenges, but will provide the bedrock for the decisions that will have to be made. As we move from handling more familiar environmental pressures to major questions of resource and energy use, the next generation of environmental lawyers will need to be even more imaginative in devising appropriate legal responses. I hope that some of the thoughts here will assist in stimulating these future debates.

I am grateful to Martin Hession, Michael Woods, Varena Magnar and Stefan Mayr, who were co-authors on a number of the pieces reproduced here.

Finally I would like the staff at Hart Publishing, and especially Tom Adams and Mel Hamill, for their unfailing good humour, efficiency and professionalism – qualities that epitomise the business that Richard and Jane created and nurtured over the years.

Richard Macrory
University College
July 2014

Acknowledgements

The publishers and the author would like to acknowledge the following for giving permission to reproduce material in this collection:

Brill/Nijhoff   Chapter 12

Bruylant   Chapter 26

Chancery Law   Chapter 17

Dartmouth   Chapter 15

ENDS Reports   Chapters 9, 20, 21, 22

Europa Law Publishers   Chapters 13, 27, 30

Frank Cass Publishers   Chapter 23

Global Information Group   Chapter 29

Haymarket Media Group   Chapters 19, 20, 21, 22

International Comparative Guide   Chapter 29

Kluwer Law International   Chapter 28

Oxford University Press   Chapters 3, 4, 5, 8, 11, 24

Norwegian University   Chapter 10

Universitetsforlaget, Norway   Chapter 10

University of Capetown   Chapter 14

Wiley & Sons   Chapter 25

Note on Updates

Some of the material here is deliberately of its time, and I have resisted trying to update all of the legal references. But I have inserted some new footnotes pointing out recent developments or legislative changes where this seemed especially helpful to the contemporary reader. Where this has been done it should be apparent from the context.

RM

About the Author

Richard Macrory is a barrister with Brick Court Chambers and Professor of Environmental Law at University College, London. He was legal adviser to Friends of the Earth between 1975 and 1978, and then joined Imperial College where he became the first Professor of Environmental Law in the United Kingdom in 1991. Richard Macrory was the first chairman of the UK Environmental Law Association, and founding editor of the Journal of Environmental Law. He has been Standing Counsel to the Council for the Protection of Rural England, a member of the Royal Commission on Environmental Pollution for 11 years, and was chair of the steering board of the European Environmental Advisory Councils in 2011–02. Professor Macrory has been a specialist adviser to select committees in both the House of Commons and House of Lords, was a board member of the Environment Agency England and Wales between 1999 and 2004, and was Hon President of the National Society for Clean Air and Environmental Protection in 2004–05. In 2005 he was appointed by the Cabinet Office to conduct the Review on Regulatory Sanctions, and the core recommendations of the Review were enacted in the Regulatory Enforcement and Sanctions Act 2008. He was chairman of Merchant Ivory film productions for almost 20 years. In 2000 he was awarded a CBE for services to the environment, and in 2008 appointed an honorary QC for his work on the development of environmental law. In 2010 he was elected a Bencher of Gray's Inn.

Contents

Table of Cases

Part I

Regulatory Reform

Modern environmental law is dominated by regulatory controls. Before the industrial revolution, legal protection for the environment in the United Kingdom largely rested on the availability of common law legal remedies such as the action in nuisance which could be employed by private landowners to protect their property from pollution and other forms of environmental degradation. Private legal remedies can still be of significance, and recent case law, including the important 2014 Supreme Court decision in *Coventry v Lawrence*, considered in Part IV, demonstrates that the judiciary are still developing common law principles to meet contemporary demands. But by the mid-nineteenth century Parliament and government had recognised the weaknesses of wholesale reliance on private legal action as a means of environmental protection. Individuals may not have the stamina or resources to engage in legal action. Private litigation requires the identification of a defendant who clearly caused the damage, and is less appropriate where there are multiple potential contributors, or where pollution is diffuse. Where the environment concerned falls outside private ownership (such as wild animals, the atmosphere, public waters), the common law may simply provide no protection since there is no obvious claimant whose legal interests have been affected. The remedies may have a deterrent value, but hardly represent a sophisticated instrument designed to ensure preventative action or the gradual tightening up of protective measures and improvement of the quality of the environment. The need for intervention by the state in the form of regulatory requirements concerning the environment therefore became apparent, and now plays a key role in contemporary legal machinery.

Regulation in the environmental field can take many forms – from the imposition of fixed product standards, such as vehicle emission requirements, the requirement of a licence or permit for particular activities, with detailed conditions set by an authorisation body, to various types of trading emission regimes and other forms of economic incentive. *Reforming Regulatory Sanctions* (2007) and *Regulatory Justice – Making Sanctions Effective* (2006) do not deal directly with evaluating the different types of regulatory instrument available, but instead are focused on the sanctions that are available where regulatory requirements are breached. Regulation of economic enterprises almost by definition is needed where the market cannot be relied upon by itself to achieve the policy goals desired by society, and an ineffective enforcement and sanctioning regime will undermine a regulatory system. It does not follow that a policy of no tolerance and excessive punishment is necessarily the most effective means to ensure compliance, and most modern regulators dealing with legitimate businesses sensibly adopt enforcement policies based on advice and persuasion in the first place, and preserving formal legal sanctions for more serious or repetitive breaches where persuasion has had little effect.

One of the distinctive features of UK environmental law, present for over 100 years, has been the prevalence of the criminal law as the dominant formal legal sanction. In nearly every area of environmental regulation, breach of a regulation is made a criminal offence. Many environmental regulators have the power to serve a formal notice or enforcement order requiring compliance within a specified period, but breach of the notice is also sanctioned by a criminal offence. Mainstream criminal law generally requires evidence of intention or recklessness before an offence is committed, but in the regulatory field offences have commonly been drafted in terms such that the mere act of the breach is sufficient to secure conviction. Offences can be committed even where the immediate cause of the breach was the action of a trespasser or the event was caused by an unforeseen accident, as the 1998 decision of the House of Lords in Empress Cars demonstrates.[1] The so-called strict liability offence clearly reduces the evidential burden on the prosecutor and was developed in the nineteenth century when enforcement bodies were considered to lack the capability to investigate the internal complexities of business operations. An added advantage for the prosecutor is that a company can be readily convicted of such an offence where the breach was caused by the action or inaction of one of its employees, or failures of equipment or other systems operated by the company. In contrast, where intention or recklessness is an ingredient of an offence, a company can generally only be convicted where a senior manager or director has shown such intention or recklessness.

The system is a tough one, though not unique to the United Kingdom.[2] In theory, potential injustice can be moderated by the discretion of the enforcement body in deciding whether or not to prosecute for a particular breach in the first place, and if a case reaches court in the sentencing practice of the courts that should reflect the perceived culpability of the defendant. Yet there remains intense academic debate on the justification and theory of strict liability offences,[3] and the pervasiveness of the principle in British regulatory law has been memorably described as the 'closest to unsophisticated pre-Enlightenment notions of criminal responsibility'.[4] But in the environmental field there was also increasing public debate in the 1990s in the United Kingdom as to the effectiveness of the ordinary criminal courts in handling such regulatory offences. Bodies such as the Environment Agency responsible for the enforcement of key areas of environmental law such as industrial pollution control, water management, and waste controls, have criticised the apparent low level of fines handed down by magistrates' courts when cases reached them. Legitimate companies who complied with regulatory requirements had sometimes felt that competitors were making money from non-compliance or that where they had breached regulatory requirements through an oversight or accident they were being unfairly lumped together with the truly criminal. In a significant public lecture, 'Are the Judiciary Environmentally Myopic?',[5] the then Lord Chief Justice, Lord Woolf, called for the creation of a single specialist environmental court to handle criminal, civil, and administrative issues arising from breaches of environmental law. This gave rise to a

---

[1] *Environment Agency (formerly National Rivers Authority) v Empress Car Company (Abertillery) Ltd* [1998] 1 All ER 481 – see Chapter 20 below, p 397.

[2] See Faure and Heine, *Criminal Enforcement of Environmental Law in the European Union* (The Hague, Kluwer Law International, 2005). Within Europe, criminal liability of corporations is also familiar in Denmark, France, and the Netherlands and more recently Belgium and Finland. Concepts of criminal law do not allow for criminal liability of corporations in countries such as Austria, Germany, Italy, and Spain.

[3] For a recent study see Simester (ed), *Appraising Strict Liability* (Oxford, Oxford University Press, 2005).

[4] J Spencer and A Pedain, 'Strict Liability in Continental Criminal Law' in Simester, ibid, 276.

[5] Woolf, 'Are the Judiciary Environmentally Myopic?' (1991) 4(1) *Journal of Environmental Law* 1.

number of studies and reports concerning the possible creation and functions of specialist environmental courts and tribunals, discussed further in part II.

Those considering reforms to the UK systems of environmental sanctions were well aware that many other jurisdictions, both in common law and continental countries, used a wider range of sanctions beyond simply the application of the criminal law. The US Environmental Protection Agency, for example, makes extensive use of administrative penalties, with the Department of Justice using criminal prosecutions for the most serious breaches.[6] German law has also long used administrative penalties as a core sanction for regulatory offences. Powerful critiques were made for the need for extending the range of sanctions available to British environmental regulators.[7] Regulators need enforcement measures that are both efficient in terms of using the minimum of scarce regulatory resources, and effective in terms of deterrence.[8] Yet one of the most difficult challenges for those in the environmental field seeking a change in traditional approaches was the question why should environmental regulation be treated so differently from other forms of regulation? With the exception of the regulation of the financial sector, the use of the criminal law as the core formal legal sanction permeates nearly every of regulation from trading standards to health and safety and food regulation. Arguments could be made that distinguish the environment from other fields of regulation,[9] but they were not wholly convincing, or, rather, not sufficiently compelling to ensure political backing for a legislative change.

Enter the Hampton Review. The Review, led by Sir Philip Hampton, was commissioned by the Treasury to examine the relationship between regulators and the regulated community, and encompassed over 60 national regulators as well as local government. His final Report, published in 2005,[10] recognised the importance of regulation but identified unnecessary burdens on industry in terms of an excessive number of regulators, and overlapping inspections and data requirements. Hampton advocated that regulators should avoid a 'tick-box' mentality towards enforcement, and should adopt a stronger risk based approach that focused resources on where they would have greatest impact, and keeping the need for securing outcomes at the forefront of their enforcement strategy. To be fair, regulators such as the Environment Agency had already begun implementing such an approach, but Hampton found that generally there were inconsistencies in practice across the board. Hampton advocated advice and persuasion as the first approach towards securing compliance, but recognised the underlying importance of an effective sanction regime. He was concerned that over-reliance on the criminal law often appeared to lead to disproportionate results, and recommended that government initiate a special Review that focused on the issue of sanctions.

I was commissioned by the Cabinet Office in 2005 to lead that Review, with the final Report published in 2006. *Reforming Regulatory Sanctions* (2007) is a revised version of the 2007 Brodies Environment Lecture, and contains a broad analysis of the context of my Review but with a particular focus on its implications for the enforcement of envi-

---

[6] See Mushal, 'Reflections upon American Environmental Enforcement Experience as it may Relate to Post-Hampton Developments in England and Wales' (2007) 19(2) *Journal of Environmental Law* 201.

[7] See, eg Ogus and Abbott, 'Sanctions for Pollution – Do We Have the Right Regime?' (2002) 14(3) *Journal of Environmental Law* 283.

[8] Gunningham, 'Regulating Small and Medium Sized Enterprises' (2002) 14(1) *Journal of Environmental Law* 3.

[9] See Chapter 6 below.

[10] *Reducing Administrative Burdens: Effective Inspection and Enforcement* (London, HM Treasury, March 2005).

ronmental law in this country. I noted that historically significant environmental reforms have often come about from what Lord Ashby, the first chairman of the Royal Commission on Environmental Pollution, described as an 'ignition' event – some well publicised environmental scandal or disaster. But major changes can also occur from what I describe in the paper as an unexpected alignment, where policy developments in a wholly unconnected field happen to provide opportunities for real policy advance in another field – in this case there were two such alignments: the Treasury-led Hampton Review, driven out of concern of excessive regulatory burdens on industry, and, quite unconnected, a major reform taking place to the Tribunal system.

Regulatory Justice – Making Sanctions Effective (2006) is the text of the final Report of the Review. The Review's remit, as was Hampton's, went well beyond the field of environmental regulation and covered some 61 national regulators as well as local government. The financial regulators and the economic regulators of privatised utilities were not within the scope of the Review, though we had extensive discussions with these regulators since generally they possessed sanctioning powers under modern legislation which were not so dependent on the criminal law. In examining such a wide range of laws and regulatory practice, it would have been all too easy to sink in a morass of detail, and it therefore seemed sensible to articulate a set of general penalty principles which should underline the design of a regulatory sanctions regime. These provide a basis for critiquing the adequacy of the present system, and for assessing any proposed reforms. Perhaps the two key principles were that first a sanctioning regime should not be designed to punish per se (though sometimes punishment was necessary) but to ensure that the offending business was brought back into compliance, and second, that an effective regime should ensure that no economic gains are made from non-compliance.

Against those principles, the present system of sanctions in England and Wales was found wanting. The Review did not deny the importance of the criminal law in dealing with certain types of regulatory offender, and made suggestions for improving the criminal system, including extending the range of sanctions available to criminal courts. But it concluded that essentially we were asking a criminal offence to do much work in this area. The single criminal sanction had to handle both the truly egregious 'rogue' trader as well as legitimate businesses who through oversight or carelessness breached regulations but in circumstances that required more than simply a warning or caution. There was a real danger that the stigma of the criminal law was being devalued by being overused. So it was necessary to propose that regulators had a far richer range of sanctions, including the use of administrative penalties without the necessary intervention of a criminal court, and the use of enforceable undertakers offered by the offending business.

During the Consultation, it became clear that while many recognised the attractiveness of this direction, there was equal concern that it would give even greater sanctioning discretion to regulators with a real danger that the powers could be abused, or used oppressively. As a consequence, governance issues concerning regulators assumed far greater importance during the development of the Review and form a major plank of the final Report. For example, the choice of sanction should always be determined by the core penalty principles rather than extraneous factors or perverse incentives such as internal targets. The revenue from many administrative penalties should never go directly to the regulator, even if ring-fenced for enforcement. Regulators need to act transparently as to the use of their sanctioning powers, and to provide regular reports of their use set against outcomes.

Gratifyingly, the Government accepted all the recommendations in the Report. Part III of the Enforcement and Sanctions Act 2008 provides a core framework of administrative sanctions which can be drawn down by secondary legislation to specific areas of regulation. Other recommendations, such as those dealing with the criminal law and restorative justice, should be pursued separately. Many of the specific sanction proposals in the Review are not totally novel. They have been used in the financial sector in this country, and have been applied in countries such as Canada and Australia in regulatory fields such as the environment and health and safety at work. But the setting of the sanctions within a clear set of principles together with the emphasis on issues of regulatory governance is novel, and the Report is increasingly being well received in jurisdictions outside the United Kingdom. The six principles that should underline an effective sanctions systems are now widely used as a starting point in the discussion and development of sanctions.

Reforming Regulatory Sanctions was written at a time the government appeared committed to implement all the recommendations in the review and introduce primary legislation. Six years on, *Sanctions and Safeguards – the Brave New World of Environmental Enforcement* (2013) provided an opportunity to reflect on the implementation of the Review in practice and the lessons learnt. As I note, 'Even where the government has accepted the proposals, translating the ambitions of a Review that cuts across such a broad spectrum of departmental and regulatory interests into legislative reality is fraught with difficulty'. Most of the progress was made with giving new powers concerning civil sanctions and improving the practice of regulatory governance – far less in coordinating improvements in criminal sanctioning. Perhaps naively, I had assumed that most regulators and their sponsoring departments would eagerly wish to acquire the new range of sanctioning, but I underestimated the conservatism of many such bodies, and the industries they regulated – the familiar world of the magistrates courts and the criminal law still has attractions. Nevertheless, such bodies as the Environment Agency, which can use the new sanctions in a limited range of areas, such as packaging regulations, report a positive experience. In fact, to date, the Environment Agency has not yet had to impose a formal variable civil penalty but has been able to rely entirely on enforcement undertakings, where the industry itself proposes what is in effect their own sanction.

I was well aware during the Review that there were dangers in giving regulators powers to impose sanctions without going through the courts – the experience in areas such as rail fare penalties and parking fines is hardly encouraging. This was one of the reasons for the emphasis on governance principles – rights of appeal, transparency and similar issues. The Review, though commissioned under a Labour government, was intended to be non-party political, but the coalition government that came into power in 2010 was concerned that regulators could be tempted to bully individuals and smaller companies into paying civil penalties. In its view, larger companies could exercise rights of appeals but smaller one might not have the time or resources to do so. Accordingly, in 2012 the government announced that in future new civil sanction powers would generally only be given in respect of companies with more than 250 employees. On the other hand, they welcomed far greater use of enforcement undertakings whatever the size of the business concerned. It is too early to know whether this change of policy represents simply a small blip on any further development down this road or the early demise of an interesting experiment. My own view is that we will now not return to an almost wholesale reliance on criminal law as a formal sanction in the regulatory area, but lessons from the actual practice of the new regimes will prove vital in their future acceptance and wider application.

Regulating in a Risky Environment (2002) is similarly focused on environmental regulation, but goes beyond the issue of enforcement and sanctions, and considers the nature and justification of environmental regulation as such. Over the last decade or so, direct regulation of the traditional type has been subjected to intense criticism as stifling innovation and being inefficient. There were powerful advocates of alternative, market based solutions, such as trading regimes and voluntary agreements, and indeed, at the time of the analysis, based on my inaugural lecture at University College, even the term 'regulation' was hardly acceptable currency in governmental circles. My analysis acknowledged that the varied and unpredictable nature of contemporary environmental challenges had of necessity seen the development of a whole new range of policy instruments in place of more conventional regulatory approaches. Yet, I was equally concerned that the division between so-called regulatory and non-regulatory approaches did not stand up to real scrutiny. Fiscal taxes are equally a form of regulation. Emissions trading regimes need underpinning regulatory structures to ensure confidence in the market, albeit one of a different nature than those traditionally used. Even the term 'command and control', so often used to disparage traditional regulation, was over-simplistic, and I advocated the more nuanced concept of 'determine and direct' to reflect contemporary regulatory challenges. As I noted,

> 'Direction' (rather than 'control'), reflects the need to ensure that as far as possible regulation is designed which is outcome-focused and which harnesses the inventive power of industry and the market to determine solutions but within clearly defined boundaries endorsed by legal sanction. 'Determination' implies that it remains the ultimate responsibility of government, rather than of science or economic theory, to decide the goals of environmental policy.

Probably rather naively, I hoped at the time that 'determine and direction' would soon become a new paradigm in contemporary regulatory language confining 'command and control' to past history, but it has not proved to be the case. In retrospect, it was a mistake to have kept the idea almost to the end of the lecture, and I now wish I had been rather bolder and more upfront with the concept. But I remain clear that regulation comes in many forms, and new forms of regulatory instrument should be considered with an open mind. But it is important that their use is subjected to the same level of rigorous scrutiny for effectiveness and efficiency as would be applied to more traditional forms of regulation. Equally, it seemed to me in 2002 – and still does – that their development should not be permitted to sacrifice the qualities of transparency, accountability and enforceability now inherent in elements of more formal legal structures.

1

Reforming Regulatory Sanctions[1] (2007)

Unexpected Alignments

Lord Ashby was a distinguished scientist and first chairman of the Royal Commission on Environmental Pollution in the early 1970s. One of his concerns was how major advances in environmental policy took place. The Royal Commission was and remains[2] concerned with the rational and detached analysis of environmental issues and their policy solutions. But however convincing its approach, that was not necessarily sufficient to win political support for legislative change. Ashby considered that generally there had also to be what he described as an ignition event before such change would take place. An ignition event on its own was likely to lead to a knee-jerk political reaction and often ill considered laws. It was only when this was combined with a pre-existing and well-thought-out analysis that truly effective changes in environmental law and policy took place.

Two examples in the development of British environmental law can be given that will illustrate his hypothesis. Smoke and the burning of coal was the curse of the British urban environment since the nineteenth century. The causes and the policy solutions were understood, and indeed draft legislation had been prepared since the early 1900s but nothing happened.[3] It was only with the ignition event of the Great London Smog of 1952 that saw the first Clean Air Act four years later. The second example concerns waste disposal. During the 1950 and 1960s there was no specialised law regulating the disposal of waste in Britain. Land use planning controls and reactive statutory nuisance controls provided the core legal controls, but their unsuitability for dealing with the complexities of modern waste management issues was well recognised by the late 1960s.[4] Experts committees had recommended what needed to be done to fill the legislative gap, but again nothing happened. Again it needed the ignition event of the well publicised illegal dumping of waste

---

[1] A revised version of the 2007 Tercentenary Brodies Environmental Law Lecture, delivered at the University of Edinburgh, March 2007.

[2] The Royal Commission on Environmental Pollution, established in 1970, was dissolved by the coalition government in 2011 as part of spending cuts.

[3] For a lucid history, see Ashby and Anderson, *The Politics of Clean Air* (Oxford, Oxford University Press, 1981).

[4] See, eg Report of the Technical Committee on the Disposal of Toxic Solid Wastes. Ministry of Housing & Local Government and Scottish Development Department, *Disposal of Solid Toxic Wastes* (London, HMSO, 1970).

contain cyanide near schools in the Midlands in the early 1970 to force the pace. Stop gap waste legislation[5] was passed within three days, and formed the foundation of the first bespoke waste management regulation system under Part I Control of Pollution Act 1974.

An ignition event might always suggest some sort of environmental catastrophe or major pollution scandal. But I think there is another sort of ignition that can take place and which can also provide the impetus for profound change. I would call this the *unexpected alignment*. By this I mean the quite fortuitous concurrence of a number of distinct drivers for policy and legislative change, each of which in themselves might be insufficient but which in combination provide a powerful impetus. I will use one of the Royal Commission's own reports to illustrate this. The Commission's Fifth report published in 1976[6] was initially concerned with the relationship of land use planning and air pollution control. The motivation for the study was some well documented *cause célèbres* involving poorly sited smelters causing local air pollution and where the then regulator, the central government Alkali Inspectorate, though technically highly competent, was failing to address contemporary concerns for greater transparency and public engagement. As often happens with a Commission study, detailed investigation of one issue throws up other problems. The Commission found itself examining how Britain regulated emissions from industrial processes generally, and was greatly concerned at the number of different regulatory agencies dealing with air emissions, water pollution and waste disposal under distinct legislation and with little coordination. As the Commission noted,

> Unless an industrial pollutant can be eliminated as opposed to being transformed, it must be disposed of elsewhere. It is sensible that the form and medium of disposal should be chosen to ensure the least environmental damage overall. This optimisation obviously calls for co-operation between the controlling authorities and we were surprised to find from our enquiries that there appears at present to be virtually none.[7]

The Commission called for the creation of single unified pollution inspectorate to regulate all emissions from key industrial processes. It would operate an integrated permit system and apply the criterion of the best practicable environmental option to determine to best solution. The Commission's recommendations are not binding, and the belated government response was that the analysis was compelling but that it did not relish institutional reorganisation[8]. Instead, it advocated greater cooperation between the existing regulatory bodies, a solution the Commission had considered but rejected. That was in 1975 and nothing happened for a decade. In 1984, the Commission in its 10th Report[9] criticised the government's advocacy of a pragmatic and cooperative approach – 'the danger, as we see it, is that such extreme open-mindedness and pragmatism may, in the absence of a more positive lead, generate much discussion but lead to little practical outcome'.[10] Essentially everyone knew the current arrangements were sub-optimal, but there was no ignition event in the sense of some environmental catastrophe, or major breakdown in the regulatory machinery, sufficient to ensure the issue was high on the political agenda.

---

[5] Deposit of Poisonous Wastes Act 1972.

[6] Royal Commission on Environmental Pollution, *Air Pollution Control – An Integrated Approach*, Fifth Report, Cmnd 6371 (London, HMSO, 1976).

[7] Ibid, para 265.

[8] Department of the Environment, *Air Pollution Control*, Pollution Paper No 18 (London, HMSO, 1982).

[9] Royal Commission on Environmental Pollution, *Tackling Pollution – Experience and Prospects*, Tenth Report, Cmnd 9149 (London, HMSO, 1984).

[10] Ibid, para 3.32.

But in 1986 an unexpected alignment occurred. The Enterprise and Deregulation Unit of the Cabinet Office published a study concerning business regulation[11] and felt that the number of pollution permits and consents businesses had to obtain to operate from different regulators was inefficient and an excessive bureaucratic burden on industry. It called for a one-stop consent system and a single inspectorate. The analysis and motives were not driven by environmental imperatives but purely on the need to reduce administrative burdens on business. But the unexpected alignment with the Royal Commission's previous analysis conducted from an environmental perspective was the push that was needed. Shortly afterwards the government created a unified pollution inspectorate, and 1990 saw legislation creating the first integrated pollution control system with a single consent covering emissions into air and water and onto land from prescribed industrial processes,[12] with the best practicable environmental option as the core underlying concept for decision making. This is not the place for an exploration of the effectiveness of the new system, the struggle to find robust methodologies for determining BPEO, and indeed the missed opportunities. But it was undoubtedly an important step change in how we approach pollution regulation, and one that later heavily influenced the development of the EC Directive on Integrated Pollution and Prevention Control, which has now succeeded Integrated Pollution Control. In this context, the significant aspect of the environmental reforms that took place was that, as with the examples of clean air and waste, there was already a pre-existing powerful analysis of the policy problem before the unexpected alignment took place.

I am going to focus on the way that we have treated sanctions for breaches of environmental law in this country. For at least a decade there has been growing concern about the effectiveness of our existing sanctions and the legal and institutional arrangements within which they operate. Under-enforcement, low fines in the courts, and a judiciary that is often unfamiliar with the detailed complexities and dynamics of modern environmental regulation. Despite all the analyses and recommendations, nothing substantially changed. And it is difficult to locate an ignition event that would force a major policy shift. There are well publicised cases of apparently poor sanctions – for example, an Oxfordshire man fined £30,000 for dumping 184 drums of toxic waste. He had been paid £58,000 for doing so, and it cost the waste authorities £167,000 to incinerate them properly.[13] But these sparks were not sufficient to catch light.

But now through quite unexpected and fortuitous alignments of different concerns – and two strands in particular – which were quite unconnected with the environmental agenda we may be on a cusp on a sanctions revolution. One that in a decade hence might see the criminal courts focused on real environmental crimes, imaginative and effective sentencing techniques, the use of far more effective economic sanctions dealing with legitimate businesses who fail to comply with regulatory requirements, and a specialised environmental tribunal providing sophisticated and responsive judgments in environmental matters.

---

[11] Cabinet Office, *Inspecting Industry: Pollution and Safety*, Efficiency Scrutiny Report (London, HMSO, 1986). For a general background see see O'Riordan and Weale 'Administrative Reorganisation and Policy Change: The Case of Her Majesty's Inspectorate of Pollution' (1989) 67(3) *Public Administration* 277.

[12] Environmental Protection Act 1990, Part I. Her Majesty's Inspectorate of Pollution was later subsumed into the Environment Agency under the Environment Act 1995.

[13] Quoted in Cabinet Office, 'Regulatory Justice: Sanctioning in a Post-Hampton World', Consultation Document of the Macrory Review of Regulatory Sanctions (Better Regulation Executive, May 2006) para 2.6.

For the last 10 years there have been reports and articles written about the apparent low level of fines in the magistrates' courts dealing with environmental offences. The Court of Appeal has issued guidelines urging a tougher approach. Nevertheless, the Environment Agency and SEPA have continued to argue that sentencing is often insufficiently robust. Other methods of bringing pressure to bear have been developed – notably the publication of annual 'naming and shaming' league tables of fines, itself a controversial matter, and something incidentally that would be disallowed in Germany where stronger privacy laws protect the naming of companies even where they have been sanctioned for a regulatory breach.

At the same time there have been calls for the development of a specialised environmental court system. 15 years ago Lord Justice Woolf in a notable lecture entitled 'Are the Judiciary Environmentally Myopic?'[14] called for the creation of a specialised court that would adopt an integrated approach to an environmental pollution incident, handling in one court criminal, civil, judicial review and regulatory matters. This was followed by a major study by Professor Malcolm Grant, then of Cambridge University, which was commissioned by the Department of the Environment.[15] He was asked to examine various environmental courts and tribunals in other parts of the world – notably Sweden, New South Wales, and New Zealand, and tasked with identifying various models that might be adopted in this country, but without firm recommendations. His report had all the virtues and weaknesses of an academic study – comprehensive, detached, and analytical, but immensely long and with too many options for politicians to make a clear choice. Although many environmental groups continued to argue for a 'big bang' solution to create an environmental court, it was clear that there was no political appetite for such a radical initiative – and as with any major institutional change, costs and benefits loomed large.

Enter the Royal Commission on Environmental Pollution again. In 2002 it presented its 23rd Report entitled 'Environmental Planning'.[16] In some way this was a throw-back to the 5th Report on air pollution in that it was concerned with the relationship of land use planning and environmental protection, but now dealing with a raft of new environmental policies and regulations, new institutional bodies, and a much wider perspective than simply pollution, covering all aspects of environmental protection from habitat protection to climate change. Tucked away in the chapter entitled 'Strengthening Public Confidence' was a section concerning environmental courts and tribunals[17]. The Commission noted the previous calls for single environmental courts, but felt that there was no compelling case for reforming judicial review arrangements. Equally, whilst it recognised the need to strengthen the criminal system, it did not feel it sensible to transfer environmental crimes to a new court. But where it did see a great deal of inconsistency at present was in the arrangements for handling various administrative appeals under environmental regulations. Land use planning appeals have long been handled by a planning inspectorate, but when it came to appeals under environmental regulations such as waste licensing, contaminated land, or packaging regulations there seemed a great deal of confusion. Some went

---

[14] Woolf, 'Are the Judiciary Environmentally Myopic?' (1991) 4(1) *Journal of Environmental Law* 1.

[15] Grant, 'Environmental Court Project', Final Report (Department of Environment, Transport and the Regions, 2000).

[16] Royal Commission on Environmental Pollution, *Environmental Planning*, Twenty-third Report, Cm 5459 (London, HMSO, 2002).

[17] Ibid, paras 5.30–5.39.

to the planning inspectorate, some to the county court or magistrates' courts, some to the Secretary of State. The Commission recommended the establishment of an environmental tribunal to consolidate all these appeals, and bring greater expertise and consistency to the area. A recommendation that was less dramatic perhaps than a new environmental court but one that merited examination.

The Royal Commission was not able to investigate the subject, but a year later the Centre for Law and the Environment at UCL was commissioned by DEFRA to examine the case for such a tribunal in more detail.[18] We examined over 50 different appeal provisions in current legislation and confirmed the lack of apparent consistency.

We looked at possible ways of improving adapting existing appeal bodies but felt that the establishment of a dedicated tribunal was the best way forward, both for dealing with existing and future environmental laws. Setting up a new tribunal is a costly and complex business, and we tried to estimate the likely number of appeals there would and what this would cost, using the Lands Tribunal as a model – probably around £2m a year. Much more difficult was to determine whether this would bring economic benefits though one could quantify time saved from transfers from existing bodies.

There were two main challenges, though. First, looking at the number of appeals on regulatory matters, it was quite difficult to be sure of the 500 or so appeals which seemed the sort of figure needed to warrant a new tribunal. We raised in the report the possibility of introducing civil penalties for environmental offences where appeals might also be routed to the proposed tribunal. This was not simply a way of boosting business for a new tribunal. For some years I have been interested in the question of environmental sanctions – how, for instance, the US Environmental Protection Agency largely relied on administrative penalties as a method of enforcement, avoiding the use of the courts and in this country similar methods used and available in fields such as competition law and economic regulation but never applied generally in the context of the environmental field.

The issue of civil penalties as a possible enforcement tool in for environmental regulations was examined in more detail in a further study commissioned by DEFRA[19]. The second major intellectual challenge was to face the question if the environment, why not other areas of regulation? Was the environment so really different from say health and safety regulation, or trading standards, or food safety? As a good advocate I constructed what seemed to me a reasonably compelling case why environmental regulation did indeed have distinctive characteristics warranting special treatment.[20]

Seven features characterised much of contemporary environmental law – complex scientific and technical issues, often featuring underlying scientific uncertainties; a challenging and rapidly developing legislative and policy base; overlapping remedies in criminal, civil, and public law; a powerful and increasing body of European legislation, together with jurisprudence from the European Court of Justice; a substantial body of international environmental treaties; the development of fundamental environmental principles such as the precautionary principle and the polluters pay which need to be understood by courts or tribunals; the emergence of principles concerning public partici-

---

[18] Macrory and Woods, *Modernising Environmental Justice: Regulation and the Role of an Environmental Tribunal* (Centre for Law and the Environment, University College, London, 2003). See ch 2, where the Report is reproduced.

[19] Woods and Macrory, 'Environmental Civil Penalties – A More Proportionate Response to Regulatory Breach' (Centre for Law and the Environment, University College, London, 2004).

[20] *Modernising Environmental Justice*, above n 18, paras 8.1–8.2.

pation and access by the public to legal remedies, epitomised by the Aarhus Convention[21]; and finally, the emergence of the overarching principle of sustainable development which underpins contemporary policy approaches – a challenging concept with contestable interpretations but one which nevertheless a court or tribunal needs to be familiar with. Individually many of these features will be found in other areas of regulatory law, but it was their combination which appeared distinctive in the field of environmental law, and which posed particular challenges for conventional judicial bodies. The argument for distinctiveness and a specialist approach did not find favour in all quarters.[22], and at times it felt like special pleading.

Nevertheless, the report on environmental tribunals was well received by DEFRA and others, and provided valuable groundwork. But it was not as dramatic and therefore perhaps politically less exciting than proposals for a full-blown environmental court. And some months later, another study[23] which had also been commissioned by DEFRA rejected this model as insufficiently radical and called for a new environmental court. The government, faced with apparent competing views even within the environmental law community felt justified in not proposing any significant institutional reform.

Reviewing Sanctions

At this stage, I thought the political momentum for any reform had now passed, and there was unlikely to be a dramatic ignition event of the sort described by Ashby – such a series of scandalously poor decisions by the planning inspectorate. But enter the first of the two unexpected alignments. In 2004 the Treasury commissioned Philip Hampton, now chairman of Sainsburys, to conduct a review of administrative burdens on business in the regulatory field. The Hampton Report,[24] *Effective Inspection and Enforcement*, published in 2005 was not motivated by environmental concerns but more on how to regulate more sensibly, and reduce inappropriate burdens on legitimate business.

Hampton was particularly concerned at the large number of different regulatory bodies – at national level and outside the economic field over 60 different national regulators – and recommended the integration a large number of these bodies. But he was equally concerned at the extent to which many regulators appeared to following a rather tick-box approach to enforcement, and advocated a much stronger risk based approach. In essence this meant using limited resources more wisely, and focusing on the difficult and recalcitrant businesses rather than carrying out inspection for its own sake. Hampton certainly

---

[21] Convention on Access to Information, Public Participation in Decision Making and Access to Justice in Environmental Matters 1988.

[22] See, eg the 2006 Consultation Document of the Scottish Government at para 2.99: 'We acknowledge the special characteristics listed by Macrory and Woods and accept that they are features of environmental law. However, we are not persuaded that these features, or indeed this combination of features is unique to environmental law and it could be argued that similar statements could be made equally about other areas of law such as health, health & safety and employment none of which have specialist courts/jurisdiction.' Scottish Government, 'Strengthening And Streamlining: The Way Forward for the Enforcement of Environmental Law in Scotland' (November 2006).

[23] Environmental Law Foundation, World Wildlife Fund, and Leigh Day and Co, 'Environmental Justice' (March 2004).

[24] P Hampton, *Reducing Administrative Burdens – Effective Inspection and Enforcement* (London HM Treasury, 2005). Since 2009 he has been chairman of the Royal Bank of Scotland.

was not against regulation, nor did he want lighter sanctions. But he was concerned with evidence of the slow processes of criminal courts coupled with often apparently light fines which did not appear to reflect economic gains made from non-compliance and was unfair to legitimate businesses. He advocated quicker and tougher penalties. Nevertheless, he recognised that the whole issue of sanctions raised complex legal and institutional questions which he was unable to explore fully in his Review, and recommended that the government initiated a further review focused on sanctions for regulatory offences.

This was when I was invited to conduct the sanctions review in 2005[25], a sort of son of Hampton. In terms of policy advance, one of the real benefits of the Hampton approach was the ability to stand back and look at the regulatory system as a whole, rather than seek special pleadings for particular fields of law. Regulation involves complex areas of different specialised laws, some more technical that others, and some strongly influenced by European Community law, and others less so. There are a range of different types of enforcement agency, ranging from elected local authorities, government departments, specialised national agencies such as the Health and Safety Executive and the Environment Agency, and national bodies such as the Food Standards Agency that work in partnership with local government enforcement bodies. But despite all these complexities, there were common principles underlying the regulation of business that cut across all these specialised areas. My remit included some 61 national regulators ranging from the familiar Environment Agency, HSE, and the Food Standards Agency to more esoteric bodies such as the British Potato Council, as well as local authorities responsible for such areas as building regulations, local nuisances, and trading standards. But as with Hampton, it because clear that that when it came to the question of enforcement and sanctions, there were many similar legal techniques and approaches being adopted across the board, and many similar problems occurring with the current system.

In understanding my analysis and recommendations, it is worth emphasising what I was not doing, although it was clear from some of those submitting evidence that they hoped I would stray into these areas. It was not my task to propose any restructuring of the regulators, since this was an issue dealt with by Hampton. I did not intend to prescribe how regulators should exercise their enforcement discretion, since they were far better placed to do so. But I wished to give them more options as to the sanctions available, though this would imply acting in a rather more transparent way than was sometimes the case. Again, where cases reached the courts, it would have been inappropriate to interfere with the sentencing discretion of courts, though again I would propose giving them a richer range of more sanctioning options. I considered whether the existing legislation prescribing regulatory offences should be restructured, but rejected this as an unnecessary burdensome task – the existing offences could remain, but allow for a broader range of responses where breaches occurred. Finally, it was not my role to question the substance of the regulatory requirements – that is a matter for government.

Regulatory intervention in the business world exists because government cannot be certain that the market by itself will achieve the public policy goals it desires. Even if a substantial proportion of the market will head towards that direction, there exist a proportion who will not and thereby gain unfair competitive advantage. Like Hampton, I believe that advice and incentives are generally the first and preferable way to induce compliance. But regulatory sanctions remain essential to a regulatory system. At the very

---

[25] Macrory, *Regulatory Justice: Making Sanctions Effective* (London, Cabinet Office, 2006).

least, the existence of formal sanctions underpins regulator's authority to give advice. The availability of formal sanctions act as a deterrent, and where breaches occur they should ensure no economic gain from non-compliance, deter future breaches, and in appropriate cases impose a societal stigma on the person or company in breach.

Early on in the Review, it seemed helpful to articulate a set of principles that should underline the construction of any sanctions regime. These principles were not intended to be translated in the law or be used as the basis of a legal challenge to any particular enforcement action, but they were originally designed to help provide an underlying basis to assess our existing system and for making any proposed recommendations. Six principles were identified.[26] First, the core aim of a sanctioning system should not be to punish per se but to change behaviour. Changing behaviour does sometimes require punishment, but not always. Equally we need a system that should at a minimum ensure that any financial gain from non-compliance is eliminated. This is fair to those industries that do comply, and sends the right signals. Penalties systems need to be responsive to the particular circumstances and the character of the regulated body and allow for a proportionate response. Where there is actual harm caused by non-compliance whether to individuals or the environment, the system should, if at all possible, aim to restore harm caused. And ultimately the aim of a sanctioning system should be deter future non-compliance.

Assessing the Criminal Law

When one looks at the current system of regulatory sanctions in this country, be it environmental, trading standards or health and safety, it is remarkable how narrow the range of sanctions are. Essentially the threat of criminal sanctions. In many areas regulators possess the power to service various forms of enforcement or improvement notice, but ultimately these are backed up by the criminal law. Where a regime includes a licensing requirement – and not all do – there may be power to revoke a licence but this is rarely used. Regulators may also possess to power to seek injunctions, but again these are reserved for extreme cases.

As to the criminal law, nearly all the key offences are drafted in strict liability terms, implying that intention or recklessness is not an ingredient of the offence. The use of the criminal law in regulatory area can be traced back to first developments of regulatory systems in the nineteenth century where essentially there were no specialised agencies or tribunals, and the local magistrates' courts were prepared to take on the role as the watchdogs and sanctioners.[27] The strict liability offence was introduced as a better deterrent and out of a recognition that probably only the industries themselves understood their internal workings and it would be near impossible for a prosecutor to prove intention or recklessness. For some offences there are defences available for due diligence or some similar wording, and on standard principles it is up to the defendant to prove his defence but on the balance of probabilities. As part of the Review, Professor Andrew Simester of Nottingham University was commissioned to analyse the availability of this defence across

---

[26] Ibid, para 2.11.
[27] See Sullivan, 'Strict Liability and the European Convention on Human Rights' in Simester (ed), *Appraising Strict Liability* (Oxford, Oxford University Press, 2005) 201.

a range of regulatory offences to see if any principles emerged as to its usage. His analysis[28] revealed great inconsistency, both in the actual language of the defence used, and in the offences covered. Even within the same area of regulation, there appeared little in the way of rationale for the use of the defence. For example, the principal water pollution offences are truly strict[29], while the equivalent waste pollution offences contain a defence of due diligence.[30] As so often with law, these differences can probably only be explained by chance and historical development rather than a true underlying principle.

It was also clear from the evidence submitted to the Review that in almost every area of regulation there is a broad spectrum of offenders – from what one might describe as the truly criminal, the fly by night operators who know exactly what they are doing and are often making calculated estimates of the money to be made and the likelihood of being caught, to the poorly managed companies who have other overriding priorities, to legitimate companies who through carelessness or an oversight breach the regulations, but perhaps with serious consequences.

Against this background, the single criminal offence has to do an awful lot of work. The range of culpability is in part reflected in the enforcement discretion of the regulator, and also in the sentencing powers of the courts. But there was a real concern that we were over-using the criminal law. The criminal courts themselves are confused as to the type of law, which is being dealt with – strict liability offences are sometimes described as not criminal in the true sense. Personally, I view an intentional fly-tipper making money out of illegal waste disposal as being as much a criminal as a shoplifter or burglar, but there was a danger that by over-relying on the criminal law as the core, formal regula-tory sanction, we ended up devaluing the impact of the criminal law. And we had many examples of where magistrates' courts gave apparently low fines compared to economic gains. Equally a criminal prosecution is, rightly so, a time consuming process that is not to be undertaken lightly, and there was concerns that this could lead to under-enforcement.

The criminal processes could certainly be improved, and the Report contained a number of recommendations for so doing; for example, better training for court officials, and focusing regulatory offences on particular courts within a regional area so that both magistrates and the courts develop specialist knowledge. In England and Wales, there is heavy use of lay part-time magistrates, and it has been estimated that on average a magistrate might hear an environmental offence once every eight years. It is not surprising there that may be a lack of familiarity with the detail and nature of regulatory offences. Legal research had shown the extent to which defence counsel often make great play of the strict liability nature of the offences, and can confuse the court as to whether it is dealing with criminals or mere technical breaches.[31] But the Review also recommended sanctions that moved beyond the simple imposition of a fine. For example, where clearly defined profits had been made from the regulatory breach – such as the failure to pay a licence or registration fee – a profits order be imposed by the court. At present this may or may

---

[28] Strict Liability in UK Regulation Appendix E, 'Regulatory Justice: Sanctioning in a Post-Hampton World', Consultation Document, Macrory Review (London, Cabinet Office, May 2006) available on web only at http://webarchive.nationalarchives.gov.uk/20060731065559/http://cabinetoffice.gov.uk/regulation/reviewing_regulation/penalties/index.asp (accessed June 2014).

[29] Water Resources Act 1991, s 85.

[30] Environmental Protection Act 1990, s 33. But the defence is not available for breaches of the Waste Permitting (England and Wales) Regulations 2010, which now govern licensed waste facilities.

[31] See, eg P De Prez, 'Excuses, Excuses: The Ritual Trivialisation of Environmental Prosecutions' (2000) 12(1) *Journal of Environmental Law* 65

not be reflected in the overall fine but is sometimes difficult to tell. A profits order would simply remove the profits element of the offence in, as it were, a neutral manner, leaving the fine representing the degree of culpability the court considers to have been present.

Of current outcomes for regulatory offences 96% result in fines, and again the Review called for a more imaginative approach. When we deal with individual criminals, we have moved a long way from the courts being able to impose only fines or imprisonment, and there now exists a richer range of possibilities such as community service orders or probation designed to bring back offenders into compliance where a fine or imprisonment may be inappropriate. We should be thinking of a similar approach for businesses, and the Review recommended the development of what we described as corporate rehabilitation orders. The enforcement body would recommend to the court that the corporate rehabilitation order was appropriate, and supervision would no doubt rest with the regulator concerned. It might be especially suitable for smaller and medium sized enterprises where, say, managers are required to undergo training or carrying out audits and so on. Some Australian states have developed a Publicity Order under which the court can order a company to take out publicity adverts in the papers.[32] A company, say, that causes a local pollution incident might be required to take out an advertisement in the local press explaining why the incident took place, what the company was doing to prevent it taking place again, that it apologised, and was donating £5,000 to a local community project. Companies do not necessarily relish the prospect of such publicity, but it may be something the affected local community would find more satisfactory that the simple imposition of a fine.

Enriching the Sanctions Response

So we certainly can improve the criminal processes, but the analysis was that this was not sufficient in itself. There seemed many instances where criminal prosecution was still potentially inappropriate and heavy handed, but where a sanction was required. For instance, a company that had caused a significant water pollution incident through an act of carelessness, or a company that had failed to register under a regulatory requirement through an oversight rather than ill-intention. A formal warning might simply be an insufficient response in such circumstances, while a formal criminal prosecution might appear to be excessive. Here the concept of administrative penalties, familiar in areas of economic regulation and used in many other jurisdictions in the context of environmental regulation, seemed a positive addition to sanctioning powers.

The Review recommended that for certain minor breaches a fixed penalty system might be useful, but the key recommendation was for the use of variable penalties. A regulator would calculate the appropriate penalty using guidelines it had developed which would include negative factors such as the seriousness of the breach, its consequences, whether it was a repeat or not, but also credits to be given for cooperation, and any compensation given to victims if there were any. In the field of competition law, where such penalties can be imposed, there is an upper limit of 10% of the company's turnover[33]. That in itself

---

[32] See Abbot, 'The Regulatory Enforcement of Pollution Control Laws: The Australian Experience' (2005) 17(2) *Journal of Environmental Law* 161.
[33] See Competition Act 1998, s 36.

can lead to complications, and I recommended no upper limit, but with a proviso that if the original offence was a summary only offence, the variable penalty should not exceed that amount. The purpose of this reform was not to introduce higher financial sanctions by the back door as it were, but a different form of penalty that did not involve a criminal prosecution.

It would be possible to redraft existing offences, distinguishing those offences which gave rise to criminal prosecution and those that gave rise to an administrative penalty. That might happen in the design of future legislation. But in my view it was simpler not to reframe existing offences, but to allow each to give rise to either a criminal prosecution or an administrative penalty. It would then up to the regulator having satisfied itself as to the existence of the offence and the need for a formal sanction to determine which was then the most appropriate sanction route. The choice of sanction would be influenced by the penalty principles, and it is vitally important that perverse incentives are not created which might determine the choice of sanction. For that reason I emphasised strongly that no revenue from administrative penalties should go directly to the regulator, even if it were to be ring-fenced and used only for enforcement purposes. It was clear from much of the evidence that the concept of administrative penalties has been corrupted for many through the direct experience or, perhaps, urban myths with parking enforcement and fixed penalties.[34] Many local authorities privatised enforcement with targets and incentives for the amount of penalties imposed, and some consciously introduced a no tolerance policy, balanced, they hoped, with a generous right of appeal after the event. That seems to me to be almost entirely contrary to the risk based approach towards enforcement. Regulators are tightly squeezed for resources and if ever there was a perception that the choice was being determined by the attraction of earning extra revenue, the system and the relationship between regulator and regulatee collapses.

That said, administrative penalties have considerable advantages. I do not believe that they will lighten the demands on investigation of potential breaches by regulators. Investigation will continue to be done by criminal standards, and only later will the choice of sanctioning route be taken. In the absence of any express legislative provision, the standard of proof for an administrative penalty will be on the balance of probabilities, though some regulators have indicated that they would be happy to have a criminal standard of proof.[35] The Review received no evidence that that there was a pent up demand for prosecutions which failed on the standard of proof required. But what the new approach offered was the possibility of the regulator imposing a sanction reasonably swiftly, and should the offender not wish to appeal for the matter to be finalised equally quickly. Criminal prosecution is a lengthy and serious business, and there was a real concern that its implications can lead to under-enforcement. A good example might be where an enforcement or improvement notice is served on a business requiring compliance within a specified period. Breach of the notice is currently a criminal offence but if the company complies, with four fifths of

---

[34] As one of the trade association responses to the Consultation Document noted, Administrative Penalties 'could become a nice little earner for the Council'.

[35] In fact the implementing legislation provided that, before serving a variable or fixed penalty notice, the regulator must be satisfied beyond all reasonable doubt that the relevant offence has been committed (Regulation Enforcement and Sanctions Act 2008, ss 39 and 42). This is a higher test that in normal criminal proceedings, where the duty to comply with the criminal standard of proof rests on the court, not the prosecutor. The prosecutor, including bodies such as the Environment Agency, must comply with the Code for Crown Prosecutors, where the evidential test for bringing a prosecution is that the prosecutor is satisfied 'there is sufficient evidence to provide a realistic prospect of conviction'.

the requirements, it is unlikely that a regulator will consider it worthwhile prosecuting for the remaining parts still in non-compliance. Here the availability of an administrative penalty is likely to ensure 100% compliance.

An administrative penalty is nevertheless a serious sanction, and it is clear that businesses must have the right to appeal to an independent court or tribunal both as to the merits and as to the amount of the penalty. Some argued that the simplest method was to allow appeals back to the criminal courts. Magistrates in England and Wales do have some jurisdiction in some civil matters, and should be able to distinguish between whether they were dealing with civil or criminal matters. But the evidence we had – especially from Germany where appeals against administrative penalties go back to the criminal magistrates – was that this was not the optimum choice. The distinction between criminal and administrative penalties would become blurred, and the criminal stigma was bound to pervade. In fields such as competition or taxation law, appeals against administrative penalties go to a specialised tribunal established for the purpose. My preference was to keep the criminal and administrative routes entirely separate but by itself it was unlikely the government would relish establishing a new tribunal just for these purposes.

Enter here my unexpected alignment No 2. A few years before the Macrory Review, Sir Andrew Leggatt, a former Court of Appeal Judge, had been charged with reviewing our whole tribunal system in England and Wales. Rather than each and every tribunal being established under new primary legislation, he recommended[36] a much more flexible tribunal system where tribunals could be established as and when needed, share many facilities, and have a proper system of appeal first to an Upper Tribunal, and then to the Court of Appeal. His reforms are now being implemented under the framework of the Tribunals, Courts and Enforcement Act 2007.

The prospect of this new system made it much easier and more attractive to recommend that appeals from administrative penalties should, assuming the regulatory system in question did not contain a more appropriate specialised tribunal, go to a new regulatory tribunal within the new system. The government has accepted this recommendation. This is not yet quite the environmental tribunal that I originally envisaged, and it is likely that initially it will take the form of a regulatory tribunal handling appeals concerning administrative penalties in whatever area of law. But the system is flexible enough that it will give birth to a more specialised environmental tribunal or other specialised tribunals if the numbers of appeals warrants it. And as the system matures, it may be that government will realise that appeals concerning licences and enforcement notices and similar administrative elements of the regulatory machinery are best handled by this body.

The Report also recommended a number of other sanctioning responses which can provide appropriate approaches in certain cases. Undertakings in lieu of a formal sanction have been used in other jurisdictions notably Australia. In such a case the company concerned offers a formal undertaking laying out how it will respond to a particular breach, and the regulator may accept this rather than prosecuting or imposing a penalty. This is likely to be most suitable for a legitimate business that causes a breach through oversight or carelessness. The regulator would have to specify in its enforcement policy the sort of circumstances when it might consider an undertaking and the discretion whether or not to accept should rest with the regulator. But the advantage is that it gives an opportunity to

---

[36] Leggatt, 'Tribunals for Users – One System, One Service', Report of the Review of Tribunals (London, Department for Constitutional Affairs, 2001).

the company itself to think out how best to deal with a breach. It is not necessarily a soft option and I was very clear that any undertaking would have to be a document on public record, rather than a private arrangement between the regulator and regulated.

Finally, I should mention restorative justice. The concept has many different connotations, but essentially reflects a need to involve victims of crimes in the process of sanctioning to a far greater extent that happens at present. It is currently being used extensively in England and Wales in the context of juvenile crime,[37] and results are generally positive.[38] The Review suggested that some of the concepts and approaches ideas might be transferred to the area of business regulation. There are examples in other jurisdictions where it has proved extremely effective. A well reported case in Australia involved the financial sector and the mis-selling of insurance policies. The company concerned could have been prosecuted, but as an alternative the regulator, the Trade Practices Commissioner, facilitated meetings with senior managers and the victims of those who has been pressurised by their salesmen. The victims were mostly poor aboriginals in remote communities, and apparently the meetings had a powerful effect on the CEO and top management who were based in Sydney. Some 80 employees were sacked, new training procedures introduced, a compensation package agreed, and new company policies designed to ensure it never happened again. It is certainly possible to think of cases where this might be valuable in the context of regulatory breaches, though with the environment it may of course be less easy to identify clear victims. The Review recommended that pilot schemes be undertaken and monitored.

The underlying thrust of the report is therefore to increase the range of sanctioning options available to a regulator. If and when regulators have access to these powers it is difficult to predict the pattern of sanctions that will be employed in the future. I would suspect that the number of criminal prosecutions will fall and be largely reserved for the truly egregious, where there is evidence of clear intent or recklessness, or the repeat offender. For legitimate businesses who breach through negligence or oversights but where the seriousness demands more than a warning letter, we will see much greater use of administrative penalties, and/or undertakings. But there will never be a clear divide. There may be circumstances where, say, a small illegal operator seems undeterred by criminal convictions and where the regulator judges that the rapid imposition of a large financial penalty will have a greater effect in changing behaviour. Alternatively, the results of an accident caused by a legitimate operator may be so serious that the public demand the stigma of a criminal prosecution rather than an administrative sanction, however large.

Nevertheless, given the greater discretionary powers being given to regulators, an important element of my report concerns issues of governance. The Cabinet Office has already indicated that regulators should not have access to these powers unless they can demonstrate that they are adopting a risk based approach to regulatory enforcement. My recommendations concerning governance echo and develop this approach. All regulators should have a published enforcement policy which gives signals as to how it will approach enforcement and the likely sanctions routes it will adopt – but not drafted in such absolute terms as to tie the regulator's hands in any particular case. Of the 61 national regulators within my review only 17 had such a published policy. New enforcement policies will

---

[37] See Home Office, 'Restorative Justice: the Government's Strategy' (London, Home Office, 2003).

[38] See, eg Hoyle et al, 'Proceed with Caution: An Evaluation of the Thames Valley Police Initiative in Restorative Cautioning' (Joseph Rowntree Foundation, 2002). More generally see A von Hirsch et al (eds), *Restorative Justice and Criminal Justice: Competing or Reconcilable Paradigms?* (Oxford, Hart Publishing, 2003).

have to reflect the new range of sanctions available, and indicate, say, the sort of circum-stances in which the regulator is likely to impose an administrative penalty or consider an undertaking from the business concerned. Regulators should publish annual figures of the different types of enforcement actions they take, so that one can monitor trends as the use of the powers develop. That is the outputs. But equally important is the measurement of outcomes. If, say, the number of water pollution prosecutions drop and the number of administrative penalties rise, that does not greatly concern me provided that the number of serious water incidents has dropped during the same period or at least not increased. I appreciate that robust outcome measurements are easier in some areas of environmental protection than others, but nevertheless it is important they are developed.

As I mentioned, one of the values of the original Hampton approach and the task I was given was that it required one to cut across different regulatory systems. During my Review, we had a large number of meetings where regulators from quite different fields including the financial sector were able to share experiences and it was clear this was a valuable forum for all concerned. I therefore recommended that the Cabinet Office con-tinue to facilitate meetings which will be especially important as regulators begin to think about issues such as constructing enforcement policies to reflect new sanction options or developing penalty calculation schemes. On a similar cross-cutting theme, I recognised that departmental parliamentary select committees provide a useful accountability system for regulators falling within the particular departments accountable to each committee. But again it would be valuable if there were also a cross-cutting parliamentary committee concerned with regulators and regulatory techniques so that one could conduct robust comparative inquiries across different fields of regulations.

The government accepted all the recommendations in the Macrory Review and the Regulatory Enforcement and Sanctions Bill[39] will initially take forward the proposals for administrative penalties and undertakings. Regulators and Departments will not be forced to acquire these new sanctioning tools, and some are already indicating that they are satisfied with the effectiveness of their existing powers. I accept that this may be the case, but I think that in future the burden will be very much on regulators to demon-strate why a richer range of legal responses. as used by many other regulators both in this country and in other jurisdictions, should not be available in their field. Anyone involved in government reviews will know that there is many a slip between acceptance and imple-mentation. But I am confident that we are at the foothills of what will eventually be a significant change in the way we approach the enforcement of environmental and other areas regulation – and in the environmental field at least one that will help to secure better environmental outcomes.

---

[39] Announced by the Prime Minister in his Legislative Programme Statement, 11 July 2007 Now the Regulatory Enforcement and Sanctions Act 2008.

2

Regulatory Justice – Making Sanctions Effective[1] (2006)

Executive Summary

Introduction

E.1 I have looked at sanctioning regimes and penalty powers in detail over the last twelve months with the aim of identifying a set of fit for purpose sanctioning tools that can be used effectively, fairly and proportionately by regulators and those enforcing regulations in situations of regulatory non-compliance. I have considered the work of 56 national regulators and 468 local authorities.

E.2 I have published two previous reports as part of this review, a discussion paper, incorporating a call for evidence, which was published in December 2005 and a consultation document laying out options for reform in May 2006.[2] Both papers introduced many sanctioning options for consideration including administrative sanctions, venues for hearing regulatory cases, as well as alternative sanctions to be used by the judiciary such as reputation related sanctions or corporate rehabilitation, and the role for restorative justice. I present my final conclusions on these and other sanctioning tools in this report.

E.3 The regulators within the scope of the review (see paragraph 1.07) carry out more than 3.6m enforcement actions each year. These regulators carry out at least 2.8m inspections per year, hand out at least 400,000 warning letters, 3,400 formal cautions, 145,000 statutory notices and take forward at least 25,000 prosecutions.[3] These enforcement actions are taken across businesses of all sizes often with small businesses and legitimate businesses feeling more of a regulatory burden than larger companies, or those firms engaged in rogue trading activity. This strikes me as counterintuitive, and repeat offenders as well as those that have an intentional disregard for the law should, under a risk based system, face tough sanctions.

E.4 I am therefore recommending that Government should consider:

[1] R Macrory, *Regulatory Justice: Making Sanctions Effective* (London, Cabinet Office, 2006) (Macrory Review).
[2] R Macrory, 'Regulatory Justice: Sanctioning in a Post-Hampton World', December 2005 and May 2006.
[3] Data submitted to Macrory Review, September 2006.

- Examining the way in which it formulates criminal offences relating to regulatory non-compliance;
- Ensuring that regulators have regard to six Penalties Principles and seven characteristics when enforcing regulations;
- Ways in which to make sentencing in the criminal courts more effective;
- Introducing schemes of Fixed and Variable Monetary Administrative Penalties, available to those regulators who are Hampton compliant, with an appeal to an independent tribunal rather than the criminal courts;
- Strengthening the system of Statutory Notices;
- Introducing pilot schemes involving Restorative Justice techniques; and
- Introducing alternative sentencing options in the criminal courts for cases related to regulatory non-compliance.

E.5   The current regulatory sanctioning system, including both criminal sanctions and non-criminal sanctions, is a system that has developed over time and as such there are variations between the powers and practices among regulators. The reforms the review proposes are designed to bring consistency into the sanctioning toolkits across the system, reflecting the risk based approach to regulation and the broader regulatory reform agenda. These proposals will provide regulators and industry with greater flexibility whilst ensuring that regulatory outcomes, such as increased compliance, are not compromised.

E.6   The Hampton Review found that penalty regimes are cumbersome and ineffective.[4] I have taken forward Philip's findings and have considered options that could add to the regulators' enforcement toolbox, broadening the flexibility available to both regulators and the judiciary to better meet regulatory objectives and improve compliance. These options would also benefit industry, by providing a transparent system with appropriate sanctions that would aim to get firms back into compliance, ensure future compliance, provide a level playing field for business and enable regulators to pursue offenders who flout the law in a more effective manner.

Problems with the Current System of Regulatory Sanctions

E.7   Regulatory sanctions are an essential feature of a regulatory enforcement toolkit and are central to achieving compliance by signalling the threat of a punishment for firms that have offended. Sanctions demonstrate that non-compliance will not be tolerated and that there will be a reprimand or consequence that will put the violator in a worse position than those entities that complied with their regulatory obligations on time.

E.8   It is important for Government to ensure that regulators have a flexible and proportionate sanctioning toolkit which also ensures the protection of workers, consumers and the environment. That toolkit should provide appropriate options to handle the regulatory needs of legitimate business as well as those businesses that intentionally and knowingly fail to comply with regulatory obligations on time.

---

[4] P Hampton, *Reducing Administrative Burdens: Effective Inspection and Enforcement* (London, HM Treasury, March 2005).

E.9   Evidence submitted to the review suggests that many regulators are heavily reliant on one tool, namely criminal prosecution, as the main sanction should industry or individuals be unwilling or unable to follow advice and comply with legal obligations. Criminal prosecution may not be, in all circumstances, the most appropriate sanction to ensure that non-compliance is addressed, any damage caused is remedied or behaviour is changed. The availability of other more flexible and risk based tools may result in achieving better regulatory outcomes.

E.10   Many of the review's recommendations are a continuation of current Government proposals and reforms. The Home Office is exploring the role of restorative justice in areas such as corporate manslaughter and youth offending; whilst Defra is currently consulting on the introduction of administrative penalties in the area of fishing and marine activities.

E.11   Whilst the UK has a leading position in the area of regulatory reform and we have made advances in the development of sanctioning regimes in some areas of regulation, little has been done to evolve the sanctioning toolkit across all regulatory bodies. Across the board, we have failed to keep pace with the innovations being introduced in other leading OECD nations such as Australia and Canada, countries which share some of our legal tradition. The review believes that the UK must address this area in order to ensure that the Government's better regulation agenda, including the recommendations of the Hampton Review and the Better Regulation Task Force's report *Less is More*, is realised.[5]

My Recommendations

E.12   The review has considered a broad spectrum of sanctioning tools, ranging from persuasive methods, such as warning letters or the use of informal, pragmatic means like advice and persuasion, to criminal prosecution at the top end of the enforcement pyramid [see annex A]. The review has also considered the major motivations for non-compliance and I have recommended that suitable sanctioning options should be available to allow regulators to deal appropriately with each type of offender, including the rogue trading element present in some industries.

E.13   My recommendations are discussed throughout this document and summarised in chapter six. They include recommendations around the following areas:

- A list of Penalties Principles and a framework for regulatory sanctioning;
- The role of the criminal prosecution as a regulatory sanction;
- The role of Monetary Administrative Penalties;
- Statutory Notices and other innovations such as Enforceable Undertakings and Undertakings Plus;
- The role of Restorative Justice in regulatory non-compliance; and
- Alternative sentencing options that could be available in criminal courts.

E.14   Chapter one outlines the role of regulatory sanctions within the regulatory system setting out the context and scope of my review. Chapter two presents the underlying principles relating to regulatory sanctions, their purpose and function as well as

---

[5] Better Regulation Task Force, 'Less is More' (March 2005).

the principles themselves. Chapters three and four set out the tools that I believe should be available in an expanded regulatory enforcement toolkit. This includes recommendations on Monetary Administrative Penalties, Statutory Notices, restorative justice and alternative sanctions within a criminal setting. I present some case studies to give examples of the way in which these tools could be used. Chapter five makes recommendations around issues of transparency and accountability for regulators and enforcers who use the enforcement toolkit. Finally, chapter six summarises all of my recommendations.

The Review's Work

E.15   The Penalties Review, as part of the implementation of the Hampton Report, was commissioned by the Chancellor of the Duchy of Lancaster in September 2005, and its terms of reference are set out in 'Regulatory Justice: Sanctioning in a post-Hampton World', December 2005. Annex B contains more details.

Publications

E.16   The review published a discussion paper, 'Regulatory Justice: Sanctioning in a post-Hampton World', in December 2005 with a corresponding call for evidence.

E.17   The review published a consultation document, 'Regulatory Justice: Sanctioning in a post-Hampton World', with specific policy proposals for consideration in May 2006.

E.18   Following the publication of the interim report, the review team has been consulting extensively with key stakeholders and experts with a focus on the preparation of this final report.

Conclusion

E.19   The reforms suggested by this review are not intended to transform sanctioning systems overnight, but to bring into them the flexibility, efficiencies and responsiveness that can facilitate the full implementation of the Hampton agenda. This will result in better deterrence options for regulators, better compliance for business and better outcomes for the public.

Box E1 List of Recommendations

1.   I recommend that the Government initiate a review of the drafting and formulation of criminal offences relating to regulatory non-compliance.

2.   I recommend that in designing the appropriate sanctioning regimes for regulatory non-compliance, regulators should have regard to the following six Penalties Principles and seven characteristics.

Six Penalties Principles

A sanction should:

1. Aim to change the behaviour of the offender;
2. Aim to eliminate any financial gain or benefit from non-compliance;
3. Be responsive and consider what is appropriate for the particular offender and regulatory issue, which can include punishment and the public stigma that should be associated with a criminal conviction;
4. Be proportionate to the nature of the offence and the harm caused;
5. Aim to restore the harm caused by regulatory non-compliance, where appropriate; and
6. Aim to deter future non-compliance

Seven Characteristics

Regulators should:

1. Publish an enforcement policy;
2. Measure outcomes not just outputs;
3. Justify their choice of enforcement actions year on year to stakeholders, Ministers and Parliament;
4. Follow-up enforcement actions where appropriate;
5. Enforce in a transparent manner;
6. Be transparent in the way in which they apply and determine administrative penalties; and
7. Avoid perverse incentives that might influence the choice of sanctioning response.

3.   I recommend that in order to increase the effectiveness of criminal courts for regulatory offences, the following actions should be implemented:

- Prosecutions in particular regulatory fields be heard in designated Magistrates' Courts within jurisdictional areas, where appropriate; and
- Regulators provide specialist training for prosecutors and discuss with the Judicial Studies Board (JSB) contributing to the training of the judiciary and justices' clerks.

4.   I recommend that with regards to Monetary Administrative Penalties:

- Government should consider introducing schemes for Fixed and Variable Monetary Administrative Penalties, for regulators and enforcers of regulations, who are compliant with the Hampton and Macrory Principles and characteristics. This can include national regulators as well as local regulatory partners;
- Appeals concerning the imposition of an administrative penalty be heard by a Regulatory Tribunal, rather than the criminal courts;
- Fine maxima for Fixed Monetary Administrative Penalties (FMAP) schemes should be set out and not exceed level five on the standard scale; and
- There should be no fine maxima for Variable Monetary Administrative Penalties (VMAPs).

5.   I recommend that for an improved system of Statutory Notices:

- Government should consider using Statutory Notices as part of an expanded sanctioning toolkit to secure compliance beyond the regulatory areas in which they are currently in use;

- Regulators should sytematically follow-up Statutory Notices using a risk based approach including an element of randomised follow-up;
- In dealing with the offence of failing to comply with a Statutory Notice, regulators should have access to administrative financial penalties as an alternative to criminal prosecution. This power should be extended by legislative amendment to existing schemes of Statutory Notices; and
- Government should consider whether appeals against Statutory Notices should be routed through the Regulatory Tribunal rather than the criminal courts.

6.   I recommend that the Government should consider introducing Enforceable Undertakings and Undertakings Plus (a combination of an Enforceable Undertaking with an administrative financial penalty) as an alternative to a criminal prosecution or the imposition of VMAPs for regulators that are compliant with the Hampton and Macrory Principles and characteristics.

7.   I recommend that Government should consider introducing pilot schemes involving the use of Restorative Justice (RJ) techniques in addressing cases of regulatory non-compliance. This might include RJ:

- as a pre-court diversion;
- instead of a Monetary Administrative Penalty; and
- within the criminal justice system – as both a pre or post sentencing option.

8.   I recommend that the Government consider introducing the following alternative sentencing in criminal courts:

- Profit Order – Where the profits made from regulatory non-compliance are clear, the criminal courts have access to Profit Orders, requiring the payment of such profits, distinct from any fine that the court may impose;
- Corporate Rehabilitation Order – In sentencing a business for regulatory non-compliance, criminal courts have on application by the prosecutor, access to a Corporate Rehabilitation Orders (CRO) in addition to or in place of any fine that may be imposed; and
- Publicity Order – In sentencing a business for regulatory non-compliance, criminal courts have the power to impose a Publicity Order, in addition to or in place of any other sentence.

9.   I recommend that to ensure improved transparency and accountability:

- The Better Regulation Executive should facilitate a working group of regulators and sponsoring departments to share best practice in enforcement approaches, the application of sanction options, development of outcome measures and transparency in reporting. Regulators and sponsoring departments should work with the Executive to include outcome measures as part of their overall framework of performance management; and
- Publish Enforcement Activities – Each regulator should publish a list on a regular basis of its completed enforcement actions and against whom such actions have been taken.

I. The Role and Importance of Sanctions within the Regulatory System

This chapter sets out the importance of sanctions in a modern regulatory system and discusses the scope and context of my review as well as an assessment of the current sanctioning system.

This review was set up following recommendation eight of the Hampton Review. Hampton set out in his principles:

- No inspection should take place without a reason;
- Businesses should not have to give unnecessary information, nor give the same piece of information twice;
- Regulators should provide authoritative, accessible advice easily and cheaply; and
- The few businesses that persistently break regulations should be identified quickly and face proportionate and meaningful sanctions.

This review has considered the last of these principles with a view to ensuring that a level playing field is created for all businesses because there is no financial gain from failing to comply. In such a risk based system most breaches will face penalties that are quicker and easier to apply while there will be tougher penalties for rogue businesses which persistently break the rules.

Introduction

1.1   This review was established to consider appropriate sanctions that could become part of an extended enforcement toolkit available to regulators and Government departments. This would be in addition to the existing sanctions of criminal prosecution and Statutory Notices set out in the relevant regulatory legislation.

1.2   This chapter gives some background on the work of the review and the sanctioning regimes I have been investigating.

The Macrory Review is Integral to the Hampton Agenda

1.3   Philip Hampton in his report, 'Reducing Administrative Burdens: Effective Inspection and Enforcement', published in March 2005, recommended that the Government establish a comprehensive review of regulators' penalty regimes.[6] Following this recommendation, the Macrory Review was established under my leadership in September 2005.

1.4   The Hampton report identified the cumulative burden of regulation – multiple inspections and overlapping data requirements as well as inconsistent practice and decision making between and within regulators – as the main burden faced by the regulated community. Philip Hampton, in his recommendations, concluded that regulators should use risk assessment as an essential means of directing resources where they can have the maximum impact on outcomes. He went on to say that

---

[6] Hampton, above n 4, Recommendation 8.

by eliminating unnecessary inspections, more resources should be directed at compliance advice to the regulated community. Lastly, he suggested Government develop better practice to reduce the administrative burden.

1.5   The Hampton Review also found that regulatory penalty regimes can be cumbersome and ineffective. The following features were identified as shortcomings:

- Penalties handed down by courts are not seen as an adequate deterrent to regulatory non-compliance as the level of financial penalty can often fail to reflect the financial gain of non-compliance with regulatory obligations; and

- The range of enforcement tools available to many regulators is limited, giving rise to disproportionate use of criminal sanctions, which can be a costly, time-consuming and slow process.

1.6   I have taken forward Philip's findings and I am recommending a suite of sanctions that could be added to the regulators' enforcement toolbox, broadening the flexibility available to regulators, the judiciary and business to better meet regulatory objectives, improve compliance and ensure a level playing-field for all.

Scope

1.7   In this report, references to 'the regulators' refer only to those regulators that are within the scope of this review as mentioned at the start of Annex C. This includes regulatory bodies at both national and local level. Over 60,000 people work for over 650 regulatory bodies within the scope of my review and have a combined budget of approximately £4 billion.[7]

1.8   The division of responsibility between national and local bodies varies. In certain areas, such as environmental regimes, responsibilities are split between national and local regulators; in the area of food standards, a national agency sets standards and Local Authorities enforce them; while in the area of health and safety, Local Authorities enforce regulation on some businesses and national regulators enforce the regulations on other businesses.

1.9   My review did not examine regulators that are the responsibility of the devolved administrations in Scotland, Wales and Northern Ireland, but did consider the operation of UK wide regulators there. Many of the underlying principles, though, are likely to be applicable within the devolved administrations. Where I have referred to penalties available to economic regulators, such as the Financial Services Authority, this is solely for the purposes of comparison. Specific terms of reference for the review are presented in more detail in Annex B.

1.10   In my review I have concentrated on the sanctioning tools available to regulators. The process by which regulatory legislation is made and enforced is not strictly within the scope of the review and does not feature in my recommendations, although it has been commented on in various places in this report. Nor was it within my remit to consider the actual substance of the regulatory legislation, though it is evident that sensibly drafted and appropriate substantive law is vital to the effectiveness of any regulatory system.

[7] Ibid, Recommendation 6, 12–13.

The Role of Sanctions

1.11   The focus of my concern is with regulations that apply to businesses, whether individuals, partnerships, or companies, rather than to individual householders or consumers. Almost by definition regulations are introduced where Government cannot be confident that the whole of the sector covered will voluntarily comply with the standards or achieve desired outcomes. I accept, as did the Hampton report, that advice and incentives should play a key role in ensuring regulatory compliance, and should normally be the first response of regulators. Nevertheless, an effective sanction regime plays an equally vital role in a successful regulatory regime. It underpins the regulator's advisory functions, and its very existence will often act as an inducement to compliance without the need to invoke the formal sanctions.

1.12   Where regulatory non-compliance occurs, sanctions can ensure that businesses that have saved costs by non-compliance do not gain an unfair advantage over businesses that are fully compliant. Where breaches result in damage or other costs to society, sanctions can assist in ensuring that those in breach provide proper recompense. Sanctions can equally represent a societal condemnation of the regulatory breach, acting as a deterrent to the sanctioned business against future breaches, and sending a wider message to the regulated sector.

My Assessment of the Current System

1.13   As part of my study to develop recommendations for an effective and proportionate sanctioning system, I have assessed the current regulatory sanctioning regimes in two prior publications.[8] Those documents highlight some of my findings in respect of the perceived shortcomings of the current system, which I summarise in the section below.

Heavy Reliance on Criminal Sanctions

1.14   Regulators have a range of responses to regulatory breaches, including issuing warning letters, giving advice, and serving various forms of Statutory Notices. But I found that ultimately there is heavy reliance on criminal sanctions as a formal response to regulatory non-compliance. I suggest that, although criminal sanctions are in some circumstances an effective tool, too heavy reliance on criminal sanctions in a regulatory system can be ineffective for the following reasons:

- Criminal sanctions currently are often an insufficient deterrent to the 'truly' criminal or rogue operators, since the financial sanctions imposed in some criminal cases are not considered to be a sufficient deterrent or punishment. Where businesses (as opposed to individuals) are prosecuted, criminal courts have a limited range of sanctioning options available beyond a fine, and must take into account the financial means of business concerned in setting a fine;

- In instances where there has been no intent or wilfulness relating to regulatory non-

---

[8] Macrory, above n 2.

compliance a criminal prosecution may be a disproportionate response, although a formal sanction rather than simply advice or a warning, may still be appropriate and justified. However, regulators may not have any alternative available to them in their toolkit and so must prosecute, even where a different type of sanction may be more effective;

- Heavy reliance on criminal sanctions leads to some non-compliance not being addressed at all. Criminal sanctions are costly and time-consuming for both businesses and regulators. In many instances, although non-compliance has occurred, the cost or expense of bringing criminal proceedings deters regulators from using their limited resources to take action. This creates what has come to be known as a *compliance deficit*;
- Criminal convictions for regulatory non-compliance have lost their stigma, as in some industries being prosecuted is regarded as part of the business cycle. This may be because both strict liability offences committed by legitimate business, and the deliberate flouting of the law by rogues is prosecuted in the same manner with little differentiation between these two types of offender; and
- Since the focus of criminal proceedings is on the offence and the offender, the wider impact of the offence on the victim may not be fully explored. There has been a limited

Table 1.1 Range of Sanctions Used by Some Regulators

	Inspections Carried Out	Warning Letters	Formal Cautions	Statutory Notices	Prosecutions	Fixed Penalties
Environmental Health[1]	2,029,793	232,023	*	105,681	*	
Trading Standards and related services[2]	203,697	40,806	2,486		4,692	
Environment Agency[3]	140,528		413	515	883	
Health and Safety Executive[4]	59,865			8,445	712	
Companies House[5]					7,570	190,945
Vehicle and Operator Services Agency[6]	134,164	1,078		16,666	10,642	
Meat Hygiene Service[7]		6,285	24	2,053	17	
Forestry Commission[8]	12,744	1,695		20	17	

Sources: CIPFA Trading Standards Statistics 2004, CIPFA Environmental Health Statistics 2003-04, Environment Agency, Health and Safety Executive, Companies House, Department for Transport, Rural Payments Agency, Meat Hygiene Service, and The Forestry Commission.
*Figures for Environmental Health Formal Cautions and Court summons for 2003/04 was 11,704 and is only available as an aggregate figure.
[1] 2003/04 figures, England and Wales only. Includes figures for Pest Control services.
[2] 2004 figures, apart from 'Inspections carried out' which is taken from 2003.
[3] 2005 figures.
[4] 2004/05 figures.
[5] 2004/05 figures.
[6] 2004/05 figures.
[7] 2004/05 figures apart from warning letters that relates to the calendar year 2004.
[8] 2005/06 figures.

evolution of the rights and needs of victims in the area of regulatory non-compliance which I have explored in more detail in my consultation paper.[9]

Limited Range of Enforcement Tools

1.15   Over the course of my review, I have received evidence and submissions from many stakeholders including regulators, businesses, academics and many others that have supported my view that regulators have a limited range of enforcement sanctions within their toolkits.

Defra supports the widely held view, espoused also in Hampton, that the current system is not sufficiently responsive, targeted and sensitive to ensure that appropriate penalties are applied in all cases. To this end, the department accepts that there is room for improvement but restates its basic tenet that a robust penalties framework should encompass different types and levels of sanctions depending on the nature, frequency and seriousness of non-compliance.

Source: Response from Defra to the Macrory Review, February 2006

1.16   Criminal prosecutions remain the primary formal sanction available to most regulators. While this sanction is appropriate in many cases, the time, expense, moral condemnation and criminal record involved may not be appropriate for all breaches of regulatory obligations and is burdensome to both the regulator and business. While the most serious offences merit criminal prosecution, it may not be an appropriate route in achieving a change in behaviour and improving outcomes for a large number of businesses where the non-compliance is not truly criminal in its intention.

1.17   Table 1.2 sets out the sanctions that regulators are currently able to access through their relevant legislation. The sanctions that the majority of regulators have access to are either a warning letter at the informal end of the spectrum or a criminal prosecution at the other. In some cases, they have access to civil injunctions. Most regulators have limited access to administrative penalties and other intermediate sanctions as a further step before escalating to prosecution or licence suspension or withdrawal as indicated in the table.

Financial Penalties Sending the Wrong Signal

1.18   Evidence presented to me over the course of the review has demonstrated that, in some instances, the fines handed down in court often do not reflect the financial gain a firm may have made by failing to comply with an obligation. This means that these penalties do not act as a deterrent and, in effect, give businesses an incentive to continue to fail to comply in return for a profit. In some cases fines do not fully reflect the harm done to society.

1.19   These apparently low financial penalties could be seen as an acceptable risk by businesses that have chosen to be deliberately non-compliant. In these instances it

---

[9] Ibid; see chapter five of my interim report.

Table 1.2 Mapping of Regulators' Enforcement Tools

	Financial Services Authority[a]	Health Safety Executive	Food Standards Agency	Environment Agency[b]	Competition House[c]	Charity Commission[d]	Defra Core Department Regulators[e]
Criminal prosecution	•	•	•	•	•	•	•
Licence revocation	•	•	•	•	N/A	N/A	•
Licence suspension		•	•	•	N/A	N/A	•
Admin financial penalty	•						
Fixed admin financial penalty				•	•		
Statutory Notices		•	•	•	•	•	•
Warning letter	•	•	•	•	•	•	•
Persuasion	•	•	•	•	•	•	•

Source: Responses from regulators to the Macrory Review, February 2006
[a] Financial Services and Markets Act 2000, sections 126 and 127 for warning and decision notices and Part XXV, sections 380 and 382 for injunctions and restitution orders. The FSA does not provide for the use of Statutory Notices such as enforcement notices which require compliance on the part of a firm or a person, but the FSA does issue warning notices, decision notices and final notices. The FSA has access to other enforcement options, which are not in the table, and can for example seek injunctions, make restitution orders and make prohibition orders against persons who are not fit and proper.
[b] Many regulators including the Environment Agency can issue Cautions. These are formal written admissions of guilt which obviate the need for a prosecution.
[c] Companies House does not operate a licence regime. Therefore the licence suspension and licence revocation sanctions are not applicable.
[d] The Charity Commission does not operate a licence regime. Therefore the licence suspension and licence revocation sanctions are not applicable.
[e] Defra core departmental regulators include regulators operating in the areas of Environmental Impact Assessment (uncultivated land), Cattle Identification Scheme, Horticulture (classification of imported fruit and vegetables), Pesticides Safety, Waste Management, and Fisheries.

Box 1.1 Examples of fines that do not reflect the inancial benefit or seriousness of the offence (environment regulation)

- An Oxfordshire man was fined £30,000 for abandoning 184 drums of toxic waste. The man received £58,000 for disposing of the material, and the Waste Authorities had costs of £167,000 to incinerate the waste properly.
- A fine of £25,000 was handed down to a small waste disposal company which was operating without a licence. The company saved £250,000 by operating illegally over a 2 year period.

Source: Examples submitted to the Macrory Review by the Environment Agency, March 2006

---

might be assumed that financial penalties in the current system are failing to achieve even the most basic objectives of an effective sanctioning regime.

1.20　If regulators are pursuing, as they should, a risk based compliance orientated enforcement strategy, prosecution will be a sanction applied for the most serious cases of regulatory non-compliance. When prosecutions do take place, it is reasonable to assume that they are for the most serious offences and offenders. Sentencing should also reflect this level of seriousness and be a strong deterrent signal for others in the regulated community.

1.21　This lack of an effective deterrent compromises the effectiveness of the regulatory relationship. Without credible and meaningful sanctions, regulators are forced to pursue a more burdensome and bureaucratic enforcement policy. Regulators are deterring non-compliance through their inspection activities. Effective sanctioning is an important signal in achieving deterrence. If criminal prosecutions sent out a strong signal of deterrence, then regulators would be able to impose less onerous burdens on legitimate business by conducting fewer inspections. However, currently legitimate businesses see their unscrupulous competitors cut corners, and gain competitive advantage, without facing serious financial or other consequences.

1.22　Information from my call for evidence suggests that the average fines handed down by magistrates are relatively low, when compared to the fine maxima available. As set out in Table 1.3 below, average fines for businesses ranged from as little as £488 to £6,855. In environmental and health and safety cases, the average fines are in the range of £5,000 to £7,000. This does indicate that the deterrent effect of fines is likely to be limited for all but the smallest businesses.

1.23　The level of fines seen in criminal courts tend to be small in relation to the size and financial position of large businesses. For example, the largest fine handed down to date for a health and safety offence is £15 million imposed against Transco (for breaches of regulations that resulted in the death of four members of the same family in a gas explosion). The financial penalty, while significant in absolute terms, represented five percent of after-tax profits and less than one percent of annual revenues for the company.[10] This shows that even large fines can be absorbed by companies and may not carry the necessary deterrent effect or motivate a change in a firm's behaviour although Transco began an accelerated programme of pipe replacement as an outcome of the incident and did change its behaviour.

1.24　There is also evidence that for some offences the average fines are considerably below the maximum available fine. For example, the average fine for non-compliance with the Trade Descriptions Act 1968 was £1,524 against a maximum fine available in the legislation of £5,000. Offences under the Health and Safety at Work etc. Act 1974 led to fines of £6,014 on average, against a maximum fine up to £20,000 depending on the offence.[11] Finally, the maximum penalty available in a magistrates' court for non-compliance with controls on the transport of waste is currently £5,000, but the average fine is just £530.[12] These are only a few examples and are not meant to suggest that courts should always aim for the maximum penalty available. I do

---

[10] *Transco v HSE* August 2005, Edinburgh High Court.
[11] Data from the DCA, selected offences in magistrates' courts during 2004.
[12] Average fine awarded by the magistrates' courts in the 156 successful prosecutions taken in 2003.

Table 1.3 Level of Financial Penalties 2004/2005

Health and Safety Executive[a]	1,267	999	£6,855[b]
Environment Agency[c]	887	876	£5,007
British Potato Council[d]	246	28	£488
Companies House	5,867	2,944	N/A
Financial Services Authority[e]	6	6	£75,500
Pesticide Safety Directorate	3	1	£1,800
Food Standards Agency	570	458	N/A

Source: Data submitted by regulators to the Macrory Review, Spring 2006.
[a] Figures for 2005.
[b] Sentencing handed down in courts reflects many factors including the ability to pay (JSB Adult Court Bench Book, pg 33). There is generally a band within which some fines will be small and others will be large. This figure excludes the convictions with fines of over £100,000. Of those excluded, there was one fine of £2,000,000; three fines at £300,000 or above; and thirteen fines of between £100,000 and £300,000. If these seventeen convictions were included, the average for 2004/05 rises to £12,642.
[c] Figures for 2005.
[d] Figures for 2003/2005. Of those businesses who receive a notification for summons, most decided to provide the requested information before the cases actually proceeded to Court. All cases that proceeded to court resulted in a successful conviction.
[e] Figures since 2000, under the Financial Services and Markets Act 2000.

believe, though, that these examples are indicative of the level of fines currently handed down by the criminal courts for particular offences.

Previous Comments on Low Financial Penalties

1.25   I am not the first person to recognise that financial penalties handed down in the criminal courts may not be sending a strong deterrence signal.

1.26   The Government has previously recognised that in the area of health and safety, courts are in need of greater sentencing power and that there is scope for extending maximum fines available in the health and safety legislation.[13]

1.27   In 2004, the House of Commons Environmental Audit Committee found, in its sixth report, that the level of sentences given in courts for environmental crimes is too low and recommended the introduction of alternative sentencing powers such as adverse publicity orders and environmental service orders.[14] In its response, the Government noted the Committee's concerns and agreed that imaginative methods of dealing with offenders are necessary.[15] In addition to my report, new approaches have been considered by the Defra-led Review of Enforcement in Environmental Regulation, which was tasked with identifying obstacles to effective environmental enforcement

---

[13] Department for Environment Transport and Regions, 'Revitalising Health and Safety' (June 2000) 24.
[14] House of Commons Environmental Audit Committee Sixth Report, 'Environmental Crime and the Court' (2004) Introduction, para 15, available at www.publications.parliament.uk/pa/cm200304/cmselect/cmenvaud/126/12604.htm.
[15] http://www.publications.parliament.uk/pa/cm200304/cmselect/cmenvaud/cmenvaud.htm.

and ways to overcome them. The report from the environmental review includes the suggestion that variable administrative penalties, financial and non-financial, would have the potential to create stronger incentives for compliance in a new balance with criminal prosecution. The report also sets out ideas for relating environmental penalties more transparently to the purposes of enforcement: removing financial gain from non-compliance; making damage good; making restitution to adversely affected communities; and exposing culpability where it exists.[16]

1.28 The academic literature on penalties often reaches similar conclusions. For example, a study of penalties for environmental offences found that, with the exception of the Netherlands, fines were generally low in the European Union. Low judicial and public awareness of the harmful consequences of pollution were among the reasons for this, in addition to a lack of familiarity with environmental law on the part of the judiciary.[17]

1.29 I acknowledge that the financial circumstances of each firm and their ability or means to pay a fine must be taken into account by a court in determining the appropriate financial penalty. However, the low level of average financial penalties indicates that the deterrent effect of these penalties will be less meaningful for all but the smallest of businesses.

Resolution of Criminal Cases Takes Time and Money

1.30 Criminal prosecutions are time and resource intensive for business and for regulators. It may be that they are currently used in the absence of other formal sanctions, rather than because they are an appropriate response. For instance, the long and resource intensive process of taking a criminal prosecution through court may seem inappropriate for a company that is being prosecuted for a strict liability offence. The Environment Agency reported that, in its experience, cases take an average of seven months from discovery of non-compliance to when proceedings are commenced. The Health and Safety Executive (HSE) estimated that, from offence to approval of prosecution, about 20 per cent of cases are approved for prosecution within three months of the offence date, and by 12 months from the offence date four out of five cases will have been approved for prosecution.

1.31 For a business this means that, although the time spent preparing and investigating a case is necessary, a rectified regulatory non-compliance can still be an issue several months on. Industry and the regulator may prefer a timelier and less costly resolution to appropriate cases of regulatory non-compliance as the delay and uncertainty of prosecution is burdensome for both.

1.32 Furthermore, regulators may not choose to pursue cases for prosecution because of the low expected outcome. Enforcers may not pursue cases because the level of penalty is not seen to justify the time, effort and resources that will need to be deployed in order to bring a successful prosecution.

---

[16] http://www.defra.gov.uk/environment/enforcement/.
[17] M Faure and G Heine, 'Criminal Enforcement of Environmental Law in the European Union' (IMPEL Working Group on Criminal Prosecution in Environmental Cases, 2000).

Is there a Compliance Deficit?

1.33   I believe that in many sectors compliance levels in the UK are generally high. However, it can be frustrating for both regulators and businesses when regulatory non-compliance is not addressed because the regulator lacks the appropriate enforcement mechanism. This problem creates what is known as a *compliance deficit*: where non-compliance exists and is identified but no enforcement action is taken because the appropriate tool is not available to the regulator.

1.34   It is difficult to assess the general level of compliance in the UK because not every firm is inspected and not every incidence of regulatory non-compliance is identified. Tangible data is absent in this area. However, I have attempted to get some indication from regulators on the overall effectiveness of enforcement strategies on compliance levels. This was a difficult process, as most regulators are able to comment on their outputs such as numbers of prosecutions or number of Statutory Notices imposed, but are unable to draw any conclusions on what impact this has on overall compliance. The results of this are discussed in my consultation document.[18]

Important Issues Beyond my Remit

1.35   It was clear from the responses to the consultation paper that there were certain subject areas that respondents wanted me to comment on, but which are outside of the remit of my review. I am constrained by the subject matter of regulatory legislation. It is outside the scope of this review to comment on the substance of regulatory requirements and I therefore have adopted the working assumption that regulations are sensible and necessary. Government should be regularly reviewing existing regulations to ensure this is the case.

1.36   In addition, it is not within my scope to comment on the structure of enforcement agencies. Philip Hampton recommended a change in regulatory structures with 35 regulators being merged into nine by April 2009.

1.37   At the conclusion of this review, I am not laying down prescriptive rules as to how regulators should respond to individual breaches of regulation, but I am suggesting that a more flexible range of sanctioning options is made available to them. I also suggest what safeguards should be present alongside an extended toolkit. Regulators will still retain the discretion as to how best to respond, and to choose the most appropriate sanction to ensure positive outcomes.

1.38   I do not wish to trespass on the sentencing discretion of the criminal courts. This report does not intend to make recommendations that will impinge on this discretion. I am, however, recommending options that enhance the sanctioning choices available to the criminal courts. I also make recommendations concerning specialisation and training which I believe will improve their effectiveness when dealing with criminal prosecutions for regulatory non-compliance.

1.39   Lastly, I am not prescribing changes to the legal framework or status of current offences relating to regulatory non-compliance. Offences relating to regulatory non-

---

[18] Macrory, above n 2, 36.

compliance come in many forms: some impose true strict liability, some allow for defences like taking reasonable precautions or similar wording, some require proof of knowledge or intent. The rationale for the differences is not always clear. This is a subject that I believe will merit further investigation in the future. Some interesting work relevant to this has been done in the course of my review. At Annex D and E of my interim report, I discuss the role of strict liability offences in the regulatory field. Some consultation responses have supported my view that there may be a case for decriminalising certain offences thereby reserving criminal sanctions for the most serious cases of regulatory non-compliance. It is however outside my terms of reference to consider this in great detail. My review has started a debate in this area and it may be something that the Government wishes to investigate further.

> We support the view that a distinction must be drawn between matters of regulation and criminal offending. There is a pressing need to avoid expensive court time being taken up with matters that are better suited to an administrative penalty.
>
> *The Criminal Sub committee of the Council of HM Circuit Judges*

Recommendation 1

I recommend that the Government initiate a review of the drafting and formulation of criminal offences relating to regulatory non-compliance.

1.40   My recommendation above relates to exploring options for distinguishing whether some offences could now be better sanctioned administratively.

The Following Chapters

1.41   In the following chapters I recommend an extension to the range of sanctioning options available to enforcement agencies where formal sanctions are considered appropriate to deal with the regulatory non-compliance. This is a response to the findings of my review both from the analysis of original evidence presented to me and from further consultation with stakeholders.

1.42   I believe that the recommendations presented in this review constitute a blueprint of sanctioning tools that is fit for a risk based regulatory society. They present flexible and proportionate sanctions that will help to close the compliance deficit and do so in an effective and coherent manner.

1.43   In chapter two, I outline the underlying principles that my blueprint of sanctions should be based on. In chapters three and four, I recommend a suite of sanctions that I believe will be the blueprint and I describe how they will work. These are:

- Recommendations to improve the effectiveness of the criminal courts;
- Recommendations to introduce Fixed and Variable Monetary Administrative Penalties;
- Recommendations introducing an independent regulatory tribunal for the appeal of administrative sanctions;

- Recommendations for strengthening the system for Statutory Notices;
- Recommendations introducing Enforceable Undertakings and Undertakings Plus;
- Recommendations introducing Restorative Justice; and
- Recommendations introducing further sentencing options for the criminal courts.

1.44   I believe that these recommendations will bring a paradigm shift to the way in which regulatory sanctions are designed and used, making them more flexible and encouraging compliance.

Transparency and Accountability

1.45   The range of sanctions that are being recommended is wider than the current powers that are generally available. They would give many regulators sanctioning options that they will not have had before. This wide range of powers requires appropriate safeguards to prevent misuse of the system, as a disproportionate use of these powers could damage constructive relationships between regulators and legitimate business.

1.46   Consequently, in chapter five, I have set out my recommendations for making this a transparent system with appropriate frameworks for regulator accountability. I believe these proposals will be vital to the effectiveness and acceptability of the sanctioning system I am advocating.

1.47   Finally, chapter six sets out all of my recommendations for easy reference.

II. Underlying Principles for Regulatory Sanctions

This chapter sets out the 'Penalties Principles' that underpin my recommendations. I also describe the characteristics of the framework within which the principles must operate to ensure successful and consistent application across all regulators.

Introduction

2.1   My recommendations not only widen the range of regulatory sanctions, but deliberately shift some of this activity away from the criminal courts to regulatory bodies themselves. This means that regulators will have new and increased powers. Given this expanded role, I believe it is necessary to provide regulators and their sponsoring departments with guidance on the parameters within which an extended sanctioning toolkit should operate. I have done this by identifying a series of principles and characteristics. These are consistent with the Hampton principles as well as the Five Principles of Good Regulation.[19]

---

[19] Better Regulation Task Force, 'Principles of Good Regulation' (2003).

2.2 I have also considered the Criminal Justice Act 2003 and the guidance it gives the criminal courts when considering a sentence.[20] It refers to five purposes of a sentence that the courts must have regard to when determining a sentence. I have attempted to mirror these five purposes in my own principles. These five purposes are summarised below:

- The punishment of offenders;
- The reduction of crime (including deterrence);
- The reform and rehabilitation of offenders;
- The protection of the public; and
- The making of reparation by the offenders to those persons affected by their offences.

The Need for Principles

2.2 My vision of a contemporary sanctioning regime for regulatory non-compliance is underpinned by a set of Penalties Principles that I defined and invited comments on in my interim report. I believe offering regulators a new suite of sanctions brings with it a need to provide guidance on how these sanctions should be applied.

2.3 My principles are primarily intended to set out the underlying rationale for my analysis and detailed recommendations. They will help build a common understanding of what a sanctioning regime should achieve amongst regulators and the regulated community, and in turn will act as a framework for regulators when considering what sort of sanction or enforcement action to take. This will provide a safeguard that the new sanctions will be used fairly and consistently. This is particularly important during the transition phase, as my recommendations are introduced and regulators develop capacity and understanding of a newer and wider toolkit.

2.4 Consultation responses were broadly supportive of the principles described in my interim report. However, some concern was expressed that the principles should be applied flexibly, taking in to account circumstances of individual cases, the relevant legislative frameworks within which regulators in the UK operate, and existing practice and policy of regulators.

2.5 A general concern amongst consultation respondents was that restrictive application of the principles may lead to adverse outcomes. I discuss an example in the box below.

---

[20] Criminal Justice Act 2003, Part 12, s 142.

Application of Penalties Principles

In relation to **Principle #5**: sanctions should include an element of ensuring that the harm caused by regulatory non-compliance is put right.

The Financial Services Authority (FSA) suggest that although the principle *is* a relevant consideration, not all cases can or should include a restorative element. For example, in some cases it may not always be possible to quantify the losses suffered by an identifiable person and in others individual losses as a result of regulatory breaches are more efficiently and effectively redressed through individuals directly pursuing claims with the firm concerned (through the Financial Ombudsman Services or through the Financial Services Compensation Scheme). The FSA suggest that Principle #5 be qualified to make it clear that regulators need only consider whether a sanction should include a restorative element.

Financial Services Authority (FSA)

2.6   I believe that the Financial Services Authority make a valid point and I want to emphasise that the principles should be taken into consideration only where appropriate. Following on the example in the box above, not all cases may have caused harm to a party. In these instances, restoration to a person or community may not be necessary or appropriate. In other instances, some of the other principles may not be relevant. It may not be appropriate for all of the principles to apply in every single case, but there is a need for a consistent approach in that the principles should always be considered when a regulator is taking an enforcement action, or designing a specific sanctioning scheme.

2.7   In addition, I wish to emphasise that the Penalties Principles should be regarded as the underlying basis of regulators' sanctioning regimes in order to achieve consistency, rather than legally binding objectives in themselves. To this end, I have qualified some of the original principles, expressing them as aims rather than absolutes.

Using the Principles

2.8   I envisage that the principles I have set out will be of particular value to:

- Government departments in the design of detailed regulatory structures should they accept the recommendations in my report;
- Enforcement agencies in the design and implementation of enforcement policies;
- Regulators when deciding what sanction to impose;
- The regulated community in that the principles provide clarity overlaying specific sanctioning policies and reassurance that non-compliance will be dealt with appropriately; and
- All stakeholders in the future assessment of sanctioning regimes.

2.9   Regulators need to have the flexibility to impose the sanction they believe is appropriate, and my principles aim to provide a framework for deciding what type of sanction is suitable in individual circumstances. The spirit of my recommendations around the Penalties Principles is that they are there for guidance and should not be a basis for specific legal challenges. I do not prescribe a particular priority with regard to the individual principles as I believe, regulators should have the discretion to when particular principles are more appropriate or relevant.

2.10 Fundamental to the Penalties Principles is the notion that the underlying regulation is fit for purpose and provides for a greater social objective such as correcting a market failure or the protection of consumers, workers, or the environment.

The Six Penalties Principles

2.11 Consultation responses generally supported the six principles I detailed in my interim report. The principles that I recommend are therefore as follows:

Principle #1 – Changing Behavior

A sanction should aim to change the behaviour of the offender. This means that a sanction is not focused solely on punishment but should also ensure that the offender changes its behaviour and moves back into compliance. Changing behaviour could involve culture change within an organisation or a change in the production or manufacturing process to ensure that regulatory non-compliance is minimised. When choosing between different sanctions, regulators should consider how best to achieve changes in behaviour.

Principle #2 – No Financial Benefit

A sanction should aim to eliminate any financial gain or benefit from non-compliance. Firms may calculate that by not complying with a regulation, they can make or save money. They may also take a chance and hope that they are not caught for failing to comply with their regulatory obligations or for deliberately breaking the law. Some firms may even believe that if they are caught, the financial penalties handed down by the courts will usually be relatively low and they will probably still retain some level of financial gain.

If, however, firms know that making money by breaking the law will not be tolerated and sanctions can be imposed that specifically target the financial benefits gained through non-compliance, then this can reduce the financial incentive for firms to engage in this type of behaviour. For firms that persist in operating this way, removing financial benefits will ensure that, in future, the financial gains are not enough of an incentive to break the law. I accept that determining the financial benefit is a difficult process in some instances, and that there may be some areas of regulation where the notion of identifiable profits gained from non-compliance is not applicable. But I believe it is a challenge that can be met as demonstrated by the methodologies developed by several leading regulators in the UK and abroad including the Canadian Border Services Agency, the US Environmental Protection Agency and the Federal Office of Consumer Protection and Safety in Germany.

Principle #3 – Responsive Sanctioning

A sanction should be responsive and consider what is appropriate for the particular offender and the regulatory issue, which can include punishment and the public stigma that should be associated with a criminal conviction. The regulator should have the ability to use its discretion and, if appropriate, base its decision on what sort of sanction would help bring the firm into compliance. It may be that some firms would respond better to a sanction such as an administrative penalty combined with advice regarding best practice, while other firms may need to be sanctioned by way of a criminal prosecution. It is important that among other factors, the regulator also considers the size of the individual firms when deciding which sort of sanction is most likely to bring about a change in a firms' behaviour.

Ultimately, a regulator is obliged to uphold the public interest and maintain a credible enforcement and sanctioning regime. It should have the flexibility to apply a sanction for punitive reasons even though a lesser sanction could be applied. This may be necessary for so-called 'repeat offenders' who have been given previous opportunities – alongside advice and guidance – to comply, but have deliberately and intentionally failed to do so. Similarly, a punitive sanction may be appropriate for a single contravention with very serious external consequences.

The regulator should also consider the needs of victims and the public when determining what enforcement action is necessary in any particular case. Responsiveness is a positive quality and I believe that as long as procedural fairness is maintained and regulators pursue consistent policy objectives, regulatory outcomes will be improved.

Punitive Sanctions

Postcomm (Postal Services Commission) commented that whilst it is in agreement with the six principles in my interim report, it suggested that some contraventions may be so serious that they deserve a serious public mark of disapproval through imposing a substantive financial penalty and that the principles need to recognise this.

Principle #4 – Proportionate Sanctioning

A sanction should be proportionate to the nature of the offence and the harm caused. Whilst the previous principle is concerned with addressing the reasons for the failure to comply, this principle takes into account the nature of the non-compliance and its consequences. Inclusion of these factors will ensure that firms are held accountable for the impact of the actual or potential consequences of their actions and that these are properly reflected in any sanction imposed. The sanction should reflect the individual circumstances of the firm and the circumstances surrounding the non-compliance.

Overlap between the Penalties Principles

In their consultation response the FSA (Financial Services Authority) commented that there was some overlap between Principles #3 and #4. Although I agree that, on a wide interpretation, some of the principles can be construed as overlapping, I nonetheless believe that there is a distinct element in each principle I have identified and a value in setting these out separately.

Principle #5 – Restore the Harm Caused

A sanction should aim to restore the harm caused by regulatory non-compliance, where appropriate. This principle encompasses the needs of victims as well as ensuring that business offenders take responsibility for their actions and its consequences.

Principle #6 – Deterrence

A sanction should aim to deter future non-compliance. Sanctions should signal to others within the regulatory community that non-compliance will not be tolerated and that there will be consequences. Whether this is by a criminal prosecution or some other sanction would remain at the discretion of the regulator, within the scope of the powers available to it in relevant legislation, but firms should never think that non-compliance will be ignored or that they will 'get away with it'.

Framework for Operation of the Penalties Principles: The Seven Characteristics

2.12   It is important, particularly from the perspective of the regulated community, that there is a consistent approach to sanctioning across all regulators. To help ensure this my interim report proposed a framework within which the Penalties Principles should operate. It would be for regulators themselves to establish this framework. Consultation responses were positive towards the seven characteristics of this framework I described in my interim report.

Characteristic # 1 – Enforcement Policy

Regulators should publish an enforcement policy. This will improve transparency and accountability from regulators by signalling to business and society the kind of responses and standards they can expect from regulators in dealing with non-compliance. A public enforcement policy will also show that regulators will use their sanction powers in a proportionate and risk based way. The regulator would need to be able to justify any departure from its own enforcement policy. Research carried out for my review indicated that currently only 17 out of 56 national regulations have a published enforcement policy. Enforcement policies will need to incorporate the new range of sanction options that I recommend and should be consistent, where appropriate, with the Regulators' Compliance Code to be issued under Part Two of the Legislative and Regulatory Reform Act 2006.

Characteristic # 2 – Measure Outcomes

Regulators should measure outcomes not just outputs. Regulatory outputs are quantitative measures such as the number of prosecutions, or the number of Statutory Notices imposed by a regulator, whereas a regulatory outcome seeks to measure what impact regulatory outputs may have had. Measuring outcomes will enable regulators and the public to know what impact the enforcement actions are having, whether these have improved compliance, or remedied the harm caused by regulatory non-compliance, and whether there needs to be any modification to the balance between different types of enforcement actions to get better results. I acknowledge this may not be an easy exercise and there may be difficulties in determining these measures, but I maintain that regulators and government departments should make every effort to identify and measure regulatory outcomes.

Characteristic # 3 – Justify Choice of Enforcement Actions

Regulators should justify their choice of enforcement actions year on year to stakeholders, Ministers and Parliament. I recommend that regulators should be required to justify overall what their general enforcement strategy is and why they have chosen the enforcement actions that make up their strategy in any given year. This will not just provide protection for legitimate business, but increase public and private sector confidence and understanding in the way regulatory non-compliance is dealt with. I consider this in more detail in chapter five when I discuss accountability and transparency.

Characteristic # 4 – Follow-up Enforcement Actions

Regulators should follow up their enforcement actions where appropriate. This is of particular importance for low-level enforcement actions such as warning letters or enforcement/improvement notices, where I am concerned that lack of follow-up on the part of regulators means that they are not taken seriously and credibly by firms. However, I recognise that follow-up activity is dependent on the resources available to individual regulators and must be consistent with a risk based approach to regulation. I do take account of other priorities faced by regulatory bodies operating with finite resources, who may not want to dedicate any resource to following up minor enforcement actions. I suggest that in order to make these enforcement actions credible, some follow-up is necessary, even if this is done on a random selection basis. One outcome measure that might be adopted is whether enforcement action has been effectively brought a business into compliance – systematic follow-up by regulators would be one way of measuring the extent to which such an outcome measure has been achieved.

Characteristic # 5 – Be Transparent in What Enforcement Actions Have Been Taken

Regulators should enforce in a transparent manner. Regulators should disclose to key stakeholders and the wider public when and against whom enforcement action has been taken. This should not be isolated to criminal prosecutions, but should also be used for other enforcement action such as administrative penalties, enforcement or improvement notices or any other formal sanction, where appropriate. This information should be easily accessible and serves as a safeguard for firms, the regulator and the public interest. I talk more about the importance of transparency in chapter five.

Characteristic # 6 – Be Transparent in the Methodology for Determining or Calculating Administrative Financial Penaltie

Regulators should be transparent in the way in which they apply and determine administrative penalties. Regulators should disclose the methodology for calculating variable administrative fines including the relevant mitigating and aggravating factors firms should be aware of. Regulators should also publish a schedule of fixed administrative fines if operating an FMAP scheme. I discuss this further in chapter three.

Characteristic #7 – Avoid Perverse Incentives Influencing the Choice of Sanctioning Response

Regulators should avoid perverse incentives that might influence the choice of sanctioning response. Regulators should, for example, avoid any rise of perverse incentives when determining the appraisal and evaluation schemes of enforcement staff. It is important that regulators do not have targets for different types of enforcement actions or any correlation with salary bonuses or similar incentives. This might incentivise staff to pursue certain enforcement actions inappropriately. Secondly, while there is already Government guidance on revenue from administrative penalties, I would emphasise that regulators should not retain the revenue from Monetary Administrative Penalties, or exercise any control over how that revenue should be spent. I describe these arrangements more fully in chapter three.

Link with the Compliance Code

2.13 The Legislative and Regulatory Reform Act 2006, contains a power which will enable some of the Hampton principles of regulatory enforcement (see section 2.92 of the Hampton review 'Reducing administrative burdens: effective inspection and enforcement') to be placed on a statutory footing through a statutory Code of Practice (the 'Regulators' Compliance Code'). I would envisage, subject to consultation, that the section of the final version of the Code relating to proportionate and meaningful sanctions for businesses that consistently breach regulations will be consistent with the Macrory Penalties Principles. Regulators should be able to demonstrate transparency in process and procedures in order to comply with the Code and I would expect regulators' enforcement policies to be consistent with both the Code and the Penalties Principles.

Link with the 'Five Principles of Good Regulation'

2.14 The consultation response from the Better Regulation Commission (BRC) highlighted that we already have the Five Principles of Good Regulation and the ten Hampton principles of inspection and enforcement.[21] The Commission expressed concern that adding further principles and providing too much guidance risked confusing both regulators and those they regulate.

2.15 I should like to make it clear, if I have not previously done so, that the wider purpose behind my review is to further the better regulation agenda as a whole and build on the good work already completed or underway. To this end I share the BRC's concern that the regulatory regime remains light-touch and I acknowledge that so-called 'principles proliferation' risks duplication and dilution. However, I believe

---

[21] The five principles are proportionality, accountability, consistency, transparency and targeting; see http://www.brc.gov.uk/publications/principlesentry.asp.

that my Penalties Principles, set in the context of regulatory sanctioning, are a natural extension of the Commission's own work. Although I agree that some of my Penalties Principles may be construed as an application of the existing Five Principles of Good Regulation, I believe that there is a need to set them out separately.

2.16   The radical changes I am proposing need to incorporate safeguards for industry and the public. By identifying a series of principles and characteristics, I have specified what I think regulators should have regard to when extending their toolkits. I have taken the concerns of stakeholders seriously, and have attempted to provide a workable framework within which regulators should operate when expanding their sanctioning toolkits and have sought to limit the scope for any inappropriate behaviour by regulators, such as over-zealous parking ticket writing, through the drafting and application of a series of common principles.

Recommendation 2

I recommend that in designing the appropriate sanctioning regimes for regulatory non-compliance, regulators should have regard to the following six Penalties Principles and seven characteristics.

Six Penalties Principles

A sanction should:

1. Aim to change the behaviour of the offender;
2. Aim to eliminate any financial gain or benefit from non-compliance;
3. Be responsive and consider what is appropriate for the particular offender and regulatory issue, which can include punishment and the public stigma that should be associated with a criminal conviction;
4. Be proportionate to the nature of the offence and the harm caused;
5. Aim to restore the harm caused by regulatory non-compliance, where appropriate; and
6. Aim to deter future non-compliance.

Seven Characteristics

Regulators should:

1. Publish an enforcement policy;
2. Measure outcomes not just outputs;
3. Justify their choice of enforcement actions year on year to stakeholders, Ministers and Parliament;
4. Follow-up enforcement actions where appropriate;
5. Enforce in a transparent manner;
6. Be transparent in the way in which they apply and determine administrative penalties; and
7. Avoid perverse incentives that might influence the choice of sanctioning response.

2.17   I believe that only when regulators can demonstrate that they are compliant with a Hampton risk based approach to regulation, should they be allowed by Government to use the toolkit I propose later in this document.

III. My Vision for Contemporary Sanctioning Regimes: Financial Sanctions

The previous chapter outlined my Penalties Principles and characteristics, which I believe provide the necessary framework and parameters for an expanded sanctioning toolkit. This chapter sets out my recommendations for what types of sanctions should become available to regulators and enforcers in order to be more flexible, effective and better meet the compliance needs of industry and the public with a specific focus on Monetary Administrative Penalties and improvements of financial penalties in the criminal courts.

Introduction

3.1   The reformed sanctioning system that I propose is designed to increase public confidence, give greater awareness of the needs of victims and ensure that business non-compliance is met with a proportionate response both by regulators and in the courts. It will do this by providing a transparent system with sanctions that encourage and assist firms to comply with their regulatory obligations while ensuring that the most serious acts of regulatory non-compliance are dealt with appropriately and effectively by the criminal justice system.

3.2   The reforms that I suggest are not intended to transform regulatory sanctioning regimes overnight. Rather, they are to bring into them the flexibility, efficiencies and responsiveness that can facilitate the full implementation of the Hampton agenda, resulting in better deterrence options for regulators, better compliance for business and better outcomes for society as a whole.

3.3   I consulted upon suggestions for reform that were outlined in my interim report and in this report I publish my final recommendations with regards to alternative sanctions for both regulators and the courts.

A Vision for the Future

3.4   I consulted upon a richer range of sanctioning tools to be made available to regulators which would permit a range of regulatory offences to be handled other than by means of criminal prosecution, leaving the most serious cases to be dealt with by the criminal courts. Making such options available would itself reinforce a more appropriate role for the criminal courts, where in turn I propose recommendations for improving effectiveness of criminal prosecution for regulatory non-compliance.

3.5   My vision of sanctioning options for a risk-based sanctioning system, based upon risk based enforcement is illustrated in Figure 3.1. Regulators would, against the

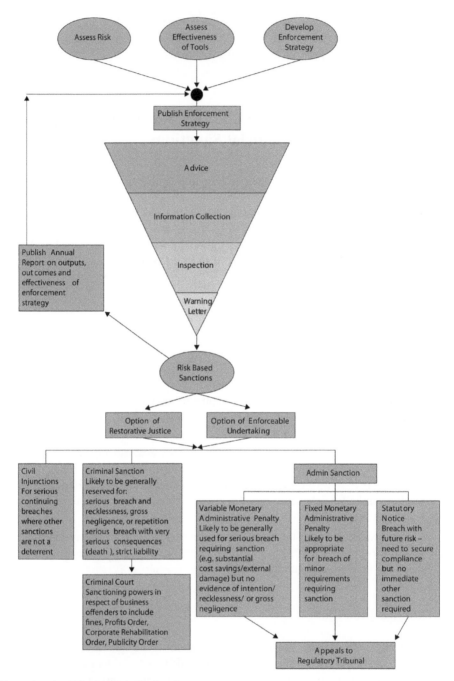

Figure 3.1 An Effective Sanctioning System.

background of their enforcement policy and the proposed Compliance Code and having regard to my principles, continue to exercise discretion as to when it is appropriate to apply a sanction, and the choice of the sanction would be determined by the nature and circumstance of the regulatory non-compliance. With the availability of additional administrative sanctions, I would expect to see some shift in the current use of sanctions.

3.6   As part of this vision, the use of criminal prosecutions would remain appropriate for serious breaches where there was evidence of intentional or reckless or repeated flouting of the law. Regulators may decide within their discretion that criminal proceedings are justified where there is evidence of gross negligence and/or where the actual or potential consequences of the breach are so serious (such as a death or serious injury) that the public interest demands a criminal prosecution.

3.7   Some incidents of non-compliance with regulatory requirements would, I believe, be generally more effectively dealt with by the use of fixed or variable penalties (giving the offender an opportunity to have the case heard before an independent tribunal). Thus, breaches involving, for example, carelessness or negligence but still requiring a sanction (because, say, a substantial financial gain has been made or where there has been an external impact) are likely to be more appropriate for administrative sanctions rather than criminal proceedings.

3.8   Enforceable Undertakings may be introduced as an additional sanction for cases where the regulator has the necessary evidence to proceed to a criminal prosecution or the imposition of a Monetary Administrative Penalty, but where the business has committed to address the issues surrounding the regulatory non-compliance through an undertaking. These may offer business a less punitive sanction leading to a desirable change in behaviour and outcomes within the business.

3.9   I emphasise again, that I do not believe that all regulatory breaches require the imposition of a formal sanction. Warnings, advice and Statutory Notices will continue to play a key role in ensuring compliance. But where (in accordance with its enforcement policy) a regulator decides a formal sanction is justified, my proposals offer a richer range of appropriate response that is currently available.

3.10 I have given some views as to when each of the sanctioning options above might be appropriate. It is not possible to set out detailed factors for choosing between the options and it is ultimately up to regulators to decide what the appropriate response is in any particular case. The views I have expressed above may indicate a direction in which sanctioning regimes might develop. I accept, that there will be instances, for example, where a regulator feels that an offender who has been subjected to several prosecutions without changing their behaviour and may be more appropriately sanctioned with an administrative penalty. Conversely, there will be instances where a company has committed a strict liability offence giving rise to such serious consequences that a criminal prosecution is justified even though accidental circumstances or inadvertence was involved. Given this, any enforcement policy, while giving signals of a likely response, should allow for some degree of flexibility.

Specific Recommendations

3.11 Following the above discussion on my overall vision, I detail specific recommendations in several areas relating to penalties. These are presented as follows:

- Improving the effectiveness of criminal courts for cases of regulatory non-compliance;
- Introducing Fixed and Variable Monetary Administrative Penalties with appeals heard through an independent Regulatory Tribunal;
- Strengthening and extending the system of Statutory Notices in cases of regulatory non-compliance;
- Introducing Enforceable Undertakings and Undertakings Plus for cases of regulatory non-compliance;
- Introducing Restorative Justice for cases of regulatory non-compliance; and
- Introducing alternative sanctioning options for cases of regulatory non-compliance heard in the criminal courts.

Improving the Effectiveness of Criminal Courts for Cases of Regulatory Non-compliance

3.12   More than two million cases are heard annually in the Magistrates' Courts in England and Wales.[22] A small proportion of these relate to cases of regulatory non-compliance. I have some recommendations which should improve the effectiveness of the courts when working with cases of regulatory non-compliance.

Sentencing Guidelines

3.13   The Government should invite the Sentencing Guidelines Council to produce sentencing guidelines for cases of regulatory non-compliance. These would be of great value to magistrates in the UK. The legal advisers in many of the local courts the review visited had prepared their own guidance documents and I think it would be beneficial for central guidance documents to exist. These guidelines could be high-level and focused on the principles that should be taken into consideration for sentencing cases of regulatory non-compliance.

Make the Financial Case Clear

3.14   Magistrates from around the UK commented to me that many prosecutors failed to provide adequate information to the court regarding the significance of the regulatory regime they are dealing with, the financial benefit gained through or financial circumstances surrounding cases of regulatory non-compliance. Prosecutors must make such matters clear to the court in order to better inform the courts so that the sanctions handed down can reflect more closely the financial and social impact of the case.

---

[22] HM Court Service, http://www.hmcourts-service.gov.uk/infoabout/magistrates/index.htm.

Focus Cases

3.15   Studying the existing practice of certain courts and regulatory areas, I believe it is sensible to consider consolidating certain types of regulatory non-compliance cases in a particular geographic area where possible. Focusing offences in this way gives greater opportunity for both magistrates and court officials to gain expertise and familiarity in the area of regulation concerned. This type of consolidation is already happening in certain areas of regulatory non-compliance. For example, in Greater London, health and safety prosecutions are initiated in the City of London Magistrates' Court. The British Potato Council, because of its location, concentrates prosecution in the Oxford Magistrates' Court and prosecutions for many regulatory offences under company law are heard before Cardiff Magistrates, reflecting the location of Companies House in Cardiff. It would appear sensible if further moves in this direction were taken. There must be limits – not least because of fairness implications for offenders who might be forced to travel long distances to a criminal court – to the extent this can be taken, but within the jurisdictional areas of magistrates, there may be further opportunities for particular magistrates' courts to take the lead in handling different types of regulatory offences. I believe the Government should consider this type of consolidation as part of the overall direction of Her Majesty's Court Service.

Training Legal Advisers

3.16   Almost all criminal prosecutions for cases of regulatory non-compliance against businesses are heard in the magistrates'courts.[23] There are over 28,000 magistrates at present in England and Wales, and I do not think it would be an effective use of time and resources to expect all Magistrates to have specialised training concerning cases of regulatory non-compliance. But I believe that there should be more systematic training made available which could be focused on district judges, prosecutors and justices' clerks who advise magistrates, and on those courts where it has been decided to focus particular regulatory prosecutions. The Judicial Studies Board (JSB) is responsible for judicial training. Regulators and sponsoring departments should discuss with the JSB the development of specialist training for district judges, justices' clerks and Magistrates where there is a sufficient volume of cases to merit this effort.

---

[23] 15,369 cases are heard in the magistrates' courts of a total of 15,445 cases of regulatory non-compliance committed by companies. HM Court Service.

Recommendation 3

I recommend that in order to increase the effectiveness of criminal courts for regulatory offences, the following actions should be implemented:
- The Government should request the Sentencing Guidelines Council to prepare general sentencing guidelines for cases of regulatory non-compliance;
- Prosecutors should always make clear to the court any financial benefits resulting from non-compliance as well as the policy significance of the relevant regulatory requirement;
- Prosecutions in particular regulatory fields be heard in designated magistrates' courts within jurisdictional areas, where appropriate; and
- Regulators provide specialist training for prosecutors and discuss with the Judicial Studies Board (JSB) contributing to the training of the judiciary and justices' clerks.

Monetary Administrative Penalties (MAPs)

3.17 Monetary Administrative Penalties, in the context of my recommendations, are monetary penalties that are applied directly by a regulator, and I refer to them below as MAPs. Criminal courts do not play a part in the MAP process, and are generally not involved in issuing or enforcing such penalties. The recipient of a MAP has a right to appeal through an administrative appeals mechanism which usually takes the form of an administrative specialist tribunal. For example, a recipient of an administrative penalty under the Financial Services and Markets Act 2000 is entitled to a complete rehearing of their case before the Financial Services and Markets Tribunal.

Current Use of Administrative Penalties

3.18 Administrative penalties are widely used in countries such as the US, Australia and Canada. In addition, many European countries, including Germany and Sweden, make extensive use of administrative penalties especially in areas of environmental regulation, health and safety, financial services and within other regulatory regimes, such as the regulation of utilities and water.

3.19 The UK experience with administrative penalties is largely limited to the financial regulators. The Financial Services and Markets Act 2000 gives the Financial Services Authority (FSA)[24] a broad range of civil, administrative and criminal sanctioning powers, including the power to issue monetary administrative penalties. The majority of FSA cases are dealt with by using administrative routes. Since 2000 more than 70 cases have been concluded with an administrative penalty. Only six cases have been pursued through the criminal court system.

---

[24] The FSA was abolished under the Financial Services Act 2012 with effect from 1 April 2013, and its responsibilities split between the Prudential Regulation authority, the Financial Conduct Authority and the Bank of England.

3.20 The Competition Commission can impose financial penalties under the Enterprise Act 2002 (set out in sections 109–111) in relation to its investigation powers. The penalties can either be a fixed amount, not exceeding £20,000 or calculated as a daily rate, not exceeding £5,000 per day.[25]

3.21 The Office of Fair Trading (OFT) has access to financial penalties for non-compliance with competition law. The OFT has discretion to impose financial penalties that can be severe, but may not exceed ten percent of turn over.[26] This power is set out in section 36 of the Competition Act 1998.

3.22 While the use of administrative penalties in the UK regulatory context is not unprecedented, they have tended to be used for cases of civil regulatory non-compliance rather than criminal regulatory non-compliance. The Hampton Review identified that out of the 60 regulators in scope only 15 were able to impose administrative penalties.[27] Of these 15, the majority only have access to fixed penalties which are for a low financial amount. I believe that the introduction of monetary administrative penalties, both fixed and variable, in more regulatory regimes, whether civil or criminal, would serve to help fill the gap that exists in the current enforcement toolkit of many UK regulators, where there is a lack of intermediate sanctions.[28]

The Effectiveness of Monetary Administrative Penalties

3.23 I have considered the academic literature, international experience and the responses provided to me through the consultation process and have found that administrative penalties are an effective way of ensuring regulatory compliance whilst reserving criminal prosecutions for the most serious of cases of regulatory non-compliance.

3.24 As discussed in my interim report, administrative penalties can provide an intermediate step between the formal, costly and stigmatising action of criminal prosecution and the more informal means of advice and persuasion to get firms back into compliance.[29] I believe that breaches of regulatory requirements can take in circumstances that require a formal sanction but not necessarily a criminal prosecution.

3.25 Well designed administrative schemes can also be flexible and take a more customised approach in dealing with regulatory non-compliance, especially in cases of variable penalties. For example, compliance history, the seriousness of the offence and its impact on the external environment or community can be taken into consideration. This flexibility can allow the regulator to ensure that the level of the MAP is appropriate to reflect the various aggravating and mitigating factors, encourage future compliance and be reflective and proportionate to the size of the business. Such a system could motivate offenders to take actions to move into compliance

---

[25] As provided for in the Competition Commission (Penalties) Order 2003 (SI 2003/1371).

[26] As defined in the Competition Act 1998 (Determination of Turnover for Penalties) (amendment) Order 2004 (SI 2004/1259).

[27] Hampton, above n 4, 23.

[28] See paras 1.33–1.34 on the compliance deficit.

[29] Macrory, above n 2, 45, para 3.9.

and provide a sanctioning option for those cases where it may not be appropriate to prosecute the offender and where previous advice or Statutory Notices have not been effective.

Overall responses to my consultation document showed that over 70 percent of respondents believed regulators should have access to Monetary Administrative Penalties as part of their enforcement toolkits.

Fixed & Variable Monetary Administrative Penalties

3.26   In my interim report *Regulatory Justice: Sanctioning in a Post Hampton World* I set out three models of Monetary Administrative Penalties. The majority of consultation responses supported my preferred option, in which regulators have access to Fixed and Variable Monetary Administrative Penalties with business being able to appeal to an independent Regulatory Tribunal.

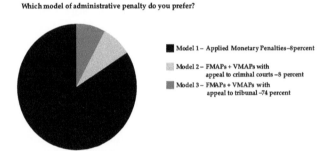

Which model of administrative penalty do you prefer?

■ Model 1 – Applied Monetary Penalties–8 percent

Model 2 – FMAPs + VMAPs with appeal to criminal courts –8 percent

■ Model 3 – FMAPs + VMAPs with appeal to tribunal –74 percent

Figure 3.2 Models of Administrative Penalties. These figures do not include individuals who responded in order to avoid undue distortion. I accept that because of the differences in size and expertise of the organisations involved these tables ate indicative only of the general thrust of the responses

Source: Macrory Review, Consultation August 2006.

3.27   This is the model that I have chosen to recommend because I believe that there are a number of advantages to this option which I mentioned in my interim report. I discuss the appeal mechanism for this system of fixed and variable penalties in the following section.

Fixed Monetary Administrative Penalties (FMAPs)

3.28   Fixed Monetary Administrative Penalties (FMAPs) are generally fines for a relatively low fixed amount that are applied in respect of low level, minor or high-volume instances of non-compliance. They can be applied directly by the regulator, where a business has been found to have failed to comply with regulations. Legislation specifies both the nature of the offence as well as the maximum amount of the fine. The regulator does not have discretion as to the level of the financial penalty, but does have discretion in whether or not to apply a penalty in the first instance.

> There are a number of offences for which a fixed monetary administrative penalty would be appropriate across the range of enforcement functions in local authorities, including Health and Safety, Food Safety and Trading Standards. This type of sanction may be particularly useful in tackling 'low-level, minor, high volume instances of non-compliance'.
>
> *Glasgow City Council*

> We believe FMAPs could be available in circumstances where the outcomes of the breach have little effect on consumer protection. Such examples might include late filing of accounts because the deadlines in one sense are 'arbitrary'.
>
> *Cattle PLC*

3.29   As FMAPs are for relatively minor amounts, they may not be appropriate for more serious or deliberate cases of regulatory non-compliance or where a firm has made significant financial gains or where the public interest would be best served by a criminal prosecution. However, international practice suggests that they can still be meaningful and significant as a sanctioning tool. As set out in the box below, in the area of health and safety in New South Wales, Australia, the on-the-spot fine scheme in operation by WorkCover, ranges in level of fine from A$80 to A$1,200 (£30–£500). The average fine is A$550 (£220). The schedule for the penalties is set out in the relevant legislation (Occupational Health and Safety Act 2002).

Scaling the FMAP

3.30   Small as well as large businesses could be liable for FMAPs but each type of business can have significantly different abilities to pay and absorb financial penalties. I believe it would be beneficial if the FMAP could reflect the size of the firm, relying on factors such as the number of employees or annual turnover, where small firms would get a fixed penalty and larger firms would get the same fixed penalty, but scaled up by a certain factor. This would ensure that regardless of the size of a business, an FMAP could still represent an effective deterrent.

Current Use of Fixed Monetary Penalties

3.31   FMAPs already exist as an enforcement option in the UK for certain offences, for example Her Majesty's Revenue and Customs can issue fixed penalties of £100 for failure to deliver a self assessment tax return when required or if the delivered tax return is incorrect. They can also issue a fine of an amount up to a specified limit per day, for example up to £60 a day for continued failure to deliver a self assessment form.[30] The Clean Neighbourhoods and Environment Act 2005 enables authorised

---

[30] The penalty is set out in s 93 of the Taxes Management Act 1970, as amended by s 196 and para 25 of Schedule 19 of the Finance Act 1994 (in relation to the year 1996/97 and subsequent years of assessment in accordance with s 199(2) of the 1994 Act).

Box 3.1 Fixed Penalty Notices – A case study – WorkCover, New South Wales, Australia

The health and safety regulator, WorkCover, in New South Wales, Australia, uses fixed penalty notices as an enforcement tool against employers. The options include penalty notices, an on-the-spot-fine handed down to businesses where the inspector is of the opinion that advice or direction is not sufficient. WorkCover considers penalty notices are an effective method of dealing with less serious breaches of the legislation.

Inspectors will consider various factors when determining whether to issue a penalty notice.

These factors include:

- whether the breach can be remedied quickly
- whether the issuing of a penalty notice is likely to have the desired deterrent effect
- whether the breach is a one-off situation or part of an ongoing pattern of non-compliance

The Occupational Health and Safety Act 2002 identifies a range of offences and determines a corresponding penalty. Fines range from A$80 to A$1,200. (£30-£500) The average fine is A$550 (£220).

The schedule of breaches with corresponding fixed financial penalties secures that there is transparency when the decision is taken to impose an on-the-spot-fine on a business.

A person served with a penalty notice may elect not to pay the penalty and to have the matter dealt with by the court. The procedure for making an election is set out on the back of the penalty notice.

Source: WorkCover compliance policy and prosecution guidelines, WorkCover, New South Wales, March 2004.

---

officers of a local authority to issue fixed penalty notices for failure to comply with some of the requirements of the Act, for example £100 for nuisance parking offences.[31] Companies House can also impose a penalty notice against a company because company accounts were not received on time. Companies House operates a scale of penalty that is dependent on how late the accounts are and whether the company is a private firm or a publicly listed company. These range from £100 to £5,000.[32]

Variable Monetary Administrative Penalties

3.32   Variable Monetary Administrative Penalties (VMAPs) are sanctions applied by the regulator where the amount is at the discretion of the regulator. Instead of being for a relatively small fixed amount whose maximum is pre-determined by legislation (as with FMAPs above), a variable penalty can, where appropriate and proportionate, be

---

[31] The Clean Neighbourhoods & Environment Act 2005, Part 2, s 6(1). In 2004/5, Local Authorities issued 15,582 fines for litter, 2,296 for dog fouling, 19 for graffiti, 52 for fly-posing and 1 for noise.
[32] http://www.companieshouse.gov.uk/infoGuide/faq/lateFilingAppeal.shtml Companies Act 1985, s 242a.

Companies House is a regulator with access to FMAPs under the Companies Act 1985. Companies House can levy a Late Filing Payment (LFP) for the late submission of company accounts. These were introduced in 1992. The Registrar of Companies House has discretion of not collecting a LFP in exceptional circumstances.

In 1991, the compliance rate for accounts was 86 percent. With the introduction of the late filing penalty regime in June 1992 the rate immediately increased to 92 percent and has continued to increase to a level of around 96 percent. There is no doubt, therefore that the penalty regime has achieved two major effects. Not only has it secured an initial significant increase in the level of compliance, but it has also maintained that level of compliance at that high percentage of companies.

Source: Companies House submission to Macrory call for evidence, February 2006.

for a more significant amount initially determined at the discretion of the regulator in accordance with a published scheme. Relevant mitigating or aggravating factors, the specific circumstances of the offence and the means of the non-compliant business must be taken into consideration by the regulator when determining the amount of the penalty in any particular case. I discuss these factors in the following sections.

Yes, we agree that it would be a good idea for VMAPs to be made available to all regulators. The situations in which the FSA can impose VMAPs includes breaches of FSA rules by authorised firms, misconduct by FSA approved individuals, breaches of FSA listing rules by listed companies or certain other persons, and market abuse by any person whether regulated or not. We find our VMAP powers operate very effectively for us. They allow us a degree of flexibility with which to respond to different cases, and ensure that the penalty matches the misdemeanour.

Financial Services Authority

Yes, VMAPs should be available to regulators as part of a mixed system. A variable fine allows the regulator to operate flexibly and proportionately.

British Chamber of Commerce

It is important VMAPs are available. In high profitability areas, the costs of FMAPs could simply be built into business plans. This is certainly the case in the premium rate industry where even substantial fines (£100,000) can be simply written off as a business expense. Therefore VMAPs must be an option to ensure the principle of removing the benefit from the crime can be upheld. The consultation provides some good illustrations that can be used to good effect in preference to prosecution – it is a case of using the right tools for the right job.

South West England Coordination of Trading Standards

Relationship between Criminal Offences and VMAPs – Parallel but Connected

3.33   As I have indicated in chapter one, I do not envisage a root and branch reform of existing offences relating to regulatory non-compliance. For those existing criminal offences where it is decided that a VMAP is an appropriate alternative sanction, the legislation would need to be amended to allow for the imposition of a Monetary Administrative Penalty. A regulator would then have the option, in line with its enforcement policy, and my suggested principles, to choose in appropriate cases the sanction of a VMAP rather than a criminal prosecution. A regulator would investigate a potential offence as usual and if satisfied that the evidence of a breach exists, then decide the most appropriate sanctioning route.

3.34   Criminal sanctions and VMAPs will be available as sanctions for the same regulatory non-compliance. The elements of the regulatory non-compliance would need to be proved to the requisite evidential standard. Where a criminal sanction is pursued, the regulator would need to meet the criminal standard of beyond reasonable doubt. Should the regulator choose to pursue a VMAP, the evidence should meet the civil standard of the balance of probabilities.

> In the CBI's view, administrative fines may be viewed simply as a 'cost of doing business' for the deliberately non-compliant firm. There is also concern within the business community that introducing more administrative fines will foster a 'parking ticket' type mentality amongst inspectors, which will fundamentally change the existing relationship between inspectors and businesses – at a time when the aim should be to encourage more co-operation and flexibility and discussion between inspectors and businesses.
>
> *Confederation of British Industry*

> We reject the view that the application of penalties in such cases helps to secure compliance. Nothing could be more calculated to enhance tick a box inspections than the desire to levy such on the spot fines for instances that would almost certainly today be ignored or subject to advice. The plain fact is that compliant businesses would willingly act on such advice and introduce any necessary procedures to mitigate the chances of the offence recurring. On the other hand rogue traders would be more likely to be compliant with the threat of a court action than with an administrative fine that could be considered part of the costs of doing business.
>
> *British Retail Consortium*

3.35   I recognise that there are concerns in some of the business community that this may unfairly encourage the use of VMAPs in place of current prosecutions and that smaller businesses may not have the financial resource to challenge a VMAP, but I do not believe these are sufficiently convincing to outweigh the advantages that the VMAP would bring as an alternative sanctioning route. I would note that the civil standard of proof does have adequate safeguards to protect the rights of the accused. The regulator would still need to ensure that the investigation process and the imposition of the VMAP protects the procedural rights of the recipient of the administrative penalty. These proposals are not about making it easier to penalise businesses but to create a system of sanctions that is more responsive and proportionate to the nature of the non-compliance.

3.36 The choice between criminal prosecution and the imposition of a VMAP should be based upon the principles I have set out in chapter two rather than on the applicable evidential standard. Regulators should consider which is the most appropriate sanctioning route relying on factors such as ability to change behaviour, ability to eliminate financial gain, and proportionality, I consider that VMAPs are a more responsive and appropriate sanction than criminal prosecution in a wide range of cases. Criminal prosecution should however be reserved for serious breaches of regulatory obligations such as cases of deliberate, reckless or repeated non-compliance.

3.37 It should be noted that these proposals are not about 'letting off' businesses for their regulatory non-compliance. While the imposition of an administrative fine such as VMAPs may not have the same stigma as a criminal conviction, the imposition of a VMAP can represent a significant sanction. One of the aims of VMAPs is to remove the financial gain made from the regulatory non-compliance – something a criminal conviction may not always achieve. This will help create a level playing field for compliant businesses and deter rogue businesses from non-compliance in the future.

Level of Financial Penalty

3.38 I have carefully considered the issue of the level of financial penalties for both FMAPs and VMAPs and there are advantages and disadvantages to setting a fine maxima in both instances.

FMAPs

3.39 In the case of FMAPs, I believe that these should have a statutory maximum level which should be set out in the relevant underlying legislation. By definition, FMAPs are for low level breaches and the financial penalty should be for a relatively low amount. I believe it makes sense for the maximum level of FMAPS to not exceed level five on the standard scale.[33] This is currently set at £5,000.

VMAPs

3.40 I have carefully considered the advantages and disadvantages of setting an upper limit to VMAPs in underlying legislation and in particular whether some cap such as a 10 percent turnover maximum should be provided in the legislation. I believe that to impose such an upper limit would pose undue legal complexity on the system, and could encourage regulators to set VMAPs at inappropriately high levels. I want

---

[33] Criminal Justice Act 1982, s 37.

to ensure that regulators have the flexibility and ability of capturing the financial benefit businesses may have acquired through a regulatory breach. I do not believe the legislation should specify an upper limit.

3.41   The business community clearly will need to be confident that such a scheme is not being used inappropriately or irresponsibly by a regulator. I have some recommendations that will seek to give business transparency into the way in which VMAPs are calculated.

Box 3.2 Aggravating and Mitigating Factors That Should Be considered for VMAPs

In a system with Variable Monetary Administrative Penalties regulators would be required to develop and publicise a method for calculating the penalty for regulatory non-compliance. The following are examples of aggravating and mitigating factors which regulators could take into account when determining the appropriate level of Variable Monetary Administrative Penalty, although this list is not exhaustive and each decision will depend on the circumstances of the individual case:

Aggravating Factors

- Seriousness of the regulatory non-compliance, e.g. the harm or potential for harm to human health or the environment, the duration of non-compliance etc.;
- Evidence of intention (if any) behind the regulatory non-compliance;
- Disciplinary record or history of non-compliance of the business;
- Financial gain made by the business as a result of non-compliance with regulations;
- Size and financial resources of the firm that failed to comply with regulations;
- The conduct of the business after the regulatory non-compliance has come to the attention of the regulator; and
- Previous actions taken by the regulator, or other regulators, to help the business into compliance.

Mitigating Factors

- Actions taken to eliminate or reduce the risk of damage resulting from regulatory non-compliance;
- Actions taken to repair the harm done by regulatory non-compliance;
- Co-operation with the regulator in responding to regulatory non-compliance;
- Fast and accurate reporting of regulatory non-compliance;
- Size and financial resources of the firm that failed to comply with regulations;
- The conduct of the business after the regulatory non-compliance has come to the attention of the regulator; and
- Vicarious liability for failures by employees including the adequacy of management controls and the extent to which the employee was acting outside of his or her authority.

Who Makes the Decision to Impose the Sanction?

3.42 While Monetary Administrative Penalties could be a valuable addition to the enforcement toolkit, it is important that the regulatory relationship between business and the regulator is not compromised. I believe it is essential that I comment on what level of decision-maker should be involved in decisions of whether or not to impose a MAP so as to provide guidance to regulators. It is important that decision makers have sufficient experience and authority to impose MAPs. This would serve to maintain the current pragmatic relationship many within the regulated community have come to value with their enforcers.

3.43 FMAPs, because they are generally imposed for low-level, minor offences and for a low financial amount, could be issued by lower levels of staff within a regulator who have undergone the appropriate training. However, I want to assure the regulated community that such a regime should not bear resemblance to the 'parking-ticket' mentality mentioned to me by many respondents in my consultation. In order to avoid FMAP training becoming a tick-box exercise, I believe regulators should look to on-going monitoring in order to test that the FMAPs are being used appropriately and I make further suggestions concerning transparency and accountability in chapter five.

3.44 As VMAPs can be for more significant sums, decisions should be taken independently from field staff or inspectors. Regulators may also want to consider seeking representations from a business on the penalty proposed in advance of it being imposed. The field staff could make a recommendation on whether a VMAP should be imposed or not and recommend a level of penalty, but I believe the final decision should be taken by more senior officials within the regulator. This would serve to ensure that the relationship between the inspector and the business is not compromised. In addition, it would encourage consistent behaviour from the regulator since decisions on imposing VMAPs would be taken by the same group within a regulator. This would provide a good check on what VMAPS are being imposed, against whom and for how much.

Fines Would Not Be Accessed by the Regulator

3.45 Many of the concerns from the business community regarding MAPs is due to an uncertainty as to whether regulators will financially benefit from imposing administrative penalties. I have reflected this concern in my principles and characteristics. MAPs should not be viewed by regulators as a means to raise revenue from the businesses they regulate. I want to avoid creating any perverse financial incentives for regulators that might influence their choice of sanctioning tool. This view is already entrenched in relevant section of HM Treasury's Consolidated Budgeting Guide and I echo their views on the separation of revenue streams in order to eliminate perverse incentives.[34] I have also emphasised that regulators must avoid creating perverse incentives (such as staff appraisal criteria) that will

---

[34] HM Treasury, 'Consolidated Budgeting Guidance from 2006–07' (13 December 2005) ch 3.

encourage the use of financial penalties without regard to the regulatory outcomes to be achieved.

Recovery of Costs to the Regulator

3.46   I am aware that bringing any form of enforcement action generates costs for regulators. Regulators are able to recover some of their costs in pursuing the prosecution. I believe a similar system should exist for regulators that choose to use the MAP system. I do not think it is right that regulators should be incentivised to use the criminal system and I want to mention this so that cost recovery is a part of the consideration of any MAP scheme. Cost recovery should include the cost of collection of an administrative penalty, which I discuss in the next paragraph.

Enforcement of Monetary Administrative Penalties

3.47   In order for any administrative penalty regime to have credibility, businesses must know that when an administrative penalty is imposed, it will be enforced and that the regulator will pursue the collection of the penalty. If a business refuses to pay the penalty without initiating an appeal, then regulators should be able to pursue the payment of this penalty through ordinary civil debt recovery procedures.

Administrative Penalties and Private Prosecutions

3.48   Some regulatory schemes permit private prosecutions. In theory, someone other than a regulator, who feels that the regulatory non-compliance justifies a criminal rather than an administrative sanction could also initiate a private prosecution for the same offence. This, of course, can happen under current arrangements where a regulator decides, in line with its enforcement policy, to issue, say, only a warning in response to an offence. A private prosecution could still be initiated in such circumstances. As a matter of general policy, I believe that the existence of the power of private prosecution can be a valuable check on regulator behaviour. There exist a number of mechanisms (such as the right of the Director of Public Prosecutions to take over a private prosecution) designed to prevent abuse or vexatiousness of private prosecutions.

3.49   I recognise that where a VMAP has been imposed on a business, it needs to be insulated from the risk of double jeopardy which a private prosecution might impose, and additional procedural checks (such as leave of a court before a private prosecution can be initiated in such circumstances) may be required. I have received very little evidence on this issue, and do not think it appropriate for me to make detailed suggestions as to the most appropriate mechanisms needed. But I recommend that when designing the legislative scheme of VMAPs, the Government needs to consider whether existing mechanisms are sufficient to prevent this form of double jeopardy, and if not, what would be the best way of handling the issue.

Recommendation 4

I recommend that with regards to Monetary Administrative Penalties:

- Government should, introduce schemes for Fixed and Variable Monetary Administrative Penalties, for regulators and enforcers of regulations, that are compliant with the Hampton and Macrory Principles and characteristics. This can include national regulators as well as local regulatory partners;
- Appeals concerning the imposition of an administrative penalty be heard by a Regulatory Tribunal, rather than the criminal courts;
- Fine maxima for Fixed Monetary Administrative Penalties (FMAP) schemes should be set out and not exceed level five on the standard scale. FMAPs should also be scaled to differentiate between small and large firms; and
- There should be no fine maxima for Variable Monetary Administrative Penalties (VMAPs).

3.50   In order for these administrative penalties to be effective, it is important that prior to regulators expanding their toolkits, regulators should be compliant with the Hampton Principles and demonstrate an ability to comply with the Macrory Principles and characteristics. Compliance with the principles and characteristics will be considered for regulators who want to gain access to these sanctions prior to the new sanctions being awarded, including both national and local regulators. This role will likely fall to the Better Regulation Executive and some national regulators (who use local regulatory partners) to ensure that regulators gaining access to the expanded sanctioning toolkit are compliant and operate in a risk based manner.

3.51   Regulators who want to use administrative penalties should ensure the following:

- Clearly identify the persons within their organisation who are authorised to impose a Fixed and Variable MAP;
- Publish the way in which VMAPs will be calculated; and
- Regulators should not make any financial gains from the imposition of Monetary Administrative Penalties, but they should be entitled to some cost recovery.

3.52   In addition, the Government should consider whether additional provisions are needed to prevent the risk of double jeopardy from a private prosecution initiated for an offence that has been sanctioned by a VMAP.

Appeal Mechanisms and an Independent Regulatory Tribunal

3.53   In my consultation document, I set out three models for the application of Administrative Monetary Penalties. The key differences in these models related to the mechanism for access to a fair and timely appeal.[35]

---

[35] Macrory, above n 2.

An Independent Tribunal as a Route to Appeal

3.54 It is important that any administrative penalty system where decisions are taken by public officials, acting as part of a Government department or agency, carries with it the necessary protections for any person or business served with a penalty notice. Having access to an effective and quick appeal route is an absolute necessity when referring to administrative financial penalties. The Department for Constitutional Affairs' White Paper on *Complaints Redress and Tribunals* states that 'where mistakes occur we are entitled to complain and to have the mistake put right with the minimum of difficulty; where there is uncertainty we are entitled to expect a quick resolution of the issue'.[36]

3.55 The tribunal I recommend could serve as an appeals mechanism for all administrative sanctions including MAPs as well as other administrative sanctions. The Regulatory Tribunal would provide the regulated community with a chance to have its say before an independent body in cases where there is disagreement over the imposition or conditions of an administrative sanction. It would also hold regulators accountable for the imposition of an administrative sanction and ensure that regulators follow their own enforcement policies and procedures when imposing sanctions. I detail further accountability mechanisms in chapter five.

3.56 For those regulators who already operate schemes of Fixed and Variable Monetary Administrative Penalties with appeals being heard with an existing tribunal, I believe that these appeals can continue to be heard in the existing tribunal. There is no need to shift any of these cases to the Regulatory Tribunal, unless a sponsoring department and regulator agree that the Regulatory Tribunal would be more appropriate.

> We believe that an independent specialist tribunal composed of members with specialist expertise is a good idea and would minimise the burden on the magistrates' court.
>
> *Trading Standards Institute*

> A tribunal would have the specialist skills and experience to deal with a new evidential test and procedure that would be required to make the MAP option work efficiently. MAPs should be viewed as an entirely separate sanction to prosecutions and the distinction could be blurred if appeals were to progress through the criminal courts.
>
> *Office of Rail Regulation*

Why Did I Choose to Create Another Tribunal?

3.57 The evidence presented to me consistently commented that there was a need to separate out those cases of regulatory non-compliance that would be better sanctioned outside of the criminal setting. It follows that if administrative sanctions are to be most effective, then it is necessary to remove appeals relating to these cases

---

[36] DCA, 'Transforming Public Services: Complaints, Redress and Tribunals', Cm 624 (July 2004) 3.

from the criminal courts. This would also avoid creating a hybrid system with no distinct separation between administrative and criminal sanctions.

3.58 Operating a hybrid system with appeals of both administrative and criminal sanctions going to a criminal court would raise some of the same issues that I have previously highlighted in my interim report when considering cases of regulatory non-compliance within a criminal setting.[37] These include:

- Low deterrence can sometimes be the outcome of a criminal prosecution as levels of fines can fail to remove the financial benefit arising from non-compliance.
- Appeals of administrative sanctions would be heard alongside mainstream violent and anti-social crime cases.
- Cases of regulatory non-compliance make up less than one percent of all cases head in magistrates' courts making it difficult to provide specific training to magistrates and legal advisers.[38]

3.59 I recognise that magistrates' courts in some areas already handle both criminal and civil matters, and as a matter of administrative simplicity it would be tempting to refer all appeals concerning MAPs back to the magistrates' courts. Given the proposed creation of the new unified tribunal system (see paragraph 3.67 below), I believe it would be a wasted opportunity not to incorporate a dedicated Regulatory Tribunal which would be better suited to handling these issues, and would clearly separate criminal and administrative processes. In my consultation report I suggested that there would be two advantages to a separate tribunal for appealing administrative sanctions. First, that the tribunal could be composed of members with both legal and specialist expertise in the subject matter, providing the tribunal with a fuller understanding of the issues. Second, a tribunal would not consider regulatory cases alongside cases of conventional crime which constitute the main workload of the criminal courts. A Regulatory Tribunal would also be a flexible and accessible appeal mechanism.

3.60 Overall, in cases of administrative sanctions, I believe that a tribunal would continue to provide sufficient procedural safeguards necessary to protect the needs of the regulated community and regulators. An independent tribunal would also allow for the differentiation and sanctioning of some cases of regulatory non-compliance outside of the criminal setting.

Appeal Route for an Administrative Sanction

3.61 Ultimately, it is for a regulator and sponsoring department to determine what the best appeal arrangements would be for its particular area of regulation provided that the minimum standards which I outline in this section are met. However, I would encourage all regulators who have an administrative sanctioning scheme to consider using the Regulatory Tribunal because it can be designed to be flexible enough to address regulatory issues in more than one particular regulatory field. I discuss this more in detail in the following section.

---

[37] Macrory, above n 2.
[38] Ibid, 89.

> This would allow for such appeals to be heard in a timely manner and will help consistency, as the criminal and civil courts are already 'over-burdened'. The tribunals should be given adequate sentencing powers, in order that they are seen by regulators, consumers and legitimate business as being a worthwhile and punitive measure.
>
> *Yorkshire and Humberside Trading Standards*

Overall Appeal Process for FMAPs

3.62   The first stage of any appeal process in relation to FMAPs should be an internal review of the case carried out by the regulator. This would not involve the tribunal. Having access to an internal review process would give the regulated industry the opportunity to question the regulator's decision and present any information that the regulator may not have had access to at the time the sanction was originally imposed. Following an internal review, the regulator could either affirm its decision and uphold the sanction, or cancel and impose a lesser sanction if appropriate.

3.63   If the member of the regulated community is not satisfied with the outcome of the internal review, an appeal of that decision could be taken forward to the Regulatory Tribunal. The appeal could either be for a complete re-hearing of the issue where the member of the regulated community believes no sanction should have been applied in the first instance because the circumstances of the breach have not been made out (including any defences available for the offence in question) or that the regulator has acted unreasonably in imposing the FMAP. The appropriate grounds for appeal will be determined in legislation. A tribunal case could be conducted on the basis of papers alone if this was agreed to by both parties, or by an oral hearing. As the tribunal will be reviewing the application of administrative sanctions, it will apply the civil standard of proof.

Overall Appeal Process for VMAPs

3.64   As VMAPs would be for more significant financial amounts, I believe that the regulator should give notice to a business that it intends to propose a VMAP, providing the business with an opportunity to make representations to the regulator for consideration. Following this process, a regulator may impose a VMAP by issuing a penalty notice.

3.65   If a business is not satisfied with the level of the VMAP or believes the VMAP should not have been imposed, it has the right of taking this matter to the Regulatory Tribunal for consideration. The appeal could either be a complete re-hearing, or pertain to a specific point of law and should take the form of an oral hearing. The appropriate grounds for appeal will be determined in legislation. Similar to the process outlined above for FMAPs, the tribunal would work on the civil standard of proof, as it is reviewing the application of an administrative sanction.

3.66   It would be up to the regulator and sponsoring department to consider what would constitute an appropriate panel and there are many models that exist. In general, I believe that the Regulatory Tribunal for VMAPs should consist of a panel of three made up of a legal expert, which could include members of the judiciary or lawyers, a relevant expert in the area of regulation before the tribunal, and a member from a relevant stakeholder group such as the industry or another relevant stakeholder.

3.67   Depending on the timing of legislation, the Regulatory Tribunal would either be a new, bespoke tribunal or would form part of the new First-tier Tribunal, proposed in the draft Tribunals, Courts and Enforcement Bill, which was published on 25 July 2006. The Bill sets out a new statutory framework for a unified tribunal system. The tribunal system will have two new, generic tribunals, the First-tier Tribunal and the Upper Tribunal. They are intended to be adaptable institutions, able to take on any existing or new jurisdictions. For those parties that are not satisfied with the outcome of an appeal to the Regulatory Tribunal, there would be a right of appeal on a point of law (and with permission) to the Upper Tribunal. The Tribunals Service, a new Department for Constitutional Affairs agency launched in April 2006, will provide common administrative support to the unified tribunal system.[39] The flexibility of the new unified tribunal system will ensure that the relevant panel of experts need only sit when there is a case to be heard in a particular regulatory area. It will also ensure a good geographical distribution so that cases can be heard in appropriate locations.

Funding

3.68   Funding and set up costs for the Regulatory Tribunal should be provided by the sponsoring departments whose regulators are using the tribunal as part of their appeal for administrative sanctions including MAPs. It is important that any tribunal fees that might be introduced in no way inhibit the right of appeal against Monetary Administrative Penalty which I believe is inherent to a fair system.

IV. My Vision for Contemporary Sanctioning Regimes: Non-financial Sanctions and Alternatives for the Criminal Courts

The previous chapter presented my recommendations for improving the effectiveness of criminal courts in addressing cases of regulatory non-compliance. It also presented my recommendations on the introduction of both Fixed and Variable Monetary Administrative Penalties. This chapter looks at non-financial sanctions such as Statutory Notices, Enforceable Undertakings and Undertakings Plus. It also presents recommendations for alternative sentencing in the criminal courts.

---

[39] http://www.tribunals.gov.uk/.

Introduction

4.1   I am aware that monetary penalties may not be effective in every instance and I want to ensure that regulators have access to a broad range of tools. This chapter sets out some reasons why financial penalties alone may not always achieve the best regulatory outcomes and presents some recommendations for sanctions that are less reliant on financial censure and include broader considerations such as rehabilitation.

Why Monetary Penalties Alone are not always Sufficient

4.2   In my interim report, I showed that 96 percent of the sentences handed down against corporations in Magistrates' Courts were financial penalties.[40] Financial penalties, whether imposed as a result of a criminal prosecution or through an administrative system, may not always be the most appropriate sanction to bring a business into compliance. In some instances, the regulator need only 'persuade' the firm through advice or an informal warning letter, and move it into compliance by explaining the merits of the regulation or explaining what it is the firm would need to do in order to comply. In other instances, where the provision of advice and guidance has failed and where a prosecution or a financial penalty is not appropriate, the regulator may need access to other types of sanctions.

Box 4.1 Some limitations of financial penalties

A body of research has developed over the past two decades that has raised some of the limitations of relying on fines alone to change business behaviour.[1] I highlight some of the shortcomings that a strategy of enforcing by fines alone could include:

Deterrence: I have previously mentioned that unless the financial penalty is of the optimal amount, it may be the case that small financial penalties can be easily absorbed by a large company and become a part of doing business, for example, treating them like overhead costs, with limited impact on the day-to-day decision making on compliance made within a business. On the other hand, smaller firms, may not have the means to pay a fine that would be large enough to deter future lawbreaking.[2]

Getting the level of the fine right is essential to their effectiveness and I believe this will continue to be a challenge for both the courts and regulators. I believe regulators may be better placed, through administrative sanctions to determine the most effective level of financial penalty, which can be subject to review by the Regulatory Tribunal. The regulator can have access to information and consider all of the relevant details when determining the level of a VMAP. Courts may have a more difficult time as the judiciary is often reliant on the prosecution for providing the relevant information. I have heard evidence which suggests that in many instances, prosecutors fail to impart this information to the court.

---

[40] The focus in this chapter is on the sentencing of businesses for regulatory non-compliance. Sentences for individual offenders not pertaining to regulatory non-compliance are not considered.

Spill over: Fining a corporation may also fail to change business behaviour because the company can pass on the financial cost to third parties such as shareholders, employees, creditors and customers, and deferring responsibility away from company management. Shareholders experience losses resulting from fines through falls in the value of shares and reduced future dividends. The cost of a fine also spills over to consumers through increases in the prices for the firm's goods and services, and to employees through adverse effects on wages and staffing.[3]

Discrimination/Unequal impact: Fines tend to impact more upon small businesses whose operations are generally more vulnerable to monetary penalties.[4] The reliance on fining in the sanctioning of a business could also be perceived as representing discriminatory and unfair practice against individual offenders who arguably face far more serious sentences (such as imprisonment).[5]

Reflecting the harm caused: The reliance on financial sanctions alone also suggests that the harm caused by corporate criminal regulatory breaches is financial. However, harm might also include physical, psychological or environmental damage and, financial sanctions alone, may not always result in the best outcomes.

Lack of rehabilitation: Lastly, financial penalties alone may not incentivise businesses to take appropriate measures to address procedures within the business that gave rise to the offence. Instead of taking the necessary steps to build long-term compliance corporate managers may decide to treat fines as recurrent business losses. This can be reinforced if non-compliance results in large financial gains and fines that are imposed do not adequately withdraw the financial benefit.

---

[1] See for example – Sentencing options against corporations, B. Fisse, *Criminal Law Forum* 211, 1990; 'Sanctions Against Corporations: Economic Efficiency or Legal Efficacy?' Sydney University Transnational Corporations Research Project Occasional Paper No 13, 1986; 'Sentencing: Corporate offenders', *New South Wales Law Reform Commission*, 2003; 'Principled Regulation: Federal, Civil and Administrative Penalties in Australia', *Australian Law Reform Commission*, 2002.

[2] 'No Soul to Damn: No Body to Kill: an Unscandalised Inquiry into the Problem of Corporate Punishment', J. Coffee, 79 *Michigan Law Review* 386 refers to this as the 'Deterrence Trap' – where the fine necessary to render future compliance the 'rational' choice for amorally calculating businesses is beyond the means of the business being punished.

[3] *Sanctions Against Corporations: Economic Efficiency or Legal Efficacy*, B. Fisse, n 58 above.

[4] Small businesses find it more difficult than large businesses to absorb a fine due to the constraints on their finances and credit. These constraints make it difficult for a small business to stay afloat through the payment period of a substantial fine.

[5] 'Sentencing: Penalties', Discussion Paper 30, Australian Law Reform Commission, 1987.

4.3   Non-financial administrative penalties could be used to deal with firms that want to comply but may have some gaps in their management system or are small firms with limited resources. They could also be appropriate for offenders who may be in severe economic difficulties and may not be able to pay even small fines. In some cases the offending business or individual might be able to, and have a desire to, undertake activities which aim to restore the harm that has been done.

4.4   For these reasons I have considered sanctions that look beyond the imposition of monetary penalties.

Statutory Notices

4.5   In some instances of regulatory non-compliance, regulators will decide to issue a Statutory Notice. An example could be in instances where a company has failed to carry out, prepare, record and implement a suitable and sufficient risk-assessment addressing the risks that could arise from the use of workplace transport.

4.6   These notices require the recipient to do or refrain from a particular behaviour. They specify the steps a business must take in order to be compliant and the timescale for these changes. Depending on the statutory provision, a Statutory Notice may also include remediation provisions relating to the damage caused by the failure to comply with regulations. Failure to carry out the actions laid out in the notice may also be a criminal offence.

4.7   Although many regulators may have recourse to this sanction, the precise forms of Statutory Notices and their conditions of use vary between regulatory areas. My report *Regulatory Justice: Sanctioning in a post-Hampton World*, published in December 2005, identified examples of different types of Statutory Notices that businesses can be subjected to by the regulator.

Box 4.2 Types of Statutory Notices

- Improvement Notices – demanding certain improvements to work practices while allowing time for the recipient to comply;
- Prohibition/Suspension Notices – prohibits an activity until remedial action has been taken in order to prevent serious harm from occurring;
- Works Notices – to prevent or remedy water pollution; and
- Enforcement Notices – served where it is believed that a breach of regulatory consent or licence has occurred. The notice specifies the steps to rectify the breach and the timescale for these changes, and, depending on the statutory provisions, may include remediation provisions relating to the damage caused by the breach.

Source: R Macrory, 'Regulatory Justice: Sanctioning in a Post-Hampton World' (December 2005).

4.8   In the majority of cases, failure to comply with the terms of a Statutory Notice is an offence in its own right, punishable either by a fine or imprisonment. For example, if the terms of an Improvement/Prohibition Notice imposed by the Health and Safety Executive are not met, this is an offence that may be prosecuted. This demonstrates the seriousness of a notice, but may also deter a regulator from pursuing action against businesses that fail to comply with a notice. A regulator may view the stigma and potential imprisonment as a disproportionate response to the underlying breach.

An enforcement notice should be the preferred form of action over penalties. The enforcement notice system works well for business because there is an emphasis on prevention of injury or harm rather than on prosecution.

Confederation of British Industry.

Scope for Strengthening the Statutory Notices System

4.9   In my consultation report, I presented several ideas for strengthening the system of Statutory Notices. I elaborate on these in the following discussion. My recommendations could apply to both new and existing notices. Such a strengthened system of Statutory Notices should be used in a wider range of regulatory non-compliance.

Notices That are Fit for Purpose

4.10   A number of regulators already have access to some kind of Statutory Notice, but there has been some innovation and development of the design of notices over time. New types of notices have been created and some regulators may benefit from updating their system of Statutory Notices to ensure that their system of notices is up to date and appropriate for a risk based approach to regulation. For example, in the area of consumer protection, Part Eight of the Enterprise Act 2002 gives Local Authority regulators access to Enforcement Orders, which are a type of Statutory Notice. Enforcement Orders are injunctions granted by the court to restrain breaches of specified law, but enforcers can accept agreed undertakings as an alternative to being taken to court. These replace and expand the scope of what were called 'Stop Now Orders' and are used in many areas of consumer protection such as in cases of giving customers written notification for cancelling contracts. This represents an example of an appropriate and effective Statutory Notice.

Box 4.3 Statutory Notices

Statutory Notices need to be improved in the following ways:
- Statutory Notices should be made available as a tool for all regulators to use, in order to ensure consistency.
- Regulators should follow up Statutory Notices through a risk based approach, in order to ensure that Statutory Notices are complied with.
- An appeal mechanism should be made available through independent review and the tribunal system.
- Breaches of notices should be able to be sanctioned by the regulator through Monetary Administrative Penalties, in order to give them strength as a sanction.

Failure to Comply with a Notice

4.11   Failure to follow up notices to check that compliance has been reached can undermine Statutory Notices as a sanctioning tool, and could encourage reluctant businesses not to take them seriously. Furthermore, without follow-up, regulators are not in a position to evaluate the outcomes obtained by using notices. I believe it would be good practice for regulators, as part of evaluating their enforcement activities and outcome measurement to include some assessment of their notice system beyond just reporting on the number of notices issued. I also believe it is important for regulators to follow-up notices on a risk-adjusted basis.

> If business gains the impression that such notices are not enforced, it will damage the credibility of the enforcement regime. Failure to do so would penalise the vast majority of business who have taken action and incurred expense to ensure they have complied.
>
> *Small Business Service.*

4.12   Non-compliance with a Statutory Notice is usually a criminal offence, but as with other cases of regulatory non-compliance, I believe it would be helpful if regulators had greater flexibility in how to sanction the non-compliance with a Statutory Notice, such as applying a MAP rather than solely relying on criminal prosecution for non-compliance. It should remain at the discretion of the regulator whether it would be more appropriate to sanction the failure to comply with a Statutory Notice, in the particular circumstances of a case, with a MAP or a criminal prosecution, and their enforcement policy should indicate the factors that will guide their discretion.

4.13   Regulators may decide that non-compliance with a Statutory Notice always justifies prosecution because an intentional act is implied, or that this should be reserved, say, for repeated non-compliance. But I believe there will be circumstances where the use of a MAP will be a more appropriate and effective sanctioning tool to ensure compliance with a statutory notice. For example, where a business has clearly saved money by delaying compliance but the behaviour does not justify a criminal prosecution. Or where a business has complied with most of the requirements of a notice, with the knowledge that a regulator is unlikely to consider that the costs and time of a prosecution is justified to deal with a small proportion of outstanding issues.

4.14   Lastly, I suggest that regulators ensure that the notice itself is clear in its language and make those who receive such notices aware of the legal status of each notice and the consequences of not complying with the terms of the notice.

Appeals of Statutory Notices

4.15   Most statutory provisions concerning Statutory Notices allow for the right of appeal against the service of the notice (including its requirements). As research undertaken for my review demonstrates the current appeals routes are varied – many provide for appeals to the magistrates' courts, but Health and Safety legislation, for example, provides for appeals to an Employment Tribunal.[41] Where a regulator decides to impose a VMAP in response to a breach of a Statutory Notice, any appeal of the VMAP would, in accordance with my recommendations, be to the Regulatory Tribunal rather than the criminal courts or other fora.

---

[41] C Parker, 'Health and Safety at Work Act 1974, s 24(2), Restorative Justice in Business Regulation? The Australian Competition and Consumer Commission's Use of Enforceable Undertakings' (2004) 67(2) *Modern Law Review*.

4.16   Strictly my terms of reference are concerned with sanctions, but I would recommend that government consider whether any existing appeals against Statutory Notices would be more effectively and speedily handled by the Regulatory Tribunal rather than magistrates' courts. This may not be appropriate in all areas of regulation (it has been argued, for example, that the local knowledge possessed by local magistrates may be especially valuable for dealing with statutory noise nuisance appeals), but appeals against notices are essentially administrative in nature, and may raise complex technical issues where the more specialist make-up of the tribunal would provide a more effective forum.

Recommendation 5

I recommend that for an improved system of Statutory Notices:
- Government should consider using Statutory Notices as part of an expanded sanctioning toolkit to secure future compliance beyond the areas in which they are currently in use;
- Regulators should systematically follow up Statutory Notices using a risk based approach including an element of randomised follow up;
- In dealing with the offence of failing to comply with a Statutory Notice, regulators should have access to administrative financial penalties as an alternative to criminal prosecution. This power should be extended by legislative amendment to existing schemes of Statutory Notices; and
- Government should consider whether appeals against Statutory Notices should be routed through the Regulatory Tribunal rather than the criminal courts.

Enforceable Undertakings

4.17   I have previously commented that the current system of regulatory sanctions lacks both financial and non-financial intermediate sanctions. Regulators have access to informal sanctioning through advice or warning letters, or extremely serious sanctions such as criminal proceedings, but there is a gap relating to intermediate sanctions. Regulators have limited sanctions for cases that are not serious enough to be prosecuted and too serious to just receive an informal warning. For this reason, I am suggesting the addition of some sanctions to fill this gap. As well as MAPs and, where appropriate, Statutory Notices, a further sanction, which I have called Enforceable Undertakings, should be introduced into the enforcement toolkit, for those instances where a non-financial intermediate sanction may be more suitable. I also make recommendations to combine both non-financial and financial administrative elements of a sanction, which I refer to as Undertakings Plus.

4.18   Enforceable Undertakings and Undertakings Plus introduce an intermediate sanction with elements of restoration into the enforcement process. If adopted in the UK, they could facilitate negotiations between regulator, business and, in appropriate cases, the victims of regulatory non-compliance. They represent a powerful alternative to traditional coercive, regulatory enforcement action, and have the potential of imposing fit-for-purpose sanctions which are more satisfying for both offender and the victims of non-compliance.

What are Enforceable Undertakings?

4.19   Enforceable Undertakings (EUs) are a flexible sanction that enable regulators to tailor their enforcement response to individual circumstances taking industry considerations and resources, such as management capacity and willingness to restore harm, into account. They represent a valuable alternative to traditional regulatory enforcement action because they can address the needs of several parties involved in, or affected by, the wrongdoing as well as correcting and preventing breaches and their underlying causes.

4.20   EUs, in the form in which I am recommending them, are a sanction not currently available in the UK. Although some elements of EUs do exist in other contexts, their application across the regulatory landscape would be an extension of regulators' existing enforcement toolkits.[42]

4.21   EUs have proven successful abroad and I have discussed these experiences in more detail in chapter four of my interim report.[43] A report for the Australian Competition and Consumer Commission – cited by the Australian Law Reform Commission in its review of regulatory penalty schemes – concluded that Enforceable Undertakings provide a quicker and more cost-effective mechanism for resolution of regulatory non-compliance than court proceedings. The Commission also quoted businesses which observed that undertakings are a 'nice way' of warning and giving the regulated business 'another chance'. Businesses also stated that Enforceable Undertakings can encourage greater candour and promote compliance.[44]

4.22   EUs are legally binding agreements between the regulator and business, under which the business agrees to carry out specific activities to rectify its non-compliance. An EU could include a commitment to future regulatory outcomes, including steps to ensure that a specific type of incident does not re-occur. EUs would be most effective when monitored closely by the regulator and where non-compliance with an EU is not tolerated.

4.23   EUs could be more effective in cases where a financial penalty or criminal conviction is likely to be absorbed by the business with a limited impact on the culture or management of the firm. They are also likely to be more effective in securing a change in businesses' behaviour when compared to warning letters or other means of persuasion currently available to the regulator. This is due to the way in which an EU is designed. Warning letters and advice are imposed by a regulator and specify what actions need to be taken by a business. The business may not have bought into the actions required. With EUs, it is the businesses who would apply for an EU and come up with their own list of conditions, and take ownership of the regulatory

---

[42] The Competition Act 1998, s 31A; the Enterprise Act 2002, ss 73 and 82.

[43] Macrory, above n 2, 70.

[44] Australian Law Reform Commission, 'Principled Regulation: Federal, Civil and Administrative Penalties in Australia' (2002) ch 16.

Box 4.4 Undertakings in lieu of Enforcement Orders

1. Under Part Eight of the Enterprise Act 2002, the power is given to certain regulators to apply for Enforcement Orders from the court. Enforcement Orders are final orders given by a court to require the cessation of, or otherwise prohibit the infringement of certain legislation, where the infringement harms the collective interests of consumers.

2. The regulators that can use this power are General Enforcers (OFT, local weights and measures authorities, Department of Enterprise, Trade and Investment in Northern Ireland), Designated Enforcers (bodies designated in a Statutory Instrument by the Secretary of State) and Community Enforcers (only enforcers from other EEA states).

3. A business is usually given a period of at least 14 days consultation regarding such an action and may seek to make undertakings to the regulator during that time. These may be to rectify any infringement made by the business.

4. The regulator may accept or reject the undertakings made. If rejected, then the application for an Enforcement Order proceeds. If accepted, then the steps that the business makes to comply with the undertakings are monitored. If they are complied with then no further action will be taken.

5. If undertakings are not complied with then the regulator may apply to court for it to issue an Enforcement Order. The court may choose instead to accept the undertaking from the business. If the undertakings accepted by the court are breached after this then it is deemed to be a contempt of court. The process is outlined in Figure 4.1.

Figure 4.1 Enforcement Orders in the UK.
Source: Enforcement of Consumer Protection Legislation Guide on Part 8 of The Enterprise Act, OFT, March 2005.

solution presented. Conditions that form part of the EU would be proportionate to the underlying breach and would hold business to account for their non-compliance.

4.24   Business responses to my call for evidence and consultation strongly supported the notion that there is a need for more flexible sanctions. EUs would allow for regulators to use a more flexible and individually tailored approach, which takes business considerations into account when determining how best to deal with cases of regulatory non-compliance. My recommendations here are very much in line with the Hampton ideas focusing on improving behaviour and moving firms into compliance through advice and persuasion.

> Enforceable Undertakings focus strongly on behaviour change and damage restitution. The IoD has also been impressed by the Australian experience of using EUs.
>
> *Institute of Directors*

> EUs may work well not only as an alternative sanction but also as an additional sanction to our current regulatory tools. We particularly see the benefit of Enforceable Undertakings in larger organisations or major outbreaks of food borne disease or major food incidents. An Enforceable Undertaking Agreement would allow proportionality with the breach and the defendant's resources. Small duty holders may also be encouraged by the principal of agreeing a strategy that is clear, objective and measured. Enforceable Undertakings could provide scope and benefit to agree restorative and community elements. Enforceable Undertakings could also be a powerful tool to deliver sustained compliance. The Enforceable Undertaking option promotes openness of organisations and transparency of the enforcement process and fits well with the Agency's developing enforcement strategy.
>
> *Food Standards Agency*

How Enforceable Undertakings Could Work in the UK

4.25   Enforceable Undertakings should be available to regulators as an alternative to imposing a VMAP, or taking court action and prosecuting a business for regulatory non-compliance. It will be for individual regulators or their sponsoring departments, to determine which of the offences set out in their regulatory legislation, and in what circumstances an EU might be an appropriate sanctioning response. A key benefit of EUs is that the system offers the industry concerned the opportunity to demonstrate how it proposes to respond to a regulatory breach and to make open and binding commitments accordingly.

4.26   I believe that EUs should be a sanction that the regulator could consider in cases where they have the necessary evidence to bring an enforcement action. Regulators may prefer to accept an application for an EU in cases where they believe the EU will better deliver:

- the best regulatory outcomes which could include redressing the harm caused by the breach; and/or
- the motivation for the necessary change in behaviour that could be brought about through an EU.

4.27 The specific actions required of a company that could be set out in Enforceable Undertakings include provisions for compensation, reimbursement or redress to affected parties. Actions may also include requirements that the offender does a service to the community, such as funding or implementing a compliance education program, and can also include a restorative element. I believe that once an Enforceable Undertaking has been agreed, there must be a consequence for the failure to comply with it.

4.28 If regulators have EUs as part of their toolkit, it will be important to make businesses aware that it is a sanctioning option. It would be helpful for regulators to provide guidance as to what might constitute an acceptable EU in order to avoid businesses offering too little. This could be included as part of a regulator's enforcement policy.

4.29 I do not intend to set out, in this report, the detail of exactly how Enforceable Undertakings would operate, as the details would be best left with by those responsible within government for the implementation of such a sanction. However, I do believe there are some key features, based on the experience of this sanction in other jurisdictions that are necessary to ensure the effective operation of this new regime, which I outline in the section below.

Enforceable Undertakings in Practice

Application

- A regulator's enforcement policy should indicate the type of circumstances in which it would consider accepting an EU rather than pursuing another sanction. In cases where a business has received notification that it is being prosecuted for an alleged breach of regulation, the business may decide to apply for an Enforceable Undertaking. When the regulator receives an application for an EU, legal proceedings connected with the alleged breach are put on hold. If the application for an EU is not accepted, prosecution will proceed.
- Where the regulator has decided to impose a VMAP on a business, and where the business may not have the financial resources to pay the administrative penalty, the business may decide to apply for an EU. When the regulator receives an application for an EU, proceedings connected with the breach and the imposition of the VMAP are put on hold. If the application for the EU is not accepted, the imposition of the VMAP will proceed.
- I suggest that business is not guaranteed a right to an Enforceable Undertaking; it would be granted at the discretion of the regulator.

Content

- Enforceable Undertakings could take the form of a written agreement between the regulator and the business. This would clearly set out the specific action(s) for the business.
- The actions set out in the EU should be proportionate to and bear a clear relationship with the underlying breach. The time period within which compliance with actions is required should be defined.

- Regulators could also consider the impact on and, in some cases, consult third parties that have been affected by the regulatory non-compliance when deciding whether to accept the Undertaking.
- One of the conditions of an EU could include a financial element through a Monetary Administrative Penalty ('Undertaking Plus') *see s 4.30 below*.

Process

- Enforceable Undertakings would require an increased monitoring role for the regulator, as it will be involved in following up EUs to ensure that the conditions are carried through.
- Where a regulator has accepted an EU, the Undertaking should be made available publicly. This is important to secure public confidence in the regulatory enforcement system, but businesses who have agreed undertakings will also benefit since it will demonstrate that it is taking responsible action in relation to a breach.

Non-compliance

- There should be consequences for the business if it fails to comply with the EU. Having agreed and accepted the Undertaking as an appropriate response to specific regulatory non-compliance, if a business fails to comply with the conditions of an EU, the regulator could apply for a court order directing compliance with the undertaking or directing the payment of a fine.

'Undertakings Plus'

4.30   A regulator may consider that while an undertaking offered by the business may be appropriate, the circumstances of the breach also require the payment of a financial penalty, and I think the system of EUs should be sufficiently flexible to incorporate this. This might be appropriate where, for example, the business has made a clear financial gain from non-compliance. The financial element of an Undertaking Plus would be based on the same principles as I described earlier in this chapter when discussing Fixed and Variable Monetary Administrative Penalties, and any revenue from the penalty would not go direct to the regulator. The Undertaking Plus would also be a voluntary but legally binding agreement. Both the financial element and the conditions of the EU would need to be agreed upon by both the company and the regulator. If a company did not agree with the level of the financial penalty, then it would choose not to enter into the EU and the regulator would decide what, if any enforcement action should be taken.

Guidance in the enforcement policy

4.31   Regulators would need to prepare guidance on when and under what circumstances EUs and Undertakings Plus might be considered and this should be reflected in and be part of the regulators' enforcement policy. This policy, in turn, will be subject to the statutory Compliance Code.

Recommendation 6

I recommend that the Government should introduce Enforceable Undertakings and Undertakings Plus (a combination of an Enforceable Undertaking with an administrative financial penalty) as an alternative to a criminal prosecution or the imposition of VMAPs for regulators that are compliant with the Hampton and Macrory Principles and characteristics.

Box 4.5 Case study of EUs in Australia and USA

Australia

In 2006, Black & Decker admitted a potential contravention of Australian law by selling a product with packaging which represented that it was made in Australia when it was, in fact, imported. After negotiation with the Australian Competition and Consumer Commission (ACCC) the company provided a court enforceable undertaking that it would (1) refrain from making misleading and false representations in regards to its products, (2) take remedial action in relation to stock held by retailers, and (3) implement a compliance programme to ensure future conduct did not contravene Australia law.

Source – ACCC Public Undertakings Register

USA

In June 2005, the Environmental Protection Agency reached an agreement with Saint-Gobain Containers Inc. to resolve Clean Air Act allegations. The agreement required Saint-Gobain to install state-of-the-art pollution control and monitoring equipment at a cost of approximately $6.6 million. Saint-Gobain was also required to pay a civil penalty of $929,000 and spend $1.2 million for an environmental project to operate and maintain the new equipment. In addition, Saint-Gobain agreed to immediately comply with interim air pollution limits, obtain proper air permits, install pollution control equipment on its furnaces, and donate approximately $1 million worth of emission credits generated by the emission reductions.

Source – Compliance and Enforcement Annual Results 2005, Environmental Protection Agency, Office of Enforcement and Compliance Assurance, November 2005

Restorative Justice

4.32   Restorative Justice (RJ) is a philosophy that views harm and crime as violations of people and relationships. It is a holistic process that addresses the repercussions and obligations created by harm with a view to putting things right. When compared with current models of punishment, RJ requires a paradigm shift in thinking about responses to harm. RJ is different from retributive justice. It is justice that puts energy into the future, not into what is past. It focuses on what needs to be restored or repaid and what needs to be learned and strengthened in order for the harm not to re-occur.[45]

4.33   The basic principles of RJ are focused around harm and relationships such as the harm caused to individuals by injury at a workplace or a financial loss to a consumer because of mis-selling. Harms to the environment could include industrial spills or emissions into the environment. There are several definitions of RJ that I have come across although none is universally accepted. A frequently used and common definition of RJ which I have adopted in this Review is:

Restorative Justice is a process whereby those most directly affected by a wrongdoing come together to determine what needs to be done to repair the harm and prevent a reoccurrence.[46]

Benefits of an RJ Approach

4.34   **Outcomes** – The use of RJ has the potential to give good long-term outcomes for both victims and offenders. Victims show consistently greater levels of satisfaction in systems using Restorative Justice when compared to those relying on court-based justice, and many studies have strongly suggested that the re-offending rate of offenders is lower if they have undergone an RJ process.[47]

4.35   **Flexible response** – An RJ process is also flexible, as there is no pre-conceived notion of what 'restoration' is. It is a dynamic process reflecting the needs and capabilities of the stakeholders involved.

4.36   **RJ is focused on restoring the harm** – A restorative style approach will have a slightly different focus than the criminal justice system, which is more concerned with fault and punishment. In contrast, RJ is focused on the harm caused and on what can be done to make things right.

These positive aspects of RJ are reflected in the experience of its use in the UK within non-regulatory areas of the UK justice system. This has included work in areas such as Youth Justice and prisons.

RJ in Regulators' Sanctioning Toolkits:

4.37   In my interim report I outlined the case for using RJ in regulators' sanctioning toolkits as a further alternative to criminal prosecution, administrative fines or statutory notices. This case relied on evidence from Australia of the successful application of RJ to regulatory matters, discussed the use of RJ in the UK justice system, and put forward options for consultation.

---

[45] The Centre for Restorative Justice, Simon Fraser University, Vancouver, 'Introduction to Restorative Justice', available at http://www.sfu.ca/crj/introrj.html.
[46] 'Restorative Justice and Practices', paper presented at 'Restorative Justice in Action…into the Mainstream', The 3rd International Winchester Restorative Justice Group Conference, 29–30 March 2006, London.
[47] J Latimer, C Dowden and D Muise, 'The Effectiveness of Restorative Practices: A Meta-analysis' (2005) 85 *The Prison Journal* 127; Restorative Justice Consortium, 'The Positive Effect of Restorative Justice on Re-offending' (January 2006).

4.38   Respondents to the consultation document on this review shared my positive outlook on the potential for Restorative Justice in this area.

RJ used in conjunction with other enforcement tools may provide a good framework to proportionately match the breach, and involve and meet the needs of victims e.g. rehabilitation, workers retraining, reassurance and support, closure and public support. RJ would enable an organisation to do the right thing quickly. RJ may well result in improvements in health and safety outcomes in businesses as well as educate the organisation and managers.

Health and Safety Commission

There are many areas of regulatory non-compliance where restorative justice may well be appropriate. These will include Financial malfeasance, environmental damage and injury or risk to members of the public.

Trades Union Congress

We consider Restorative Justice (RJ) to be an innovative means of imposing sanctions on a particular business. RJ has the potential to educate where a strict financial penalty would not. It would also ensure a satisfactory outcome for the victims of regulatory non-compliance.

British Chamber of Commerce

4.39   Overall, 74 percent of respondents believed that RJ could be applied to the area of regulation, 24 percent believed that it could not be applied to this area. Furthermore the responses were favourable on the potential use of RJ in all three potential options for its use raised in the consultation document.

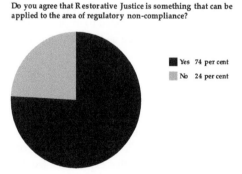

Figure 4.2 Consultation Response to RJ proposals

Recommendation 7

I recommend that Government introduce pilot schemes involving the use of Restorative Justice techniques in addressing cases of regulatory non-compliance. This might include RJ:

* as a pre-court diversion;
* instead of a Monetary Administrative Penalty; and
* within the criminal justice system – as both a pre or post sentencing option.

Some Considerations to make RJ Effective as a Regulatory Sanction

RJ Practitioners

4.40   RJ events can have very serious consequences for all stakeholders involved. Victims will often be very raw and sensitive about the physical, emotional, or financial harm that has been inflicted upon them. Offenders, on the other hand, will often be very nervous about facing those who they have harmed. Furthermore, the result of an RJ event will be an agreed remedy for the harm that has been caused. This agreement could amount to a significant burden on the offender, for example, financial compensation or a commitment to undertake unpaid work.

4.41   Given the importance of these potential consequences, and the sensitivities on both sides that need to be respected, RJ must be carried out by trained experts. I understand that Skills for Justice, the standards setting body for the justice sector, will be publishing Occupational Standards by the end of this year and these will form the basis of any professional qualifications for such experts.

RJ Best Practice

4.42   There is a good body of work on the use of RJ in the UK that provides many good points of learning that will provide safeguards for participants and give RJ the best chance of success. Any schemes introduced to implement RJ in the area of regulation should use this Best Practice guidance as the basis for designing RJ procedures.[48]

Piloting RJ

4.43   Pilots could help capture for the regulatory system, the positive experience of RJ in other non-regulatory areas. Building on the Government's evidence-based approach to RJ policymaking I believe the best way to take forward the use of RJ in the area of regulation is through the use of pilots. The evidence from the use of RJ in the UK in non-regulatory areas, and the positive experience from Australia of the use of RJ in regulation show that there could be a use for RJ in regulatory sanctioning in the UK. I believe it would be good practice for a few pilot schemes to be undertaken to better develop RJ in the context of regulatory sanctioning.

---

[48] Home Office, 'Restorative Justice Guidance: Best Practice for Practitioners, their Case Supervisors, and Line Managers' (December 2004).

Alternative Sanctions in the Criminal Courts

4.44 Throughout this chapter, I have recommended a number of non-financial administrative sanctioning options to supplement the regulators' enforcement toolkit. Finally, in this last section, I look at expanding the sanctioning options available to the judiciary in cases of criminal prosecution.

Introduction

4.45 In recent years, the criminal justice system in England and Wales has seen innovations in sentencing options for individual offenders beyond the traditional options of financial penalties or imprisonment. This is evident in the range of community sentencing options made available to judges in the Criminal Justice Act (CJA) 2003. Amongst these options are Unpaid Work Requirements, Curfew Requirements, Supervision Requirements, and Electronic Monitoring.[49] While these examples are not directly applicable to regulatory legislation, I mention them to demonstrate the flexibility in sanctioning of individuals.

4.46 There has been very little development in relation to the sanctioning of businesses for cases of regulatory non-compliance as the options I mentioned under the CJA 2003 are only available for individuals. I believe that there are existing tools that could be developed to effectively sanction the regulated community in cases that lead to a criminal conviction.

My Recommendations for Alternative Sentencing in Criminal Courts

4.47 I believe criminal courts should have more flexibility in the sanctions available to them in cases of regulatory non-compliance. I discuss several options that could be adopted in legislation by regulators and departments to better achieve increased compliance when sanctioning through a criminal prosecution in the section below.

Box 4.6 Holistic use of Alternate Sanctioning in Australia

In November 2004, Vilo Assets Management was convicted by the Environmental Protection Agency (EPA) of the explosive discharge of over 6,500 litres of partially reacted bio-diesel. A number of people were injured and property on other sites damaged due to the incident. The company was ordered to pay $20,000 towards an indigenous planting project within 30 days of the court order and to provide the EPA with proof of the payment within 45 days of that order. The business was prohibited from referring to the payment without also referring to the fact that they were ordered to do so by the court as a result of their regulatory non-compliance. The order also required Vilo to publish in the local and metropolitan media a notice about the offence and its impact in a manner specified by the court.

Source – EPA media release November 2004 – Vilo Assets Management Pty Limited v EPA (Victoria) 2004

---

[49] As defined in ss 199, 204, 213 and 215 of the Criminal Justice Act 2003.

Profit Orders

4.48   Evidence has been presented in the course of both the Hampton Review and this review that clearly demonstrates that current levels of fines do not appear to reflect the gains from non-compliance with regulatory requirements in most cases.[50] As I discuss with regard to VMAPs and setting of the fines in Box 3.2, I believe that there are many factors that should determine the level of a financial penalty. These factors include whether the business has gained a financial benefit as a result of the non-compliance.

4.49   Fine levels imposed by the criminal courts should take into account any savings made by non-compliance, but in cases where the savings are clear (such as the failure to pay licence fees for a number of years) I believe that it would be preferable if the criminal courts had the power to impose a Profit Order that is separate from any fine imposed. The Profit Order would be a non-judgmental sanction in that it reflected solely the profits made from non-compliance, while the fine imposed would reflect the court's assessment of the seriousness with which they regard the breach. Thus it would be perfectly possible for a court to impose a substantial Profit Order where the savings were large, but impose a small fine because it considered the business had acted carelessly rather than with intent or recklessness. Identifying and removing the financial benefit from a regulatory breach is something I believe would strengthen enforcement and send a clearer signal to industry that it is not acceptable to make financial gain from non-compliance. It also seeks to provide a more level playing field for business and provides a deterrent for non-compliant businesses. Adding this level of differentiation and transparency and separating out financial benefits from punitive fines would ensure that businesses did not feel subject to large punitive sanctions unnecessarily and would guard against those types of accusations.

Box 4.7 A New Sanctioning Tool: Profit Orders

Profit Orders would aim to ensure that the criminal offender should not gain from committing an offence and would seek to remove any financial gain that arose as a result of the non-compliance.

In effect, the Profit Order would seperate the financial gain from the fine (the punitive sanction representing social and moral condemnation). Financial gains can include direct financial benefits as a result of non-compliance as well as deferred costs.

The Profit Order should reflect the actual gain made and should not be subject to any statutory limit. Nevertheless, in assessing both the fine and Profit Order imposed, the courts would be required to take into account the financial means of the offender.

4.50   To my knowledge, there is no similar scheme in operation in the UK at present, but there have been some attempts to remove the financial gains from wrongdoing. Most often, this takes the form of Confiscation Orders, which are made after conviction to deprive the defendant of the benefit that has been obtained from crime as set out in the Proceeds of Crime Act 2002. The Assets Recovery Agency uses the Proceeds

---

[50] Hampton, above n 4, 6, para 17.

of Crime Act 2002 to disrupt organised criminal enterprises and recover criminal assets.[51] It appears that Confiscation Orders have generally been used against individuals. Magistrates do not currently have access to Confiscation Orders and must refer cases up to the Crown Court to have access to this sanction. In addition, Confiscation Orders are strict in that they can only be used to capture acquisitive benefits such as profits that result from an offence. This benefit does not currently include provision for costs avoided, deferred or saved, which is a substantial part of the financial benefit obtained as a result of regulatory non-compliance.

Box 4.8 Criminal Convictions and Confiscation Orders

When deciding how to sanction a business who has not complied with regulatory requirements, the regulatory authority should also consider the power of the court to make a Confiscation Order under the Proceeds of Crime Act 2002 in the event of a conviction. For offences committed up to 24 March 2003, the relevant legislation is the Criminal Justice Act 1988 (as amended).

When a defendant (including a corporate body) has benefited from an offence and the prosecution asks the court to proceed, the court must make an Order for the offender to pay the amount by which they have benefited from the criminal conduct, or the available amount, whichever is the lesser.

In cases of offending by a corporate body, the starting point for calculating the defendant's benefit may be the gross turnover of the business during the period of the offence, i.e. deductions are not made for legitimate expenditure and so the amount of the Confiscation Order may be considerably greater than the net profit during the relevant period.

In deciding whether to prosecute an offender, the likelihood of a Confiscation Order being made in the event of a conviction is a public interest factor in favour of prosecution in the Code for Crown Prosecutors.

4.51   It would be up to the prosecution to apply for a Profit Order. They will not be appropriate in all cases of regulatory non-compliance, but suitable where the profits or financial gains made are clear. It would be at the discretion of the court whether or not to impose such an order.

Corporate Rehabilitation Orders (CROs)

4.52   Financial penalties represent the main sanction available to criminal courts in dealing with businesses who have not complied with regulatory obligations. Even where courts have access to a Profit Order as recommended above, the level of any financial penalty imposed will always take account of ability to pay which may account for some of the apparent low level of fines imposed on smaller businesses. In dealing with individual offenders, criminal courts now have access to a wide range of sanctions beyond fines and imprisonment, designed to bring home to the offender the consequences of the breach or secure rehabilitation. I believe that in

---

[51] Proceeds of Crime Act 2002; the Act deals with Confiscation Orders in Part 2 in relation to England and Wales, Part 3 for Scotland and Part 4 for NI.

Box 4.9 Use of POCA in the Regulatory Context by UK Local Authorities

Evidence from UK Local Authorities shows that POCA (Proceeds of Crime Act 2002) has been successfully used to remove illegal profits from rogue traders such as counterfeiters. Three examples that have been submitted to the review are:

- Counterfeit Goods – The London Asset Recovery Team (RART) secured a confiscation order of £1,077,700 against an offender from Leyton working with Hackney Trading Standards Authority. The offender was also sentenced to 18 months' imprisonment after he was convicted of selling counterfeit goods, including well known brands to various retail outlets across London. (see http://cms.met.police.uk/met/news/convictions/forgery/1million_confiscation_order)
- Counterfeit Goods – Brent and Harrow Councils Trading Standards Departments secured the first confiscation order against a limited company. Trading Standards, with the Police and the London Regional Asset Recovery Team raided the premises of the offending company (a handbag wholesalers) and found over 1,700 counterfeit items which breached trademarks belonging to Louis Vuitton, Celine and Versace. The company's business records, accounts and computer hard drives were searched to determine the extent of the financial benefit from selling counterfeit goods. Following a successful prosecution, the company was ordered to pay £400,000 in August, this year.
- Clocking Cars – Northamptonshire County Council – A financial investigation by Northamptonshire Police established that the defendant had benefited to an amount of £180,507 and identified realisable assets amounting to at least £123,472. A confiscation order in the sum of £25,611 was made, together with an order for costs in the sum of £15,000 and compensation orders totalling £10,404. The Crown Court judge accepted the prosecutor's submission that in calculating the benefit he should make a confiscation order in respect of all 33 cars. The judge also accepted that the method of calculating the benefit submitted by the prosecution (i.e. the *Glass's Guide* true mileage price for the vehicle less the Guide's lower mileage price) was appropriate. Two alternative methods were suggested by the defendant but application for leave to appeal was dismissed. The Court of Appeal found that the method adopted by the prosecutor was not unjust and indicated that the benefit may even have been aptly assessed by reference to the gross proceeds of the sale of the 'clocked' cars.

Source: LACORS response to Macrory Review consultation

---

dealing with regulatory breaches by businesses, the criminal courts should also have access to a more flexible range of sanctioning tools beyond the simple imposition of a financial penalty.

4.53   Corporate Rehabilitation Orders, as they are currently used in Australia, contain provisions to enable a court to require a company to undertake specific actions or activities during a specified period, such as one or two years. Corporate Rehabilitation Orders, as implied by their title, aim to rehabilitate the offender by ensuring tangible steps are taken that will address a company's poor practices and prevent future non-compliance. They involve a period of monitoring of the activities, policies and procedures of a business, with a view to organisational reform.[52]

4.54   Activities specified in the order could include training of personnel in regulatory related matters, the adoption and implementation of action plans to address regulatory non-compliance or taking steps to remedy the harm caused by regulatory non-compliance.

4.55   I believe a similar model could be introduced in the UK. Although I do not want to be too prescriptive in the models set out because different regulatory areas will have different needs, I do outline the way in which these could work in practice here in the UK.[53] CROs give criminal courts access to a sanction similar to Enforceable Undertakings.

- On conviction the company would be invited to put forward to the court a plan of action to remedy the matter which caused the harm. This could include a community project or a compliance audit;
- The court, in consultation with the regulator would either approve that scheme or appoint its own experts (who would be paid by the company) to design a more robust plan;
- The court would make its order;
- The relevant regulator would monitor compliance with this order; and
- Failure to comply with the order would lead to the company being brought back to court and sentenced in an alternative way, with the court taking into consideration, failure to comply with the CRO.

4.56   Corporate rehabilitation is an effective means of rehabilitating an offending firm and reducing the likelihood of future harm. The imposition of this sanction goes beyond what a fine can achieve in this respect by identifying tangible steps that a company must take and binding that company to their implementation. In taking steps to solve a company's compliance problems (as opposed to simply fining) there is also a greater chance that the individuals responsible will be identified and be held to account for their offences. A CRO will often replace a fine imposed, but in appropriate cases courts should retain the discretion to impose a fine in addition to the order.

Community Projects

4.57   The range of requirements that could form the elements of Corporate Rehabilitation Orders should be flexible, reflecting both the circumstances of the regulatory breach and the nature of the defendant. It could, for example, include a requirement for the business to complete an appropriate community improvement project within a specified period and for a specified value related to the underlying harm or benefit that has been caused or obtained by the offender. Community projects would enable the business community to take responsibility for its actions within a local community and restore the harm it may have caused to the community or individuals. The project symbolises the restitution of the loss to the community that

---

[52] New South Wales Law Reform Commission, 'Sentencing: Corporate Offenders', Report 102 (2003).
[53] M Jefferson 'Corporate Criminal Liability: The Problem of Sanctions' [2001] *Journal of Criminal Law* 65.

Box 4.10 Case Study for Corporate Rehabilitation Orders

US v World Air Conditioning Inc

On October 30, 1997, US Federal Court found World Air Conditioning Inc. guilty of failing to report income in federal tax returns, obstruction of justice and mail fraud. The defendant was ordered to pay $1.5 million in fines and several conditions of corporate probation, including co-operation with the IRS (Internal Revenue Service) and periodic reports of financial condition and periodic investigations of the company's records by independent experts were imposed on it.

Source – US Department of Justice press release October 1997

US v Royal Caribbean Cruises Ltd

On September 17, 1998, Royal Caribbean Cruises Limited was sentenced to a $1 million criminal fine for dumping oil and lying to the US Coast Guard. In addition the court imposed a period of corporate rehabilitation of five years, during which the conduct of the company will be closely monitored, with periodic reports to the court and the Government, detailing the company's environmental compliance and including the results of independent audits.

Source – US Department of Justice press release September 17, 1998

---

corporate crime involves, and could be appropriate where the business does not have the ability to pay a large financial penalty.

4.58   Examples of community projects include funding and delivering an education campaign in a specific subject or funding and delivering a project in the built environment, such as a park or a garden, or making some donations to the local community of time or resource as our examples in Box 4.11. More generally, the projects should be:

- Carried out in addition to something the company is already legally obliged to do;
- The firm should not be allowed to use the project for its own public relations purposes; and
- The community project could be used where the defendant is not in a position to pay a high financial penalty.

4.59   International experience with such community requirements has been positive. Australian environmental and health and safety legislation provides broad powers to judges to order businesses to carry out specified projects to either restore the environment or improve health and safety respectively. Not only do the projects deliver tangible benefits to the local community where the offence was committed, but it has also engaged the business more so than a financial penalty would, for example, to ensure that future compliance is secured. This engagement would enhance the rehabilitative element of the sentence as the offender recognises the serious harm that has been caused.

Box 4.11 Examples of Community Projects

Six bakeries convicted of price fixing in the US were excused from paying substantial portions of the fines imposed on condition that they provided baked goods to various organisations assisting the needy for one year. The court identified several reasons for making the order:[1]

Avoidance of 'spill over' – Imposing fines commensurate with the gravity of the offence would have bankrupted the bakeries. This would have caused a large spill over effect through creating widespread unemployment amongst the bakeries' production-line employees.

Reflecting non-financial aspect of the crime – The community project required the firm to make symbolic restitution for their offences by doing something more onerous and thought-provoking than merely paying fines.

Publicity – The community project brought the offences to the attention of the public, thereby increasing deterrence without harming the needs of employees, consumers or communities that would otherwise be affected by a fine.

This example illustrates some of the added value that a community project can deliver in comparison to a simple fining approach.

In February 2002, Rosedale Leather pleaded guilty to one charge of air pollution after offensive odours from its tannery affected local residents. As part of the sentence handed down by the magistrates' court the company was ordered to pay $20,000 to a local community project to aid in the implementation of streetscape beautification works in the town of Rosedale.

Source: EPA media release February 2002 (Rosedale Leather v EPA (Victoria) 2002)

[1] *United States v Danilow Pastry Co* (1983) 563 F Supp 1159 at 1166-1167.

Mandatory Compliance Audits

4.60   The power to compel companies to undertake an 'audit' is common in Australian states, especially in the area of environmental regulation.[54] This type of sanction is designed to remedy deficiencies in the business's management and may be appropriate where systemic organisational change would help to better achieve future compliance. Bringing in external expertise could get the business the help it needs to identify how to improve its operations and meet its regulatory objectives.

4.61   A Mandatory Compliance Audit, by an accredited third party, ordered by the court, would identify the necessary changes to a business, to protect the public and also provide a framework to ensure that the changes would be made.[55] Audits by third parties would be systematic, documented and objective reviews of a business' facilities, operations and product lines.[56] The outcome of such a review would be an

[54] Macrory, above n 2.

[55] M Berlin, 'Environmental Auditing: Entering the Eco-information highway' [1998] *New York University Law Journal* 2.

[56] JT O'Reilly, 'Environmental Audit Privileges: The Need for Legislative Recognition' (1994) 19 *Seton Hall Legislative Journal* 119.

action plan of what corrective actions would be necessary to bring the business back into compliance.[57] The court could then direct the regulator to monitor the business to ensure it takes all of the necessary corrective action.

4.62   Mandatory audits have the potential to be wide ranging in their operation; in Australia they can be sought not only in relation to the premises and operation where the original offence was committed or brought to the regulator's attention, but to all sites and operations carried out by the defendant.[58] The scope of audits can also include an examination of both physical and managerial activities.[59]

4.63   I believe that as part of a Corporate Rehabilitation Order, the court should have discretion on whether such an audit is appropriate, seeking guidance from the regulator and its prosecutors on whether it is appropriate. The regulator could keep a list of accredited agents who could carry out the audit, with the costs of this met by the non-compliant business. If a business contested and a court agreed that the business did not have the means to pay, then such a sanction would not be appropriate.

Box 4.12 International Use of Mandatory Compliance Audits

In August 2002, the Environmental Protection Agency fined Shell Refining Australia Limited for three separate incidents of oil discharges to Corio Bay beach. After a number of other cases of pollution were taken into consideration the EPA issued a clean up order and after discussion with the company initiated a number of independent environmental audits to identify and fix problems at the refinery.

Source – EPA media release 2 August 2002 [Shell Refining (Australia) Pty Limited v EPA Victoria 2002]

On 10 May 2006, the US Environmental Protection Agency (EPA) brought a civil action for injunctive relief and civil penalties against AgriProcessors Inc. for numerous violations of federal environmental laws. The consent decree required the company to pay an administrative fine as well as undergo a Compliance Audit, carried out according to provisions set out in the consent decree, by an independent auditing firm. The purpose of the audit was to determine and achieve the firm's compliance with federal environmental legislation and was at the expense of the defendant. Provisions of the Compliance Audit included stipulations for a audit work plan, what the audit report should contain and the timing of when the audit report has to be submitted to the EPA.

Source US Department of Justice – www.usdoj.gov

---

[57] Berlin, above n 54.
[58] NSW Environmental Protection Agency, 'Guidelines for Seeking Environmental Court Orders'.
[59] O'Reilly, above n 55.

Publicity Orders

4.64 Reputation is an important asset to many businesses. When thinking about how to motivate firms to change their behaviour, reputational sanctions can have more of an impact than even the largest financial penalties. The use of reputational sanctions is already in practice in some areas of UK regulation as I outline in Box 4.14.

4.65 Publicity Orders are an effective means of deterring regulatory non-compliance as it can impact the public reputation of a business. A company's reputation and prestige is an important and valuable asset. The consequences of damaging a firm's reputation can potentially exceed the effect of a maximum fine that a court could impose.[60] A company that loses its reputation even for a short time can suffer significant damages to consumer confidence, market share and equity value.[61]

4.66 Publicity Orders can also make a business's behaviour more public and really hold it to account for its regulatory failures. The threat of this type of sanction may encourage firms contemplating not complying with regulatory objectives to re-consider, even if the non-compliance would generate significant financial benefit.

4.67 Adverse publicity could also trigger other non financial consequences such as interest from other regulatory agencies as well as consumers and they can be applied without limitations of a business' ability to pay.[62] Small and large firms with regard to their reputation could be sanctioned without the constraints that a financial sanction would impose which could be effective in some instances of regulatory non-compliance.

Box 4.13 Example of Publicity Orders in the US

Under Federal sentencing guidelines a judge may order a convicted company to publicise, at its own expense, its conviction and what steps it is putting in place to avoid future non-compliance. For example, the American Caster Corporation was found guilty of the illegal dumping of 250 deteriorating drums of solvents. The company's officers pleaded guilty to the charges and were ordered to take out a full page advertisement in the *Los Angeles Times* at a cost of $15,000. In addition, the company also had to pay $20,000 for the cleaning of the site and the president and vice president received a six month custodial sentence.

Source: New York Times, 17 February 1985 (Polluter Purchases Ad to Tell of its Illegal Toxic Dumping)

4.68 I believe that the requirements of a CRO should be flexible, reflecting both the circumstances of the offence and the nature of the business and could include mandatory audits and the carrying out of community projects. The regulator would,

---

[60] A Cowen, 'Scarlet Letters for Corporations? Punishment by Publicity under the New Sentencing Guidelines' [1992] *Southern California Law Review* 2387.

[61] C Fombrun, *Reputation: Realizing Value from the Corporate Image* (Boston, MA, Harvard Business School Press, 1996).

[62] C Abbot, 'The Regulatory Enforcement of Pollution Control Laws: the Australian Experience' (2005) 17(2) *Journal of Environmental Law* 161.

Box 4.14 Reputation as a Motivation for Regulatory Compliance

UK regulators already recognise and utilise policies of 'naming, faming and shaming' both good and bad practice. The Health and Safety Executive currently discloses details of its enforcement actions on its Web site which the CBI has said 'puts peer pressure on those firms that have issues to address and threatens adverse impact on their reputation' (evidence submitted to the Macrory Review, Spring 2006). In addition, the Financial Services Authority accompanies a penalty with a press release giving details of the non-compliance and the size of penalty as does the Environment Agency who issues press releases for successful prosecutions to local and national media.

Recommendation 8

I recommend that the Government consider introducing the following alternative sentencing in criminal courts:

- Profit Order – Where the profits made from regulatory non-compliance are clear, the criminal courts have access to Profit Orders, requiring the payment of such profits, distinct from any fine that the court may impose;
- Corporate Rehabilitation Order – In sentencing a business for regulatory non-compliance, criminal courts have on application by the prosecutor, access to a Corporate Rehabilitation Order (CRO) in addition to or in place of any fine that may be imposed; and
- Publicity Order – In sentencing a business for regulatory non-compliance, criminal courts have the power to impose a Publicity Order, in addition to or in place of any other sentence.

under appropriate guidance from the court, be responsible for supervising the carrying out of the CRO.

4.69 For Publicity Orders, I believe that this type of order would enable a court, to order that a notice (with wording agreed by the regulator and the business) to be placed in an appropriate publication, such as a local or national newspaper, a trade publication or another appropriate media outlet such as radio or television, or in a company's annual report within a specified period. The notice would state the background to the offence, the steps taken by the offender to prevent repetition and any remedial or compensatory measures taken by the offender. While some regulators have a strategy for 'naming and shaming', the recommendation on Publicity Orders differs in that they would be imposed by the court, an independent third party, and not by the regulator. This would ensure that the business has a received a fair and objective assessment of the offence.

Conclusion

4.70 Chapters three and four have gone through my main recommendations regarding the types of sanctions that I think should be available to regulators. These represent additional tools and are not meant to replace criminal prosecution as a regulatory sanction. The additional sanctions may be more appropriate in some cases that are currently prosecuted. They provide a range of administrative financial and non-financial options where criminal prosecution is not appropriate. Furthermore, I have also made recommendations for more flexible sanctions for cases of regulatory non-compliance that are sentenced within the criminal courts. The addition of these sanctioning tools to a regulator's and courts' toolkit will make them more effective when it comes to enforcement and this will strengthen the entire regulatory regime of advice, inspection and enforcement.

4.71   The next chapter focuses on transparency and accountability mechanisms that I believe are necessary for a well functioning and effective sanctioning system that includes financial and non-financial sanctions.

V. Transparency and Accountability

The previous two chapters presented a blueprint for an effective sanctioning system that reinforces and is consistent with a risk based approach to regulation. This chapter discusses the transparency and accountability frameworks that are necessary to support this blueprint.

Introduction

5.1   Regulators wield power over the regulated community and have been entrusted to act on behalf of the public to maintain and safeguard certain obligations or requirements. There is a strong culture of good governance within the UK regulatory system that acts as a check on these powers.

5.2   Some of my recommendations in the previous two chapters involve extending regulators' enforcement options, thereby giving some of them access to powers they have not previously held. Both regulators and industry have expressed some concern on how new powers of enforcement will be introduced and used in the coming years. However, some UK regulators, most notably the economic regulators, already use most of the sanctions that I have suggested should be part of an extended toolkit.[63] There is much good practice already in existence here, in particular strengthened transparency and accountability frameworks such as open board meetings.

5.3   Although standards of accountability and transparency amongst UK regulators in general are already high, I believe these systems must be developed further in order for a more flexible sanctioning system to be effective and credible. I detail some recommendations for these areas in the following discussion.

---

[63] These regulators include FSA, OFGEM, OFT and the Competition Commission.

Transparency

5.4   Transparency is something that the regulator must provide to external stakeholders, including both industry and the public, so they have an opportunity to be informed of their rights and responsibilities and of enforcement activity. However, it is also important for the regulator itself, to help ensure it uses their sanctioning powers in a proportionate and risk based way.

5.5   I have set out recommendations relating to an increased level of transparency for regulators through:

• The publication of an enforcement policy;
• Publicly disclosing who enforcement actions have been taken against; and
• Publishing information on the outcomes of enforcement action.

Accountability

5.6   Regulators see their primary accountability to Ministers and elected officials whether in Parliament or at local level and this relationship is already strong. In addition, regulators are making some good progress on increasing their accountability to those who they regulate and those on whose behalf they are regulating. Some of my recommendations will strengthen the answerability of regulators to stakeholders further. I also propose that Ministers and Parliament should also look more closely at the enforcement and sanctioning activities of regulators, rather than focus mainly on financial accountability in order to provide a complete overview of a regulator's activities including enforcement.

What Do I Mean by Transparency?

5.7   Being transparent is necessary to ensure that business knows what consequences it could face for failure to comply with regulatory requirements. Transparency can be achieved in several different areas, for example transparency in procedural decision making also ensures high standards when the regulator makes its enforcement decisions. Broadly speaking, regulators should be able to outline the process by which decisions are arrived at, the types of factors that may influence a regulator's enforcement decisions, and what types of enforcement action could be taken in what circumstances.

5.8   The culture of transparency is strong in those national regulators who have published enforcement policies available to the public and regulated communities. At present, however, the use of enforcement policies is patchy amongst UK regulators. Internal research I commissioned for my review showed that only 17 of the 60 national regulators surveyed had a publicly accessible enforcement policy.

5.9   Other agencies may have policies available for internal reference, but these are not easily available publicly. For local authority regulators, 96 percent have signed up to the Enforcement Concordat, which articulates general 'Principles of Good

Enforcement'.[64] Although this is a good starting point, more specific guidance on its enforcement practice in particular regulatory areas should be produced beyond the Concordat by those local regulators who want to use an expanded sanctioning toolkit. Businesses should have a clear idea what they need to do in order to comply with regulations. In addition, where local authority regulators are enforcing on behalf of a national regulator, they should do so following the national regulators' policy guidelines.

Transparency through Enforcement Policies

What are Enforcement Policies?

5.10   An enforcement policy is a public document setting out what action the public, and the regulated community, can expect from a regulator when a regulatory breach has been identified. This will specify the range of enforcement options available to the regulator, when enforcement action is likely to be taken and in what circumstances. It should also talk about the regulator's policies for risk based enforcement, enforcement action in cases of conflicting regulations, the provision of advice and information it requests from business.

Characteristics of a Good Enforcement Policy

5.11   Enforcement policies must always retain a degree of flexibility, since I believe the choice of sanctioning response can never be a purely mechanical exercise. But if they are to be of real value to the regulated community, it is important that they are drafted with reference to the specific area of regulation to which they relate, rather than expressed in over-generalised terms, although I expect there would be some over-arching principles which would apply to all areas.

5.12   The language in an enforcement policy should not however be over-specific on what a business should expect when found in each and every potential type of breach. This would be arduous and bureaucratic and would bind a regulator's discretion too tightly leading to an overly rigid enforcement system that would not be beneficial for the regulator, the regulated community, or the public. Flexibility remains a cornerstone of a good enforcement system.

Positive Influence of Published Enforcement Policies

5.13   **Consistent decision making** – public enforcement policies both facilitate and incentivise regulators to make decisions on a fair and consistent basis. They facilitate consistency by giving enforcers a reference point – applicable to all their enforcement activity – for how they should react to different circumstances. This delivers consistent decisions as regulators act in the knowledge that when formal enforcement proceedings are pursued this should happen in a manner consistent

---

[64] http://www.cabinetoffice.gov.uk/regulation/documents/pst/pdf/concord.pdf#search=%22enforcement%20 concordat%22.

with the public policy. It would also require the regulator to explain and justify any significant departure from its public policy.

5.14 **Safeguards for stakeholders** – public enforcement policies provide a valuable safeguard for businesses against the misuse of regulators' powers. Likewise they provide reassurance for the public that decisions on enforcement are made consistent with public policy.

5.15 Given that some regulators already have experience in publishing enforcement policies I suggest the sharing of best practice here which could be co-ordinated by the Better Regulation Executive. Each policy should:

- Have regard to the Principles of Good Regulation, the Enforcement Concordat, the Compliance Code (when established) and the Macrory Penalties Principles;
- Set out what a regulator may do to bring businesses into compliance without the need for taking punitive action;
- Explain the range of enforcement options available to the regulator;
- Explain the criteria upon which decisions are made when choosing what specific enforcement action to take in each case of non-compliance, including any aggravating or mitigating factors the regulator might take into account before applying a particular sanction;
- Where a regulator has FMAP powers – outline the scheme for imposing these sanctions detailing, for example, relevant time limits, the scale of charges, and methods of paying FMAPs, and complaints and appeals procedures;
- Where a regulator has VMAP powers – outline the calculation mechanism for deciding the appropriate fine including aggravating and mitigating factors that will impact on the level of VMAP, and give relevant details relating to payment of the VMAP;
- Where a regulator has FMAP and/or VMAP powers – outline complaints and appeals procedures;
- Where a regulator has access to Statutory Notices – outline the circumstances under which these might be appropriate and the consequences of non-compliance; and
- Where a regulator has access to Enforceable Undertakings or Undertakings Plus – outline the scheme for entering into these agreements, for example, the relevant time limits, application process, types of conditions and consequences for non-compliance.

5.16 Enforcement policies should be clearly identified and readily accessible on the regulator's own website. They may take the form of separate documents addressing each sanction individually provided that there is overall transparency about the regulator's sanctioning options.

5.17 Enforcement policies once published should not be subject to constant change, but regulators should ensure that they are subject to periodic review, to ensure that in the light of experience they are fit-for-purpose and up-to-date. While I do not propose any formal assessment of regulators' enforcement policies, actions taken by the regulator will be held against the policies when it reports on outputs and outcomes, which I discuss in the next section.

Transparency through Reporting Outcomes

5.18 As I discussed in my interim report, I have found that most regulators, when reporting on enforcement activity or compliance, focus on the outputs of this activity, for example, the number of prosecutions or the number of Statutory Notices that have been issued. This information is important, but there is very little evidence on what the actual result, or outcomes, of these enforcement actions are. I think that regulators should be encouraged to measure and communicate their regulatory outcomes and objectives in addition to the outputs.

5.19 Reporting on these measures through existing reports to stakeholders or Parliament, would let the regulated community and the public know what activities the regulator is engaged in. It also is an indication of the effectiveness of the regulator in discharging its statutory duties, thereby holding it to account.

Measuring Outcomes

5.20 Appropriate outcome measures will vary in different areas of regulatory activity, but are essentially concerned with the expected consequences and goals of the regulator's enforcement activity rather than an account of the amount and type of enforcement activity it undertakes. In some cases, the regulatory requirements themselves may clearly identify a policy goal. In other cases, it may be appropriate to formulate an outcome that can be measured, such as the quantifiable reduction of pollution incidents or reduction in deaths and serious injuries. Evaluating the extent to which non-compliant businesses become compliant could also form an outcome measure. Determining the appropriate outcome measures and the methodology by which they should be measured are challenging tasks. However, it is only by measuring outcomes that regulators, the regulated community, and the public will begin to know what impact enforcement actions are having on regulatory outcomes and whether these have improved compliance. It will also highlight for the regulator if there needs to be any modification to its choice of enforcement actions in order to better meet regulatory objectives.

5.21 During the course of the review, it became apparent how little information is available on the effectiveness of sanctioning regimes. If government accepts my recommendation, I would suggest that sponsoring departments and/or regulators use the opportunity of introducing new sanctioning tools to study and develop information, including commissioning independent research, relating to the sanctions and their effectiveness especially during the transition period. This will be very helpful to many within the regulatory sector.

5.22 Alongside providing the regulatory community with greater information, a focus on outcomes will also ensure that industry is better served. Regulators will need to demonstrate that their enforcement actions are having a measured impact. Simply publishing the number of enforcement actions, will no longer suffice as a demonstration of the effectiveness of a regulator in meeting its regulatory objectives. Business should be reassured because the regulator will need to go one step further in supporting its enforcement strategy. It will, for example, need to demonstrate that

The Office of Fair Trading has established an evaluation programme into how effective enforcement (and non enforcement) methods, such as information campaigns, are at changing business and consumer behaviour. It is also planning work on establishing appropriate performance measures in consumer regulation enforcement and market studies work. It will be working with academics and other competition authorities internationally to set baseline and success criteria that will enable a robust evaluation of performance and impact.

Source: http://www.oft.gov.uk/NR/rdonlyres/F704C245-D32B-4E17-854D-715C23073A6D/0/ AnnualPlan07.pdf

imposing administrative sanctions is improving regulatory outcomes compared with sanctioning by criminal prosecutions alone.

5.23 I do recognise that regulation is not an exact science and that regulatory outcomes are not the only measure of a regulator's success. Nonetheless I believe that measuring outcomes has been a neglected area of reporting within the regulatory community that is essential to the credible functioning of a modern regulatory system and I would like to see regulators strive towards achieving this.

5.24 Regulators and sponsoring departments should in their annual reports:

• Summarise the relevant regulatory output measures for the relevant period;
• Summarise the relevant regulatory outcome measures during the relevant period; and
• Comment on the relationship between the outcomes and the outputs.

Transparency through Publishing Enforcement Actions

5.25 When regulators make a decision to enforce and impose a formal sanction, I believe that this should be a matter of public record. This will:

• Ensure that the public knows that the regulator is taking action in cases where regulatory non-compliance has occurred;
• Demonstrates to industry that the regulator will take action and is doing so against firms that do not comply; and
• Publicly hold industry to account for its behaviour.

5.26 A number of regulators have made this part of their current practice and I think this is something that others should also adopt. For example, the HSE has a database of enforcement actions available on its website for prosecutions that the agency has taken forward and where Statutory Notices have been applied. I believe that disclosure of when and against whom enforcement action has been taken should not be isolated to criminal prosecutions but should also be used for other enforcement action such as administrative penalties, enforcement or improvement notices or any other formal sanction in order to be consistent and transparent in the approach to enforcement and publishing sanctions.

5.27 I believe that making public outcome measures, success in achieving them, and information concerning the number and types of enforcement sanction pursued provides one source of performance accountability of regulators. But I also believe that more formal channels of accountability should be strengthened and I discuss this in the section below.

Accountability

5.28 A previous study of independent regulators found that, when asked to whom they are accountable, most national regulators suggested that it is to ministers and parliament.[65] This is an important mechanism of accountability, especially where the regulator is funded either in full or in part, by public money. Rigorous financial accountability mechanisms are a crucial part of a well-functioning, effective and credible regulatory system. There are currently a number of good accountability mechanisms in place including:

- All regulators have an accounting officer;
- They have to produce annual accounts – available to everyone;
- They can be audited by the National Audit Office or the Audit Commission;
- They can be subject to value for money examinations by the National Audit Office; or
- They can be called to appear before the relevant House of Commons or Lords select committee to answer for their actions.

5.29 Local Authority regulators are accountable through their management structures to the chief executive and ultimately to the elected councillors. All authorities will have a corporate complaints procedure to deal with complaints about the service and local authorities are also governed by the Local Government Ombudsman. All local authorities also have their own independent auditors plus a range of government inspectors and reporting requirements to central government.

5.30 Whilst accountability to Parliament and Ministers is important, it is equally important that regulators are clearly answerable to those that they regulate, and those on whose behalf they are regulating. Such accountability would assist in reassuring the regulated community that non-compliance is dealt with effectively. My recommendations on improved transparency will serve to strengthen regulators' accountability to the public and the regulated community through the publication of their enforcement policies and outcomes of their enforcement actions.

5.31 Many regulators are making real progress in their efforts to become more answerable to their stakeholders. Some examples of these include:

- Corporate plans (sets out priorities and details of how these will be achieved);
- Open meetings;
- Accessible and affordable appeal mechanisms;
- Open consultation exercises and feedback;
- Publication of board agendas, papers and minutes where appropriate;
- Regulatory impact assessments presented alongside proposed legislation; and
- Comprehensive and easy to use websites.

The Better Regulation Executive (BRE)

5.32 Many of my recommendations may pose a challenge to regulators and I believe the BRE is the right body to facilitate the introduction of many of my recommendations, given its oversight of the better regulation agenda.

[65] Better Regulation Task Force, 'Independent Regulators' (October 2003) 22.

5.33   The Better Regulation Executive is the central government body that promotes delivery of the government's regulatory reform agenda. As such, it plays a key role in working with government departments and regulators to improve performance on better regulation, embedding the principles of better regulation and identifying areas of best practice. This work should continue and be extended to include the implementation of the extended sanctioning toolkit.

5.34   The Better Regulation Executive should facilitate a working group of regulators and sponsoring departments to share best practice in enforcement approaches, the application of sanction options, development of outcome measures and transparency in reporting. Regulators and sponsoring departments should work with the Executive to include outcome measures as part of their overall framework of performance management.

5.35   This working group would consist of regulators, departments, industry representatives where appropriate, and BRE staff with an interest and expertise in enforcement related issues. Its aims could be to share best practice on many issues relating to enforcement including risk assessment, designing appropriate sanctioning schemes and providing support and guidance to enforcers more generally on the better regulation agenda. It could also assist regulators and departments in the development of regulatory outcome measures and enforcement policies.

5.36   The working group would exist to facilitate the exchange of best practice and assist regulators and sponsoring departments in developing expertise and competence in the extended range of sanctions. It could work alongside other expert groups such as the Whitehall Prosecutors Group and the Joint Regulators Group.

Accountability for Specific Enforcement Decisions

5.37   My proposals envisage that regulators will have a wider range of sanctioning responses to particular instances of regulatory breach, but that their enforcement discretion is exercised in the context of strengthened overall transparency and accountability. However, it is also important to consider what protective mechanisms exist to deal with allegations of abuse or poor practice in individual cases.

5.38   Where a regulator imposes an administrative penalty, I have proposed a right of appeal to a regulatory tribunal in order to provide a speedy and cost-effective protection for those who feel that the imposition of a sanction is unjustified, or the circumstances do not amount to a breach. The tribunal could also censure the regulator where there had been abuse or poor practice thereby also holding the regulator to account.

Third Parties Can Improve Accountability

5.39   Third parties such as non-governmental organisations, victims or consumers can provide an important challenge and accountability function. They act to ensure that regulators are carrying out their public duties with due care. If a regulator is not seen to be carrying out its public duties, then third parties can challenge the regulator and hold the regulator to account for its actions. I outline some of these mechanisms below.

5.40 Judicial review is a check on the lawfulness of actions and decisions of public bodies, examining the way in which a decision has been made.

5.41 The expanded toolkit I recommend in this review will not change recourse to judicial review for third parties. However, given that my recommendations will improve the transparency of regulators' enforcement procedures and policies, I envisage this in turn will reduce the need for regulatory cases to be referred to the Administrative Court.

5.42 Finally there is the option of bringing a private criminal prosecution, which individuals may do in most areas of regulation even where the regulator has decided not to commence prosecution. Although the powers are rarely exercised in the regulatory field, I believe the right of private prosecution represents a valuable public safeguard. Mechanisms already exist to prevent abuse and vexatiousness, but I have recommended that in the design of any scheme for VMAPs the Government ensure that businesses are protected from double jeopardy.

A Further Role for Parliament

5.43 As I mention above, regulators are currently accountable to Ministers and Parliament. However, I have some specific suggestions I believe will strengthen these relationships. Many of my recommendations in this area have been previously mentioned by other reports or reviewers and I want to add my endorsement for these. I fully recognise that these recommendations will be for Parliament rather than government to consider, and I have therefore not formulated them as formal recommendations. Nevertheless, I hope that they will be addressed by Parliament in the context of my other proposals.

Departmental Select Committees

5.44 Departmental Select Committees are the parliamentary bodies responsible for scrutiny of each Government department. Their role is to examine 'the expenditure, administration and policy' of the relevant department and its 'associated public bodies' and they are the leading bodies assessing the work of independent regulators with sponsoring departments. They serve to challenge and consider annual reports and specific ad hoc issues which are deemed of importance. Departmental Select Committees are widely perceived amongst the regulatory community to be the most important body holding regulators to account.

5.45 However, as highlighted in a report by the House of Lords Select Committee on the Constitution, this scrutiny function could be improved further.[66] In the first instance, I would hope that Departmental Select Committees could systematically review the enforcement performance of regulators sponsored by the departments which they

---

[66] House of Lords Select Committee, 'The Regulatory State: Ensuring its Accountability' (May 2004).

scrutinize. My recommendation that regulators publish outcome measures should facilitate this process. To facilitate the scrutiny process by Select Committees, the Better Regulation Executive could, through the Enforcement Working Group I have recommended, work with regulators to create some models of good practice on reporting regulatory outcome measures and enforcement activity, which may make the material more intelligible and user-friendly.

Select Committee on the Regulatory System

5.46   Departmental Select Committees work on issues relevant to their specific government department. While this sector specific scrutiny is appropriate in many instances, the cumulative impact of regulatory issues is difficult to capture under such governance arrangements. Both the Hampton Review and my own review have demonstrated that, despite very different legislative structures and institutional arrangements, there are many common issues and challenges in the regulatory field that cut across sectoral boundaries. I support the view of the House of Lords Select Committee in recommending that a joint Parliamentary Select Committee be created to focus on overarching regulatory issues. This recommendation was also endorsed by the Hampton Review.[67]

5.47   Such a committee could make a substantial contribution on the evaluation of the extended sanctioning toolkit, and issues pertaining to the regulatory system as a whole. It would not duplicate the work of Departmental Select Committees in examining individual regulators, but would assist in investigating both good and bad practice across the regulatory spectrum, and, in the context of my report, help assess the effectiveness of different sanctioning approaches.

5.48   The Parliamentary Select Committee should preferably be a joint committee of both Houses. The functions of this committee could include the right to be consulted over proposals to confer statutory powers and enforcement powers on a new or existing regulator with enough time for its comments to be taken into account during pre-legislative scrutiny.

5.49   This committee could also take on additional functions, which fall outside of my remit, but I suggest some options for Parliament to consider.

- Having regard to issues such as the potential duplication or overlap of regulatory activities, the clarity of the hierarchy of regulatory objectives with specific attention to the development of a 'whole of Government' view of regulation;
- Identify and promote good practice in its role as the Parliamentary counterpart of the Better Regulation Executive within the Cabinet Office;
- Monitor the consistency and effectiveness of regulators in complying with the Principles of Good Regulation, the Compliance Code (when established) and my Penalties Principles; and
- Focus on annual reports of regulatory bodies with a view to maintaining the consistency and co-ordination of Parliamentary scrutiny.

---

[67] Hampton, above n 4, 77 at 4.119.

5.50   I believe it is important for such an over-arching committee to exist in order to institutionalise this scrutiny function over regulators and sponsoring departments across a wide number of regulatory fields. The business community usually interacts with several regulators. At present, the accountability mechanisms that exist are often narrow and sectoral in scope, and therefore have difficulty in assessing the wider consequences of regulatory requirements and their enforcement, both for those that are regulated and society as a whole.

Recommendation 9

I recommend that to ensure improved transparency and accountability:
- The Better Regulation Executive should facilitate a working group of regulators and sponsoring departments to share best practice in enforcement approaches, the application of sanction options, development of outcome measures and transparency in reporting. Regulators and sponsoring departments should work with the Executive to include outcome measures as part of their overall framework of performance management.
- Publish Enforcement Activities – Each regulator should publish a list on a regular basis of its completed enforcement actions and against whom such actions have been taken.

5.51   To further emphasise the importance of transparency and accountability I refer readers back to chapter two where I reinforce two of the characteristics I mentioned. Regulators should:

- Publish an enforcement policy – this policy should be drafted in consultation with both the regulated community and wider stakeholder groups where appropriate.
- Outcome measures – regulators alongside sponsoring departments should work, in consultation with stakeholders, to determine meaningful outcome measurements which can assist in the achievement of regulatory objectives. These outcome measures and the extent to which they have been achieved should be reported in the regulator's annual report.

5.52   Where I suggest publishing enforcement activities, this can be in the form of a database on a website, through a press release, or other appropriate means for the dissemination of such information, in accordance with the relevant data protection rules. This can further promote the risk based approach to regulation as there would be more information on compliant and non-compliant businesses and this would better inform risk assessment frameworks. The increased information on compliant and non-compliant businesses will further promote transparency, by providing regulators with more information to take targeted enforcement actions on business that break the rules and allowing good businesses a light touch.

VI. Summary of Recommendations

This chapter is a summary of my recommendations.

Introduction

6.1   This chapter summarises my recommendations that have appeared in the previous five chapters of this report. I want to highlight that reforms to the sanctioning regimes are an essential feature of a risk based approach to regulation envisaged by Philip Hampton in his report. Having an effective and credible sanctioning system should result in the need for fewer routine inspections on compliant businesses and allow regulators to focus attention on those businesses who fail to comply with the law. Most breaches identified in a risk based system, should face penalties that are quicker and more proportionate to the offence, while there will continue to be tough criminal sanctions for those offenders who persist in rogue trading activity.

6.2   The recommendations in this report suggest that regulators should have access to a more flexible sanctioning toolkit. It is important that only regulators who are following the risk based approach should gain access to these sanctions. That is why I have qualified many of my recommendations with a need for regulators to demonstrate that they are compliant with both the Hampton and Macrory Principles. The Regulators' Compliance Code takes Hampton's seven principles, which support a risk based approach to regulation (such as inspections being risk based, regulators sharing data between them, sanctions being proportionate and meaningful) and puts them on a statutory footing under Part Two of the Legislative and Regulatory Reform Act 2006). Regulators will have a statutory duty to have regard to the Compliance Code as it relates to their enforcement activity. The government intends to issue the Code and accompanying guidance after further consultation with regulators and the regulated community and after necessary Parliamentary scrutiny (as laid out in the Act).

6.3   The Better Regulation Commission have recently published a report on risk, entitled *Risk, Responsibility and Regulation – Whose risk is it anyway?* Recommendation Four of this report has commented on the need to identify what are the principal risks regulators are protecting against and what regulatory outcomes regulators are trying to achieve. This is very much in line with my own thinking and I have also recommended that regulators look beyond outputs to also consider measuring outcomes. Outcome measures will represent a challenge for regulators to identify and determine, but I believe that this is something that government should strive towards.

Summary of Recommendations

I. THE ROLE AND IMPORTANCE OF SANCTIONS WITHIN THE REGULATORY SYSTEM

1.   I recommend that the Government initiate a review of the drafting and formulation of criminal offences relating to regulatory non-compliance.

II. UNDERLYING PRINCIPLES FOR REGULATORY SANCTIONS

2.   I recommend that in designing the appropriate sanctioning regimes for regulatory non-compliance, regulators should have regard to the following six Penalties Principles and seven characteristics.

Six Penalties Principles

A sanction should:

1.   Aim to change the behaviour of the offender;

2.   Aim to eliminate any financial gain or benefit from a non-compliance;

3.   Be responsive and consider what is appropriate for the particular offender and regulatory issue, which can include punishment and the public stigma that should be associated with a criminal conviction;

4.   Be proportionate to the nature of the offence and the harm caused;

5.   Aim to restore the harm caused by regulatory non-compliance, where appropriate; and

6.   Aim to deter future non-compliance

Seven Characteristics

Regulators should:

1.   Publish an enforcement policy;

2.   Measure outcomes not just outputs;

3.   Justify their choice of enforcement actions year on year to stakeholders, Ministers and Parliament;

4.   Follow-up enforcement actions where appropriate;

5.   Enforce in a transparent manner;

6.   Be transparent in the way in which they apply and determine administrative penalties; and

7.   Avoid perverse incentives that might influence the choice of sanctioning response.

III. MY VISION FOR CONTEMPORARY SANCTIONING REGIMES: FINANCIAL SANCTIONS

3.   I recommend that in order to increase the effectiveness of criminal courts for regulatory offences, the following actions should be implemented:

• The Government should request the Sentencing Guidelines Council to prepare general sentencing guidelines for cases of regulatory non-compliance;

• Prosecutors should always make clear to the court any financial benefits resulting from non-compliance as well as the policy significance of the relevant regulatory requirement;

- Prosecutions in particular regulatory fields be heard in designated magistrates' courts within jurisdictional areas, where appropriate; and
- Regulators provide specialist training for prosecutors and discuss with the Judicial Studies Board (JSB) contributing to the training of the judiciary and justices' clerks.

4.   I recommend that with regard to Monetary Administrative Penalties:

- Government should, consider introducing schemes for Fixed and Variable Monetary Administrative Penalties, for regulators and enforcers of regulations, that are compliant with the Hampton and Macrory Principles and characteristics. This can include national regulators as well as local regulatory partners;
- Appeals concerning the imposition of an administrative penalty be heard by a Regulatory Tribunal, rather than the criminal courts;
- Fine maxima for Fixed Monetary Administrative Penalties (FMAP) schemes should be set out and not exceed level five on the standard scale. FMAPs should also be scaled to differentiate between small and large firms; and
- There should be no fine maxima for Variable Monetary Administrative Penalties (VMAPs).

IV. MY VISION FOR CONTEMPORARY SANCTIONING REGIMES – NON-FINANCIAL SANCTIONS AND ALTERNATIVES FOR THE CRIMINAL COURTS

5.   I recommend that for an improved system of Statutory Notices:

- Government should consider using Statutory Notices as part of an expanded sanctioning toolkit to secure future compliance beyond the areas in which they are currently in use;
- Regulators should follow-up Statutory Notices using a risk based approach including an element of randomised follow-up;
- In dealing with the offence of failing to comply with a Statutory Notice, regulators should have access to administrative financial penalties as an alternative to criminal prosecution. This power should be extended by legislative amendment to existing schemes of Statutory Notices; and
- Government should consider whether appeals against Statutory Notices should be routed through the Regulatory Tribunal rather than the criminal courts.

6.   I recommend that the Government should consider introducing Enforceable Undertakings and Undertakings Plus (a combination of an Enforceable Undertaking with an administrative financial penalty) as an alternative to a criminal prosecution or the imposition of VMAPs for regulators that are compliant with the Hampton and Macrory Principles and characteristics.

7.   I recommend that Government introduce pilot schemes involving the use of Restorative Justice techniques in addressing cases of regulatory non-compliance. This might include RJ:

- as a pre-court diversion;
- instead of a Monetary Administrative Penalty; and
- within the criminal justice system – as both a pre or post sentencing option.

8.   I recommend that the Government consider introducing the following alternative sentencing in criminal courts:

- Profit Order – Where the profits made from regulatory non-compliance are clear, the criminal courts have access to Profit Orders, requiring the payment of such profits, distinct from any fine that the court may impose;
- Corporate Rehabilitation Order – In sentencing a business for regulatory non-compliance, criminal courts have on application by the prosecutor, access to a Corporate Rehabilitation Order (CRO) in addition to or in place of any fine that may be imposed; and
- Publicity Order – In sentencing a business for regulatory non-compliance, criminal courts have the power to impose a Publicity Order, in addition to or in place of any other sentence.

V. TRANSPARENCY AND ACCOUNTABILITY

9.   I recommend that to ensure improved transparency and accountability:

- The Better Regulation Executive should facilitate a working group of regulators and sponsoring departments to share best practice in enforcement approaches, the application of sanction options, development of outcome measures and transparency in reporting. Regulators and sponsoring departments should work with the Executive to include outcome measures as part of their overall framework of performance management.
- Publish Enforcement Activities – Each regulator should publish a list on a regular basis of its completed enforcement actions and against whom such actions have been taken.

Annex A

Sample Enforcement Pyramid

A.1 The sample 'enforcement pyramid' below, illustrates the range of sanctioning and penalty powers exercised by regulators. The sample enforcement pyramid does not correspond to the sanctioning powers of any particular regulator, but is a generalised model. Individual regulators have specific and different sanctioning options, depending on the powers provided by the underlying legislation.

Figure A.1 Sample Enforcement Pyramid.

A.2 The enforcement pyramid indicates a range of sanctioning options starting at the least severe at the base of the pyramid. As one moves towards the apex, the enforcement actions increase in severity. Regulators usually choose which level of the pyramid to commence their enforcement action depending on the nature of the offence, the seriousness of the consequences, and the level of intent of the offender.

3

Sanctions and Safeguards – The Brave New World of Environmental Enforcement[1] (2013)

The Regulatory Sanctions Review

The Regulatory Sanctions Review[2] was launched by the Cabinet Office in 2005 and all the recommendations in the final report[3] were accepted by the government. During the last six years, core proposals in the Review have been reflected in primary legislation,[4] followed by secondary legislation granting powers to regulators to impose civil sanctions in a limited number of fields,[5] publication of a Statutory Code of Practice for regulators[6] and the establishment of a new sanctions appeals body in the form of an environmental tribunal within the General Regulatory Chamber of the First-tier Tribunal,[7] and since 2012 regulators have begun to exercise their new sanctioning powers. This was followed at the end of 2012 with a reappraisal by the coalition government of its policy, resulting in a fresh policy approach towards the further extension of new sanctioning powers.[8]

---

[1] R Macrory, 'Sanctions and Safeguards – The Brave New World of Environmental Enforcement' (2013) 66(1) *Current Legal Problems* 233.

[2] Hereafter the Sanctions Review or the Review.

[3] R Macrory, *Regulatory Justice: Making Sanctions Effective* (London, Cabinet Office, 2006).

[4] Regulatory Enforcement and Sanctions Act 2008, Part III.

[5] The most extensive developments have been in the broad area of environmental law. See, eg Environmental Civil Sanctions (England) Order 2010, SI 2010/1157; Environmental Civil Sanctions (Miscellaneous Amendments) (England) Regulations 2010, SI 2010/1159; Environmental Civil Sanctions (Wales) Order 2010, SI 2010/1821 (W178); Environmental Civil Sanctions (Miscellaneous Amendments) (Wales) Order 2010, SI 2010/ 1820 (W 177); Eco-design for Energy-Related Products Regulations 2010 SI 2010/2617; Single Use Carrier Bags Charge (Wales) Regulations 2010, SI 2010/2880 (W 238); Energy Information Regulations 2011, SI 2011/1524; Marine Licencing (Civil Sanctions)(Wales) Order 2011, SI 2011/924 (W 133); Green Deal Framework (Disclosure, Acknowledgment, Redress etc.) Regulations 2012, SI 2012/2079; Climate Change Agreements (Administration) Regulations 2012, SI 2012/1976; Greenhouse Gas Emissions Trading Scheme Regulations 2012, SI 2010/3038.

[6] Department of Business Innovation and Skills, 'Statutory Code of Practice for Regulators' (BISS, 17 December 2007). The Code was approved by both houses of Parliament in accordance with Legislative and Regulatory Reform Act 2006, s 29 and applies to regulatory functions specified by Order made under s 24(2) of the Act. See Legislative and Regulatory Functions Reform (Regulatory Functions) Order 2007, SI 2007/ 3544. Under s 22 of the Act Reform (Regulators Functions) Order 2007, SI 2007, those to whom the Code applies must have regard to the Code in determining general policy and principles in exercised specified functions.

[7] http://www.justice.gov.uk/tribunals/environment (accessed on 23 March 2013).

[8] Written statement, The Minister of State, Department for Business, Innovation and Skills (HC Deb, 8 November 2012, Col 43 WS).

The Sanctions Review extended well beyond environmental law regulation, covering some 61 national regulators as well as local authorities and areas of law as diverse as building controls, food standards, health and safety, and trading standards. In this respect it mirrored the scope of the Hampton Review,[9] which was largely concerned with the relationship of regulators and the businesses they regulated. Hampton recognised the significance of regulatory sanctions and recommended that the Better Regulation Executive (then within the Cabinet Office) 'should undertake a comprehensive review of regulators' penalty regimes, with the aim of making them more consistent'.[10] It was this recommendation that gave rise to the Sanctions Review, and its concern was not so much with the substantive content of existing regulations, the type of regulatory instrument chosen (such as permitting regimes, regulatory standards, or economic instruments) or, indeed, whether regulation in a particular area was needed at all; rather, the Review sat within a growing body of literature exploring the rationale for businesses to comply with regulatory requirements where formal sanctions may play only one element in what is a complex picture.[11] Nevertheless, the Review's focus was deliberately confined to what happens when a sanction is needed and whether the existing system was adequate in this respect. Hampton argued that regulators should 'provide improved advice, because better advice leads to better regulatory outcomes, particularly in small businesses',[12] and in many instances when dealing with legitimate businesses, the best way of securing compliance is likely to be persuasion and advice in the first instance. The Review strongly endorsed this approach: 'Advice and incentives should play a key role in ensuring regulatory compliance, and should normally be the first response of regulators'.[13] But even then, some form of formal sanction will still be a necessary ingredient of any regulatory system, both to deal with those who ignore such advice and to provide an incentive for others to take the advice of regulators seriously. As Ayes and Braithwaite observed, 'Regulatory agencies have maximum capacity to lever cooperation when they can escalate deterrence in a way that is response to the uncooperativeness of the firm, and to the moral and political acceptability of the response'.[14]

The Review proposed six core principles, which it recommended should characterise an effective sanctioning system: (i) sanctions should aim to change the behaviour of the offender; (ii) sanctions should aim to eliminate the any financial gain or benefit from non-compliance; (iii) sanctions should be responsive, and should consider what is appropriate for the particular offender and regulatory issue, which can include punishment and the public stigma that should be associated with a criminal conviction; (iv) sanctions should

[9] P Hampton, *Reducing Administrative Burdens: Effective Inspection and Enforcement* (London, HM Treasury, 2005).

[10] Ibid, Recommendation 8.

[11] See, eg Greenstreet Berman Ltd, 'Business Perspectives on Approaches to Securing Compliance', Report to Defra and the Environment Agency GSB Ref CL2463 (Greenstreet Berman, 2011) and studies cited therein; R Baldwin and J Black, 'Really Responsive Regulation' LSE Working Paper 15/2007 (LSE, 2007); I Ayres and J Braithwaite, *Responsive Regulation: Transcending the Deregulation Debate* (Oxford, Oxford University Press, 1992); N Gunningham and R Kagan (eds), 'Regulation and Business Behaviour' (2005) 27(2) *Law and Policy* special issue; D Thornton et al, "General Deterrence and Corporate Environmental Behaviour" (2005) 27(2) *Law and Policy* 262. In the environmental field see W Benson et al, 'The Effectiveness of Enforcement of Environmental Legislation', Defra 7208 (Department of Food Environment and Rural Affairs, 2006); C Abbot 'The Regulatory Enforcement of Pollution Control Laws. The Australian Experience' (2005) 17(2) *Journal of Environmental Law* 161.

[12] Hampton, above n 9, para 29.

[13] Sanctions Review, para 1.11.

[14] Ayres and Braithwaite, above n 11, 36.

be responsive to the nature of the offence and the harm caused; (v) sanctions should aim to restore the harm caused by regulatory non-compliance, where appropriate; and (vi) sanctions should to aim to deter future non-compliance. Set against this framework, the existing range of sanctions available to many regulators in England and Wales was found to be wanting, and the Review recommended that a much richer range of sanctions be made available but against a number of proposals to improve the transparency and accountability of regulators. It is not the purpose of this analysis to provide a full account of the recommendations in the Review or the provisions of the Regulatory Enforcement and Sanctions Act which implemented many of the core recommendations.[15] Instead, it will present the underlying rationale for the proposals made in the Review, and explore how, despite acceptance by the government of all the recommendations, the process of translating these recommendations into legislation meant that the outcomes did not necessarily reflect the conclusions of the Review. For reasons that will be explained, most of the legislative initiatives to date have been focused on the introduction of civil sanctions, but the Review contained a much broader analysis of regulatory sanctions and how they could be made more effective. The author was appointed the reviewer,[16] and the account will contain at times what are unashamedly personal insights into what happened and why.

Criminal Law and Strict Liability Offences

Despite the very different nature of the laws that fell within the scope of the Review, it became clear that when it came to sanctions the criminal offence, usually drafted in strict liability terms, remained ubiquitous. The strict liability offence has a long history in British regulatory law, with the 1846 decision of *Regina v Woodrow*[17] generally acknowledged as the first clear decision of the courts accepting the notion of criminal liability without the need to prove intention or recklessness. A retailer in tobacco had been found to be holding tobacco that was cut with a small quantity of sugar and other substances. There was a criminal offence under the Excise Act 1840 for a retailer to have in his possession adulterated tobacco, but in this case the evidence was that the adulteration had taken place during manufacture, and that the retailer had bought the tobacco in all innocence and had no reasonable way of knowing it was not pure. Yet he was still held criminally liable. All three members of the court held that, on construction of the statute, all that was required for criminal liability was possession, and knowledge, intention or recklessness was not an ingredient. As Baron Parke put it,

---

[15] For a general account of the Review and its recommendations see R Macrory, 'Reforming Regulatory Sanctions' in Oliver, Rawlings and Prosser (eds), *The Regulatory State* (Oxford, Oxford University Press, 2010). For an analysis of the legislation, see J Norris and J Phillips, *The Law of Regulatory Enforcement and Sanctions* (Oxford, Oxford University Press, 2011).

[16] The Review was not carried out by a committee, but instead the author was appointed as a single independent reviewer, supported by a small secretariat of seconded civil servants. This form of review was heavily promoted by Gordon Brown when Chancellor of the Exchequer (1997–2007), and has continued under the present administration: see http://www.hm-treasury.gov.uk/independent_reviews_index.htm (accessed on 24 March 2013).

[17] 15 M & W 404 (Exch 1846).

> The legislature has made a stringent provision for the purpose of protecting the revenue and have used very plain words. It is very true that in particular instances it may produce mischief because an innocent man may suffer . . . but the public inconvenience would be much greater if in every case the officers were obliged to prove knowledge.[18]

Despite its long tradition, the justification and the effectiveness of strict liability especially in criminal law continues to divide contemporary scholars.[19] It is a concept described memorably by Spencer and Pedain in 2005 as the 'closest to unsophisticated pre-Enlightenment notions of criminal responsibility'.[20] Various forms of strict liability are not unknown in continental jurisdictions, including evidential and similar presumptions, but the extent to which the strict liability offence has permeated and underpinned our regulatory systems appears to be distinctive to the United Kingdom. During the early years of the industrial revolution, when there was little in the way of specialised regulators or specialised courts, it is understandable why the strict liability criminal offence became the sanction of default and the criminal courts the forum for enforcement. But it may be that we took a wrong turn at that point, and the extent to which criminal sanctions have dominated our regulatory landscape emerged as one of the more important concerns in the 2005 Cabinet Office Review of Regulatory Sanctions.

The initial consultation document of the Sanctions Review[21] tentatively touched on the issue of strict liability offences and suggested that 'The use of criminal prosecution should be maintained to sanction serious regulatory non-compliance where there is evidence of intentional or reckless behaviour or where the actual or potential consequences are so serious that public interest demands a criminal prosecution'.[22] Annex D contained my own analysis of strict liability, where I summarised the justification of such offences but also raised concerns that the concept could misrepresent the seriousness of the conduct involved, with courts sometimes characterising such offences as not truly 'criminal'. For example, in an empirical study of environmental prosecutions, de Prez concluded that strict liability 'acts as a cloak for many defendants, for, as the prosecution is not required to prove "fault", this leaves defence counsel plenty of room to deny culpability in order to attract the sympathy of the bench'.[23]

Regulators have the discretion whether or not to prosecute,[24] and in practice enforcement policies often ensure that prosecution is reserved for the more egregious offender,

---

[18] Ibid, [417].

[19] See generally A Simester (ed), *Appraising Strict Liability* (Oxford, Oxford University Press, 2005); A Ashworth, *Principles of Criminal Law*, 6th edn (Oxford, Oxford University Press, 2009) 160–70; Simester et al, *Criminal Law: Theory and Doctrine*, 4th edn (Oxford, Hart Publishing, 2010); Simester, 'Is Strict Liability Always Wrong?' in Simester, *Appraising Strict Liability*, ibid. For arguments in favour of and against strict liability offences in the field of pollution control, see Hilson, *Regulating Pollution* (Oxford, Hart Publishing, 2000) 134–37.

[20] J Spencer and A Pedain, 'Approaches to Strict and Constructive Liability in Continental Criminal Law' in Simester, *Appraising Strict Liability*, ibid, 276.

[21] Cabinet Office, 'Regulatory Justice: Sanctioning in a Post-Hampton World', Consultation Document of the Macrory Review of Regulatory Sanctions (Better Regulation Executive, May 2006).

[22] Ibid, Proposed elements for reform of the penalties systems Box E1, 7.

[23] P de Prez, 'Excuses, Excuses: The Ritual Triviliasation of Environmental Prosecutions' (2000) 12(1) *Journal of Environmental Law* 65. In the field of consumer law, a similar empirical study reached the same conclusions: H Croall, 'Mistakes, Accidents and Someone Else's Fault' (1988) 15 *Journal of Legislative Studies* 293: 'Successful performers were able to use the law, legal representation, and strict liability to neutralize moral blameworthiness by routinely masking the severity of offences and elements of blame potentially involved in offending' (293).

[24] As confirmed recently by the High Court in *Moss and Sons Ltd v Crown Prosecution Service* [2012] EWHC 3658 and by the Court of Appeal (Criminal Division) in *A v R* [2012] EWCA Crim 234. See R Macrory, 'Regulators' Enforcement Policies and the Courts' (2013) 457 *ENDS Report* 47.

thereby mitigating an overly zealous application of strict liability. But the Sanctions Review also revealed considerable variations in the structure of strict offences. Some offences were truly strict in that no statutory defence was available,[25] while others have various forms of defences built in, essentially based on taking reasonable care or some similar formulation,[26] and with the burden on the defendant to prove on the balance of probabilities. It is often hard to determine why a defence has been made available in one instance but not in another, especially where closely related activities are involved – for instance, the classic water pollution offence under the Water Resources Act 1991[27] contains no defence of reasonable care, whereas the offence of illegal waste disposal did.[28] The Review therefore commissioned Professor Simester of Nottingham University to undertake a more systematic analysis of strict liability offences in a range of regulatory areas including trading standards, environmental protection, food standards, health and safety, and vehicle licencing, and to determine if there was any principle underlying the differences in the defences available or not, and the choice of actual wording of defences.

Not surprisingly he found the state of the law confused, and a product of history rather than rationality. Simester concluded that the availability of some form of due diligence defence

> helps to ensure that the innocent are not labelled as criminals; at the same time, by reversing the onus, the law relieves regulators of some of the costs of proving guilt. As things stand, however, the law is inconsistent both in making the defence available and in formulating a clear and consistent standard for exculpation.[29]

When it comes to defences, Horder has argued that in certain cases courts should have the power to imply a defence of due diligence.[30]

There is considerable force in the proposal that strict liability offences should always contain a due diligence defence, and should preferably use the same language so that case law and precedent can develop consistently. In the final analysis, however, the Sanctions Review concluded that it was straying beyond its terms of reference to propose such fundamental changes to the structure of criminal law, and recommended instead that 'Government initiate a review of the drafting and formulation of criminal offences relating

---

[25] The courts, however, have accepted that automatism is a defence to strict liability offences: A Ashworth, *Principles of Criminal Law*, 6th edn (Oxford, Oxford University Press, 2009) 160.

[26] For example, Trade Descriptions Act 1968, s 24 provides that 'In any proceedings for an offence under this Act it shall, subject to subsection (2) of this section, be a defence for the person charged to prove – (a) that the commission of the offence was due to a mistake or to reliance on information supplied to him or to the act or default of another person, an accident or some other cause beyond his control; and (b) that he took all reasonable precautions and exercised all due diligence to avoid the commission of such an offence by himself or any person under his control.'

[27] Water Resources Act 1991, s 85.

[28] Environmental Protection Act 1990, s 33(7). No such defence applies for a breach of a permit under Environmental Permitting (England and Wales) Regulations 2010, SI 2010/675, which is replacing waste management provisions under the 1990 Act.

[29] Simester, 'Patterns of Strict Liability and Reverse Onus Defences', unpublished report to the Regulatory Sanctions Review (2005). An extract of this report was contained in Annex E of the Consultation Document of the Sanctions Review, available at http://webarchive.nationalarchives.gov.uk/20071001175030/http://bre.berr.gov.uk/regulation/documents/pdf/macrory_annexes.pdf (accessed on 24 March 2013).

[30] J Horder, 'Whose Values?' in Simester, *Appraising Strict Liability*, above n 19. He uses as his example Education Act 1996, s 444, which imposes an apparent strict liability offence on parents for children in truancy from school, and quotes with approval the dissenting judgment of Elias J in *Barnfather v London Borough of Islington Education Authority* [2003] EWHC 418, who was prepared to read in a due diligence defence into s 444: 'Any problems of proof could in large part be dealt with by imposing as reverse burden of the parent to require him or her to demonstrate what steps had been taken and to satisfy the court that they were reasonable' [52].

to regulatory non-compliance.'[31] This recommendation led to the Law Commission subsequently carrying out a review on criminal liability in regulatory contexts, where the Commission proposed that the courts 'should be given the power to apply a due diligence defence to any statutory offence that does not require proof that the defendant was at fault in engaging in the wrongful conduct'.[32]

Extending the Range of Criminal Sanctions

Despite the concerns over strict liability offences, the Sanctions Review concluded that the criminal law would still be central to any regulatory system. It was clear from most of the evidence that in nearly every field of activity there were at one end of the spectrum people or companies operating consciously in breach of regulations and making money in so doing. Significant recommendations for improving the current criminal process were made. For example, the Sanctions Review proposed[33] that classes of regulatory offence could be concentrated on designated magistrates courts in areas or regions, giving both the magistrates and the court staff an opportunity to become far more familiar with the regulation concerned.[34] It recommended that the Sentencing Council produce guidelines for cases of regulatory non-compliance.[35]

The Sanctions Review went on to recommend that a far richer range of sanctions for regulatory offences should be made available to the criminal courts. Essentially, where a business was concerned the only sanction was a financial penalty, with the occasional possibility of directors being held personally liability and subject to imprisonment. The Review recommended the use of Publicity Orders,[36] widely used in Australia,[37] which allow a court to require the company concerned to take out advertisements in the national or local press apologising for the offence and explaining what they would do to avoid it happening again. The Review also saw a role for what was rather ungainly called 'corporate rehabilitation orders', whereby directors or other officers in a convicted company might be required to undergo some form of training course in the area of regulation concerned. This would be equivalent to the speed awareness courses introduced by the Department for Transport in 2006[38] as an alternative to a fine and points on the driving licence. Research indicates that these courses have benefits to the majority who attend them, at least in the

---

[31] Sanctions Review, 98.

[32] Law Commission, 'Criminal Liability in Regulatory Contexts – A Consultation Paper', Consultation Paper No 195 (Law Commission, 2010) para 8.14. At the time of writing, there appears to have been no follow-up to the Commission's proposals.

[33] Sanctions Review, para 3.15.

[34] This is already the practice in some regulatory areas. For example, by arrangement, health and safety prosecutions in the Greater London area are all initially commenced in the City of London Magistrates Court. See http://www.hse.gov.uk/enforce/enforcementguide/pretrial/procedure-jurisdiction.htm (accessed 22 January 2013).

[35] Sanctions Review, para 3.13. In March 2013 the Sentencing Council published a consultation document on sentencing guidelines for environmental offences: 'Environmental Offences Guideline Consultation' (Sentencing Council, 2013).

[36] Sanctions Review, paras 4.64–4.69.

[37] See C Abbot, 'The Regulatory Enforcement of Pollution Control Laws: The Australian Experience' (2005) 2 *Journal of Environmental Law* 161, 173–76. The Corporate Manslaughter and Corporate Homicide Act 2007, s 10 now gives a court power to order a Publicity Order is respect of an organisation convicted under the Act.

[38] Department for Transport, 'Effective Interventions for Speeding Motorists', Report No 66 (DfT 2006).

short and medium terms.[39] The Review also recommended that criminal courts should be able to make a profits order where clearly identifiable financial gains made from the regulatory non-compliance[40] could be removed, leaving the fine itself to reflect the level of blame attached. Finally, the Review was struck by the potential power of restorative justice procedures, whereby the victim of a crime at some point takes part in the process and ideally meets the perpetrators involved. In this country this has been used mainly in the field of juvenile crime, but the Sanctions Review felt that the government should examine how it might be applicable to business regulation.[41]

It was therefore clear that the criminal law would continue to play a significant role in any system of regulatory sanctions, but it was equally apparent that in the current system the criminal law had to cope with an enormous spectrum of activity. Warnings or more formal cautions may be the appropriate response for many non-intentional breaches. But what if there was an unexpected breakdown of equipment that had serious consequences, such as a pollution incident, or if there was a company that inadvertently secured a financial gain through non-compliance with a regulatory scheme? Warnings without any additional penalty to the business concerned in such circumstances would be an ineffective response, and would be unlikely to command the confidence of the public or other businesses that were compliant with the regulatory requirements. But the use of the criminal law in such circumstances could equally seem heavy handed, and there was a real danger of its stigmatic value being undermined by being used too broadly. Enforcement notices giving businesses a time limit for coming back into compliance appeared to be a valuable regulatory tool, appropriate for the type of regulatory breach which is continuing (rather than, say, the one-off pollution incident) and where the business concerned has not behaved intentionally or recklessly. The Review recommended that the powers to serve such notices be available to all regulators.[42] Yet in most current laws, non-compliance with an enforcement notice is a criminal offence. Given that the business concerned will have been made aware of the breach and given a time limit for compliance, then a criminal sanction may seem appropriate, but the Review heard how less scrupulous companies sometimes complied with 90% of a notice or stretched the time limits, knowing full well that the regulator was unlikely to invest in a prosecution in such circumstances.

Hence the need to supplement the criminal law with forms of non-criminal sanctions, described in the legislation as 'civil sanctions' and discussed further below.[43] But

[39] See, eg Brainbox Research, 'Evaluation of the National Speed Awareness Course', report commissioned by The Association of Chief Police Officers of England, Wales and Northern Ireland, National Driver Retraining Scheme and the Association of National Driver Improvement Service Providers (Brainbox Research, 2011).

[40] Sanctions Review, paras 4.48–4.50. The recommended Profits Orders would be similar to Compensation Orders made under Powers of Criminal Courts (Sentencing) Act 2000, ss 130–33, but there would be no requirement to prove any 'personal injury, loss or damage' resulting from the offence, simply that a profit had been made.

[41] See J Shapland et al, *Restorative Justice: Does Restorative Justice Affect Reconviction*, Research Series 10/08 (Ministry of Justice, 2008). In 2010 the Ministry of Justice advocated extending restorative justice schemes to adult offenders: Ministry of Justice, *Breaking the Cycle Effective Punishment, Rehabilitation and Sentencing of Offenders* (Cm 7972, 2010) paras 78–81. For a general examination of restorative justice concepts see G Johnstone, *Restorative Justice – Ideas, Values, Debates*, 2nd edn (London, Routledge, 2010).

[42] Sanctions Review, paras 4.5–4.16.

[43] The Sanctions Review consistently used the term 'administrative penalty', reflecting the vision that this was a penalty that was initially imposed administratively and with any appeals handled outside the criminal courts. For some reason, which was never made clear, the terminology was changed in the Regulatory Enforcement and Sanctions Act 2008 to the term 'civil penalty'. This term seems rather confusing in that it suggests the realm of civil law and compensation, and can confuse as to appropriate standards of proof, but since it now appears in the legislation it will be used here.

an underlying vision of the Sanctions Review was an integrated enforcement system that looked at the range of criminal and civil sanctions as a single continuum of response to regulatory breaches. In devising particular recommendations, the Sanctions Review often drew on best practice on other parts of the world, but this concept of an integrated system combining criminal and civil sanctions was arguably the most distinctive contribution of the Review. It was here, however, that effective implementation of this approach hit the buffers of the unexpected.

Unravelling the Vision

The Review was commissioned by the Cabinet Office and carried out under its auspices. The fact that all the recommendations in the Review were accepted by the government on publication did not happen by chance, nor was it due to the immediate compelling logic of the recommendations. The Cabinet Office officials who were seconded to the Review were extremely adept in carrying out the appropriate internal consultation with the many different government departments that potentially had an interest in the issue. Once the basic structure and the proposed core recommendations became clear, many hours were spent in the final months of the Review discussing the implications with officials and groups in different departments, such as the Home Office, the then Department of Constitutional Affairs and the then Department of Trade and Industry. The key was to ensure that when the Review was published there were no surprises within the machinery of government to those that mattered.

The Cabinet Office is uniquely placed to handle departments across Whitehall, and in many ways the Review, cutting across so many different sectorial areas, both required and was ideally suited this cross-departmental perspective. Once the Review was published, the expectation was that the Cabinet Office would then take the lead on implementation. At the time, there was much talk of the then Department of Trade and Industry being disbanded as having no useful function as a separate government department.[44] Undoubtedly a lot of rear-guard battles took place and, to the surprise of many, on 28 June 2007, a new Department of Business Enterprise and Regulatory Reform (BERR) was created. One of the first tasks it took on was implementing the recommendations in the Review.

BERR was successful in guiding the Regulatory Enforcement and Sanctions Act 2008 through its parliamentary passage. But the transfer of the responsibility to implement the Review's recommendations from the Cabinet office to BERR had a number of unfortunate consequences. First, and most seriously, BERR felt it had no remit to take a lead on reform in the criminal arena, so this was left to the recently created Ministry of Justice[45] and the Home Office. Instead, BERR's focus would be on the creation of non-criminal

---

[44] In September 2002, for example, Vince Cable, currently Secretary of State for Business, Innovation and Skills, had called for its abolition at the Liberal Democrat Conference. 'Scrap the DTI says Liberal Democrat Spokesman', *The Guardian (London)*, 25 September 2002, available at http://www.guardian.co.uk/business/2002/sep/25/libdems2002.liberaldemocrats (accessed on 13 January 2013).

[45] The ministry was formed in 2007, when some functions of the Home Office and the Department of Constitutional Affairs were combined. For a critical view over the way the new ministry had been created see House of Commons Constitutional Affairs Committee, 'The Creation of the Ministry of Justice: Sixth Report of Session 2006–07', HC 466 (The Stationery Office, 2007).

sanctions and the reform of the regulatory culture. The result has been that there has never been the equivalent coherent push for the reform of regulatory criminal sanctions and processes in line with the recommendations of the Review. It is true that there have been occasional glimpses – for instance, the introduction of publicity orders and a form of rehabilitation order, but only in the field of corporate manslaughter and homicide,[46] and coming from a different agenda. The more recent proposals for deferred prosecution agreements in serious fraud again echoes some of the Review's proposals on enforceable undertaking, but is similarly underpinned by a distinct agenda, that of reducing lengthy and complex fraud trials.[47] So, rather than looking on the criminal and civil system as an integrated whole, the result of the shift to BERR as the lead department was that core attention has focused on the civil side. At the same time, the reforms proposed in the Sanctions Review inevitably caught up within a deregulatory agenda being pursued within BERR – for instance, at times there were what appeared to be overly optimistic predictions emerging from BERR of the proportion of regulation offences which would be removed from the criminal courts.

The Sanctions Review proposed not that the new range of sanctions be imposed on unwilling regulators and their sponsoring departments, but that they should acquire them should they feel the need. The primary legislation would provide a core framework with common principles and procedures, but the actual powers would be drawn down by regulation. I had assumed that nearly all regulators and their departments would welcome the new powers as a sensible addition to their existing system, but in hindsight this underestimated the deep conservatism that exists within many institutions. By carrying out extensive internal Whitehall consultation before the Review was published, the Cabinet Office ensured that other departments did not block the recommendations, but it did not follow that the departments would necessarily implement them with alacrity. If the responsibility for seeing the reforms through had remained in the Cabinet Office, more pressure would have to brought to bear on individual departments, and in effect the burden would have been on them to justify why they did not wish to take on the new approach to sanctions.[48] As it turned out, the impression was that BERR – and its current successor, the Department of Business, Innovation and Skills[49] – was left with negotiating with and persuading other departments on a much more equal footing – a relationship where other departments are inevitably inclined to protect their own turf and indeed may positively resent other departments of an equal status from undue interference with established practices.

The final consequence of the transfer from the Cabinet Office to BERR concerned institutional memory. During the twelve-month period of the Sanctions Review, there had been a small team of around half a dozen Cabinet Office staff working closely with the reviewer, analysing written evidence, attending meetings of interest groups and helping

---

[46] Corporate Manslaughter and Homicide Act 2007, ss 9–10.

[47] See Ministry of Justice, 'Consultation on a New Enforcement Tool to Deal with Economic Crime Committed by Commercial Organisations: Deferred Prosecution Agreements', Consultation Paper CP9/2012 (Ministry of Justice, 2012); Ministry of Justice, 'Deferred Prosecution Agreements Government Response to the Consultation on a New Enforcement Tool to Deal with Economic Crime Committed by Commercial Organisations (Ministry of Justice, 2012).

[48] According to the description on its website, the Cabinet Office has responsibility for 'supporting collective government, helping to ensure the effective development, coordination and implementation of policy': https://www.gov.uk/government/organisations/cabinet-office/about (accessed on 28 March 2013).

[49] Created in 2009 by merging BERR with the Department for Innovation, Universities and Skills.

sell the basic message across Whitehall. As soon as the Review was published, most of the secretariat rapidly moved onto other functions and responsibilities. This meant that the BERR implementing team, however competent, had, beyond the text of the Sanctions Review itself, little instinctive insight for the way the Review had worked or the rationale for the choices made. Some of these difficulties might have been overcome if there had been a strong minister who really understood the significance of the proposals, the vision of a new type of sanctions regime and the fact that it was potentially something of a world leader in regulatory design. There was general ministerial support, but the subject of sanctions are not the most politically engaging of issues, especially in a climate where even the term 'regulation' is challenging in many quarters. The usual practice for a reviewer or chairman of an independent inquiry is to drop out of the picture once the final report is published and let the written analysis do the work. However, here I became concerned that much of the underlying philosophy of the Review would be lost through the institutional shifts that had taken place, and offered my services to the BERR legislative team to contribute to the detailed implementation process on a voluntary and non-party political basis. During the process, issues emerged that were not necessarily covered in the Review itself, and it was possible to provide answers based on the principles underlying the Review.

Maintaining the Distinction between Sanction Responses

The Sanctions Review envisaged that at some point the regulator must use its professional judgment to decide what is the most appropriate response to any particular breach – a criminal prosecution, a warning, a caution, and now the imposition of a civil penalty or acceptance of an enforceable undertaking.[50] One model proposed during the Sanctions Review both by some regulators and some industries was one where the regulator would propose a civil penalty, but if this was not accepted it would then prosecute for the criminal offence. An industry faced with such a penalty could equally reject it and face prosecution instead. In many ways it was an attractive model, similar to, say, the familiar fixed penalty system for minor motoring offences,[51] and one with the least disruption to the existing system. The defendant always retained the right, as it were, of being prosecuted, with the burden resting on the regulator, and did not have to initiate an appeal to challenge the penalty.

The Sanctions Review concluded that this model was sub-optimal. From the regulators' perspective, it had the uncomfortable tinge of blackmail – 'pay up or we prosecute'. From the defendant's perspective, there were scenarios of long negotiations on a civil penalty proposed by the regulator, with the defendants knowing full well that they were often in a good bargaining position, since undertaking prosecutions remains a serious commitment of resources by a regulator. More fundamentally, this model did not deal with the issue of whether only certain types of breach were appropriate for a criminal response in

---

[50] Here the regulator, rather than imposing a penalty, accepts an undertaking from the company concerned which may involve the payment of money to third parties. See further O Pederson, 'Environmental Enforcement Undertakings and Possible Implications: Responsive, Smarter, or Rent Seeking?' (2013) 76(2) *Modern Law Review* 319.

[51] Road Traffic Offenders Act 1988, Part 3.

the first place. The vision in the Sanctions Review was for a system where the regulator operating against a set of core principles, an enforcement policy and a deep knowledge of the regulated sector in question made a judgement as to the appropriate response to a breach, then stayed with that choice. In this respect, the approach somewhat differed from the well-known and highly influential graduated response pyramid, promoted by Ayres and Braithwaite in the 1990s.[52] This suggested, at least in its visual representation, that the appropriate response to a regulatory breach was to start with informal warnings and gradually work up the scale, depending on the reaction of the regulated body concerned. As the authors note, 'Every escalation of noncompliance by the firm can be matched with a corresponding escalation in punitiveness by the state'.[53] That might be applicable to some types of industry, but in reality the response of the regulator needed to reflect the very different circumstances of different breaches and the form of the breach – in some a warning was appropriate, others would require the imposition of a civil penalty without any warning, while in other cases an immediate criminal response was appropriate. The diagram promoted in the Review[54] therefore deliberately avoided a hierarchical representation of different sanctions, but instead reflected a vision that all should be equally available, depending on the nature and circumstances of the regulatory breach concerned.

Integrating the Standard of Proof

A core recommendation of the Sanctions Review was that the choice of sanction should as far as possible be undistorted by factors other than the judgement of what type of sanction would best achieve core goals – regulators should 'avoid perverse incentives that might influence the choice of sanctioning response'.[55] This raised the question of the standard of proof. The Sanctions Review itself assumed that the civil standard of proof would apply, though the issue was not examined in any real depth. Clearly, companies might be concerned at the prospect of being faced with large financial civil penalties imposed on the basis of far lower evidential standards than in the criminal courts. For a number of years, the courts had been hinting that higher evidential standards than simply the balance of probabilities might be appropriate in some types of civil case where there were grave consequences for the defendant, but the concept of an 'enhanced standard of proof' has now being firmly rejected by the House of Lords in cases such as *Secretary of State for the Home Department v Rehman*[56] and *In Re C D (Original Respondent and Cross-Appellant) (Northern Ireland) Appellate Committee*,[57] where Lord Carswell quoted with approval the proposition made by Richard LJ in *R (N) v Mental Health Review Tribunal (Northern Region)*:[58]

> Although there is a single civil *standard* of proof on the balance of probabilities, it is flexible in its *application*. In particular, the more serious the allegation or the more serious the conse-

---

[52] Ayres and Braithwaite, above n 11.
[53] Ibid, 37.
[54] Sanctions Review, 37.
[55] Sanctions Review, para 2.16.
[56] [2003] 1 AC 153.
[57] [2008] UKHL 33.
[58] [2006] QB 468, 497–98.

quences if the allegation is proved, the stronger must be the evidence before a court will find the allegation proved on the balance of probabilities. Thus the flexibility of the standard lies not in any adjustment to the degree of probability required for an allegation to be proved (such that a more serious allegation has to be proved to a higher degree of probability), but in the strength or quality of the evidence that will in practice be required for an allegation to be proved on the balance of probabilities.

This 'flexible approach' in application seemed to provide some protection, and the Review noted that, 'the civil standard of proof does have adequate safeguards to protect the rights of the accused'.[59]

Nevertheless, at some point during the preparation of the Regulatory, Enforcement and Sanctions bill the decision was taken that the same standard of proof – beyond all reasonable doubt – would apply to both criminal and civil penalties. This approach appears to be unique compared to other jurisdictions employing civil penalties, and I am now convinced it is the right model and, indeed, a key element for the effectiveness of the new system. Why is this solution so significant? The Sanctions Review received little evidence that the standard of proof was the core problem in enforcement – the real difficulties in the criminal law were the lengthy timescales involved, the often poor familiarity of the criminal courts with the area of regulation concerned and the inappropriateness of the criminal law for handling certain types of breaches. With the same standard of proof for criminal and civil sanctions, investigation of a potential offence will be carried out to the same criminal standards as now and by the same team, following the requirements of the Police and Criminal Evidence Act 1984 and any other requirements of the criminal law designed to protect the rights of suspects. As the Review noted, the proposals for civil sanctions 'are not about making it easier to penalize businesses but to create a system of sanctions that is more responsive and proportionate to the nature of the non-compliance'.[60] In those institutions where the standards of proof are different from criminal and civil responses, such as the United States, the system of environmental enforcement almost inevitability leads to different teams of investigators who may well not fully cooperate with each other or integrate their response.[61] A further advantage of an integrated system of investigation is that it avoids problems where incidents are initially investigated to civil standards of proof but the regulator later deems that a criminal prosecution is more appropriate then finds that during initial investigation the defendants were not afforded the appropriate protective measures for the criminal law.

Various forms of civil or administrative penalties have already been introduced in this country to supplement or replace criminal law responses – whether in economic regulation, the use of control orders, penalty fares on transport or fixed penalties for litter and other social behaviour – but there appears to be little in the way of developed principle in design. In an important paper for the Bingham Rule of Law Centre published in 2011[62] Michael Fordham QC argues that recent terrorism legislation has deliberately blurred the line between criminal and civil, threatening the rule of law. As already noted, the courts

---

[59] Sanctions Review, para 3.35.

[60] Ibid.

[61] In the US, the Department of Justice handles prosecutions for Federal environmental criminal prosecutions, while the Environment Protection Agency has power to impose administrative penalties. During discussions in the US with enforcement officials in 2010, one officer from the US Department of Justice memorably told me 'We give our weak puppies to the EPA'.

[62] M Fordham, 'The Rule of Law and Civil Constraint: Cheating the Criminal Law' (Bingham Centre for the Rule of Law, 2011).

have now rejected the 'enhanced standard of proof' in civil cases, and the trend is now in favour of applying the criminal standard if appropriate,[63] and especially where liberty is affected. As Fordham notes,

> The ability to focus on the true question – what basic protections are minimum standards on which the rule of law will insist in the particular context – can be a breath of fresh air. It treats questions of label or classification as incidental matters, distractions even.

By clearly stating that the criminal standard of proof applies to civil penalties,[64] the Regulatory Enforcement and Sanctions Act 2008 reflects that more explicit approach, and one that is in keeping with the overall vision of the Sanctions Review.[65] In providing that the regulator must be satisfied beyond all reasonable doubt that the offence has been committed before imposing a civil sanction, the Act has actually imposed a higher standard on the regulator than in criminal cases, where the Code for Crown Prosecutors provides that a prosecutor must be satisfied there is enough evidence to provide a 'realistic prospect of conviction',[66] leaving it to the court to decide whether the case is proved beyond all reasonable doubt.

In practice, this may impose little extra evidential burden on a regulator, which is unlikely to a launch a prosecution unless it is satisfied that it can prove its case beyond reasonable doubt. But the drafting in the legislation could raise potential problems. An example would be a case where the facts are secure but there is an issue of law – the definition of waste, say – that is worth pursuing, and where it might be reasonable for a regulator to initiate a criminal prosecution to test the point. But the regulator might consider a civil penalty to be a more appropriate response in the circumstances of the case. If counsel advised that, because of the legal uncertainties, there was a 70% chance of winning on the point of law should there be an appeal, would the regulator have met the statutory test that they are satisfied beyond reasonable doubt that an offence had been committed? If application of the requirement meant that legally they could not impose a civil sanction, this could lead to perverse consequences in that issues involving more difficult legal questions would revert to the magistrates courts rather than having the benefit of the more specialist appeal tribunal for civil sanctions.

---

[63] Ibid, para 21: 'Subsequent cases have rejected the notion that there is in the law some intermediate "hybrid" civil standard (see *In re D* [2008] UKHL 33 [2008] 1 WLR 1499). But that is not to say that the "criminal" standard is incapable of being applied in a "civil" case. Rather, it is to grasp the nettle of avoiding references to "the civil standard flexibly applied" and identify "civil" cases where a "beyond reasonable doubt" standard is called for: see *In re D* at §49 (Lord Brown); and see *Birmingham CC v Shafi* [2008] EWCA Civ 1186 [2009] 1 WLR 1961 at §49 (confirming the criminal standard as applicable to ASBOs under the decision in McCann).'

[64] Eg Regulatory Enforcement and Sanctions Act 2008, s 42(2): 'Provision [to confer powers on a regulator to impose discretionary requirements] under this section may only confer such a power in relation to a case where the regulator is satisfied beyond reasonable doubt that the person has committed a relevant offence'.

[65] Frustratingly for the development of this more coherent approach, departments have since produced regulations under powers other than the Regulatory Enforcement and Sanctions Act containing civil sanctions which are silent as to the standard of proof and where presumably the balance of probabilities standard will apply in the absence of a court or tribunal ruling. See, eg the Greenhouse Gas Emissions Trading Scheme Regulations 2012, SI 2012/3038.

[66] 'The Code for Crown Prosecutors', 7th edn (Crown Prosecution Service, January 2013) para 4.4.

An Independent Appeals Body

A robust appeal system was clearly going to be essential to any civil sanctions regime. Let alone any requirements for such an independent body to satisfy the requirements of the European Convention on Human Rights, provision for the right to appeal was essential as a matter of fairness and acceptability of the new system. The Review considered having appeals reverted to the ordinary courts, but experience in some of the jurisdictions looked at, such as Germany, suggested that this was not an optimal model. Setting up a wholly new specialist court or tribunal would have probably been unduly expensive and politically unacceptable but, fortuitously, at the time of the Review the Tribunal System was being completely reformed following the Leggatt Review.[67] Essentially, under the framework of the Tribunal and Courts Act 2007 it is now much easier to establish new tribunals, there is a common and more coherent structure for appeals from tribunals, and the tribunals are now clearly part of the independent judiciary. In the context of appeals against civil penalties, the tribunal model had considerable attractions. The Sanctions Review appreciated that, unlike in criminal prosecutions, the civil penalties system shifts a burden onto defendants who wish to challenge a regulator's decision in that it is the defendant who must initiate an appeal. Any system needed to both command confidence and be user-friendly, especially to smaller businesses.[68] As Leggatt noted,

> Choosing a tribunal to decide disputes should bring two distinctive advantages for users. First, tribunal decisions are often made jointly by a panel of people who pool legal and other expert knowledge, and are the better for that range of skills. Secondly, tribunals' procedures and approach to overseeing the preparation of cases and their hearing can be simpler and more informal than the courts, even after the civil justice reforms.[69]

So the decision to recommend in the Review that, as a matter of principle, any appeals should go to the new First-tier Tribunal was not a difficult choice.[70]

Part III of the Regulatory Enforcement and Sanctions Act reflects this appeals structure, but there were important areas where the statutory provisions appeared to be defective, and remain so. The Sanctions Review was clear that an appeal should be possible both as to the amount of any penalty imposed by the regulator and to the circumstances of the alleged offence. Essentially, it should be a full merits appeal with no constraints, and providing no fewer rights than would be available to a defendant in criminal proceedings. The Act seemed to provide this. For example, section 42 of the Act, on variable penalties, states that any order conferring powers on the regulator must include as minimum appeal grounds:

(a) that the decision was based on an error of fact;
(b) that the decision was wrong in law;
(c) that the amount of the penalty is unreasonable;

---

[67] A Leggatt, 'Tribunals for Users – One System, One Service', Report of the Review of Tribunals (London, Department for Constitutional Affairs, 2001).

[68] 'Where mistakes occur we are entitled to complain and to have the mistake put right with the minimum of difficulty; where there is uncertainty we are entitled to expect a quick resolution of the issue': Department of Constitutional Affairs White Paper, 'Transforming Public Services: Complaints, Redress and Tribunals' (DCA, July 2004) 3.

[69] Leggatt, above n 69, para 1.2.

[70] Sanctions Review, paras 3.54–3.61.

(d) that the nature of any requirement is unreasonable; or

(e) that the decision was unreasonable for any other reason.

At first reading this seemed broad enough to encompass a full merits appeal, but in practice there could be aspects of a regulator's decision that were neither strictly fact nor law (a professional judgement as to what is 'significant' pollution, say). Unless one could show that the regulator had been unreasonable in its finding (ie ground (e)), then in those circumstances[71] there would not be a full right of appeal.[72]

The rationale may have been that, with the fixed and variable penalties, a person served with a notice has the opportunity to make representations to the regulator. But this is a second consideration by the regulator rather than a true appeal, and the restricted right of appeal was contrary to the vision in the Review, let alone probably being contrary to Article 6.1 of the European Convention on Human Rights, discussed further below.[73] The Act, however, explicitly states that these are minimum grounds of appeal, and the first orders[74] introducing civil penalties for limited environmental offences have included an extra ground of appeal – 'any other reason' – thus avoiding any concerns concerning restricted appeal rights. Unless and until the primary legislation is amended, this means that any secondary legislation granting powers to regulators will need to be checked to ensure that the minimum appeal grounds have been extended in this way.

The second area of concern related to the burden of proof on appeals. The Sanctions Review did not explicitly address this question, but a system of civil penalties is deliberately designed to bypass the courts if no appeal is made. For someone who questioned whether there had been a regulatory breach to be faced with the burden of proving their innocence would offend notions of fairness, and would probably be contrary to the presumption of innocence under Article 6.2 of the European Convention.[75] During the preparation of the Regulatory Enforcement and Sanctions Bill, I argued for this to be made explicit on the face of the Bill, but was told by BERR lawyers that such a provision would be trespassing on the jurisdiction of the appeals tribunal, and that it would be up to the tribunal to create such principles should it wish to do so. In fact, the first orders granting civil sanction powers in respect of certain environmental offences make it clear that, in appeals against civil penalties where the commission of an offence is an issue requiring determination, the burden is on the regulator, who must prove that offence according to the same standard

---

[71] I am grateful to Judge Nick Warren, currently President of the Regulatory Tribunal, who first brought this point to my attention

[72] This analysis appears to be confirmed by the provisions for appeal under s 47 relating to stop notices. These include error of fact, wrong in law and unreasonable decision, but then adds a further ground, that 'the person has not committed the relevant offence or would not have committed it had the stop notice not been served'. It thus appears that the draftsman had clearly made a deliberate distinction between the minimal grounds of appeal against the core penalty sanctions and stop notices.

[73] 'In the determination of his civil rights and obligations or of any criminal charge against him, everyone is entitled to a fair and public hearing within a reasonable time by an independent and impartial tribunal established by law.'

[74] The Environmental Civil Sanctions (England) Order 2010, the Environmental Sanctions (Misc Amendments) (England) Regulations 2010, the Environmental Civil Sanctions (Wales) Order 2010 and the Environmental Civil Sanctions (Miscellaneous Amendments) (Wales) Regulations 2010.

[75] See further below. Under US legislation concerning appeals against civil penalties imposed by the Environmental Protection Agency, the burden is on the regulator to establish that the violation took place: 40 CFR Part 22.34 (2012).

of proof as in a criminal prosecution.[76] But, once again, unless the primary legislation is amended, each and every subsequent order will need to be checked to ensure that it includes this requirement.

European Convention on Human Rights

The Review was fully alive to the implications of the European Convention on Human Rights for any new system of civil penalties. Article 6.1 provides that, in the determination of his civil rights and obligations or of any criminal charge against him, everyone is entitled to a fair and public hearing within a reasonable time by an independent and impartial tribunal established by law. Article 6.2 goes on to provide that where a criminal charge is involved there are further rights, including the presumption of innocence. As is well known, the European Court on Human Rights has held that deciding whether proceedings are criminal or civil under the Convention is not a matter of choice by the national authority or how national legislation describes the relevant provisions, but will depend on a series of factors, including the seriousness of the sanction being imposed.[77] As Long Bingham, noted in *Secretary of State for the Home Office v MB*:[78]

> The language of article 6(1) is to be given an autonomous Convention meaning, that is, a Council of Europe-wide meaning applicable in all member states whatever their domestic laws may provide. Consistent with its constant principles of preferring substance to form and seeking to ensure that Convention rights are effectively protected, the European court is concerned to ascertain whether a proceeding is, in substance, civil or criminal: see, for example, *Öztürk v Germany* (1984) 6 EHRR 409, para 53; *Lauko v Slovakia* (1998) 33 EHRR 994, para 58. It is recognised that member states may have many reasons for choosing to treat as civil proceedings which are in substance criminal. It is the substance which matters. More significant in most cases are the second and third Engel criteria, the nature of the offence and the degree of severity of the penalty that the person concerned risks incurring.

The extent which civil sanctions under the Regulatory Enforcement and Sanctions Act should be classified as criminal or civil under the European Convention will no doubt eventually be a matter for determination by the courts. My personal view has long been that at least the variable penalties, as proposed by the Sanctions Review and contained in section 42 of the Regulatory Enforcement and Sanctions Act, should be considered criminal for the purposes of the European Convention.[79] The financial penalties are potentially very high, and under the system are intimately linked to defined criminal offences.

Some have argued that if this is the case it follows that the RESA system is fundamentally incompatible with Article 6.1 in that it is the regulator, and not an independent and

---

[76] See, eg Environmental Civil Sanctions (England) Order 2010 SI 2010/1157, 10(2): 'In any appeal (except in relation to a stop notice) where the commission of an offence is an issue requiring determination, the regulator must prove that offence according to the same burden and standard of proof as in a criminal prosecution.'

[77] See *Engel v Netherlands (no 1)* (1976) 1 EHRR 647; *International Transport Roth GmbH v SSHD* [2003] QB 728; *Albert and LeCompte v Belgium* (1983) 5 EHRR 533.

[78] *Secretary of State for the Home Office v MB* [2007] UKHL 46, 19.

[79] The European Court of Human Rights has never said that the standard of proof in criminal cases must be beyond all reasonable doubt, and the Convention has played no part in my views on the advantages of having the same standard of proof for both criminal and civil sanctions.

impartial tribunal, that is making the determination.[80] Norris and Phillips, for example, argue that 'At the very least, the regime could be said to offend against the twin guarantees permitting the opportunity to defend himself in person and to examine witnesses adverse to his case',[81] and that 'It is also arguable that the regime fails to protect the presumption of innocence'.[82]

Again, we may eventually have to wait for a judicial determination on the issue, but my own view is that the system is compatible. The European Convention does not say that an independent tribunal must determine *all* such rights and obligations – rather that everyone is *entitled* to such a determination. The opportunity of appeal to an independent court or tribunal, provided it contains no restrictions on the grounds of appeal and reflects the presumption of innocence, would appear to be compatible with Article 6.

This conclusion is supported by the 1984 decision of the European Court of Humans Rights in *Ozturk*.[83] One of the most developed systems of administrative penalties in Europe is that in Germany under its regulatory offences legislation, first developed in the early 1950s. *Ozturk* concerned administrative penalties created for certain traffic offences, with fines being imposed by the police and an appeal to a district court. The defendant was Turkish and argued that, since the offence was in reality a criminal offence, he should have been entitled to a free interpreter in the court under Article 6 of the Convention when he appealed. In the actual case the court charged him for the services.

The European Court held that this was indeed a criminal matter and that the Article 6 criminal rights came into play, and the failure to provide a free interpreter was therefore a breach. But in an important passage, the court noted that it would be wrong if, by a simple act of national categorisation, the state could remove the Article 6 right which guarantees everyone charged with a criminal offence the right to a court and a fair trial. It then observed that in this case these rights were not jeopardised since the legislation granted perpetrators 'the faculty – of which the appellant availed himself – of appealing to a court against an administrative decision'.[84] The decision implies that the availability of an appeal to an independent tribunal ensures consistency with the Convention when looked at as a whole. But it equally follows that the tribunal must comply with the obligations of the Convention – it must be able to handle the appeal 'within a reasonable time', there must be a right to cross-examine witnesses and legal aid must be provided 'when the interests of justice so require'. Some of this will be readily achievable within the arrangements;[85] others requirements, such as legal aid, which is not generally available in the tribunal system, may be more of a challenge. But if not addressed, the system will be vulnerable to a legal challenge based on the Convention.

---

[80] See, eg R Macrory and J Maurici, 'Rethinking regulatory sanctions – Regulatory Enforcement and Sanctions Act 2008 – an Exchange of Letters' (2009) 21(4) *Environmental Law and Managemen* 183.

[81] Norris and Phillips, above n 15, chap 4, para 22(i).

[82] Ibid 4.22(ii).

[83] *Öztürk v The Federal Republic of Germany* (1984) 6 EHRR 409.

[84] Ibid, [53].

[85] The Tribunal Procedure (First-tier Tribunal) (General Regulatory Chamber) Rules 2009, SI 2009/1976, do not give appellants an explicit right to cross-examine witnesses, though such rights could be granted under the tribunal's general discretionary powers under the rules concerning the conduct of hearing. The Employment Appeal Tribunal has held that the Art 6.1 ECHR rights to cross-examination were not engaged in an employment discrimination case since this was not a criminal matter: *Power v Greater Manchester Police* (UKEAT/ 0087/10/ JOJ, 29 April 2010).

Regulatory Governance

A system that allows greater use of civil penalties gives more power to regulators and deliberately bypasses the automatic involvement of independent courts or tribunals in each and every case. The whole issue of what might be termed regulatory governance therefore became more and more important during the Review. The last thing the Review wished to encourage was officious regulators who would impose immediate penalties for the most minor of breaches without exercising any sensible discretion, though this was a concern of some of those submitting evidence.[86] It was important to avoid the sorts of criticism that have dogged existing systems of administrative or civil penalties, such as those imposed under parking restrictions[87] or on public transport for incorrect tickets.[88]

It thus became vital to construct some core governance principles. The first was that the regulator imposing the penalty should received no direct economic benefit,[89] and this is now written into section 69 of the Regulatory Enforcement and Sanctions Act.[90] With government grant-in-aid being increasingly reduced, regulators will not have welcomed this provision, but, given the amount of enforcement discretion available, public confidence would weakened if there were any suspicion that the reason for imposing a sanction is to make up financial shortfalls in income.

The second core principle was that regulators should publish a clear enforcement policy indicating how they went about determining what sort of sanction was appropriate for what sort of breach. A policy gives important signals to the regulated community to ensure improved compliance, and assists in making the regulator more accountable. The Environment Agency has long published such an enforcement policy and at the beginning of the Review I had assumed that this was common practice amongst all regulators. However, the Review commissioned a survey of the 61 national regulators falling within its remit and found that only 15 had such a policy.[91] Published policies can provide valuable

---

[86] Eg the evidence of the Association of Master Bakers submitted to the Review: 'We believe there is a massive potential for abuse and misuse. It hands a massive amount of power to the enforcing officer with, in reality, virtually no compensatory checks and balances to prevent abuse' [16] (author's collection).

[87] See House of Commons Select Committee on Transport 7th Report of Session 2005–6 Parking Policy and Enforcement (House of Commons HC 741 206): 'Whilst not in crisis, decriminalised parking enforcement is certainly in need of steps to raise performance to a consistently high standard throughout the country' (para 36); 'Local authorities have shown poor judgement and a lack of professionalism in failing to publish and highlight their parking polices and objectives, performance measurements, financial information, and an appropriately complete range of relevant statistics' (para 47); 'Incentive schemes in parking enforcement contracts are utterly misguided. Why these should have ever been considered to be compatible with sensible enforcement of parking measures as a tool of street management is a mystery. That some local authorities should have started them, in the face of common sense and sound administration, is deeply disappointing' (para 69).

[88] Eg House of Commons Transport Select Committee 5th Report Session 2007–8 Ticketing and Concessionary Travel on Public Transport (House of Commons HC 84): 'The current appeals procedures for bus and rail are not sufficiently independent. The consequences of being accused of fare dodging can be serious and it is important that the procedures are just and rigorous. The current principal rail appeal panel is associated with the rail industry and this undermines its credibility as a truly independent arbiter, sitting equidistant from the passenger and the train operating company. The bus industry appeals body has no regulatory backing. The Government should consult on new arrangements' (Recommendation 11).

[89] Sanctions Review, para 3.45.

[90] Regulatory Enforcement and Sanctions Act 2008, s 69(1): 'Where pursuant to any provision made under or by virtue of this Part a regulator receives— (a) a fixed monetary penalty, a variable monetary penalty or a non-compliance penalty under section 45(1), (b) any interest or other financial penalty for late payment of such a penalty, or (c) a sum paid in discharge of liability to a fixed monetary penalty pursuant to section 40(2)(b), the regulator must pay it into the [Consolidated] Fund.'

[91] Cabinet Office, above n 21, para 1.36. As a comparison, in 2009 in the Australian state of Victoria, 55%

signals on the sort of behaviour that will give credit (such as early voluntary compensation to those affected by a breach) and the sort of behaviour that will not (such as a failure to report an incident), and these signals form a valuable element of effective enforcement, let alone helping to provide transparency and consistency.

The Review therefore recommended that all regulators should have a statutory duty to publish an enforcement policy that would cover all of their enforcement activity, including both criminal and civil.[92] This obligation is reflected in the Regulatory Enforcement and Sanctions Act, but because the Act did not deal with criminal matters, the duty is confined to regulators acquiring the new sanction powers and relates only to civil sanctions. However, the statutory Code of Practice for Regulators issued on 17 December 2007 requires regulators to whom the Code applies to publish an enforcement policy, without confining this to civil sanctions.[93]

The third core principle concerning governance was that regulators using these powers need to report on their activity in the form of output measures.[94] It is important to understand trends – the numbers and types of enforcement actions being taken and the type of sanction being used. The Regulatory Enforcement and Sanctions Act now incorporates this obligation for those regulators using the powers, but, as with the duty on enforcement policies, because of the way the legislation was developed, it is confined to civil sanctions[95] rather than encompassing, as the Review envisaged, all the sanctions imposed, including criminal prosecutions and the use of warnings and cautions.

Information on outputs by themselves is fairly meaningless, since they say little about the real impact of the sanctions regime, and the Review called for the greater use of outcome measures. As the Sanctions Review noted, 'Appropriate outcome measures will vary in different areas of regulatory activity, but are essentially concerned with the expected consequence and goals of the regulator's enforcement activity rather than an account of the amount and type of enforcement activity'.[96] There are pitfalls, though, especially in the choice of measures. Information can be misleading or manipulated in favour of the regulator. For example, the 2007 Annual Performance Report of the US Environmental Protection Agency[97] combined both output and outcome information by stating that the total penalties for that year amounted to $137m and that pollution had been reduced by 890 million pounds of pollutants. A year later, the General Accountability Office heavily criticised the quality of some of these performance measures: there was no adjustment of penalties for inflation over time, thus undervaluing past achievements; there was no men-

---

of major regulators had published enforcement policies: A Frieberg, *The Tools of Regulation* (Annandale, NSW, Federation Press, 2010), 206.

[92] Sanctions Review, paras 5.10–5.17 and Summary of Recommendations p 100.

[93] Department of Business Innovation and Skills, above n 6. Compared to the duties under the Regulatory Enforcement and Sanctions Act 2008, the obligations under the Code are less direct from a legal perspective in that the Legislative and Regulatory Reform Act 2006, s 22 requires that regulators to whom the Code applies must '*have regard to*' the Code in determining general policy and principles in exercised specified functions (author's emphasis).

[94] Sanctions Review, paras 5.25–5.27.

[95] The Regulatory Enforcement and Sanctions Act 2008, s 65 requires that where a regulator acquires powers under the Act, it must 'from time to time publish reports specifying—(a) the cases in which the civil sanction has been imposed; (b) where the civil sanction is a fixed monetary penalty, the cases in which liability to the penalty has been discharged pursuant to section 40(2)(b); and (c) where the civil sanction is a discretionary requirement, the cases in which an undertaking referred to in section 43(5) has been accepted from a person'.

[96] Sanctions Review, para 5.20.

[97] Environmental Protection Agency, *Performance and Accountability Report for Fiscal Year 2007* (Washington DC, EPA, 2007).

tion that three exceptional large penalties had distorted the figures; and the quantities of pollutants reduced made no distinction between hazardous and non-hazardous.[98]

The Sanctions Review recommended that Regulators and sponsoring departments should work with the Better Regulation Executive to include outcome measures as part of their overall framework of performance management[99] while acknowledging that 'Determining the appropriate outcome measures and the methodology by which they should be measured are challenging tasks'. The difficulties involved may account for the lack of any statutory obligation concerning outcome measures in the Regulatory Enforcement and Sanctions Act, although the statutory Compliance Code requires regulators 'to measure outcomes not just outputs'.[100] There are no easy answers,[101] but it is important to recognise that the choice of any particular outcome measure is contestable and may involve value choices. As such, it is a choice that should not be left solely to the decision of the regulator or government department, but should first involve open discussion with the regulated community and the wider public before final decisions are made.

But even where a sophisticated outcome measure is used, can this provide useful information on the effectiveness of different types of sanctions? As Sparrow states in the *Character of Harms*,[102] the really difficult question inherent in regulation is whether one can ever move beyond correlation to causality. Can one assign credit to particular functions within the regulator? And, crucially, is it possible to measure prevention? The Sanctions Review noted that, 'During the course of the Review it became apparent how little information is available on the effectiveness of sanctioning regimes'.[103] Too often there are far too many variables to identify any particular factor as significant. Comparing pollution incidents, say, between England (mainly using criminal sanctions) and Germany (largely administrative penalties) is unlikely to prove the effectiveness of either regime, since different cultures and different legal regimes are likely to provide too much background noise to single out individual factors.[104]

In 2012 the Cabinet Office published an important paper analysing the weaknesses of the traditional approach of judging effectiveness of policies simply by implementing policy and observing outcomes.[105] The sort of randomised controlled trials it argued for which would allow for a more robust comparison to be made between the effectiveness of the new policy intervention and no change may not be entirely appropriate for dealing with different forms of regulatory sanction. However, in the field of environ-

---

[98] General Accountability Office, *EPA Needs to Improve the Accuracy and Transparency of Measures Used to Report on Program Effectiveness*, GAO-08-1111R (GAO, 2008).

[99] Sanctions Review, Summary of Recommendations p 101.

[100] Department of Business Innovation and Skills, above n 6, para 8.4.

[101] See, eg E Mazur, 'Outcome Performance Measures of Environmental Compliance Assurance: Current Practices, Constraints and Ways Forward', OECD Environment Working Papers No 18 (OECD Publishing, 2010).

[102] M Sparrow, *The Character of Harms* (Cambridge, Cambridge University Press, 2008) 136–43.

[103] Sanctions Review, para 5.21. A more recent study including of review of over 80 articles concerning businesses' regulatory compliance behaviour concluded that 'The literature review identified no evidence that considered the effectiveness of specific powers available to environmental regulators.' Greenstreet Berman, above n 11, 2.2.2.

[104] The Sanctions Review identified one study which provided a robust comparison between two provinces in Canada applying the same laws to similar industries, but with one regulator using criminal sanctions and the other administrative sanctions. The study, however, focused on the process rather than the outcomes. RM Brown, 'Administration and Criminal Penalties in the Enforcement of Occupational Health and Safety Legislation' (1992) 30(3) *Osgoode Hall Law Journal* 691.

[105] L Haynes et al, 'Test Learn and Adapt – Developing Public Policy with Randomized Controlled Trials' (Cabinet Office, 2012).

mental regulation, in this country there will soon be opportunities for a more robust comparative evaluation of different forms of sanctions regime in different areas of the United Kingdom. At present in England and Wales, the Environment Agency has new sanctioning powers in only limited areas, while Natural England has more extensive sanctioning powers. The most recent policy position of the government is that in future any extension of civil sanctions (other than enforcement undertakings) will generally only be available to large businesses. Scotland, in contrast, is developing its own more comprehensive regime in the environmental sector, but one where the civil standard of proof is likely to apply to civil sanctions.[106] Northern Ireland equally has a regulatory reform agenda under way where new forms of sanctions are likely to play one element.[107] The Review indicated a dearth of robust research on the effectiveness and impact of sanctioning regimes, and advised that, 'sponsoring departments and/or regulators of introducing new sanctioning tools to study and develop information, including commissioning independent research, relating to sanctions and their effectiveness especially during the transition period'.[108] The way in which the types of sanctions are available in different areas and sectors of the United Kingdom may be uncomfortably asymmetric, but equally they could provide significant opportunities for investing in well-constructed, independent and comparative research at this critical time of implementation.

Obligations concerning enforcement policies and the provision of information concerning outputs and outcomes are important in providing increased transparency and accountability of individual regulators. The Sanctions Review, however, cut across myriad areas of regulatory laws and identified common issues and challenges whatever the differences in the detailed substance of the laws concerned. Questions such as the design of enforcement statements, the choice of output and outcome and evaluative research cut across many areas of regulatory law. The Department for Business Innovation and Skills is pursuing, through its regulatory reform agenda, initiatives on improving regulatory enforcement in particular sectors,[109] but outside government there is little in the way of institutional mechanisms whereby the performance of regulators can be compared and held accountable across the board. Existing departmental Parliamentary Select Committees deal only with regulators falling within the departmental silos, making it difficult to compare, say, output measures of the Environment Agency and of the Health and Safety Executive in a common forum. The Sanctions Review therefore called for the setting up of a Parliamentary Committee on Regulators, which could perform this type of function. In fact, the House of Lords Select Committee on the Constitution had begun to address this issue in 2004 in its report on the regulatory state,[110] though the focus was mainly on the economic regulators. An ad-hoc select committee was then established which examined economic

---

[106] Scottish Government, 'Consultation on Proposals for an Integrated Framework of Environmental Regulation' (Scottish Government, May 2012).

[107] Northern Ireland Department of the Environment, 'Environmental Better Regulation White Paper' (DOENI, March 2011).

[108] Sanctions Review, para 5.21.

[109] For example, a recently announced regulatory reform package concerning the chemical industry where the Environment Agency and the Health and Safety Executive would integrate their inspection regimes. Department of Business Innovation and Skills, 'Smarter Enforcement of Regulation to Cut Red Tape in the Chemical Industry', 6 February 2013, available at www.gov.uk/government/news/smarter-enforcement-of-regulation-to-cut-red-tape-for-chemicals-industry (accessed on 24 March 2013).

[110] House of Lords Select Committee on the Constitution, 'The Regulatory State: Ensuring Its Accountability, 6th Report of Session 2003–04' HL Paper 68-1 (Stationery Office, 2004).

regulators, but its report in 2007[111] called for the establishment of a Joint Committee or, failing that, a House of Lords Committee: 'The question of who regulates the regulators has not been answered and will not go away. There is a need for a committee to pursue cross-sector best practice.'[112] The government's response to the recommendation was that this was a matter for Parliament rather than government,[113] and there the matter appears to have rested.

Conclusions

We are at the foothills of a fundamental change in the way we think about regulatory sanctions. The Sanctions Review picked up on some of the best of current practice taking place in such jurisdictions as Australia and Canada, but proposed a distinctive system. Two special features stand out. First, placing criminal and civil sanctions into a single integrated system, which that gives the regulator the responsibility of choosing the most effective routes. Secondly, it should be a system which lays emphasis on the need to address issues of regulatory governance, including accountability and transparency, and the importance of reducing to a minimum those factors that can unwittingly distort the regulatory choices being made.

The principles proposed in the Review were designed to provide a coherent framework for the overall development of the regulatory sanctions and the way in which they are handled by regulators. These at least are now reflected in the Statutory Code for Regulators.[114] But, as this analysis has shown, even where the government has accepted the proposals, translating the ambitions of a review that cuts across such a broad spectrum of departmental and regulatory interests into legislative reality is fraught with difficulty. There are lessons to be learnt for future such initiatives. Even where there is cross-department support in principle, proposals that combine reforms in both the area of criminal law and civil sanctions are particularly challenging to implement in a coherent way where there appears to be a powerful division of responsibilities between different government departments. In the case of the Sanctions Review, once responsibility for implementation had moved from the Cabinet Office to the revived Department of Business and Regulatory Reform, it was almost inevitable that there would be a distortion of effort, with the greater emphasis on the introduction of civil sanctions, and to some extent with the proposed reforms now being seen within a general regulatory reform agenda designed to cut back on regulation as much as improving the system of sanctions. A strong ministerial champion might have helped in redressing the balance and promoting the message of a coherent approach to reform, but the subject of sanctions is not the most politically attractive aspect of the regulatory reform agenda. Once a review is completed, the members of the secretariat who were intimately involved in the analysis of evidence and the development of arguments are

---

[111] House of Lords Select Committee on Regulators, 'UK Economic Regulators, 1st Report of Session 2006–07', HL Paper 189-1 (Stationery Office, 2007).

[112] Ibid, para 1.29.

[113] Department of Business Enterprise and Regulatory Reform, 'Government Response to the House of Lords Select Committee on Regulators – Economic Regulators' (Better Regulation Executive, 2008) 16.

[114] Department of Business Innovation and Skills, above n 6, para 8.4.

often rapidly dispersed, and it is valuable if the reviewer can remain involved to explain the rationale behind proposals and deal with the unexpected.

The Sanctions Review expected that the legislative framework provided in the Regulatory Reform and Sanctions Act would provide a set of procedures and principles concerned with issues such as grounds of defence, standards of proof and appeal procedures that would bring order to the existing muddled picture of regulatory sanction powers and procedures. However, there is still a long way to go on this journey. On 8 November 2012, the government announced in Parliament that in future powers to impose fixed or variable penalties would only be applicable where the transgressing company has more than 250 employees. Other powers under Part III of the Regulatory Enforcement and Sanctions Act 2088, including enforceable undertakings and stop notices, will be available in respect of any size of company.[115] The underlying intention was a perception that smaller sized companies could be unfairly treated by overzealous regulators and would not have access to suitable legal resources to mount effective appeals. It is a danger to which I was fully alive during the Review, and the announcement has been criticised as failing to recognise some of the core features of the new system, including a user-friendly appeal tribunal.[116] It will be fascinating to discover whether in future small and medium-sized enterprises feel deprived or relieved in being denied access to the new sanctions. The government announcement may suggest a change of direction or even that there will be a truncated journey in England and Wales. But ultimately the quest for more effective systems of regulatory sanctions is a journey I believe worth taking.

[115] Written statement, above n 8.

[116] UK Environmental Law Association, Letter to Minister of State for Business and Enterprise, 20 December 2012.

4

Regulating in a Risky Environment[1]
(2002)

In October 2000 the Prime Minister delivered a major speech on the environment.[2] For those concerned with environmental policy, it was a politically significant occasion in that it was his first speech on the subject as prime minister. But for British lawyers who over the past two decades or so have studied and contributed to an extraordinary development of what is now known as environmental law there was an equally intriguing aspect: regulation as a policy tool received just one scant mention in the whole speech.[3]

Regulation is a notoriously difficult concept to define with precision. One commonly used definition refers to the 'sustained and focused control exercised by a public agency over activities that are socially valued',[4] though, as Hilson notes,[5] this does not necessarily capture all those undesirable activities which one could also expect to be controlled by environmental regulation. For the purpose of my analysis, a further key essential is that regulation is clearly enforceable by a legal sanction,[6] distinguishing it from many forms of economic intervention by government. What is clear is that there is a number of challenges facing contemporary environmental regulation and my underlying concern is with the extent to which governments have lost confidence in regulation as an instrument of environmental policy. We need to understand the reasons for this, whether they are sound, and, I would argue, explore mechanisms for revitalizing its role. For a country such as the United Kingdom, where traditionally one might have expected the clear location of responsibility for designing environmental regulation to rest with central government, in part any present discomfort with regulation can be attributed to the uncertainties brought about by a general realignment of formal powers away from central government, with supra-national 'pressures' for 'concerted' international action competing with continuing and sometimes contradictory pressures for increased decentralisation. The environment

---

[1] R Macrory, 'Regulating in a Risky Environment' in M Freeman (ed), *Current Legal Problems 2001* (Oxford, Oxford University Press, 2002) 619–48.

[2] Prime Minister, 'Richer and Greener', speech to the CBI/Green Alliance Conference on the Environment (London, 24 October 2000).

[3] The one reference to regulation in the speech is 'On regulation, our aim must be to raise environmental standards without imposing unnecessary burdens on business'.

[4] G Majone, 'The Rise of the Regulatory State in Europe' (1994) 17 *West European Politics* 77, 81; P Selznick, 'Focusing Organisational Research on Regulation' in R Noll (ed), *Regulatory Policy and the Social Sciences* (Berkeley, 1985).

[5] C Hilson, *Regulating Pollution: A UK and EC Perspective* (Oxford, 2000), ch 1.

[6] For the purposes of the present analysis, whether sanctions take the form of criminal penalties, civil penalties as extensively used in the United States, or administrative sanctions such as the withdrawal of a licence is a second-order question, which is not further explored here, though clearly significant in the design of effective regulation.

is a particularly complex policy field, and poses especially difficult challenges for the allocation of government responsibilities. Traditional models of federal or quasi-federal constitutions which attempt to articulate a clear separation of powers in the environmental field are unlikely to reflect the physical and political dynamics of the issue.[7] Such questions concern what might be described as the vertical allocation of powers, but, as Peter Hain has forcefully argued in a recent study,[8] the realities of global capitalism and an increasingly articulate citizenship create new challenges for the traditional authority of national governments: 'power is also moving outwards into new configurations that have little to do with governments at any level, or with the physical boundaries that define where they hold sway'.[9]

These considerations form a background to the exercise of regulatory power in any policy field by contemporary government at whatever level. But environmental regulation has been subject to a distinctive and sustained intellectual challenge in recent years, and it is on a number of those themes that I intend to focus. In doing so, I will test the validity of theory against a number of case studies in recent United Kingdom policy, and draw on my personal experience as a member of the Royal Commission on Environmental Pollution[10] and a board member of the Environment Agency.[11]

Market Failure and Regulatory Prescription

There are two important underlying presumptions concerning environmental regulation, both of which can be challenged. The first is that the justification for environmental regulation is solely based on the concept of market failures in a free economy: the dominant economic theory is that the sum of individual consumer choices in a free market will maximise collective welfare, and the role of areas of law such as property, contract, and tort is to define the rights and responsibilities of these economic actors. In certain areas,

---

[7] R Macrory, 'The Environment and Constitutional Change' in R Hazell (ed), *Constitutional Futures: A History of the Next Ten Years* (Oxford, 1999), where I discuss some of the difficulties in the context of current constitutional reform in the United Kingdom. For a recent study of the challenges of locating power in the context of federal systems and particularly that of the United States, see R Ravesz, 'Environmental Regulation in Federal Systems' in H Somsen (ed), *Yearbook of European Environmental Law* (Oxford, 2000) 1.

[8] P Hain, *The End of Foreign Policy? British Interests, Global Linkages and Natural Limits* (London, 2001) ch 5.

[9] At the time of writing the author was Minister of State at the UK Foreign and Commonwealth Office, but the concerns of a practising politician clearly reflect themes of the authority of government explored by contemporary political sociologists such as Ulrich Beck and Anthony Giddens; see in particular U Beck, *Risk Society: Towards a New Modernity* (London, 1992); A Giddens, *The Consequences of Modernity* (Cambridge, 1990). For insightful British accounts see P Macnaughten and J Urry, *Contested Natures* '(London, 1992); D Goldblatt, *Social Theory and the Environment* (London, 1997), especially ch 5, where the author questions the applicability of some of Beck's analysis to a number of British environmental issues.

[10] The Royal Commission on Environment Pollution was established in 1970 'to advise on matters, both national and international, concerning pollution of the environment; on the adequacy of research in the field; and the future possibilities of danger to the environment'. It is the only remaining standing Royal Commission in the United Kingdom, and produces major reports around every 28 months. (The Commission was dissolved by the coalition government in 2011 as part of government financial cut-backs.)

[11] The Environment Agency was established in 1995 under Part I Environment Act 1995 as a non-departmental public body with extensive responsibilities in England and Wales for the regulation of waste, water pollution and water resources, fisheries, radioactive wastes, and key industrial processes. In addition, the Agency has operational functions concerning land drainage and flood management. The views expressed in this article are personal, and do not necessarily represent the collective views of the Royal Commission or the Agency.

though – and the environment is an obvious example – there will be market failure in that costs can be externalised and imposed on others than the actor concerned, and hence the need for government intervention, traditionally in the form of regulation. The analysis, of course, has a powerful logic. Furthermore, it provides a driver and justification for seeking methods other than legal regulation to perform functions equivalent to interventionist regulation. The redefinition of property rights provides one example, while current proposals to develop tort principles concerning civil liability for environmental damage as a tool of public policy provide another example.[12]

Yet there are deficiencies in the argument. For a start the model consciously avoids attributing any moral dimension to regulation. Yet few would attempt to argue that many areas of criminal law are based solely on market failure, nor would the various legal principles concerning, say, rights and obligations that have been developed in the area of family law be described as a response to market failure. As well as economic considerations, environmental issues do raise important moral and value questions of our relationship with the environment,[13] or our relationships with each other and with future generations. In this context, environmental regulation reflects questions of value as well as market failure, and merely adjusting notions of private property or internalizing external costs are unlikely to satisfy those aspirations.

Even within its own terms, the theory has serious problems. In its pure form it provides a justification for seeking to determine and to quantify in financial terms the economic costs imposed by environmental externalities. But it seems unlikely that we will ever succeed in measuring environmental costs with such a degree of precision that they can be imposed on relevant economic actors in a way that will allow us to rely upon market forces alone. Two recent examples illustrate the difficulties involved. In 1997 Andrew Stirling of Sussex University collated over thirty studies published between 1979 and 1995 estimating in monetary terms the environmental externalities of modern coal-fired power stations.[14] The results of individual studies were often expressed in extremely precise terms and with considerable confidence, but when presented collectively the variations were so immense as to throw doubt on their validity as a policy tool: values on the lowest estimates were less than 4/100 of a cent per kilowatt hour with the highest around $20 per kilowatt hour, a factor of more than fifty thousand. Deriving a workable and acceptable set of fiscal instruments to internalise such an uncertain range of costs would have proved near impossible, or have involved so many political choices as to undermine the intellectual grounding of the exercise.

The second example concerns transport. In its 18th Report on Transport the Royal Commission on Environmental Pollution attempted to estimate the external costs imposed by transport in the United Kingdom.[15] Some costs, such as property damage were quantifiable with a reasonable degree of certainty. Others, such as global warming, are based on

---

[12] At European Community level see in particular European Commission, *White Paper on Environmental Liability,* COM (2000) 66 final. For a recent legal analysis see M Wild, 'The EC Commission's White Paper on Environmental Liability: Issues and Implications' (2001) 13 *Journal of Environmental Law* 21. In the same issue Peter Cane provides a powerful critique of the use of civil liability mechanisms as an instrument of public policy goals: P Cane, 'Are Environmental Harms Special?' (2001) 13 *Journal of Environmental Law* 3.

[13] A valuable collection of recent material written on the subject of ethical value and the environment is contained in R Elliot (ed), *Environmental Ethics* (Oxford, 1993).

[14] A Stirling, 'Limits to the Value of External Costs' (1997) 25 *Energy Policy* 517.

[15] Royal Commission on Environmental Pollution, *Transport and the Environment,* 18th Report, Cm 2674 (London, 1994) ch 7.

arguable assumptions, and in any event contain an enormous range of uncertainty. When considering damage from transport in the form of, say, visual intrusion, loss of habitats, and severance of communities, the Commission, rightly in my view, eventually concluded that the methodologies were so suspect that any numerical figures would not produce useful results. Instead, it was felt preferable to start with a judgment of the environmental goals one wished to secure, and then to consider the most cost-effective ways of achieving them. This does not mean that an exercise in estimating external costs in general terms is without value. In that case it provided a broad-scale picture of the extent of external damage imposed by transport, and highlighted substantial discrepancies between the costs paid by private motorists and heavy goods vehicles. But it also revealed the enormous difficulties facing those who wished to internalise external costs. The problem of the logic was underlined by the fact that in relation to private motorists, at least, it was not easy to show that their external environmental costs in fact exceeded the actual costs paid in the form of both direct and indirect taxes. If motorists were prepared to pay such costs, did it then follow that all was well with the market-based approach and that society should accept that consequential environmental damage was being paid for?

The second prevailing presumption concerns so-called command and control regulation. The term is often used rather loosely and as a pejorative to attack all traditional forms of environmental regulation, particularly in the field of pollution control. As Gunningham and Grabosky have observed, the term 'command and control' has now largely replaced the more traditional term of direct regulation.[16] Much of the sustained criticism of command and control has come from the legal and economic literature in the United States over the past decade or so,[17] and a central concern is that by prescribing the details of technical solutions, such command and control regulation stifles innovative solutions and leads to inefficient outcomes.

Yet an analysis of the form of regulation that has developed in practice reveals a considerably richer picture. In the field of pollution control, where much of the criticism has been focused, one can identify three broad approaches in the design of regulation: true technical standards which prescribe particular forms of technical solutions; emission- or performance-based standards which are outcome-focused and are concerned with prescribing levels of pollutants which may be discharged; and finally, ambient-based controls which relate to the quality of the receiving medium and may be set either on a single medium basis (air, water, etc.) or on a more integrated multi-media basis. In relation to the first, type. technical standards, as the distinguished US environmental lawyer, Turner T. Smith Jr, has noted, even in the United States:

> other than (1) management standards for transportation, storage and disposal of hazardous waste and (2) limited case of US work practice rules, virtually all of the technology based air and water standards and some of the hazardous waste treatment standards are not command and control in the sense of expressly requiring use of a specific type of technology.[18]

Such standards are clearly related to technological solutions, but industry is free to

---

[16] N Gunningham and P Grabosky, *Smart Regulation: Designing Environmental Policy* (Oxford, 1998) 39.

[17] Examples include B Ackerman and R Stewart, 'Reforming Environmental Law: The Democratic Case for Market Incentives' (1988) 13 *Columbia Journal of Environmental Law* 171; R Stewart, 'Models for Environmental Regulation: Central Planning versus Market Based Approaches' (1992) *Boston College Environmental Affairs Review* 547; S. Breyer, *Regulation and its Reform* (Cambridge, MA, 1992).

[18] TT Smith Jr and R Macrory, 'Legal and Political Considerations' in P Douben (ed), *Pollution Risk Assessment and Management* (Chichester, 1998) 406.

choose its most effective method of achieving them, whether by process management or alternative technologies. The same analysis can be made of much of the environmental legislation in Europe, where at European Community level there have been long standard philosophical disputes between the merits and weaknesses of emission and quality ori-entated standards.[19] Yet true technological standards which prescribe particular forms of technology remain rare. It is true that recent European Community legislation such as the IPPC Directive makes reference to the 'Best Available Technology', yet even here it is clear that the legislative intent is to focus on the production of emission standards rather than particular forms of technology.[20] See, for example, paragraph 4 of Article 9, which states that:

> emission limit values and the equivalent parameters and technical measures referred to in paragraph 3 shall be based on the best available techniques without prescribing the use of any technique or specific technology.

The attack on command and control regulation as a form of law that prescribes forms of technical solution is therefore somewhat misplaced, and has sometimes been promoted by those who fail to appreciate the flexibilities that even apparently tough environmental regimes can provide.[21] Nor should one ignore the very real achievements of direct regula-tion in the last twenty years or so. In its recent report on the state of the environment in England and Wales,[22] the Environment Agency notes significant progress in the improve-ment of air and water quality over the last decade, but a decline in the quality of soil, an area where in comparison with water and air there has been a signal lack of dedicated environmental regulation. Despite this background, direct regulation remains a politically vulnerable instrument of policy, and over the last decade or so two key forms of policy tool have been promoted as alternatives to regulation: economic instruments and volun-tary agreements.

Economic Instruments and their Weaknesses

The use of economic instruments has a powerful theoretical basis if one believes that the root cause of environmental problems is market failure. As the 1996 Government Annual Report on the UK's Sustainable Strategy put it:

> Economic instruments use the efficiency properties of markets to attain environmental objec-tives in the most cost-effective way. Moreover this cost-effective solution is achieved through the operation of market mechanisms themselves, dispensing with the need for a regulator.[23]

Economic instruments in the form of taxes or charges appear to be consistent with the 'polluter pays' principle and to provide a mechanism for government to influence the

---

[19] N Haigh, *EEC Environmental Policy and Britain,* 2nd edn (London, 1987) 20–23.
[20] G Lübbe-Wolff, 'Efficient Environmental Legislation: On Different Philosophies of Pollution Control in Europe' (2001) 13 *Journal of Environmental Law* 79.
[21] See, eg N Hanley, J Shogren and B White, *Environmental Economics in Theory and Practice* (Basingstoke, 1992), quoted in Lübbe-Wolff, ibid. At 58 the authors appear to characterise command and control regulation as imposing 'technological restrictions such as mandated abatement methods'.
[22] Environment Agency, *Environment 2000 and Beyond* (Bristol, 2001).
[23] United Kingdom, 'This Common Inheritance', Cm 3188 (London, 1996) para 147.

direction of behaviour without determining solutions. But where the aim is to achieve articulated policy goals, their effectiveness is less certain, and we are entitled to test their seductive theory against practical experience. Three recent examples from the United Kingdom suggest a need for some degree of scepticism.

The differential taxes on leaded and unleaded petrol were for many years promoted as a prime example of an effective economic instrument. Yet as the table from the second assessment of the European Environmental Agency indicates,[24] a comparison of the United Kingdom reduction rates with other European countries hardly inspires unqualified confidence in the ability of the instrument to achieve policy goals. Comparing reductions of lead emissions from petrol between 1990 and 1996 Britain's reduction is half that of Scandinavian countries and comes between Georgia and Lithuania.

The next example relates to the landfill tax, introduced in the United Kingdom in October 1996, initially applying a tax of £7 per tonne of waste, with various reductions and exemptions.[25] To anyone who is critical of direct regulation because it can consist of complex, legally binding rules, the lengthy regulations required to implement the landfill tax clearly illustrate that economic instruments equally require mandatory rules, and often of similar density. The policy intention behind the landfill tax, namely to increase the cost of landfill so that other waste disposal methods including minimisation, recycling, and incineration became more economically attractive options, is environmentally persuasive. Yet markets behave in unpredictable ways. The cost of landfill did indeed rise considerably, but also led to a substantial diversion of waste to other destinations which were not included in the preferred options: increased fly-tipping, and more seriously the substantial diversion to, and possible abuse of various form of disposal exempted under current regulations. As the (ENDS) report noted:

> Within months of the landfill tax taking effect in 1996, reports came rolling in that golf courses and farms had become prime destinations for the disposal of construction and demolition waste.[26]

A government-commissioned report suggested that land filling of inert wastes had fallen from around 66 million tonnes before the introduction of the tax to about 30 million tonnes in 2000.[27] The Environment Agency itself was hampered in effective supervision, partly because its revenue streams in relation to waste derived from charges on licensed landfills, and it is only recently that the government is seriously addressing the need to tighten up the exempted routes. A key lesson from the saga was the danger of assuming that a market instrument by itself could achieve desired policy goals. Without a powerful and adequately enforced regulatory framework, unexpected consequences can arise. This, of course, is particularly the case when dealing with an issue such as waste which generally has negative economic value for producers, and where the cheapest diversion route will have a powerful attraction. In that context, economic instruments need to be supportive rather than substitutive of regulation.

Whether the landfill tax by itself, even against a background of strengthened regulation against undesired diversion, would have had the desired outcome of reducing landfill is

---

[24] European Environment Agency, *Europe's Environment: A Second Assessment* (Copenhagen, 1998) 27.
[25] Landfill Tax Regulations, SI 1996/1527; Landfill Tax (Qualifying Material) Order, SI 1996/1528; Landfill Tax (Contaminated Land) Order, SI 1996/1529.
[26] *ENDS Report*, 'Inertia over Inert Waste Embarrasses Ministers and Agency' (2000) 303 *ENDS Report* 22.
[27] Ecotec, *Effects of the Landfill Tax* (London, 2001).

difficult to judge. What is now clearly going to have a far more substantial impact on shifting the hierarchy of waste management options is the European Community Landfill Directive,[28] which came into force in July 2001, and which imposes direct bans on overall quantities of waste going into landfill over the next decade or so.[29] The Landfill Directive represents a form of command and control instrument, albeit one at supranational level. Again, far from prescribing in detail forms of technological choice, it leaves considerable discretion to choose the most effective means to achieve the prescribed goals. The government may well choose a form of market instrument, permits tradeable between local authorities,[30] as a method of achieving the requirements, but against the backdrop of a regulatory instrument. Now that the European Court of Justice possesses the power to impose sanctions in the forms of penalties or fines for member states who fail to comply with its judgments, directives have come to resemble classical legal forms of regulation, though developed at supranational level and directed at national governments. The power of the court to impose direct sanctions[31] – a unique ability among international courts – was introduced under the Maastricht amendments with the strong support of the UK government. At the time it was being proposed, the House of Lords Select Committee on the European Communities investigated the whole issue of the implementation of Community environmental law[32] and, as one of the specialist advisers to the Committee, I admit entertaining misgivings about the prospective power of the European Court. At its crudest, it appeared to denigrate the rule of law by accepting that governments need to be threatened with financial sanctions to ensure compliance with judgments of a court. Despite the Committee's reservations at the time, the power was introduced, and we have since seen the first case in which the Court of Justice imposed a fine,[33] at the same time endorsing the Commission's policy documents explaining its approach towards establishing the level of appropriate penalty.[34] Evidence to date suggests that even the threat of the sanction has had a considerable effect in concentrating the minds of governments to ensure proper implementation.[35]

My third example again concerns transport. A key concern of the Royal Commission's 18th Report on Transport was the continuing contribution of carbon dioxide emissions from road transport. Carbon dioxide (CO_2) is the main greenhouse gas affected by human activity, and UK emissions from transport have been rising over the past quarter century. Twenty-five per cent of UK CO_2 emissions are attributable to transport, with the vast proportion coming from road transport.[36] With CO_2 emissions likely to reduce from other major sources such as heavy industry, transport's contribution is likely to rise in

[28] EC Directive on the Landfill of Waste 99/31/EC OJL 182, 17 July 1999.

[29] Amongst other requirements, biodegradable municipal wastes must be reduced to 75% of 1995 levels by 2010, 50% by 2013 and 35% by 2020.

[30] Department of the Environment, Transport, and the Regions, 'Consultation Paper on Tradeable Landfill Permits' (London, 2001).

[31] Art 228, European Community Treaty.

[32] House of Lords Select Committee on the European Communities, 'Implementation and Enforcement of Environmental Legislation', 9th Report Session 1991–2, HL Paper 53 (London, 1992). In its subsequent report, 'Community Environmental Law: Making It Work', 2nd Report Session 1997–8, HL Paper 12 (London, 1997) the Committee held a more positive view towards the sanction powers of the court: para 98.

[33] *Commission v Greece* (C-387/97) [2000] ECR I-5047. For a discussion see R. Macrory, 'Greece gets first fine for breach of EC environmental laws' (2000) 306 *ENDS Report* 47.

[34] EC Commission Communications of 1996 and 1997: [1996] OJ C242/6 and [1997] OJ C63/2.

[35] See L Kramer, *EC Environmental Law*, 4th edn (London, 2000) 291–92.

[36] Royal Commission on Environmental Pollution, 'Transport and the Environment: Developments since 1994', 18th Report, Cm 3752 (London, 1997) para 2.34.

future years. In contrast to many other forms of pollutant emissions, it is not practicable to remove carbon dioxide from individual motor vehicles, and since the amount of carbon dioxide is broadly proportional to the amount of fuel used, a reduction of total fuel consumption is an obvious route towards achieving policy goals. Yet it was clear in 1994 that very large improvements in fuel efficiency could be achieved using known technology, and evidence from government indicated that it was technically possible to improve the weighted average fuel efficiency of new cars by 40 per cent over the next ten to fifteen years.[37] It was equally clear, however, that there was a trend for cars to become heavier and more powerful, more than compensating for any trends in improved efficiency. The average fuel consumption of new cars registered in the United Kingdom fell by about 20 per cent between 1978 and 1987.[38]

Faced with such a challenge, what is the most appropriate policy response? As the Commission noted, without policy intervention, improved design of the scale required would not come by itself:

> It is unlikely to be applied in practice unless government provides appropriate signals to influence decisions by manufacturers and the behaviour of the general public as purchasers and drivers.[39]

Regulatory instrument in the form of mandatory efficiency standards represents one form of policy mechanism. Corporate Average Fleet Economy Standards have been mandatory in the United States since 1976, and though starting from a higher point than European averages produced a 25 per cent reduction in fuel consumption between 1970 and 1990.[40]

The Commission, however, was eventually persuaded that the use of economic instruments, in the form of an annual fuel escalator, might achieve the same effect, sending a sustained signal to car manufacturers to introduce greatly increased efficiencies. Such an escalator was introduced by the government, but when the Commission revisited the subject of transport in 1997[41] and again in its 2000 report on Energy[42] it was apparent that while there had been some reductions of CO_2 emissions from the average new car, there had been no reduction in overall fuel consumption. Improvements in engine efficiency had been more than offset by increased sales of larger vehicles (including four-wheel-drive vehicles) and increases in vehicle weights. At the same time the intended price signals of the fuel escalator tax had been weakened by fluctuations in the price of crude oil, with prices at the pump failing to match increases in the tax. The sudden escalation in crude oil prices revealed the political vulnerability of the escalator, and the Chancellor of the Exchequer announced its abandonment in November 1999 stating that any future fuel duty increases would be determined on a budget-by-budget basis. A striking feature of the initial political response to fuel demonstrations was the failure to justify the fuel escalator as a policy instrument for improving efficiency. Instead it was presented as an important source of government income for sectors such as education or health which would otherwise have to be raised from other forms of taxation.

[37] Ibid, para 8.39.
[38] Ibid, para 8.36.
[39] Ibid, para 8.59.
[40] Ibid, para 8.50.
[41] Ibid, para 2.35.
[42] Royal Commission on Environmental Pollution, 'Energy: The Changing Climate', Cm 4749 (London, 2000) para 6.110.

In a 1996 study on European political responses to climate change[43] Professor Tim 'O'Riordan, described the then emerging fuel price escalator as 'a real piece of policy innovation'. Yet he was also sufficiently perspicacious to note that:

> The test will come in the political determination to continue the increase, year in and year out, and the manner in which the additional revenue is spent.[44]

The demise of the fuel escalator demonstrates the potential vulnerability of relying solely on an economic instrument as a means of securing policy goals, whatever the underlying theory. Its intended effect lacked precision, its impact was subject to many external economic forces outside the control of government, and its original purpose could be easily forgotten and overtaken by the attractions of its value to government as a revenue stream. In comparison to the sorry saga of the fuel escalator, one may conclude that direct regulation in the form of mandatory efficiency standards with sufficient advance notice to manufacturers would have had a greater effect on achieving key policy goals.[45]

Indeed, in its Energy Report last year the Royal Commission came very close to endorsing the need for such standards.[46] That they did not do so was because in the meantime another form of policy instrument had been employed. In 1998 the European Commission and the European Automobile Manufacturers Association reached an agreement under which the average fuel consumption of new cars within the European Union would reduce by 25 per cent between 1995 and 2008.[47] The agreement was presented as a political breakthrough, but as with economic instruments, while voluntary agreements offer considerable attractions to government, their use raises a number of significant concerns.

Voluntary Agreements

The automobile agreement was by no means unique, and the past decade has seen the increasing use in both Europe and the United States of voluntary agreements between governments and industry as a means of handling environmental challenges, and as an alternative to direct regulation. According to a study in 1997 by the European Environment Agency, by 1996 more than 300 environmental agreements had been concluded at the national level within the European Union, with the Netherlands leading the way.[48] The underpinning of such approaches in the United States can again be traced to trenchant

---

[43] T. O'Riordan and J Jager (eds), *Politics of Climate Change* (London, 1996).

[44] Ibid, 249.

[45] Efficiency standards, of course, deal with only one aspect of the transport issue, and increased efficiencies in individual vehicle performance may be offset by overall increased usage. Government projections published in 2000 suggest that overall road traffic volumes will increase by 16–29% between 1996 and 2010, but on the assumption that voluntary agreements between the European Commission and vehicle manufacturers are complied with projected decreases in overall CO_2 emissions of between 1 and 10% in the same period: Department of the Environment, Transport, and the Regions, 'Tackling Congestion and Pollution: The Government's First Report under the Road Traffic (National Targets) Act 1998' (London, 2000).

[46] Royal Commission on Environmental Pollution, above n 36, para 6.123.

[47] Similar agreements between the Commission and Japanese and Korean car manufacturers were reached at the same time.

[48] European Environment Agency, 'Environment Agreements, Environmental Issues', Series No 3 (Copenhagen, 1997).

criticisms by lawyers such as Richard Stewart of the perceived failures and shortcomings of traditional regulatory approaches.[49] Continental lawyers have developed a deeper underlying theory of reflexive law according to which the perceived inadequacies of goal-orientated and instrumental public law is replaced by an emphasis on using law to encourage actors to assess critically and to determine their own environmental performance.[50]

Voluntary agreements clearly represent one form of such reflexive law. They come in many forms, including agreements made between private parties, such as industries and non-governmental organisations. My concern, though, is with agreements with government and sectors of industry or of a particular industry, since these more starkly reflect a conscious decision by government to develop an alternative to direct regulation. Even within this class we can distinguish several different forms of voluntary agreement currently being employed. Some forms of voluntary agreement are heavily encased within a public law framework: in this country agreements with landowners under the Wildlife and Countryside Act 1981 are a strong example. Other agreements may be made after a clear threat by government to use existing powers of enforcement or to introduce legislation if agreements are not forthcoming. Some appear to have no enforcement mechanism attached to them.

In the same year as the publication of the report by the European Environment Agency, the distinguished German environmental lawyer, Ekhard Rehbinder, described environmental agreements as a 'new instrument of environmental policy'.[51] It is true that in continental Europe various forms of environmental agreements were first employed in France and Germany in the early 1970s,[52] but for British environmental lawyers the idea of agreements being novel is somewhat surprising. While the post-War development of British environmental law lacked the more sophisticated theoretical underpinning of continental law, voluntary agreements were a clear feature of government environmental policy until the 1980s – so much so that in 1983 the then Chief Scientist of the Department of the Environment could describe as one of the key features of British environmental policy before joining the European Community the 'acceptance, where possible, of a voluntary approach where Government relies on a polluting industry to impose its own measures'.[53]

Some reflection on that experience suggests that concern about the current use of environmental agreements is justified. A key example relates to pesticide control, where from 1954 until 1983 the regulation of the marketing and use of pesticides in the United Kingdom was largely achieved under a voluntary arrangement between government, manufacturers, and distributors: the Pesticide Safety Precaution Scheme.[54] Essentially the parties agreed to ensure that new pesticides were subject to risk assessments initiated under the scheme and to withdraw from the market pesticides that had raised environmental or health concerns. In many ways the scheme illustrated the attractions of voluntary arrangements: it was

[49] See, eg B Ackerman and R Stewart, 'Reforming Environmental Law' (1985) 37 *Stanford Law Review* 1333.

[50] See in particular G Teubner, 'Substantive and Reflexive Elements in Modern Law' (1983) 17 *Law and Society Review* 239; in the context of environmental law see G Teubner, L Farmer and D Murphy (eds), *Environmental Law and Ecological Responsibility: The Concept and Practice of Ecological Self-Organization* (Chichester, 1994).

[51] E Rehbinder, 'Environmental Agreements: A New Instrument of Environmental Policy', Jean Monet Chair Paper RSC 97/45 (Florence, 1997).

[52] E Orts and K Deketelaere (eds), *Environmental Contracts* (London, 2001) 22. The volume as a whole provides some excellent studies of contemporary practice in the United States and Europe.

[53] M Holdgate, 'Environmental Policies in Britain and Mainland Europe' in R Macrory (ed), *Britain, Europe and the Environment* (London, 1983).

[54] For a history of the scheme see R Macrory and D Gilbert, *Pesticide Related Law* (Farnham, 1989).

reasonably efficient, could act speedily where needed, and industry was fully engaged in the process. But it also underlined real structural weaknesses which eventually led to its replacement by a statutory scheme under the Food and Environment Act 1985. Participation in the scheme was limited to government and industry, and wider public interests, especially those of agricultural workers and environmental bodies, were excluded from the process. There was a lack of transparency in the information and assumptions being used to justify decisions, and the role of the independent scientists and government officials involved was unclear. Finally, and most crucially, the scheme depended on the complete involvement of all manufacturers and wholesalers; voluntary agreements cannot tolerate nor are they compatible with free riders. Britain's accession to the European Community in 1973 meant that this voluntary-scheme was unlikely to be compatible with the right of free movement of goods by foreign pesticide manufacturers and distributors:[55] hence its transformation in 1985 into a statutory regulatory scheme.

The Pesticide Safety Precaution Scheme was perhaps the most comprehensive and long-lasting example of a voluntary arrangement between government and industry in British environmental policy. Yet the development of post-War British environmental law exhibited a similar tendency towards a consensual system and a largely closed system of regulation. Even where a legal framework existed, such as that under the old Alkali Act 1863 dealing with atmospheric emissions from certain industrial processes, it tended to be expressed in broad terms, leaving the details of licensing standards to be negotiated between those responsible for regulation and those whom they regulated. The heart of the protection system for Sites of Special Scientific Interest under the Wildlife and Countryside Act 1982 was based on the negotiation of agreements between landowners and bodies responsible for nature protection, a system later memorably summarised by Lord Mustill in the first decision of the House of Lords on the legislation:

> It needs only a moment to see that the regime is toothless for it demands no more from the owner or occupier of a Site of Special Scientific Interest than a little patience.[56]

The courts were rarely involved-in interpreting legislation. To take one example, the key legal criterion for industrial air pollution – employing the 'best practicable means' to prevent or minimise emissions – which existed for almost one hundred and fifty years until the introduction of the new system of integrated pollution control under Part I of the Environmental Protection Act 1990 – never once received authoritative interpretation from the courts, despite each word in that phrase being rich in ambiguity. Outside the Town and Country Planning legislation, opportunities for public consultation and public access to information were minimal or non-existent.

The development during the 1970s and 1980s of what I have described as the 'new formalism' in British environmental law[57] led to a transformation of legal structures in the United Kingdom: more comprehensive rights of public consultation, public registers of information, greater use of explicit environmental standards, and the application of procedural safeguards developed in public law. The causes are diverse and include: sustained criticisms by bodies such as the Royal Commission on Environmental Pollution and by individuals such as Nigel Haigh of the Institute of European Environmental Policy, the

---

[55] The issue was never tested in the courts, though there were threats of legal challenges.
[56] *Southern Water Authority v Nature Conservancy Council* [1993] 5 *Journal of Environmental Law* 109.
[57] R Macrory, 'Environmental Law: Shifting Discretions and the New Formalism' in O Lomas (ed), *Frontiers of Environmental Law* (London, 1991).

privatisation of key public utilities such as the water and electricity industries, and the need to transpose European Community obligations into national legislation consistent with doctrines developed by the European Court of Justice.[58]

There is a certain degree of irony in the fact that the United Kingdom has transformed its legal structure of environmental law in this way at a time when other countries in Europe are discovering and promoting voluntary arrangements as an instrument of environmental policy. Yet many of the concerns which led to changes in the nature of British environmental law still dog the development of contemporary voluntary agreements. There is no guarantee that wider public interests will be engaged in the process, nor any legally guaranteed rights in that respect. It is true that some countries, such as the Netherlands and Belgium, have developed more systematic procedures of consultation leading to agreements which are binding under private contractual law.[59] Dutch practice, and in particular the intervention of the Dutch Supreme Court, has attempted to elaborate in far more detail than has happened to date in this country the relationship between public law and the appropriate use of environmental agreements.[60] But this structured approach begins to resemble regulation, albeit a system where standards and goals are subject to intense negotiation prior to their legal enactment. And it is an approach which is still the exception. Danish legislation in 1991 established the possibility of voluntary agreements encased in law, but industry and government appear still to prefer non-legal agreements.[61] This is hardly surprising since the more that voluntary agreements are encased in legal frameworks, the more they lose the very qualities of flexibility and consensuality which were their initial attraction. In contrast to the details of regulatory requirements or individual licences or consents, there is no guarantee that the terms of voluntary agreements will be publicly available, nor is there systematic monitoring of their success. The 1997 study by the European Environment Agency reported that in most of the sample agreements studied it was impossible to make a quantitative assessment of their effectiveness due to the lack of reliable monitoring data and consistent reporting.[62] In 1996 the UK government concluded agreements with five industrial sectors concerning the reduction of certain products containing greenhouse gases, but according to ENDS Report in 1998 nothing was known about their success or otherwise.[63]

[58] As Derrick Wyatt QC noted, before the development of the ECJ's doctrines on formal transposition the early phase of the. UK's implementation of Directives 'was characterised by a tendency towards regarding EEC Directives as helpful if eccentric recommendations to be gently eased into the United Kingdom scheme of things, ideally by government circular rather than legislation and ideally without cost': D Wyatt, 'Litigating Community-Environmental Law' (1998) 10 *Journal of Environmental Law* 1.

[59] But as Seerden notes, in relation to collective environmental agreements in the Netherlands between industry sectors and government there appears to be no example of court actions concerning their enforcement: 'This paucity of litigation may be due in part to the fact that many agreements, though formally written as private law contracts, function also as an expression of internalised behaviour': R Seerden, 'Legal Aspects of Environmental Agreements in the Netherlands' in Orts and Deketelaere, above n 52, 193.

[60] See the discussion of the 1990 *Windmill* decision of the Dutch Supreme Civil Court and subsequent case law in Seerden, ibid, 180.

[61] G Calster and K Deketelaere, 'The Use of Voluntary Agreements in the European Community's Environmental Policy' in Orts and Deketelaere, above n 52, 239, where the authors report that only one such agreement under the legislation has been made to date.

[62] European Environment Agency, above n 48, 9.

[63] (1998) 281 *ENDS Report* 39.

It is nevertheless clear that the use of voluntary agreements still holds attractions for policy-makers both in this country[64] and at European level.[65] At their extreme, the use of voluntary agreements represents a new form of corporatism under which governments bargain with key interest groups, avoiding the use of formal legal powers. Yet it is equally clear that their use may threaten important qualities inherent in contemporary regulatory approaches: transparency, enforceability, monitoring, and public involvement in the form of both participation and accountability.[66] A similar structural criticism can be made of the use of economic instruments.[67] The dilemma is that it is the very avoidance of these legal and procedural complexities which may be seen as a benefit to the parties involved and to the efficiency of the instrument. The more they are incorporated into the negotiation and implementation of agreements, the less the apparent advantages of agreements over regulation. Indeed, in a recent review by Professor Gaines of Houston University and Cliona Kimber,[68] the authors, who treat voluntary agreements as one example of reflexive law, go so far as to conclude that policy makers have over the last decade or so misdirected their efforts on self-regulation in areas of industrial pollution control as a substitute for regulatory machinery. In their view, voluntary approaches are certainly not without validity, but would be better directed towards areas where there has traditionally been a lack of regulatory machinery and where reorientation of environmental behaviour is desirable even though precise goals are difficult to determine: the activities of private households and public service organisations are given as examples. The argument has attractions; if nothing else, it forces a re-evaluation, from an environmental perspective, of potentially important uses of agreements which do not threaten or devalue the positive aspects of existing regulatory structures.

Scientific Risks

The political attractions of alternative mechanisms to direct regulation cannot however, simply be attributed to advocates of a free or less regulated market. In the environmental field one of the prime unsettling influences for governments in recent years has been a reassessment of the contribution by science to government policy underlying regulatory systems. Where difficult decisions of judgment are involved, one approach for govern-

---

[64] Department of Environment, Transport, and the Regions, 'Sustainable Business', Consultation Paper (London, 1998). See also UK government, 'A Better Quality of Life: A Strategy for Sustainable Development for the United Kingdom', Cm 4345 (London, 1999), though the endorsement seems rather more muted at para 5.11: 'The Government will continue to consider the scope for voluntary agreements with industry'. In the context of climate change, by April 2001 more than 40 negotiated agreements had been concluded between government and industry: see 'Looking to the Future with Negotiated Agreements' (2001) 315 ENDS Report 6.

[65] European Commission, Communication on Voluntary Agreements, COM (96) 561 final (Brussels, 1996). For further discussion of the development of Commission policy in this area see J Verschuuren, 'EC Environmental Law and Self-Regulation in the Member States: In Search of a Legislative Framework' in Somsen, above n 7, 103.

[66] For a recent review of UK experience see Green Alliance, Signed, Sealed and Delivered? The Role of Negotiated Agreements in the UK (London, 2001).

[67] In the context of New Zealand, see B Richardson, 'Economic Instruments and Sustainable Management in New Zealand' (1998) 10 Journal of Environmental Law 21. The author concludes at 38 'Economic instruments cannot be applied without regulatory frameworks, and the choice of mechanisms and situations in which they are applied must be governed by public consultation processes to ensure that equity and ethical issues are not inappropriately excluded from management decisions'.

[68] S Gaines and C Kimber, 'Redirecting Self-Regulation' (2001) 13 Journal of Environmental Law 167.

ment is to divest responsibility to other bodies. Contemporary areas of environmental law such as private and public nuisance, of course, do just that, leaving individual judges to determine the environmental standards to be applied in particular instances, against a background of general principles. Despite the recent decision of the House of Lords in the *Alconbury*[69] case, calls will continue for the setting up of an independent planning or environmental tribunal to act as the final decision maker on individual decisions, and no doubt, whatever the stated public position, there will be some in government who would welcome decisions on, say, the more intractable and sensitive planning cases being handled by a body other than themselves. An alternative approach, which is in line with the theories of reflexive law, is to focus the attention of environmental legislation on procedural requirements rather than outcomes, leaving the goals of the regulation to be determined through a guided process of decision making.[70]

We are likely to continue to see initiatives along those lines but, for very good reasons, the tendency in the last thirty years has been to elaborate detailed environmental standards or goals in the body of legislation itself. Courts tend to be uncomfortable with handling preventative issues; industry requires a degree of certainty in advance for forward investment; there is greater public demand for legal certainty in the environmental standards they can expect to enjoy; in a European Community context, the goal of a free and competitive market provides a key driver for explicit standards in the field of products, and more controversially for processes. At the same time as these developments were being made one of the key underlying principles consistently advocated by governments was that environmental policy must be based on 'sound science'.[71] To the extent that science was perceived by policy makers and the public to provide certainty and undeniable objective truth, legal standards based on science could be said to derive an authority over and above that of the law itself. We are now of course aware that this is a very simplistic and misleading picture, particularly in the field of the environment. As concerns move from acute problems of human health to more chronic and less direct effects, from individual to synergistic effects, and increasingly to impacts on the natural environment, the uncertainties of contemporary scientific knowledge have become increasingly apparent. Even within different scientific disciplines relevant to environmental issues there may be distinct biases and assumptions which can be obscured in more simplistic scientific evaluations.[72]

For the policy maker, and indeed the lawyer, not trained in science, the growing appreciation of certain inherent uncertainties in science is uncomfortable. Yet as the Royal

---

[69] *R v Secretary of State for the Environment, Transport, and the Regions ex parte Hilding & Barnes, ex parte Alconbury, ex parte Legal and General Assurance* (conjoined appeals) House of Lords May 2001 [2001] UKHL 23. If the House of Lords had agreed with the High Court that the Secretary of State could not be both a policy maker and a decision maker in planning cases in order to comply with the Human Rights Act, the argument for a new independent body, or at least for complete delegation of all planning decisions to the planning inspectorate, would have been overwhelming.

[70] Reflecting Mashaw's 'accommodatory' rather than 'determinate' model of decision making. See J Mashaw, 'An Overview: Two Models of Regulatory Decision' in J Nyhart and M Carrow (eds), *Law and Science in Collaboration: Resolving Regulatory Issues of Science and Technology* (Lexington, 1983).

[71] See, eg the 1990 White Paper on environmental policy: 'United Kingdom, This Common Inheritance: Britain's Environmental Strategy', Cm 1200 (London, 1990) HMSO, where it is stated 'We must base our policies on fact not fantasy and use the best evidence and analysis available'. See also 'United Kingdom, This Common Inheritance: UK Annual Report', Cm 3188 (London, 1996): 'It is, however, fundamental to achievement of sustainable development that decisions should proceed from the basis of sound science, with an assessment of the likely costs and benefits (environmental and economic alike)' (para 176).

[72] D Fisk, 'Environmental Science and Environmental Law' (1998) 10 *Journal of Environmental Law* 3.

Commission tried to demonstrate in its study of Environmental Standards,[73] science is not a matter of certainties but of hypothesis and experimentation. 'Sound' science possesses qualities of transparency, scepticism, and peer review.[74] It can and should lead to greater understanding, but not necessarily to the certainty for which a policy-maker may wish. What is equally clear is that a decision concerning a particular environmental standard is a political choice: in stark terms the role of scientific assessment is to describe a dose-effect curve but not to determine a legally defined standard of acceptability. This will be informed by other considerations including economic and technological appraisal and ultimately value judgments, and it follows that scientific committees should ideally present to a decision-maker options rather than solutions.[75]

In the field of environmental policy-making there have been two important institutional and policy responses to this growing understanding of the nature and extent of scientific uncertainty. First, and still far more apparent at international level, the development of the type of elaborate exercise in scientific assessment epitomised by the Intergovernmental Panel on Climate Change.[76] The extent to which such .an exercise can be replicated with the same degree of legitimacy and general public confidence in other fields of environmental controversy, such as genetically manipulated organisms, remains to be seen.[77] The second key development has been the emergence of the precautionary principle as an underlying norm in decision making, explicitly recognised in the 1992 Rio Declaration on Environment and Development,[78] increasingly articulated in international environmental treaties, and a principle of European Community environmental policy.[79] Far from being a political or anti-scientific approach, the Royal Commission on Environmental Pollution endorsed it as a perfectly rational principle which was consistent with the inherent quali-

[73] Royal Commission on Environmental Pollution, 'Setting Environmental Standards', 21st Report, Cm 4053 (London, 1998). See also R Macrory, 'Environmental Standards: New Procedures for New Paradigms' (1999) 56 *Science in Parliament* 6.

[74] See A Stirling, *On Science and Precaution in the Management of Technological Risk*, vol 1, EUR 19056 EN (Seville, European Commission Institute for Prospective Technological Studies, 1998). In addition to the qualities of sound science listed above, the author includes systematic methodologies, independence, accountability, and learning in the sense that understanding is open to continuous change and challenge. See also Office of Science and Technology, *The Use of Scientific Advice in Policy Making* (London, 1997), where the then Chief Scientific Advisor to the government, Sir Robert (now Lord) May notes at para 11 'Scientific advice will often involve an aggregation of a range of scientific opinion and judgment as distinct from statements of assured certainty'. The advice of government departments was updated in 2000: Office of Science and Technology, *Guidelines 2000: Scientific Advice and Policy Making* (London, 2000).

[75] In this respect I probably go somewhat further than the conclusions of the Phillips report on BSE which appears to concede that it may be appropriate for government to ask scientific advisory committees, to advise on a policy option, though it is noted at 14.1290 that 'Where a policy decision involves the balancing of considerations which fall outside the expertise of the committee, it will normally not be appropriate to ask the committee to advise which policy option-to follow': 'Report of the Inquiry into the Emergence and Identification of Bovine Spongiform Encephalopathy (BSE) and Variant Creutzfeldt-Jakob' Disease (vCJD) and the Action Taken in Response to It Up to 20 March 1996' (London, 2000). My view is that, at least where a decision on environmental standards is involved, there will be considerations which will *always* be outside a scientific committee's expertise.

[76] The Intergovernmental Panel on Climate Change (IPCC) was established by the World Meteorological Organization and the United Nations Environment Programme in 1988. The role of the IPCC is to assess the scientific, technical and socio-economic information relating to the understanding of the risk of human-induced climate change, and the Panel has produced three assessments to date.

[77] See 'Government Proposal for Global GM Panel Runs into Fire'(2000) 305 *ENDS Report* 6, where some leading UK environmental observers are strongly critical of any analogy between the IPCC model and the government's proposal for a similar exercise in the field of GMOs.

[78] Principle 15 of the Rio Declaration: 'Where there are threats of serious irreversible damage, lack of full scientific certainty shall not he used as a reason for postponing cost-effective measures to prevent environmental degradation'.

[79] Art 174.2, Treaty Establishing the European Community.

ties of science.[80] It is, though, hardly surprising that operationalising the principle is far less straightforward and more open to contention than simply stating it.

Yet for the development of environmental law these important shifts in process and understanding raise significant challenges for legal process. The procedures of scientific assessment and open peer review developed by the Inter-governmental Panel on Climate Change have yet to be adopted at national or regional level. This is particularly so in the case of European Community legislation where many decisions on environmental standards are effectively made by management and regulatory committees under rules of comitology,[81] processes which are frequently obscure and little understood by the wider public and where the line between scientific and political decision making is often opaque. The precautionary principle raises issues concerning the development of appropriate standards of legal review. If one of the main functions of public law is to restrain inappropriate or irrational behaviour by government, how should principles be applied in a situation where the application of the precautionary principle implies a lack of substantive scientific evidence supporting a decision?[82] As the House of Lords acknowledged in the recent *Alconbury* decision, basing a decision on no evidence or on a wrong factual basis, can now be considered a ground for judicial review in British law.[83] At the level of international trade disputes we have already noted the unease of the GATT panel in handling issues of scientific uncertainty in trade and environment disputes, and where the invocation of the precautionary principle by a national government can clearly more readily disguise less legitimate motivations for restricting trade. Recent decisions of the Appellate Body, though, are beginning to display greater sensitivity to the problem of scientific uncertainty.[84]

Yet until we have developed more consistent and transparent procedures for the appropriate application of the precautionary approach by government to any given situation,[85] there is the danger that the function of judicial review as a restraint on irrational behaviour by government is inhibited. From that perspective, the precautionary principle may be beneficial to the environment but is not necessarily so to the rule of law. Above all, the appreciation that in many environmental areas the old model of scientific certainty will

[80] See Royal Commission on Environmental Pollution, above n 73, paras 4.41–4.48. The European Commission's *Communication on the Precautionary Principle*, Com (2000)1 (2 February 2000) echoes much of the analysis of the Royal Commission on Environmental Pollution. According to the accompanying explanatory text (IP/00/96), 'The Communication makes it clear that the precautionary principle is neither a politicisation of science nor the acceptance of zero-risk but that it provides a basis for action when science is unable to give a clear answer'.

[81] See J Falke and G Winter, 'Management and Regulatory Committees in Executive Rule Making' in G Winter (ed), *Sources and Categories of European Union Law* (Baden-Baden, 1996) ch C.ll. The authors note at 542 that in 1996 the Council of Ministers adopted 468 legislative acts, while in the same period the Commission, acting under delegated powers, adopted 7034 acts. The number of Committees listed in the Community budget increased four times between 1975 and 1995.

[82] As David Fisk notes, above n 72, 'it is a fallacy to assume, that the absence of evidence to support a proposition can be taken as equivalent to [the presence] of evidence that refutes it'.

[83] Per Lord Slynn in *Alconbury*, above n 69, para 55. See also *Smith, Woolf, and Jowell's, Judicial Review of Administrative Action* (London, 1995) 288.

[84] See the decision of the Appellate Body in the *Beef Hormones* case, *EC Measures against Meat and Meat Products* AB-1997-4, 16 January 1998. At para 194 the Appellate Body note that 'In most cases, responsible and representative governments may act in good faith on the basis of what, at a given time, may be divergent opinion coming from qualified and respected sources'.

[85] For a recent review of the development and application of the principle see O MacIntyre and T Mosedale, 'The Precautionary Principle as a Norm of Customary International Law' (1997) 9 *Journal of Environmental Law* 221. The authors discuss emerging practices including precautionary assessment, though not in the context of my own concern here which is the alignment of the principle with those concerning the rule of law and appropriate judicial restraint against its. misuse.

no longer provide the policy maker with an underlying legitimacy for his decisions raises issues concerning the authority of law itself: As Raz has argued,[86] this in part rests on the authority of the institutions responsible for developing and making law. In contemporary environmental politics, governments, faced with difficult and complex policy decisions, can now less easily hide behind a cloak of science, and will constantly need to develop new approaches and procedures to reestablish their legitimacy.

Handling Enforcement Risks

If direct regulation is to maintain its key role in many areas of environmental protection, inadequate enforcement will clearly undermine its effectiveness as an instrument for motivating behaviour. Inconsistent enforcement will give rise to cynicism and distrust. Indeed, one of the attractions of both economic instrument and voluntary agreements is that they are perceived to be largely self-enforcing, while enforcement by regulatory bodies can be portrayed as expensive, never adequately funded, arbitrary, and never complete. At the European level, recognition has been growing of the significance of implementation and enforcement, and in 1996 the European Commission promoted the concept of the 'chain of regulation' which correctly acknowledges that effective implementation of legislation depends as much on the quality of legislative drafting, appropriate training, adequate funding, and feed-back mechanisms as on the actual enforcement of legal rules.[87] The analysis is sound, and is applicable at the national as well as the European level, though we remain some way from the ideal picture presented.

At national level we have progressed considerably from the period in the 1970s when environmental regulators possessed a wholly unfettered and largely untransparent discretion towards enforcement. It was only the efforts of legal scholars such as Keith Hawkins and Genevra Richardson,[88] whose research, particularly in the water industry, revealed to the wider public some of the motivations behind the decisions as to whether or not to prosecute for non-compliance. As with any bureaucracy, motivations for non-prosecution were not always driven by sound environmental policy reasons. But in 1998 the Environment Agency made its first public statement on enforcement and prosecution policy, though recent internal audits reveal considerable regional variations in its interpretation and application.[89] Nevertheless, despite the self-imposed difficulties of ensuring consistent

---

[86] See J Raz, *Authority of Law* (Oxford, 1993), where he argues that one of the origins of the autonomous authority of law is the authority of the institution with the power to make laws. My argument here is that in the context of environmental law institutional authority based on old models of scientific certainly has been substantially weakened.

[87] European Commission, *Implementing Community Environmental Law,* COM(96) 500 (Brussels, 1996). A similar expression of the 'chain of regulation' is the concept of 'compliance-orientated regulation' as defined in a recent OECD study of regulatory compliance generally: 'An outcome-orientated approach to promulgating and revising regulation where regulatory drafting, implementation, monitoring and enforcement are all designed to maximise the potential for compliance with substantive regulatory goals'. C Parker, 'The State of Regulatory Compliance: Issues, Trends and Challenges', report prepared for the Public Management Service of OECD, para 7 (Paris, 1999).

[88] G Richardson, A Ogus and A Burrows, *Policing Pollution – A Study of Regulation and Enforcement* (Oxford, 1982); K Hawkins, *Environment and Enforcement: Regulation and the Social Definition of Pollution* (Oxford, 1984).

[89] 'Agency Flounders on Prosecution Policy' (1991) 315 *ENDS Report* 3.

enforcement practices, the publication of such a statement is an important advance in providing greater accountability and improved signals to those who are required to comply with regulation.

But much remains to be improved. Legislators could take a more systematic interest in the successes and failures of implementation. Risk management techniques, properly applied, can play an important role in using limited regulatory resources to target inspection and enforcement.[90] Regulation could be more outcome-orientated, and where this involves the adoption of ambient environmental standards, regulators need to be more transparent in the assessment of methodologies used to calculate and assign load responsibilities of individual contributors.[91] Modern technology can be harnessed to provide extensive warnings of regulatory noncompliance. Continuous monitoring equipment providing an automatic alert of non-compliance is already extensively used in the field of water pollution control[92] and can be extended in the future. In the field of land use, satellite imaging is already used by government departments to monitor compliance by farmers with set-aside requirements, and has been used in the fields of marine oil pollution and fisheries control. The use of such techniques is not appropriate for all forms of environmental regulation, and they raise significant legal questions, notably about their consistency with principles of privacy.[93] Yet their contribution towards establishing a more secure and consistent compliance regime has scarcely yet been tapped, especially given the rapidly developing higher resolutions of the most recent satellites.[94] A major recent European research project[95] has suggested that such imaging could be employed in the enforcement of a broad range of environmental legislation, including damage to habitats, breaches of planning law, and illegal waste disposal.

In a democratic society it is important that the information concerning the results of regulation are made as accessible as possible, and that imaginative uses of modern information technology are employed to the fullest extent to achieve these goals. To take one example, we are still a long way from making publicly available in a systematic way the results of prosecutions for breaches of environmental law. The position has improved from a decade or so ago when information in areas such as waste was scattered among local authorities, and Home Office statistics were insufficiently detailed.[96] Bodies such as the

---

[90] In 1997 the Environment Agency introduced an Operator and Pollution Risk Appraisal (OPRA) in relation to industrial processes falling under the Integrated Pollution Control regime: (1997) 271 *ENDS Report* 32. A similar scheme is being discussed in relation to waste management sites: Department of the Environment, Transport, and the Regions, 'Waste Management Licensing Risk Assessment Inspection Frequencies' (London, 1999).

[91] T Smith Jr and R Macrory, 'Legal and Political Considerations' in Douben, above n 18, 402.

[92] A Mumma, 'Use of Compliance Monitoring Data in Water Pollution Prosecutions' (1993) 5 *Journal of Environmental Law* 191.

[93] R Purdy, 'Legal and Privacy Issues of Spy in the Sky Satellites' (1999) 3 *Mountbatten Journal of Legal Studies* 33. It is likely, though, that their most useful value will be as a warning to regulators of potential non-compliance rather than as direct evidence in court proceedings.

[94] To date the most widely used satellites have been SPOT and LANDSAT, with resolutions of 20 and 30 metres, respectively, and repeating coverage of most areas of the world every two to three weeks. More recent satellites such as IKONOS II have far greater resolution and can be programmed to obtain images at predetermined locations. More high-resolution satellites were launched in 2002, some with resolutions of as little as 0.5 metres.

[95] APERTURE Project (1998–2000) (Environmental Typological Space Mapping Facilitating the Implementation of European Legislation) http://www.iis. gr/aperture/.

[96] For an early attempt to review information in one field of environmental law see R Macrory and S Withers, 'Application of Administrative and Criminal Punishments with Regard to Hazardous Wastes in England', report to the European Commission (London, 1985). The report was a contribution to a comparative European study for the European Commission. With the exception of Italy, the other countries within the study, including France

Environment Agency have produced reports summarising the results of key prosecutions, though not without controversy,[97] and any such exercise inevitably involves difficult judgements concerning the appropriate benchmarking criteria to be adopted by the regulator. But it is technically feasible to develop a far more open system where the results of all environmental cases heard before the courts are systematically collated, and retrievable from a database by free-form searches. Such a system would allow any individual to obtain information on regulatory enforcement concerning, say, an individual company, a region, or a particular substance.[98] It would not obviate the need for interpretation by official bodies, but would 'democratise' core data to wider and potentially richer critiques

'Determine and Direct': a New Regulatory Paradigm?

These technological possibilities are to some extent operational issues, though of immense importance to the future design and application of environmental regulation. They hint at future possibilities of remedying some of the key deficiencies in regulatory implementation. But there remain what at times seem utterly irreconcilable views of the role of direct regulation. Traditional forms of regulation can be presented as stifling of innovation, over-bureaucratic, and incapable of handling more than the most direct impacts of human intervention on the environment. The environmental challenges facing society are immense, varied, and often unpredictable, and it is hardly surprising that the last decade has seen experimentation with a whole range of new forms of policy instruments in place of the more conventional approaches founded on old paradigms. Yet it remains equally important to ensure that the qualities of transparency, accountability, and enforceability inherent in the more formal legal structures are not lost in the process. Similarly, however pressing the environmental concerns, it would be a backward step if new instruments allowed governments to side-step the discipline both on themselves and on agencies of government of contemporary principles of the rule of law.

Lawyers need to be innovative and forward-looking, but perhaps the time has also come to be less defensive about the positive qualities of environmental regulation. Continuous critical evaluation of the existing effectiveness of regulation remains vital, but we are equally entitled to impose the same level of scrutiny on the true environmental effects of non-regulatory initiatives. It may well be that the term 'command and control' is now burdened with so much critical baggage that new terminology should be developed to provide the space for a more detached appreciation and relocation of the appropriate role and development of future environmental regulation. My own preference would be 'determine and direct'. 'Direction' (rather than 'control'), reflects the need to ensure that as far as possible regulation is designed which is outcome-focused and which harnesses the inventive power of industry and the market to determine solutions but within clearly defined boundaries endorsed by legal sanction. 'Determination' implies that it remains the

and Germany, revealed equal difficulties in obtaining comprehensive data.

[97] House of Commons Select Committee on Environment, Transport, and Regional Affairs, *The Environment Agency*, HC 289 (London, 1999).

[98] To my knowledge, the only country in Europe which has attempted to develop such a comprehensive database is Italy at the Center Ellettronico, Corte Suprema di Cassazione. See A Postiglione, *La Giurisprudenza Ambientale Europea a la Hanca Dati Enlex Della* (Milan, 1987).

ultimate responsibility of government, rather than of science or economic theory, to decide the goals of environmental policy. In the contemporary political climate, it may well be that governments or agencies can no longer simply 'command' but need to develop new procedures and more sensitive processes for securing legitimacy and understanding of the policy choices that are made. But that does not detract from the requirement to make those choices. It is true that instruments such as fiscal measures and voluntary agreements can and should equally involve the articulation of policy choices, but crucially, in my view, not necessarily with the same degree of precision, and nearly always involving no legal compulsion or accountability. We are in a process of social transition which is making ever more apparent the political nature of the decisions involved in designing and applying environmental regulation; in that context, avoiding hard policy choices by diminishing the role of regulation or transferring those decisions to other spheres is clearly an attractive option, but it is ultimately a derogation of political responsibility.

Part II

Institutional Reform and Change

It is all too easy for politicians to initiate change to the structures of government as a substitute for the delivery of effective policy. Yet there are times when it becomes necessary to acknowledge that the existing shape of institutions inhibits the achievement of contemporary environmental goals, and change is needed. Equally, major reforms occurring for other reasons may have a significant impact on the way that environmental policies are determined and delivered, and need to be evaluated.

Changes in law and policy may affect the workings of the courts, but have little to say about their actual structure. In the United Kingdom, environmental cases, be they concerned with criminal law, civil disputes or public law, have in the past been handled by the ordinary courts dealing with areas of law. Yet for nearly 20 years there has been discussion and reviews in this country on whether there is the need for some form of specialised court dealing with environmental cases. Similar discussions have taken place in many other jurisdictions, with a 2009 study reporting that there were now over 350 forms of specialised environmental courts or tribunals in 41 countries, over half of them being created since 2004.[1] In 2010, England and Wales joined the list, when, with remarkable little fanfare, a specialised environment tribunal was established. The Long and Winding Road (2013) considers the lengthy saga of the creation of the court and the lessons it tells about policy development. Looking back, it is all too easy to see a logical coherence to the story and the steps that took place. Rational analysis of the underlying problems and their solutions remained vital, but equally important were unexpected alignments where developments in policy areas completely unrelated to environmental requirements proved significant drivers. As I try to demonstrate, however, securing major policy change often requires the sensitivity to perceive where, within the complex machinery of government, the core nexus of policy development and change resides at any particular time. At times there was a degree of opportunism by key players involved in the debate who were alive to the politics of the time.

The first explicit mention of a specialist environmental court appears to have been in 1989, when Robert (now Lord) Carnwath proposed the idea of combining various courts and tribunals dealing with land use planning and environmental protection into a single jurisdiction[2] Two years later, Patrick McAuslan of the London School of Economics published a provocative article calling for the establishment of a court-like body 'with wide decision-making, advisory and regulatory powers in the environmental field', while at the same time criticising the 'intellectual poverty' of most British environmental lawyers of the

---

[1] G Pring and C Pring (2009) Greening Justice : Creating and Improving Environmental Courts and Tribunals Access Initiative, 2009.

[2] R Carnwath (1989) Enforcing Planning Controls Department of the Environment, April 1989.

153

time.[3] In the same year the then Lord Chief Justice, Lord Woolf, put forward the idea of a single environmental court that might handle all the legal issues, be they criminal, civil or public, that could arise from an environmental dispute or incident.[4] Professor Malcolm Grant was subsequently commissioned by government to examine the workings of specialist environmental courts in other jurisdictions such as New South Wales and Sweden, and to propose possible models for this country.[5] Six alternative models were identified, ranging for a new planning appeals tribunal to a new division of the High Court. At the time, however, the government was not convinced that the costs of significant institutional upheaval would be outweighed by any benefits resulting, and in any event any proposals would be premature prior to the outcome of major reviews of the criminal and tribunal system then being undertaken.

In 'The Long and Winding Road' I describe this period, roughly between 1989 and 2000, as one of reflective analysis. The debate continued during the next period, between 2001 and 2004, but here reports and publications were rather more designed to influence policy making, and in doing so revealed more explicitly diverging visions of the nature and role of a specialised environmental jurisdiction. In 2002, I was commissioned by the Department of the Environment, Food and Rural Affair to re-examine the case for an environmental tribunal in England and Wales, resulting in the report Modernising Environmental Justice (2003), co-authored with my researcher, Michael Woods. The focus of the research was concerned with administrative appeals under environmental legislation. Under planning legislation, developers have long had the right to appeal against a decision of local government to central government, with appeals now conducted and largely decided by an agency of government, the Planning Inspectorate. Similar rights of appeal now pervaded environmental legislation where licences and similar permits were sought, but it became clear that there was little coherence in the choice of bodies for determining such appeals – some went to the planning inspectorate, some to the Secretary of State, some to local courts, with apparently little rationale for the choice of fora.

Our proposal for a single environmental tribunal to handle such appeals was certainly more modest than some of the earlier ideas for a full-blown division of the High Court handling all environmental legal issues. Although there was clearly a case for improving the way that existing criminal courts handled environmental cases, I felt that criminal environmental prosecutions should remain in the criminal courts rather than being given special treatment. Again, I was not convinced that the civil litigation in the environmental field such as nuisance cases raised such distinct issues as warranting a special court, nor that judges in the Administrative Court were incapable of handling environmental public law issues effectively, though undoubtedly issues concerning costs and the expense of judicial review needed to be tackled.

Intellectually, then, it seemed justifiable in Modernising Environmental Justice to focus on a more modest reform to the judicial system. But it was also clear at the time that government did not have the appetite for a major institutional upheaval, and my study was equally influenced by a realistic assessment of the politics of the possible. The drafting of the report deliberately avoided an overly academic approach, and was written in a style that would be accessible and intelligible to Ministers and senior civil servants, including

---

[3] P McAuslan (1991) The Role of Courts and other Judicial Type Bodies in Environmental Management 3 JEL (2) 195-208.

[4] H Woolf (1991) Are the Judiciary Environmentally Myopic? 4 JEL (1) 1-14.

[5] M Grant (2000) Environmental Court Project Final Report Dept of Environment, Transport and the Regions.

the provision of a succinct executive summary. We consciously examined the implications of different options including 'do nothing' or adapting existing bodies, and in the contemporary style of policy analysis considered the cost implications and possible financial savings that would result from the different options. The report was generally well received as representing a practicable step forward. A core question facing anyone calling for an environmental court or tribunal is what is so distinctive about environmental law that warrants special treatment. Modernising Environmental Justice addressed this by identifying some distinctive features of modern environmental law, but not all bodies were convinced that it was so different from areas such as health and safety law or consumer regulation, where there were no specialised courts. Furthermore, the proposal for a fairly focused new tribunal handling administrative appeals under environmental legislation did not sit well with the aspirations of those looking for a more radical institutional change. Another study, commissioned by Defra,[6] and published the next year rejected the modest approach and called for a specialist environmental court. The environmental NGO perspective was more concerned with access to justice for environmental litigants, and the proposal for a Tribunal did not deal with this question directly. Faced with such divergent views even from within the environmental law community, government was able to refrain from taking positive action.

At this time it looked as though the debate on a specialised court or tribunal was now stalled for another generation. Then, quite unexpectedly – and for reasons quite unconnected with environmental policy demands – came the Hampton Review on the relationship between business and regulators,[7] and my own Review on Regulatory Sanctions,[8] reproduced in Part I of this book. In the Review I called for the introduction of new regulatory sanctions in the form of civil penalties, and it was clear that there would need to a right of appeal to an independent judicial body as a matter of procedural fairness, let alone compliance with the European Convention on Human Rights. I was anxious to keep any system of civil penalties away from the ordinary courts, and the tribunal system seemed an obvious location for an appeal body. When Modernising Environmental Justice was published, setting up a new tribunal would have required new legislation, but in the meantime the Tribunals and Courts Act 2007 had introduced a far more coherent and flexible system of tribunals, and one where it was relatively easy to create a new tribunal without the need for new primary legislation. I therefore recommended the establishment of a regulatory appeals tribunal within the new system.

As I describe in Part I, rather to my surprise, regulators were not queuing up eagerly to acquire the new powers under the Regulatory Sanctions and Enforcement Act that followed the Sanctions Review. It so happened that the Environment Agency and its sponsoring department, Defra, were first off the mark, acquiring the new sanctioning powers in a limited range of areas in 2010. Appeals from the new civil penalties duly went to the Tribunal system, and by a simple act of internal administrative restructuring a First-tier Tribunal (Environment) was created as part of the Regulatory Chamber of the Tribunal System. Conspiracy theorists might surmise that my proposals for a regulatory appeals tribunal in the Sanctions Review were motivated by my so far frustrated desire to set up an

---

[6] Environmental Justice Environmental Law Foundation, World Wildlife Fund, and Leigh Day and Co, March 2004.

[7] Philip Hampton (2005) Reducing Administrative Burdens – Effective Inspection and Enforcement (HM Treasury).

[8] Richard Macrory (2006) Regulatory Justice: Making Sanctions Effective (Cabinet Office).

Environment Tribunal, but that was not the case. It is true that the research for Modernising Environmental Justice had made me more aware of the attributes and advantages of the tribunal system than I might otherwise have been, but there was a compelling logic in using the tribunal system as the location for an appeals body for civil penalties. The Sanctions Review covered some 61 national regulators as well as local authorities, and I had no idea that it was the environmental field where the running would be made. As I have mentioned subsequently, if the British Potato Council (one of the bodies falling within the scope the Sanctions Review) had been a first mover on acquiring civil sanctioning powers, we might now be discussing a First-Tier Tribunal (Potatoes).

The Environment Tribunal was duly set up with new legal and non-legal members, but its only initial jurisdiction was hearing appeals against civil penalties introduced in a limited range of environmental regulation. But even here there was no work for the Tribunal since the Environment Agency has to date found the use of Enforcement Undertakings agreed with industry as effective as the imposition of penalties. No formal penalty has yet been served and therefore no appeal to the Tribunal. The then Senior President of Tribunals, Robert Carnwath, clearly realised there was now a body without business and commissioned me to revisit and update my 2003 study to see if there was still a case for the new Tribunal to handle a greater range of statutory appeals. Consistency and Effectiveness: Strengthening the New Environment Tribunal (2011) was the result. If anything the position concerning appeals presented an even more confusing position than in 2003. It was true that more environmental appeals falling within the remit of the Department of Environment Food and Rural Affairs were being handled by the Planning Inspectorate, but other government departments, including the Department of Energy and Climate Change, created in 2008, and Business, Innovation and Skills, created in 2009, had significant responsibilities in areas of environmental regulation, and each were creating their own mechanisms for statutory appeals. Since an environmental tribunal now existed, it was no longer necessary to repeat the arguments for a special treatment of environment law, but the case for consolidating appeals under existing and new environmental legislation to the First-Tier tribunal was compelling. The proposals in the 2003 Report were largely driven by what was felt to be beneficial for the environment. The 2011 Report emphasised that the proposals were also consistent with the current regulatory reform agenda promoting the simplification and modernisation of regulatory structures. A single set of procedural rules would govern all environmental appeals, and the tribunal would sit within a structure that can be expected to command confidence among the regulated community and the public. The government accepted the basic thrust of the report, and an increasing number of statutory appeals, from nitrate zones to emissions trading, have been transferred to the new Tribunal. In 2013, the system was given an important endorsement by the High Court[9] which refused to hear a judicial review concerning the legality of environmental variation notice, arguing that the party concerned should have exercised its rights of appeal to the Environment Tribunal as provided for in 2011 regulations. As the court noted, 'The tribunal system looked at as a whole is not only able to deliver justice as well as the court system but, for the types of cases assigned to it, sometimes better'.

Environmental Regulation as an Instrument of Constitutional Change (2011) considers environmental law in the broader context of constitutional developments in the

---

[9] R on the Application of Great Yarmouth Port Company v Marine Management Organisation [2013] EWHC 3052 (Admin), analysed in Chapter 22, p 417.

United Kingdom. The environment provides a clear example of the complex web of the connections between and the roles of different levels of government that are now part of contemporary reality for achieving policy goals – international, the European Union, national, local, and devolved administrations – and well as the interface between regulatory and non-regulatory actors. But it seemed to me that there was a more significant consequence of the extraordinary development of environmental law in this country in the last thirty years or so. On reflection, it becomes apparent how many features of what we might now describe as the contemporary constitutional settlement between citizens and the state were often first driven and given legal reality in the environmental field. Environmental law in this country has pioneered concepts of legal rights to information held by public authorities, broad rights to participation in decision-making, rights of access to justice, new approaches to regulatory sanctions, and the more systematic accountability of regulatory authorities. Many legal initiatives first seen in the environmental field have subsequently been applied more generally. The environment, as I concluded has 'provided a laboratory and impetus for deeper changes in our legal and constitutional system.'

Yet these development seen by many to be beneficial for the environment have created real policy tensions within government, especially in the content of current economic challenges. In this context, the 1998 Aarhus Convention to which both the United Kingdom and the European Community are now parties, has been highly significant. Under the Convention, members of the public and non-governmental organisation are given the right to challenge the legality of environmental decisions of government and public bodies before an independent court or tribunal under procedures which must be 'equitable, timely, and not prohibitively expensive.' The British courts proved themselves more sensitive than government to the implications of these access to justice Aarhus provisions, and have, within their limits of their own powers, signalled new approaches to costs provisions, such as a more generous application of Protective Costs Orders, limiting in advance a party's exposure to costs should they lose. Government for some years remained convinced that our current system satisfied Aarhus requirements, but faced with condemnation by the Aarhus Compliance Committee,[10] and infringement proceedings taken by the European Commission before the European Court of Justice[11] eventually in 2013 introduced changes to the Civil Procedure Rules, introducing automatic capping and upper limits for costs exposures in Aarhus claims.[12]

In 2012 and 2013 saw a different development, when the government proposed major changes to judicial review procedures,[13] designed to part to prevent what it saw as a misuse of litigation for overtly political purposes. At the same time it was anxious that judicial reviews concerning land-use planning procedures were holding up development and taking too long. Significant proposals included more restrictive standing rules, stricter time-limits for bringing claims, and tougher leave procedures. The government

[10] Findings and Recommendations of the Aaarhus Convention Compliance Committee with regard to Communication ACCC/C/2008/33 concerning compliance by the United Kingdom (Port of Tyne Complaint), 2010.

[11] In February 2014, the Court found the UK costs regimes as applied in May 2010 was in breach of Aarhus obligations contained in EU environmental legislation – Case C 530/11 *European Commission v United Kingdom of Great Britain and Northern Ireland* Court of Justice of the European Union 13 February 2014. It remains unclear whether the new costs rules introduced by the government satisfy Aarhus.

[12] Civil Procedure (Amendment) Rules 2013 (SI 2013/262) introducing new Rule 45.41-44 CPR and Practice Direction 45 Fixed Costs.

[13] Ministry of Justice (2012) Judicial Review – Proposals for Reform, Cm 8515 December 2012; Ministry of Justice (2013) Judicial Review – Proposals for Further Reform, Cm 8703 September 2013.

also floated the possibility of transferring planning and environmental Judicial Reviews from the Administrative Court to the Upper Tribunal. Interestingly, the government by then accepted the implications of Aarhus, and noted that its proposals concerning more restrictive standing and protective costs orders could not apply to Aarhus environmental claims. My own response to the Consultation document, Judicial Review – Proposals for Further Reform (2013) argued that in practice it would be difficult to separate out many planning Judicial Review from Aarhus environmental challenges – any planning JR, for example, concerning with environmental assessment would inevitably engage Aarhus. I also felt it unwise to restrict standing rules, and felt that the judiciary could be trusted to exclude claim where the legal process was being abused. On a positive side, I felt that the transfer of planning and environment JRs to the Land Chamber of the Upper Tribunal had real merit. The Upper Tribunal has flexible procedural rules, combines legal and other professional expertise in its members, and has the capability of encouraging mediation and other interventionist techniques designed to help focus on the real issues in dispute. There was an opportunity to create a bold, new Land, Planning and Environment Tribunal, hearing both Judicial Reviews and appeals from the First-Tier Environment Tribunal. Statutory appeals now form the bulk of the work of the First-Tier Tribunal, but such rights of appeals have always remained restricted to the individual or business seeking the licence, challenging conditions imposed by the regulator, or similar action. Third parties such as neighbours or local amenity groups have never had equivalent rights of appeal but have to rely upon Judicial Review. I remain concerned that formal Judicial Review procedures, even with cost-capping, do not readily sit well with the vision of Aarhus for wide and rapid access to independent review procedures, and that the British procedures are excessively 'gold-plated' compared to practice in many other European countries. My response therefore floated the idea of limited third party rights of appeal on grounds of substantive or procedural illegality to the First-Tier tribunal – a sort of rapid and more economical form of judicial review. Not surprisingly in the current climate the idea has yet to find favour with government, though counter-intuitively it might well reduce overall delays and costs. In its response to the Consultation,[14] the government announced in 2014 that it would not change standing rules.[15] But instead of transferring planning Judicial Reviews to the Upper Tribunal, it proposed establishing a new Planning Court within the High Court. This may be the correct response if the primary aim of government to speed up decision-making, but I suspect in the longer run it is a lost opportunity to have created a judicial body truly capable of handling the complexities and demands of future environmental challenges.

[14] Ministry of Justice (2014) Judicial Review – Proposals for Further Reform: The Government Response Cm 8811, February 2014.

[15] Ibid, para 35: 'The Government is clear that the current approach to judicial review allows for misuse, but is not of the view that amending standing is the best way to limit the potential for mischief. Rather, the Government's view is that the better way to deliver its policy aim is through a strong package of financial reforms to limit the pursuit of weak claims and by reforming the way the court deals with judicial reviews based on procedural defects.'

5

The Long and Winding Road – Towards an Environmental Court in England and Wales[1] (2013)

Twenty-five years before the *Journal of Environmental Law* was first published, an unusual conference on law and science was held in the Temple. Co-chaired by a Law Lord, it brought together scientists, judges and lawyers and was focused on environmental issues.[2] Many of the subjects considered then have remained depressingly familiar over the succeeding years – river pollution, pesticide control, transboundary air pollution and the conservation of marine resources. Other concerns considered then, such as the potential effect of rockets on the climate, failed to materialise, although this perhaps could be seen as an early reflection of contemporary discussions on the potential environmental impact of geo-engineering.[3] There was considerable discussion about the adequacy of the existing laws, but interestingly very little reflection on the extent to which the judicial institutions were capable of handling the complexities of modern environmental challenges. But the launch of the *Journal of Environmental Law* in 1989 happened to coincide with the first serious proposal for some sort a specialised environmental court in England and Wales. The intervening period has seen numerous reports and conferences on the subject, often reflected in the pages of the journal, and leading eventually to the establishment of an environmental tribunal in 2010. It is too early to judge its real impact on the development and implementation of environmental law, although quite fortuitously its first significant decisions are likely to be seen during this twenty-fifth anniversary year of the journal.

The long saga of how the Environment Tribunal came into being is significant for a number of reasons. The often competing visions of the role that such a court or tribunal could play provide important insights on the nature of deeper concerns on the relationship of law and the environment over the last 25 years, and how these have evolved over time. Equally importantly, it provides lessons on how significant policy changes can come about. In 1977 the first chairman of the Royal Commission on Environmental Pollution suggested that the effective changes to environmental policy and law required two preconditions:[4] a detached analysis of the underlying problem and the solutions needed, coupled with

---

[1] R Macrory, 'The Long and Winding Road – Towards an Environmental Court in England and Wales' (2013) 25(3) *J Environmental Law* 371.

[2] Report of Conference on Law and Science, chaired by Lord Hodson and Kenneth Lindsay (David Davies Memorial Institute of International Studies, 1964).

[3] See, eg Royal Society, *Geoengineering the Climate: Science, Governance and Uncertainty* (Royal Society, 2009).

[4] E Ashby, *Reconciling Man and the Environment* (Stanford University Press, 1978).

what he described an 'ignition event', some sort of high-profile scandal, such as a major pollution incident. Ashby's analysis clearly applies to some significant developments in environmental law that have taken place – one of the most obvious being the first modern piece of specialised legislation concerning waste disposal, the Deposit of Poisonous Wastes Act 1972, passed through Parliament in a month and following highly publicised incidents of illegal dumping of cyanide. But with a subject such as environmental courts it is far less easy to identify an ignition event of this sort. For over 20 years there had been growing concerns with the adequacy of institutional arrangements, but these never amounted to the sort of scandal that would raise the subject high on the political agenda. At one stage, despite extensive analysis from both academia and practitioners, progress on creating a new form of specialised environmental court or tribunal appeared to have ground to a halt. What eventually gave rise to the creation of an environmental tribunal in England and Wales was caused in part by what I have described as unexpected alignments, where policy developments wholly unconnected with the environmental agenda happened to coincide and reinforce the case for change. At the same time, there was a degree of opportunism by key players involved in the debate. Securing significant policy change often requires a sensitivity to perceive where, within the complex machinery of government, the core nexus of policy development and change resides at any particular time. In retrospect, it is all too easy construct a rational analysis and explanation for legal development, but the reality at the time is that chance and opportunism are often critical elements that drive significant change. As a recent study has noted, 'The more one delves into the reality of policy making, the more that policy cycles and their like resemble a comforting narrative that imposes specious order on a complex reality'.[5] The history of the creation of the environment tribunal provides a compelling example of the significance of the chance and the unexpected in securing policy goals.

The Core Stages

It is not the purpose of this article to provide a detailed account of the critical studies that have influenced the debate on environmental courts and tribunals over the past 25 years. Elsewhere I have suggested that there seem to be two key periods.[6] The period from 1989 to 2000 can be described as one of reflective analysis, with reports and articles providing a substantive but sober examination of the issue. This was followed by a second period, from 2001 to 2004, that was dominated by more overtly policy-influencing responses, which at the same time laid bare significantly diverging analyses of the problems and solutions. Still no change took place, and it was only in a third period, roughly from 2005 to 2008, that unexpected alignments and opportunism came into play and led to institutional innovation.

The comprehensive land-use planning system introduced into the United Kingdom in 1947 has long played a powerful role in environmental protection, quite distinct from many

[5] M Hallsworth, with S Parker and J Rutter, *Policy Making in the Real World* (Institute for Government, 2011).
[6] R Macrory 'Environmental Courts and Tribunals in England and Wales – A Tentative New Dawn' (2010) (3)1 *Journal of Court Innovation* 61. See also R Macrory 'The Role of the First-Tier Environment Tribunal' (2012) (17)1 *Judicial Review* 54.

other jurisdictions. Indeed, the Planning Inspectorate, to whom most appeal decisions have been delegated by the Secretary of State, provides an early example of a quasi-independent specialist tribunal operating in this field. It is thus not entirely surprising that the first significant proposal for a specialised environmental court in this country appeared in the context of discussions on reforming land-use planning controls. Most of the recommendations in Robert Carnwath's 1989 report on the enforcement of planning controls[7] were concerned with improving the machinery for enforcing land-use planning controls. But he also made a cautious case for a new form of environment tribunal:

> there may be a case for reviewing the jurisdiction of the various courts and tribunals which at present deal with different aspects of what might be called 'environmental protection' (including planning) and seeking to combine them in a single jurisdiction.

A seed was sown. Two years later, Patrick McAuslan of the London School of Economics published a provocative article in the *Journal of Environmental Law*, 'The Role of Courts and Other Judicial Type Bodies in Environmental Management'.[8] McAuslan felt there was

> a strong case for the establishment of a court-like body with wide decision-making, advisory and regulatory powers in the environmental field to develop our systems of environmental management in a principled and expert manner and so contribute to both to our and to international environmental jurisprudence.[9]

McAuslan's contribution at the time to the environmental court debate has never been given the attention it deserved, perhaps because his analysis strayed well beyond a confined legal straightjacket and touched upon fundamental issues of philosophy, science and governance. At the same time it makes uncomfortable reading, in that he did not shrink from criticising 'the intellectual poverty' of British environmental lawyers for failing to grasp the nettle of what was needed. A year later, however, the subject was taken up by a leading figure of the legal establishment, when Lord Woolf gave the annual Garner environmental law lecture under the arresting title, 'Are the Judiciary Environmentally Myopic?'[10] For the then Lord Chief Justice to be showing such an interest in environmental law at the time when a new momentum for raising the profile of the subject was still in its infancy[11] was especially noteworthy. Recognising that one of the challenges of environmental law is that it does not sit neatly within familiar structure of criminal and civil law, or private and public law, Lord Woolf argued that, 'There could be great benefits in having a Tribunal with a general responsibility for overseeing and enforcing the safeguards provided for the protection of the environment which is so important to us all.'[12] But it was clear that his vision was not just for another specialist court or tribunal but something quite different:

> It is a multi-faceted, multi-skilled body which would combined the services provided by the existing courts, tribunals, and inspectors in the environmental field. It would be a 'one-stop'

---

[7] R Carnwath, *Enforcing Planning Control* (Stationery Office, 1989).
[8] (1991) *Journal of Environmental Law* (2)195.
[9] Ibid, 207.
[10] H Woolf, 'Are the Judiciary Environmentally Myopic' (1992) (4)1 *Journal of Environmental Law* 1.
[11] The UK Environmental Law Association, which organised the lecture, had been formed just three years before.
[12] Woolf, above n 10, 13.

shop which should lead to faster, cheaper, and more effective resolution of disputes in the environmental area.[13]

There was no immediate political response to Lord Woolf's proposal, but the Department of the Environment, Transport and the Regions commissioned Malcolm Grant, then head of Department of Land Economy, University of Cambridge, to study the concept of an environmental court, and in particular to examine examples of specialist environmental courts that were emerging in other jurisdictions such as Sweden, New Zealand and Australia. Grant's terms of reference were to analyse options rather than make recommendations. He rejected the idea that the systemic problems that existed could be met without structural change, and proposed six possible models of an environmental court ranging from a planning appeals tribunal to a separate two-tier Environmental Court.

Grant's report had all the virtues of the best of academic analysis – rigorously detached, massively detailed (the report ran to nearly 500 pages) and conceptually challenging. But these very qualities meant there was no simple message or clearly articulated solution to engage the political machinery, and in any event not all leading practitioners were wholly convinced. Stephen Tromans, for example, in his review of Grant's report in *Journal of Environmental Law*, concluded, 'I am open to persuasion that we need an environment court, and am not yet persuaded'.[14] In the debate on the subject in the House of Lords, Lord Bach for the government echoed these sentiments: 'The government welcomes the opportunity to debate this issue. We are not persuaded of the need for an environmental court, certainly not on its possible shape.'[15]

The tone of the reports and articles during the period from 2001 to 2004 somewhat changed and seemed more clearly designed to influence the political and policy agenda, with more marked criticism and focused solutions. A highly critical article in the *New Law Journal* written by three leading environmental law practitioners concluded that

> Our system for environmental protection has evolved in a piecemeal way over hundreds of years. The framework which has been patched together has so many weaknesses that now is the time to scrap it and replace it altogether with a mechanism designed to protect the environment in the new Millennium.[16]

A year later the Royal Commission on Environmental Pollution produced its report on environmental planning,[17] and in a section concerning public confidence in decision making suggested that there was a case for a specialised tribunal to handle various appeals under environmental regulation, then handled by a disparate array of bodies, including magistrates courts, the Secretary of State and the planning inspectorate. The wider vision of the Commission concerning environmental planning fell on stony ground at the time, but in relation to the environmental tribunal the government responded by commissioning the present author, who had been a member of the Royal Commission, to carry out a detailed study of existing environmental appeals to test the soundness of the Royal Commission's proposal.

[13] Lord Woolf later pursued in the idea in the 1997 Lord Morris Memorial Lecture, 'The Courts' Role in the Protection of the Environment'.

[14] S Tromans, 'Environment Court Project: Final Report' (2001) 13(3) *Journal of Environmental Law* 423.

[15] Hansard HL Deb 9 October 2000 col 97.

[16] M Day, R Stein and W Birtles, 'An Environmental Court' [2001] *New Law Journal* 638.

[17] Royal Commission on Environmental Pollution, Environmental Planning 23rd Report, Cm 5459 (Stationery Office, 2002).

Modernising Environmental Justice[18] provided a compelling snapshot of the haphazard arrangements for statutory appeals in over 50 examples of environmental laws, including a number of significant areas where, aside from judicial review, there was no right of appeal. The report concluded that a new specialist tribunal would bring greater legal authority and coherence, and improved confidence in environmental regulation for direct users, the regulatory authorities and the general public. The report acknowledged that the proposals were more modest than the sort of one-stop shop advocated by Lord Woolf, but the authors were acutely conscious of what was politically achievable at the time and, as Lord Justice Carnwath (as he then was) noted in the foreword to the report, 'The authors show how (if we concentrate for the moment on the regulatory and civil aspects of public environmental law), we can devise a structure which would be manageable and economical and would build on the best features of current practice'.

But despite a generally positive reception, there were criticisms. On the one hand, there were those who were not convinced that environmental law as a regulatory area deserved special treatment – if a specialised tribunal for environmental appeals, then why not one for health and safety, trading standards and other areas of regulation?[19] Equally, there were those who argued the proposals were far too modest, and that a more radical solution was required. The Department of Environment Food and Rural Affairs had commissioned at the same time a study of environmental law issues by a coalition of non-governmental organisations including legal practitioners.[20] Their concerns were driven more from the perspective of environmental litigants often faced with an unsympathetic judiciary and an unacceptable risk of high costs exposure. In their view, the UCL proposal for an environmental appeals tribunal failed to address these issues:

> We do not, however, believe that a tribunal of such limited scope as identified in the UCL Report is, in itself, sufficient to achieve access to environmental justice. Moreover, we are concerned that the establishment of a tribunal limited to regulatory appeals could fill the 'window of opportunity' to improve access to environmental justice at a time when more fundamental reform is clearly necessary.[21]

The Environmental Justice Project proposed a more radical solution – the establishment of a specialist environmental court within the High Court with jurisdiction to handle all civil environmental cases, including judicial reviews, statutory applications and appeals to the High Court, and environmental claims relating to nuisance, property damage, impairment of human rights and 'toxic tort' or chemical poisoning personal injury/nuisance claims.

---

[18] R Macrory with M Woods, *Modernising Environmental Justice: Regulation and the Role of an Environmental Tribunal* (Centre for Law and the Environment, Faculty of Laws University College London, 2003).

[19] See, eg the response of the Scottish Executive: 'We acknowledge the special characteristics listed by Macrory and Woods and accept that they are features of environmental law. However, we are not persuaded that these features, or indeed this combination of features is unique to environmental law and it could be argued that similar statements could be made equally about other areas of law such as health, health & safety and employment none of which have specialist courts/jurisdiction.' Scottish Executive Environment Group, 'Strengthening and Streamlining The Way Forward for the Enforcement of Environmental Law in Scotland' (Scottish Executive, 2006) para 2.99.

[20] WWF, Environmental Law Foundation (ELF) and Leigh Day & Co, 'Environmental Justice Project: A Report' (DEFRA 2004)

[21] Ibid, 12.

The Unexpected Alignments

Faced with competing solutions even within the specialised environmental law community, the government not unexpectedly did nothing. Aside from a general disquiet with existing arrangements, there was no clear 'ignition event' to secure political traction, and the momentum for any new form of environmental tribunal or court appeared to have run its course for the time being. However, a year later, the Treasury launched a review concerning regulators and their relationship with the business community, an initiative that had little to do with environmental concerns but was part of a general regulatory reform agenda. The Hampton Report[22] covered some 61 national regulators, including the Environment Agency, as well as local authorities, and encompassed an enormous range of regulatory areas, including trading standards, building regulations, environmental protection, food standards, and health and safety. Hampton argued that many regulators appeared to adopt a 'tick box approach' to regulatory enforcement, and advocated the greater use of risk-based strategies. Although Hampton felt that in most cases the best way to secure compliance from legitimate business was advice and persuasion, he recognised the importance of the sanctions that were available to regulators should this approach be inappropriate or ineffective.

Hampton therefore called for a more detailed study of regulatory sanctions, and as a result the present author was appointed by the Cabinet Office to lead a review on the subject (the Sanctions Review). As with Hampton, the Sanctions Review covered an enormous spectrum of regulatory fields, well beyond environmental law, but found that when it came to sanctions there were surprisingly common patterns. To a large extent, criminal offences, often drafted in strict liability terms, predominated. As with Hampton, the final report[23] acknowledged that 'Advice and incentives should play a key role in ensuring regulatory compliance, and should normally be the first response of regulators'.[24] It recognised that criminal offences would continue to play a significant role in regulatory enforcement, but felt that essentially the criminal law was being made to do too much work, dealing with both the truly egregious as well as legitimate businesses that had failed to comply with regulatory requirements through an oversight or negligence at the worse. Building on developments in jurisdictions such as Australia and Canada, the Review proposed that regulators should also have a richer range of sanctions, including the power to impose civil sanctions[25] in the form of financial penalties, ensuring that no financial gain was made from regulatory non-compliance but without imposing the full stigmatic weight of the criminal process.

Any system of civil penalties requires a robust and independent appeal procedure, both as a matter of basic fairness and a protection against overzealous regulators, let alone the

---

[22] P Hampton, *Reducing Administrative Burdens: Effective Inspection and Enforcement* (London, HM Treasury, 2005).

[23] R Macrory, *Regulatory Justice: Making Sanctions Effective* (London, Cabinet Office, 2006). For a general account of the Review and its recommendations see R Macrory 'Reforming Regulatory Sanctions' in Oliver, Rawlings and Prosser (eds), *The Regulatory State* (Oxford, Oxford University Press, 2010); R Macrory, 'Sanctions and Safeguards – The Brave New World of Regulatory Enforcement' (2013) 66(1) *Current Legal Problems* 233.

[24] Ibid, para 1.11.

[25] Eventually described as 'civil sanctions' under the Regulatory Enforcement and Sanctions Act 2008 (RESA).

need to comply with the European Convention on Human Rights.[26] Appeals could have gone back to the ordinary courts, but another unexpected alignment presented itself. Following the Leggatt Review,[27] the whole tribunal system had been substantially reorganised. Under the overall framework of the Tribunal and Courts Act 2007, a far more coherent structure was introduced, making tribunals clearly part of the independent judiciary and making it much easier to establish new tribunals without the need for primary legislation. The Sanctions Review envisaged an appeals system that would command confidence and be user-friendly, and proposed that appeals against administrative sanctions should be handled by a new regulatory appeals tribunal within the new system. The government accepted all the recommendations in the Sanctions Review, and Part III of the Regulatory Enforcement and Sanctions Act 2008 provided the framework for the proposed new civil sanctions, including the right to appeal to the new First-tier Tribunal.[28]

A New Environmental Tribunal

The Regulatory Enforcement and Sanctions Act 2008 deliberately did not impose the new sanctioning powers on regulators but left it to the discretion of regulators and sponsoring departments to determine whether they were needed in their field, using secondary legislation to acquire the powers. A number of significant regulators, such as the Health and Safety Executive, considered their existing powers to be sufficient.[29] The reforms had not been driven by the environmental agenda, and in practice any regulator might have been the first mover. As it turned out, it was the two main national environmental regulators, the Environment Agency and Natural England, that first acquired the powers to impose the new range of administrative sanctions. Secondary legislation was made in 2010[30] that covered a limited number of environmental offences and, in line with the principles of the Regulatory Enforcement and Sanctions Act, the legislation granted rights of appeal to the First-tier Tribunal. Within the General Regulatory Tribunal,[31] an Environment Tribunal was established by means of internal administrative reorganisation, with its members being both lawyers and others with specialist skills: with remarkable little publicity, and after more than 20 years of debate, the first specialist Environment Tribunal in the United Kingdom had come into being.

The Tribunal's initial jurisdiction was confined to hearing appeals against the imposition of civil sanctions, but to date neither the Environment Agency nor Natural England

---

[26] Art 6.1 of the Convention provides that, in the determination of his civil rights and obligations or of any criminal charge against him, everyone is entitled to a fair and public hearing within a reasonable time by an independent and impartial tribunal established by law.

[27] A Leggatt, 'Tribunals for Users – One System, One Service', Report of the Review of Tribunals (London, Department for Constitutional Affairs, 2001).

[28] For an analysis of the legislation, see J Norris and J Phillips, *The Law of Regulatory Enforcement and Sanctions* (Oxford, Oxford University Press, 2011).

[29] Health and Safety Executive, 'The Macrory Review of Penalties' (HSE, 2007), available at http://www.hse. gov.uk/aboutus/meetings/hsearchive/2007/040407/b48.pdf (accessed on 24 April 2013).

[30] Environmental Civil Sanctions (England) Order 2010, SI 2010/1157; Environmental Civil Sanctions (Miscellaneous Amendments)(England) Regulations 2010, SI 2010/1159; Environmental Civil Sanctions (Wales) Order 2010, SI 2010/1821 (W178); Environmental Civil Sanctions (Miscellaneous Amendments)(Wales) Order 2010, SI 2010/ 1820 (W 177)

[31] The First-tier Tribunal has been structured with six chambers, including the General Regulatory Tribunal.

has imposed a financial civil sanction.[32] At the time of writing there has been one appeal against a remediation notice served by the Marine Management Organisation under section 91 og the Marine and Coastal Access Act 2009. The outcome was a detailed order by consent, and both of the barristers involved reported that 'The Tribunal's specialist experience proved invaluable in achieving and guiding the final order'.[33]

The next significant stage in the development of the Tribunal's jurisdiction took place in 2010, when the then Senior President of Tribunals, Sir Robert Carnwath, commissioned the present author to revisit the UCL Environment Tribunal report and determine if there was still a case for consolidating statutory appeals in environmental legislation (such as appeals against refusal of consents) to the new Tribunal. The ensuing report[34] found that, if anything, the picture had become more confused since the original study. A number of environmental appeals falling within the remit of the Department of Environment, Food and Rural Affairs had been transferred to the Planning Inspectorate, but other government departments, such as Energy and Climate Change, and Business Innovation and Enterprise and Skills, now also dealt with important areas of environmental regulation, and had developed their own appeals procedures. The report recommended that, given that there now existed a new Environment Tribunal, many such appeals could be usefully transferred to the Tribunal, and that in any new environmental legislation there should be a presumption that statutory appeals be heard by the Tribunal. As the report noted, 'Over the years we have developed a system of environmental appeals which is complex and confusing. There is now a unique opportunity to make the current system more coherent, simple, and effective.'[35] The government accepted the general thrust of the report, and in the last two years a range of statutory appeals have been transferred to the Tribunal, including the designation of Nitrate Vulnerable Zones, Climate Change Agreements and various provisions of the Greenhouse Gas Emissions Trading scheme. Further transfers are proposed.[36]

Conclusions

At the time of writing, the Environment Tribunal remains a largely untested new institution, but with a wide range of appeals now falling within jurisdiction,[37] 2014 is likely to

---

[32] Sanctions have been threatened, but the Environment Agency has to date found it more fruitful to use enforcement undertakings, also provided under s 50 RESA, under which the company in question agrees to take appropriate action, including the payment of sums of money to thirds parties. Since such undertakings are made by agreement, there is no appeal provision unless there is disagreement that the undertaking has been fulfilled.

[33] Essex Street Chambers, 'Justine Thornton and James Burton appeared against each other in the first ever case to come before the First Tier Tribunal, General Regulatory Chamber (Environment)', available at http://www.39essex.com/resources/news_listing.php?id=163 (accessed on 24 April 2013).

[34] R Macrory, 'Consistency and Effectiveness – Strengthening the New Environment Tribunal' (Centre for Law and the Environment, UCL, 2011), Chapter 7 of this volume.

[35] Ibid, 6.

[36] Department of Environment Food and Rural Affairs, 'Environmental Permitting Consultation on draft Environmental Permitting (England and Wales) (Amendment) Regulations 2013' (Defra, February 2013).

[37] As of April 2013, appeals under the following: the Environmental Civil Sanctions (England) Order 2010, the Environmental Sanctions (Misc Amendments) (England) Regulations 2010), the Environmental Civil Sanctions (Wales) Order 2010, the Environmental Civil Sanctions (Miscellaneous Amendments) (Wales) Regulations 2010,the Ecodesign for Energy-Using Products (Amendment) (Civil Sanctions) Regulations 2010, the Ecodesign for Energy-Using Products (Amendment) Regulations 2009, the Ecodesign for Energy-Using

prove the year that its impact and value will first be felt. It clearly is not designed to fulfil some of more radical visions for environmental courts promoted in England and Wales over the last quarter century, including a new Environmental Division of the High Court or the sort of one-stop interdisciplinary shop advocated by Lord Woolf. Major pollution civil claims will still be heard by the civil courts, criminal environmental cases by the ordinary criminal courts and environmental judicial reviews within the Administrative Court of the High Court. In many ways the Tribunal's remit is more akin to the proposals first aired by Robert Carnwath in 1989, though it remains to be seen whether the Planning Inspectorate will ever be transferred into the new tribunal system. Policy development hardly ever takes place in a vacuum, and since the first arguments concerning the nature of an environmental court there have been significant developments in how other areas of environmental law are handled. Most notably there has been sustained pressure on government to modify the strict application of the costs in the cause principle in environmental judicial reviews in the light of the Aarhus convention.[38] This may help explain why there was not the same opposition from NGOs and other environmental lawyers to the setting up of the Environment Tribunal, since the solutions to their concerns were now being sought elsewhere.

But the saga also reveals how, whatever the extent and quality of rational analysis, chance and opportunism can play a significant role in securing change where there is no obvious scandal or ignition event to drive the debate. The Hampton Review was not directly concerned with environmental issues but led directly to the Sanctions Review, which provided the legal framework for civil sanctions with appeals to a tribunal. The Leggatt Reforms, again totally unconnected with environmental issues, meant that establishing a new tribunal was now much less costly and simpler that in earlier years, when primary legislation would have been required. And if the Department of Environment Food and Rural Affairs and the national environmental regulators it sponsored had not decided to press for the new administrative sanctions in the area of environmental regulation, a specialist environmental tribunal might never have been set up. Once established, the Tribunal could clearly provide an attractive home for many statutory environmental appeals, well beyond the field of administrative sanctions, and the then Senior President of Tribunals, who happened to have a special interest in environmental law, recognised in 2010 there was a timely opportunity to explore the issue further. From its fairly humble beginnings, the tribunal is now well placed to develop further and play a significant role in

Products Regulations 2007, the Ecodesign for Energy-Related Products (Amendment) Regulations 2011, the Energy Information Regulations 2011, the Single Use Carrier Bags Charge (Wales) Regulations 2010, the Marine Licensing (Notices Appeals) Regulations 2011, the Marine Licensing (Civil Sanctions) (Wales) Order 2011, the Marine Licensing (Notices Appeals) (Wales) Regulations 2011, the Flood and Coastal Erosion Risk Management Information Appeal (Wales) Regulations 2011, the Waste (England and Wales) Regulation 2011, the Nitrate Pollution Prevention (Amendment) Regulations 2012, Coast Protection England and Wales, Environmental Protection England and Wales, Flood Risk Management England and Wales, the Designation of Features Appeal Regulations 2012,the Green Deal Framework (Disclosure, Acknowledgment, Redress etc) Regulations 2012, the Climate Change Agreements (Administration) Regulations 2012, the Greenhouse Gas Emissions Trading Scheme Regulations 2012, the Single Use Carrier Bags Charge Regulations (Northern Ireland) 2013.

[38] See especially Report of Working Group on Access to Environmental Justice (Sullivan Report), 'Ensuring Access to Environmental Justice in England and Wales' (2008); Ministry of Justice, 'Cost Protection for Litigants in Environmental Judicial Review Claims', Consultation Paper CP16/11 (Ministry of Justice 2012); Ministry of Justice, 'Cost Protection for Litigants in Environmental Judicial Review Claims: Outline Proposals for a Cost Capping Scheme for Cases which Fall Within the Aarhus Convention Response to Consultation' (Ministry of Justice, 2012).

the handling of environmental law in this country. In future years its decisions are likely to be subject to critical analysis in the *Journal of Environmental Law* alongside those of other courts, though how the journal will assess its overall contribution in 25 years' time is one prediction that the present author will wisely duck.

6

Modernising Environmental Justice – Regulation and the Role of an Environmental Tribunal[1] (2003)

Procedures have grown up haphazardly with no apparent underlying principle, and we consider they fail to provide a system appropriate for contemporary needs. We recommend the establishment of Environmental Tribunals to handle appeals under environmental legislation other than the town and country planning system.

Royal Commission on Environmental Pollution, 23rd Report, 'Environmental Planning' (2002)

We express our conviction that the deficiency in the knowledge, relevant skills and information in regard to environmental law is one of the principal causes that contribute to the lack of effective implementation, development and enforcement of environmental law.

Johannesburg Global Judges Symposium 2002

In order to contribute to the protection of the right of every person of present and future generations to live in an environment adequate to his or her health and well-being, each Party shall guarantee the rights of access to information, public participation in decision making, and access to justice in environmental matters in accordance with the provisions of this Convention.

Aarhus Convention 1998

Key Messages of the Study

1.   This study is concerned with modernising the ways in which we handle environmental regulation. It stems from a recent recommendation of the Royal Commission on Environmental Pollution that a specialist environmental tribunal system be set up to consolidate and rationalise a range of environmental appeal mechanisms which are currently distributed amongst an array of different courts and other bodies.

---

[1] R Macrory with M Woods, *Modernising Environmental Justice: Regulation and the Role of an Environmental Tribunal* (Centre for Law and the Environment, Faculty of Laws University College London, 2003).

2.   The right of applicants for planning permission to appeal to the Secretary of State is a familiar and developed feature of our land-use planning system. Land-use planning appeals are handled (and most cases now decided by) the Planning Inspectorate. Similar rights of appeal have been built into many existing environmental laws, ranging from waste management licensing to the service of statutory nuisance abatement notices. But the institutions that determine such appeals are many and varied. This study has examined over 50 different appeal provisions in contemporary environmental legislation, with appeal bodies ranging from the Secretary of State and the Planning Inspectorate under delegated powers, to the magistrates' courts, county courts and the High Court. There are also examples where the applicant has no right to question regulatory decision other than by way of judicial review.

3.   The system that has developed is complex, and not one easily intelligible to direct users, let alone the general public. It lacks any underlying coherence, and fails to reflect contemporary developments in environmental law. The system's haphazard nature can only be explained by the fact that as new environmental regulatory requirements have been introduced, decisions as to the choice of appeal route have been made on a pragmatic basis from a diversity of existing bodies which were not originally established for such purposes.

4.   Pragmatism can often be a virtue. But evidence from existing users of the system (including regulatory bodies) suggests unease with the current arrangements. It is questionable whether local magistrates' courts are the best fora for handling technically complex appeals brought by trade and industry under statutory nuisance provisions, and even more so, appeals under the emerging contaminated land regime. The Planning Inspectorate appears to be coping effectively with the relatively small number of environmental appeals that it now handles, but there are concerns about how it deals with difficult legal issues, the accessibility of its decision letters, and the fact that it is not a suitable forum for providing authoritative decisions on environmental appeals which can then be used as more general guidance for the better application of environmental regulation. There are also glaring gaps in the existing legislation where no appeal route is provided.

5.   The study has also considered pressures on existing judicial review procedures. An examination of over 50 case files over the past three years has indicated that judicial review applications concerning environmental decisions are brought as much by industry as by members of the public or environmental organisations, and are frequently merits driven rather than concerned with purely legal grounds. Failure to tackle the existing weaknesses and gaps in appeal mechanisms will only increase the pressure on judicial review as a default appeal route to which it is not best suited.

6.   One way forward is based on the adaptation of current arrangements, and the study identifies a number of possible improvements which could be made to existing institutions. This includes the transfer of contaminated land remediation notice appeals to the Lands Tribunal, and the strengthening of legal and environmental expertise within the Planning Inspectorate.

7.   However, this is likely to be very much a second-best solution. A key concern is whether such a 'pick and match' approach can be sustained in the light of future demands. On the horizon there is a range of new and challenging sets of environmental requirements, often involving smarter regulatory concepts than

more traditional approaches – examples include end of life vehicles, carbon dioxide emissions trading, agricultural waste and environmental liability to name but a few. An appeals system based on a specialised tribunal, bringing heightened legal authority and coherence to the system, would significantly improve confidence in future environmental regulation for direct users, the regulatory authorities, and the general public.

8.   The need for a specialised jurisdiction is reflected in the distinctive characteristics of contemporary environmental law, and it is possible to identify a core environmental jurisdiction that could fall within a new Environmental Tribunal system. Estimates of the current numbers of environmental regulatory appeals being made indicate that that they could be transferred to a single Environmental Tribunal operating along similar lines to the current Lands Tribunal, with establishment costs of under £2m. This would provide a secure basis for any extension of jurisdiction to meet future requirements. Such a tribunal would fall within the new unified Tribunals Service, and benefit from being associated with the government's reform programme for tribunals.

9.   The need for a new institutional framework is all the more pressing given the changing context of the role of environmental regulatory appeals. The Aarhus Convention, in particular, promotes the concept of a more active environmental citizenship, and introduces a new concept of environmental justice. This includes the right to legal review mechanisms for members of the public and non-governmental organisations that are fair, equitable, timely and not prohibitively expensive. An Environmental Tribunal is likely to provide a more appropriate basis for meeting the aspirations of Aarhus than relying on current procedures.

10.   The model of the Environmental Tribunal considered in this study is more modest than earlier proposals for a 'one-stop' environmental court or a land and environment tribunal. Yet it is also one that offers a manageable and viable solution, with a core structure that could be established without undue cost or administrative upheaval. Regulatory appeal mechanisms are only one element of our system for delivering and implementing environmental law, but they play a vital role, and their potential benefits have been largely ignored to date. A new appeal body in the form of such an Environmental Tribunal would bring greater coherence and authority to the development of the legal and policy dimensions of environmental regulation, and would make a significant contribution to our justice system.

The Report

1.   The Context

1.1   Environmental law has grown rapidly in its scope and content in this country over the last two decades. It is a subject that is being continually developed to face new environmental challenges. Much effort is currently being focused on ensuring that the design of modern environmental regulation is proportionate, intelligible for the user, and effective in achieving beneficial outcomes. This study, though, is not concerned with the substantive content of regulation – it is equally important that we have in place the most appropriate legal machinery to resolve environmental disputes in a way that is fair, attracts public confidence, and provides an authoritative and coherent approach to environmental law and policy. This led us to concentrate on certain key aspects of the current arrangements for administering and implementing environmental regulation.

1.2   This challenge of institutional design is not unique to the United Kingdom. Other countries have developed or are thinking about new legal machinery for handling the interpretation and application of environmental law. In this country, various models for change have been proposed during the last decade or so. The 1989 Carnwath Report on Enforcing Planning Control argued the need to review the jurisdictions of the various courts and tribunals dealing with different aspects of what might be called 'environmental protection' (including planning), and saw merit in combining them in a single jurisdiction.[2] In his 1991 Garner Lecture 'Are the Judiciary Environmentally Myopic?', Lord Woolf spoke of the benefits of a specialist tribunal with a general responsibility for overseeing and enforcing safeguards provided for the protection of the environment.[3] Professor Malcolm Grant's major study on Environmental Courts, commissioned by the government and published in 2000,[4] identified six alternative models, ranging from a planning appeals tribunal to an environmental court as a new division of the High Court. But at the time, the government was not convinced of the need for change, and were particularly concerned about the institutional upheaval involved in introducing such models. In the Parliamentary debate on the issue, the government minister noted the apparent lack of consensus on the types of environmental issues that might be included in a new jurisdiction, as well as the diversity of courts that could currently deal with what might be described as environmental disputes.[5] Any significant institutional change was also considered premature prior to the outcome of major reviews of the criminal and tribunal systems then being undertaken.

1.3   More recently, there has been much increased international discussion and co-operation amongst the judiciary in the search for new approaches to environmental law and the mechanisms for delivering effective results. In August 2002, senior members of the judiciary from sixty countries met at the Global Judges Symposium as part of the Johannesburg World Summit. They affirmed the Johannesburg Principles on the Role of Law and Sustainable Development,[6] stressing the vital role of the judiciary and environmental law in the enhancement of the public interest in a healthy and secure environment. This has been followed by meetings of the judiciary in London last year, and most recently in Rome in May 2003, where the establishment of a European Judicial Forum was confirmed. Key substantial issues identified at the Rome meeting for further work included:

---

[2] R Carnwath QC, *Enforcing Planning Control* (Department of the Environment, April 1989).
[3] Woolf LCJ, Garner Lecture, 'Are the Judiciary Environmentally Myopic' (1991) 4(1) *Journal of Environmental Law* 1.
[4] M Grant, Department of the Environment Transport and the Regions (UK), Environmental Court Project Final Report (2000).
[5] House of Lords, Hansard, 9 October 2000, col 97.
[6] The full text of the Johannesburg Principles is reproduced in (2003) 15(1) *Journal of Environmental Law*.

- the pros and cons of establishing specialist environmental courts or tribunals.
- the ability of citizens to obtain access to the courts to further enhance the effective implementation, compliance with, and enforcement of environmental laws.
- consideration of environmental scientific evidence and the fashioning of appropriate remedies, including restoration of the environment.

2. The Report of the Royal Commission on Environmental Pollution

2.1 The most recent significant UK study dealing with these issues, and which provides the context for this report, was the 23rd Report of the Royal Commission on Environmental Pollution (RCEP), entitled *Environmental Planning* and published in 2002.[7] Much of the RCEP's study was concerned with improving strategic planning for the environment, but it also included recommendations dealing with current institutional arrangements for handling planning and environmental disputes.

2.2 Following the recent establishment of the Administrative Court, the RCEP did not consider that there now exists a compelling case for creating a specialist environmental division of the High Court to handle environmental judicial reviews. It was of the view that criminal environmental offences were probably still best handled by ordinary criminal courts, though it recommended improved training for magistrates. The RCEP also recognised that in respect of applicants for planning permission, we have a well developed system of appeal procedures under the town and country planning legislation as handled by the Planning Inspectorate.

2.3 But when the RCEP examined current arrangements for dealing with environmental appeals outside the planning system, such as appeals against the refusal of a waste management licence, or the service of a statutory nuisance abatement notice, it concluded that the present system lacked consistency and coherence, both as to whether there are any rights of appeal on merits, and as to which forum decides such appeals. It therefore recommended the establishment of a new environmental tribunal system to consolidate and rationalise the handling of such appeals. Although the RCEP recognised that there might be merit in bringing all environmental appeals under the jurisdiction of the Planning Inspectorate, it considered that it would be preferable to establish a specialist environmental tribunal system in order to provide a more visible focus for the development and application of environmental law and policy, and to avoid environmental appeals being treated as a sub-set of the much greater number of planning appeals.

3. The Purpose of this Study

3.1 The aim of this project has been to test the merits of the RCEP proposal in greater detail, and to provide more extensive underlying data to allow a rigorous analysis of some of the important questions that need to be addressed if the proposal is to be taken forward:

[7] Royal Commission on Environmental Pollution, Environmental Planning 23rd Report, Cm 5459 (London, Stationery Office, 2002).

- How coherent is the present system for appeals?
- Are there concerns with how current arrangements operate in practice, and could these be met by incremental adaptation rather than a new tribunal system?
- Will the current arrangements be able to handle the new environmental legislation on the horizon?
- Would there be a viable jurisdiction for an Environmental Tribunal?
- What would be the likely workload, and what are the costs and benefits involved?
- What are the current pressures on judicial review procedures, and to what extent could these be addressed by a new Environmental Tribunal?
- Would a specialist Environmental Tribunal improve confidence in the application and enforcement of environmental law?
- Would such a Tribunal contribute towards meeting the aspirations of active environmental citizenship underlying the Aarhus Convention?

3.2   The research also needs to be seen in the context of wider concerns about the current effectiveness of environmental law, including the adequacy of criminal penalties and enforcement mechanisms. The RCEP model did not envisage an environmental tribunal system directly handling criminal cases, which would remain as now with the criminal courts. We will argue that a coherent regulatory appeals system is in any event an important element for the more effective enforcement of environmental regulation, but we also consider later in the report the extent to which an Environmental Tribunal system might take on more overt enforcement functions.

3.3   The current regulatory arrangements now need to be tested against the provisions of the 1998 Aarhus Convention on Access to Information, Public Participation in Decision-Making and Access to Justice in Environmental Matters. The Convention (which is in the process of implementation within the European Community) promotes the concept of an active environmental citizenship to ensure sustainable and environmentally sound development, including public participation, transparency, and accessible and effective judicial mechanisms. Governments are required to establish and maintain 'a clear, transparent and consistent framework' to implement the Convention's requirements. We have to consider the extent to which a new Environmental Tribunal system might contribute to fulfilling both the letter and spirit of Aarhus.

3.4   Our study should also be viewed in the context of the government's current reform programme for tribunals, following the 2001 Leggatt Report, 'Tribunals for Users'.[8] The government has recently announced its intention to create a unified Tribunals Service responsible to the Lord Chancellor as part of its wider agenda for reforming the country's legal systems and public services. Current plans envisage the establishment of such a service in incremental stages, and a White Paper should be published later this year. The Leggatt Report was largely concerned with existing tribunals rather than the creation of new jurisdictions, but contains a valuable set of principles against which changes to the current system of environmental appeal procedures can be judged. It is clearly important that any proposals for change are consistent with the proposed reforms of the tribunals system as a whole.

---

[8] Leggatt, 'Tribunals for Users – One System, One Service', Report of the Review of Tribunals (London, Department for Constitutional Affairs, 2001) (Leggatt Report).

3.5   This report is focused on the legislation and appeals procedures in England and Wales only. Nevertheless, we suspect that many of the underlying concerns and the arguments for change will be of relevance to Scotland and Northern Ireland as well.

4.   Environmental Appeals under Existing Legislation

4.1   A key part of the research has been to establish in more detail the range of what might legitimately be described as environmental appeals provided for in existing legislation, as well as the current numbers of such appeals taking place. The types of appeals that we have considered fall into two broad categories:

(i)   appeals against the refusal of a licence/permit (or against conditions imposed in a licence/permit) required under environmental legislation

(ii)   appeals against some form of notice served under environmental legislation requiring remedial action or the cessation of activities

4.2   We describe these as 'regulatory appeals' in part to distinguish them from judicial review applications. The appeals are distinct from legal actions between private parties such as private nuisance actions, in that they are concerned with resolving disputes between the citizen (whether an individual or a company) and the state (in the form of central government, a specialised agency, or local government). This is described in the Leggatt Report as the typical jurisdiction of most tribunals. One distinction, though, from the range of work carried out by many existing tribunals is that the majority of regulatory decisions in environmental law that might be subject to appeal are likely to involve companies and businesses rather than private individuals. Statutory nuisances are an exception where many appeals, such as those relating to noise nuisance or housing conditions, involve domestic premises. Importantly, where such rights of 'regulatory appeal' exist, they currently rest with the person or business immediately affected (i.e. the licence applicant or the person served with the notice), and other members of the public have no general right of appeal other than by way of judicial review, and subject to normal standing requirements. The question of whether third party rights of appeal should be introduced within an Environmental Tribunal system is considered more fully later in this study.

4.3   Where grounds of appeal are provided in the legislation, they are typically very broad, covering both the factual merits of the original decision, procedural questions, and questions of law. In other cases, appeals are effectively based on the right to a *de novo* decision. Regulatory appeals are therefore in effect full merits appeals, often involving questions of fact and law, and should be treated as distinct from judicial review applications where more restricted grounds of review apply – though we consider later in the study the extent to which judicial review procedures in environmental matters are in practice being used a default merits appeal route.

4.4   The regulatory appeals that we have described are concerned with resolving disputes concerning the validity of the action of a governmental body rather than the prosecution of environmental offences. We discuss further on in the report whether any Environmental Tribunal system could usefully incorporate enforcement functions in addition to determining regulatory appeals, but in any event there is an intimate connection between a regulatory appeals system and environmental enforcement. Non-compliance with an environmental licence or permit, or with notices such as those served under statutory nuisance or contaminated land legislation, is generally deemed to be a criminal offence, and under contemporary environmental legislation there are now few 'stand-alone' environmental criminal offences, i.e. nearly all such offences are at least indirectly connected with the type of licence or notice handled by the environmental regulators as described above. A regulatory appeals system which can deliver effective, consistent, and authoritative rulings on the interpretation and application of regulatory requirements can therefore be seen as an essential building block – though not the only one – in ensuring improved compliance with, and the enforcement of environmental legislation.

4.5   The government's agenda for the reform of public services emphasises the need for modern, user-focused services, and any critique of the current arrangements for handling environmental appeals should be seen from the perspective of the user. The direct users of the current appeal system are the individuals or companies who are subject to environmental regulation and would legitimately expect the opportunity to question the factual and legal basis of administrative decisions directly affecting them. But in the environmental field there are also other interests involved whose perspectives need to be taken into account, and might best be described as 'indirect' users. They include:

- Bodies responsible for implementing environmental regulation who should be able to rely on an appeals system that delivers decisions with consistency and authority, even where individual decisions are made against them (e.g. the Environment Agency and English Nature).
- Members of the public who are indirectly affected by environmental decisions taken by regulatory bodies (e.g. owner/occupiers in the vicinity of a proposed landfill site). Whilst the main impact of administrative decisions in fields such as social security entitlement or immigration is likely to be on the individual seeking entitlement, the environmental field is distinctive in that decisions taken by regulatory bodies may also have real or perceived impacts on the health and physical environment enjoyed by a wide group of third parties.
- Companies seeking to comply with regulatory requirements who do not necessarily wish to exercise rights of appeal, but need to be assured that where competitors do appeal, decisions are made fairly and consistently.
- The general public, who have a stake in a system that delivers effective environmental outcomes in a manner in which they can have confidence.

5.   Legislative Analysis

5.1   We have conducted a systematic analysis of legislation to determine the extent of current appeal provisions and their decision forums. Determining the boundaries of 'environmental' legislation with precision is always a question of judgment, but we have excluded from the analysis at one end of the spectrum, town and country planning and transport legislation, legislation broadly concerned with amenity questions (such as tree preservation orders or hedgerow appeals), valuation appeals and the type of land dispute that falls within the jurisdiction of the Lands

Tribunal; and at the other end, we exclude health and safety, and similar workplace controls.

5.2   We do not claim this to be a complete exercise, nor that all such appeals should necessarily be handled by a single Tribunal system. Nevertheless, Appendix A[9] lists over 50 different appeal routes under specialised environmental legislation that fall within these parameters. Broadly, we can categorise the different routes of appeal under the following headings:

(a)   Appeals to local magistrates' courts (mainly in respect of notices served by local authorities under statutory nuisance and contaminated land provisions).

(b)   Appeals to the Secretary of State but formally delegated to the Planning Inspectorate (mainly Integrated Pollution and Prevention Control (IPPC) consents, waste management licences, and water discharge consents, plus contaminated land notices for 'special' sites designated by the Environment Agency).

(c)   Appeals to the Secretary of State which are handled by the Planning Inspectorate but with the final decision resting with the Secretary of State.

(d)   Appeals to the Secretary of State where no specific procedure may yet have been identified.

(e)   Appeals to the High Court on merits grounds (a rag-bag set of provisions, often dealing with off-shore activities).

(f)   Miscellaneous appeals to a variety of other courts and tribunals (including, for instance, the County Court in respect of charging notices served under the contaminated land regime)

(g)   Cases where no right of merits appeal is provided under the legislation (typically where the initial decision is made by the Secretary of State such as on GMO licences; in some cases the procedures allow for further representations to be made on proposed decisions, but otherwise it is necessary to use judicial review as a default means of appeal)

(h)   The use of arbitration (as introduced in respect of decisions by the Secretary of State under recent voluntary agreements concerning carbon emission reductions to avoid the likelihood of judicial review)

5.3   The only existing appeal route against the refusal by a public body to release environmental information under the Environmental Information Regulations has to date been by way of judicial review. A Consultation Paper was issued by government in November 2002, proposing an appeal route in respect of environmental information to the new Information Commissioner with a further right of appeal to the Information Tribunal established under the Freedom of Information Act 2000. Against this background, we do not consider this area of law further in the report.

5.4   The pattern of appeal routes clearly presents a complex picture and one not easily intelligible to the expert, let alone the ordinary citizen. Even within some discrete regimes, such as contaminated land, there is more than one appeal body involved. It is not easy to discern any underlying principles that determine the

---

[9] The appendices are not reproduced in this volume.

choice of appeal forum, though some rationale can be identified in particular cases. Statutory nuisance provisions, for example, were based on structures originating in nineteenth century public health legislation and were already locked into the magistrates' courts system before appeal provisions against notices were introduced (first for noise nuisances in 1974 and then for other statutory nuisances in 1990). Statutory nuisance abatement notice appeals may be argued to involve the need for local knowledge where magistrates are considered to have expertise. The new contaminated land provisions were modelled on the statutory nuisance provisions, justifying the choice of magistrates' courts rather than any other forum for dealing with appeals in respect of local authority sites. IPPC and waste management consents are usually associated with land based projects which perhaps explains the choice of the Planning Inspectorate as the body for handling appeals. Three examples of key legislative appeal mechanisms are provided in Box 1.

Box 1 Examples of Key Legislative Appeal Mechanisms

Waste

Waste management on land in the UK is regulated under Part II of the Environmental Protection Act 90 and related regulations, on order to comply with the EC Waste Framework Directive. This legislation set up a waste management licensing system to cover the keeping, treatment and disposal of controlled waste, under the supervision of the Environment Agency. There is a right of appeal to the Secretary of State in relation to decisions by the Environment Agency on licence applications , including their transfer or surrender. This right of appeal is available to the applicant, the holder or a proposed transferee of a licence. The appeals can take the form of a hearing or written representations, and are delegated to the Planning Inspectorate. Such delegation is normally carried out as the need arises, by way of a formal letter with legally binding effect. The Government is currently consulting on the proposed End of Life Vehicles (Storage and Treatment) (England and Wales) Regulations 2003, which will implement (in part) the EC End of Life Vehicles Directive. These Regulations will require some operators of sites who currently comply with the waste management licensing system, to obtain a permit if they wish to continue to undertake recovery activities on end of life vehicles before existing pollutants have been removed. A right of appeal would be available against decisions taken by the Environment Agency to the Secretary of State, or her appointee.

Contaminated Land

The new contaminated land regime is covered by Section 78A of the Environmental Protection Act 1990 (introduced by the Environment Act 1995) and related regulations. Local authorities are under a duty to inspect their areas in order to identify contaminated sites so that remediation can be addressed. The local authority is then to serve a remediation notice on those parties it considers should be responsible for carrying out the remediation. This will mainly be the person who 'caused or knowingly permitted' the contamination to take place, but if such a person cannot be found, then liability may rest with the current owner or occupier. The local authority will need to allocate liability where a number of parties have contributed to the contamination. Local authorities also have default powers to carry out remediation work and then recover their costs. If a site is more seriously contaminated, then it will be designated a 'special' site, in which case, the Environment Agency takes responsibility for addressing the remediation process. Parties served with a remediation notice have a right of appeal. If the notice was served by a local authority the appeal will be heard by the local magistrates' court. If the notice was served by the Environment Agency then the appeal is to the Secretary of State. Such appeals can take the form of a hearing or written representations, and are currently delegated to the Planning Inspectorate. In addition, there is a right of appeal to the county court in respect of a charging notice served by a local authority in order to recover its costs in carrying out remediation work itself. There is also a right of appeal to the Secretary of State regarding a determination by an authority to hold confidential information relating to the affairs of an individual or business on a public register for contaminated sites.

Genetically Modified Organisms

The deliberate release and contained use of Genetically Modified Organisms (GMOs) are controlled under separate legislation designed to implement relevant EC requirements. Under the new Genetically Modified Organisms (Deliberate Release) Regulations 2002, the Secretary of State can authorise the release of GMOs into the environment. Applications for commercial releases need a collective decision by all the EC Member States, but decisions on releases for certain research purposes can be taken by the Secretary of State without the same level of EC involvement. Such decisions are handled by Defra officials in practice, based on EC consultations, expert advice and any public representations. However, no formal right of appeal is provided in the Regulations, and applicants would have to use judicial review to challenge the decision. The Genetically Modified Organisms (Contained Use) Regulations 2000 cover the use of GMOs in laboratory and similar conditions where there is a barrier to contact with the public. Applications for authorisations are processed by the Health and Safety Executive, and decisions are made by the Secretary of State and the Health and Safety Executive acting jointly. There is a right of appeal available to the Secretary of State.

5.5   Nevertheless, one must suspect that as new environmental requirements have been introduced, choices as to appeal routes have been made on a pragmatic basis from the array of existing fora, leading to the haphazard nature of the present arrangements. A senior judge told us: 'Some environmental legislation is extraordinarily deficient in terms of the sufficiency or availability of appeal mechanisms...but pressures from the Human Rights Act and for third parties' rights will change this...' Complexity in itself is not necessarily a justification for change, but a drawback of the current disparate structure is that it may inhibit consistent approaches to resolving environmental appeals, and the development of environmental decision making that will attract both business and public confidence. An effective appeals system is equally important for the confidence of those public bodies charged with the responsibility for delivering environmental regulation, and as we have noted, is closely linked to more effective criminal enforcement.

5.6   In addition, we need a system that will meet future environmental regulatory requirements. This need is particularly driven by developments in the European Community (EC), and Box 2 provides a selective list of anticipated EC legislation, requiring transposition into UK law, much of which will require new appeal procedures. Looking to the future, a key policy choice has to be taken as to whether it is preferable to continue to make pragmatic choices as to appeal routes on an ad hoc basis by loading the variety of existing institutions with new responsibilities, or if it would be better to establish a more specialised Environmental Tribunal system with the expertise and capability to handle both current and future requirements.

6.   Current Numbers of Environmental Appeals

6.1   Our research has also explored the numbers of environmental appeals currently taking place under the environmental legislation identified above. There are no comprehensive statistics maintained by government, which is perhaps not surprising given the variety of routes that exist. We would recommend at the very least that government pays greater attention in the future to monitoring the number of environmental appeals being made on a more systematic and complete basis than is currently the case. Details of the figures we have been able to acquire are contained in Appendices B and C,[10] and are focused on statutory nuisance appeals heard in magistrates' courts and those environmental appeals handled by the Planning Inspectorate. For other appeals such as those to the county court or the more specialised routes to the High Court, we suspect that the numbers are small, or that in some instances appeal rights have not yet been exercised.

6.2   For statistical purposes, the Planning Inspectorate includes hedgerow appeals under its category of 'environmental appeals', but as indicated we have excluded them from our list of environmental regulatory appeals as being more akin to land-use planning and amenity issues. In the twelve month period between April 2002 and March 2003, the number of environmental appeals as we have defined them received by the Planning Inspectorate was 233, with the vast majority (211) relating to water discharge consents. Other categories of appeals included: waste management regulation (8); Integrated Pollution Control and Air Pollution Control under Part I of the Environmental Protection Act 1990 (8); water abstraction (3); and anti-pollution works in respect of water (3).[11] During this 12 month period, 68 appeals were withdrawn or turned away as invalid or out of time, and there were eight decisions issued. There is also a very large backlog of appeals relating to water discharge consents (755), and our understanding is that these are either still the subject of negotiation between the parties and the regulatory authority, or have been held up pending policy advice being provided by the Department for Environment, Food and Rural Affairs (Defra).

6.3   For contaminated land, the procedures are insufficiently mature to predict the typical numbers of appeals that might be made. For 'special' sites handled by the Environment Agency, 13 sites had been designated by the end of 2002 with a target

---

[10] These appendices are not reproduced in this volume.
[11] Planning Inspectorate, personal communication.

BOX 2 – Selected New And Anticipated EC Legislation			
STATUS	ISSUE	TYPE OF MEASURE	PURPOSE
Adopted	Emissions Ceilings	Directive	Sets national emissions ceilings for SO_2, NO_x, VOCs and NH3 to be reached by 2010, requiring the extension of air pollution controls through IPPC to ammonia emissions from agriculture and in particular the dairy sector
Adopted	Waste Electrical & Electronic Equipment (WEEE)	Directive	Requires that producers (manufacturers, sellers, distributors) will be responsible for financing the collection, treatment, recovery and disposal of WEEE from private households which are deposited at collection facilities (and from non-households from 2005)
Adopted	Restriction of Hazardous Substances in Electrical and Electronic Equipment (ROHS)	Directive	Restricts the use of certain hazardous substances in the manufacturing of new electrical and electronic equipment
Adopted	End of Life Vehicles (ELVs)	Directive	Requires that producers reduce the use of hazardous substances and increase the quantity of recycled materials in the manufacture of vehicles and (from 2007) pay the costs of free take-back of zero or negative value vehicles to authorised treatment facilities
Adopted	Water	Framework Directive	Requires that all inland and coastal waters reach 'good status' by 2015 by establishing a river basin district structure within which environmental objectives will be set, including ecological targets for surface waters

set of 80 sites by 2007. To date 47 sites have been designated by local authorities, but information on predicted numbers is still difficult to obtain. One leading expert on the subject whom we interviewed, predicted a growing number of appeals, rising to around 100 a year in ten year's time, mainly in respect of local authority notices.

6.4   For statutory nuisance appeals, there are no current comprehensive statistics available on a national basis. With the assistance of the Chartered Institute of Environmental Health, we have therefore surveyed all local authorities in England and Wales, and the response rate has been sufficient to form a general picture of overall numbers. Details of the survey are provided in Appendix B. There is clearly a variable picture across the country with some local authorities having no appeals, whilst others experience considerable numbers. From the returns we estimate that around 14,700 statutory nuisance notices are issued each year, with about 3,000 being served on trade and industry. There appear to be around 1,000 appeals made each year to magistrates' courts. Many of these are likely to involve domestic noise nuisances or housing repairs, but we estimate that around 135 are made by trade and industry.

6.5   Compared to land-use planning appeals (running at around 14,000 per year) the total number of environmental regulatory appeals currently being made is therefore not large. Such a workload is clearly much less than that undertaken by the first tier tribunals such as the Appeals Service or the Immigration Appellate Authorities, but is comparable to some of the smaller, specialised tribunals. The Lands Tribunal, for example, which acts both as a first tier and appellate body, disposes of around 600 cases a year. Assuming at least the inclusion of the environmental appeals currently handled by the Planning Inspectorate, contaminated land remediation notice appeals and those statutory nuisance abatement notice appeals involving trade and industry, we estimate that under current legislation an Environmental Tribunal system could be handling a comparable figure to the Lands Tribunal, at around 500 appeals a year. This does not take into account future legislative requirements or the possible incorporation of some form of third party right of appeal. These numbers do not undermine the case for an Environmental Tribunal, but instead can be seen as a positive advantage when considering the costs and benefits of establishing a new discrete Tribunal. We would also note that:

- small numbers of appeals may indicate unease with or under-use of current procedures; for example, we were informed by one expert on the new contaminated land procedures that there was likely to be a reluctance amongst local authorities to make full use of the remediation notice powers because of unease with the capacity of local magistrates to handle such appeals.
- there remain significant 'gaps' under present environmental legislation where there are no rights of regulatory appeal other than by way of judicial review. We discuss the pressures on judicial review in section 9 below, and the extent to which this has become a surrogate means of merits appeal.
- the need for an effective and efficient appeal procedure is likely to increase as environmental requirements assume more public significance.
- those regulatory appeals which do take place are very often technically complex and therefore more time consuming.
- there is also a clear advantage in anticipating the future climate of environmental law resulting from European and international requirements. This is particularly significant in the context of the implementation of the Aarhus Convention which introduces the concept of 'equitable, timely, and not prohibitively expensive' appeal procedures for members of the public and environmental organisations in respect to specified licensing procedures (as discussed further in section 10 below). Scale as well as substance is also

significant. For example, IPPC licensing requirements are being extended to around 1,600 pig and poultry operations; new permitting will be required for around 2,500 sites as a result of the End of Life Vehicles Directive; and the extension of waste legislation to cover agricultural waste is likely to require around 8,500 new licences, together with waste exemptions extending to 170,000 farms.[12]

6.6   A concern with previous proposals for combined planning and environmental courts or tribunals was that the major institutional upheaval involved would outweigh the advantages that might flow from the proposals. The more focused model of an Environmental Tribunal system being considered here would require the transfer of appeal functions from the existing bodies identified above, but given the numbers involved, this should not cause significant disruption to those institutions. The size and costs involved are likely to be comparable to those for the Lands Tribunal. We consider in more detail, in section 15 below, a possible model and the likely costs involved. Even though there will be cost savings from reducing the pressure on existing appeal bodies, establishing a new Tribunal system is unlikely to be wholly cost neutral. However, it is clear from the existing numbers of appeals that we are talking of a manageable institution and one that can develop focus and coherence in a key area of public policy. It would also provide greater confidence in anticipating future environmental regulatory requirements. The policy gains from such a discrete initiative may be hard to quantify but could be very large.

7.   Concerns about Existing Appeal Procedures

7.1   Within the project time-scale, research on the quality of existing procedures has been necessarily limited, and largely confined to interviews with a number of senior members of the judiciary, experienced environmental law practitioners representing users of the system, and policy makers and officers in regulatory bodies with experience of the current system. Our survey of local authorities also invited comments on the quality of the present arrangements. These reflections are therefore bound to be somewhat impressionistic, but valuable insights have nevertheless emerged.

7.2   There does appear to be concern at the ability of lay magistrates to handle highly technical issues such as the definition of 'Best Practicable Means' (BPM) in statutory nuisance appeals involving trade and industry. Again, in relation to statutory nuisances, there are worries that appeal procedures are often used by trade and industry as a delaying tactic, and that appeals take too long to come to court (nine months was quoted as a typical figure). Appeals appear to be given a lower priority by court administrators by being reserved for infrequent 'local authority' days. A senior environmental health officer also commented that, 'cases take a long time because appeals are treated no differently by the courts to prosecutions.' Many environmental health officers do appear to favour the improved decision making which an Environmental Tribunal might bring, but would not wish to see the loss of local knowledge in such decision making. There is clearly a tension in environmental adjudication between the need for local fact finding and the need for expertise in

---

[12] Environment Agency, personal communication.

handling technical issues. It may be possible to distinguish between more technically complex issues (such as BPM) and more straightforward environmental issues (such as neighbourhood noise nuisance) when considering whether there would be benefit in transferring jurisdiction for statutory nuisances appeals to a specialised tribunal.

7.3   Our interviews have also indicated a real concern as to whether current arrangements will deliver an effective appeals system in respect of remediation notices served under the contaminated land regime introduced by the Environment Act 1995. As detailed in Box 1, appeals for local authority sites will be made to local magistrates' courts, and current regulations specify 19 separate grounds of appeal, often involving highly complex issues of both a technical and economic nature. Appeals for the smaller number of 'special' sites identified by the Environment Agency are made to the Secretary of State and will be handled by the Planning Inspectorate. As mentioned above, this system was largely based on the model for statutory nuisance procedures, which justified the use of the magistrates' courts for appeals in respect of local authority sites, but as the writers of the leading guide to the legislation have noted: 'It must be questioned whether the magistrates' court is a suitable forum for resolving such appeals, and whether the civil procedures in the magistrates' court are adequate for the purpose. It also seems strange that there should be two entirely different modes and forms of appeal for ordinary remediation notices and for those relating to special sites.'[13] A key objective in introducing the new contaminated regime was to increase the consistency of approach taken by different authorities, and there is understandable concern that the current appeal routes will undermine that goal. As one of the leading experts in the area told us: 'Consistency in judgement is the key to transparency in the contaminated land regime.'

7.4   We should stress that our analysis of environmental appeals currently heard in Magistrates' Courts is not intended to detract from the integrity or commitment of individual magistrates, or to question their concern to ensure the effective application of environmental law. Rather, it raises questions as to whether it is the best use of their time and the qualities they can bring to the justice system, if they are required to handle the sorts of issues involved in these types of environmental appeals.

7.5   We have noted that in addition to the more familiar land-use planning appeals, the Planning Inspectorate now handle a range of environmental appeals on behalf of the Secretary of State. These are mainly concerned with pollution related licences dealt with by the Environmental Agency. The Planning Inspectorate will also be responsible for appeals under the contaminated land regime relating to 'special' sites. A leading barrister with experience of environmental appeals handled by the Planning Inspectorate commented favourably on their approach and expertise: 'The strengths of the Planning Inspectorate are individual technical expertise, good legal awareness, good procedures, and flexibility'. However, he noted that difficult points of law could be a problem, and that greater use of legal expertise within the Planning Inspectorate would be valuable if the current system were continued, but also appreciated the wider advantages of bringing environmental matters into one forum by way of rationalisation. At present, our understanding is that where necessary, the Planning Inspectorate seeks legal advice on environmental law issues

---

[13] Tromans and Turrall-Clarke, *Contaminated Land – The New Regime* (London, Sweet & Maxwell, 2000).

from the government. Another leading environmental solicitor noted that the Planning Inspectorate 'does seem to be a default appeal forum for environmental matters but it is not the right place as the Inspectors are not generally legally trained'. He also questioned whether the Planning Inspectorate was the right forum for environmental appeals because of the distinctive nature of the legal and technical issues often involved: 'Environmental regulation is different from planning control as the former often focuses on whether active harm is being caused.'

7.6   Officials from regulatory bodies who had experienced environmental appeals handled by the Planning Inspectorate were reasonably favourable about the procedures, though there was concern that Inspectors may have problems in understanding specialist areas of the law, for example IPPC/PPC or concepts such as 'Best Available Techniques'. As one noted: 'In an ideal world, I would like there to be a specialist appeal body, but one could also improve the panel of environmentally trained Inspectors'. There was also concern at the difficulty in accessing decision letters from the Planning Inspectorate: 'PINS is opaque or worse when it comes to accessing decision letters, though my experience of appeal hearings is relatively favourable.' Regret was also expressed that individual decisions of the Planning Inspectorate do not have sufficient gravitas to be used as general guidance in the application of regulation: 'Proper reporting of cases is needed and PINS decisions don't carry the proper weight.'

7.7   Even if within their individual jurisdictions, the current arrangements for appeals were considered satisfactory by existing users – and the comments we have received suggest some distinct unease in certain areas – this fails to meet what are probably the more important deficiencies. There are significant gaps in the system where no appeal routes lie other than by way of judicial review, and there is a need to ensure an adequate and coherent basis for appeal mechanisms under future environmental regulation. The Aarhus Convention will require a framework that is clear, transparent and consistent, and review mechanisms for citizens that are fair, equitable, timely, and not prohibitively expensive. The current haphazard structure is based on a piecemeal and old fashioned approach towards the application of legislation concerning the environment, and fails to reflect the need for greater expertise and consistency brought about by the special characteristics of environmental law which are now emerging. As one leading solicitor commented: 'Trade and industry want consistency of approach even if the decision-makers are therefore tougher on them.' We consider the nature of these special features of environmental law in the following section.

8.   Does Environmental Law Warrant a Special Jurisdiction?

8.1   We have identified a broad range of appeals which can be described as environmental, but to warrant the establishment of a single form of tribunal to handle most or all of them, we need to establish whether there are sufficiently special features of environmental law which would justify such an approach. We feel it is possible to identify a number of distinctive elements:

(a)   Evidential and judgmental issues involving complex technical/scientific questions, usually of a quite different sort to those found in planning/amenity type decisions. The nature of the science involved in many environmental and public health questions (such as pathways of exposure to pollutants, or effects of chemicals on human health) is often characterised by inherent uncertainties distinct from those found in disciplines such as engineering or surveying. As the RCEP pointed out in its 21st Report, Setting *Environmental Standards*: 'In a scientific assessment of an environmental issue there are bound to be limitations and uncertainties associated with the data at each stage.'[14]

(b)   A challenging legislative and policy base, which as demonstrated above, is rapidly developing.

(c)   The overlapping of remedies (civil and criminal) as well as interests (public and private). We have pointed out how the validity of licences and regulatory notices in environmental law are critically connected with the subsequent enforcement of environmental standards under criminal law. In relation to the interests involved, one environmental lawyer told us: 'Environmental law is qualitatively different from other areas of the law in terms of the values and interests that are engaged – many of which are not properly represented.'

(d)   A powerful and increasing body of EC legislation and a growing number of interpretative judgments of the European Court of Justice (notably in areas such as IPPC, waste management, water pollution, genetically modified organisms and habitats protection). The density of the European Community policy and legislative background in the environmental field is far greater than, say, in town and country planning (with the exception of environmental assessment requirements) or health and safety. Not all regulatory appeals in the environmental field will explicitly raise issues of EC law, but those charged with the responsibility of determining such appeals are likely to need to be fully familiar with this dimension and the underlying policy objectives of the legislation.

(e)   A substantial body of international environmental treaties and law covering issues such as trade in endangered species, pollution of marine waters, transnational shipments of hazardous waste and climate change. The intensity of this international dimension, which influences the content and interpretation of both EC and national environmental law, is again of a quite different scale to that found in planning or health and safety law.

(f)   The development of certain fundamental environmental principles such as the precautionary approach, polluter-pays, prevention at source, and procedural transparency. The extent to which these are yet binding legal principles and how they are to be put into practice is still being developed, but they have now entered the common language of environmental law and policy.

(g)   The emergence of principles concerning third party access to environmental justice, and the requirement under the Aarhus Convention for review procedures that are timely and not prohibitively expensive. These aspects are discussed further in section

---

[14] Royal Commission on Environmental Pollution, 21st Report 'Setting Environmental Standards', Cm 4053 (London, Stationery Office, 1998).

10 below, but are now a significant backdrop to thinking about structures that will meet future public expectations.

(h)   The emergence of the overarching principle of sustainable development which underpins contemporary policy approaches. This is not a straightforward concept and is subject to differing interpretations, but it is a policy dimension that increasingly requires appreciation by those handling environmental law disputes.

8.2   Technical and legal complexity is not in itself a compelling reason for a special jurisdiction, and can be found in other areas of the law. Some of the above features will be more apparent in certain applications of environmental law than others, and they may not be of equal significance in any particular decision. But it is the combination of all these factors which is of particular importance.

9.   Judicial Reviews and Stated Cases

9.1   One of the arguments made by the RCEP was that in the absence of a specialised tribunal, there was likely to be increased pressure on the judicial review system as a surrogate means of undertaking merits appeals, both by third parties and those directly affected. Conversely, the creation of a more specialised and comprehensive tribunal appeal system could reduce the pressure on the higher courts handling such judicial review cases.

9.2   To test this argument in more detail, we have examined the judicial review applications and stated cases heard by the High Court involving environmental legislation over the past 3 years. We excluded town and country planning cases, and in particular those involving environmental assessment. There is inevitably some difficulty in categorising cases, but the overall numbers were in the order of 60-70 environmental judicial review applications and 25 stated cases arising over the 3 year period. The number of judicial reviews in 2001 was slightly higher than 2002, but we believe this was caused by a 'spike' of cases concerning foot and mouth controls, and overall the trend does appear to be upwards. It can therefore be predicted that under current legislation an average of some 25-30 environmental judicial review applications per year will arise. Further details of these figures are provided in Appendix D.[15]

9.3.   We examined in detail some 55 case files from the last three years, and it is apparent that, despite the publicity given to a number of high profile cases brought by environmental groups, the current system is as much driven by companies and industry. The applicants were companies or industries in 28 cases, while in 22 cases the applicants were individuals and environmental or similar associations. For related reasons, only in a minority of cases was legal aid involved, with reference being made to the Legal Services Commission in the files for only four cases. The decision-makers being challenged included government departments in 27 cases and the Environment Agency in 16 cases. The average time for cases to reach a full hearing in court was six months from the date of lodgement to a final court order, and the average duration of the main hearing before court was 1.3 days. This does

---

[15] Not reproduced in this volume.

not take into account the time spent in pre-hearing procedures, nor judicial time spent in making decisions solely on written material and affidavits.

9.4   Only 4 out of the 55 environmental judicial reviews examined were successful. Otherwise 18 cases were dismissed, 13 withdrawn, and leave for judicial review refused in 12 cases. The remaining cases were still outstanding at the time of examination. This seems to be consistent with the views of the RCEP, as well as the judges and lawyers whom we interviewed, who indicated that judicial review applications in environmental cases frequently appear to be merits driven, with a tendency to build cases on the permitted but restrictive grounds for judicial review. Our own examination of the files suggested that around two thirds were essentially merits-driven i.e. seeking a substantial rehearing of the facts. It also appears clear from the figures that only a small minority of judicial reviews followed a previous merits appeal. In 36 out of the 55 files examined, there had been no previous appeal, mainly because there was no merits appeal route available (as will have been the case for most of the 22 actions brought by third parties), or in a small number of exceptional cases, where leave was granted despite the non-exercise of an appeal right.

9.5   The overall picture of current judicial reviews in the environmental field suggests that a considerable amount of judicial time in the High Court is being spent on handling applications which are largely merits-driven; the numbers of environmental judicial reviews are increasing steadily (though not dramatically); and that the users are as much regulated businesses as individuals and other third parties.

9.6   The picture is a little different for the stated cases from magistrates' courts, in relation to which we examined 22 case files from the past three years. Sixteen of these cases followed on a criminal prosecution, and the remaining six related to the service of notices. Companies brought half of the cases, with the other half brought by individuals or local authorities. Just over half the cases related to statutory nuisance provisions. The average length of time to complete the proceedings was around the same as for judicial review (five months), but the average length of the hearing in open court considerably less, at around two and a half hours. However, the 'success' rate was considerably higher with the applicant succeeding in half the cases. This may support the comments in section 7 regarding the suitability of magistrates' courts for handling more complicated environmental issues.

9.7   It is less straightforward to predict the extent to which improvements to the current regulatory appeals system might reduce the number of applications for judicial review. Unless third parties have some access to a merits appeal route, third party judicial reviews will continue, though these do not represent the majority of current environmental judicial review applications. On the other hand, should a first-tier appeal body in the form of an Environmental Tribunal have both specialised environmental legal and technical expertise, then the decisions it takes should be manifestly more legally and technically sound, thereby reducing the likelihood of applications for judicial review. In a case concerning a Social Security appeal,[16] the Court of Appeal noted that where a tribunal structure is sufficiently expert to be able to take an independent and robust view, the Court could afford to be circumspect in

---

[16] *Cooke v Secretary of State for Social Security* [2001] EWCA Civ 734.

entertaining further appeals. This case concerned statutory appeal rights rather that judicial review, but a similar approach is likely to be taken.

9.8   For similar reasons, if regulatory appeal rights to an Environmental Tribunal were provided where none exist at present other than by way of judicial review, this must also be predicted to reduce the pressure on the judicial system. There is the example of environmental information rights where the only current appeal route against the refusal by public bodies to disclose information is by way of judicial review. The proposal for the Information Commissioner/Tribunal to handle such disputes would fill a significant gap in the availability of an appropriate appeal mechanism. Furthermore, if an effective first-tier appeals structure were created, it would become more legitimate to build in stronger filter procedures whereby leave for judicial review against the decision of a regulating body would not be granted unless the right of appeal to the first-tier appeal body had already been exercised. This is consistent with the views of the Law Commission and the Leggatt Report,[17] and from the judicial review files we examined, it was rare for leave to be granted unless an available appeal right had previously been exercised.[18]

9.9   For stated cases from the Magistrates' Courts, the majority related to criminal matters, and unless this jurisdiction were changed, the current numbers are likely to continue. It could be suggested that provision be made in relation to these cases for obtaining advisory opinions from a specialist Environmental Tribunal, this being in effect what the High Court does at present in many cases. We could also expect that the decisions of a specialised Environmental Tribunal dealing with a novel policy point or a set of new environmental regulations, would contain sufficiently authoritative guidance and be sufficiently publicised to be of value to fora such as the Magistrates' Courts and the County Courts, so reducing the number of stated cases where the substantive meaning of the legislation is at issue.

9.10   One of the attractions of creating a specialised first-tier Environmental Tribunal is that it could now be integrated into the government's proposals for modernising the tribunal system following on the Leggatt Report. One of the recommendations of the Leggatt Report was for a unified tribunal appeal system, which would replace judicial review to the High Court as a route of appeal against tribunal decisions. Our understanding is that the government intends to create such a unified appellate body, possibly on a divisional basis. As noted in the Leggatt report, 'The aim of the new Appellate Division will be to develop by its general expertise and the selective identification of binding precedents, a coherent approach to the law. In this, although operating with greater procedural flexibility and informality than may be found in the High Court, as well as being considerably cheaper to approach, it will be comparable in authority to the High Court so far as tribunals are concerned.'[19]

9.11   The Leggatt report also recognised that it would be valuable if the proposed Appellate Division had first-tier jurisdiction in particularly complex cases, in much the same way that the Lands Tribunal has a mixture of first instance and

---

[17] Leggatt Report, above n 8, para 6.29.
[18] See *R on the Application of Great Yarmouth Port Company v Marine Management Organization* [2013] EWHC 3052 for a recent application of this principle, analysed in Chapter 22 (p 419) of this volume.
[19] Ibid, para 6.32.

appellate cases. We could see this model working well for environmental appeals. Where, for example, an appeal concerned the interpretation of provisions of new environmental regulations or the application of a novel or controversial policy, a rapid decision of the Appellate Division would be of value to all users of the system.

10. Access to Justice and the Aarhus Convention

10.1 The Aarhus Convention has been signed by the United Kingdom and is currently awaiting ratification by the European Community. It contains important principles concerning public participation and access to justice. The key provisions on access to justice are detailed in Box 3. In relation to rights of access to environmental information (which largely reflect the provisions of the existing EC Directive on the subject), the Convention guarantees that members of the public who claim to have been refused information by a public authority should have access both to court review procedures, and a free or inexpensive expeditious procedure for reconsideration of the matter by a public authority or review by an independent and impartial body other than a court of law. As we have noted in paragraph 5.3 above, under existing legislation concerning environmental information, review procedures have previously only been possible by judicial review, but if introduced, the proposals by the government to integrate environmental information appeals procedures into those provided under the Freedom of Information Act should now meet these concerns.

Box 3 The Aarhus Convention on Access to Information, Public Participation in Decision Making and Access to Justice in Environmental Matters

The Aarhus Convention was adopted on 25 June 1998 in the Danish city of Aarhus (Århus) by the UN Economic Commission for Europe, and entered into force on 30 October 2001 following its ratification by sufficient member state Parties.

Considered to be the most forward thinking international treaty on public participation yet completed, it places obligations on the member state Parties to ensure the availability in their national law of procedural rights for the public based on the three 'pillars' described in the Convention's title.

Key provisions of the Convention relating to access to justice are as follows:

Article 1 Objective

In order to contribute to the protection of the right of every person of present and future generations to live in an environment adequate to his or her health and well-being, each Party shall guarantee the rights of access to information, public participation in decision making, and access to justice in environmental matters in accordance with the provisions of this Convention.

Article 3 General Provisions

1.   Each Party shall take the necessary legislative, regulatory and other measures…
      to establish and maintain a clear, transparent and consistent framework to
      implement the provisions of this Convention.

Article 9 Access to Justice

1.   Each Party shall, within the framework of its national legislation, ensure that
      any person who considers that his or her request for information under Article
      4 [dealing with Access to Information] has been ignored, wrongly refused…
      or otherwise not dealt with in accordance with…that Article, has access to a
      review procedure before a court of law or other independent and impartial body
      established by law.

2.   Each Party shall, within the framework of its national legislation, ensure that
      members of the public concerned: (a) having a sufficient interest…have access
      to a review procedure before a court of law and/or another independent and
      impartial body established by law, to challenge the substantive and procedural
      legality of any decision, act or omission subject to the provisions of Article 6
      [dealing with Public Participation in Decisions on Specific Activities] and,
      where so provided for under national law…of other relevant provisions of the
      Convention.

3.   In addition…each Party shall ensure that, where they meet the criteria, if any,
      laid down in its national law, members of the public have access to administrative
      or judicial procedures to challenge acts and omissions by private persons and
      public authorities which contravene provisions of its national law relating to the
      environment.

4.   In addition…the procedures referred to in paras 1, 2 and 3 above shall provide
      adequate and effective remedies, including injunctive relief as appropriate, and be
      fair, equitable, timely and not prohibitively expensive.

In order for the European Community (and therefore the UK) to be able to ratify
the Convention, amending legislation has been and will be adopted to ensure the
consistency of the EC environmental regulatory framework with the provisions of
the Convention. The Government will also have to amend existing UK legislation in
various respects.

   A replacement Directive on public access to information has been adopted and a
new Directive has been proposed on public participation in respect of the drawing up
of certain plans and programmes. A consultation process has also been commenced by
the European Commission for a Directive on access to justice.

10.2   The Aarhus Convention also guarantees the right of public participation in a range
       of consent procedures for projects specified in the Convention, which largely follow
       those currently the subject of mandatory environmental assessment under EC
       legislation. Article 9 of the Convention also requires that members of the public 'with
       sufficient interest' should have access to a review procedure before a court of law or
       other independent body 'to challenge the substantive and procedural legality' of the

consent related decisions covered by the Convention. What constitutes sufficient interest is to be determined with the objective of giving the public concerned wide access to justice. Non-governmental organisations promoting environmental protection and meeting any requirements under national law are deemed to have such an interest.

10.3   The grounds for such rights of appeal are confined to 'the substantive and procedural legality' of the decision in question, and the drafting is clearly rather narrower than the full review procedure required under the Convention for environmental information. The present view of the government is that this phrase is consistent with the grounds for review currently provided in this country by judicial review. There are, though, other views that while the Aarhus Convention may not provide third parties with a full merits appeal, the phrase 'substantive and procedural illegality' implies a rather more intense scrutiny than that traditionally provided for by judicial review. Whatever the answer on this point, the Convention also provides that the review procedures provided must be 'fair, equitable, timely, and not prohibitively expensive', and there have to be concerns whether existing judicial review procedures can meet all these criteria. One experienced environmental lawyer told us that the potential costs of judicial review and the risk of uncapped adverse cost orders appeared to prevent many cases being commenced. Under the Convention, governments must also provide public information on access to administrative and review procedures, and consider appropriate assistance mechanisms to remove or reduce financial and other barriers to access to justice. The European Community is itself a party to the Convention and a proposed Directive on access to justice will implement the Convention with respect to areas covered by EC environmental legislation. The draft Directive would require such review procedures to be 'expeditious' and 'not prohibitively expensive'.

10.4   The longer-term significance of the Aarhus Convention is that it explicitly introduces new concepts of access to justice in environmental decision making, and the need for inexpensive review procedures to be made available to members of the public and environmental organisations. As one environmental lawyer suggested to us, the Convention is based on establishing a system 'rooted in broad and deep citizen participation and access to justice'. As such it is quite different from the more familiar regulatory appeal models which have been largely developed to provide protection to the interests of applicants or those directly subject to regulation. Governments are required to publicise the legal remedies that are available, and without any change to current structures, existing pressures on judicial review procedures are therefore only likely to grow. There may also be benefit in making regulatory changes in order to enhance compliance with the spirit of Aarhus rather than allow the United Kingdom to rest on what was characterised to us as 'the lowest common denominator interpretation' of the strict letter of the Convention.

10.5   In the past, members of the public or environmental organisations unable to afford the costs involved in legal challenges have often made use of the complaint procedure to the European Commission when possible breaches of EC law are raised. This quasi-administrative procedure can lead to investigations by the Commission, and possible enforcement action by the Commission before the European Court of Justice. There is a heavy administrative burden involved and a backlog of cases, especially where the non-application of Community law is raised (rather than claims that formal transposition into national law is defective). The Commission may in future require that all national legal remedies are exhausted before considering such a complaint, this being more in line with the practice of the European Commission on Human Rights, and arguably consistent with the principle of subsidiarity. The number of environmental complaints received by the Commission varies tremendously from Member State to Member State, though the United Kingdom has consistently produced some of the highest numbers. The comparative figures probably reveal less about the extent of compliance than they do about the accessibility of national dispute mechanisms and the strength of non-governmental organisations.[20] But any introduction of a principle of exhaustion of national remedies within Commission procedures, suggests that there be will be even greater pressure on existing national procedures (especially those of judicial review), and therefore strengthens the case for developing new approaches. Against this background, we consider in the next section, whether there is case for introducing some form of third party right of appeal within the current environmental regulatory system.

11.   Third Party Rights of Appeal

11.1   The RCEP considered that there was a strong case for a specialised environmental tribunal system, whatever the position on third party rights of appeal. Nonetheless, it went on to recommend that in the interests of public confidence, the concept of third party rights of appeal should be introduced in both planning and environmental decision making. The government has to date rejected the implementation of third party rights of appeal within the land-use planning system, and it is not the purpose of the study to revisit this particular issue.

11.2   However, the question of third party appeals in the context of environmental rather than planning regulation has received rather less examination. Whatever the position in town and country planning legislation, there are a number of distinctive special features in the environmental field which suggest that the issue should be addressed seriously:

• A key argument of the government in rejecting third party rights of appeal in planning matters is that the public have the opportunity to participate in the land-use plan-making process, and that community based involvement should be revitalised and encouraged in that arena. In relation to the sort of environmental decision making to which third party rights of appeal might be applied (such as GMO or IPPC licensing) there is generally no equivalent and developed plan-making context involving the public. The selective introduction of such third party rights into environmental decision making would therefore not undermine the government's preferred approach to land-use planning.
• A second important argument against the introduction of third party rights of appeal within the planning system is that the majority of decisions are made by elected local

---

[20] Macrory and Purdy 'The Enforcement of EC environmental law against Member States' in Holder (ed), *The Impact of EC Environmental Law in the United Kingdom* (Chichester, Wiley, 1997).

authority members who are directly accountable to the local electorate. But in contrast to land-use planning, many of the key decisions in contemporary environmental regulation are made by the specialist agencies of government, such as the Environment Agency or English Nature. In relation to decisions made by such bodies, the arguments concerning the direct local political accountability of the decision-maker are less compelling.

• As noted in section 10 above, in relation to permitting decisions for a large number of specified projects, the Aarhus Convention and the EC implementing legislation will require review procedures for members of the public and non-governmental bodies that are fair, equitable, timely, and not prohibitively expensive. As we will discuss below, the Convention may provide a workable basis for a 'filtered' appeals system.

11.3   These factors suggest that the question of third party rights of appeal should be seriously addressed in the context of environmental regulation and a possible Environment Tribunal system. As one senior environmental lawyer commented to us: 'The Rubicon has been crossed in relation to third party rights of appeal but standing still needs to be addressed.'

11.4   The RCEP acknowledged that, even with the use of strict time-limits for making appeals, the introduction of third party rights of appeal could increase the time and cost of procedures, but concluded this was a price worth paying for improved public confidence and ensuring that environmental considerations are given their proper weight. We would also expect that a specialist Environmental Tribunal would have the ability to act speedily and effectively to handle such appeals, including the use of flexible procedures and mediation techniques where appropriate.

11.5   The RCEP also recognised that the introduction of wholly unrestricted merits based rights of third party appeal was unlikely to be practicable, and that filtering mechanisms should be developed. In relation to town and country planning, the government considered these would be difficult to devise with any precision, but for environmental regulation, the provisions of the Aarhus Convention may now provide an effective basis. Third party appeals could be restricted to members of the public and non-governmental organisations as defined in the Convention; confined to licensing procedures relating to projects defined in the Convention; and made only on grounds of substantive or procedural illegality as prescribed in the Convention. These grounds, as we noted in section 10 above, may require rather closer scrutiny than those traditionally applied in judicial review, but certainly should not raise the spectre of a full merits review by third parties across the board.

12.   The Human Rights Act And Access to an Independent Tribunal

12.1   Following the entry into force of the Human Rights Act 1998, many commentators considered that the introduction of a more comprehensive system of independent tribunals deciding merits appeals would be a legal precondition for both planning and environmental regulation in order to satisfy the requirements of Article 6 of the European Convention on Human Rights. This requires that that in the determination of civil rights, 'everyone is entitled to a fair and public hearing within a reasonable time by an independent and impartial tribunal established by law.'

12.2 There has now been a fair amount of case law, both nationally and before the European Court of Human Rights, testing the application of Article 6 in the context of the type of regulatory procedures considered in this report. See for example *R (Alconbury Developments Ltd) v Secretary of State for the Environment, Transport and the Regions* [2001] 2 WLR 1389 (on the role of the Secretary of State in planning decisions);[21] *R (Aggregate Industries UK Ltd) v English Nature* [2002] EWHC 908 (regarding the designation of Sites of Special Scientific Interest by English Nature); *R v Rhondda Cynon Taff CBC* [2002] Env LR 15 and *Bryan v United Kingdom* [1995] 21 EHRR 342 (considering the function of Planning Inspectors and judicial review).

12.3 The generous interpretation of what is meant by 'civil rights' developed by the European Court of Human Rights (and now adopted by the British courts) implies that in most of the areas of environmental regulation considered in this report, civil rights (within the meaning of the Convention) will be engaged in respect of applicants for licences or permits, or those served with enforcement notices or similar requirements. Rather less clear as yet, is the extent to which third parties indirectly affected by such decisions can be said to have their civil rights determined by such decisions.

12.4 The legislative analysis in Appendix A indicates that in certain areas of environmental law, full rights of merits appeal against a decision of a governmental body are available to what is clearly an independent court such as a magistrates' court. It is also clear from the case law that an appellate body such as the Planning Inspectorate or the Secretary of State does not in itself represent the independent court or tribunal required by Article 6. However, the courts have established that, even where any appeal to a court is restricted to legal grounds or judicial review, this can still be sufficient to satisfy Article 6 by looking at the procedures as a whole (the composite approach) and by considering the nature of the decision at hand. Essentially, the more that an administrative decision involves the exercise of discretion against a policy background, the less it is necessary that appellate procedures before a court or tribunal are required to stray beyond judicial review grounds to incorporate a full merits review. As Lord Hoffmann noted recently in *Begum v London Borough of Tower Hamlets* [2003] UKHL 5: 'The question is whether, consistently with the rule of law and constitutional propriety, the relevant decision making powers may be entrusted to administrators.'

12.5 We cannot be sure that all of the existing environmental appeal routes outlined in Appendix A satisfy Article 6 requirements, and certainly the establishment of an Environmental Tribunal handling merits appeals would guarantee a better degree of certainty of compliance. But it does now seem reasonably clear from the case law that in many areas, a fully independent review tribunal is not absolutely essential to ensure compliance with Article 6. The need to introduce an Environmental Tribunal has therefore to be justified by reasons other than securing compliance with the European Convention.

12.6 We should note, however, that the approach being taken in the current case law, which essentially preserves the remedy of judicial review, may put greater pressures

---

[21] Analysed in Chapter 20 (p 395) of this volume.

on those procedures. Some of the recent human rights case law hints that where judicial review is the only independent appellate remedy, courts may be justified in exercising a rather more intense scrutiny than has traditionally been the approach in judicial review. Our study of recent environmental judicial review cases indicates the extent to which the process is already being driven by the desire to achieve merits reviews. In this context, an Environmental Tribunal may provide a more appropriate forum for handling such issues.

13.   Separating Land Use Planning and Environmental Appeals?

13.1   The model of the environmental tribunals proposed by the RCEP envisaged that (initially at any rate) the proposed tribunals should handle only environmental regulatory appeals, whilst town and country planning appeals would remain within the well-established jurisdiction of the Planning Inspectorate. On the surface this appears to run counter to much of the thrust of the RCEP critique, which was about ensuring a greater connection between land-use and environmental planning. However, the main concerns in this respect were addressed more at the strategic planning level than the handling of individual permissions and licences.

13.2   At present, a number of appeal procedures mainly in the field of pollution control (IPCC, water discharge consents, etc.) are in practice handled by the Planning Inspectorate, and transferring that jurisdiction to a separate Environmental Tribunal might inhibit a closer integration of land-use planning and environment regulation. For some years, there have been calls for the 'twin tracking' of planning application and environmental licence procedures, but in practice this has proved very difficult to achieve. The political accountability and the application of political policy in decision making inherent in the planning system is also seen by some as a positive factor which might be lost in a more independent tribunal structure. We also recognise that, especially since the introduction of environmental assessment procedures within the town and country planning system, environmental factors are now an integral element of many land-use planning decisions.

13.3   Based on this recognition of the close connection between land-use planning and environmental protection, a combined planning and environmental tribunal (one of the models in the original Grant report) may still be an attractive option. Alternatively, more environmental appeals could be transferred to the Planning Inspectorate (as has happened with IPPC and other pollution related consents) in effect transforming the body into a Planning and Environmental Inspectorate. But there remain compelling arguments in favour of a specialist Environmental Tribunal dealing solely with the type of environmental appeals identified in Appendix A:

• As indicated in section 5 above, there are a number of distinctive features in environmental law, the combination of which calls for special treatment; these features are not so apparent in land-use planning.

• Although the Planning Inspectorate at present handles a number of environmental appeals, the total number and range of environmental regulatory appeals that currently exist and are likely to arise under environmental legislation in the future will be much greater; a full-scale transfer of jurisdiction to the Planning Inspectorate would therefore require the development of additional legal and new types of specialist technical expertise. Given other current pressures on the Planning Inspectorate and its focus on land development issues, the extension of their jurisdiction to cover all such appeals may not be attractive.

- Whilst the Planning Inspectorate may handle discrete environmental appeals effectively at present, it is less suited than a specialised tribunal to provide authoritative decisions which can serve as guidance on the meaning and application of regulatory requirements. A specialised tribunal could assist the development of environmental law and policy in a way that is beneficial to both business and public interests.

- As the RCEP report indicated, the most significant challenge for securing improved integration in land-use planning and environmental policy lies not in the area of individual planning or regulatory decisions but in the area of strategic plan and policy making which provides the context for discrete decisions.

- Environmental considerations are so pervasive that drawing a line for jurisdictional purposes is never perfect, but for practical purposes the core land-use planning remit of the Planning Inspectorate does provide a useful and practical line of demarcation.

- The major administrative upheaval which would be involved in setting up a new Planning and Environmental Tribunal might simply outweigh any policy advantages to be gained; conversely, we have identified a number of real gains which could be achieved by establishing a dedicated Environmental Tribunal system operating within the proposed new Tribunals Service.

14. Options for the Way Forward

14.1 Our research has identified the complex and haphazard array of appeal routes that exist in contemporary environmental legislation; particular problem areas; and the possible advantages to be gained from a more coherent approach. Based on our research and findings, there appear to be a number of key options:

14.2 Carry on with the current system: undertaking no change at all would not meet some of the specific problems with current arrangements identified in this report. Pressures on judicial review as a default appeal route will continue. As a senior judge noted to us: 'Unless something is done now the pressures will manifest themselves through third party claims especially in the High Court'. Magistrates' Courts will have to contend with the complex contaminated land regime. The Planning Inspectorate will have to accommodate an increasingly complicated environmental jurisdiction driven by new legislation at the EC and international levels. Difficulties will be faced in adapting to new requirements for access to environmental justice, leading to increased public discontent with the system.

14.3 Incrementally adapt and improve existing structures: improvements could certainly be made to the current arrangements to meet some of the problems identified in our research. We can identify a number of steps that might be appropriate, though this is by no means a complete list:

- The Planning Inspectorate could ensure the availability of greater legal and specialist technical expertise for handling its existing environmental appeals.

- The Planning Inspectorate could do more to ensure that key environmental appeal decisions are readily accessible and given wider publicity.
- Existing 'gaps' in the range of appeal mechanisms could be filled, so reducing the dependence on judicial review as a 'surrogate' means of appeal.
- Contaminated land appeals could be transferred from the Magistrates' Courts and the Planning Inspectorate to the Lands Tribunal, which might be considered a more appropriate body to develop the particular expertise necessary to handle these issues.
- The greater use of District Judges in Magistrates' Courts for handling the more complex statutory nuisance appeals could be formalised; where there is no District Judge in an area, clerks to the justices could be encouraged to apply for one.
- Further specialised training and advice for magistrates in the application of environmental law could be provided, perhaps along the lines of the 'Costing the Earth' toolkit recently produced by the Magistrates' Association and the Environmental Law Foundation to assist sentencing practice in environmental cases.
- Ways of reducing the costs involved in judicial review procedures could be considered.

14.4   Nevertheless, there remain drawbacks to this incremental approach. Whilst it might improve arrangements for existing appeals, it fails to provide a secure basis to properly meet future demands. This more limited and ad hoc approach would sacrifice the opportunity to develop more coherent approaches towards the interpretation and application of environmental law and policy in what is a rapidly developing field. As new environmental requirements were implemented, decisions would still be needed each time as to the most appropriate forum for handling new appeals, by choosing from the existing array of bodies. The development of new and more flexible procedures for handling access to justice issues would also be more difficult to achieve within existing structures.

14.5   Establish a specialised Environmental Tribunal within the proposed unified Tribunals System: as the Leggatt report has noted, tribunals combining both legal and specialist expertise and an understanding of underlying policy issues, can be particularly effective in dealing with the mixture of fact and law which is often required to review decisions taken by administrative or regulatory authorities.

14.6   Although the RCEP envisaged a system of part-time tribunals operating on a regional basis, our research indicates that in order to meet the current levels of environmental appeals being made, it would be more feasible to establish a single Environmental Tribunal, operating in a similar way to the Lands Tribunal. The Lands Tribunal has a single President, three expert members and a legally qualified member, and disposes of nearly 600 cases a year, this being equivalent in number to the environmental regulatory appeals currently being made. Although based in London, the Lands Tribunal sits outside London where this is more convenient to the parties, and we understand that in practice almost half its cases are heard in this way, normally sitting in local courts.[22] We would expect a single Environmental Tribunal to have a similar flexibility of approach, hearing cases out of London where appropriate. Interlocutory matters or appeals raising more straightforward technical issues might be dealt with by the non-lawyer specialist members, leaving appeals raising more complex legal issues or new regulatory requirements to be heard by

---

[22] Lands Tribunal, personal communication.

the full Tribunal. Again this is in line with the practice of the Lands Tribunal, where we understand about half of the cases are handled in this way.[23] Operating within the proposed new unified Tribunal Service, appeals from such an Environmental Tribunal would be made to the Tribunals Appellate Division rather than by way of judicial review.

14.7 Unlike the Lands Tribunal, though, an Environmental Tribunal would not need to be a court of record with a status equivalent to the High Court. It would not handle private party disputes, nor would we envisage it handling appeals from other tribunals or judicial bodies.

14.8 Through its incorporation within the government's proposed unified Tribunal Service, the new Environmental Tribunal would benefit from being associated with the general modernisation programme now under way. We would expect the Tribunal to develop procedures that are fair, economic, proportionate and speedy, and to make the fullest use of modern case management systems and information technology. The use of alternative dispute resolution procedures, including mediation and arbitration, would be encouraged and adopted within its procedures where appropriate.

14.9 This new way of handling environmental appeals would also benefit from being grounded in the government's key objectives for delivering an improved tribunal system:

- To provide the user with a focused modern service in line with the government's agenda for the reform of public services.
- To ensure better information for and support to users.
- To encourage common standards of service and deliver all the efficiencies and economies to be gained from bringing services together.
- To allow the findings of tribunals to be a positive voice in the reviewing and shaping of policy and standards of administrative decision making.

15.   A New Environmental Tribunal in Practice

15.1 If the model of a single Environmental Tribunal were adopted, its precise jurisdiction must ultimately be a matter for the government. The core initial jurisdiction could involve the transfer of appeal functions from existing bodies covering the majority of regulatory environmental appeals currently being made, and might consist of:

- Appeals relating to decisions of specialised environmental agencies, such as the Environment Agency and English Nature.
- Appeals in respect of industrial processes regulated by local authorities.
- Appeals in respect of the contaminated land regime.
- Appeals in respect of statutory nuisance abatement notices involving trade and industry.

15.2 We see attractions in appeals relating to abatement notices served in respect of domestic premises (such as noise nuisances) remaining with local Magistrates' Courts, but perhaps with the greater use of District Judges where appeals raise difficult technical or evidential issues. Current legislation provides for special

---

[23] Ibid.

grounds of appeal in respect of notices served on trade and industry and includes the use of 'Best Practicable Means', a concept involving expert technical judgment. We feel that statutory nuisance appeals involving trade and industry would be a sensible part of the jurisdiction for the Environmental Tribunal. Criminal offences for non-compliance with such notices would remain with the magistrates' courts. We note that the current legislation also provides trade and industry with a special defence of 'Best Practicable Means' to such criminal prosecution. Given that an appeal on these grounds can already be made against a notice, we feel that the opportunity should be taken to remove what appears to be anomalous duplication. Magistrates dealing with non-compliance with a valid notice would then able to focus on the determination of fact.

15.3   As the Environmental Tribunal developed experience and reputation, the opportunity could then be taken to transfer further existing appeals in order to clear up anomalies under existing legislation, and reduce the pressure on judicial review. The Tribunal would also provide the natural forum for appeals arising under future environmental legislation. Examples include proposed EC legislation concerning environmental liability and emissions trading. Where there is discretion as to whether to establish appeal mechanisms for such new legislation, the principles contained in the Leggatt Report are valuable: 'Where any legislation establishes a statutory scheme involving decisions by an arm of government, the responsible minister should explicitly consider whether a right of appeal is required, on the basis that there should be strong specific arguments if an appeal route is not to be created, and that a tribunal route, rather than redress to the courts, should be the normal option in the interests of accessibility.'[24]

15.4   Our model for the Environmental Tribunal envisages that the Planning Inspectorate would continue to handle appeals under planning legislation, and we recognise that there would need to be close liaison between the two institutions. Under current procedures, a considerable number of planning judicial reviews are concerned with the interpretation and application of environmental assessment requirements in relation to development projects, a subject underpinned by the EC legislation and case-law. The opportunity could be taken to transfer jurisdiction relating to the legal challenges concerning environmental assessment to the new Environmental Tribunal.

15.5   Environmental appeals often raise both legal and policy issues, and as with many other existing tribunals, we would expect the Environmental Tribunal to be fully conversant with relevant policy dimensions and to apply them in their decisions. We would hope that the government would have sufficient confidence in the Tribunal to allow it to determine the vast majority of individual appeals, including those of a controversial nature. Nevertheless, there may be cases of such significance that the government would wish to retain the right of final decision along the lines of recovered jurisdiction in planning appeals. We see it as perfectly feasible that such a mechanism could be applied to the Environmental Tribunal, provided suitable guidelines were issued and cases kept to a minimum. In such cases, the Environmental

---

[24] Leggatt Report, above n 8, para 1.13.

Tribunal would in effect be making a recommendation to the government rather than exercising the final decision.

15.6   We also recognise that the operation of an Environmental Tribunal may encourage the government to publish more developed statements on environmental policy objectives, to provide a more explicit policy context for the decision making role of the Tribunal, as has happened in the town and country planning field. We feel this would be a positive development, and is in line with recommendations of the RCEP in its 23rd Report on this subject. We would also anticipate that the Environmental Tribunal would be allowed to make direct references to the European Court of Justice under Art 234 (formerly Art 177) in appropriate cases.

15.7   We have argued that serious attention should be paid to the question of introducing some form of third party right in relation to environmental appeals, both as a matter of principle, and in order to be more consistent with the concept of environmental citizenship and access to justice implied by the Aarhus Convention. Such appeals would fall within the jurisdiction of the Environment Tribunal. But we would emphasise that there is a good case for such a Tribunal even within the confines of current procedures, and we would be reluctant to see any initiative become stalled or delayed because of the issue of third party rights. In any event, we would expect the Tribunal to adopt sufficiently flexible rules of procedure and approach to incorporate the views of third parties where appropriate.

15.8   Appendix E[25] provides more details of the possible costs and benefits involved in establishing such an Environment Tribunal. As to the direct costs of establishment, based on the initial lines we have suggested, the costs of the Lands Tribunal are calculated in the background papers to the Leggatt Report at £1.25 M a year, and this provides a useful benchmark given that we are thinking of a comparable case-load and size. If the Environment Tribunal's jurisdiction were extended with the introduction of appeals under new environmental legislation, the costs would be likely to be neutral since they would otherwise have to be borne by other appeal bodies.

15.9   We have listed in Appendix E some of the direct cost-savings that are likely to result, though we leave it to others to quantify these in detailed financial terms if that is possible or indeed necessary. In respect of governmental costs, these include, for example, a reduction of the current work-load of the Planning Inspectorate and Magistrates' Courts; reduced pressure on High Court and Court of Appeal time in handling judicial reviews; and the freeing up of governmental time currently taken up in advising the Planning Inspectorate on environmental law and policy issues. We would also expect that the coherence and authority the Tribunal would bring to the current system would be of direct benefit to the regulatory bodies concerned with the implementation and enforcement of environmental law. As we have indicated, the overall public policy gains from this proposal, in terms of increased public confidence and improved environmental outcomes, are likely to be considerable, though difficult to quantify in straightforward financial terms.

15.10 Two case-studies may give a better idea of how the Tribunal might operate in practice:

[25] Not reproduced in this volume.

A Ltd operate a foundry works in an urban area. Following complaints of noise and dust pollution from local residents, the local authority serve a statutory nuisance notice under Part III of the Environmental Protection Act 1990. A Ltd appeal against the notice on the grounds that they are operating the 'Best Practicable Means' in respect of the noise and dust. The appeal is made to the Environmental Tribunal rather than the local magistrates' court. The Tribunal operates an up-to-date case management system, and the local authority request that because of a history of poor compliance, and a suspicion that this is a holding appeal to allow operations to continue, the matter is dealt with expeditiously. The case papers indicate that the issues are largely technical rather than legal, and the case is assigned to a specialist member of the Tribunal rather than the full Tribunal. The appeal is heard in the local area, and with the co-operation of the parties, informal procedures are adopted. The validity of the notice is upheld by the Tribunal. A Ltd later fail to comply with the notice, and the prosecution for non-compliance is heard before the local magistrates' court. The defence of 'Best Practicable Means' is no longer available, and the court is concerned only with the assessing the factual evidence of non-compliance.

B Ltd operate an industrial site requiring a licence from the Environment Agency under new Pollution Prevention and Control Regulations recently introduced under an EC amending Directive. B Ltd appeal against licence conditions imposed by the Agency, and the appeal is heard by the Environmental Tribunal (rather than the Planning Inspectorate as now). The case raises new legal and policy issues, and is one of the first of its kind under the new Regulations. The case is therefore heard in London before the full Tribunal. Because of the distinctive features of the case, the Tribunal permits an intervener representation by a non-governmental organisation with a track record of interest in the area. In making its decision in favour of the Agency, the Tribunal takes the opportunity of providing more general guidance on the interpretation and application of the regulations against the policy background. The analysis in the Tribunal's determination is sufficiently legally watertight and convincing to deter any judicial review application or appeal to the Appeals Division of the Tribunal Service. The decision of the Tribunal is immediately posted on the Tribunal's website, which is regularly accessed by the regulatory bodies, trade associations, non-governmental bodies and interested members of the public. As a result of the decision, a number of similar pending appeals by other industries are withdrawn.

15.11 The position in which the Environmental Tribunal might fit into the existing court structure is shown in Box 4.

16. A More Direct Enforcement Role for an Environmental Tribunal?

16.1 This report has largely been confined to considering the role of an Environmental Tribunal system in handling environmental regulatory appeals. On this model, the hearing of criminal environmental cases and the application of penalties to ensure compliance with environmental law would remain with the ordinary criminal courts. We are aware of current concerns over the effectiveness of current environmental enforcement regimes, and various initiatives have already been made to improve

Box 4 The Environmental Tribunal in Relation to the Current System

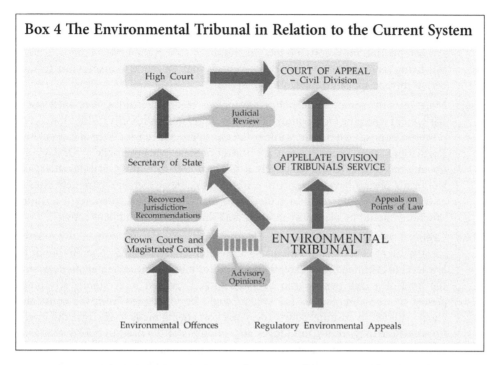

training and sentencing practice in the criminal courts. Specific research projects have recently been commissioned by Defra on enforcement and sentencing in the criminal courts in relation to environmental offences, and it would be inappropriate to anticipate their outcomes.

16.2   We need to recognise, however, that the model of an Environmental Tribunal handling regulatory appeals, though perhaps not as ambitious as earlier conceptions of a 'one-stop' specialist environmental court, is still likely to have a beneficial impact on ensuring the more effective application and enforcement of environmental regulation. Licences and enforcement notices of the type identified in this report form the core basis of contemporary environmental law. We would expect the specialist Environmental Tribunal to develop the capacity to issue authoritative interpretations and rulings on environmental law, especially where new, complex regulations are involved, and this will again assist the application of environmental regulation in the context of criminal law.

16.3   Nevertheless, there are arguments that were an Environmental Tribunal system established, its remit could be extended to include some form of enforcement function. It is beyond the scope of this research to explore this issue in detail, but we raise three areas for future consideration.

16.4   Administrative or civil penalties: There is growing interest in the possible value of the imposition of civil financial penalties as an additional enforcement tool to criminal prosecution. In this country civil penalties have not previously been used in the field of environmental law, and instead the traditional use of strict liability criminal offences as the final sanction prevails. In British law, the use of civil penalties is more familiar in areas of fiscal regulation such as competition and tax. For example under

Section 36 of the Competition Act 1998, the Director General of Competition may impose a penalty on an undertaking which has intentionally or negligently infringed key competition provisions, up to a maximum of 10% of the undertaking's turnover, this being recoverable as a civil debt. Appeals may be made to a specialist tribunal with a further appeal to the Court of Appeal.

16.5   More recently, some of the policy advantages of civil penalties were spelt out in Parliament when the Occupational Pensions Regulatory Authority (OPRA) was given power to impose civil penalties under the Occupational Pension Schemes (Penalties) Regulations 2000. According to the Minister of State (Mr Jeff Rooker): 'OPRA could operate more quickly and effectively if it had power to impose civil penalties, as it would not always have to resort to criminal penalties which are extremely onerous as they must be enforced under the Police and Criminal Evidence Act... Criminal sanctions should be used only in open-and-shut cases of fraudulent activity.'[26]

16.6   Criminal sanctions could remain for the most serious environmental cases, but greater use of civil penalties might be a method for unravelling concerns about the low level of criminal fines currently imposed for many environmental offences, since the level of a civil penalty can be more directly related to economic advantages gained by non-compliance. The system could be uncoupled from the constraints clearly still felt in criminal courts (despite efforts being made to increase the level of fines), where magistrates and judges are conscious of the need to ensure that levels of fines are not totally out of step with those imposed for other criminal offences. Magistrates and judges may also sense that punitive sanctions are less appropriate for strict liability offences where no intention or recklessness is involved.

16.7   Civil penalties are familiar as a modern enforcement tool for environmental law in other countries. In the United States, for example, most Federal environmental statutes authorise the Environmental Protection Agency to apply civil administrative penalties against industries that fail to comply with legal requirements, and these are assessed against published rules of practice. Appeals against such penalties can be made to the courts, while criminal offences are reserved for the most serious violators. In 1999, the US Environmental Protection Agency recovered $166.7 million in civil penalties, compared to $61.6 million in criminal fines. Germany has a developed system of administrative offences (*Ordnungswidrigkeiten*) where financial sanctions are considered distinct from criminal fines, and where appeals against such sanctions are made to administrative tribunals rather than criminal courts.[27] To take one example in the environmental field, the German Federal Emission Control Act dealing with industrial air emissions provides for an administrative offence leading to a fine for failure to comply with operator requirements under the Act, while criminal offences are provided under the Criminal Code for more serious failures which are likely to injure human health, animals, plants or other objects of value.

16.8   The question of the introduction of civil penalties in the context of environmental enforcement was beyond the precise terms of reference of this study, and we have therefore not considered, for example, whether it would be appropriate to confine

---

[26] House of Commons Standing Committee on Delegated Legislation, 8 March 2000.

[27] A Ogus and C Abbot, 'Sanctions for Pollution: Do We Have the Right Regime?' (2002) 14(3) *Journal of Environmental Law* 283.

their use to certain specialist authorities such as the Environment Agency. We recognise that in Europe, the requirements of the Human Rights Act on potential criminal liability may also need to be incorporated into their application, reducing some of the procedural flexibility. However, there do appear to be attractions in using civil penalties, and we hope that the government will consider the issue further. If the power to impose civil penalties was introduced, the Environmental Tribunal could play a central role in their development and consistent application. The standard model of a penalty system enables the enforcement agency to impose a penalty for non-compliance with regulatory requirements, and allows a right of appeal against the assessment. In other fields of law, where civil penalties are used, tribunals operate as the first-tier appellate body, and the Environmental Tribunal rather than a conventional criminal or civil court, would be the more appropriate body for hearing appeals against the imposition of such penalties.

16.9 Criminal enforcement: In addition to its powers to determine environmental appeals, the jurisdiction of the Environmental Tribunal could be extended to handling designated criminal environmental offences. The Tribunal might, for example, deal with environmental offences currently considered in magistrates' courts, leaving the Crown courts, as now, to handle the most serious cases. This is a more radical approach, and would require a more elaborate system than the single Tribunal we have proposed. Again it is an issue that was beyond the particular terms of reference of this report, but we considered it should at least be raised.

16.10 A combined civil and criminal jurisdiction would acknowledge that many of the distinctive characteristics of environmental law identified in this report are arguably also relevant to the application and interpretation of criminal environmental offences. The specialist Tribunal would bring a deeper appreciation of the environmental policy background and the significance of regulatory compliance than is often possible in ordinary criminal courts. It could also command greater confidence from those charged with enforcement responsibilities, as well as providing greater assurance to the majority of industries and individuals who comply with environmental requirements, that transgressors are being treated in an effective and consistent manner.

16.11 Some models of environmental court in other countries include a criminal jurisdiction. The New South Wales Land and Environment Court, for example, hears certain criminal cases, though this aspect of their work has not been without controversy. The drawback of including a criminal jurisdiction is that criminal law of necessity involves greater procedural formality, different evidential requirements and the incorporation of specific safeguards for the defendant. It is less clear whether the model of Environmental Tribunal, which we are recommending, could readily handle these distinctive requirements of the criminal process.

16.12 Other judicial enforcement powers: If a more direct enforcement role were considered appropriate for the Environmental Tribunal, it would be necessary to address the assignment of powers such as the award of injunctions, interlocutory relief, and other similar judicial remedies. In this context, the Aarhus Convention requires that procedures concerning the rights of appeal by the public and non-governmental organisations shall provide 'adequate and effective remedies, including injunctive relief as appropriate.' We also note that the Stop Now Orders (EC

Directive) Regulations 2001 have introduced new powers for enforcement bodies to apply to the courts for a 'Stop Now' orders to speed up action against businesses which breach a number of existing consumer protection laws. If such powers were extended to environmental regulation, the Environmental Tribunal might provide the most appropriate forum for handling them.

17. Conclusions

17.1   The current system of environmental appeals is haphazard and lacks coherence. It reflects an outmoded approach to environmental law, and is unlikely to provide a sound basis for handling future regulatory demands in a convincing manner. Existing structures could continue to be adapted as has been done in the past, but we see considerable benefits in establishing a new system based initially on a single Environmental Tribunal. The costs and administrative changes involved in setting up such a Tribunal to handle the majority of existing appeals would be modest compared to the policy gains to be made. Such a Tribunal would bring a greater consistency of approach to the application and interpretation of environmental law and policy. The improvements in authority and specialist knowledge would also foster increased confidence in those subject to environmental regulation, the regulatory authorities, and the general public. For these reasons, even without any direct enforcement functions, the Environmental Tribunal would substantially improve the application of environmental regulation.

17.2   Operating within the proposed Tribunals System, the Environmental Tribunal would have the flexibility to develop innovative and cost-effective approaches in the resolution of disputes, as well as greater inherent capacity to adapt to the developing principles on access to environmental justice. Incorporating rights of appeal for concerned members of the public or non-governmental organisations, based on grounds of substantive and procedural illegality as defined in the Aarhus Convention, would be consistent with the vision of the Convention, and provide a more cost-effective appeal route than judicial review procedures. Both in Europe and internationally, it would mark the United Kingdom as a leader in the design and practice of modern environmental governance.

17.3   The functions and jurisdiction of the Environmental Tribunal considered in this study are rather more modest than some of the earlier proposals for environmental courts or land use and environmental tribunals. We do not claim its introduction would resolve all the challenges involved in delivering effective and modern environmental regulation, but it does appear to offer an attractive and viable model which fits well with the current reform agenda for public services. The Environmental Tribunal would lead to the better application of current environmental law and policy, a more secure basis for addressing future challenges, increased public confidence in how we handle environmental regulation, and the improved environmental outcomes which should follow.

7

Consistency and Effectiveness – Strengthening the New Environmental Tribunal[1] (2011)

Summary

1. The report is concerned with regulatory appeals in England and Wales – the rights of individuals or business to challenge decisions made government departments or regulatory agencies by means of an appeal to another body. This is distinct from judicial review in the courts, which is concerned with the legality of decisions. Regulatory appeals allow someone to have their case reheard on the merits.

2. Regulatory appeals have long been a significant feature of our legal system. Decisions of government bodies and other regulatory agencies can affect the livelihood of individuals or businesses (eg by refusal a licence to do something) or impose significant direct financial costs (eg the service of a civil penalty or an enforcement notice requiring remedial action). It has been considered right and fair that in many cases the individual or company directly affected should be protected by having the right of appeal to another body who can decide the case afresh.

3. This review has examined the provision for environmental appeals which appear in over 60 pieces of current legislation relating to the environment, from water pollution to emissions trading. It has found that appeals go to a wide range of different bodies, including the High Court, Magistrates Courts, the Planning Inspectorate and different government departments. The system lacks common procedure and intelligibility. There is little in the way of underlying principle in choice of the appeal body.

4. In 2010 a specialised tribunal dealing with appeals concerning new environmental sanctions was established as part of the new First-tier Tribunal. Judges and expert members have now been appointed to the new Environment Tribunal, which has a great deal of flexibility in where it sits and how it conducts its procedures. More straightforward cases can be heard by a single member, while those raising complex legal and technical issues can be heard by a panel of three with a legal chair and two

---

[1] R Macrory, 'Consistency and Effectiveness – Strengthening the New Environment Tribunal' (Centre for Law and the Environment, UCL, 2011), reproduced in Chapter 6.

expert members. There is an emphasis on flexible and low-cost procedures where appropriate, and the encouragement of alternative dispute resolution.

5. The existence of the Environment Tribunal now provides an opportunity for consolidating environmental appeals across a wide range of existing laws. This is entirely in line with the current regulatory reform agenda, which promotes the simplification and modernisation of regulatory structures. It will allow the development of expertise in both law and technical issues needed to handle many contemporary environmental appeals in an effective way. The Tribunal operates under a set of procedural rules which will be clear and common to all involved, and sits within a structure that can be expected to command confidence among the regulated community and the public. Unlike many forms of appeal body, it has the capacity to provide wider guidance in its decisions, which can greatly assist both regulators and the regulated, and reduce the likelihood of future disputes and consequent costs involved.

6. The report does not advocate the transfer of all appeals under environmental legislation to the Tribunal: those with significant land-use connections remain best handled by the Planning Inspectorate. Statutory nuisance appeals should continue to be made to magistrates courts, but those courts should have the power to refer particularly complex appeals to the Tribunal.

7. A set of priorities for transfer to the Tribunal is identified, starting with appeals against environmental civil sanctions imposed by regulators. These are important new powers which avoid the unnecessary use of the criminal courts, but an effective appeals process is vital to prevent abuse. We are already seeing different appeals bodies being developed under different laws, and there is a real danger of losing the opportunity for a more coherent appeals process.

There also exist significant examples where the legislation provides no right of regulatory appeal, other than by judicial review. This is often the case where the primary decision-maker is a government department, but even here the picture is by no means consistent. Appeals or other forms of review are provided in some cases but not others, and there is little in the way of coherence in the current system. Evidence suggests that the absence of the right to a regulatory appeal leads to greater pressure of judicial reviews which are ill-suited for such cases. The report recommends a systematic review of current provisions where no appeal is provided to identify whether there are good grounds for continuing the present situation.

8. For new environmental legislation, the report recommends that, where such laws give powers to a government body or agency to affect someone's rights or impose obligations, there should be a presumption that there is a right of regulatory appeal to the Environment Tribunal.

9. Over the years we have developed a system of environmental appeals that is complex and confusing. There is now a unique opportunity to make the current structures more coherent, simple and effective.

The Context

1. In October 2010 I was asked by Lord Justice Carnwath, Senior President of Tribunals, to examine the current system of administrative appeals under environmental laws in England and Wales and to determine whether there was a case for making greater use of the new First-tier Tribunal (Environment) in handling them. This is my report to him.

2. In 2003 I conducted a similar exercise for the Department of Environment, Food and Rural Affairs. This was at a time of considerable discussion about the need for a new environmental court or tribunal in this country, but with a range of different views as to its form and jurisdiction. These extended from a 'one-stop-shop' court handling criminal, civil and regulatory issues arising from a single incident, such as a major pollution spill, to a new division of the High Court, to a more modest extension of appeals powers of the Planning Inspectorate. My research at that time focused on what could be broadly termed as regulatory appeals where legislation gives, say, an applicant for a licence or someone served with an enforcement notice the right to appeal the decision of the regulator to another body. Unlike judicial review, these appeals are normally unrestricted in that the appellant can have the merits of the decisions re-examined afresh by the body determining the appeal. In the remainder of this report I will use the term 'regulatory appeal' to describe this type of appeal and to distinguish it from judicial review.

3. My report *Modernising Environmental Justice*[2] examined over 50 pieces of environmental regulation, and found a complex array of appeal routes, including magistrates courts, county courts, the Planning Inspectorate (PINS), the Secretary of State and the High Court. In some cases there was no right of appeal other than by way of judicial review. It was difficult to determine any coherent principles that determined the choice of appeal route.

4. *Modernising Environmental Justice* recommended that a new environmental tribunal be established as a single body to handle regulatory appeals under most environmental legislation. It was hoped that this would lead to more consistent and effective decision making, and be an appropriate body to deal with future developments in environmental regulation, both at national and European Union level.

5. Although generally well received, the recommendations in the report were not implemented by the government. There were three particular challenges at the time. First, was it really the case that environmental law was so different from other areas of contemporary regulation, such as health and safety, that it warranted its own appeals body? The report argued that there were distinct characteristics of modern environmental law that marked it out for special treatment, but not everyone agreed with this.[3] Secondly, the report was arguing for a fairly modest though significant

---

[2] R Macrory with M Woods, *Modernising Environmental Justice: Regulation and the Role of an Environmental Tribunal* (Centre for Law and the Environment, Faculty of Laws University College London, 2003).

[3] Eg Environment and Rural Affairs Department, Scottish Government, 'Strengthening and Streamlining: The Way Forward for the Enforcement of Environmental Law in Scotland' (2006): 'We acknowledge the special characteristics listed by Macrory and Woods and accept that they are features of environmental law. However, we are not persuaded that these features, or indeed this combination of features is unique to environmental law and

reform of just one aspect of the environmental regulatory system. It expressly rejected the idea of a new division of the High Court or similar model on grounds of both principle and political pragmatism. But others in the environmental law world were not convinced that this proposal would deal with the costs and risks involved in environmental litigation generally (especially judicial review), and in another report, commissioned by Defra at the same time, the proposal of an environmental appeals tribunal was rejected as insufficiently ambitious.[4] Finally, the report was advocating the setting up of a wholly new tribunal that was likely to involve considerable establishment costs, and raised questions as to whether there would be a sufficient number of environmental appeals to justify the costs and upheaval involved in creating a new institutional body.

Changes since 2004

6.   The most significant change since the publication of *Modernising Environmental Justice* is that in 2010 a First-tier Tribunal (Environment) was established as part of the new Tribunal System. For the sake of succinctness, I will refer to this as the Environment Tribunal in the remainder of this report. It was set up because the Environment Agency and Natural England were the first regulators to acquire civil sanctioning powers under Part III of the Regulatory Enforcement and Sanctions Act 2008, which provides that appeals against the imposition of sanctions must in principle be made to the First-tier Tribunal. It means that two of the key arguments addressed in *Modernising Environmental Justice* are no longer relevant. It is not necessary to continue to argue that environmental law requires special treatment in institutional terms since the Environmental Tribunal now exists. Nor is it necessary to justify the costs of setting up a wholly new tribunal since this has already occurred.

7.   One of the major reasons why some of the environmental groups rejected the proposal of an environmental appeals tribunal in 2004 was that the proposal failed to address explicitly concerns at the costs of litigation, especially in judicial review. A new environmental division of the High Court was considered by many to be a preferred solution to these problems. But since 2004 there has been a great deal of movement on this issue, with the publication of the Sullivan Report on Access to Environmental Justice,[5] the Jackson Review on Civil Litigation,[6] the Sullivan follow-up report,[7] enforcement action by the European Commission against the

---

it could be argued that similar statements could be made equally about other areas of law such as health, health & safety and employment none of which have specialist courts/jurisdiction' (para 2.99).

[4] WWF, Environmental Law Foundation (ELF) and Leigh Day & Co, 'Environmental Justice Project: A Report' (Defra, 2004), 'We do not, however, believe that a tribunal of such limited scope as identified in the UCL Report is, in itself, sufficient to achieve access to environmental justice. Moreover, we are concerned that the establishment of a tribunal limited to regulatory appeals could fill the 'window of opportunity' to improve access to environmental justice at a time when more fundamental reform is clearly necessary' (Executive Summary, para 12).

[5] Report of the Working Group on Access to Environmental Justice, 'Ensuring Access to Environmental Justice in England and Wales' (2008) (the Sullivan Report).

[6] *Review of Civil Litigation Costs: Final Report* (2009) (the Jackson Report).

[7] 'Ensuring Access to Environmental Justice in England and Wales: Update Report' (2010).

United Kingdom for excessive costs with a Reasoned Opinion issued in 2010,[8] condemnation of the existing British system by the Aarhus Compliance Committee,[9] and judicial intervention, including a revisit of the existing limitation on Protective Costs Orders[10] and the more recent referral by the Supreme Court to the European Court of Justice on the meaning of requirement that costs must not 'not prohibitively expensive' as used in EU environmental legislation and reflecting obligations under Aarhus.[11] Given all these developments, I do not think that strengthening and extending the regulatory appeals jurisdiction of the new First-tier (Environment) Tribunal will now be seen as a diversionary threat to the challenge of dealing with costs issues in environmental litigation generally.

Review of Regulatory Appeals Provisions under Environmental Legislation

8.   This review has re-examined and updated the provisions for appeals under the environmental legislation first considered in *Modernising Environmental Justice*. It is never easy deciding a precise boundary between environmental and other related legislation, but, as with *Modernising Environmental Justice*, town and country planning legislation is excluded, as is food standards, health and safety, built heritage and hedgerow protection. One example of the powers to impose orders relating to agricultural diseases is included as representative of many other regulations in this area..

9.   Appendix 1 contains nearly 70 examples of regulatory appeals in the environmental field arranged under subject area. Appendix 2 arranges the information by appeal body. *Modernising Environmental Justice* noted the complexity of the appeals provisions with a range of different bodies involved, including PINS, magistrates courts, county courts and the High Court, and with little in the way of underlying principle guiding the choice. In some ways, the picture has become more complex since 2004 since, in addition to Defra, two government departments, the Department of Energy and Climate Change (DECC) and Department of Business Innovation and Skills (BIS), now take a lead on significant areas of environmental regulation such as greenhouse emissions trading and electrical waste. They have developed their own form of appeals arrangements. DECC, for example, has appointed a senior barrister as Emissions Trading Scheme Appeals Officer to hear appeals and made recommendations to the Secretary of State.[12] In 2009 two appeals under the Waste Electrical and Electronic Equipment Regulations 2006 were conducted by a senior BIS lawyer who made his decision on behalf of the Secretary of State. In addition to relating to the civil sanction powers of the Environment Agency and Natural

---

[8] European Commission press release, 'Environment: Commission Warns UK about Unfair Cost of Challenging Decisions', 18 March 2010.

[9] 'Findings and Recommendations of the Aarhus Compliance Committee with regard to Communication' ACCC/C/2008/33 (24 September 2010).

[10] *Garner v Elmbridge Borough Council* Court of Appeal (Civil Division) [2010] EWCA Civ 1006, 29 July 2010.

[11] *R (on the application of Edwards and another) v Environment Agency and others* [2010] UKSC 57, 15 December 2010.

[12] Three such appeals have been reported to date: http://www.decc.gov.uk/en/content/cms/what_we_do/change_energy/tackling_clima/emissions/eu_ets/legislation/legislation.aspx.

England, the First-Level Tribunal (Environment) is beginning to acquire appeal functions in other areas of environmental regulation. Finally, as was the case in 2004, there continue to be instances where there is no right of appeal against a regulatory decision other than by way of judicial review. This is particularly the case where the initial decision-maker is the Secretary of State, though even here the position is not consistent, with some regulations allowing for an appeal to, say, the High Court and others none at all. This issue is discussed further in paragraph 19 below.

10.   A good example of the complexity of appeal provisions that can exist even within a single set of regulations is contained in the recent REACH Enforcement Regulations 2008/2852. In less than two pages, Schedule 8 provides for four separate appeal routes – decisions on notices served by the Environment Agency being appealed to the Secretary of State, notices served by the Health and Safety Executive to an Employment Tribunal, notices served by local authorities to the magistrates court, and finally notices served by the Secretary of State to the High Court. The choice of appeals route is clearly being largely determined by the body making the initial decision rather than the underlying nature of the regulations themselves. This is understandable, but sacrifices any consistency that might come from a single appeals body dealing with a common set of regulations, and providing a common approach towards their interpretation.

The Environment Tribunal

11.   The Environment Tribunal was established in 2010 and sits as part of the General Regulatory Chamber of the First-tier Tribunal.[13] At present there are six appointed judges, all with at least seven years' professional experience, together with 10 non-legal members with a wide range of expertise. Members sit part-time, and the tribunal has a great deal of flexibility in how it handles cases. A judge and two non-legal members can be appointed to handle more serious or complex cases, but it is perfectly possible for a case to be heard by a single judge or a single non-legal member. The Tribunal is not based in a single location but can sit wherever it is needed, taking advantage of the common approach to administrative support provided by the new tribunal system. Procedures are governed by the Tribunal Procedure (First-tier Tribunal) (General Regulatory Chamber) Rules 2009 as amended,[14] and there is a fast-track procedure for handling appeals against Stop Notices.[15]

12.   As is common practice in tribunal appeals, each party normally bears their own costs, although the 2009 Rules allows for a tribunal, acting either on its own initiative or in response to an application, to make an order for costs where, for example, it considers a party has acted unreasonably in bringing, defending, or conducting proceedings. The Rules also require that, where appropriate, the tribunal must bring to the attention of the parties any appropriate alternative dispute resolution

---

[13] See generally http://www.tribunals.gov.uk/environment/.
[14] SI 1976 (L.20).
[15] Practice Direction 9 April 2010.

procedure and, if the parties wish, help facilitate this procedure.

13.   The jurisdiction of the Environment Tribunal was originally limited to hearing appeals against civil sanctions imposed by environmental regulators created under regulations made under the Regulatory Enforcement and Sanctions Act 2008.[16] Other environmental appeals have now been added to his jurisdiction, notably appeals against decisions of the National Measurement Office concerning civil sanctions under eco-design regulations[17] and appeals under the new Welsh plastic bag regulations.[18] The first appeals under these various regulations are likely to be heard sometime in 2011.

Advantages of the Environmental Tribunal as an Appeals Body

14.   There are a number of advantages in having appeals under a range of environmental laws being handled by a single appeals body. Such a body can develop an expert understanding of the complexities of contemporary environmental legislation and policy, and can provide a consistency of interpretation across the board where appropriate. Challenging concepts, such as the precautionary principle, now permeate many areas of environmental law, as do provisions of European Union and international environmental law, and it is not easy to develop expertise or familiarity where appeals are scattered across too many different fora. The Tribunal sits in public, has its own infrastructure where hearings are held and can provide a single portal for the reporting of appeal decisions. There exists an Upper Tribunal, established as a court of record, which provides for the hearing of appeals from the First-tier Tribunal.

15.   The Environmental Tribunal[19] should provide a natural home for many of these appeals in that it is now functioning, has a wide range of legal and other expertise available to it, and operates under an established set of procedural rules. From discussion with its judicial members, it is clear to me that the Tribunal is fully aware that, in addition to dealing with the appeal before it, its decisions can play a valuable role in providing wider guidance to regulators and the regulated community, and can be couched accordingly. This is likely to be particularly important where one is dealing with a wholly new area of law and policy, such as environmental civil sanctions, and where a substantial number appeals can be expected in the early years of operation as the new system is tested. Consolidating a large number of existing diverse regulatory appeal routes within a single clear structure is entirely consistent with the government's regulatory reform agenda designed to simplify and modernise regulatory structures.

---

[16] The Environmental Civil Sanctions (England) Order 2010, the Environmental Civil Sanctions (Miscellaneous Amendments) (England) Regulations 2010, the Environmental Civil Sanctions (Wales) Order 2010, the Environmental Civil Sanctions (Miscellaneous Amendments) (Wales) Order 2010.

[17] Eco-design for Energy Using Products (amendment) (Civil Sanctions) Regulations 2010.

[18] The Single Use Carrier Bags Charge (Wales) 2010 No 2880 (W 238).

[19] The Tribunal heard its first appeal on 22 October 2012 – an appeal against a remediation notice served by the Marine Management Organization, and stayed on terms of a settlement agreed by the parties: http://www.marinemanagement.org.uk/news/news/121112.htm (accessed on 10 May 2014).

Comparative Costs of Appeals Bodies

16. Especially in the current economic climate, the comparative running costs of different appeals bodies may strongly influence the choice of body made by the government. Under various internal financial arrangements, the costs of the body are generally charged to the department responsible for the policy area in question. I have seen various different daily figures quoted, generally with the costs, say, of a Planning Inspector or a single barrister appointed as appeals officer being rather less that the Environmental Tribunal. Ultimately it is for the government to decide the significance of these costs, but I would make two general points. First, it is important that the figures to be relied upon are calculated on the same basis, and I am not convinced that is always the case at present. The costs of accommodation and meeting rooms should to be taken on board, and it needs to be recognised that the Environment Tribunal may often sit with a single judge or expert member if this is appropriate for the appeal in question, which would significantly reduce the daily costs. If a new appeals body or appeals officer are proposed, the costs of advertising and interviewing candidates must be taken on board, as should the time spent by such a person in developing their own rules of procedure. Secondly, in the longer term it may prove a false saving if one automatically chooses the option with the cheapest daily costs. As I have indicated, the Tribunal can play an important role in providing wider legal and policy guidance in its decision making in a way that is less easy for some of the other appeals bodies, and this can help decrease the subsequent number of appeals, leading to an overall reduction in costs and delays.

Secretary of State Appeals

17. I am aware that the legislative structure underlying existing environmental appeals to the Secretary of State varies, and this will be an important factor in deciding how easy it is to transfer such appeals to the Environment Tribunal. In some cases, an appeals body such as PINS may be making recommendations to the Secretary of State, who makes the final appeal decision. I do not believe it would be acceptable for the Tribunal to be making recommendations to the Secretary of State in this way. There are examples where the primary legislation identifies the Secretary of State as determining the appeal, and amendments to the legislation would be needed if the Tribunal were to assume this role. In other cases, the primary legislation leaves the position flexible, in which case the choice of appeals body can be defined in regulations.[20] Sometimes, the primary legislation may give the Secretary of State the formal power to delegate his appeals functions to another body under regulations,[21] or to refer the appeal to another body. If that is the case, then it seems acceptable for him to formally delegate powers or refer the appeal to the Environment Tribunal without the need for new primary legislation.

---

[20] For example, in relation of trading schemes under Climate Change Act 2008, Part 3, Sched 2, para 31(3) provides that regulations must 'specify the court, tribunal or person who is to hear and determine appeals in relation to a trading scheme'.

[21] See, eg Town and Country Planning Act 1990, Sched 6 and The Town and Country Planning (Determination of Appeals by Appointed Persons) (Prescribed Classes) Regulations 1997.

18. There may be a reluctance on the part of the Secretary of State to formally delegate individual regulatory appeals to an independent body over which he has no control. I can understand that in the case of, say, a major infrastructure decision concerning a new nuclear power station it may be appropriate that the Secretary of State takes the decision. But for the types of environmental appeals considered here, I think it preferable that decisions on individual appeals are handled by an independent body, operating against the background of regulatory and policy framework determined by the government. If the government is uncomfortable with the policy implications of an individual appeal decision, then it has the option of changing the policy. If the appeals body interprets the relevant legislation in a way that is contrary to government expectation, then equally it can change the legislation.

19. In some cases, notably where the Secretary of State is the primary decision-maker, there is no right of appeal other than by way of judicial review. There may be doubts as to whether the complete absence of an administrative appeal is consistent with the Article 6.1 of the European Convention on Human Rights,[22] but in any event I think that, as a matter of principle and good practice, a merits appeal to an independent tribunal should generally be made available. An absence of appeal is likely to increase pressure on judicial reviews to handle what are in effect merits appeals – see further on this point in paragraph 26 below. In any event, the current position does not appear to be consistent with different mechanisms being employed. Some regulations (eg leaded petrol permits) formally allow for an appeal against the decision of the Secretary of State but to the Secretary of State, and it is dubious whether this is truly an appeal right rather than a right of review. Others, especially those relating to offshore activities, allow for an appeal to the High Court with no restriction on the grounds that may be raised. The 2009 Environmental Damage Regulations provide that, where the Secretary of State is the enforcing authority, any appeal to him against his enforcement action must be referred for decision to someone appointed by him. The 2005 Greenhouse Gas Emissions Trading Regulations contain a rather odd reciprocal arrangement under which the Secretary of State is the appeal body against decisions of the Environment Agency, including the imposition of civil penalties, but, where the Secretary of State is the primary enforcement body (in relation to offshore installations), the Environment Agency acts as the appeal body against the Secretary of State's decisions. Frankly, I can find little in the way of an underlying rationale for the distinctions being made, both as to whether there should be some sort of regulatory appeal and to what form it should take, other than historical accident or uncoordinated individual choices being made by departmental lawyers in drafting regulations.

20. The list in Appendix 1 of regulations where there are no appeals indicates that this is not simply confined to cases where the primary decision-maker is the Secretary of State. As a matter of principle, I think there should generally be a right of appeal in such cases, and would recommend that the current list be reviewed and the absence of appeal justified if appropriate.

---

[22] 'In the determination of his civil rights and obligations or of any criminal charge against him, everyone is entitled to a fair and public hearing within a reasonable time by an independent and impartial tribunal established by law.' See further *R v Secretary of State for the Environment, Transport and Regions ex parte Holdings & Barnes plc* (Alconbury) [2001] UKHL 23; *Tower Hamlets LBC v Begum* [2003] UKHL 5; *Tsfayo v United Kingdom* [2007] European Court of Human Rights BLGR 1.

Appeals Held by PINS (Planning Inspectorate)

21.   PINS already handles a very large number of appeals under the town and country planning legislation, and in many ways operates as a form of tribunal with the hallmarks of independence and expertise. In the longer term it might be sensible to formally incorporate PINS within the new tribunal system, but that is beyond the scope of this report. PINS also handles a number more specialised environmental appeals, including water abstraction and discharge appeals, and Appendix 4 provides figures on the current numbers.

22.   There is always going to be a fine judgement as to what sort of appeals are truly environmental or not. My view is that appeals with clear land-use implications, such as hedgerow and listed buildings appeals, should continue to be handled by PINS, while it would make far less sense for environmental appeals with little connection with land-use planning – such as electrical waste or emissions trading – to be assigned to PINS. Appeals under environmental permitting regulations are somewhat of a borderline case, and I recognise that PINS has already developed considerable expertise in some of these areas which should not be jeopardised by any change. But my recommendation is that in future appeals under environmental permitting regulations should be handled by the Environment Tribunal. The issues involved often raise a combination of complex technical and legal issues (often involving underling EU legislation) for which the Tribunal should be especially well placed. Individual planning inspectors who have developed experience and expertise in environmental appeals should be considered for appointment as tribunal members.

23.   I do not think this goes against the recommendations of the Penfold Review[23] or the government's response to the Review,[24] and indeed in many ways the proposals here are consistent with the thrust of the Review. Penfold called for changes that would speed up processes, reduce duplication of non-planning consents, and improve the interaction of planning and non-planning consents. However, it did not recommend any further unification of planning and other consent regimes as a viable option for the time being. As to appeals, the Review noted the benefits of greater standardisation of appeals and inquiries, especially those handled by PINS, but again did not call for a single unified system. It also noted the benefits of

> attempting to resolve objections or disputes without the need for an inquiry, such as by written procedure; ensuring that inquiries are focused on the key elements in dispute as opposed to the scheme as a whole; and timetabling when key actions and decisions are taken.[25]

The proposals in this report are clearly designed to seek far greater standardisation and simplification in the environmental appeals structure, and it is equally clear to me that the Environment Tribunal is fully alive to the benefits of different ways of handling appeals (such as by written representation, alternative dispute resolution) in appropriate cases, and will do so in practice. There may be rare cases where it

---

[23] 'Penfold Review of Non-Planning Consents Final Report' URN 10/1027 (July 2010), available at www.bis. gov.uk/penfold.
[24] 'Government Response to the Penfold Review of Non-Planning Consents' (Department for Business Innovation and Skills, November 2010).
[25] Penfold Review, above n 22, para 3.25.

would be sensible to hear a planning appeal and an environmental regulatory appeal simultaneously, and, given the flexibilities in administrative arrangements now available to the Tribunal Service, I see no reason why it should not be possible to organise a joint appeal held by both PINS and the Environmental Tribunal in such cases.

Statutory Nuisances

24.   Appeals concerning statutory nuisances are heard by the magistrates courts, and can vary enormously in scope and length, from a neighbourhood noise dispute to an appeal involving a business and highly complex legal and technical issues, sometimes lasting days. Appeals involving businesses often involve examination of the difficult concept of 'best practicable means'. In practice, more complex technical appeals may well be transferred from lay magistrates to a district judge, but the evidence of the United Kingdom Environmental Law Association raises real concerns as to the suitability of magistrates courts to handle these sorts of complex statutory nuisance appeals.

25.   There may be a case for transferring all statutory nuisance appeals to the Environmental Tribunal, which can sit locally as and when needed, but it appears to be those appeals raising very complex technical issues that present the greater challenges at present. It is difficult to define in advance classes of statutory nuisance appeals that should be heard by magistrates courts or the Environmental Tribunal. My recommendation therefore would be that statutory nuisance appeals continue to be heard by magistrates courts but that in any particular appeal the magistrates court (or district judge) should have the power to transfer the appeal to the Environment Tribunal, either on application by one of the parties or on the court's own initiative.

Third Party Appeals

26.   The traditional UK approach in the design of regulatory appeals has been to confine the right of appeal to the person or body being regulated. Third parties such as neighbours or non-governmental organisation have no right of regulatory appeal but can challenge decisions of the regulators by way of judicial review, and subject to standing issues. Third party rights of appeal exist in some jurisdictions, such as New Zealand, and in its 23rd Report Environmental Planning[26] the Royal Commission on Environmental Pollution recommended that third party rights of appeal be introduced in a limited number of planning and environmental decisions.

27.   This is an issue that should be kept under review. At first sight, extending rights of appeal to third parties might appear to impose unacceptable new costs and delays, but equally, introducing such a right may reduce the pressures on judicial review. In *Modernising Environmental Justice* some 55 judicial review files involving

---

[26] Royal Commission on Environmental Pollution, Environmental Planning 23rd Report, Cm 5459 (Stationery Office, 2002) paras 5.40–5.47.

environmental legislation[27] and heard between 2000 and 2002 were examined. Only four cases were successful, and the files suggested that around two-thirds of the cases were essentially merits-driven, where the party was in reality seeking a substantial rehearing of the case, though the case had to be couched in judicial review terms. Over half of the judicial reviews were brought by industry rather than individuals or non-governmental organisations, and in two-thirds of the cases there had been no previous administrative appeal either because the applicant was a third party or because there was no right of regulatory appeal in the legislation in question. The evidence suggested a pent-up need for a right of administrative appeal which was currently being met by having to use the judicial review procedure.

28.   Judicial review is inevitably a costly process, and can lead to substantial delays. Current proposals to change costs rules associated with judicial review could well lead to an increased number of applications. Introducing new rights of regulatory appeal that could reduce the pressure on judicial reviews could clearly bring benefits to all parties concerned, and I believe that the Environmental Tribunal could develop efficient and fair procedures for handling such appeals, and with the minimum of delays.

Presumptions and Priorities

29.   It is clear that the present system of administrative appeals under environmental legislation has developed in a haphazard fashion, with little in the way of underlying principle. The establishment of an environmental tribunal in 2010 now offers the opportunity of greater consolidation of existing appeals procedures and would lead to improved consistency and effectiveness. I do not recommend an immediate transfer of all existing environmental appeals identified in this report, and in some cases changes to primary legislation would be required. It seems preferable to adopt an incremental approach, and I would suggest the following as a basis for priorities.

30.   **New legislation relating to the environment:** I recommend that anyone seeking a licence or similar right should normally have the right of an unrestricted appeal to the Environment Tribunal. There should be the same expectation for anyone served with a notice or similar order imposing an obligation on them. This principle would apply whether the decision-making body was a local authority, a national regulator such as the Environment Agency, or the Secretary of State, and any departure from this presumption should be explicitly justified. Expressed more formally: there should be a presumption that, where under new legislation relating to the environment a government department or other public body has power to make a decision affecting a person's rights or imposing an obligation on a person, that person should have an unrestricted right of appeal to the First-tier Tribunal (Environment).

31.   **Existing environmental legislation:** I appreciate that some transfers may be easier to achieve than others, and that in some cases a change to primary legislation would be required. These factors are likely to influence the choice of initial candidates, but, all things being equal, I would recommend the following order of priorities for transfer to the Environment Tribunal:

---

[27] Town and country planning judicial reviewss (including those involving environmental assessment) were excluded.

(a)   Appeals against the imposition of civil financial penalties which do not currently go to the Environment Tribunal.

(b)   Appeals against the imposition of other administrative orders requiring action (eg clean up) or suspending or imposing restrictions on activity.

In both these cases, a regulatory body has been given the power to impose immediate sanctions on an individual or business, and it is appropriate that these powers are keep under review in the form of an appeals procedure to an independent tribunal. Civil financial sanctions, in particularly, are increasingly being used in many areas of environmental regulation, and there are likely to be many common issues of principle emerging which would be better handled by a single tribunal rather than scattered through different forms of appeal body.

(c)   In the case of statutory nuisance appeals, however, appeals should remain with the magistrates court, but a court should have the power to refer any appeal to the Environment Tribunal on grounds of technical/legal complexity, on application by one of the parties or on its own initiative.

(d)   Appeals against other administrative decisions (eg refusal of a licence or registration) under environmental legislation should be systematically reviewed, and a case for continuing to provide no regulatory appeal in any particular instance justified.

(e)   Appeals against administrative decisions in environmental legislation, whether or not there are land-use connections, where the legal and technical complexity involved in the field of law concerned would be appropriately handled by the Environment Tribunal.

Expertise already built up by individuals handling appeals in environmental legislation should not be jeopardised by any transfer to the Environment Tribunal, and their appointment as members of the Tribunal should be considered.

Appendix 1

Appeals Body (England only)

Information Rights Tribunal

The INSPIRE Regulations 2009/3157 and The Environmental Information Regulations 2004/339 (information and enforcement notices)

NVZ Appeals Panel

The Nitrate Pollution Prevention Regulations 2008/2349 (England) (designation of zones)

S of S (Environment Food and Rural Affairs)[28]

Clean Air Act 1993 (smoke control areas etc)

Environmental Protection Act 1990 Part IIA and the Contaminated Land (England) Regulations 2006/1380 (England) (remediation notice and exclusion of confidential information on registers)

The Environmental Protection Act 1990 Part IIA, the Radioactive Contaminated Land (Enabling Powers) (England) Regulations 2005/3467 and the Radioactive Contaminated Land (Modification of Enactments) Regulations 2006/1379 (England) (identification of land, remediation notice and exclusion of confidential information)

Genetically Modified Organisms (Contained Use) Regulations 2000/2831 (authorisations and exemption certificates)

Wildlife and Countryside Act 1981 and Countryside Rights of Way Act 2000 (consents and management notices relating to SSSIs)

The Conservation of Habitats and Species Regulations 2010/490 (consents – referrals)

Control of Pollution (Amendment) Act 1989 (registration of carriers)

Environmental Protection Act 1990 (c 43) Part II (authorisations, enforcement and prohibition notices)

Control of Major Accident Hazard Regulations 1999/743 (information to the public)

The Persistent Organic Pollutants Regulations 2007/3106 (derogations)

The REACH Enforcement Regulations 2008/2852 (enforcement notices etc by EA)

The Environmental Permitting (England and Wales) Regulations 2010/675 (recovered appeals)

Anti-Pollution Works Regulations 1999/1006 (service of notice by EA)

---

[28] Legislation simply specifies the 'Secretary of State'. The assignment of policy and decision-making responsibilities to specific Secretaries of State will change from time to time, though I believe the following is accurate at the time of writing.

Control of Pollution (Oil Storage) (England) Regulations 2001/2954 (service of notice by EA)

The Water Resources (Control of Pollution) (Silage, Slurry and Agricultural Fuel Oil) (England) Regulations 2010/639 (service of notices etc by EA)

The Producer Responsibility Obligations (Packaging Waste) Regulations 2007/871 (registration/accreditation decisions by EA)

Planning (Hazardous Substances) Act 1990 and regulations (consents by LA – recovered appeals)

PINS

The Environmental Damage (Prevention and Remediation) Regulations 2009/153 ((liability to remediate and remediation notice)

The Environmental Permitting (England and Wales) Regulations 2010/675 (licences/consents – delegated appeals)

Planning (Hazardous Substances) Act 1990 and regs (consents by LA – delegated appeals)
Marine and Coastal Access Act 2009 (marine licence – proposed)

S of S (Transport)

Motor Fuel (Composition and Content) Regulations 1999/3107 Leaded petrol permits (appeals against own decisions by S of S)

S of S (Energy and Climate Change)

The Greenhouse Gas Emissions Trading Scheme Regulations 2005/925 (permits, notices, certifications, civil penalties)

The Greenhouse Gas Emissions Data and National Implementation Measures Regulations 2009/3130 (information and civil penalty notices)

The CRC Energy Efficiency Scheme Order 2010/768 (enforcement notices and civil penalties)

The Aviation Greenhouse Gas Emissions Trading Scheme Regulations 2010/1996 (benchmarking plan approval, information notices, civil penalties)

The Transfrontier Shipment of Radioactive Waste and Spent Fuel Regulations 2008/3087 (consents by EA)

S of S (Business Innovation and Skills)

The Export of Radioactive Sources (Control) Order 2006/1846 (appeals against own decisions by S of S)

The Waste Electrical and Electronic Equipment (WEEE) Regulations 2006/3289 (approval of compliance schemes etc by EA)

The Waste Batteries and Accumulators Regulations 2009/890 (decisions by EA on compliance schemes)

High Court

Offshore Combustion Installations (Prevention and Control of Pollution) Regulations 2001/1091

The Renewable Transport Fuel Obligations Order 2007/3072 (civil penalties)

Offshore Petroleum Activities (Conservation of Habitats) Regulations 2001/1754 (directions by DECC to reduce or eliminate adverse effects)

The REACH Enforcement Regulations 2008/2852 (enforcement notices by S of S)

Offshore Chemicals Regulations 2002/1355

County Court

Environmental Protection Act 1990 Part IIA and the Contaminated Land (England) Regulations 2006/1380 (England) (charging notice)

The Environmental Protection Act 1990 Part IIA, the Radioactive Contaminated Land (Enabling Powers) (England) Regulations 2005/3467 and the Radioactive Contaminated Land (Modification of Enactments) Regulations 2006/1379 (charging notice)

Magistrates Court

Clean Air Act 1993 (LAS requirements on fireplaces)

The Environmental Protection (Controls on Ozone-Depleting Substances) Regulations 2002/528 (enforcement/prohibition notices)

The Fluorinated Greenhouse Gases Regulations 2009/261 (enforcement/prohibition notices)

The Persistent Organic Pollutants Regulations 2007/3106 (enforcement notices)

The REACH Enforcement Regulations 2008/2852 (suspension notices by LA)

Control of Pollution Act 1974 s 60/61 (construction site notices)

Environmental Protection Act 1990, Noise and Statutory Nuisance Act 1993 (statutory nuisance notices)

The Private Water Supplies Regulations 2009/3101 (England) (enforcement notice by LA)

Environmental Protection Act 1990 Part IV (litter) (LA litter notices and consent to distribute free material)

The Transfrontier Shipment of Waste Regulations 2007/1711 (service of enforcement notices by EA or S of S)

Person Appointed by S of S

Biocidal Products Regulations 2001/880 (product authorisations etc by HSE on behalf of S of S)

Person Agreed by Parties

The Ecodesign for Energy-Using Products Regulations 2010/2617 (non-conformity notice)

The Merchant Shipping (Prevention of Air Pollution from Ships) Regulations 2008/2924 (detention by Harbour Master)

The Merchant Shipping (Prevention of Pollution by Sewage and Garbage from Ships) Regulations 2008/3257 (ship detention notice)

Director General of Water Services

Water Industry Act 1991 (undertaker consents for discharge of effluent into sewers)

Environment Agency

The Greenhouse Gas Emissions Trading Scheme Regulations 2005/925 (permits, civil penalties for offshore installations where S of S primary decision-maker)

Employment Tribunal

Control of Major Accident Hazard Regulations 1999/743 (enforcement and prohibition notices)

The REACH Enforcement Regulations 2008/2852 (enforcement notices etc by HSE)

First-Level Tribunal (Environment)

Environmental Civil Sanctions (England) Order 2010, Environmental Sanctions (Misc Amendments) (England) Regulations 2010), Environmental Civil Sanctions (Wales) Order 2010, Environmental Civil Sanctions (Miscellaneous Amendments) (Wales) Regulations 2010 (civil penalties for specific environmental offences)

The Ecodesign for Energy-Using Products Regulations 2010/2617 (civil penalties)

The Single Use Carrier Bags Charge (Wales) Regulations 2010/2880 (civil penalties)

Marine and Coastal Access Act 2009 (civil penalties when regulations made)

No Regulatory Appeal

The Environmental Protection (Controls on Ozone-Depleting Substances) Regulations 2002/528 (decisions of S of S and Port Health Authority)

Sustainable Energy Act 2003 (modifications of distribution licence by S of S)

Energy Act 2004 (imposition of charges etc by Nuclear Decommission Authority, and numerous powers including nuclear transfer schemes, modification gas and electricity licences, construction of renewable energy installations in waters)

The Renewable Transport Fuel Obligations Order 2007/3072 (issue and revocation of RTF certificates by Renewable Fuels Agency – to be transferred to the Department of Transport on abolition of the RWA)

The Community Emissions Trading Scheme (Allocation of Allowances for Payment) Regulations 2008/1825 (but internal review by Treasury provided for)

The Renewable Obligation Order 2009/785 (issue and revocation of renewable obligations certificates by GEMA)

The Electricity and Gas (Community Energy Saving Programme) Order 2009/1905 (determination of reduction obligations etc by GEMA)

The Storage of Carbon Dioxide (Licensing etc) Regulations 2010/2221 (grant, modification, revocation of storage permits and approval of site-closure plans by DECC)

Environmental Protection Act 1990 Part VI and Genetically Modified Organisms (Deliberate Release) Regulations 2002/2443 (issuing and revocation of release and marketing consents by Defra)

Wildlife and Countryside Act 1981 and Countryside Rights of Way Act 2000 (notification of SSSIs by Natural England but right of representation provided before Natural England)

The Conservation of Habitats and Species Regulations 2010/490 (making of Special Nature Conservation Order by S of S but inquiry/hearing must be held if proposed order opposed)

Offshore Petroleum Activities (Conservation of Habitats) Regulations 2001/1754 (consent for surveys by DECC)

Control of Major Accident Hazard Regulations 1999/743 (approval of reports by HSE/EA)

The Large Combustion Plants (National Emission Reduction Plan) Regulations 2007/2325 (verification of annual emissions and determination of allowances on closure by EA)

The Merchant Shipping and Fishing Vessels (Port Waste Reception Facilities) Regulations 2003/1809 (direction to remedy waste facilities etc)

The Offshore Marine Conservation (Natural Habitats, &c) Regulations 2007/1842 (designation of site and granting of consents)

Water Industry Act 1991 (review and issue of notice by EA concerning special effluent discharges into sewers)

Water Resources Act 1991 (making of drought order by S of S but inquiry must be held if objections)

The Private Water Supplies Regulations 2009/3101 (England) (refusal by LA to authorise different standards)

The Water Supply (Water Quality) Regulations 2000/3184 (England) (refusal by S of S to authorise temporary supply that is not wholesome)

The End-of-Life Vehicles (ELVs) (Producer Responsibility) Regulations 2005/263 (decisions by S of S to ascribe responsibility, approve collection systems, and service of compliance notice)

The Batteries and Accumulators (Placing on the Market) Regulations 2008/2164 (service of compliance notice by BIS or NMO)

The Bluetongue Regulations 2008/962 (England) (designations, licences to move animals etc)

Appendix 2

The appeals listing by subject matter is not reproduced in this volume.

Appendix 3

Appeal Bodies in Environmental Civil Penalty Schemes

In paragraph 31 of the report, I recommend that a high priority should be to ensure that all appeals against civil penalties imposed under legislation related to the environment should be heard by the First-tier Tribunal (Environment). This is the current position.

First-tier Tribunal (Environment)

Environmental Civil Sanctions (England) Order 2010, Environmental Sanctions (Misc Amendments) (England) Regulations 2010, Environmental Civil Sanctions (Wales) Order 2010, Environmental Civil Sanctions (Miscellaneous Amendments) (Wales) Regulations 2010 (civil penalties for specific environmental offences)

The Ecodesign for Energy-Using Products Regulations 2010/2617 (civil penalties)

The Single Use Carrier Bags Charge (Wales) Regulations 2010/2880 (civil penalties)

Marine and Coastal Access Act 2009 (civil penalties when regulations made)

S of S (Energy and Climate Change)

The Greenhouse Gas Emissions Trading Scheme Regulations 2005/925

The Greenhouse Gas Emissions Data and National Implementation Measures Regulations 2009/3130

The CRC Energy Efficiency Scheme Order 2010/768 (enforcement notices and civil penalties)

The Aviation Greenhouse Gas Emissions Trading Scheme Regulations 2010/1996

Environment Agency

The Greenhouse Gas Emissions Trading Scheme Regulations 2005/925 (civil penalties served by S of S in respect of offshore installations)

High Court

The Renewable Transport Fuel Obligations Order 2007/3072

Appendix 4 Planning Inspectorate Environment Appeals 2006–10

	2006–07	2007–08	2008–09	2009–10
Water discharge consents (including enforcement)	69	21	39	21
PPC Regs	65	37	18	1
Landfill Regs 2002	9	7	2	
EP Regs 2007	–	=	42	14
Waste	22	14	4	5
Anti-pollution works	1	1	0	0
Water abstraction	0	0	0	0
Hazardous Substances	3	1	0	0
IPC/Part I EPA	1	0	0	0
Total received	173	88	106	41
Total withdrawn	339	195	267	332
Decisions/reports	29	39	7	20

Figures supplied by PINS to Macrory 2010.

8

Environmental Regulation as an Instrument of Constitutional Change[1] (2011)

Less than a generation ago the Chief Scientist of the then Department of the Environment and Transport could argue, with some justification, that one of the defining characteristics of the British approach to environmental policy was a preference for voluntary arrangements between government and industry rather than legal compulsion.[2] Even in areas where there were explicit legal frameworks, the substantive legislation was often expressed in extremely broad terms, allowing the regulators and the regulated to negotiate solutions without the intervention of legal process and the courts. To take one example, long familiar to British environmental lawyers, the core legal requirement concerning atmospheric emissions from major industrial processes was to use the 'best practicable means' to prevent or minimise emissions, a statutory expression that remained in force 100 years from 1875 until 1990 – despite the heavily open-textured language of that central duty, there is not a single reported case in the higher courts concerning its interpretation throughout that period. The translation of the legal obligation into practical reality was largely the result of a dialogue and negotiation between chemical engineers and other technically qualified staff working within the regulated industry and the national regulatory body, the Alkali Inspectorate, and its successor, the Industrial Air Pollution Inspectorate. These distinctive characteristics of environmental regulation in this country no longer hold true. The last 40 years has seen an extraordinary expansion in the depth and scale of substantive legislation bringing about a fundamental change in the prevailing legal culture operating in this field.[3]

This chapter, though, deals with environmental law not in order to analyse the reasons behind the massive expansion of the law in this area, still less to consider in any detail the substance of contemporary environmental regulation – rather, the subject serves as a useful illustration of two aspects of constitutional change. First, the environment provides a clear example of the web of complex constitutional connections between different branches of government and different levels of government (local, central and the European Union) and between other regulatory and non-governmental bodies. Secondly, the environment serves as an illustration of how one area of law, policy, and public

---

[1] R Macrory (2011) 'The Environment as an Instrument of Constitutional Change' in J Jowell and D Oliver, *The Changing Constitution* (Oxford, Oxford University Press).

[2] M Holdgate, 'Environmental Policies in Britain and Mainland Europe' in R Macrory (ed), *Britain, Europe and the Environment* (Imperial College Centre for Environmental Technology, 1983) 6–18.

[3] See R Macrory (1991) 'Environmental Law: Shifting Discretions and the New Formalism', reproduced as Chapter 12 of this volume.

administration can engage practice and principle in a way that bring about changes to the overall constitutional structure. This chapter should therefore be seen a case study of constitutional interaction and change. Indeed, I will argue that the real significance of the developments over the last 30 years – and in hindsight the one with the most long-lasting impact – is the extent to which environmental law and regulation has proved to be at the forefront in articulating principles and precedents that are central to a contemporary constitutional settlement. Legal rights to public information and participation in decision-making, access to justice and the accountability of regulatory authorities are issues that have a universality and help define the relationship between citizen and state. In all of these areas environmental law has played a key role in pioneering concepts and practice, and continues to do so.

The Context

Why should environmental law have proved a fruitful area for driving legal innovation concerning fundamental principles? The roots of contemporary environmental regulation can be traced back to the nineteenth century, and the policy response to unacceptable side effects of the industrial revolution. The first non-governmental organisations concerned with environmental issues were formed in the latter half of that century, with specialised laws and regulatory agencies becoming well developed by the post-war period. Yet it was the growth of modern environmental groups from the 1970s onwards that posed profound challenges to familiar ways of handling issues. Rather than dealing with environmental issues on a topic-by-topic basis, as was typically reflected in the legislation of the time (air pollution, water and so on), the new wave of organisations demanded a more holistic approach that looked at environmental impacts as a whole and pressed for more preventative solutions beyond the more immediate amelioration of pollution impacts. Concern at the urgency and enormity of the environmental challenges implied a rejection of the cautious gradualism which appeared to characterise policy development. More recently the concept of sustainable development became a familiar part of the language of the policy debate, but is equally subject to differing interpretations and competing visions. A simple balancing of environmental, economic and social agendas is pitched against a vision that would argue that, without a secure environmental basis, economic and social progress will prove unattainable. Others have promoted a more politically challenging vision of sustainable development incorporating ideas of greater economic and social justice both within and between generations, and a revitalisation of local and community identities.[4] It took some years before the environmental dimensions of the UK legal structure were seriously addressed in this debate – the UK Environmental Law Association, for example, was not formed until 1987. But the restless challenge to long-established ways of thinking about and handling policy issues that have been such an integral part of the modern environmental movement provided a potent basis for treating environmental law as a significant engine for constitutional change. Regulatory practices and styles of policy making were

---

[4] See generally T O'Riordan and H Voisey, *Sustainable Development* in *Western Europe: Coming* to *Terms with Agenda 21* (London, Frank Cass, 1997).

subject to sustained scrutiny and critiques in a way not experienced before. Fundamental re-evaluations provide a powerful engine for innovation.

Public Access to Information and Participation

General rights of public access to information in the UK as enshrined in the Freedom of Information Act 2000 are now a familiar part of the constitutional landscape. Such broad rights were first enshrined in British law in the environmental field some eight years before, and these in turn found precedent in individual areas of environmental law from the 1970s, deriving from a lengthy period of intellectual and policy argument conducted in the environmental policy community. Registers of regulatory consents in fields such as water pollution had existed since the 1950s, but they were open only to persons 'interested' in the register, interpreted narrowly to mean someone with a legal interest, such as an owner of fishing rights in the waters concerned, rather than a member of the general public. Industry in particular fought hard to restrict wider access on the grounds of confidentiality. The Royal Commission on Environmental Pollution, established in 1970,[5] was the first official body to seriously raise the issue, which it did in its Second Report,[6] urging the government 'to devise measures which will increase the availability and flow of information on the production and disposal of industrial effluents and wastes'.[7] Largely as a consequence of the report, one of the first major environmental statutes of the time, the Control of Pollution Act 1974, mainly dealing with the regulation of waste, water pollution and noise, contained provisions concerning registers of applications for consents, consents and monitoring results which were to be open to any member of the public. The Royal Commission demonstrated the value of being a standing commission by constantly returning to the subject of openness over the next 12 years in a number of different reports, and arguing consistently that a presumption of public access would lead to improved environmental protection. In its Tenth Report,[8] published in 1984, the Commission carried out an extensive analysis of the arguments for and against greater access to environmental information, and concluded that, while some progress was being made in more recent individual laws, insufficient priority was being given to the principle. It concluded with a statement that could have formed the rallying call for general freedom of information legislation:

> A guiding principle behind all legislative and administrative controls relating to environmental pollution should be a presumption in favour of unrestricted access for the public to information which the pollution control authorities obtain or receive by virtue of their statutory powers, with provision for secrecy only in those circumstances where a genuine case for it can be substantiated.[9]

The underlying principle of open access to environmental information was also beginning to gain momentum with the European Community, and in 1990 the Community

---

[5] The Commission was dissolved by the coalition government in 2011 as part of government financial cutbacks.
[6] (1988). Royal Commission on Environmental Pollution, 'Three Issues in Industrial Pollution', Cmnd 4894 (1972).
[7] Ibid, para 9.
[8] Royal Commission on Environmental Pollution, 'Tackling Pollution – Experience and Prospects', Cmnd 9149 (1984).
[9] Ibid, para 7.8.

adopted a directive on the subject, the first sector of Community policy where such a general right was granted.[10] The Directive was framed in the language of a human right, and gave broad rights to anyone, including non-governmental associations, to acquire environmental information held by public authorities and other bodies performing public functions. There was no precondition of holding a legal or other special interest in the matter concerned, a challenge to the administrative practice in many Member States.[11]

Transposition of the Directive required the UK to move beyond its then practice of incorporating public registers in specific environmental laws to promoting legislation giving much broader rights in the form of the Environmental Information Regulations 1992.[12] Though containing various exemptions in line with the Directive, the regulations created a precedent in the concept of general access to information held by public authorities.[13] The Freedom of Information 2000 Act acknowledges the distinctive and independent nature of the environmental rights, essentially by providing that any information falling with the terms of the Directive and implementing regulations is treated as not covered by the Act as 'exempt' information.[14] Indeed, it is arguable that the scope of exemptions is narrower under the environmental information regulations than the Freedom of Information Act 2000[15] and the EU dimension means that the European Court of Justice has jurisdiction in the area, and has already given a strongly progressive, liberal interpretation of the Directive.[16]

The environmental field can also be seen to have developed important legal principles concerning rights of public participation in decision making, though its contribution is perhaps somewhat more subtle. The UK had long established opportunities for public participation in certain fields, particularly in town and country planning, where public inquiries were regularly held into planning appeals and formed a familiar part of the administrative landscape.[17] Indeed, in the 1970s and 1980s it was the planning inquiry that was seen by many in the modern environmental movement as a unique forum where new ideas and ways of looking at development proposals could be articulated and raised, leading to a number of major inquiries involving the exploration of complex issues of public policy well beyond the narrow confines of land-use planning.[18] More specialised

[10] Council Directive (EEC) 90/313 on Freedom of Access to Information on the Environment [1990] OJ L56/58 (the Directive), replaced by Council Directive (EC) 2003/4 on Public Access on Environmental Information [2003] OJ L41/126.

[11] L Kramer (2007), *EC Environmental Law*, 6th edn; see generally R Hallo (ed), *Access to Environmental Information in Europe – The Implementation and Implications of Directive 90/313/EEC* (The Hague, Kluwer Law International, 1997).

[12] SI 1992/3240, replaced by Environmental Information Regulations 2004 (SI 2004/3391).

[13] One of the first laws granting general rights to information was in fact the Local Government (Access to Information) Act 1985, giving rights to access to agendas and background papers for meetings of local authorities.

[14] Freedom of Information Act 2000, s 39.

[15] See, eg D Hughes, *Environmental Law*, 4th edn (2002) 163.

[16] C-321/96 *Mecklenburg v Kreis Pinneberg-Der Landrat* [1998] ECR I-3809. For a recent example of the European Court continuing to give a liberal interpretation of the Directive, see Case T-545/11 *Stichting Greenpeace Nederland and Pesticide Action Network Europe v European Commission*, 8 October 2013). An analysis of the case is contained in Chapter 20 of this volume.

[17] *Report of the Committee on Administrative Tribunals and Inquiries* (Franks Report) Cmnd 218 (1957). The *Report of the Committee on Public Participation in Planning: People and Planning* (The Skeffington Report) (1969) was a significant endorsement of the public policy value in engaging with the public in land use plan development.

[18] See, eg D Pearce, I Edwards and C Bennet, *Decision-making for Energy Futures: A Case Study of the Windscale Inquiry* (1979); T O'Riordan, R Kemp and M Purdue, *Sizewell B: An Anatomy of an Inquiry* (1988); J Jowell, 'Policy, Inquiries, and the Courts' in R Macrory (ed), *Commercial Nuclear Power – Legal and Constitutional Issues* (Imperial College Centre for Environmental Technology, 1982).

environmental legislation, such as the Control of Pollution Act 1974, reflected a growing demand for participation rights by including provisions for rights of participation in various pollution consent procedures.[19] But, as with rights of information, it was at European level that such rights were first expressed in law with a more general application. The 1985 Directive on Environmental Assessment,[20] applying to consent procedures for numerous types of development proposals from transport and energy projects to waste disposal and deforestation, incorporated consultation with the general public as part of the assessment process. It was the first piece of EC environmental legislation to have incorporated such public participation rights, and indeed probably the first EC law in any field to have done so. It took some years before the British courts fully appreciated the significance of these participation rights as an integral and obligatory element of European-style environmental assessment,[21] with Lord Hoffmann eventually declaring in *Berkeley v Secretary of State for Environment, Transport and Regions:*[22]

> The directly enforceable right of the citizen which is accorded by the Directive is not merely a right to a fully informed decision on the substantive issue. It must have been adopted on an appropriate basis and that requires the inclusive and democratic procedure prescribed by the Directive in which the public, however misguided or wrongheaded its views may be, is given the opportunity to express its opinion on the environmental issues.

The 1998 United Nations Economic Commission for Europe (UNECE) Aarhus Convention (the Convention)[23] developed the participation principle even further by containing a second pillar wholly devoted to participation, and requiring parties to the Convention to ensure that the general public had opportunities to participate in consent procedures for individual projects, plans and programmes relating to the environment, and environmental rule-making and legislative drafting.[24] Considerable discretion is left to the parties as to the precise form of participation that is offered, but the underlying principles are clear. The provisions in the Convention concerning access to justice, considered in the next section, are posing the most immediate challenge to current UK practice, but it would be rash for the government to ignore the implications of the Convention's participation provisions, especially those concerning plans and rule making. *R on the application of Greenpeace v Secretary of State for Trade and Industry*[25] concerned a challenge to the government's consultation procedures on nuclear energy policy. The court found the government's own procedures to have been flawed, but it is significant that Sullivan J noted that even if the government had not committed itself to the widest possible consultation should the nuclear option be reopened, it might have been obliged to do so because of its obligations under the Convention.

---

[19] R Macrory and B Zaba, *Polluters Pay – The Control of Pollution Act Explained* (1978), an example of a citizen's guide to the new legal rights contained in the 1974 Act.

[20] Council Directive (EC) 85/337 on the Assessment of the Effects of Certain Public and Private Projects on the Environment [1985] OJ L175/40.

[21] The EC legislation had been inspired by the US legislation on environmental impact statements under National Environmental Policy Act 1970, s 102, but, while the US law was focused on the production of a written assessment by public officials, the EC law was deliberately focused on procedural requirements, including public participation.

[22] [2001] 2 AC 603.

[23] Convention on Access to Information, Public Participation in Decision-Making and Access to Justice in Environmental Matters (25 June 1998).

[24] The Convention, Arts 6–8.

[25] [2007] EWHC 311 (Admin). For an analysis see Chapter 23 of this volume.

Access to Justice

Disputes before the courts involving environmental issues have a long history, and Victorian law reports are littered with cases involving conflicts between private rights, such as the use of water or intrusive pollution, or testing the ambit of new public health legislation. It was not, however, until the 1980s that environmental organisations and affected individuals began to use the courts more regularly to explore issues of public law. Those bringing a claim for judicial review must demonstrate that they have 'sufficient interest' in the issue at hand,[26] a phrase that was once interpreted very restrictively by the courts, largely confining it to those with a defined legal interest at stake. Contemporary practice shows a far more liberal approach, and a number of the leading cases involving public interest groups involved questions of environmental law,[27] reaching a sort of apotheosis in *R (Edwards) v Environment Agency*,[28] where a homeless individual was still granted standing to challenge the legality of a permit for a local cement works because he breathed the potentially polluted air. Standing in the environmental field will rarely prove a hurdle in the contemporary judicial climate,[29] and the debate has moved on to the question of the exposure to costs in public law cases where the general costs in the cause rule, developed in the context of disputes between private parties, is applied by the courts. Legal aid is increasingly constrained, and in any event is not available to a non-governmental organisation.

In recent years the courts themselves have acknowledged that the 'loser pays' principle developed in the context of private law disputes may not always be appropriate in the context of public law, where it may be in the general public interest for the law to be tested. In a non-environmental case, the Court of Appeal in 2005[30] revived the more general use of protective costs orders (PCOs), under which a claimant in judicial review would in the early stages of litigation be limited as to the amount of costs they could be exposed to even if the case were lost. The *Corner House* principles were, however, only to be applied if five factors were present:

> (i) the issues raised are of general importance; (ii) the public interest requires that those issues should be resolved; (iii) the claimant has no private interest in the outcome of the case; (iv) having regard to the financial resources of the claimant and the respondent(s) and to the amount

---

[26] Supreme Court Act 1981, s 31(3).

[27] Eg *R v HM Inspectorate of Pollution ex parte Greenpeace Ltd (No 2)* [1994] 4 All ER 329 doubting the more restrictive earlier decision of *R v Secretary of State for the Environment ex parte Rose Theatre Trust* [1990] 1 All ER 754; *R v Secretary of State for Trade and Industry ex parte Greenpeace* [1998] Env LR 415, where Laws J noted that this type of public interest litigation was now an 'accepted and greatly valued dimension of the judicial review jurisdiction'.

[28] [2004] Env LR 43.

[29] But not necessarily the political climate. In 2013 the Ministry of Justice consulted on the possibility of restricting standing in judicial reviews due to potential 'misuse' of the courts, though acknowledged that the proposals could not apply to Aarhus environmental claims because of the way both the Convention and EU implementing legislation define standing in such cases. But in its response published in February 2014 the government decided that amending standing rules was not the best way to 'limit the potential for mischief', preferring instead to tighten up financial procedures to reduce weaker claims and strengthen the powers of a court to throw out a claim based on procedural defects which the court considers would have made no difference to the final outcome: Ministry of Justice, 'Judicial Review: Proposals for Further Reform, The Government Response', Cm 8811 (February 2014). See Chapter 9 below.

[30] *R (Corner House Research) v Secretary of State for· Trade and Industry* [2005] 1 WLR 2600.

of costs that are likely to be made it is fair and just to make the order; (v) if the order is not made the claimant will probably discontinue the proceedings and will be acting reasonably in so doing.

Expressed as such, the principles were clearly seen as an exception to the general rule concerning costs, and PCOs were expected to be made in only a small number of cases each year.[31] Nevertheless, the general approach might have made a limited but valuable contribution towards reducing the freezing effect of costs exposure in public litigation, and one that would have been legally sound had it not been for developments in the environmental field, both internationally and at the European level.

The origins of the Aarhus Convention can be traced back to the 1992 Rio Declaration on Environment and Development, which was produced after the major UN Conference known as the Earth Summit. Principle 10 of the Declaration emphasised the importance of citizen participation in environmental issues, both in terms of access to information and active participation in decision making, but also included a tentative reference to access to judicial remedies and redress.[32] Three years later, a pan-European conference adopted the Sofia Guidelines, which fleshed out some of the principles, particularly in relation to access to information and participation. This, in turn, led to the UNECE preparing a convention on the subject involving more than 40 countries, though with the notable exceptions of the USA and Canada.[33] The draft Convention was initially confined to provisions concerning access to information and public participation, and had this continued to be the case the provisions would probably have posed little in the way of challenge for the UK, where generally such principles in the environmental field were by now well developed. Early on in the negotiations, however, it was agreed to include a so-called 'third pillar' relating to questions of access to justice, and Article 9 of the Convention gives rights to members of the public and environmental non-governmental organisations to challenge the legality of decisions by public authorities granting consent for a wide range of projects as well as other acts or omissions 'which are contrary to the provisions of national laws relating to the environment'. Again, the liberal approach to standing expressed in the Convention would pose little problem for a jurisdiction such as the UK, but Article 9(4) requires that parties ensure that procedures for rights of access must 'provide adequate and effective remedies, including injunctive relief as appropriate and be fair, equitable, timely, and not prohibitively expensive'. The UK, along with all other Member States with the exception of Ireland,[34] duly signed and ratified the Convention, as did the European Community.

The legal commitment to ensure access to judicial procedures that are not 'prohibitively expensive' has subsequently come to drive the debate in the UK and prove a potent source of change which will spread well beyond the field of environmental law. It is still somewhat unclear why the UK found itself agreeing to a commitment containing such potentially

---

[31] *R (on the application of Bullmore) v West Herts Hospital NHS Trust* [2007] LTL, 27 June 2007; *River Thames Society v First Secretary of State* [2006] EWHC 2829 (Admin).

[32] 'Environmental issues are best handled with the participation of all concerned citizens, at the relevant level. At the national level, each individual shall have appropriate access to information concerning the environment that is held by public authorities, including information on hazardous materials and activities in their communities, and the opportunity to participate in decision-making processes. States shall facilitate and encourage public awareness and participation by making information widely available. Effective access to judicial and administrative proceedings, including redress and remedy, shall be provided.' See www.unep.org/Documents.MultilinguaIlDefault.asp?doeumentid=78&articleid=1163.

[33] J Jendroska, 'Public Information and Participation in EC Environmental Law – Origins, Milestones and Trends' in R Macrory (ed), *Reflections on 30 Years of EU Environmental Law* (2006) 63, 69–71.

[34] Ireland signed the Convention in June 1998 but did not ratify it until 20 June 2012.

unsettling implications. Given that nearly all of the obligations in other parts of the Convention could be readily met and that in many ways the Convention was politically viewed at the time as a means of raising the standards of Eastern European countries to those of the West, it may have just been conveniently ignored. At the same time there was a view that the reference in Article 9(4) referred only to court fees rather than any exposure or risk of exposure to litigation costs, and the official government line was that UK procedures met the obligations.[35] The restrictive interpretation of Article 9(4) was given some support by the Irish High Court in 2007,[36] but it is a view that appears increasingly untenable. In 2004 the Court of Appeal[37] had already noted the difficulties of the conventional costs principles in judicial reviews meeting up to the aspirations of the Convention, and it clearly felt that Article 9(4) was not confined to the court fees:

> If the figures revealed in this case were in any sense typical of the costs reasonably incurred, in litigating such cases up the highest level, very serious questions would be raised as to the possibility of ever living up to the Aarhus ideals within our present system.

If the Convention had retained the characteristics of a more conventional public law convention, it may well have been the case that a national government could have resisted pressures for change even where breaches occurred. But this was not the case for a number of reasons.

First, a number of senior members of the judiciary made it increasingly clear that they were sensitive to the implications of the Convention, and expressed concerns both judicially and extra judicially that the UK might not be in compliance. The Court of Appeal, for example, doubted that the principles concerning PCOs developed in *Corner House* which excluded PCOs where a private interest was involved were applicable to environmental cases.[38] The Court reached a clear conclusion that it disagreed with the government's view that the Article 9(4) obligation was confined to court fees.[39] Pressure continued to mount with a judicial-led initiative to establish a committee to suggest how the Convention principles could be implemented within current procedures, chaired by a High Court judge and including representatives from environmental practitioners and non-governmental organisations. The resulting report[40] made a powerful case for improving procedures in judicial review cases and extending the use of PCOs.

The second source of pressure was the enforcement procedures developed under the Convention itself. The Convention was, as with many international conventions, rather vague about compliance mechanisms, but required parties to establish compliance arrangements that were of a 'non-confrontational, non-judicial, and consultative nature'.[41] The first meeting of the parties went on to establish a Compliance Committee with powers to hear

---

[35] 'Our administrative and judicial systems are fully compliant with the requirements for access to review'. Summary of Implementing Measures to Achieve Compliance with the UNECE Aarhus Convention, available at www.defra.gov.uk/environment/policy/internationallaarhus.

[36] *Sweetman v An Bord Pleanala and the Attorney General* [2007] 1 EHC 153.

[37] *R (on the applications o(Sonia Burkett) v London Borough of Hammersmith and Fulham* [200] 1 EWCA Civ 1342, [76] *per* Brooke LJ.

[38] *R (on the application of England) v Tower Hamlets* [2006] EWCA Civ 1742.

[39] *Morgan and another v Hinton Organics (Wessex) Ltd and others* [2009] EWCA Civ 107: 'The requirement of the Convention that costs should not be "prohibitively expensive" should be taken as applying to the total potential liability of claimants, including the threat of adverse costs orders', [47] *per* Carnwath LJ.

[40] Working Party Group on Access to Environmental Justice (Chair Mr Justice Sullivan), 'Ensuring Access to Environmental Justice in England and Wales' (2008). The Group issued a follow-up report in 2010.

[41] The Convention, Art 15

complaints both from parties to the Convention and members of the public, described by one of the leading architects of the Convention as 'strong and unprecedented'.[42] In 2010 the Compliance Committee published draft findings in two cases from the UK which directly raised the compatibility of costs principles in judicial reviews with Article 9(4) of the Convention, and in both found that British practice did not meet the requirements of costs not being prohibitively expensive.[43]

A finding by the Compliance Committee of a breach might well be politically embarrassing, but there are no formal sanctions available under the Convention. However, the final distinctive nature of the Article 9 provisions was the fact that the European Community was party to the Convention and had implemented the provisions on access to justice by including the wording under amendments to two core environmental directives, the Directive on Environmental Assessment and the Directive on Integrated Pollution and Prevention Control.[44] Within the context of those directives, the obligation that access to justice procedures is not prohibitively expensive is now one of EU law, bringing with it the implications of the distinctive enforcement procedures available to the European Commission, leading to potential action before the European Court of Justice and a financial sanction for failure to comply with its judgments. In relation to the Assessment Directive, the European Commission had already commenced infringement procedures against the UK following a complaint from a coalition of environmental non-governmental organisations, and in 2010 issued a Reasoned Opinion, the last stage before action before the European Court of Justice.[45] In April 2011 the case was referred to the Court of Justice.[46]

---

[42] Jendroska, above n 33, 63, 72; V Koester, 'Review of Compliance under the Aarhus Convention: A Rather Unique Compliance Mechanism' (2005) 2 *JEEPL* 31; V Koester, 'The Compliance Committee of the Aarhus Convention – An Overview of Procedures and Jurisprudence' (2007) 37(2) *EPL* 83.

[43] Aarhus Compliance Committee Draft Findings ACCCIC/2008/27, and in particular ACCCIC/2008/33, para 133: 'The Committee concludes that despite the various measures available to address prohibitive costs, taken together they do not ensure that the costs remain at a level which meets the requirements under the Convention. At this stage, the Committee considers that the considerable discretion of the courts in deciding the costs, without any clear legally binding direction from the legislature or judiciary to ensure costs are not prohibitively expensive, leads to considerable uncertainty regal ding the costs to be faced where claims are legitimately pursuing environmental concerns that involve the public interest.' In December 2010 the Committee confirmed that the United Kingdom had failed to comply with Art 9(4) of the Convention by essentially relying too much on the discretion of the judiciary, and the Committee also concluded that the UK was in breach of Art 3(1) in not having a clear, transparent and consistent framework to implement the provisions of the Convention. The Committee recommended that the United Kingdom 'Review its system for allocating costs in environmental cases within the scope of the Convention and undertake practical and legislative measures to overcome the problems identified' (United Kingdom ACCC/C/2008/33, ECE/MP.PP/C.1/2010/6/Add.3, December 2010).

[44] Council Directive (EEC) 85/337, above n 20, and Council Directive (EC) 96/61 concerning integrated pollution prevention and control [1996] L257/26 (now codified under Council Directive (EC) 2009/1 on integrated pollution prevention and control [2008] OJ L24/8).

[45] http://europa.eu/rapid/pressReleasesAction.do?reference=IP/10/312&type=en. The European Environment Commissioner Janez Potonik said, 'When important decisions affecting the environment are taken, the public must be allowed to challenge them. This important principle is established in European law. But the law also requires that these challenges must be affordable. I urge the UK to address this problem quickly as ultimately the health and wellbeing of the public as a whole depends on these rights' (press release, March 2010).

[46] European Commission Press Release 8/11/439, Brussels, 6 April 2011. Advocate General Kokott gave her Opinion in September 2012 and proposed that, based on the procedures in the United Kingdom as of May 2010, the Court should declare that the discretion given to the courts and the criteria applied was inconsistent with the objective nature of Aarhus provisions contained in the EU directives. C 530/11 *European Commission v United Kingdom* Opinion of Advocate General, 12 September 2013. Her Opinion was upheld by the CJEU on 13 February 2014. Since the proceedings commenced, the government introduced amendments to the Civil Procedure Rules, which came into effect on 1 April 2013 and reduced the judicial discretion concerning protective costs orders in Aarhus environmental claims: see Civil Procedure Rules, rules 45.43 and 45.44; Practice Direction 45, paras 5.1 and 5.2.

It is difficult to see how this three-way pressure from the judiciary, the international convention and the European Union will not lead to significant change, even at a time of restrictions on public expenditure. In its most recent decision on Aarhus,[47] the Court of Justice of the European Union has held that the Aarhus Convention now forms 'an integral part of the legal order of the European Union'. As such, it applies to all areas of environmental protection covered by EU environmental law, and, in relation to access to justice, there is a duty on national courts 'to interpret, to the fullest extent possible, the procedural rules relating to the conditions to be met in order to bring administrative or judicial proceedings' in fights with the objectives of the Convention. In the arguments concerning a specialist environmental court considered below, one ground for resisting change was that it was inappropriate to make a special case for the environment compared with other fields of law. The same argument has been made in the context of the Convention, but, because the legal obligation to implement within the environmental field is a reality, far from providing a ground for maintaining the status quo, it has had the reverse effect of creating pressure for change in all areas of judicial review. Both the difficulties of defining the boundaries of the Convention and the unfairness of confining its principles to one area of law have been acknowledged by the courts.[48] Jackson LJ's major review of civil litigation costs published in 2010[49] recognised the significance of the Convention but similarly argued that any change in the costs principles should apply to all judicial reviews. He recommended a solution of 'qualified one way costs shifting', where essentially the defendant pays the claimant's costs if the claim is successful but the claimant does not pay the defendant's costs if the claim is unsuccessful. Jackson was prepared to allow for exceptions, giving considerable judicial discretion and taking into account the financial resources of the parties and their conduct in connection with the proceedings. A follow-up report of the Sullivan Working Party[50] welcomed the general thrust of the Jackson proposals but recommended a rule that involved less judicial discretion and uncertainty, 'An unsuccessful Claimant in a claim for judicial review shall not be ordered to pay the costs of any other party other than where the Claimant has acted unreasonably in bringing or conducting the proceedings'. The implication of the proposed shifts in approach is that the permission stage of judicial review will become more significant in weeding out unmeritorious claims rather than the potential exposure to costs acting as a surrogate filter to frivolous action. The fundamental reappraisal of costs principles in judicial review, initiated rather cautiously by the judiciary in *Corner House*, is now largely being driven by obligations and perspectives created within environmental law.[51]

---

[47] Case C-240/09 *Lesoochranarske zoskupenie VLK v Ministerstvo zivotneho prostredia Slovenskej republiky*, 8 March 2011.

[48] *Compton v Wiltshire Primary Care Trust* [2008] EWCA Civ 749, [20]; *R (Buglife – The Invertebrate Conservation Trust) v Thurrock Thames Gateway Development Corporation* [2008] EWCA Civ 1209, [17]; *Morgan v Hinton Organics (Wessex) Ltd* [2009] EWCA Civ 07, [33].

[49] www.judiciary.gov.uk/publications-and-reports/reports/civil/review-of-civil-litigation-costs.

[50] Working Group on Access to Justice (Chair Lord Justice Sullivan), 'Ensuring Access to Environmental Justice in England and Wales – Follow Up Report' (2010).

[51] See the rules on protective costs orders for Aarhus claims introduced in April 2013 imposing fixed exposure costs for Aarhus environmental claims: Civil Procedure Rules, rules 45.43 and 45.44; Practice Direction 45 paras 5.1 and 5.2. In its 2014 proposals to reform PCOs and other financial provisions for judicial review claims in order to prevent misuse of the courts in judicial review, the government acknowledges that they cannot apply to Aarhus claims until the final judgment of the Court of Justice in the infringement proceedings brought by the European Commission. 'Once the outcome is known, intends to examine whether the approach to PCOs in environmental cases should be further reviewed': Ministry of Justice, 'Judicial Review – Proposals for Further Reform: The Government Response', Cm 8811 (February 2014) para 59.

Reforming Regulatory Sanctions

Despite a long history of regulatory controls in the environmental field, the way in which they were actually enforced remained somewhat obscure until the early 1970s. Discretion and secrecy permeated the enforcement role of regulators, and specialised government agencies, such as the Alkali Inspectorate regulating air emissions from key sectors of industry, preferred a policy of gentle persuasion rather than aggressive legal action. Pressure from the new wave of non-governmental organisations in the 1970s began to shed light on how these bodies actually operated, and this was followed by a series of sophisticated socio-legal research studies designed to analyse how individual enforcement officers exercised their enforcement discretion in dealing with regulatory breaches.[52] Criminal law with offences mainly drafted in strict liability terms dominated the structure of environmental laws, but it was clear that, whatever the strict letter of the law, officers often exercised their own sense of judgement as to what constituted or did not constitute criminal behaviour before deciding whether to prosecute or not.

The creation of new national regulatory bodies in the 1990s, such as the Environment Agency, was motivated in part by the desire of industry in particular to see a more consistent approach to the implementation and enforcement of controls across the country. This desire for consistency was not confined to the setting of consents and licences but affected the strategy for enforcement as well, with the result that the Environment Agency became the first national regulatory body to publish a detailed enforcement policy setting out the core principles as to how it would respond to regulatory breaches and the circumstances in which it was likely to prosecute or not.

Nevertheless, the range of sanctions available to environmental regulators still remained fairly narrow – warning letters, a formal caution or an actual prosecution. Many regulators possessed powers under different environmental laws to serve notices requiring the industry concerned to take the necessary steps to come back into compliance, but sanctions for breach of such notices remained equally narrow and in the last step were based on the criminal law. There was criticism both of the apparently small sentences (mostly fines) imposed by the lower criminal courts in dealing with environmental offences and the opportunity that strict liability offences allowed lawyers to persuade lay magistrates to downplay the seriousness of offences[53] – a somewhat ironic development, given that the strict liability offence had originally been developed in the nineteenth century expressly to make prosecution of industry and businesses simpler. This was coupled with critiques of the limited range of sanctions available and the heavy reliance on criminal law, especially compared with the practice in the field of environmental law in other jurisdictions such as Germany and Australia.[54]

---

[52] Examples include K Hawkins, *Environment and Enforcement: Regulation and the Social Definition of Pollution* (1984); G Richardson, A Ogus and P Burrows, *Policing Pollution: A Study of Regulation and Enforcement* (1982); BM Hutter, *The Reasonable Arm of the Law? The Enforcement Procedures of Environmental Health Officers* (1988).

[53] P de Prez, 'Excuses, Excuses: The Ritual Trivialization of Environmental Prosecutions' (2000) 12(1) *Journal of Environmental Law* 277.

[54] J Abbott, 'The Regulatory Enforcement of Pollution Control Laws: The Australian Experience' (2005) 17(2) *Journal of Environmental Law* 161.

In 2004 a report commissioned by the Department for Environment, Food and Rural Affairs[55] called for environmental regulators to be given the power to impose civil financial penalties as an additional form of sanction to criminal prosecution, and most likely to be appropriate to the normally responsible operator who, through carelessness or an oversight, had caused a serious regulatory breach. Civil penalties of this sort were not unknown in British law and were extensively used in fields such a financial regulation and competition law, but would have been an innovation in more traditional areas of business regulation. Although well received, the report did not attract sufficient political support to justify change. Industry in particular was alarmed at the prospect of suddenly shifting from a familiar system of regulatory prosecution, with criminal burdens of proof resting on the regulator, to one where the regulator could impose large financial penalties on a civil standard of proof and bypass the courts, leaving the burden on industry to raise any defence by appeal. Given that it was the more responsible end of industry that would most likely be at the receiving end of civil penalties, with the criminal law reserved for the more egregious offenders, this seemed potentially doubly unfair. The report laid important groundwork but failed to address in sufficient detail those wider issues of regulatory governance that would be necessary to secure political purchase. More fundamentally, a convincing case had to be made out for singling out the environment for special treatment compared to many other areas of regulation, such as health and safety and trading standards, that would appear to be susceptible to the same analysis.

The debate concerning environmental sanctions appeared to have ground to a halt, and the impetus for what would eventually prove the decisive shift came from a quite unexpected and unconnected government initiative. In 2004 the Treasury commissioned a wide-ranging review of the administrative burdens imposed on business by regulatory enforcement. The Hampton Review, published in 2005,[56] argued that too many regulators, especially at local government level, had adopted an excessively 'tick-box' mentality to enforcement, losing sight of the overall aims of regulation. Hampton called for a greater emphasis on a risk-based approach to regulatory enforcement, focusing resources on the clearly non-compliant, and adopting a more enlightened and cost-effective approach towards legitimate business. The Review acknowledged that that excessive reliance on the criminal law appeared inimical to a philosophy of a more nuanced relationship between the regulators and the regulated, and recommended the government to initiate a special review of regulatory sanctions.

The subsequent Macrory Review on regulatory sanctions reported in 2006.[57] As with Hampton, the Macrory Review encompassed an enormous spectrum – some 61 national regulators as well as all local authorities, covering areas such as health and safety, planning, trading standards, environment, and food standards. Despite very different sets of laws in such a diverse range of regulations, common patterns emerged, with the core formal sanction under nearly all areas being a criminal offence, usually drafted in strict or semi-strict terms. It was equally clear that there were very similar patterns in the range of non-compliant actors, whatever the field of regulation. At one end of the spectrum,

---

[55] M Woods and R Macrory, *Environmental Civil Penalties – A More Proportionate Response to Regulatory Breach* (2004).

[56] P Hampton, *Reducing Administrative Burdens: Effective Inspection and Enforcement* (London, HM Treasury, 2005).

[57] R Macrory, *Regulatory Justice: Making Sanctions Effective* (London, Cabinet Office, 2006), reproduced in Chapter 2 above.

there were the truly egregious individuals or companies who knew exactly what they were doing and were often making large sums of money out of breaking the law. At the other end were responsible businesses who unintentionally committed a breach – an unexpected equipment breakdown, for example. The middle ground covered a range of different circumstances, involving carelessness or a failure to give sufficient priority to regulatory compliance but lacking direct intention or recklessness. British enforcement practice has never required the police or regulators to prosecute for every offence, and in many instances warnings or a more formal caution might be an effective response at least where responsible businesses were concerned. However, even unintentional breaches might give rise to significant harm or the risk of such harm, and in such circumstances a formal sanction would be appropriate and, indeed, expected by the public. It was questionable, though, whether the criminal law was appropriate, and Macrory argued that the criminal law was in effect being made to do too much work within the regulatory system – indeed, there was a danger that the criminal law itself was being devalued in the process.

The Macrory Review advocated six core penalty principles that should underline the design of any effective regulatory sanctions system. A sanction should: (i) aim to change the behaviour of the offender; (ii) aim to eliminate any financial gain or benefit from non-compliance; (iii) be responsive and consider what is appropriate for the particular offender and regulatory issue; (iv) be proportionate to the nature of the offence and the harm caused; (v) aim to reverse harm caused by regulatory compliance; and (vi) aim to deter future non-compliance.

The current system dominated by the criminal law was found wanting against these principles. The Review argued that regulators should have access to a much wider range of non-criminal sanctions, including civil penalties, familiar in areas such as competition and economic regulation but far less common in other areas. Civil penalties allow a regulator to calculate and impose a financial sanction without the intervention of a court unless the offender decides to appeal.

For many, these proposals could represent an unacceptable shift of discretionary powers to regulators, and the Review addressed these issues in a rather more sophisticated way than in previous studies. First, regulators were to be given power to offer enforcement undertakings as an alternative to the imposition of a civil penalty. Here the business itself would in effect design its own self-imposed sanction, which could then be accepted by the regulator. The Review was insistent that such undertakings were made available to the public to avoid the impression of secret deals between the regulaters and the regulated, but they offered an attractive form of sanction for the legitimate business that had made a one-off serious regulatory breach. Perhaps rather surprisingly there was very little evidence presented to the Review that the criminal standard of proof presented a significant hurdle in detection and enforcement – the problem with the criminal law was more its inappropriateness for certain types of breaches, the slowness of procedures and the frequent lack of knowledge amongst lay magistrates. The Review therefore recommended no change to the existing regulatory offences and that the same standard of proof – the criminal standard of beyond all reasonable doubt – should apply whether or nor a criminal or civil penalty was imposed.[58] In practice, regulators would continue to

[58] Actually, I was mistaken to say this. The Review advocated an integrated approach to inspection and enforcement but accepted that civil standards of proof would apply to civil penalties. The Regulatory Enforcement and Sanctions act 2008 introduced criminal standards of proof for civil penalties. See pp 119–21 above.

investigate to criminal standards and with all the procedural protections of the criminal law, and only then, assuming that a case could be proved and that a formal sanction necessary, determine whether a criminal or civil response was appropriate. This approach was intended to avoid problems that have plagued many other regulatory systems, where there can be lack of coordination between different bodies responsible for criminal and civil investigation or where a civil response may be considered to be reserved for weaker cases. In pure legal terms, this aspect of the proposed design was probably the most innovative element of the Review and offers the prospect of a truly integrated sanctions system not found in other jurisdictions. Finally, the Review contained recommendations designed to diminish the opportunities of abuse by regulators. These principles – termed 'characteristics' in the Review – provide something of a constitutional bedrock in the design of regulatory systems. Regulators who acquired the powers would be legally obliged to publish enforcement policies spelling out the circumstances in which they were likely to impose different sorts of sanction,[59] as well as guidance on how they proposed to calculate civil penalties. Regulators should regularly make public reports on both outputs (the number of enforcement actions taken and so on) and outcomes (the extent to which key policy goals are being secured). Internal practices and procedures that might inadvertently distort the choice of sanction route should be avoided, and in particular the regulator should never receive directly any income from civil penalties – the Review was well aware that the perception, whether justified or not, that regulators were financially interested in the enforcement of regulatory requirements had undermined public credibility in such areas of regulation as traffic parking or speeding.

Many of the arguments concerning the limitations of wholesale reliance on the criminal law as a regulatory sanction had already been rehearsed in the environmental field, but by looking at regulatory sanctions across such a wide spectrum, the Review did not have to make any special pleading for any particular field of law. Instead, it was able to articulate common principles that should be adopted in all areas and, largely as a result, all the recommendations in the Review were accepted by the government. Part III of the Regulatory Enforcement and Sanctions Act 2008 provided the framework for the core powers concerning civil sanctions as well as the recommendations on regulatory governance. The Review did not advocate that all regulators should be obliged to acquire the new powers – it would be up to ministers to draw them down by regulations – and in 2010 two national regulators, the Environment Agency and Natural England were the first to acquire the new powers.[60] Since then the Environment Agency has published its proposed guidance on how to calculate civil penalties, and a revised enforcement policy incorporating the new powers with the first civil penalties was introduced in 2011.

Other regulators have expressed interest, but it is clear that it is in the environmental field that the first serious experience of the new regime will be tested and evaluated. It is too early to predict the real impact of these reforms, but a significant shift in thinking about the design of regulatory sanctions in the UK has begun to take place. Regulators and their departmental sponsors are more than ever conscious of financial pressures on public resources, and a critical element in the eventual success of the reforms is likely to

---

[59] At the time of the Review, some regulator bodies, including the Environment Agency, had already published an enforcement policy, but only 17 out of 60 national regulators had a policy that was publicly available: Macrory, ibid, paras 5.7–5.17.

[60] The Environmental Civil Sanctions (England) Order 2010 (SI 2010/1157) and the Environmental Sanctions (Misc Amendments) (England) Regulations 2010 (SI 2010/1159). Similar regulations have been made for Wales.

be their impact on cost savings. The new system deliberately does not lighten the costs of investigation by regulatory bodies, but where a civil penalty is proposed it should make it simpler or faster to resolve the issue without the need for the involvement of a court or tribunal. It is, however, possible to envisage regulators in practice becoming overconfident or ambitious in applying proposed civil sanctions, followed by protracted negotiations and arguments between the regulators and the regulated, coupled with an extensive number of appeals. If that were to happen, regulators and their ministers might conclude that in pure economic terms the traditional criminal enforcement system was preferable, and the system would revert back to its familiar pattern of relying on the criminal law.[61]

This scenario is possible but unlikely, not least because the sanctions review has now set in train a substantial review of the use of criminal law in the regulatory system. The Review itself did not advocate the abandonment of criminal law, and made important recommendations concerning the improvement of the current system, including giving criminal judges a wider range of sanctions where a case had been proved. These include publicity orders, corporate rehabilitation orders and orders that could speedily remove a financial gain made from non-compliance with regulatory requirements. Yet the Review also questioned the continued reliance on offences drafted in strict liability terms, allowing companies to be held vicariously liable for acts they knew nothing about or had even prohibited.[62] It fell shy of making blanket recommendations concerning the future structure of the criminal law but recommended that the government initiate a review of the drafting and formulation of criminal offences relating the regulatory non-compliance. As a result, the Law Commission launched a study on the subject, and published an initial consultation paper in 2010.[63]

An Environmental Court

Legal cases involving environmental issues in the UK have long been heard in the ordinary courts appropriate for the type of action brought. Environmental judicial reviews are handled by the Administrative Court, though clearly with some degree of specialisation developing amongst the judges who are assigned particular cases. Similarly, the prosecution for criminal offences concerning the environment has taken place before the ordinary criminal courts, with private civil actions, such as nuisance or negligence arising from pollution, being handled by the civil courts. But for over 20 years in the UK there has been intense debate on a possible role of a specialised environmental court or tribunal, though

---

[61] There are also concerns within the coalition government as to whether regulators rather than the courts should have the power to impose financial sanctions: 'Civil Sanctions Regime is "Intolerable" says Minister', *ENDS Report*, 7 April 2011. On 12 November 2012 the government announced a new policy on civil sanctions in a written statement to Parliament by Rt Hon Michael Fallon, Minister of State for Business and Enterprise; Department for Business, Innovation and Skills, who said that in future powers to imposes financial penalties under Part III of the Regulatory Enforcement and Sanctions Act would 'only be granted where their used is restricted to undertakings with more than 250 employees'.

[62] The combination of strict and vicarious liability was described by Glanville Williams as a 'tyrannous combination' and quoted by Simon Brown LJ in *National Rivers Authority v Alfred McAlpine Homes East Ltd* [1994] 4 All ER 286.

[63] The Law Commission, 'Criminal Liability in Regulatory Contexts', Consultation Paper No 195 (2010).

often the arguments have been dogged by very different visions of what the concept might entail in practice.

The first official recommendation for an environmental court appears to have been contained in a report by Sir Robert Carnwath, then a leading planning barrister and now a judge in the Court of Appeal and the Senior President of the new Tribunal System.[64] The report was largely concerned with strengthening the enforcement mechanisms within the existing town and country planning system,[65] but Carnwath made a cautious case for combining the jurisdictions of various courts and tribunals dealing with planning and environmental protection into a single judicial forum. Three years later, the then Lord Chief Justice, Lord Woolf, provided a broader vision.[66] He argued that a distinctive feature of environmental law was the possibility of a single pollution incident giving rise to many different types of legal action heard in different legal fora – a coroner's inquest (if deaths involved), criminal prosecution where regulatory offences had been committed, civil actions for compensation, and judicial review if public authorities are involved. He felt there was a strong case for a single environmental court which would handle all the legal consequences that arose from an environmental incident or problem. Lord Woolf's vision was for a body which was not just a court or existing tribunal under another name, but something quite radically different:

> It is a multi-faceted, multi-skilled body which would combine the services provided by the existing courts, tribunals, and inspectors in the environmental field. It would be a 'one-stop shop' which should lead to faster, cheaper, and more effective resolution of disputes in the environmental area.[67]

Largely as a result of Lord Woolf's lecture, the then Department of Environment and Transport and the Regions commissioned a major study examining the experience of specialised environmental courts in other jurisdictions, and considering possible models that could be adopted in the UK. The Grant Report[68] considered six different forms of court or tribunal that might be adopted, but in essence there were two main routes that could be followed – the so-called 'big bang' approach, involving the creation of a major new environmental court, probably as a division of the High Court, or strengthening existing judicial and quasi-judicial institutions from the bottom up to develop greater expertise in environmental law. The political appetite for institutional change was, however, not present at the time.[69]

Two years later, following a recommendation of the Royal Commission on Environmental Pollution,[70] the Department for Environment, Food and Rural Affairs commissioned a further study on the subject but one with a narrower focus. The Report[71] examined over

---

[64] Robert Carnwath was appointed to the Supreme Court in December 2011.

[65] R Carnwath, *Enforcing Planning Control* (London, HMSO, 1989).

[66] H Woolf, 'Are the Judiciary Environmental Myopic?' (1992) 4(1) *Journal of Environmental Law* 1.

[67] Ibid, 14.

[68] M Grant, *Environmental Court Project: Final Report* (2000). For a review of the Report see S Tromans, 'Environmental Court Project' (2001) 13(3) *Journal of Environmental Law* 423.

[69] Lord Brennan initiated a debate on the subject in the House of Lords. According to Lord Bach, the Minister, 'The Government welcomes the opportunity to debate this issue. We are not persuaded of the need for an environmental court, certainly not on its possible shape': *Hansard*, HL, col 100 (9 October 2000).

[70] Royal Commission on Environmental Pollution, 'Environmental Planning', Cm 5459 (2002) para 5.37.

[71] R Macrory with M Woods, *Modernising Environmental Justice: Regulation and the Role of an Environmental Tribunal* (Centre for Law and the Environment, Faculty of Laws University College London, 2003), reproduced in Chapter 6 of this volume

50 sets of environmental regulations to determine the extent to which they contained statutory rights of appeal and where these appeals were heard. The town and country planning system contained a well-established appeal system for developers, with appeals heard by an executive agency of government, the Planning Inspectorate. Compared to this, the system for environmental appeals was far more muddled, with a wide range of different bodies involved, including the Secretary of State, the High Court, magistrates courts and the Planning Inspectorate. The lack of coherence appeared to simply be a matter of historical accident rather than a conscious decision by policy makers, and the Report recommended that an environmental tribunal be established to act as a single statutory appeals body.

But there were two particular challenges to the proposal. As with the initial debates on the use of civil penalties in environmental enforcement, the question that had to be addressed was whether the environment deserved special treatment. The report argued that there were a number of features that did indeed distinguish environmental law from many other legal fields – the extent to which technical and scientific questions were frequently intertwined with legal issues, the prevalence of EU environmental legislation, the emergence of core underlying legal principles such as the precautionary principle, the heavy involvement of public bodies exercising considerable discretion, the growing significance of international environmental treaties, and the developing concept of sustainable development as an underlying policy goal. Many of these features are to be found individually in other areas of law, such as workplace safety, but it was the combination of all which appeared to place environmental law in a distinctive position and required a more specialised judicial approach. But not all found this argument convincing. The Scottish Government, for example, rejected the argument:

> We acknowledge the special characteristics listed by Macrory and Woods and accept that they are features of environmental law. However, we are not persuaded that these features, or indeed this combination of features is unique to environmental law and it could be argued that similar statements could be made equally about other areas of law such as health, health & safety and employment none of which have specialist Courts/jurisdiction.[72]

The second challenge related to the proposal's rather modest vision of an environmental tribunal. This may have been workable, but at the time it did not align with the approach being promoted by environmental non-governmental organisations and lawyers in a study also funded by the Department for Environment, Food and Rural Affairs. The Environmental Justice Report[73] was particularly concerned with the costs and risk of exposure to costs involved in environmental litigation, and argued that a far more radical approach was needed in the form of a new division of the High Court with the power to hear all civil law claims with a significant environmental component. Faced with the environmental law community itself advocating very different models of a specialist environmental court or tribunal, it was hardly surprising that the government felt unable to act, and the debate appeared to have ground to a halt.

---

[72] Environment and Rural Affairs Department, Scottish Government, 'Strengthening and Streamlining The Way Forward for the Enforcement of Environmental Law in Scotland' (Scottish Executive, 2006) para 2.99.

[73] WWF, Environmental Law Foundation (ELF) and Leigh Day & Co, 'Environmental Justice Project: A Report' (Defra, 2004).

This proved to be an over-pessimistic presumption. Two years later, the Review of Regulatory Sanctions[74] had to consider the question of appeals against the imposition of the civil sanctions it was recommending. Under the European Convention on Human Rights, Article 6, there would have to be a right of appeal to an independent court or tribunal, but even if this had not been the case, the Review would have recommended such a right as a matter of fairness and a check against regulatory abuse. Appeals could have gone back to the ordinary courts, but the Review took advantage of the fact that a new, more flexible tribunal system was being created,[75] and recommended that appeals against civil sanctions should go to a new regulatory tribunal. Once the regulator had decided that a civil sanction was the appropriate route, then all procedures should remain within the administrative system rather than become possibly confused by being heard within criminal courts. The government accepted the recommendation and the Regulatory Enforcement and Sanctions Act 2008 provided that appeals should go to the First-tier Tribunal, the first level of tribunals established under the new system,[76] unless a more specialised and appropriate tribunal already existed.

As discussed above, it is the national environmental regulators that in practice have been the first bodies to acquire the new civil sanction powers, and the first orders in 2010 provided for appeals to go to a tribunal.[77] The new tribunal system had divided the first-tier level into a number of chambers, grouping together jurisdictions dealing with similar work or requiring similar skills, and was decided that sanctions appeals best fell within the General Regulatory Chamber. Since the first appeals would fall within the field of environmental regulation, in April 2010 an internal administrative decision was taken to establish an environmental tribunal within the Regulatory Chamber. With remarkably little fanfare or fuss, England and Wales gained a specialist environmental judicial body after almost 20 years of debate. Admittedly, its jurisdiction is extremely limited compared to earlier visions of an environmental court or tribunal, but the important institutional step had been taken, and in future its remit may well be extended to encompass a wider environmental remit.[78] From one perspective the creation of the environmental tribunal at this point was purely a matter of chance – if regulators in other fields had been the first movers to acquire civil sanctions the story might have been very different. Yet the initial focus on the environment was not wholly surprising. It was in the environmental field that the most substantial intellectual case for civil sanctions had been made for a number of years prior to the Regulatory Enforcement and Sanctions Act 2008, and it was in the same field of law that the arguments for a new specialist form of court or tribunal had already

[74] Macrory (2006), above n 57.

[75] The system of tribunals was reformed under the Tribunals, Court and Enforcement Act 2007 following the major review by Sir Andrew Leggatt, *Tribunals for Users: One System, One Service* (Department for Constitutional Affairs, 2001), available at http://webarchive.nationalarchives.gov.uk/+/http://www.tribunals-review.org.uk/index.htm.

[76] Appeals on points of law go to the Upper Tribunal.

[77] See n 59 above.

[78] In 2010, Lord Justice Carnwath, as he then was, commissioned in his capacity as Senior President of Tribunals a study to re-examine the issue of consolidating administrative appeals under environmental regulations. The final report, R Macrory, 'Consistency and Effectiveness – Strengthening the New Environment Tribunal' (Centre for Law and the Environment, UCL, 2011), reproduced in Chapter 7 of this volume, argued that most environmental appeals should now go to the First-tier Tribunal (Environment). As of February 2014, the Environment Tribunal had yet to hear an appeal against a civil sanction, but since its establishment it has been given power to determine an increasing number of statutory appeals under various pieces of environmental legislation. See http://www.justice.gov.uk/downloads/tribunals/environment/environment-rules-rights-appeal.pdf.

been extensively rehearsed. It remains to be seen what longer-term impact the presence of a specialist tribunal will make to the development of environmental law in this country, but it is likely to be considerable.

The Future

Disputes involving environmental law issues often display inherent characteristics that in any event do not lend themselves to easy resolution by conventional legal institutional arrangements, and this has provided some of the impetus for innovation. Lord Woolf has noted how environmental litigation tends to display an unusual combination of technical and scientific complexities, challenging policy issues, and issues that cut across traditional divides between criminal and civil law and between public and private interests.[79] In addition, the fusion of environmental obligations developed under European Union environmental law and international public environmental law has now added a distinctive and powerful pressure to the national discourse, making it difficult for the government to stonewall legal and policy change. But perhaps more significantly the search for new legal ways of doing things reflects an unease with the capability of more traditional legal and regulatory techniques in contemporary environmental challenges. The British environmentalist Tom Burke has spoken of an 'old' and a 'new' environmental agenda.[80] The older agenda encompasses such subjects as water pollution and waste disposal, where the problem is generally well understood, the science of cause and effect are reasonably settled, and the policy maker is usually faced with situations where nearly all those affected by policy change will gain – the public will generally welcome tighter environmental controls, but equally legitimate industry will often support regulation in that it drives out the sub-standard. Legal techniques that are likely to be effective are often well established and, while there will always be problems in enforcement and implementation, the basic legal toolkit is not called into question. The newer environmental agenda concerns issues such as transport, climate change, resource use and biodiversity, where the underlying knowledge and science may be far less certain, and the policy solutions by no means bring about immediate win–win situations. It is far less clear what sort of legal techniques are appropriate, or indeed what role law may play in their resolution. In this light, it is hardly surprising that in recent years much of environmental legal development has shifted from prescribing clearly defined solutions to providing more open-ended approaches where the law provides a combination of legal rights and opportunities for more extensive citizen engagement and obligations and procedures designed to make the state more accountable for what it does. One test of an effective constitutional and legal system is its ability to handle and accommodate competing visions, and to adapt to new perceptions and understandings. From this perspective, environmental law has proved remarkably creative over the past quarter of a century, and has provided a laboratory and impetus for deeper changes in our legal and constitutional system.

[79] Lord Woolf, 'Environmental Law and Sustainable Development' in H. Woolf, *The Pursuit of Justice* (2008) 391.
[80] See R Macrory, 'Maturity and Methodology – A Personal Reflection' (2009) 21(2) *Journal of Environmental Law* 251, 254.

9

Judicial Review – Proposals for Further Reform[1] (2013)

Aarhus and Access to Justice

As is noted several times in the Consultation Paper, Article 9 of the Aarhus Convention constrains the way in which the government can restrict the right of review by third parties in environmental cases. The Aarhus access to justice provisions are now reflected in two core EU environmental directives (environmental assessment and industrial emissions), and the European Court of Justice has recently gone further by stating that, since the EU is party to Aarhus, 'According to settled case-law, the provisions of that convention now form an integral part of the legal order of the European Union'.[2]

Although the Consultation Paper acknowledges that many of the proposals, especially concerning standing, will not apply to Aarhus cases, many planning judicial reviews (JRs) – involving environmental assessment, for example – will inevitably engage Aarhus, and to treat planning and environmental JRs as distinct categories is not in reality sustainable. This is all the more so given that the UK chose to implement the Environmental Assessment Directive within its existing town and country planning controls. The UK has traditionally adopted a fairly 'gold-plated' form of judicial review, and my personal view is that the vision of Aarhus for economical and speedy access to legal review for a broad section of the public, including NGOs, will require a more radical rethink of how we handle JRs, well beyond the capped costs regime introduced in April of this year.[3] Otherwise, there is a danger that the UK will face continuing challenges to the compatibility of current procedures with Aarhus, together with increasing uncertainty and delays. The need for a fresh approach could tie in with some of the proposals in the Consultation Paper which I expand upon below. I also think it is worth exploring recent reforms in how we handle environmental statutory appeals and what they might have to offer in this context.

The Aarhus provisions on access to justice do not require that such rights are exercised by judicial review before the courts – Article 9 permits review before a court of law or 'another independent and impartial body established by law'. Equally, as the Sullivan Report noted, 'Aarhus does not entitle members of the public to bring frivolous or unwar-

[1] A revised version of the submission by Professor Macrory to the Ministry of Justice during the consultation of *Judicial Review – Proposals for Further Reform*, Cm 8703 (6 September 2013).
[2] Case C-240/09 *Slovakian Bear*, 8 March 2011, para 30.
[3] Civil Procedure (Amendment) Rule 2013/262.

ranted claims'.[4] The costs in the cause principle, with the potential risk of exposure to the other side's costs should the case be lost, has in the past no doubt acted as a surrogate filter on weak or unfounded cases, counterbalancing the liberal approach to standing developed by the judiciary over the last 25 years or so. It is now accepted that costs in the cause are not compatible with Article 9 of Aarhus, but restricting standing cannot be used as an equivalent filter, since that can be equally incompatible with Aarhus. Cost capping, as recently introduced for Aarhus cases, may address the costs issues (though there remain doubts whether the lack of flexibility in the amounts specified are compatible with Aarhus), but potentially imposes significant costs on public bodies even where they win cases. Hence the need to rethink how we handle such cases and whether they could be dealt with more speedily and economically than traditional JR procedures.

It is also important to note that it is not only NGOs that can make use of JR procedures to raise legitimate concerns about legality and/or as a delaying tactic: planning and environmental JRs are also brought by rival industries and businesses, whose motives for doing so may also sometimes be questionable or are driven by their own economic interests. Given the radical nature of some of the proposals, I would have found it helpful to have had a more detailed analysis of the planning JRs brought in recent years (who were the claimant parties (developers, national NGOs, local individuals, etc), their success rate, the extent to which Aarhus was engaged, etc). The general figures in the Consultation Paper for all JRs do not indicate whether these are equally applicable to planning JRs. Below, I give more details of the analysis of environmental JRs I conducted for Defra a few years ago which provide some useful insights.

First-tier Tribunal as a Regulatory Appeals Body

In 2003 the Department of Environment Food and Rural Affairs commissioned me to examine the case for a specialised environmental tribunal. My report[5] was focused on providing a more coherent and efficient system for handling regulatory appeals in environmental regulation rather than judicial review as such, although it was clear that there was a connection between the issues. In this context, a regulatory appeal means the right of the applicant for a consent or licence or a person in receipt of some form of regulatory enforcement notice (such as a remediation notice) to appeal on merits to another body. The right of appeal against refusal of planning permission to the Secretary of State (and mainly handled by the Planning Inspectorate) has been a long-established feature of the town and country planning system. The 2003 report demonstrated that the system was far more confused in the field of environmental regulation, with appeals heard by a range of different bodies under different legislation, and sometimes there was no right of appeal. The evidence suggested that an incoherent or incomplete system of regulatory appeals was likely to increase the pressure on judicial reviews. My proposal for a new specialist

---

[4] Report of the Working Group on Access to Environmental Justice, 'Ensuring Access to Environmental Justice in England and Wales' (2008) (the Sullivan Report) para 7.

[5] R Macrory with M Woods, *Modernising Environmental Justice: Regulation and the Role of an Environmental Tribunal* (Centre for Law and the Environment, Faculty of Laws University College London, 2003). See Chapter 6 of this volume.

tribunal to handle such appeals was generally well received, but the government at the time did not act upon it.

Under Part III of the Regulation Enforcement and Sanctions Act 2008, civil sanctions were introduced for a range of environmental regulations, and as a result a specialised Environment Tribunal was established in 2010 within the Regulatory Chamber of the First-tier Tribunal. Although its jurisdiction was initially limited to appeals against sanctions imposed under Part III of RESA, no such appeals have yet been heard because enforceable undertakings (under which the regulator and the regulated business agree an appropriate response to the regulatory breach) have to date proved to be a more effective mechanism that the imposition of a sanction. In the two formal appeals to date (remediation notices imposed by the Marine Protection Agency), the Tribunal, through effective case management, has secured agreed settlements.[6] In 2010, the then Senior President of Tribunals commissioned me to re-examine whether, now that there existed an Environmental Tribunal, there was a case for the Tribunal to handle a greater range of regulatory appeals in the environmental legislation. My report[7] concluded that, if anything, the system for regulatory appeals had become more confused since the 2003 study, and I recommended that environmental appeals should as a matter of principle be consolidated within the Tribunal. This would provide a more coherent and specialised body, and be beneficial to both the regulated community and the wider public interest. The general analysis was accepted by the government, and over the past few years a large number of existing environmental appeals have been transferred to the Environment Tribunal, with more proposed. Over 400 Nitrate Zone Appeals were heard by the Tribunal this year.

Environmental Judicial Reviews

As part of the 2003 study, I was given access to judicial review files in the High Court, and examined cases involving environmental legislation over the past three years. Town and country planning cases, including those involving environmental assessment, were deliberately excluded, and inevitably some subjective judgement had to be made as to what was or was not an environmental case. Overall, there were around 60–70 such judicial reviews over the three year period, and 55 files were examined in detail.

The figures indicated that the majority of cases (28 out of 55) were brought by companies or industry, while 22 were brought by individuals or environmental groups or similar associations. Decision makers being challenged included government departments in 27 cases and the Environment Agency in 16 cases. The average time for cases to reach a full hearing in court was six months from the date of lodgement, and the average duration of the main hearing was 1.3 days.

Leave for judicial review was refused in 12 cases, indicating a higher rate of leave being granted than in the 2012 figures quoted in the consultation document. Thirteen cases were withdrawn, and of the remainder only four were ultimately successful. The figures

---

[6] The parties to the first appeal were represented by counsel from the same chambers, who have since written a joint and positive account of the procedure: http://www.39essex.com/resources/news.php?id=163.

[7] R Macrory, 'Consistency and Effectiveness – Strengthening the New Environment Tribunal' (Centre for Law and the Environment, UCL, 2011), reproduced in Chapter 7 of this volume.

quoted in the consultation document indicate a 40 per cent success rate for the claimant in adjudicated decisions, though it is not clear whether this applies equally to planning cases. One reason for the lower success rate in environmental cases (7 per cent) may be that often the decisions being challenged were those of specialised agencies, who could be expected to ensure that the legal basis of their decision was sound, or whose expertise the courts will generally respect.

Equally, however, it was clear from an examination of the files and the actual decisions of the courts that many of the cases were in reality merits driven but disguised as judicial reviews, and ultimately did not succeed for that reason. The files indicated that about two-thirds of the cases fell within this category, with the claimant essentially seeking a substantial rehearing of the facts. I have not been able to examine recent files, but, on the assumption that there has not been a significant change in the overall picture, there seem to be two responses to this analysis. One is that this confirms a view that judicial review is being used inappropriately, and that stronger case management and leave procedures might more effectively weed out earlier what are in effect merits appeals. The other is that this in fact reflects a repressed need for some form of third party merits appeal which should be addressed rather than dismissed out of hand, or otherwise pressure on JR procedures will continue. The traditional view that it is the local authority or other public agency that is seen as representing the public, thus avoiding the need for third party appeal rights, may no longer hold true.

The right of third party merits appeals (other than by way of judicial review) in planning and other areas has never been a traditional feature of the UK appeals procedure, and will not be attractive in the current climate.[8] However, one could envisage a system whereby third parties who had participated in a regulatory procedure (by objecting to a licence application, for example) could have the right of appeal to the First-tier Environment Tribunal in what would not be a full merits appeal as such, but would rather be restricted to challenging the 'substantive and procedural legality of the decision' (reflecting the wording of the access to justice provisions of Aarhus). The First-tier Tribunal, with its combination of legal and technical expertise, could be expected to handle such appeals with authority, speed and economy, and involving mediation where appropriate. In itself, the right of such an appeal would not necessarily remove the availability of judicial review, but the failure to exercise such a right would weigh heavily with the court.[9] Providing an appeal in this way to the First-tier Tribunal would be more consistent with Aarhus aspirations than JR actions, and the channelling of such challenges through the First-tier Tribunal would help to dampen unrealistic JR claims. As for frivolous or vexatious appeals, the current Tribunal Procedure Rules give the Tribunal considerable powers to strike out claims, including where it considers that 'there is no reasonable prospect of the appellant's case, or part of it, succeeding'.[10] Appeals on point of laws from the First-tier Tribunal would go to the Upper Tribunal.

---

[8] Despite calls for such rights over many years, successive governments have rejected the idea: see, eg the Planning Green Paper 2001, Thirteenth Report of Session 2001–02, HC 476–I; C Barclay, 'Third Party Rights of Appeal in Planning', Research Paper 02/28 (House of Commons Library, 2002).

[9] See, eg Lord Scarman in *R v Inland Revenue Commissioners ex parte Preston* [1985] AC 835: 'a remedy by way of judicial review is not to be available where an alternative remedy exists'.

[10] Tribunal Procedure (First-tier Tribunal) (General Regulatory Chamber) Rules 2009/1976, rule 8.

Upper Tribunal Handling Judicial Reviews

The Consultation Paper considers the possibility of establishing a Lands and Planning Chamber within the Upper Tribunal to handle planning JRs. I find considerable merit in the greater use of the Upper Tribunal to handle specialist JRs of this nature. The combination of members with specialist legal and other technical expertise appropriate to the case in hand is attractive.

The overall objectives of the Upper Tribunal Rules (SI 2008/2698), including the express duty on parties to assist the Upper Tribunal in furthering these objectives, provide a compelling set of principles for a more proportionate and modern approach to JR procedures:

> 2.
> (1) The overriding objective of these Rules is to enable the Upper Tribunal to deal with cases fairly and justly.
> (2) Dealing with a case fairly and justly includes—
> (a) dealing with the case in ways which are proportionate to the importance of the case, the complexity of the issues, the anticipated costs and the resources of the parties;
> (b) avoiding unnecessary formality and seeking flexibility in the proceedings;
> (c) ensuring, so far as practicable, that the parties are able to participate fully in the proceedings;
> (d) using any special expertise of the Upper Tribunal effectively; and
> (e) avoiding delay, so far as compatible with proper consideration of the issues.
> (3) The Upper Tribunal must seek to give effect to the overriding objective when it—
> (a) exercises any power under these Rules; or
> (b) interprets any rule or practice direction.
> (4) Parties must—
> (a) help the Upper Tribunal to further the overriding objective; and
> (b) co-operate with the Upper Tribunal generally.

Compared to the High Court, the Upper Tribunal is likely to have more flexibility in the way it develops procedures appropriate to the type of case in hand. A specialist chamber in the Upper Tribunal would provide an identifiable jurisdiction, and have access to the appropriate professional expertise to handle both the legal issues and the complex factual questions that are often involved in these types of JR. It is likely to have the ability to reach faster decisions which are both consistent and robust, reducing the likelihood of appeals against its decisions. The Upper Tribunal has the capability of encouraging mediation and other interventionist techniques to assist parties in identifying and focusing on the real core issues in dispute, and to reduce the current 'stand-off' periods (which can last many months) between the lodging of JR papers and the actual hearing, which is usually effectively dead time when everything is on hold. There may well also be a case for greater use of written submissions and a time limitation on oral argument (more akin to the Court of Justice of the European Union). Recently, the Upper Tribunal has indicated that in judicial review cases it will not feel obliged to follow the cost-shifting principles applied in the High Court.[11] Above all, the attraction of using the Upper Tribunal (Land Chamber) as the basis for the expansion of jurisdiction is that it is building upon an existing and well-established institution rather than involving the costs and upheaval of establishing a wholly new body.

---

[11] *R (LR) v FtT (HESC) and Hertfordshire County Council* [2013] UKUT 0294.

If a decision is taken to establish a specialist Planning Chamber of the Upper Tribunal in the form of a Land and Planning Chamber, I would suggest that the chamber should also include an environmental jurisdiction. This should happen whether or not the proposal above to introduce a limited right of third party appeal to the First-tier Tribunal is accepted. Defining in a transfer order what is or is not an environmental JR is less easy than defining a planning JR, but a sensible starting point would be JRs involving those areas of environmental law where there now exists a right of statutory appeal to the First-tier (Environment) Tribunal. Where an applicant for, say, an environmental permit[12] has appealed to the First-tier Tribunal, appeals on points of law are heard by the Upper Tribunal. It would make far more sense if any JR by a third party in the same area of law also went to the Upper Tribunal, rather than having two different courts potentially ruling on the same provisions. As further environmental appeals are transferred to the First-tier Tribunal, transfer orders should operate in parallel in relation to JRs in those areas. As the Upper Tribunal develops expertise and profile in such cases, the High Court may be more willing use its discretionary power to transfer individual environmental JRs not falling within a transfer order to the Upper Tribunal where it considers it 'just and convenient' to do so.[13] The proposed new chamber could be named the Land, Planning and Environmental Chamber to reflect its wider jurisdiction. The new body is likely to attract considerable confidence within the business community and the wider public.

There is clearly an argument that it would be premature to create a Land and Planning Chamber in the Upper Tribunal until more is known about the impact of Planning Fast-Track. But the Upper Tribunal has advantages in its capacity for handling specialist JRs, with a membership with combined legal and other relevant professional expertise, and greater flexibility in developing its procedures in the light of the overall objectives stated in its procedural rules. If a decision is taken to delay any role for the Upper Tribunal in the light of Planning Fast-Track, it would still be sensible in the meantime to establish a project to examine in more detail the practicalities and time-scales involved in establishing a Land, Planning and Environment Chamber within the Upper Tribunal, including any primary legislation that may be required.[14]

Procedural Defects

It would be sensible to explore whether one could introduce faster and more economic interlocutory procedures to determine the legality of alleged procedural defects that arise during administrative decision making. Often such an issue will arise but the parties will continue until the result of the final decision, and then, if it is unfavourable to them, look

---

[12] Defra has been consulting this year on transferring environmental permitting appeals to the First-tier (Environment) Tribunal, with a transfer possibly taking place in October 2013. Other areas where the Tribunal currently has appeal jurisdiction include environmental civil sanctions, energy-using products, emissions trading, energy information, carrier-bag charges, marine licencing, nitrate vulnerable zones, flood and coastal zone management, waste regulations, green deal regulations, climate change agreements, energy efficiency schemes and reservoirs.

[13] Supreme Court Act 1981, s 31A, inserted by Tribunal, Courts and Enforcement Act 2007, s 19. As far as I know, no order for such a transfer in an environmental JR has been made to date.

[14] Transferring planning s 288 statutory appeals, including the possible introduction of leave procedures, is likely to require amendments to the Town and Country Planning Act and the Planning Act 2008.

to procedural defects that might vitiate it, with the result that any JR is not heard for months after the final decision.

A lay observer would consider this a strange practice, and potentially an immense waste of time and resources. A procedure that allowed for a rapid interlocutory ruling on the legality of a procedural defect (which could then be remedied during the original decision making) would bring considerable advantages, and avoid the potentially unsatisfactory and difficult task of the judiciary having to second-guess at a later stage whether the defect in question would have made any difference to the final decision.[15] A dispute, for example, about the legality of the scope of environmental assessment information could be resolved in this way rather than waiting for the final decision. The use of the Upper Tribunal to provided rapid access to a decision could be considered. The failure of any party to exercise such a right in respect of a procedural defect of which they were reasonably aware at the time could be a ground for refusing leave for a JR at a later stage.

Standing Issues

The Consultation Paper raises issues concerning standing, and essentially questions whether the judiciary has developed too liberal an approach in its interpretation of the 'sufficient interest' test. As the paper notes, however, in relation to environmental NGOs, the Aarhus Convention (and its implementation under EU law) constrains restrictions on standing in that 'non-governmental organizations promoting environmental protection and meeting any requirements under national law' are deemed to have a sufficient interest to challenge substantive and procedural illegalities. In terms of requirements under national law, some other countries in Europe have developed more precise criteria in relation to standing, such as a minimum size in terms of membership, or that the issue at stake must fall within the purpose of the organisation.[16] However, any requirements under national law must not be contrary to the general goals of Aarhus. In 2009[17] the Court of Justice held that a Swedish requirement that an NGO had to have 2,000 members to have standing before the courts hindered effective judicial protection – the threshold has since be reduced to 100 members.[18]

Although Aarhus therefore expressly permits Member States some discretion to define standing for NGOs, there must be doubts about how far doing so will really meet the concerns expressed in the Consultation Paper. Under the existing principles of sufficient interest, courts will be reluctant to grant standing to an NGO the purposes of which are unrelated to the issue at hand. Even if new standing rules excluded an NGO, it is often possible to find a surrogate individual with clear standing to bring the case. A good example is

---

[15] Parties do sometimes apply for judicial review before the final planning decision is taken when a fundamental legal issue is raised. A good example is *R v Secretary of State for Environment, Transport and Regions ex parte Alconbury*, where parties raised during the public inquiry the compatibility of the procedures with Art 6 of the European Convention on Human Rights. The case eventually reached the House of Lords – [2001] UKHL 23 – and is analysed in Chapter 20, but it is rare for this to happen.

[16] For a recent comparative analysis see Eliantonio et al, *Standing up for Your Right(s) in Europe – A Comparative Study of Locus Standing (Locus Standi) before the EU and Member State' Courts* (Cambridge, Intersentia, 2013).

[17] Case C-263/08 *Djurgarden-Lilla Vartans Miljoskyddsforening v Stockholms kommun genom dess marknamnd* [2009] ECR I-09967.

[18] Eliantionio, above n 16, 73.

the 1983 anti-fluoridation case *McColl v Strathclyde Regional Council*,[19] in which the actual petitioner was an 'adental' elderly woman, but, as the judge noted,

> others attended Court with great regularity and it would be naive to presume that the petitioner alone has an interest in the outcome of this action or indeed that her interests in the outcome is as great as that of others who have attended regularly.

In that case, the petitioner was legally aided, but, since the abolition of champerty as a crime or tort under Criminal Law Act 1967, it is no longer illegal for an NGO to fund another person's legal action – though, subject to court discretion, they could be exposed to a third party costs order. In certain cases, judges have welcomed the value of NGOs as claimants in terms of expertise and efficiency. Otton J (as he then was) noted in *R v Her Majesty's Inspectorate of Pollution ex parte Greenpeace Ltd* (Queens Bench Division, 29 September 1993) that a neighbour or employee of British Nuclear Fuels Ltd who clearly had individual standing would have been unlikely to command the expertise at the disposal of Greenpeace: 'Consequently a less-informed challenge might be mounted which would stretch unnecessarily the court's resources and which would not afford the court the assistance it requires in order to do justice between the parties'.

Finally, when it comes to cases brought for 'political' purposes, courts are highly sensitive to this being a potential abuse of process, and will exercise the power to strike out if this is felt to be a significant motive. One of the first legal cases I was involved in as a young barrister was a tort action brought by families against oil companies producing leaded petrol. Evidence from newsletters produced by the families indicated that this was part of a political campaign, and that they hoped it would secure a great deal of publicity even if they did not win. Had it not been for the fact that the actual plaintiffs were the children of the adults involved, the judge in the lower court indicated he would have struck out the claim as an abuse of process.[20] JRs of course sometimes involve issues of high political significance, but, as illustrated, for example, in the Heathrow extension case,[21] British judges often emphasise that the courts are not the appropriate place to determine questions of policy, accepting the 'principle that Parliament and the elected Government are best place to determine what is in the public interest' (Consultation Paper, para 80). Their concern, rightly so, is with questions of law that relate to such policy.

---

[19] (1983) SLT 616.
[20] *Budden v BP et al* (1980) 124 SJ 376. The Court of Appeal did in fact strike out the claim not as abuse but as disclosing no reasonable cause of action.
[21] *London Borough of Hillingdon and others v Secretary of State for Transport and another* [2010] EWHC 626.

Part III

The Dynamics of Environmental Law

The substantive content of environmental law is constantly changing, as policy makers and legislators attempt to deal with fresh environmental challenges. A critical change in the nature of the environmental law was the degree of legal formalism and detail introduced from the early 1980s – broad legal frameworks, extensive use of policy documents and other informal methods of securing policy goals had characterised much of British environmental law for many years, but no longer could prevail. Yet beneath the detail of particular legal provisions it is possible to detect underlying patterns which reflect more substantial changes in the way that society is organised, and the role of law in that process. The chapters below explore themes such as the relationship of law and science, public engagement, and effective enforcement which have remained constant, and continue to pose.

Environmental Law: Shifting Directions and the New Formalism (1991) was an early attempt to assess profound ways in which the style of British environmental legislation was changing, and to consider the impact of this on the practice of environmental law. Environmental regulation, especially of pollution from industrial processes, had been well established in the United Kingdom for over 100 years. A core feature of the legislative structures was the large degree of discretion given to regulators, with the legislative provisions largely focusing on process and procedures rather than prescribing detailed environmental standards. The law on industrial air emissions, for example, imposed a duty to use the 'best practicable means' to control emissions; water companies had a duty to supply 'wholesome' water. Occasionally, the courts would be asked to provide greater interpretation of these open-ended phrases, but to a large degree it was left to regulators and government to convert them into practical reality as they thought best. Courts and lawyers were largely excluded from the regulatory process, a feature that caused endless bewilderment to US environmental lawyers. By the 1980s, however, it was clear that significant changes to the structure of environmental law and regulations was taking place, with far more detail in the way of the substantive environmental standards, usually expressed in precise scientific terms, being contained in the body of the law. The influence of European Community environmental legislation, the privatisation of key utilities such as water and electricity, and greater public distrust of regulatory discretion were all important factors. As *Shifting Discretion and the New Formalism* predicted, environmental regulators would soon be acting within the constraints of legal process and judicial oversight to an extent unheard of even a generation before, though perhaps it remains an open question whether this necessarily leads to improved environmental outcomes.

The earlier attempts to inject detailed substantive provisions into the body of environmental law can be contrasted in many ways with the Climate Change Act 2008, described as a world leader in climate change legislation and dealing with one of the most profound

255

of contemporary environmental challenges. In *The UK Climate Change Act – Towards a Brave New Legal World* (2012) I chose to analyse the legislation from a lawyer's perspective and to try to understand the legal significance of the legislation. The Act contains little in the way of detailed policy substance but contains important procedural mechanisms and the use of binding carbon budgets, and is the first law to explicitly recognise the importance of adaptation policies. Above all, it starts off with a deceptively intelligible long-term duty – 'It is the duty of the Secretary of State to ensure that the net UK carbon account for the year 2050 is at least 80% lower than the 1990 baseline'. Much of the language of contemporary environmental politics is about our duties towards future generations, but here the notion of inter-generational equity is transformed into a duty imposed on a future Secretary of State, perhaps unborn or just a child at the time the Act was passed. My initial view of the Climate Change Act was that it was a somewhat cynical political exercise – rather too much in the way of smoke and mirrors to be a truly enforceable legal instrument. Now, however, I hold more respect for what it is trying to achieve, and the mechanisms that were employed in the legislation. It is quite distinct in this respect from most other areas of environmental law and, as I note at the end of the analysis, it can be seen to represent a distinctive form of legislation 'the very existence of which inhibits policy makers from undue change and compromise in a field that demands long-term and sustained commitment beyond the more familiar political cycles and time horizons'.

When it comes to legal instruments for handling carbon dioxide emissions, for over a decade the European Union has placed its legal faith largely in an emissions trading regime. As yet, the low price of carbon has meant that the regime has failed to provide significant incentives for industry to invest in carbon-reducing measures. In my UCL inaugural lecture, *Regulating in a Risky Environment* (reproduced in Chapter 4), I raised general concerns about real effectiveness of economic instruments and the need to subject them to same level of critical scrutiny as more conventional regulation. *Weighing Up the Performance – Emissions Standards v Emissions Trading* (2011) was a review of a Parliamentary Committee's report on performance standards, and provided an opportunity for a more focused analysis of the debate between the emission trading and performance standards. Much of the fundamental criticism of conventional regulatory techniques emerged from the United States, and was written in the context of a different legal and administrative culture which did not necessarily equate with European systems. Emissions trading has undoubtedly proved politically attractive, yet I find it remarkable that respectable policy-makers continue to justify the effectiveness by quoting reduction levels of SO_2 from power stations under emissions trading in the United States without comparing equivalent reductions during the same periods under conventional regulation in Europe, or exploring in depth the real causes of such reductions, which may have as much to do with economic and industrial changes as with legal techniques. The 1980s saw a major debate within Europe, with the United Kingdom and Germany very much on opposing sides, in the field of water pollution control, where emissions standards and quality objectives were presented and argued about as incompatible alternatives for dealing with hazardous emissions. This type of conflict can all too readily lead to exaggerated support from each camp, with the inevitable slowing down of procedural and policy development.[1] The 2000 Water Framework Directive essentially integrated the two approaches. In the field of climate

---

[1] See further on this Macrory and Peachey, 'Underlying Themes in the Policy Process' (1983), reproduced in Chapter 31 below.

change, the challenge for the next decade may be to see how emissions trading and regulatory performance standards can be similarly employed within an integrated system.

Rights of public participation in regulatory decision making have long been a feature of British land use planning and environmental law, but have generally remained focused at the individual consent or permit stage, though land use plan making under town and country planning legislation also included provisions for public participation. The 2001 EU Directive on Strategic Environmental Assessment introduced rights of public participation at a higher level of policy and plan making, but essentially repeated the provisions on participation from the project-based 1985 Directive on Environmental Assessment. However, there is no reason to believe that the participation procedures used at one level are best suited for another, and the SEA Directive was intellectually lazy in this respect. I was a member of the Royal Commission on Environmental Pollution during its study on environmental standards.[2] Without denying the critical role of scientific information into the process of setting environmental standards, the Commission was clear that at the heart of most standard setting were questions of value which could not be resolved by technical analysis alone. The Commission was equally concerned that decision makers were often ill-equipped to gain robust information about public values. Traditional public participatory procedures were more suited to hearing views rather than exploring values, and most members of the Commission were convinced that economic appraisal techniques, such as cost–benefit analysis, were best suited to reflect preferences rather than values in the sense understood by the Commission.[3]

The Commission therefore advocated that the government should embark on new ways of exploring public values in the context of environmental policy making, but without prescribing any particular method for doing so. At the time of the publication of the Commission's report, the whole issue of genetically modified organisms was rising higher on the British political agenda, and in 2000 the government established an independent Agriculture and Environment Biotechnology Commission to advise the government on social and ethical implications of the new technology. The Commission advised the government to engage in new forms of deliberative mechanisms for public engagement, but stressed that the purpose of any such procedure was not to act as a quasi-referendum on the issue but to provide the government with a better understanding of the nature and spectrum of public views. The government accepted the advice, and in 2003 and 2004 initiated an ambitious public debate on biotechnology, involving 7 national meetings, 41 regional meetings and over 600 local meetings. *Public Consultation and GMO Policy – A Very British Experiment* (2008) is an analysis of this bold exercise in public engagement. It did not produce the result that the government probably hoped it would, and there were later criticisms of bias and design. Nevertheless, a post-hoc parliamentary review welcomed the exercise as being innovative and imaginative, but criticised the government for providing inadequate resources and setting far too ambitious a timetable. Nothing quite like it has been attempted since, but current concern over issues such as fracking

---

[2] Royal Commission on Environmental Pollution, 21st Report, 'Setting Environmental Standards', Cm 4053 (1998).

[3] Ibid, para 7.3 'We understand values to be beliefs, ether individual or social, about what is important to life, and thus about the ends or objectives which should govern and shape public policies. Once formed, such beliefs may be durable. It is also characteristic that they may be both formed and modified as a result of information and reflection. Environmental and social values, in particular, are not necessarily pre-formed or fixed but, for many people, emerge out of debate, discussion and challenge, as they encounter new facts, insights, and judgements contributed by others.'

(in the United Kingdom) and carbon storage (in a number of other European countries, including Germany and the Netherlands) suggest that the search for better ways of public engagement where new technologies are involved is by no means over.

Effective enforcement of environmental law is essential to achieve the environmental outcomes implicit in the legal requirements and to ensure public confidence in the legal system. My work on sanctions presented in Chapter 2 was concerned with extending the range of options available to enforcement bodies where regulatory breaches occur. *Technology and Environmental Law Enforcement* (2003) is concerned more with methods of supervising the implementation of regulatory requirements and the detection of breaches, another key element in the chain of enforcement. The last 15 years have seen a significant extension of the range of environmental laws for which enforcement bodies are responsible, but coupled with a constant squeeze on resources. One response to the new challenges has been to develop so-called risk-based approaches to enforcement – rather than carrying out inspections and supervision to the same level of intensity on all the activities falling within the scope of control, calculated assessments are made to focus enforcement attention on where the most risk is likely. The Environment Agency, for example, has developed a scoring tool for appraising the likely compliance risks of waste facilities and other permitted facilities PPC processes, based both on the operator's performance history and the site's environmental risks.[4] Targeting resources in this way is a sensible approach, though as with any prior assessment techniques not without its own risks should the unexpected occur. *Technologies and Environmental Law Enforcement* considers rapid developments in technologies such as automatic monitoring devices and the use of satellites, which provide complementary aids to supervision, and are likely to prove of increasing importance.

Environmental Standards, Legitimacy and Social Justice (1999), a revised version of a lecture given at the 1998 Environmental Justice and the Legal Process Conference at the University of Cape Town, is a further reflection on the implications of the increasing use of formalised, scientific standards in environmental law, which had become so apparent at both British and European Union level. Although such standards provided a comforting sense of certainty, closer examination of the underlying science revealed the degree of uncertainty involved and the value judgements that were necessarily being made in deciding on a particular standard. One legal response has been to introduce greater rights of public participation and access to information, but this tends to be most effective at a local level, dealing with discrete projects, while increasingly in reality core environmental standards are being determined at European Community or international level, often in fairly obscure committees and other forums. Nor, did it seem to me, that a rejection of the simplistic notion, often expressed in official statements, that standards were derived from 'sound science' could be replaced by an equally simplistic invocation of the precautionary approach. The study of the Royal Commission on Environmental Pollution environmental standards, discussed above and published later that year, formed much of the backdrop to the analysis. The Commission argued for a far more nuanced process for establishing standards, and one that involved new forms of public engagement. Yet the dilemmas and contradictions involved, and the challenges of devising fresh approaches, remain with us today.

---

[4] Environment Agency, 'Environmental Permitting Regulations, Operational Risk Appraisal Scheme', Version 3.8, April 2013.

Defining the scope of environmental law with any precision is extraordinarily difficult. The environment affects and is affected by so many distinct policy areas that it becomes almost a fruitless, and indeed potentially pernicious to draw precise boundaries, whether for the purposes of administrative organisation or defining a legal discipline or subject specialism. It was a key reason for avoiding the term by naming the teaching and research centre at UCL the 'Centre for Law and the Environment' rather than the 'Centre for Environmental Law', The distinguished German environmental lawyer, Gerd Winter, has argued that the contemporary challenge is not to treat environmental law as a distinct field of law which restrains or mediates the excesses of market based law such as free trade or company law but to ensure that all such law becomes 'inoculated with ecological solutions'.[5] We are still a long way from that goal, but the term 'integration' has increasingly entered the language of environmental law, as for example, in the EC Directive on Integrated Pollution and Prevention Control, and now reflected in Chapter 1 of the 2010 Industrial Emissions Directive.[6] The duty now expressed in Article 11 of the Treaty on the Functioning of the European Union, that 'Environmental protection requirements must be integrated into the definition and implementation of the Union policies and activities, in particular with a view to promoting sustainable development', adds a further dimension to the concept.[7] Yet what is implied by the concept of integration is by no means obvious. *The Scope of Environmental Law* (1996) is a reflection on the range of interpretations than can be given to the term, ranging from modest administrative co-operation between different bodies to more fundamental rethinking of legal structures and principles.

Loaded Guns and Monkeys: Responsible Environmental Law (1994) is the revised text of my inaugural lecture at Imperial College, London. It focuses on the concept of 'responsibility' as an underlying feature of liability under environmental law. The House of Lords had recently given judgment in the seminal *Cambridge Water Company*[8] case, exploring the extent to which polluters should be liable for the damage they had caused even where it was not predictable at the time, or whether some degree of negligence or reasonable foreseeability was an essential ingredient of liability. I was particularly intrigued that one of the cases quoted in the argument before the House of Lords was an 1846 decision of the High Court concerning a pet monkey which had escaped through no fault of its owner and attacked a passer-by. For the first time, the court espoused a general principle of strict liability on the owner on the grounds that the animal was known to be potentially dangerous. The analogy with the operator of a potentially hazardous installation is obvious. The notion of responsibility seemed particularly interesting in the environmental field – should designers of poorly insulated flats be responsible for noise nuisances that inevitably resulted? Did consumers of cheap flights bear any responsibility for damaging emissions from the aircraft? Four years after the lecture, Lord Hoffmann discussed the notion of causation in the *Empress Cars* decision,[9] where liability under the relevant water pollution legislation rested on the term 'causes'. Lord Hoffmann argued persuasively that the notion of causation was not, as previous courts had often treated it, a matter of common sense fact but one of legal construction: 'one cannot give a common sense answer to a ques-

---

[5] Winter, 'Perspectives on Environmental Law – Entering the Fourth Phase' (1989) 1(1) *Journal of Environmental Law* 38, 45.

[6] Directive 2010/75/EU.

[7] For a legal analysis of the integration duty, see Chapter 23 (1998) in this volume.

[8] *Cambridge Water v Eastern Counties Leather plc* [1994] 2 AC 264.

[9] *Environment Agency (formerly National Rivers Authority) v Empress Car Company (Abertillery) Ltd* [1998] 1 All ER 481. For an analysis see Chapter 20, p 397 below.

tion of causation for the purpose of attributing responsibility under some rule without knowing the purpose and scope of the rule'.

Finally, *Cycle Lore* (1979) is included in part out of sentiment as my first published legal article, but it also illustrates a number of themes echoed in later writings. The lawyer concerned with the environment should not necessarily be constrained by conventional boundaries of environmental law, but be prepared to examine areas of law such as transport or planning. It also demonstrates how the promotion of policies – here the greater encouragement of cycling – may be unwittingly inhibited by the details of existing and long-established legal frameworks. To take one example, prior to 1978 local authorities possessed extensive powers to construct 'street furniture' such as horse troughs, public lavatories, lamps stands, and bus shelters but no equivalent explicit powers to erect cycle racks. Some authorities ignored the constraint, but it was nevertheless a detail of law not without legal consequence. Street furniture erected without statutory authority would be an illegal obstruction of the highway, and someone, such as a blind person, who was injured by walking into an illegally erected stand would have the right to sue the authority concerned. As part of a transport campaign, I and my then colleagues at Friends of the Earth successfully lobbied government to change the law in 1978.[10] The delightful Victorian case law testing at what point a bicycle ceased to be a vehicle in law resonated over 100 years later in 2006 when a commuter successfully evaded a private rail operator's restrictions on the carriage of bicycles on trains by wrapping his cycle in brown paper and turning it legally into a parcel.[11] And all the earlier case law resurfaced in 2011 when the Divisional Court had to consider whether someone using a Segway personal transporter on the pavement had committed an offence.[12]

---

[10] See s 12 Transport Act 1978, which extends the power of authorities to provide parking places 'to providing, in roads or elsewhere, stands and racks for bicycles'.

[11] Macrory, 'Cycling Mad', The Times, 21 April 2006, letters page.

[12] *Coates v Crown Prosecution Service* [2011] EWHC 2032.

10

The UK Climate Change Act – Towards a Brave New Legal World?[1] (2012)

The UK Climate Change Act was passed in 2008 and has been described as a world leader in climate change legislation.[2] In broad terms, the Act contains three significant and innovative features. It imposes a legal duty on the government to achieve significant long-term carbon reductions by 2050, coupled with intermediate targets and extensive reporting requirements on progress in meeting those targets. It establishes a high-level independent expert committee to provide advice on the setting of carbon budgets and how the trajectory of reductions is best achieved, and to report on government progress. Finally, it includes, for the first time in UK national legislation, express provisions concerning adaptation to climate change, a statutory acknowledgement that, whatever reductions might be secured in the future, the level of carbon dioxide already in the atmosphere is likely to bring about impacts requiring adaptation measures. These are significant features of any new climate change legislation, but the Act contains little in the way of substantive policy, and there is an alternative view that the legislation, far from being at the cutting edge of environmental law, represents essentially nothing more than what Edelman would describe as 'symbolic reassurance'[3] – a generalised framework with little in the way of hard edged legal obligations. The truth is rather more nuanced.

The General Long-term Duty and its Legal Significance

Broad obligations relating to climate change are not without precedent in UK law. Two years earlier the Climate Change and Sustainability Act 2006 required the government to provide reports on UK greenhouse gas emissions but little more. Following a campaign initiated by Friends of the Earth Ltd in 2005, which included the production of a draft climate change law, the then Labour government agreed to promote the Climate Change Act 2008, which breaks new ground by imposing a long-term reduction duty on the government. The need for long-term climate change targets was first identified clearly by

---

[1] R Macrory, 'The UK Climate Change Act – Towards a Brave New legal World?' In Backer, Fauchald and Voight (eds), *Pro Natura* (University of Oslo, 2012).

[2] Friends of the Earth, 'Climate Law a World First', 28 October 2008, available at www.foe.co.uklnews (accessed on 12 June 2011).

[3] M Edelman, *Symbolic Uses of Politics* (1964).

the Royal Commission on Environmental Pollution, a high-level expert advisory body, in a highly influential and ground-breaking report published in 2000.[4] At that stage, government policy on climate change was largely driven by concerns to meet comparatively short-term targets, such as those in the Kyoto Protocol and accompanying European Union requirements, but the Royal Commission insisted that a longer-term view was equally needed. Decisions being taken now, such as the design of buildings and investment in new energy infrastructure, could have implications for a generation or more. The Commission therefore adopted the longer term date of 2050, which was considered not so far into the future as to make any design of policy utterly unrealistic but sufficiently far ahead to be appropriate for the challenges of climate change – the Commission in effect then worked backwards from that date, asking itself what level of temperature rise was at the margins of tolerability by that date. From that analysis, it derived a long-term reduction target of 60 per cent of carbon dioxide by 2050, a recommendation that the then Prime Minister was quick to endorse.[5]

Only eight years later a 60 per cent reduction appeared to be overly conservative in the light of developing scientific knowledge, and during the passage of the Climate Change Act through Parliament an 80 per cent reduction target was accepted by the government as more appropriate. Section 1(1) of the Act therefore begins by providing that 'It is the duty of the Secretary of State to ensure that the net UK carbon account for the year 2050 is at least 80 % lower than the 1990 baseline'.[6] It is an admirably concise and clearly drafted legal provision, and, as was noted in Parliament, a provision that imposes duties on future politicians who might well not even be born at the time the Act was passed – notions of inter-generational equity and the need to have regard for future generations have metamorphosed into legal duties imposed on the unborn. Yet what does this duty really mean from a legal perspective?

A lawyer's first reaction is to ask whether this is a public duty that is enforceable by the courts. Statutory duties expressed in the form of longer term goals are not unknown in recent UK legislation, but previous such duties have usually been expressed in qualified terms, incorporating expressions such as 'as far as possible'. The courts have then generally felt able to characterise them as target duties,[7] where the core decisions and judgements involved in the allocation of resources and elaboration of policies to achieve the targets should rest on government rather than the courts. In a recent case concerning duties under a 2000 Act of Parliament requiring the government to produce strategies to eliminate fuel poverty,[8] the Court of Appeal noted that, for the United Kingdom at least,[9] 'This style of legislation is of recent origin. Historically, central Government has announced and developed its policies primarily through political rather than statutory or legal channels

---

[4] Royal Commission on Environmental Pollution, 22nd Report, 'Energy – the Changing Climate', Cm 4749 (London, HMSO, 2000).

[5] The UK's 60 per cent reduction figure calculated by the Royal Commission was in part based on its endorsement of a contraction and convergence approach to greenhouse gas reductions as the long term goal of international negotiations. The UK government was far less committed to such a policy, and in endorsing the 60 per cent reduction appear to fail to understand its true rationale.

[6] Drafting tradition in UK legislation uses the term 'Secretary of State' essentially to embrace the government of the day.

[7] See, eg *Larner v Solihull Metropolitan Borough Council* [2001] RTR 469.

[8] Warm Homes and Energy Conservation Act 2000.

[9] In contrast, environmental legislation in jurisdictions such as the United States, where there is a much stronger division of powers between the legislature and the executive, has often imposed demanding target obligations on government.

and the consequences of failure have been political rather than justiciable'.[10] In that case, the legal provisions imposed a duty on government to produce a strategy that would 'as far as reasonably practicable' ensure that people did not live in fuel poverty by a specified date, and, drafted in those terms, the court felt justified in characterising this duty as a language of effort to achieve targets rather than a guarantee that targets would be reached. But it noted that other statutory duties might be harder edged, and indeed the duty under the Climate Change Act 2008 appears to be different. It is expressed in absolute unqualified terms, with a set date and a clear and measurable goal. As such, one could argue it is amenable to judicial review if the government were to fail to meet the target, and the question of legal enforceability was subject to considerable discussion during Parliament when the legislation was being discussed. Yet, in practice, what would happen? Illegal action was taken too early: say, five or ten years before the date, on the basis of a prediction that the target would not be reached, the courts would be likely to reject the case as premature. However, if one waited until 2049 before taking legal action, it would be difficult to know what sort of effective legal remedy would then be available – a mere declaration by the court that the government was in breach would be something of a pyrrhic victory. It is possible that the court could order the government to purchase emissions credits on the open market to make up the shortfall, but, if the current scientific predictions are correct, by that date the environmental damage will already have been done if the target is not met. In certain cases a breach of statutory duty by government has been held to give rise to a claim of damages by private parties who have suffered as a result, but it seems unlikely that the courts would be able to ascribe particular losses to individual claimants.[11] A further argument might suggest that, in any event, this is not a duty that can be enforced in a conventional way in the courts. Section 20 of the Act provides an express duty on the Secretary of State to provide a final statement to Parliament for 2050 not later than 31 May 2052, and this includes the provision that, 'If the target has not been met, the statement must explain why it has not been met'. Judges are generally loath to see their jurisdiction ousted by legislation, but here the courts might feel justified in interpreting this provision as implying that any remedy under the Act for failure to meet the duty is expressed into the form of political accountability to Parliament rather than judicial enforcement in the courts.

If the long-term target in section 1 were the only statutory duty concerning climate change, there would be a strong argument that the legislation was essentially aspirational. But in fact the Climate Change Act then goes on to provide a whole range of intermediate duties (discussed in the next section), and these provide considerable more legal bite. And even if, in strict legal terms, the long-term 2050 duty is not enforceable in the courts, this misses a number of implications of section 1 that may have greater significance than its legal enforceability. First, the duty is expressed in clear, unequivocal terms, which are readily understandable by the general public even if the fine detail of what exactly the 'net carbon account' implies leads to greater legal complexities. This contrasts with the complex and arcane language of many statutory environmental provisions. Anyone, lawyer or non-lawyer, reading section 1 can readily understand the essential government commitment being made, and the public understanding of these long-term duties and its consequent

---

[10] Lord Justice Maurice Kay in *R on the application of Friends of the Earth Ltd v Secretary of State for Energy and Climate Change* [2009] EWCA Civ 810, para 2.

[11] P McMaster, 'Climate Change – Statutory Duty or Pious Hope' (2008) 20(1) *Journal of Environmental Law* 115.

ability to maintain pressure for political action is not to be underestimated. Secondly, expressing the duty in primary legislation gives it a moral dimension and permanence which cannot be replicated in mere statements of government policy. Such policy statements can be readily changed and fudged, and while the statutory duty could be removed by a future government this would have to be done by new legislation, subject to public and parliamentary scrutiny rather than simply announcing a change of policy. In practice, the Climate Change Act received support from all political parties and has survived a change of government in 2010. It is also true that the actual figure of 80 per cent can be changed by subsequent regulation rather than amending primary legislation, but any such regulations must go through a special parliamentary procedure requiring a positive vote of approval by the legislature,[12] and can only be made in the light of significant developments in scientific knowledge, or changes to European or international law or policy.[13] Simply protecting the UK national economy would not be sufficient grounds for changing the long-term goal, and if this were invoked as justification for reducing the 80 per cent figure or extending the date, the legality of any such regulations could be challenged in the courts. Thirdly, the duty clearly places the lead policy responsibility for climate change reductions on the government – this is not an area that can be wholly delegated to the private sector. Interestingly, the equivalent Scottish legislation, which largely mirrors the Climate Change Act requirements, has gone further and extended duties on all public bodies to assist in achieving the targets.[14] Finally, the very existence of the duty, even if not directly enforceable in itself, may have indirect legal implications in that the courts may invoke the duty to interpret other legislation or judge the legality of government acts by reference to these requirements. Already we have seen one important case of judicial review,[15] discussed further below, concerning aviation policy where the Climate Change Act significantly affected the outcome.

Intermediate Carbon Budgets

The long-term duty in the Climate Change Act is innovative, but important provisions then go on to provide for regular carbon budgeting, providing political accountability for developing a realistic trajectory towards the 2050 goal, encased within a legal framework. Section 4 of the Act imposes a duty on the Secretary of State to produce a carbon budget for every five years beginning 2008–12, with section 5 providing a mid-point target of at least a 26 per cent reduction by 2020. Three consecutive carbon budgets, for the periods 2008–12, 2013–17 and 2018–22, were to be produced by 2009, and were duly made under

---

[12] Climate Change Act, ss 2 and 91(1). The Secretary of State must also consult the Committee on Climate Change and the devolved administrations in Scotland, Wales and Northern Ireland before proposing such a change: ibid, s 3.

[13] Ibid, s 6.

[14] Climate Change (Scotland) Act 2009, s 44: 'A public body must, in exercising its functions, act: (a) in the way best calculated to contribute to the delivery of the targets set in or under Parr 1 of this Act; (b) in the way best calculated to help deliver any programme laid before the Scottish Parliament under section 53; (c) in a way that it considers is most sustainable'.

[15] R on the application of the London Borough of Hillingdon and others v Secretary of State for Transport [2010] EWHC 626, 26 March 2010.

secondary legislation by that date.[16] The Act then provides that any subsequent carbon budgets must be made at least 11.5 years before the start of the budgetary period, in order to provide a reasonably level of certainly for the medium term. Carbon budgets must be set 'with a view to meeting' both the long-term 2050 target and the intermediate 2020 target, as well as any European and international obligations. The phrase 'with a view to meeting' is a deliberately qualified phrase which suggests that intention will be more important than actual achievement. But setting the budgets is not the only duty – the government is then obliged to prepare 'proposals and policies' which it feels will enable the five-year budgets 'to be met' as well as 'with a view to meeting' the 2050 goal. Here the slight difference in wording is legally significant – policies and programmes are set *with a view to meeting* the long-term target, but in relation to intermediate budgets *must enable them to be met*. This latter is a rather tougher test and, during the passage of the legislation through Parliament, the government was acutely conscious of the possibility of judicial intervention, particular when it came to the intermediate budgets:

> [A]ny failure to meet a target or budget carries the risk for the government of judicial review, like most legal duties on Government. In such a case the remedy would be at the discretion of the court. In most cases when a Government has failed to comply with a duty, courts do no more than issue a declaration, bur we cannot rule out completely the possibility of a court making a more stringent order such as ordering them to purchase credit. No Government would take that risk lightly.[17]

Nevertheless,there is some flexibility in the setting of the five-year budgets. The statutory reduction goals are drafted in respect of the United Kingdom's 'net carbon account', a term defined in the Act and meaning the amount of UK greenhouse gases reduced by amounts determined by regulations and increased by amounts similarly determined by regulations. This gives the flexibility for the UK to purchase allowances from overseas to secure the reduction goals, but, as within the European Union generally, the politics of doing so are sensitive, and the Act goes on to provide that the Secretary of State must by order, subject to confirmation by Parliament, set a limit on the net amount of carbon units that may be credited in this way. During the passage of the legislation an amendment was proposed to impose that at least 70 per cent of reductions were achieved by domestic action, but the government was uncomfortable in setting such a legislative restriction. Nevertheless, despite allowing for a percentage of reductions to be achieved by overseas purchases, the overall goal of creating a low-carbon economy within the United Kingdom prevails – although in 2011 a potential crack in this stance occurred with the fourth carbon budget. The final section in this chapter considers the implications of these developments further. Further flexibility is provided by the power to borrow from future carbon budgets between budgetary periods if there is a shortfall for any particular period, but the legislation has placed a limit of 1 per cent on the total amount that may be permitted in this way. According to the government, this 'would be consistent in the rise of emissions that may result during an unexpectedly cold winter'.[18]

As the government acknowledged in Parliament, it may be that the failure to meet an intermediate carbon budget in a particular period could be subject to judicial intervention. However, the legislation expressly imposes a duty on the government to report to Parlia-

---

[16] Carbon Budgets Order 2009 No 1259.
[17] Lord Rooker, Minister, HC Public Bill Committee (Bill 97) 2007–2008, cols 236–37, 1 July 2008.
[18] Lord Rooker, Minister, HL Deb 8 January 2008, vol 697, col 826.

ment setting out proposals and policies to compensate in future budgetary periods where in any particular period the net UK carbon amount has exceeded the carbon budget for that period, and again it could be argued that the legislation explicitly envisages political accountability of government to Parliament rather than legal accountability to the courts.

The Statutory Committee on Climate Change

A key feature of the institutional mechanisms embodied in the Climate Change Act is the establishment of a new statutory advisory body, the Committee on Climate Change. The legislation bristles with obligations on the government to report on its actions – to Parliament and to the public – with the requirement of the publication of regular budgets and plans. The existence of a high-level, expert committee adds an important dimension to this accountability. The Committee has no executive role, but the Act gives it many significant functions, both giving technical advice to government and providing detailed critiques of government progress in securing climate change reduction. As the government put it, the Committee's role is 'to provide independent and expert analytical advice to the United Kingdom Government and devolved administrations on the pathway to 2050' and to 'help hold the government and, for that matter, the country as a whole, accountable for the progress we are making towards our 2050 target'.[19] The Committee currently consists of eight expert members, a thirty strong secretariat, and an annual budget of just under £3.5 million. It is jointly sponsored by the Department of Energy and Climate Change, the Scottish Government, the Welsh Assembly Government and the Northern Ireland Executive.

The statutory functions of the Committee include providing advice on the 2050 target and whether it should be amended; advice on the intermediate carbon budgets, including 'the sectors of the economy in which there are particular opportunities for contributions to be made towards meeting the carbon budget for the period through reductions in emissions of targeted greenhouse gases';[20] and advice on whether emissions from aviation and shipping should be included within the carbon budgets.[21]

Equally important to its advisory functions, the Committee has a statutory duty to produce an annual report on the progress being made by the government to achieve both the intermediate budgets and the long-term 2050 reduction target. The government con-

---

[19] Lord Rooker, Minister, HL Deb 14 January 2008, vol 697, col 1069.

[20] Climate Change Act, s 34(1)A.

[21] Aviation and shipping emissions are not included with the original definition of the UK carbon account under the Climate Change Act, but s 30 of the Act requires the government to make a decision either to include or exclude such emissions by 2012 at the latest. In December 2012 the government made a decision under section 30 that, 'Due to the degree of uncertainty over the future shape of international agreements affecting international aviation, in particular aviation's treatment within EU-ETS, we are deferring a firm decision on whether to include international aviation and shipping emissions within the net carbon account at this time'. The government also announced it would defer any decision as to international shipping – 'although this sector is not affected directly by the uncertainties affecting international aviation, we would prefer to maintain a consistent approach to both international sectors'. Department of Energy and Climate Change, 'International Aviation and Shipping Emissions and the UK's Carbon Budgets and 2050 Target', presented to Parliament pursuant to s 30 Climate Change Act 2008, 19 December 2012, Part II, paras 3 and 5.

sciously did not provide the Committee with an explicit duty to advise on policy action needed:

> The committee has to have a role in the assessment of the overall effect of reducing emissions and the effect of policies, but we do not see that its role would be to recommend future policies. It will for the government to come up with the policies to give practical effect to advice from the Committee on Climate Change.[22]

The Committee's reports are to include views on the progress being made, on whether targets are likely to be met and on further progress that may be needed. It may be a fine balance between refraining from advising on policies and providing a critique on the adequacy of existing policies, but it is one that the legislation explicitly endorses. During the parliamentary debates there were calls for the Committee to have more executive functions, including the power to set the key targets, but climate change is about both science and politics, and the balance struck in the legislation between the responsibilities of a non-elected expert body and those of government seems correct. In many ways these arguments reflect the continuing tensions over the proper role of the European Environment Agency and the extent to which it should be confined to data collation and analysis or engage in a more active policy development role. The annual reports of the Committee will provide a critical mechanisms for holding the government to account, and the legislation goes on to provide that the government 'must lay before Parliament a response to the points raised by each Report of the Committee' within a specified time limit.[23] The failure to do provide such a response would be politically damaging, but equally would be a duty clearly amenable to judicial review.

The Climate Change Committee is established by statute to have a large degree of independence. It is true, however, that the legislation gives government the power both to issue guidance to the Committee (which the Committee must then 'have regard to' in performing its functions[24]), as well as the power to issue directions as to the exercise of its functions.[25] Any direction must be complied with by the Committee, but the legislation expressly excludes the power 'to direct the Committee as to the content of any advice or report',[26] thus preserving its integrity. In practice, the Committee has remained independent from political interference, and to date its reports have carried immense authority. Its advice on the first three carbon budgets, covering the periods 2008–12, 2013–17 and 2018–22, was accepted by the government, and enacted in secondary legislation made in 2009.[27] Only in 2011, following its advice on the fourth carbon budget, have real tensions emerged between the government and the Committee – this is discussed in the final section of this chapter.

---

[22] Lord Rooker, Minister, HL Deb 14 January 2008, vol 697, col 1121.
[23] Climate Change Act, s 37.
[24] Climate Change Act, s 42(4).
[25] Ibid, s 42.
[26] Ibid, s 42(4).
[27] Carbon Budgets Order 2009 No 1259.

Adaptation

Whatever mitigation steps are taken over the next few decades, the level of greenhouse gases already in the atmosphere implies that adaptation measures to accommodate change in the climate will be required as well. In the initial draft of the Act, adaptation was the subject of just three sections, but substantial amendments were made during the passing of the legislation, leading now to a full Part of the Act encompassing some 15 sections. This is the first time that adaptation has received express statutory recognition in national legislation, though a year before, in legislation relating only to London, a general statutory duty had been imposed on the Mayor of London and the London Assembly to take action with a view to mitigation or adaptation of climate change.[28] As with carbon budget measures, the Climate Change Act essentially prescribes a detailed framework of procedures but avoids any details of actual measures that may be needed to secure the policy goals, with the core statutory provision being to require the government to produce a report every five years assessing 'the risks for the United Kingdom of the current and predicted impact of climate change'.[29] The Committee on Climate Change again has an important role to play in this area of climate policy. The Committee is given a statutory duty to advise the government on the preparation of each of the five year reports, and its advice must be published.[30] The government has a duty to 'take in account'[31] this advice, and this provision, coupled with the public nature of the advice, implies that the government would have to explicitly and publicly justify any disagreement with the Committee.

The government's duties under the Act in relation to adaptation extend beyond simply producing a regular report on the risks for the country. The Act then requires the government to lay before Parliament 'programmes' which set out the objectives of its adaptation policy; its proposals and policies for meeting those objectives, and the timescales for introducing such proposals and policies. There is no specified time periods for introducing such programmes, nor any express duty to implement such programmes, but accountability is provided by requiring each annual report of the Climate Change Committee to contain an assessment of the progress made towards achieving the adaptation objectives, proposals and programmes.[32] In practice, the Climate Change Committee has established an Adaptation Sub-committee and, as was noted during the passage of legislation, this committee 'will examine the government's progress on delivering adaptation, provide independent and expert advice on what further action the government need to take, and deliver that advice'.[33]

This part of the Act is therefore wholly devoid of the substantive content of future adaptation polices, and this is almost certainly the correct approach. A major UK review of the challenges posed by climate change adaptation for institutional and policy machinery was contained in the 28th Report of the Royal Commission on Environmental Pollution,

---

[28] Greater London Authority Act 2007, ss 41–44.
[29] Climate Change Act, s 56.
[30] Ibid, s 57.
[31] Ibid, s 56(5).
[32] Ibid, s 59.
[33] House of Commons, Public Bill Committee (Bill 97) 2007–2008, col 322, 3 July 2008.

published in March 2010.[34] The Report noted that, while mitigation policies had defined goals to reducing greenhouse gas emissions, 'there is no defined blueprint, end-point, or programme for adaptation'.[35] The Commission identified four particular and overlapping challenges that adaptation posed for institutions and how they design appropriate responses.[36] First, the levels of uncertainties involved in predicting specific impacts meant that adaptation does not readily respond to more familiar policy approaches of managing defined risks. Decision-making must therefore incorporate a large degree of flexibility that allows strategies to develop and change in the light of improved understanding and knowledge. Secondly, there is immense complexity in the number of authorities and other bodies inevitably involved in developing responses to adaptation, especially at local level: 'Complexity may be unavoidable due to the pervasive nature of the adaptation challenge, multi-level governance and the urgent need for public engagement, but efforts should be made where possible to reduce it'.[37] The Commission's third challenge was what it described as 'path dependency'. This refers to institutional structures and existing policies that are often well defined in the interests of stability but which can inhibit the shift to new trajectories that may be required by adaptation. Path dependency in this sense can pose a special challenge to the design of substantive environmental legislation, where the demands of legal explicitness and enforceability may compete with requirements of a more flexible and adaptive response. The Commission singled out the EU Water Framework Directive[38] as a good example of legislation largely incorporating a large degree of future flexibility, though the Directive has also been criticised for those very qualities. The Royal Commission felt, however, that the approach to quantitative standards for chemical standards contained with the Directive might sit uneasily with the pressures of a changing climate, and that the British methodologies for classification and monitoring compliance with the Directive potentially were unable to cope with shifting population distributions brought about by climate change.[39] The fourth and final challenge articulated by the Commission was the problem of equity and fairness in managing the climate change impacts, not simply at a global level, but equally at a national level: 'the distributional dimension of climate change is especially acute in respect of flooding and coastal erosion, although it may arise elsewhere, for example, in increased water scarcity or reduced access to blue or green space'.[40] Institutions are generally required to secure least-cost outcomes, but the Commission warned of the dangers of employing conventional cost–benefit analysis where questions of climate change adaptation are involved, not least because of its limitations in translating in quantitative terms the long-term and often uncertain benefits.

The 2009 report of the Royal Commission underlined many of the very real challenges posed by climate adaptation to the conventional design of environmental law and policy. It welcomed the general framework contained in the Climate Change Act, and recognised that many of its immediate recommendations would fall on the Adaptation Sub-Committee of the Climate Change Committee. The next major stage in the development of

---

[34] Royal Commission on Environmental Pollution 28th Report, 'Adapting Institutions to Climate Change Cm 7843' (London, HMSO, 2010). This was the penultimate report of the Royal Commission on Environmental Pollution, which was abolished a year later as part of the coalition government's spending cuts.

[35] Ibid, para 5.7.

[36] Ibid, paras 4.5 et seq.

[37] Ibid, para 4.16.

[38] EC Council and Parliament Directive 2000/60/EC [2000] OJ L327/1.

[39] Royal Commission on Environmental Pollution 28th Report, above n 34, paras 4.21–4.22.

[40] Ibid, para 4.31.

adaptation policy will be the production of the UK Climate Change Risk Assessment, the government's first assessment under section 56 of the Act, which is due to be published in 2012, preceded by the publication of advice from the Adaptation Sub-Committee. The potential tensions between that advice and the current enormous pressures of public finances are likely to be played out in this process.

The Courts and the Climate Change Act

It may be that the primarily statutory duties concerned with securing emission reductions under the Climate Change Act will be difficult to enforce in the courts in any conventional sense, although the many procedural obligations under the legislation, such as the production of reports, clearly would be amenable to legal action if the government failed to comply with them. But it is already clear that this does not mean that the overall reduction duties and what they symbolise in terms of long-term government commitment to climate change are devoid of legal effect, and in 2010 the High Court for the first time addressed the relationship of these duties with the new planning procedures designed to speed up decision making for major infrastructure projects. The Climate Change Act proved critical in the court's analysis and decision.

R on the application of the London Borough of Hillingdon and others v Secretary of State for Transport[41] was a challenge by a local authority and other parties to the government's decision in January 2009 to commit to a new runway at London's Heathrow airport. The background to the case was the government's 2003 White Paper on the future of air transport, which in principle backed a new runway at Heathrow, but subject to conditions concerning local air quality, noise and improved public transport access being satisfied. At this stage, although the government was committed in policy terms to a 60 per cent reduction in CO_2 emissions from 1990 by 2050, international aviation was excluded from these figures.

The government began a new consultation process in 2007 which expressly excluded the climate change implications of me runway, but was limited to local environmental impacts and the other issues identified in the 2003 White Paper. In January 2009 the government announced its conclusions stating that a new runway was 'critical to this country's long-term prosperity' and that it was satisfied that the conditions concerning local environmental impacts could be met. A year before the Planning Act 2008 had been passed, mainly designed to speed up the process of major infrastructure developments and in part as a response to the enormous time – some seven years – it had taken to conduct conventional planning procedures for Heathrow's Terminal Five. A critical element of the new planning legislation was the provision for the production of National Policy Statements which would provide the policy context for major infrastructure projects and had to be followed. The government was committed to producing a National Policy Statement on aviation policy, although this had not been done by the time the case was heard, and it was clear that any new runway proposal at Heathrow would fall under these new procedures.

---

[41] [2010] EWHC 626, 26 March 2010.

Aviation emissions are not yet formally included within the 80 per cent reduction target under the Climate Change Act,[42] but in 2009 the government decided as a matter of policy rather than legal obligation it would set a target of limiting emissions from aviation in 2050 to below 2005 levels and referred the general question of how this might be achieved to the Committee on Climate Change. In 2009 the Committee advised that air traffic should not increase by more than 55 per cent between 2005 and 2050, but explicitly did not advise on the implications of this for the Heathrow proposals.[43]

In the light of all these developments, a number of local authorities challenged the legality of the 2009 announcement about the Heathrow runway. The significance of the case was underlined by the fact that it was heard by a senior Court of Appeal judge unusually sitting in the High Court for the occasion – Lord Justice Carnwath,[44] one of the United Kingdom's leading judicial figures in environmental law. He decided that the 2009 ministerial announcement had not been made under any statutory powers, and was no more than a policy statement without any direct substantive effect at this stage on the proposals. The real decisions of legal significance would come at a later stage, when a formal planning application for the runway was lodged under the new Planning Act procedures. This meant that the legal action before him was strictly premature, but Lord Justice Carnwath then went on to express what would be almost irresistible judicial pressure on the government to reconsider its policy in the light of climate change. He noted that any government policy must clearly be open to reconsideration due to changing circumstances, and this was especially significant in the context of climate change: 'Common sense demanded that a policy established in 2003, before the important developments in climate change policy, symbolised by the Climate Change Act 2008, should be subject to review in the light of these developments'.[45]

Lord Justice Carnwath, however, argued that the courts were not a suitable forum to resolve the technical debate on aviation and climate change, but stated that climate change issues were clearly something the government would have to take into account when it developed under the Planning Act its National Policy Statement on aviation. The clear implication of the judgment was that any substantial failure to address the issues in that Statement could render it vulnerable to legal challenge on the grounds of irrationality. The National Policy Statement was intended to set the policy framework for any possible subsequent planning application for the runway, and indeed would prevent any debate on national policy issues during the planning procedures, one of the purposes of the new planning legislation. But the legislation required preparation of the statement to go through a statutory consultation process and parliamentary procedure, and Lord Justice Carnwath observed that, until that process was concluded, the government could not limit any public debate on the proposed runway that took place.

In fact, shortly after the decision there was a general election and a change of government. One of the first decisions of the new coalition government was to scrap plans for the new runway at Heathrow.[46] But this is no way diminishes the longer term implications

[42] See above n 21.

[43] Committee on Climate Change, 'Meeting the UK Aviation Target – Options for Reducing Emissions to 2050' (December 2009).

[44] Lord Carnwath was promoted to the Supreme Court in 2011.

[45] Para 52 of the judgment.

[46] But this may not be a permanent decision. In September 2012 the government appointed the Airports Commission to 'maintain its status as an international hub for aviation and immediate actions to improve the use of existing runway capacity in the next 5 years'. The Commission must produce its final report by summer

of the judgment of the court. It is a clever analysis, which avoids the courts becoming over-involved in the resolution of issues more appropriate for government but emphasises that there remain legal implications to the Climate Change Act which cannot be ignored by politicians in the development of future policies. The new National Policy Statement on aviation will have to address climate change issues in order to reflect the spirit of the judgment and, by implication, many other policy statements, such as those to do with housing or other transport issues which might impact on climate change, will need to do so. The European Union Treaty was the first constitutional document in the world to include an express principle that environmental considerations be integrated into all areas of Community policy.[47] The United Kingdom famously does not have a written constitution as such, but it could be argued that the Climate Change Act emulates this integration principle – all relevant areas of policy making must now, as a matter of law, at least address the issue.

The Climate Change Committee and the Government – the 2011 Tensions

The Climate Change Act received support from all political parties, and survived the change of government in 2010. But it is less certain whether the commitment to long-term reduction targets can survive the immediate pressures on public finances in a weakened economy. Political disputes over the most recent carbon reduction budget have underlined the significance of the policy framework being so explicitly encased within a carefully constructed framework of law prescribing precise procedures.

At the end of 2010 the Committee on Climate Change published a report, as it was required to do so under the Climate Change Act, making recommendations for the fourth carbon budget, covering the years 2023–27.[48] The Committee accepted that the reduction curve for carbon budgets to the year 2050 would not be even, since early progress would be constrained by existing policies and commitments, while new technologies available in future years could increase the reductions possible at later dates. The Committee therefore based its predictions on some 62 per cent of the reductions required to meet the 2050 target being met after 2030, but the fourth budget was particularly important because it was seen as representing the minimum reductions needed if the 2050 targets were to be met. The key recommendation of the Committee was to limit UK emissions to 1950 $MtCO_2e$ (an average of 390 $MtCO_2e$ per year) for the period 2023–27, representing a 50 per cent reduction in 2025 from 1990 levels. But even these highly ambitious targets 'should be regarded as an absolute minimum, and more may be both feasible and

---

2015. One of its tasks is to include material to support the government in preparing a National Policy Statement under the Planning Act. In its Aviation Policy Framework (Cm 8584) presented to Parliament in March 2013, the government noted that, 'Should the government decide to support any new nationally significant airport infrastructure following the conclusions of the Airports Commission's work, it is likely that the next step would be to draft and consult on a National Policy Statement for Airports' (para 5.5).

[47] M Hession and R Macrory, 'The Legal Duty of Environmental Integration: Commitment and Obligation or Enforceable Right?' (1998), reproduced in Chapter 23 of this volume.

[48] Committee on Climate Change, 'The Fourth Carbon Budget – Reducing Emissions through the 2020s' (2010).

required as current uncertainties over emissions projections and abatement opportunities are resolved'.[49] Furthermore, the Committee strongly recommended that the reductions be achieved by domestic action only, rather than relying on purchases of credits in the international carbon markets. The Committee's report is no lightweight document but runs to nearly 400 pages, and contains detailed analysis of the implications of this budget for different sectors of the economy.

The advice of the Committee on previous budgets had been accepted by the government, although the legislation dearly gives the government the legal discretion not to agree should it so wish. Following the publication of the Committee's recommendation for the fourth budget, however, an unusually public row between different government departments developed. According to newspaper reports,[50] the Secretary of State for Business Innovation and Skills, supported by the Transport Secretary and the Chancellor of the Exchequer, argued that the proposed budget was not cost-effective, and that agreeing to too aggressive a reduction would be detrimental to the country's economic competitiveness. He argued for a lower target, though one that would still be in line for the 2050 goal, and incorporating, against the advice of the Committee, a greater reliance on purchasing overseas credits. The Secretary of State for Energy and Climate Change, supported by the Foreign Secretary and the Secretary of State for Environment, Food and Agriculture, apparently strongly supported the Committee's recommendations.

The matter was eventually resolved in May 2011, following intervention of the Prime Minister, with the government announcing to Parliament that it would accept the targets recommended by the Committee.[51] On the surface, this looked like a clear victory for the Committee's approach, but there were two potentially significant qualifications in the government response, which clearly reflect the outcome of complex political compromise. First, the government rejected the Committee's advice that reductions should be wholly achieved by domestic action. According to the government, it would aim to reduce emissions domestically only insofar as it was 'practical and affordable', and that it would keep the carbon trading option open 'to maintain maximum flexibility and minimize costs in the long run'.[52] Secondly, the government was acutely conscious of the United Kingdom getting out of step with the rest of the European Union. In line with the Committee's advice, it would urge the European Union to adopt a 30 per cent reduction for 2020 compared to 1990 levels, but – and here it again differed from the Committee's advice – it would review progress on achieving this change in 2014

> If at that point our domestic commitments place us on a different emissions trajectory than the Emissions Trading System trajectory agreed by the EU, we will, as appropriate, revise up our budget to align it with the actual EU trajectory.[53]

The Climate Change Act had already dealt with the possibility of UK allocations under the emissions trading regime being higher than the national carbon budget for that period by providing that regulations must be made to ensure that in those circumstances any such excess carbon units cannot be used to offset greenhouse gas emissions in the UK or

---

[49] Ibid, 12.

[50] 'Vince Cable and Chris Huhne Clash over Carbon Emissions', *The Guardian*, 9 May 2011, available at www.guardian.co.uk/politics (accessed on 12 June 2011).

[51] Department of Energy and Climate Change, 'Fourth Carbon Budget', oral ministerial statement by Secretary of State Chris Huhne, 17 May 2011.

[52] Ibid.

[53] Ibid.

elsewhere. But here the possibility of downgrading the intermediate budgets in line with EU policy being raised was something not expressly contemplated in the Act. Quite how an intermediate budget revised downwards in line with EU targets could sit easily with the long-term 80 per cent reduction target remains to be explored.

It is too early to judge precisely what the recent resolution concerning the fourth budget means for the Climate Change Act.[54] One view is that it reinforces the distinctive nature of the legislation, the very existence of which inhibits policy makers from undue change and compromise in a field that demands long-term and sustained commitment beyond the more familiar political cycles and time horizons. The fact is that the tighter budget eventually prevailed, but might well not have done had there not been such a degree of legal underpinning. A less generous view is that the outcome and the qualifications it contains represent the first signs of real doubt by politicians of the wisdom of being a first mover in a globally competitive economy, and that the flexibilities that have been built into the legislation will be exploited to the full when the going gets tough. In its report on the fourth budget, the Climate Change Committee reviewed the current state of scientific evidence, including recent errors made by the Intergovernmental Panel on Climate Change which have fuelled the arguments of climate change sceptics. The Committee's conclusions make sobering reading: 'A continued rise in emissions is likely to cause sustained global heating of a magnitude and rate unprecedented in the course of human civilization.'[55] The Climate Change Act may be said to provide legal leadership in this field, and contains mechanisms and principles that may well provide a model for climate change legislation in other jurisdictions despite different cultural and national traditions.[56] But it will be no substitute for the political leadership that will be key in the years to come.

---

[54] On 11 December 2013 the Committee on Climate Change published its review of the fourth carbon budget, and argued that there was no change in circumstances since the 2011 decision that would legally justify a revision of the budget. Section 21 of the Climate Change Act 2008 provides that the Secretary of State may subsequently alter a carbon budget, but only where 'there have been significant changes affecting the basis on which the previous decision was made'. What exactly was the 'basis' of the previous decision may well be contested.

[55] Committee on Climate Change, above n 48, 73.

[56] See generally ClientEarth, The UK Climate Change Act 2008 – Lessons for National Climate Laws (2009).

11

Weighing up the Performance:
Emissions Standards v Emissions
Trading[1]
(2011)

Policy makers have found emissions trading a powerful and attractive concept. But there is now a real concern about whether the EU trading scheme for greenhouse gases can provide the necessary incentives for securing investment in carbon reduction technology within the timescales needed. A UK Parliamentary Committee has recently endorsed the UK government's proposals for performance standards to drive down CO_2 emissions from power stations and other major emitters. They wish to see such standards work alongside the existing trading scheme, but this raises a number of complex legal issues and some challenging policy issues.

The report of the House of Commons Select Committee on Energy and Climate Change[2] is an important stepping stone in the analysis of measures needed to secure climate change reduction targets. It also has wider significance, in that it deals directly with fundamental issues concerning the design of environmental regulatory instruments, and in particular the relationship between more traditional techniques based on emissions standards and economic-based instruments such as emission trading. *Emissions Performance Standards* certainly does not resolve the debate—and perhaps it is a debate that never will be truly settled—but at least it tackles it in a rather more rounded and less partisan way than has sometimes been the case.

Emissions trading as a major tool of environmental policy was first introduced in the USA through the 1990 amendments of the Clean Air Act in order to resolve the deadlock between Congress and the Reagan administration as to how to deal with the problem of acid rain. Its theoretical justification was based on a sustained critique of conventional regulatory techniques by US lawyers and economists. The term 'command and control' regulation entered the language of environmental policy debate—one that had intentionally derogatory connotations but which also exaggerated the constraints on technology choices imposed by most US environmental regulations[3] and in any event was less relevant to the rather more flexible regulatory style prevailing in Europe.

---

[1] R Macrory, 'Weighing Up the Performance' (2011) 23(2) *Journal of Environmental Law* 311.

[2] House of Commons Select Committee on Energy and Climate Change, First Report of Session 2010–11, HC 523, *Emissions Performance Standards*.

[3] The leading US environmental lawyer TT Smith Jr has noted that, 'other than (1) management standards for transportation, storage and disposal of hazardous waste and (2) the limited case of US work practice rules, virtually all of the technology based air and water standards and some of the hazardous waste treatment

The apparent success of the US emissions cap and trade trading regime in the field of sulphur dioxide and nitrogen dioxide reduction programmes continues to be held up as justification for the extension of emissions trading to other areas of environmental policy. The 2009 Lazarowicz report, commissioned by Gordon Brown when UK Prime Minister,[4] advocated the creation of a global emissions regime for greenhouse gases and relied upon the US example as the only case study of a successful trading regime—according to the US Environmental Protection Agency, by 2004 sulphur dioxide emissions from US power stations had fallen by around 40 per cent from 1980 levels and with greatly reduced costs. Yet there still remain conflicting arguments as to the real impact of the US scheme. In a recent analysis, Keohane[5] noted that

> The two major ex post analyses of cost savings from allowance trading . . . have reached opposite conclusions. Carlson [et al, 2000][6] find that the costs of abatement during phase I were higher than they would have been under prescriptive regulation. On the other hand, a study by Ellerman [et al, 2000][7] estimates that the use of allowance trading led to savings of hundreds of millions of dollars per year.[8]

Lazarowicz then fails to mention that during the same period greater emission reductions of SO_2 from power stations were achieved in the UK, relying upon more conventional regulatory techniques and underpinned by the EC Large Combustion Directive.[9] Other factors, such as changing economic structures, may have been as important in reducing emissions in both jurisdictions—distinguishing correlation and causation in weighing up the effectiveness of different regulatory approaches in any complex and dynamic economic system remains a challenge that is fraught with difficulty.

Nevertheless, emissions trading continues to be a powerful and attractive concept to policy makers, and, following its ratification of the Kyoto Protocol, the European Union led the way in developing a cap and trade system for greenhouse gases reflected in the original 2003 Directive.[10] That development took place during a period when there was a distinct lack of confidence by European policy makers in the capacity of traditional regulatory approaches to handle contemporary environmental challenges. *Emissions Performances Standards* is now published at a time when, less than a decade later, there is a

standards are not command and control in the sense of expressly requiring use of a specific type of technology'. TT Smith Jr and R Macrory, 'Legal and Political Considerations' in P Douben (ed), *Pollution Risk Assessment and Management* (Wiley & Sons, 1998) 406.

[4] M Lazarowicz, *Global Carbon Trading: A Framework for Reducing Emissions* (The Stationery Office, 2009).

[5] N Keohane, 'Cost Savings from Allowance Trading in the 1990 Clean Air Act: Estimates from a Choice-Based Model' in J Freeman and C Kolstad (eds), *Moving to Markets in Environmental Regulation* (Oxford, Oxford University Press, 2007) 194, 195.

[6] C Carlson, D Burtrow and M Cropper, 'Sulfur Dioxide Controls for Electric utilities: What Are the Gains from Trade?' (2000) 108 *Journal of Political Economy* 1292.

[7] AD Ellerman, PL Joskow, R Schmalensee, J Montero and EM Bailey, *Markets for Clean Air* (Cambridge University Press, 2000).

[8] Keohane himself argues that the trading approach was more cost efficient compared with prescriptive regulation, though only modestly so if one assumed more flexible, emissions-based rather than technology-based standards. Clearly much depends on how the counterfactual, prescriptive regulatory approach is assumed. I am grateful to Donald McGillivray for drawing my attention to this literature.

[9] Defra, 'UK Emissions of Air Pollutants 2009 Results' (Department of Environment, Food and Rural Affairs, 2010) Fig 1. This indicates that emissions of SO_2 from large combustion plants fell by around 75 per cent between 1980 and 2005.

[10] Parliament and Council Directive 2003/87/EC establishing a scheme for greenhouse gas emission allowance trading within the Community [2003] OJ L275/32, as amended most recently by Parliament and Council Directive 2009/29/EC [2009] OJ L140/63.

similar concern with the ability of the emissions trading system to provide the necessary incentives for securing investment in carbon reduction technology within the timescales needed. As the report notes, the EU emissions trading system has not yet been successful in achieving the goal of encouraging investment in low-carbon technology 'because the carbon price generated by the System has been too low and too volatile to provide a strong enough signal to investors'.[11]

The inquiry was born out of the 2010 Coalition Agreement, which stated that the new government would 'establish an emissions performance standard that will prevent coal-fired power stations being built unless they are equipped with sufficient carbon capture and storage to meet the emissions performance standard'.[12] This was against the background of the Climate Change Act 2008 setting a nationally legally binding target to reduce the UK's emissions of CO_2 by at least 34 per cent by 2020 and by 80 per cent by 2050. The Committee felt that the current policy framework was 'grossly inadequate' and would not deliver adequate investment in new low-carbon technology over the next 20 years. Against that context, the Committee welcomed the proposed introduction of emission performance standards, but felt that the government had failed to fully consider their likely impact in relation to other existing policies.

The original EU emissions trading directive attempted a clear demarcation by amending the Directive on Integrated Pollution and Prevention Control to provide that, where an integrated pollution and prevention control (IPPC) facility covered by the Emissions Trading Scheme was concerned, 'the permit shall not include an emission limit value for direct emissions of that gas unless it is necessary to ensure that no significant local pollution is caused'.[13] In contrast to pollutants such as sulphur dioxide, it is unrealistic to conceive of greenhouse gases giving rise to local pollution, and the provision seemed expressly designed to ensure that emission trading was the sole regulatory instrument available in this area. Nevertheless, there was legal doubt whether a provision of this nature could effectively rule out the residual power of Member States to introduce non-discriminatory performance standards, especially as the Directive was based on the environmental provisions of the EU Treaty, which explicitly allow Member States the power to introduce stricter standards.[14] The 2010 Directive on Industrial Emissions, which will replace the Directive on Integrated Pollution and Prevention Control, repeats the restriction on limit values where the greenhouse emissions trading regime is concerned, but then adds enigmatically in the preamble that, in accordance with the environmental provisions of the Treaty, the Directive 'does not prevent Member States from maintaining or introducing more stringent protective requirements for example greenhouse gas emission requirements, provided these are compatible with the Treaties and the Commission has been notified'.[15] The Select Committee was uncertain whether this gives a legal carte blanche to Member States to

---

[11] *Emission Performance Standards*, above n 2, para 16.

[12] 'The Coalition: Our Programme for Government' (Cabinet Office, 2010) para 16.

[13] Parliament and Council Directive 2008/1/EC concerning integrated pollution prevention and control (codified version) [2008] OJ L24/8, Art 9.1.

[14] Under ex Art 175 EC, see now Art 192 TFEU and the derogation provision in Art 193. See, eg the Legal Opinion of February 2010 by D Wyatt and R Macrory commissioned by World Wide Fund for Nature (WWF) and made available to the European Parliament during the legislative discussion of the Industrial Emissions Directive (2010/75/EU). We argued that it is not even necessary to rely upon the environmental provisions of the Treaty since the restriction could be interpreted to relate only to IPPC permits, and does not prevent controls being introduced under other national legislation. The Opinion is available at http://www.europolitique.info/pdf/gratuit_fr/269819 (accessed on 21 February 2014).

[15] Parliament and Council Directive 2010/75/EU on industrial emissions [2010] OJ L334/17, preamble (10).

introduce national performance standards, and called for the government to clarify the position. In its response,[16] the government felt that, given the wording of the preamble, it should be possible for a national performance standard to be compatible with EU law, though this was an area where detail matters, and no definitive answer could be given until the precise content of the proposed standard was known. Ultimately, though, this is an issue that seems destined for the Court of Justice of the European Union.

The Select Committee accepted that if one Member State alone introduced CO_2 performance standards it might have no immediate impact of EU greenhouse gas levels, since industries in other EU countries could purchase the additional allocated allowances that would flow into the market. The Committee recommended that the government considered retiring an equivalent number of allowances to ensure this was not a possible outcome, yet admits there are doubts about the legality of such an action, and again called for the government to clarify the position. In its response, the government considers the impact of performance standards on the emissions trading regime, if confined to new coal-fired power stations, would be negligible, though it studiously avoids answering the legal question directly.

In the past, performance standards and emissions trading have usually been presented as either/or options. What is new in the current policy debate is the apparent willingness of government to see an emissions trading regime and performance-based emissions standards work alongside each other. Yet the full ramifications of this new policy paradigm have not been addressed. How far can a government introduce regulatory measures which assist the achievement of policy goals but do not end up undermining the essential qualities of an emissions trading regime? Both the Select Committee and the UK government continue to assert that the emissions trading regime will remain central to the policy response to climate change. Yet, in parallel to the emission performance standard, the government is also proposing to introduce a carbon price support mechanism providing a guaranteed floor price for carbon.[17] Whether such a support system can effectively operate in one Member State alone remains to be seen, but the idea has already rung alarm bells amongst those who advocate emissions trading as the most effective policy tool in this area. As the International Emissions Trading Association (IETA) has robustly observed:

> IETA does not understand why a government that has championed free markets and open trade, and lent strong support to the European Commission in the use of trading mechanisms to reach climate objectives, is now seemingly turning its back on emissions trading as a policy instrument. IETA believes that the UK proposal for a carbon price support mechanism . . . shows a serious lack of trust in the EU ETS which is the cornerstone of the EU's strategy for fighting climate change.[18]

Any regulatory intervention can also raise the spectre of unexpected consequences where a largely free market is concerned. The Committee noted that the introduction of performance-based standards for new coal-fired stations only could simply lead to a transfer of

---

[16] 'Emissions Performance Standards: Government Response to the Committee's First Report of Session 2010–11', 24 February 2011 (The Stationery Office, 2011).

[17] A 'carbon price floor' came into effect on 1 April 2013 under provisions of the Finance Act 2011, with more detailed provisions published by Her Majesty's Revenue and Customs in December 2012 as part of the draft Finance Bill 2013. According to the House of Commons Library briefing, 'The rate for 2103 is equivalent to £4.94 per tonne of carbon dioxide. From 1 April 2014, the CPS rates of CCL and fuel duty will be equivalent to £9.55 per tonne. Indicative prices have been published up to 2017. Revenue raised will be retained by the Treasury' (Carbon Price Floor House of Commons Library Standard Note SN05927, 7 November 2013).

[18] IETA, 'Response to UK Carbon Price Support Mechanism' (IETA, 2011).

investment to gas-fired power stations. Performance-based standards could be introduced for gas-fired stations too, with carbon-capture technology perhaps reducing their carbon intensity sixfold.[19] On this issue, the government response, while mostly supportive of the Select Committee's analysis, is disappointing. It firmly rejects any proposals to include gas within the proposed performance standards:

> To affect new gas generation at this stage could have significant impacts on energy security. While over the longer term the UK will need gas plant operating at baseload to be equipped with CCS if we are to meet decarbonisation objectives, unabated gas plant have an important role as we make the transition.[20]

From this perspective, energy security and climate change prevention are not necessarily objectives that reinforce each other.

We are entering an unsettled period in the design of energy strategy and appropriate regulatory instruments. In the 1980s, the UK pioneered major privatisation of the gas and electricity industries, both generators and suppliers, deliberately allowing energy policy and investment to be determined largely by the market, with the role of government regulation mainly designed to prevent consumer exploitation. The reliance on the free market to determine strategy was epitomised by the abolition in 1992 of the Department of Energy[21] as no longer being seen to have a useful function. As a result, low-cost, low-risk fossil fuel generation, largely through gas-fired generating stations, trumped technologies with high upfront capital costs and higher risks. The creation in 2008 of the new UK Department of Energy and Climate Change symbolised a re-evaluation of the role that the government should play in handling energy security and climate change for which the market by itself was ill-equipped. With the European Union pressing ahead with energy liberalisation, the Select Committee noted a degree of irony in the current UK developments, and quoted one of its witnesses, Lord Turner, chairman of the statutory Committee on Climate Change[22]:

> There is an element to which we have been so proud of our complicated energy market which was created for a particular set of purposes that we have managed to sell it to Europe and they are rolling ahead to try and make everybody have to have it just at a point where we are realizing that it is not necessarily the most efficient way to drive a low-carbon economy.[23]

The observation of the philosopher Sir Isaiah Berlin in his 1958 inaugural lecture at Oxford University that 'not all good things are compatible'[24] is nowhere more apposite than in the design of contemporary energy policy and regulation. *Emission Performance Standards* points to a number of the dilemmas and ambiguities that are already becoming apparent, and are likely increasingly to do so.

---

[19] Parliamentary Office of Science and Technology, 'Carbon Footprint of Electricity Generation' (POST, 2006), available at http:www.parliament.uk.doc/documents/post/postpn268/pdf (accessed on 20 April 2011).
[20] 'Emissions Performance Standards: Government Response', above n 12, para 12.
[21] The Department of Energy was originally created as a response to the 1973 oil crisis.
[22] Established under the Climate Change Act 2008.
[23] Emission Performance Standards, above n 2, Q 31 (Turner).
[24] I Berlin, *Two Concepts of Liberty* (Oxford, Oxford University Press, 1958).

12

Public Consultation and GMO Policy – a Very British Experiment[1] (2008)

Engaging with Public Values

In 2003–04 the UK government engaged in a novel experiment in public participation concerning policy on genetically modified organisms (GMOs) and how it should develop. Entitled *GM Nation*, the exercise came against a growing background of debate in the United Kingdom concerning the relationship of science, public values and policy both in the area of GMOs but also in other fields of environmental policy. Various forms of formal public consultation procedures, such as public inquiries and rights to make representations, have long been established features of British regulatory practice, but *GM Nation* was a conscious departure from existing practices and aimed at genuinely trying to engage the public in new forms of debate. How it actually worked out in practice has been subject to subsequent criticism that will be discussed later. Much of this criticism is justified, but this does not detract from the ambitions behind the exercise or the novelty of what was being done – as such, it still provides a valuable model for thinking about how governments should engage with the public in complex policy areas.

The starting point is the Royal Commission on Environmental Pollution (RCEP), an independent and permanent advisory body to the government.[2] The Commission had investigated the subject of GMO releases into the environment as early as 1989,[3] and its report was one of the first detailed UK study of the subject. While recognising potential benefits of GMOs technologies, the Commission called for a dedicated regulatory specific to GMOs based on a licensing system for releases. At the time, the European Commission had only recently published proposals for the first EC Directive on the subject,[4] and the Royal Commission expressed some concerns over the proposal, particularly on the degree to which a Community-wide system of regulation could be truly sensitive to local environments.

---

[1] R Macrory, 'Public Consultation and GMO Policy – A Very British Experiment' (2008) 5(1) *Journal of European Environmental and Planning Law* 95.

[2] The Royal Commission on Environmental Pollution, established in 1970, was dissolved by the Coalition Government in 2011 as part of spending cuts.

[3] RCEP, *The Release of Genetically Engineered Organisms*, 13th Report, Cm 720 (London, HMSO, 1989).

[4] European Commission (1988) 'Proposal for a Council Directive on the deliberate release to the environment of genetically modified organisms', COM (88) 160 final.

As to public participation, the Royal Commission in previous reports had consistently advocated for greater openness and the need for wider public access to environmental information than was the traditional British practice.[5] The GMO report took up the theme and argued that transparency was especially important in the area of GMOs: 'The potential benefits which we foresee are likely to arise from exploitation of genetic engineering could be frustrated by public opposition motivated by fear of the unknown'.[6]

The Commission recommended, inter alia, that there should be public registers of applications for release licences and of licences granted. Advertisements should be placed by companies or organisations seeking licences for field trials. Members of the public should be given the opportunity to comment in respect of the licence applications, and be allowed to comment on recommendations by expert committees on proposed licences. The Commission's recommendations for a dedicated regulatory regime, including provisions for public consultations and information, were largely accepted by the government and were contained in the Part VI of the Environmental Protection Act 1990. These provisions still provide the core national legal framework, though they now have to be read alongside relevant European Community legislation.

Despite the Royal Commission's advocacy of greater transparency, its recommendations in this respect in the 1989 report are of a fairly conventional nature, echoing provisions now seen in many contemporary environmental regimes – essentially public registers of licence information and the opportunity for the public to comment on individual licence applications. The report contains no discussion or recommendations concerning more imaginative methods of engaging public debate, nor any discussion of how general policy questions concerning the benefits and disbenefits of GMOs as opposed to the details of individual applications should best be discussed, especially as these are inevitably likely to raise complex issues concerning the relationship between science, technology and public trust.

Almost a decade later, the Royal Commission addressed the question of public participation again, and its analysis and recommendations demonstrated the rapid development in debate and analysis that had taken place in the intervening period. Its Report, *Setting Environmental Standards*,[7] was not concerned with GMOs as such, or indeed any specific environmental policy issue. Rather, it raised general questions of the processes by which environmental decision making was made. Its analysis and recommendations, though sometimes of a fairly abstract nature, raised fundamental questions concerning the nature of environmental science and the policy process, and in retrospect can be seen to have had profound influence on the experiment in public participation that the government later launched concerned GMOs.

The Commission's report was concerned with environmental standards generally, and it deliberately adopted a definition that went beyond the detailed numerical limits contained in the legislation, instead encompassing any considered official judgment about the acceptability of environmental modifications resulting from human activity.[8] In most cases scientific input was an essential part of the process, and a key role of any scientific

---

[5] Extensive public information and consultation rights had long existed in the land use planning system but were less developed in the 1960s and 1970s in more specialised pollution control regimes.

[6] RCEP, above n 3, para 8.22.

[7] RCEP, *Setting Environmental Standards*, 21st Report (London, HMSO, 1998).

[8] The report makes it clear that the judgment would apply to a defined class of cases, thus distinguishing it from a decision made, say, on an individual licence or consent. A 'standard' in this sense has some generic application.

assessment was to indicate to the decision maker the level and nature of uncertainties, and the effects of different levels and intensities of human intervention into the environment – in simple terms, the production of dose–effect curves. Nevertheless, the Commission was clear that when it came to a decision about the 'acceptability' of any particular level of intervention in the environment this could not be determined by scientists themselves but inevitably involved questions of public values. The decision would rest with whichever body had been given responsibility for standard setting in a particular area – perhaps an environment agency, the government, an individual minister or European institutions. But the Commission was concerned that, while decision makers might have good access to reasonably robust scientific, technological and economic data, they often lack equivalent information concerning the nature of public values.

Various forms of economic appraisal claim to provide information to decision making concerning the value that individuals place on different choices, and where cost–benefit analysis is used, the Commission accepted that the purpose of placing monetary values on items that are not traded as such was not to estimate their actual worth or price but to communicate evidence about 'the relative values which society places on different uses of resources'.[9] Nevertheless, the claims of the ability of economic appraisal to represent moral values rather than simply preferences was strongly disputed by some members of the Commission. In an important though somewhat hidden passage, the Report analyses techniques of economic appraisal and concludes that,

> To the extent that people's values (as expressions of fundamental commitments to the environment or to equity, whether within society or between present and future generations) are regarded as not answerable to economic appraisal, the question then arises whether there is any other approach that could provide additional assistance to decision making in that respect.[10]

The Commission then went on to examine various more familiar forms of seeking public views such as public opinion surveys, consultation exercises and local public inquiries. These methods will continue to play an important role, but they were not best suited, in the Commission's view, to providing an adequate method for articulating values or for providing decision makers with a greater understanding of such values. Such traditional methods provided little scope for exchanging views with others and considering issues in the light of growing understandings. In this sense, values, as opposed to opinions, are not always fixed and preformed, and the Commission felt that, for most people, it is more accurate to think of their values emerging or taking shape as they are brought to face important choices between competing options: 'A more rigorous and wide-ranging exploration of people's values requires discussion and debate to allow a range of viewpoints and perspectives to be considered, and individual values developed'.[11] It was essential that any such exercises should be held at the earliest possible stage in the policy process rather than, as often happens, being deferred to a relatively late stage, after the problem has already been defined.

Various methods have been developed to allow for greater exploration of values, including consensus conferences, which have been used in Denmark, the Netherlands, New Zealand and Switzerland, and were first used in the United Kingdom in 1994 in

---

[9] Department of the Environment, *Policy Appraisal and the Environment: A Guide for Government Departments* (London, HMSO, 1991) para 4.2, quoted in RCEP, ibid.

[10] RCEP, ibid, para 5.48.

[11] Ibid, para 7.23.

connection with plant biotechnology. Citizens' juries have been extensively used in the United States, and an early example in the United Kingdom was that conducted by the Welsh Institute for Health and Social Care in 1997 concerning genetic testing for common disorders. Other forms of deliberative institutions include focus groups and deliberative polls. The Commission was careful to avoid endorsing any particular method as providing a guaranteed solution, and warned against expecting a consensus to be reached:

> The fundamental purpose of these new approaches is not to produce a 'right answer' but to illuminate the value questions raised by environmental issues in order to identify the policies around which consensus is more likely to form and to enable decisions to be better informed and more robust.[12]

The Royal Commission's report was deliberately cast in fairly abstract terms, and did not recommend their approach be applied to any particular area, though it noted these new methods of public engagement should be applied 'primarily in connection with issues which are both complex or controversial and of broad scope'.[13] However, by the time the report was published after some two years of study, the whole issue of GMOs had become politically heightened, following a period when the subject had been dominated by science and a regulatory approach based on conventional risk evaluation.[14] At the press conference launching the Commission's report, environmental groups pressurised the Commission into recommending that their proposals be applied to the GMO policy debate, but the Commission refused to be drawn, and responded that the policy areas considered most appropriate for this sort of approach must be a matter of government choice.

The Agriculture and Biotechnology Commission

Reports of the Royal Commission are not binding on the government, but in its response to the 21st Report, published two years later,[15] it noted that it had already put some of the Commission's proposals into practice 'in difficult areas such as genetically modified organisms'.[16] It acknowledged that ethical and social considerations had to be factored into debates on scientific issues, and in 2000 had established two Commissions to provide input to its evolving strategy on biotechnology: the Human Genetics Commission[17] and the Agriculture and Environment Biotechnology Commission (AEBC). The AEBC was deliberately established to have a broader remit than simply providing expert scientific advice but was required to keep under review current and possible future developments in biotechnology with actual and potential implications for agriculture and the environment, and to advise government on the ethical and social implications from these developments and their public acceptability. The Commission was chaired by an academic professor of

---

[12] Ibid, para 7.43.

[13] Ibid, para 7.41.

[14] See Black, 'Regulation as Facilitation: Negotiating the Genetic Revolution' (1998) 61 *Modern Law Review* 621.

[15] *Government Response to the Royal Commission on Environmental Pollution's Twenty First Report*, Cm 4794 (London, HMSO, July 2000).

[16] Ibid, para 6.

[17] The Human Genetic Commissions is a multi-disciplinary expert body provide advice on social and ethical aspects of human genetics, and still exists: see http://www.hgc.gov.uk.

planning and environmental law, and, perhaps to mark a distinct break from previous exercises, included members from both the biotechnology industry and environmental groups.

The AEBC existed for 5 years during a critical period of policy debate in the United Kingdom concerning GMOs. From the beginning, AEBC acted upon principles of transparency and openness, with agendas and minutes of all its meetings available publicly, and its meetings being held in public around the country. It published a total of 17 reports, on subjects ranging from animals and biotechnology, soil science, coexistence and liability, to shaping the research agenda. The AEBC was fully alive to the need to engage the public in the debate on GMOs. For example, during the preparation of what turned out to be its final report on shaping the future agenda in agricultural biotechnology,[18] the AEBC commissioned a stakeholder and public consultation exercise in order to understand views of those who were not normally consulted during this sort of process. The exercise involved six discussion groups with 40 members of the general public, recruited by on-street and referred recruitment, ensuring a wide mix of key demographic characteristics. Scientists and non-governmental organisation activists were deliberately excluded. Parallel to this process were three discussion groups of stakeholders, including nine scientists, four field advisers and six farmers. This was followed by two further half-day workshops involving the public and a half-day workshop involving the stakeholders. The exercise was concluded with a full-day workshop involving both the public and stakeholders.

The exercise provided the AEBC with much greater insight into public and stakeholder perspectives, and influenced its overall conclusions on the research agenda. It noted that, after deliberation, almost all participants felt that the public had an important contribution to make to setting research agenda strategies, and the AEBC endorsed that view.

However, it was the AEBC's first report,[19] published in 2001, that set the agenda for the government's major public debate concerning GMOs. The report was set against the background of the farm-scale evaluations of GMO crops which the government had commenced in 1998 and which, to their surprise, had caused considerable public controversy, including many local protests and direct action. The AEBC examined the evaluation exercise as an example of a regulatory process, and noted the wide range of different opinions that existed concerning the benefits and disbenefits of GMO technology. It concluded,

> We believe that robust public policies and regulatory frameworks for GM crops need to expose, respect and embrace the differences of view which exist, rather than bury them. The appropriate development of GM technology has suffered as a result of the lack of opportunity for serious debate about the full range of potential implications of GM agriculture, on the basis of clear understandings of what is involved, away from concern that has been promoted by campaigning elements of the media.[20]

The AEBC recommended that the government initiate a broad public debate concerning GMOs involving new approaches: 'We need to harness new deliberative mechanisms, to develop participatory methods of public engagement, together with new capacities within Government and industry for digesting and responding to the implications'.[21]

---

[18] Agricultural and Biotechnology Commission, 'What Shapes the Research Agenda in Agricultural Biotechnology?', URN 05/1078 (London, AEBC, 2005).

[19] AEBC, 'Crops on Trial', URN 01/1083 (London, AEBC, 2001).

[20] Ibid, para 16.

[21] Ibid, para 68.

To its credit, the government endorsed the idea, and sought advice from the AEBC as to how such a debate might be conducted. The AEBC's advice was published in 2002 in the form of a report.[22] The advice stressed that the purpose of the debate was not to act as a quasi-referendum or to relieve the government from its responsibilities to make decisions in the light of national, European and international law; rather, its prime purpose was to assess the nature and spectrum of public views, with an emphasis on the quality rather than the quantity of the information. The AEBC advocated a range of methods, including local discussion fora linked to national and regional debates, initiated by groups assisting in framing questions for discussions. It strongly advocated that any programme should be conducted an arm's length away from the government and carried out by an independent contractor, under the guidance of a steering board appointed by the government. The proposed debate and the AEBC's advice were strongly endorsed by the Parliamentary Select Committee that looked at the issue, though it warned against the government expecting any consensus to emerge:

> We support the proposed public debate about the issues surrounding the outcome of the farm-scale evaluations and the future commercial growing of GM crops. However, we caution that the most optimistic aspirations for such a debate – that through it a clearer public consensus in favour or opposed to commercial planting will be formed – are unlikely to be fulfilled. The debate will, though, help to inform those members of the public who become aware of it about GM crops in a rational and intelligent way, and at the same time help the Government to understand public opinion rather better.[23]

The GM Debate

At the end of May 2002, the Secretary of State announced the establishment of a public debate.[24] This was in fact part of a three-stranded approach, with two parallel reviews being carried out. One concerned the economics and cost and benefits of GM commercialization, and was carried out by the Cabinet Office Strategy Unit.[25] The second was a review of the science and level of certainty, led by the government's Chief Scientific Adviser and leading to two major reports.[26] A key underlying message of the science review was that the most important effects of GMOs were not health impacts but the potential effects on wildlife and the natural environment, and that the effects were unlikely to be homogeneous across all GM crops.

As to the public debate, and in line with the AEBC's recommendation, the government established an independent steering board, chaired by the chair of the AEBC itself and including some of its members but also a broader range of expertise. The underlying aim of the debate, according to the government, was to 'promote an innovative, effective and

---

[22] AEBC, 'A Debate about the Possible Commercialization of GM Crops' (London, AEBC, 2002).

[23] House of Commons Select Committee on Environment, Food and Rural Affairs Fifth Report, 'Genetically Modified Organisms', Session 2001–2002, para 19.

[24] Press Notice, Department of Environment, Food and Rural Affairs, 31 May 2002.

[25] Cabinet Office, 'Field Work: Weighing Up the Costs and Benefits of GM Crops' (London, Cabinet Office, 2003).

[26] GM Science Review Panel First Report (2003) and Second Report (2004), 'An Open Review of the Science Relevant to GM Crops and Food Based on Interests and Concerns of the Public'.

deliberative programme of debate on GM issues, framed by the public, against a back-ground of the possible commercial production of GM crops in the UK and the options for possibly proceedings with this'.[27] Despite difficulties and a pressing timetable, the general view was that both the AEBC and the Steering Board had established a credible pro-gramme for the debate.[28] Initially nine workshops were held across the United Kingdom. These were organised by an independent consultancy with the aim of helping to framing the issues that should be the subject of debate. The formal debate took place over an intense six-week period starting in June 2003, and involving seven national meetings, 41 regional or county level meetings and 629 local scale meetings. The GM debate website received over 2.9 million hits during the period. Some 37,000 feedback forms were sent in.

An important aspect of the debate was the initiation of so-called 'narrow but deep' debates. Ten group discussions were commissioned involving members of the public who had not taken a conscious decision to participate in the debate, and excluding those working for or campaigning against the GM industry. The groups first met to be introduced to the subject, then were asked to think and research about the issue before reconvening for discussion and debate after a two-week period.

Following the debate, the Steering Board, which had conducted its own meetings with a great deal of transparency, published a summary of the findings.[29] In doing so, it expressly did not judge whether or not the public were right in their views, but concluded that there were a number of key messages about public attitudes that had emerged from the exercise. First, the predominant mood was a sense of uncertainty towards GM, but a general sense of unease. However, the more the general public engaged in the debate, the harder that attitude became. While they were more willing to accept some potential benefits from GM technology, such as medicine and for developing countries, the public became more doubtful about other benefits and the uncertainties involved. There was little support for early commercialisation, and a feeling that the technology should not proceed without further research, firm regulation, demonstrated benefits to society and not just to producers, and clear and trusted answers to unresolved questions about health and the environment. There was a widespread general distrust of both the government and the multinational companies involved in GM technology, but a broad desire to know more. The public debate was generally welcomed by those who took part, though there were deep suspicious that its results would be ignored by the government.

Certainly the government's response[30] was not as dramatically opposed to further com-mercialisation as some argued was reflected in the public debate. Its key conclusion was to reject a further moratorium but to advocate a case-by-case approach 'consistent with the precautionary principle'.[31] This was in line with the conclusions of the scientific review and the field trial evaluations, which indicated that different environmental effects could be derived from different types of GMO crops. But it went on to argue that the consumers should have the right to choose between GM and non-GM products through new label-ling rules, farmers should be protected by measures to facilitate the coexistence of GM

[27] www.gmpublicdebate.org/gmdebate/objectives,asp.

[28] See Brown, 'The Agriculture and Biotechnology Commission: Independent and Influential?' (2003) 15(2) Environmental Law and Management 85.

[29] Department of Trade and Industry, 'GM Nation: The Findings of the Debate' (London, Department of Trade and Industry, 2003).

[30] Department of Environment, Food and Rural Affairs, 'The GM Dialogue: Government Response' (London, Defra, 2004).

[31] Ibid.

and non-GM zones, and guidance should be provided to farmers wishing to establish voluntary GM-free zones. Finally, the government committed itself to considering the best ways of providing the information that the public wanted in an open and transparent way.

Evaluation and Aftermath

Whether or not the response of the government was justified, the form of public debate that preceded it broke new ground in the ways that public consultation exercises were carried out in the United Kingdom. But the way in which the exercise had actually carried out has also been subjected to criticism. The Royal Commission on Environmental Pollution, in its report on environmental standards, had warned that innovative forms of public consultation are costly,[32] yet initially the government had budgeted only £250,000 for carrying out the consultation, and it took lengthy wrangling from the Steering Committee to persuade the government to double that figure. Even then, many observers, including the Chairman of the Agriculture and Environment Biotechnology Commission, concluded that this was not sufficient for a national exercise of this nature. Again, for an issue of such complexity, an intense six-week period of debate seemed excessively short. The Agriculture and Environmental Biotechnology Commission had recommended that the exercise be carried out at arm's length from the government, but it was in fact managed by the government's Central Office of Information. Finally, a number of key reports, including the economic and scientific evaluations commissioned by the government, together with the results of the field crop evaluation studies, which could have provided invaluable background material to the public debate, were simply not completed in time for the start of the debate.

Rather more worryingly, an academic evaluation of the exercise concluded that, while it was undoubtedly innovative in terms of public engagement, the processes overestimated the strength of anti-GM feeling in the country. Those most actively engaged already had committed views, and the process had failed to properly engage uncommitted members of the public.[33] An opinion survey carried out by the same group after the debate suggested that, while 36 per cent of those survey were opposed to GM technology, nearly 40 per cent still had no firm views either way. As the leader of the research group noted,

> The devil really is in the detail here. It's no good announcing a public debate, setting up a board to oversee it, and then throwing money at it. These things need careful design, they need not to be rushed, and they probably need a little more money – but that money has to be well spent.[34]

A Parliamentary Review of the debate drew similar conclusions.[35] It welcomed the debate as an innovative and imaginative attempt in conducting such an exercise in a complex and controversial policy area, but it, too, felt that those primarily engaged were essentially a

---

[32] RCEP, above n 7, para 7.46.
[33] Horlick-Jones et al, 'A Deliberative Future? An Independent Evaluation of the GM Nation? Public Debate about the Possible Commercialization of Transgenic Crops in Britain Understanding Risk', Working Paper 04-02 (University of East Anglia, 2003).
[34] BBC Online News, 24 February 2004.
[35] House of Commons Select Committee on Environment, Food and Rural Affairs, *Conduct of the GM Public Debate*, 18th Report Session 2002–3, HC 1220 (London, HMSO, 2003).

self-selecting group rather than general members of the public. It blamed these weaknesses not on those who conducted the exercise, but on two decisions made by the government – the insufficient allocation of resources and an absurdly tight timetable. It hoped that the government would learn from the experience.

Critical also, especially in an area such as GMOs, is the relationship between a national debate on fundamental issues of values and a regulatory system operated at EU level. Early in 2003, it had already emerged that decisions concerning applications for commercial growing of GMO crops under EC Directive 2001/18/EEC which had restarted after an effective moratorium might be taken at EU level in advance of the national debate, thereby undermining its political credibility. The government responded that there would be no conflict, since final decisions on any of the applications would be unlikely to be taken before the end of the year:

> by that time we have the first set of results from our crop trials, the report of the public debate, and the information provided by the other parts of the work programme on GM that the Government has put in place.[36]

The timing was fortuitous perhaps, but it is less easy to see how such a deliberative debate could have been conducted at EU level within the EU regulatory regime, or indeed the extent to which an assessment of public concerns and anxiety, whether based on 'rational' evidence or not, can form a legitimate ground for turning down applications to commercialise GMOs with the current regulatory structures. Both the government and the courts often find it more tempting to return to the apparently more certain world of science and economics, and the concept of rational risk assessment.[37] Yet one of the challenges surely facing the future design of environmental regimes is how the concept of public values, however nebulous and difficult to ascertain, should be incorporated into a robust and fair regulatory system. In this context, the British experience with the *GM Nation* debate should be seen as the start of a process towards the development of new paradigms in public decision making, but one whose final shape is by no means certain.

---

[36] Quoted in Brown, above n 28.
[37] See M Lee (2008) 'The UK Regulatory System on GMOs: Expanding the Debate' in E Everson and M Vos, *Uncertain Risks Regulated* (London, Routledge, 2008).

13

Technology and Environmental Law Enforcement[1]
(2003)

It would be entirely wrong to deny to the law of evidence the advantages to be gained from new techniques and new advances in science[2]

Introduction

One of Gerd Winter's strengths as an environmental lawyer has been his ability to consider the legal implications of developments of technology and science and from perspectives that often fall outside the immediate concerns of more conventional environmental law. He acknowledges the potential environmental benefits of man's continual inventiveness but has been prepared to explore difficult questions concerning the role of law in creating solutions that are both transparent and lead to a more environmentally sustainable society. In his seminal article, 'Perspectives for Environmental Law – Entering the Fourth Phase',[3] he questioned the capacity of interventionist approaches which have so characterised developments in environmental law over the past thirty years to handle the demands now being made on them. He argued that a preferable approach might be to reduce such burdens while at the same time injecting an environmental dimension and reorientating substantive areas of law concerned with harnessing or emancipating the capacities of individuals and corporations, such as labour law, competition law, and company law: 'All of this must not be seen as a controlling law and administrative programme but rather as a programme which is inscribed into that body of law which at the outset releases the individual's economic energy'.[4] In a similar vein he has explored the fundamental concepts of patent law in the context of biotechnology,[5] noting that, while legal debate has largely been concerned with developing regulatory techniques to handle environmental risks, the question of reforming intellectual property law had been largely untouched. Patent law in this context can been seen as a promotional body of law which should be reconsidered

[1] R Macrory, 'Technology and Environmental Law Enforcement' in Winter (ed), *Rechtund Um-Welt* (Amsterdam, European Law Publishers, 2003) 431–46.
[2] Lord Justice Steyn, *R v Clarke* (1994) Criminal Division, Court of Appeal.
[3] (1989) 1(1) *Journal of Environmental Law* 38.
[4] Ibid, 46.
[5] 'Patent Law Policy in Biotechnology'(1992) 4(2) *Journal of Environmental Law* 167.

and refocused rather than imposing every increasing burdens on an already over worked regulatory system:

> This is not a mere doctrinal discourse, where new phenomena are subsumed under stretched old legal forms, nor is it a substantialist discourse where vitalists wage an idle war against materialist pervasiveness. Rather, it is a functionalist argument where patentability as opposed to other policy alternatives is assessed with regard to social, economic and ecological effects.[6]

Remote Sensing in Court

Effective enforcement of environmental law is a challenge facing all governments, and the almost inevitable implementation gaps that pervade the use of traditional environmental regulatory techniques have been one of the motivations for Gerd Winter's search for new ways of thinking about the law and the environment. It is entirely in keeping with his intellectual curiosity that he has more recently been concerned with the potential use of satellite technology and remote sensing as a important technological tool in the application of environmental law. With ever increasing resolution and coverage, the technology can be presented as a cost-effective and reliable tool which will dramatically improve the ability of regulatory bodies in many areas of environmental law to detect and deter. Oil pollution from sea, illegal abstractions of water, damage to special protection sites for nature conservation, and even illegal disposal of waste can all in theory be determined by the use of remote sensing. Knowledge of the capacity of such satellites and the extent to which even the current generation can provide regular and detailed information is not yet generally pervasive among regulators, judges, environmental lawyers let alone the average citizen. More significantly, in the past few years there appears to have been a step change in the capacity of the technology. The Landsat systems which have been familiar to users of remote sensing for the past 20 years or so have a spatial resolution of between 30 and 50 metres, but in 2000 there were 31 satellites in orbit with the capability of providing land cover data at spatial resolutions of 1–30 metres, while the Ikonos satellite, launched in 1999, has the capacity of 1 metre resolution, with high resolution and high frequency of revisits. Images from such resolution can distinguish, for example, individual vehicles. A new generation of satellites is planned for 2004 with 0.5 metre resolutions, and the future may well see the greater use of unmanned space vehicles which fly at 50,000 or so feet, lower than current satellites but considerably higher than an aeroplane. The potential for this technology in the assisting the implementation of environmental law is clearly enormous and of a quite different nature to what has been the experience to date; yet a more serious and intensive effort to harness this capacity in the interests of improved environmental protection raises potential conflicts with other well developed areas of law such as data protection, privacy, intellectual property ownership, and rules of evidence. Over 50 years ago the American lawyer, Thurman Arnold wrote that the law 'fulfils its functions best when it represents the maximum of competing symbols'. But unless the environmental lawyer is prepared to understand and engage with these 'competing' areas of law with their own important goals and precepts, progress with environmental law is

---

[6] Ibid, 184.

likely to be stymied. The purpose of this contribution is therefore to consider a number of the legal issues likely to be raised in the context of the use of satellite technology for improved enforcement of environmental law.[7] The focus is on Europe, and many of the more detailed aspects of the law are provided are from the United Kingdom context, though they are likely to represent issues that will be common to most developed legal systems.

One could imagine a scenario of a regulator responsible for the enforcement of laws designed to prevent damage to special nature protection areas. Where such damage occurs the relevant legislation imposes criminal liability on the owner of the land unless, say, he can prove it was caused by a third party beyond his control. The constraints on public sector finances means that regular inspection by individual officers across last tracts of lands is not possible, and it is more cost effective to monitor remote sensing images of the land in question. The regulator decides to use one such satellite image to prove before a court that damage has taken place, and an offence committed. In all jurisdictions fairly complex rules of evidence have been developed to ensure that a defendant has a fair trial, and that evidence produced is as authentic as possible. In a common law jurisdiction such as the United Kingdom the rules and principles are especially coloured by the fact of the adversarial nature of the process and the strong lay element in criminal courts with juries determining facts in serious criminal cases, and a wide use of lay magistrates in less serious offences. In the scenario outlined above the likely immediate reaction of court faced with such an image as sole evidence will be to ask why the regulator did not investigate the situation at first hand. In this context a satellite image is likely to be of greatest value as providing a warning to a regulator of a potential problem, a valuable administrative tool particularly for regulators under financial pressure and tasked with monitoring expansive or remote tracts of land or the sea. In the United Kingdom, for example, set-aside schemes under the Common Agriculture Policy are regularly monitored by remote sensing, and in at least one case have provided advance warning of fraud, later confirmed by visual inspection and leading to a successful prosecution of the farmer concerned.[8] Indeed, the use of remote sensing is positively encouraged under European Community rules concerning aid in the agricultural field, one of the few examples of Community legislation making such express reference to the technology for enforcement purposes.[9]

Nevertheless, we can also imagine situations where the relevant environmental law incorporates a temporal dimension, and where the capacity of remote sensing to build up data showing land changes over a period of years may provide the critical and only available evidence to contradict the defendant. An example might include laws requiring permits for new building but where the existence of the building for a number of years provides a good defence; or where new requirements for licences to abstract water do not apply to those who have abstracted water for a set number of years prior to the legislation

---

[7] Much of the original analysis is based on a joint project involving both legal and technological research centres across Europe and conducted for the European Commission, APERTURE, ENV4-CT97-437 final report, October 3 2000. Professor Winter led the German contribution.

[8] R Macrory and R Purdy, 'Use of Satellite Images as Evidence in Environmental Actions in Great Britain' (2001) 51 *Droit et Ville* 71.

[9] Commission Regulation EEC 3887/92 laying down detailed rules for applying the integrated administration and control system for certain Community aid schemes. See Art 6 and the preamble, which states, 'Whereas the conditions for the use of remote sensing for on-the-spot checks should be laid down and provision should be made for physical checks to be required in doubtful cases'. The Regulation provides for financial contribution from the Community 'in order to encourage Member States in their efforts to develop remote sense'.

coming into force.[10] In such cases the bank of images already obtained by remote sensing may prove critical to resolving conflicts of evidence over what took place in the past.

The use of photographs, tape-recordings, and other documentary evidence are now, of course, familiar to the criminal courts. As long ago as 1878, photography was held admissible as evidence in court proceedings:

> The photograph was admissible because it is only the visual representation of the image or impression made upon the minds of the witnesses by the sight of the person or the object it represents; and therefore, is, in reality, only another species of the evidence which persons give of identity, when they speak merely from memory.[11]

It is arguable that remote sensing from satellites is no different from the use of aerial photography, and should be treated as such. Nevertheless there are potentially significant distinctions. Rules of evidence concerning the admissibility of documents in court proceedings in the United Kingdom were largely developed on the basis that there existed an 'original' (for analogue photographs, the negative) from which all copies derived. Common law jurisdictions, in particular, have long made an important distinction between 'real' evidence, that is, some material object such as a document or photograph from which the court may draw an inference, and what is termed 'hearsay' evidence, essentially evidence not of direct observation but what a witness heard others say. Clearly, the latter evidence may be given less weight because of the greater possibility of mistake or simply because there is another intervening level of human interpretation present. In jurisdictions based on an inquisitorial system and with a judge alone determining both fact and law, the distinction is less vital and simply goes to the weight of the evidence to be determined by the judges. Indeed, in civil cases in the United Kingdom where a judge determines both fact and law, hearsay evidence is admissible. In criminal cases, however, due to the tradition of lay citizens determining facts, there have long been rules forbidding its use in such cases: 'an assertion other than one made by the person while giving oral evidence in the proceedings is inadmissible as evidence of any fact asserted'.[12] Essentially the actual writer or originator of the statement must be present in court and available for cross-examination by the defence.[13]

Such rules may have been appropriate for a simpler era which was less rich in information technology, but clearly raise immense practical problems for the administration of justice where computer and similar data sources pervade almost every aspect of life. Legislation was therefore introduced in the United Kingdom[14] which permits the use of evidence produced by a computer but under the conditions that there was no reason to

---

[10] The use of remote sensing images has already been the subject of extensive court proceedings concerned with the registration of existing water rights under the Spanish Water Act, which came into force on 1 January 1986, and is one of the few examples in Europe where the conflict between a satellite image and the evidence of an individual was directly in issue.

[11] Per Willes J, *R v Tolson* (1864) 4 F & F 103.

[12] *R v Sharp* (1988) I All ER 65. See also Howarth, 'Self-monitoring, Self-policing, Self-incrimination and Pollution Law' (1997) 60 *Modern Law Review* 200.

[13] It is arguable that the prohibition of hearsay evidence in criminal cases is implied by Art 6(3) European Convention of Human Rights, which provides that everyone charged with a criminal offence has the right 'to examine or have examined witnesses against him and to obtain attendance and examination of witnesses on his behalf under the same conditions as witnesses against him', though the European Court have not yet adopted such a strict interpretation. See C Osborne, 'Hearsay and the Court of Human Rights' [1993] *Criminal Law Review* 255.

[14] See s 69 Police and Criminal Evidence Act 1984. See also ss 23 and 24 Criminal Justice conditions, even though the writer may not be present.

believe the information was inaccurate because of improper use of the computer and that at all times the computer was operating properly. Nevertheless, the conceptual difficulty of determining whether information derived from a computer or similar technological equipment is real rather than hearsay evidence are not always easy to determine, and require judgments to be made on the level of human intervention involved. In one case, for example,[15] the Criminal Court of Appeal upheld a trial judge's ruling that evidence from a computer automatically recording telephone calls in a hotel was real evidence[16] of those facts:

> This was not a print out which depended on its content for anything that had passed through the human mind . . . What was recorded was quite simply the acts which had taken place in regard to the telephone machinery and there was no intervening human mind.

But a year later, in a case concerning shoplifting, the Appeal Court held that evidence[17] from a computer providing accumulated data from till rolls, and entered by individual till operators, was hearsay:

> In Spilby the computer was recording information automatically without the intervention of any human agency. It was that fact that as a consequence the documentary evidence did not infringe the hearsay rule. Here much of the information supplied by the till rolls was supplied by cashiers. So far as that information is concerned, it was clearly hearsay and would only be admissible if it could be brought into one of the exceptions . . .

The significance of the distinction can have immense implications as was seen in litigation concerning the use of computer records held by local authorities where local authorities sought liability orders for the failure to pay a new and politically controversial local tax. The ruling by the High Court[18] that such evidence was inadmissible as being hearsay threatened the whole viability of the enforcement system in this area, and led to the government introducing special legislative provisions to permit their use in such proceedings.

It is clear that digital images from remote sensing do raise particular evidential problems of categorisation and authenticity. There is no 'original' image, but essentially a visual representation of binary data in a computer memory, and a considerable amount of processing has taken place before that data is converted to a visual representation. Even at an initial stage, a degree of image pre-processing is likely to be conducted in order to reduce errors that were introduced during image acquisition with techniques such as geometric and radiometric correction. Image processing itself involves a large degree of manipulation by the operator, for instance, in the assignation of colours designed to reveal particular features. Although it seems likely that the image itself would be considered 'real' rather than 'hearsay' evidence, expert evidence explaining the nature and implications of such resulting images are bound to be essential. All this is very different from the 'direct' photograph of the type more familiar to courts, and is clearly potentially vulnerable to legal challenge.

Nevertheless, the challenge of digital manipulation, lack of 'originals' and authenticity is no longer confined to satellite imagery but is increasingly experienced by courts handling evidence from video recordings, CCTV, and similar surveillance systems. But a 1998

---

[15] *John Eric Spilby* (1990) 91 Cr App R 186.
[16] The argument that computer evidence was real rather than hearsay was first suggested in Smith, 'The Admissibility of Statements by Computer' [1981] *Criminal Law Review* 387.
[17] *Hilda Shephard* (1991) 93 Cr App R 140.
[18] *R v Coventry Justices ex parte Bullard and another, Times Law Report,* 24 February 1992.

Parliamentary inquiry into the use of digital images in court proceedings[19] could find no case where defence lawyers in a criminal case involving the use of video evidence had requested an audit trail – an omission which the committee attributed to a lack of technical knowledge amongst lawyers as to the nature of the technology and audits. In what continental lawyers might find a typically British pragmatic approach, the Committee nevertheless recommended against detailed legislation on the subject on the grounds that it would never keep up with technological development, and that it was best left to the courts to provide the necessary principles through case law. Already the Criminal Court of Appeal has provided ground-rules in the context of DNA evidence where it has held that a defendant must have access to all the individual stages involved in the production of such evidence, including the details of databases and specialist software upon which calculations have been based.[20]

The development of standardised procedures for audit trails in remote sensing is likely to be a crucial step in reassuring courts of the authenticity of the data presented, although as yet it is not a subject governed by legislation either in Britain or the at European level. At present, guidance has been issued by voluntary standards bodies such as the British Standards Institute concerning the best practice to be adopted in the case of computer generated evidence,[21] and though not legally binding, non-compliance with such a code could render the admissibility of such evidence vulnerable. Such a trail is likely to require the recoding of every step of enhancing and manipulating the date that the image goes through, ensuring that all processing and changes made to the document are recorded, and that the individuals who were responsible for this stages has the necessary authorisation. Although the concept of an 'original' image fits less easily into digital technology, bodies such as the British Standards Institute have recommended the hard copy original and original digital image be secured on a non-erasable image such as WORM (Write Once Read Many times), a practice now followed in financial and other business sectors. Even then such a procedure is not infallible, as in theory images could be altered and retransferred back to a second WORM, and any such alterations would be impossible to detect. Watermark or digital signatures can also be incorporated with the computer data to preserve authenticity, although even these technologies are fallible.

Technological Equipment

Legal provisions concerned with the use of evidence produced by technological equipment have been introduced in some areas of pollution law, notably section 111 of the Environment Act 1995 which permits the use of information 'by means of any apparatus' used in connection with monitoring compliance with water discharge consents. A conviction based on evidence obtained by an automatic sampling device was first obtained by the then National Rivers Authority in 1993, by a device which was remotely operated to take

---

[19] House of Lords Select Committee on Science and Technology 5th Report, 'Digital Images as Evidence', HL Paper 64 (London, HMSO, 1998).

[20] *R v Doheny, R v Adams* (1997) 1 Cr App Report 369, 669.

[21] See, eg British Standards Institution, 'Code of Practice for the Legal Admissibility of Information Stored on Electronic Document Management Systems', DISC PD0008 (1996).

effluent samples following a rise in pH levels.[22] The device, known as CYCLOPS, carried out continuous monitoring of the water quality and where consent levels were breached triggered a warning to a control centre, which permitted operators to instruct the machine to then take actual samples for potential use in a prosecution. The equipment containing the samples was opened in the presence of the defendant, and since the company in question decided to plead guilty, no legal points concerning the nature of the evidence came into play. Under section 111 of the 1995 Act where monitoring is carried out as part of a consent condition, the burden of showing that such apparatus is not recording accurately is placed on the defendant,[23] but in other cases it would be presumably be open to the defendant to question the accuracy of the device and the manner in which information is stored and processed. This does not appear to have occurred to date in criminal proceedings concerning water pollution offences, though it has be noted that there still remain legal doubts as to the precise nature of the evidence that is produced, and particularly whether it is to be categorised as real or hearsay, especially if computer equipment is involved.[24] The better view is probably that evidence from an automatic sampling device, where the only human intervention is to activate the device, would be classified as real evidence and admissible as such before the court and without the need to fall within any of the legislative exceptions.[25]

Probably the most developed use of digital imaging employed in the enforcement of criminal law is to be found in traffic speeding where remotely operated speed cameras are now extensively used in the United Kingdom. The near impossibility of comprehensive enforcement by conventional means, which required corroborative evidence from a police officer, in some respects mirrors the problems facing environmental law, but in this context more elaborate and procedural changes have now been developed. According to section 20 of the Road Traffic Offences Act 1988,[26] evidence of speeding offences may be given by the production of evidence produced by a device prescribed by the Secretary of State, accompanied by a police certificate as to the circumstances in which the record was produced. The statutory requirements relate to the type of equipment installed at the roadside, but an elaborate Code of Practice has been developed under the auspices of a government committee concerning operational requirements and the management and retention of data, especially important as digital imaging is replacing the use of conventional analogue photographic equipment originally used in the equipment. As the Code notes,

> The integrity and full acceptance of the evidence by the courts is of paramount importance. It is therefore essential this continues to be ensured by the use of data protection methods that will themselves be recognised as adequate by the courts.[27]

As indicated above, current data from remote sensing is probably of most practical value as an administrative tool to provide advanced warnings to enforcement bodies of potential legal breaches which are then to be investigated and proved in court by more conventional

---

[22] Howarth and McGillivray, *Water Pollution and Water Quality Law* (Kent, Shaw & Sons, 2001) 16.10.

[23] Environment Act 1995, s 111(3).

[24] See Mumma, 'Monitoring Data in Water Pollution Prosecutions' (1993) 5(1) *Journal of Environmental Law* 191; see also Howarth and McGillivray, above n 22, 16.12.

[25] Mumma, ibid.

[26] The use of speed cameras was recommended in the Road Traffic Law Review Report, 12 April 1988 (London, DoT and Home Office, 1988) by Peter North, who had become 'convinced that the legal issues could not sensibly be considered separately from practical considerations of enforcement and technology'.

[27] 'Home Office Police Policy Directorate' (London, Home Office, 1996) para 4.3 'Outline Requirements and Specification for Automatic Traffic Enforcement Systems'.

evidential means. Yet the new generation of satellites with vastly increased spectral and spatial resolution which is on the horizon opens up new potentials for the direct use of imaging in court proceedings. Without more standardised procedures and the development of codes of practice across the industry to maintain authenticity – as have been developed in the case of CCTV – their direct use in court is likely to be vulnerable to challenge. The examples above illustrate that legal systems can adapt and develop evidential principles to accommodate the use of new forms of technology, and it may be in future that satellite images will be as familiar and unexceptional element of evidence as traditional photographs are today.

Privacy

This new generation of high resolution satellites may indeed offer dramatic scope for the potential improvement of the enforcement of environmental law, but it also raises important issues and potential conflicts with other areas of law, notably rights to privacy.

Such issues in relation to satellite imagery have barely been considered to date by the courts, even in the United States where privacy rights have been an inherent part of the constitutional law. As Slonecker has noted,[28]

> Until recently, the level of detail has been so gross as not be to be a concern, and the intrusion is one that society generally accepts as reasonable for some greater overall purpose, such as map making, effective land-use planning, or protecting human health and natural resources.

Yet the emerging technology raises real potential confrontations with the notion of individual privacy, and the extent to which those rights are protected in law. The analysis of Warren and Brandeis[29] in their seminar article of privacy written over 100 years ago and in the context of press intrusion may well resonate in this new context:

> The intensity and complexity of life, attendant upon advancing civilisation, have rendered necessary some retreat from the world, and man, under the refining influence of culture, has become more sensitive to publicity, so that solitude and privacy have become more essential to the individual.

Within Europe, the European Convention on Human Rights provides in Article 8(1) the right of an individual 'to respect for his private and family life, his home, and his correspondence', and since the introduction of the Human Rights Act 1998, courts in Britain are increasingly being faced with challenges to the actions of public authorities based on a breach of these and other rights within the Convention. No case law exists to date concerning the application of Article 8 to possible intrusion by satellite imagery, and it seems unlikely in any event that images taken with today's generation of satellites would be considered a breach. But a world where resolution was such as to identify with certainty activities taking place on private property, vehicles, and perhaps even individuals clearly makes it a potentially live legal issue. Any analysis would have to consider first whether there was in fact a breach of Article 8(1), and second, if there were, whether it came

---

[28] Slonecker, Shaw and Lillesand 'Emerging Legal and Ethical Issues in Advanced Remote Sensing Technology' (1998) 64(6) *Photogrammetic Engineering and Remote Sensing* 589.
[29] S Warren and L Brandeis, 'The Right to Privacy' (1890) 4 *Harvard Law Review* 103.

within one of the public interest exceptions allowed for in the Convention. As for the first question, it is clear that from decisions that the European Court of Human Rights that the case law on Article 8 reflect the need to allow for different degrees of privacy according to different circumstances. The more intimate the aspect of private life being infringed, the more serious must be the legitimate grounds for interference.[30] Certainly, the court has been reluctant to confine the notion of privacy solely to aspects of family life per se. As the Court noted in *Niemitz v Germany*,

> it would be too restrictive to limit the notion [of private life] to an 'inner circle' in which the individual may live his personal life as he chooses and to exclude therefrom from the outside world not encompassed within that circle. Respect for private life must also comprise to a certain degree the right to establish and develop relationships with other human beings.

Photography in a public place was been subject to decision of the European Court where in *Friedl v Austria*[31] the court held that this would not normally be a breach of Article 8:

> the reason why the taking of photographs and the retention of the photographs were not regarded as an interference could be said to be mainly that, when the photographs were taken, the applicant was in a public place where anyone is in principle free to take photographs and where the taking of photographs can, in most circumstances, be considered a trivial act which must be tolerated by others, although some persons may indeed consider it unpleasant that someone should take their photograph.

The reasoning was elaborated in *PG and JH v United Kingdom*,[32] a case concerning listening devices used by the police and where the court made a specific reference to security monitoring in a public place:

> There are a number of elements relevant to the consideration of whether a person's private life is concerned in measures affected outside a person's home or private premises. Since there are occasions when people knowingly or intentionally involve themselves in activities which are or may be recorded or reported in public a person's reasonable expectations to privacy may be significant though not necessarily a conclusive factor. The person who walks down the street will inevitably be visible to any member of the public who is also present. Monitoring by technological means of the same public scene (eg a security guard viewing through closed circuit television) is a similar character. Private life considerations may arise however once any systematically permanent record comes into existence of such material from the public domain.

The Court of Human Rights will soon have to deal with a further elaboration of the use of CCTV images in the *Peck* case which was found admissible by the court last year.[33] In that case, security cameras in a shopping centre captured an individual attempting to commit suicide, with the result that rescue services were able to save him. The footage was subsequently sold to broadcasters by the local authority to boost the use of CCTV by showing that it could save lives, but without the individual's permission. The breach of Article 8 claimed refers not to the actual filming in the first place but to the subsequent

---

[30] *Douglas v United Kingdom* (1981) 4 EHRR 149.
[31] *Friedl v Austria* (1994) A 305-B.
[32] App No 00044787/98, 25 September 2001.
[33] See Wadham, 'Remedies for Unlawful CCTV Surveillance', *New Law Journal*, 4 and 11 August 2000; Dodd, 'Still Life: For Your Eyes Only' in 'Big Brother: The Secret State and the Assault on Privacy', *The Guardian*, 14 September 2002.

passing on of the footage for broadcasting.[34] As to the use of evidence by regulatory bodies in criminal proceedings, British courts have never gone as far as US courts in holding that illegally obtained evidence is inadmissible per se. Judges retained a discretion to exclude evidence, now codified under section 78 of the Police and Criminal Evidence Act 1984, which gives power to a judge to exclude 'unfair evidence' where the court considers that its admission 'would have such an adverse effect on the fairness of the proceedings that the court ought not to admit it'. The discretion has largely been used to exclude unreliable evidence rather than as a tool to persuade enforcement agencies to act within the law. In one case, for example, the court allowed the used of videotaped footage obtained by the police even though this was in breach of Codes of Practice and Article 8 of the European Convention,[35] and the European Court of Human Rights has similarly refrained from holding that evidence obtained in breach of the Convention is thereby inadmissible in court proceedings.[36]

Even if surveillance by satellite were considered to intrude on rights of privacy according to Article 8(1), the Convention does not grant unfettered rights. Article 8(2) provides a number of public interest justification including 'the prevention of disorder or crime', 'the protection of health or morals' and 'the protection of the rights and freedoms or others'. No specific reference to the environment is made, and although the European Court has clearly held that the right to private life may include the right to a reasonable environmental quality for that life,[37] it is perhaps less obviously clear how it would handle claims that a breach of privacy was justifiable in order to protect the environmental quality of others. Nevertheless, especially where the enforcement of criminal law concerning environmental protection was involved, it seems likely that the public interest exceptions would apply, and the Court would be faced with applying a test of proportionality, essentially asking whether the degree of surveillance involved was justified by the nature of the public interest being protected. More troubling, perhaps, is the further requirement that any such interference with Article 8 rights must 'be in accordance with the law'. The lack of specific statutory provisions authorised the use of telephone tapping in the United Kingdom was found to be in breach of Article 8[38] – authorisation by the law implied explicit and transparent legal provisions rather than administrative procedures, and the decision required the introduction of new national legislation requiring warrants for carrying out telephone surveillance in respect of public telecommunications systems.[39]

---

[34] The court gave its judgment on 28 January 2003 and held that the local authority's release of the footage was a disproportionate interference with the applicant's Art 8 rights: *Peck v United Kingdom* (2003) 26 EHRR 41.

[35] *R v Loveridge and Lee* (2001) EWCA Crim 1034. As Lord Hope noted in *R v Sargent* (2001) UKHL 54, a case concerning the admissibility of evidence from unlawful telephone tapping: 'It is in the interests of everyone that serious crime should be effectively investigated and prosecuted. There must, of course, be fairness to all sides. But in the context of the criminal law the interests of the victim and the public interest must be taken into account as well as that of the accused. A rigid rule which excluded the use in all cases of all inadmissible intercepts at a person's interview would go further than was necessary to protect the accused. It could create an imbalance in his favour which would operate against the public interest, and that of the victim, when an alleged crime was being investigated. I do not think that a rule in such absolute terms can be justified.'

[36] *Schenk v Switzerland* (1988) 13 EHRR 242. In *Khan v UK* (2000) Criminal Law Report 68-1 (illegal surveillance of conversations), the European Court held that the discretionary powers under s 78 PACE were sufficient to ensure a fair trial.

[37] *Guerra v Italy* (1988) 26 EHRR 357.

[38] *Malone v United Kingdom* (1985) 7 EHRR 14.

[39] Interception of Communications Act 1985. This has now been replaced by more comprehensive provisions under Part I of the Regulation of Investigatory Powers Act 2000, which includes both public and private telecommunications systems, and was needed to comply with the judgment of the European Court of Human Rights in *Halford v United Kingdom* (1997) 24 EHRR 523.

This approach to the need for specific statutory provisions concerning authorisations was confirmed by the European Court more recently in *Khan v United Kingdom*.[40]

Against the background of human rights provisions, controversial recent legislation in the United Kingdom, the Regulation of Investigatory Powers Act 2000, has recently been passed in order to provide a more systematic means of regulating authorisations for the use of investigatory powers and with the establishment of Surveillance Commissioners to provide independent oversight.

Part II of the Act is concerned with surveillance, and distinguishes between 'directed surveillance' defined as being carried out for the purposes of specific investigation and operation and likely to result in the obtaining of private information, and 'intrusive surveillance' which refers to surveillance carried out in relation to anything taking place on residential premises. Both types of surveillance must be 'covert' to fall within the legislation, meaning that it is carried out in such a way 'to ensure that persons who are subject to the surveillance are unaware that it is or may be taking place'.[41] Although the Act does not require authorities to obtain authorisations for such operations, it is intended to ensure that if such authorisations are in fact obtained, the authority concerned will be guaranteed to have acted in compliance with the Human Rights Act. These aspects of the legislation have raised concern, and in any event it remains doubtful as to the extent to which the use of generalised remote sensing falls within the focused concepts of covert directed and intrusive surveillance defined in the legislation. Visible CCTV cameras, for example, would not appear to be covert within the meaning of the legislation, and in many cases are operated by private bodies for general preventative purposes – see, for example, the Home Office Code of Practice,[42] which states that 'the provisions of the 2000 Act or of this code of practice do not normally cover the use of overt CCTV surveillance systems, since members of the public are aware that such systems are in use'. It is perhaps less obvious how members of the public would be aware of the existence of a surveillance satellite in the same way they are considered to be aware of (and implicitly consent to) the presence of CCTV cameras, but it is equally clear that the legislation was not drafted with the potential intrusiveness of satellite technology in mind.

Data Protection

Further legal issues of some complexity concerning privacy, data, and the use of remote sensing are to be met when considering the relevance of new data protection legislation. Under EC Directive 95/46/EC which came into force on March 1st 2000 and implemented in the United Kingdom by the Data Protection Act 1998, certain types of data processing systems must be registered, and with provisions concerning the fair obtaining of information, its retention, and the availability of copies to individual on personal data held by such systems. The Directive applies to 'personal data' meaning information relating to an identified or identifiable natural person and the 'processing of personal data' defined as

[40] See above n 35.

[41] Regulation of Investigatory Powers Act 2000, s 26(7).

[42] Home Office (2002) Code of Practice on Covert Surveillance, which came into force on 1 August 2002. The Code acknowledges that, where CCTV was being used by a public authority for specific investigatory purposes, authorisations under the Act might be necessary.

any operation performed on personal data including collection, recording and storage,[43] which has been processed by automatic means or within a filing system. Certainly in the United Kingdom, and under the domestic implementing legislation, it is accepted that CCTV systems falling within these basic concepts, and are liable to be registered with the Data Protection Registrar. It is less clear whether satellite imaging would fall within the controls, and much would depend on the interpretation of the concepts of personal data and their application to the type of images received. Again, on current resolutions, it may be dubious whether the provisions are applicable, but once such data is enriched or merged with information giving exact data on land use belong to an identified person the position might be different. Similarly, as resolutions become increasingly higher and are able to identify with precision individual parcels of land, it is arguable that the obligations are applicable.

The analogy between CCTV surveillance and the new generation of satellites, and the way in which law develops to balance the potential benefits to society from the new technology and the safeguards that individuals can legitimately expect needs is one that perhaps should not be taken too far. But there are some powerful similarities. In particular, public and private boundaries are no longer explicit, both in respect of the areas under surveillance and those responsible for operation.[44] Britain is considered to be the country with the most CCTV cameras in operations (perhaps some 300,000), and despite the developments of codes of practice, the legislative framework for their controlled use remains at an unsophisticated level, and a number of commentators expressing continuing concern with the adequacy of current arrangements.[45] Legislation such as the Regulation of Investigatory Powers Act 2000 is essentially aimed at action by public authorities rather than the private sector. Equally, the Human Rights Act 1998, implementing the European Convention, imposes duties on public authorities rather than the private sector. Here, though, the jurisprudence of the European Court of Human Rights has recognised that an artificial division between intrusions of privacy directly by public authorities and those made by private bodies would deprive the right of meaningful content, and has imposed positive obligations on the state to take action to protect those rights whatever the source of intrusion:

> The Court recalls that although the object of Article 8 is essentially that of protecting the individual against arbitrary interference by the public authorities, it does not merely compel the State to abstain from such interference: in addition to this primarily negative obligation, there may be a positive obligation inherent in an effective respect for private and family life. These obligations may involve the adoption of measures designed to secure respect for private life even in the sphere of the relations of individuals between themselves.[46]

Governments, and indeed the courts, can clearly not wash their hands of responsibility for ensuring legitimate protection of privacy even if the private sector dominates the acquisition and exploitation of data from remote sensing. Whatever the 'horizontal' duties of the state, in relation to operations by the private sector, individuals may still, though, have to

---

[43] Art 2.

[44] It is estimated, for example, that some 1000 satellites will be launched over the next decade, the vast majority being privately owned: Yaukey, 'Satellites Raise Privacy Questions', Gannet News Services, USA, 2000.

[45] See, eg C Norris and G Armstrong, *The Maximum Surveillance Society, the Rise of CCTV* (Oxford, Berg, 1999); D Lyon, *Surveillance Society* (Cambridge, Polity Press, 2001).

[46] *X v Netherlands* (1985) 8 EHRR 235, 239–40. See also M Hunt, 'The "Horizontal Effect" of the Human Rights Act' [1998] *Public Law* 423.

rely on the protection of private civil law remedies. United Kingdom law never developed an express tort of invasion of privacy, and others forms of actions, such as trespass, libel and breach of confidence, have been all been explored to protect personal privacy, particularly from the press. More recently, though, the courts have been emboldened by these provisions of the European Convention, and have apparently accepted that the invasion of privacy should be recognised as a distinct, though qualified, right by the courts.[47] In doing so, the courts have thrown doubt on a long-standing decision that a landowner had no rights of protection against aerial photographs being taken by a private commercial operator on his property without consent on the grounds that this did not amount to trespass.[48]

Gerd Winter himself has explored another legal aspect of the rich data base that is obtained through satellite technology, which, as with CCTV, is made more complex by the increasing privatisation of the industry. In 'Access of the Public to Environmental Data from Satellite Remote Sensing',[49] he explored the extent to which remote sensing information, at least where it related to environmental matters, should be regarded 'as part of the public sphere' rather than a commodity to be exploited and sold, both as a matter of international, European and national law. In a country such as the United Kingdom, the position is made more complex because since the strong introduction of market force principles from the 1980s even public sector bodies are expected to generate revenue by the commercialisation of their data sets. In its most recent report, the Royal Commission on Environmental Pollution[50] highlighted what to them seemed a short-sighted situation where some public bodies were generating almost 60 per cent of their data sales through contracts with other public sector bodies, described as 'a merry-go-round of public finances with no net benefit and high transaction costs in which the full value of environmental information is not being realised'.[51] In this context, environmental law has provided a number of progressive pointers, notably within the European Community with the principles of public access to environmental information held by public bodies under the Directive of Access to Environmental Information[52] Similarly at international level, Principles X and XI of the 1986 UN Resolution 41/65 on Remote Sensing of the Earth from Outer Space contain explicit obligations on states to disclose information to other states which could advert environmentally harmful phenomenon or natural disasters. But as Gerd Winter notes, both the EC Directive and the UN Resolution were largely cast to reflect the obligations of the public sector and the state, and are less meaningful where the private sector and the market dominates the activity of data acquisition and processing. In this context, Gerd Winter concluded that 'remote sensing information should be seen not only as an economic good but also as an important element of public discourse'.[53] These sentiments resonate even more strongly as we enter an era of far higher resolution and more pervasive sensing technology. The environmental benefits to society are potentially

[47] See especially *Douglas v Hello* (2000) 9 BHRC 543, where the Court of Appeal refused an injunction against a magazine publishing unauthorised wedding photographs but recognised that the claimants might still be able to secure damages for invasion of privacy.

[48] *Bernstein v Skyviews and General Ltd* [1997] 2 All ER 902. See in particular Sedley LJ in *Douglas v Hello*, ibid, 119.

[49] (1994) 6 *Journal of Environmental Law* 43.

[50] Royal Commission on Environmental Pollution, *Environmental Planning*, 23rd Report, Cm 5459 (Stationery Office, 2002).

[51] Ibid, para 6.18.

[52] 90/313/EEC.

[53] Winter, above n 49, 55.

immense, but unless we see concurrent developments in the legal frameworks for authenticity, privacy, and data access which anticipate both the nature of the technology and the structure of the industry, they are benefits that may not be fully realised or will be acquired at too high a price.

14

Environmental Standards, Legitimacy and Social Justice[1] (1999)

The Rise of Environmental Standards

I want to raise concerns about environmental standards in the context of the current and likely future developments in environmental law. Standards of various sorts have a critical role in many areas of environmental law yet the procedures and processes at work are revealing disturbing tensions. Inevitably my perspectives will be shaped and possibly distorted from my involvement in United Kingdom and European Community law, but many of the issues raised have more general application.

For someone who has worked in British and European environmental law for a number of years, one of the most striking features during the last decade or so has been the enormous proliferation of legally binding environmental standards of different types. British environmental law, in particular, used to be permeated by flexible legal frameworks, especially in the field of pollution regulation. These gave considerable interpretative discretion to those bodies responsible for enforcement – with the occasional nudge by the courts where litigation occurred. To take two examples, for many years the legal standard for drinking water was simply expressed as 'wholesome water'. The key criterion for air pollution control of emissions from industries was the 'best practicable means' to prevent or minimise or render harmless emissions. The formal law gave no further guidance of the meaning of those terms. Yet for operational purposes, regulatory bodies had to convert these qualitative criteria into something more precise, expressed in scientific and technological language often drawing on the work of international bodies such as the World Heath Organization.

Discretion has now given way to a large degree to legally binding environmental standards. We now see a vast array of environmental standards covering areas such as air quality, emissions from particular types of processes, water quality, chemical regulation and the like. Coupled with this has been the development of an enormously complex range of institutional machinery, for the development and making of such standards.

The underlying reasons and indeed attractions of such a development are not hard to find. Environmental standards in this context represent a rule of some general application which reflect a public judgement about the acceptability of human activities on the

---

[1] R Macrory, 'Environmental Standards, Legitimacy, and Social Justice' [1999] *Acta Juridica* 257.

303

environment. By conversion into specific terms, they provide an apparent transparency of that judgement, and assist in ensuring consistency in application. For industry or those affected by such standards they provide a benchmark for investment and performance. They remove from the realm of the courts the need for the judiciary to make complex economic and policy judgements which many would argue is not their legitimate role. In parenthesis I might add that at the height of deregulatory policies in the previous Conservative government there was rumoured to be a paper circulating cabinet sub-committees arguing that the protection of the environment should be left to private interests relying on common law remedies such as the law of nuisance, and leaving it to individual courts to determine appropriate levels of protection on a case by case basis. The complex regulatory machinery of public law could then be safely filleted. This was in retrospect one privatisation too far and was never seriously pursued.[2]

At the same time advances in scientific understanding, the development of toxicology and ecotoxicology as distinct disciplines, developments in reliable instrumentation and measurement techniques have helped develop the concept of rigorous standards expressed in quantifiable form.

Above all the impact of globalised markets has driven the development of environmental standards. Within the European Community in particular environmental policy was originally justified by the demands of market harmonisation and concerns about the distorting effects of differing standards. We are now in an era where the principle of subsidiarity potentially modifies excessive enthusiasm for complete harmonisation. At the same time explicit provisions in the Europe Treaty concerning environmental protection remove the need for what were sometimes intellectually spurious justification for environmental intervention on purely market harmonisation ground.[3] Yet the standardisation process remains powerful. One attribute of subsidiarity is the idea of national mutual recognition and reciprocity. Under such legal frameworks, authorisation by a national regulatory body in one Member State is automatically recognised and accepted by others – this principle, originally encouraged by the European Court of Justice in its famous judgments in the 1970s such as *Cassis de Dijon*,[4] is increasingly reflected in many areas of the law such as chemical regulation. Yet it demands either considerable trust by national bodies on the capacity and ability of others, or a degree of standardisation of procedures such as risk assessment. These developments can already be seen in the latest proposals for revising EC legislation concerning genetically modified organisms where greater authority will be given to national authorities to grant authorisation but against a clearer framework of approach.

This does not imply that standardisation necessarily implies uniformity of approach nor removes significant elements of discretion turning regulators into blind automatons. Many standards may be expressed as minimum rather than uniform standards giving discretion to public authorities to determine tighter standards according to particular local

---

[2] Standards, whether legally binding or not, may of course assist the judiciary when determining tests for common law nuisance, though they will only be one factor. See, eg *Murdoch v Glacier Metal Co, Times Law Reports*, 19 January 1998, where in a noise nuisance case the court made reference to World Health Organization guidelines but held that noise just above the levels did not amount to a nuisance in law.

[3] See Title XVI of the European Community Treaty, Arts 130r and following, which give express authority for Community environmental measures. The provisions were originally inserted under the 1987 amendments to the Treaty.

[4] Case 120178 *Rewe Zentral AG v Bundesmonopolverwaltung fur Branntwein (Cassis de Dijon)* [1979] ECR 6497.

circumstances. Standards expressed in the form of environmental quality standards leave discretion to regulators how to ensure they are met, often involving complex distributional judgements in dealing with individual emitters – to take one example, if an environmental quality standard for a particular stretch of water is established, should all existing dischargers be treated equally in order to ensure that the quality standard is not breached; should a safety allowance be made for potential future development and new dischargers who might arrive?

At the national level, supranational trade systems still permit a degree of discretion in developing distinct national environmental standards. Within the context of the common market, the European Treaty rules make allowance for individual Member States to determine national environmental protection standards in the absence of harmonised rules.[5] These provisions, reflected in GATT rules,[6] are constrained by rules of proportionality, necessity, and equal application to national and imported goods.

It is an area where the European Court has frequently been obliged to intervene. The court has to a large degree accepted that, even in the context of human health standards among apparently similar and neighbouring countries, differing cultural and social contexts may justify differing standards.[7] Even where environmental standards have been promulgated at European level, Treaty rules permit national derogations though again bounded by considerable restrictions.[8] The recent Amsterdam amendments to the Treaty governing directives harmonising standards based on the operation of the market in fact represent a move in favour of European standardisation and against national discretion. The national discretion to impose tighter standards remain but, if the Treaty amendments are approved, constrain that discretion considerably. Where after a harmonisation measure has been adopted at Community level, a Member State may still introduce national measures relating to the protection of the environment provided these are not a means of arbitrary discrimination or disguised restriction of trade. But they may only do so on the basis of new scientific information on the grounds of a problem specific to that Member State. So a Member State, say, concerned at the inadequacies of an EC law concerning endocrine disrupters and wishing to introduce tighter standards would be unable to introduce national laws unless there was evidence relating to specific problems in their country.

These complexities are worthy of a conference in themselves. But if we accept that in certain countries and regions at any rate the proliferation of environmental standards as I have described them has been an inherent feature in the development of contemporary environmental law I want to highlight particular concerns.

The Current Intellectual Crisis

There are a number of distinct trends which, in conjunction, are producing what might be

---

[5] Art 36 EC Treaty; *Commission v Denmark* Case 302/86 [1988] ECR 4607.

[6] See Art XX(b) GATT. For the connection between Art XX(b) GATT and Art 36 EC Treaty see Petersmann, 'Freie Warenverkehr und nationale Umweltschultz in EWG und EWR' [1993] *Aussenwirtschaft* 95.

[7] See, eg Case 272/80 *Fumicot* [1981] ECR 3277.

[8] See especially Art 100a(4) EC Treaty; Case 41/93 *France v Commission* [1994] ECR I-1829. See A Zieglar, *Trade and Environmental Law in the European Community* (Oxford, Clarendon Press, 1996) 161–67. See *Denmark v Commission* (2003), analysed on p 381 below.

described as an intellectual crisis in the conventional approaches towards environmental standard setting. Science is inherently built upon uncertainties, but the nature of contemporary environmental science is particularly complex. Moving away from pollutants affecting acute human heath to more chronic, and invidious, issues raises difficult questions of causation and correlation. Many human health standards have been based on toxicology and derived assumptions from the effects on animals to humans. But closer analysis suggests real problems. To take one well-known example, concerning the effects of dioxins on human health. Toxic tests on hamsters and guinea pigs have indicated extraordinarily different results, with guinea pigs being some 5 000 times more vulnerable than hamsters.[9] There was no convincing explanation nor, more importantly, any principles which could suggest whether humans were more similar to guinea pigs or hamsters. The classic analysis by Filov and others[10] trying to determine the effective dose of LSD that would give a trip to an elephant illustrates differing calculations depending on comparative body weight, metabolism rates, or brain weights of cats and humans reveals a 'correct' answer that varies by a factor of 1,000. Current scientific research concerning the effects of vehicle pollution on respiratory diseases, including asthma, again shows tremendous uncertainties, whatever one's intuitive experience.[11] Standards relating to the protection of the natural environment as opposed to humans used to be largely calculated by crudely applying a safety factor but again this is increasingly recognised as far too simplistic an approach. The sheer volume of activity required under some regimes is also daunting. Under European Community legislation dealing with existing chemicals on the market since 1981[12] it was estimated that over 100,000 chemicals substances exist on the market. A number of priority lists were compiled between 1994 and 1997 numbering 109, but to date only four assessments have been submitted and agreed for submission to the relevant Commission directorate generals. At this rate we are talking of 100 years to deal with just the priority list.

Finally despite the importance of scientific underpinning where appropriate, scientific committees have sometimes been misused. In simple terms it is an appropriate use of science to determine a dose-effect curve, but it cannot be a purely scientific judgement to determine at what point on that curve a standard should be set. David Fisk, Chief Scientist at the United Kingdom Department of the Environment Transport and Regions has recently argued[13] for the need to separate scientific assessment to test our current state of knowledge with all its inherent uncertainties from the process of risk assessment whose purpose is to lead to a conclusion or decision based on the assessment. Yet we have clear examples where the process is confused. More subtly, much of the contemporary scientific process involves risk assessment which in itself can reflect cultural and social perspectives often obscured. Josef Falke and Gerd Winter have provided a fascinating study of the workings of various technical committees at European Community level dealing with the regulation of dangerous substances.[14] Examining the issue of asbestos, French and German

---

[9] See Royal Commission on Environmental Pollution 17th Report, 'Incineration of Waste', Cm 2181 (London, HMSO, 1993).

[10] VA Filov et al, *Quantitative Toxicology* (New York, John Wiley & Sons, 1973).

[11] Royal Commission on Environmental Pollution 18th Report, 'Transport and the Environment', Cmnd 2674 (London, HMSO, 1994).

[12] See EC Council Directive 79/831 and EC Council Regulation No 293/93.

[13] D Fisk, 'Environmental Science and Environmental Law' (1998) 10(1) *Journal of Environmental Law* 3.

[14] J Falk and G Winter, 'Management and Regulatory Committees in Executive Rule Making' in G Winter (ed), *Sources and Categories of European Union Law* (1996).

delegates came to diametrically opposed views, mainly because the French approach to risk assessment includes in the equation a benefit comparison of the current use and need of the product while the Germans adopted the approach of considering solely the health and environmental risks.

It is hardly surprising that faith in the concept of scientific certainty is less sure than it was. Regulators and those responsible for devising environmental standards now operate in a political and social climate where professional judgements are not accepted unquestioningly. The so called 'nanny knows best' syndrome which operated in the United Kingdom for many years no longer holds true. One political and legal response has to be to open up decision making, and to allow members of the public and other interests to participate to some extent in decision making. We have seen at national level extensive new rights under environmental laws of consent applications being publicised, rights of the public to inspect public registers, and to comment on proposed decision making. Yet here we see a conundrum. During the same period as these rights were being extended at local level, many areas of the standard setting processes were moving up at a regional or international level. The pressures of the free market, the moves toward reciprocal recognition or standardisation of product standards, and in the European context at least the harmonising of many process standards in an effort to remove competition distortions has removed much of the discretionary powers and authority of national or local regulatory bodies. Public participation at a local level may still have a function but is heavily reduced, and may indeed be counterproductive in that it can raise expectations which cannot be fulfilled. Yet certainly in the European context we have scarcely begun to develop mechanisms of real transparency and participation. Much of the detail of European law making is delegated in various forms to sub-committees with a total of nearly 400 currently operating, quadrupling between 1975 and 1995.[15] Even at what might be described as primary law making, much of the procedures are still clouded in traditions of international diplomacy.

A further challenge to the concept of standard setting derives from their legal context. In the field of pollution control in particular, the setting of standards has been associated with classical forms of interventionist regulation. The last decade has seen a sustained critique of so called command and control regulation as being excessively costly, inefficient, and stifling of innovation. Other methods of environmental management,[16] from economic instruments, self-regulation, various forms of contractual arrangements,[17] and voluntary initiatives are being advocated and experimented with. For my part, I resist the simple division between legal and non-legal methods, and the over-simple characterisation of command and control. Furthermore while the use of economic instruments in particular can provide a means of achieving policy aims, I am not convinced that they can define those aims in themselves. Environmental standards will still have a key role in goal-setting even if the means of achieving those goals are varied.

This is particularly important where one is dealing with issues that move beyond the control of identifiable fixed sources. A good example is the recently introduced British national air quality standards and a legal framework requiring local authorities to devise

---

[15] The figures are derived from the annual general budget of the European Union.

[16] O'Riordan (ed), *Eco-Taxation Earthscan* (Addison-Wesley, 1997); J Bowers, *Sustainabilty and Environmental Economics – An Alternative Text* (Longman, 1997).

[17] European Environment Agency, *Environmental Agreements EEA* (1997).

strategies of achieving those standards, using a variety of instruments from land use planning controls, traffic regulation, control of industrial emitters and the like.[18]

The final challenge to the environmental standard setting process is the shift of policy goals from that of environmental protection to one of sustainable development. I have already described the difficulties of moving from human health protection to the protection of the natural environment. Sustainable development, which is already working its way into legal expression, brings in a range of other factors including social equity and economic consumption making the identification of standards all the more challenging. The shift reflects the move away from what the British environmentalist Tom Burke has described as the easy politics of the environment of the last 25 years which has dominated much of environmental law, to the much more difficult issues of the next 25 years. We are entering a more fluid world of policies and politics. In this context sustainable development reflects a trajectory rather than a fixed state or goal. Reconciling that concept with the notion of environmental standards that inherently do represent an identifiable level of protection at a particular point of time is not easy.

Ways through the Quagmire

How does one steer a route through these quagmires? It is, I think, a mistake to assume that a perfect methodology for standard setting can be devised. But some markers can be established. Scientific knowledge and understanding will still play a key element, but the idea, if ever if were true, that we can look for certainty from those quarters, or indeed have the time to do so, has to be resisted. The uncertainties and complexities involved in many contemporary environmental issues will lead to the development of new scientific procedures of arriving at scientific consensus, as witnessed in the workings methods developed by the scientific panel of the Inter-governmental Panel on Climate Change since 1988. On the other hand, rejection of the simplistic notion that environmental standards can be derived solely from 'sound science' cannot be merely replaced by an equally simplistic invocation of the precautionary principle. Almost every activity has the capacity for harm, and the principle cannot be applied without some degree of risk analysis. Distinguishing more clearly the process of scientific assessment from risk analysis, as David Fisk has argued, is vital. Economic analysis has traditionally formed a key element in decision making, and while important the blind use of cost benefit analysis has to be treated with caution. Recent examples in the UK of its use in the environmental field illustrate clearly some of the underlying weaknesses of the conceptual approach, and the large degree of assumptions that must be made and which cannot derive from the discipline itself – before figures are arrived at.[19] But in future it will be all the more important for those responsible for standard setting to draw on other disciplines which can illuminate human behaviour in areas where economists should not tread. Socio-legal studies, and cultural anthropology

---

[18] See Part IV of the Environment Act 1995.

[19] In a recent major example of the use of cost–benefit analysis for environmental evaluation, the United Kingdom Environment Agency estimated the 'value' of the River Kennet to be £13.6 million, most of which was based on 'willing to pay' figures by consumers in the whole Thames Region. The Department of the Environment. Transport and Regions revised the figure down to £700,000 by reducing the number of consumers counted. See O Tickell, 'Stream of Abuse', *The Guardian*, 4 March 1998.

have important roles to play, though not a traditional expertise which many Western governments have drawn upon.[20] To the extent that many of the future environmental and sustainable issues concern the behaviour of individuals these disciplines will be all the more important. We have to ensure that there is real feedback from the study of how laws are implemented back into the law-making processes. Too often governments devote time and effort to making new legislation with insufficient attention to the questions of implementation. As an MEP put it recently, 'We are good midwives but bad mothers'.

More significantly, it will be increasingly important to examine underlying principles behind the detail of environmental law, and be prepared to devise more rigorous mechanisms for their discussion and development. We have seen this recently in the field of biotechnology in the United Kingdom and the rest of Europe. There the complex regulatory machinery for controlled releases of Genetically Manipulated Organisms both on the market and for experimental purposes has consciously focused on the environmental risks.[21] Not surprisingly in a liberal economy the legal regulatory machinery is uncomfortable in engaging in a risk/need exercise. To that extent the procedures avoid addressing ethical concerns that are apparent, and certainly alive with the general public. The simple answer is to say this is a political issue for decision by elected politicians. Yet our current institutional machinery – and certainly my own country's Parliamentary processes – are often ill-equipped to explore such issues in a convincing and rigorous manner. The phrase 'deliberative institutions' is currently in vogue amongst political scientists. Rather like 'sustainable development', the notion is readily dismissed as lacking clarity or straightforward solutions. Yet it represents a searching for new mechanisms to handle issues of genuine public concern which conventional methodologies have avoided.

In a short space of time I seem to have travelled from a bounded field of drinking water protection to the more uncertain world of political processes. For the environmental lawyer it would be more comfortable to remain in a familiar world of dealing solely with the implementation and enforcement of environmental standards. Yet if environmental law is to develop in a sophisticated way in tune with contemporary concerns it is important to appreciate some of the underlying tensions and complexities which is now apparent, even if our discipline cannot provide all the solutions.

---

[20] Though in the United States the Environmental Protection Agency has recently drawn up a Co-operative Agreement with the Society for Applied Anthropologists – see http://www.telepath.com/sfaaleap/abouteap.html.

[21] See Part VI of the Environmental Protection Act 1990 (UK); Directive 90/220/EEC Deliberative Release into the Environment of Genetically Modified Organisms.

15

The Scope of Environmental Law[1]
(1996)

1. Introduction

Academic and practising lawyers in nearly all European countries now recognise that environmental law represents a distinctive and significant body of law and legal principle. Yet, when it comes to trying to define the boundaries of the subject, it is clear that there is little in the way of agreement. Certain commonly agreed elements exist such as the regulation of polluting activities by man and the protection of natural assets such as wildlife or landscapes, and these fields of law are what many environmental lawyers would describe as their core concerns. However, it is equally clear that there are many other areas of regulatory law such as health and safety at work, land-use planning, the protection of the manmade cultural heritage, and consumer protection law which have substantial environmental implications, even if environmental protection, as many would understand it, is not their sole focus. Looking further afield, the principles upon which apparently unconnected areas of law, such as competition or trade law, operate may be far from neutral in their potential impacts on the environment.

The need to integrate an environmental dimension into areas of policy hitherto largely unaffected by such concerns is one that is increasingly recognized by many countries, although the task is far from easy to achieve. In this chapter, I outline a number of legal considerations that appear to be involved in the challenge of integration. My underlying argument is that those who study and practise environmental law should be wary of limiting their attention to boundaries of law that are so narrowly confined that they fail to address what may prove ultimately to be far more significant issues of concern.

2. Integrated Pollution Control

In the context of environmental law and policy there are different notions of what can be implied by integration. A significant element of environmental law is the regulation of industrial pollution, most commonly by means of various forms of consents or permits. The development of this type of pollution legislation has taken place at different times in

---

[1] R Macrory, 'The Scope of Environmental Law' in G Winter (ed), *European Environmental Law* (Aldershot, Dartmouth, 1996) 3–14.

different European countries, with examples in some countries to be found in the nineteenth century but with a rapid growth in scope and complexity in the last 30 years. The initial driving force behind such pollution controls was often a concern for the protection of human health and, at a later stage, the incorporation of wider environmental considerations. But common to many national legal systems is the extent to which such pollution laws regulate discharges into the environmental media of air, water and land on a quite distinct legislative basis, with different laws often being developed at different times. The UK, for example, had legislation regulating industrial discharges into the atmosphere dating back to the mid-nineteenth century, while a detailed regulatory system controlling discharges into waters did not appear until the early 1950s. No specialist controls over waste disposal on land emerged until the 1970s. These specialist controls are frequently enforced and applied by different agencies. The drawback of such a legal structure is that it may lead to inconsistent decision making and ignore or fail to consider the cross-media impact of control strategies, leading to results which are sub-optimal from an environmental perspective.

In 1975 the UK Royal Commission on Environmental Pollution identified these concerns, and coined the term, the *Best Practicable Environmental Option* (BPEO) as an appropriate criterion for the goal of all pollution control strategies.[2] It took some 15 years for the Commission's legal and institutional recommendations for the implementation of this approach to be fully taken on board by government. Part I of the Environmental Protection Act 1990 introduced the concept of *integrated pollution control* under which discharges of pollutants from specified industries into water, air and land are regulated by a single licence issued by a single authority.

Other countries, such as the Netherlands, have introduced 'one stop' licences for industrial discharges, and in 1993 the European Commission proposed European Community legislation which would introduce integrated pollution control throughout the Union.[3] The main aim of the proposal is to protect water, air and land against pollution from certain types of industries by introducing an integrated permitting regime and, as an underlying harmonising principle, requiring industry to employ the 'best available techniques' of pollution prevention. At the time of writing the proposal has still not been agreed by Member States,[4] and it is likely to be some years before the type of integration required by the proposed Directive is converted into a legal requirement throughout Member States.

But even where distinct legislation has existed for different pathways of industrial discharges, the obligation to conduct environmental assessment procedures for new projects, as required under the 1985 European Community Directive on the subject[5] has inevitably required a degree of integration. Where the Directive applies, the type of information generally required as part of the assessment process before consent is given for the project to proceed includes, inter alia, 'an estimate, by type and quantity, of expected residues and emissions (water, air and soil pollution, noise, vibration, light, heat, radiation, etc) resulting

---

[2] Royal Commission on Environmental Pollution, *Air Pollution Control – An Integrated Approach*, 5th Report (London, HMSO, 1976). See also the Commission's follow-up report, *Best Practicable Environmental Option*, 12th Report (London, HMSO, 1988).

[3] Proposal for a Council Directive on Integrated Pollution and Control, Com (93) 230, 14 September 1992.

[4] The Directive was agreed as Council Directive 96/61/EC of 24 September 1996 concerning integrated pollution prevention and control, now replaced by Directive 2010/75 of 24 November 2010 on Industrial Emissions (integrated pollution prevention and control) (Recast).

[5] Council Directive 85/337 of 27 June 1985 on the assessment of the effects of certain private and public projects on the environment [1985] OJ L175/40.

from the operation of the proposed project'. The Directive does not oblige Member States to establish a single, unified consent procedure for projects subject to environmental assessment, but at the very least requires them to ensure improved coordination between decision-making agencies.

In countries such as the UK, where the assessment procedures were largely integrated into an existing land-use planning consent system rather than the specialist regulatory controls over pollution, the link between land-use planning and the pollution implications of land-based developments has been strengthened by the requirements.

Improved coordination between different pollution control agencies, the reorganisation of such bodies into unified agencies[6] and the establishment of 'one-stop' pollution consent procedures are developments that are now likely to take place in many jurisdictions, and represent one form, though a limited one, of integration.

3. Codification

A further development of the concept of environmental integration may now be seen in a trend towards the codification of environmental legislation. At the very least, this may involve an updated restatement of existing laws into a single body of law and the removal of the more overt inconsistencies. For example, it was only recently that the European Community passed legislation which attempted to introduce a greater degree of harmonisation and standardisation concerning the requirements under various Community environmental Directives for Member States to provide regular national reports to the Commission containing the results of monitoring in the sector covered by the Directive in question.[7] Previously there were some glaring inconsistencies between different items of legislation even within the same general field; for example, Member States had an obligation to make regular reports concerning the state of bathing waters under the Bathing Water Directive, but no similar obligation in respect of drinking water under the Drinking Water Directive.

But, as Kiss and Shelton note: 'Codification involves more than the reproduction and restatement of applicable statutory texts; instead it constitutes a systematic consolidation and revision of the law, a major legislative effort'.[8] Examples of a moderate form of integration can been seen in the type of framework legislation adopted by Portugal in 1987, the Lei de Bases do Ambiente. Current work in Belgium, undertaken by the Interuniversity Commission for the Revision of Environmental Law in the Flemish Region, represents a more ambitious approach towards codification seeking to articulate underlying principles as well as consistent procedures.[9]

Yet, however laudable, even this approach towards codification generally restricts itself to the more familiar boundaries of pollution and nature protection legislation. This is not to underrate the intellectual challenges involved in such a task but, again, it by no means represents the full implication of environmental integration.

---

[6] See, eg the creation of the French environmental agency, the Agence de l'Environnement et de la Maitrise de l'Energie, in 1990 and the establishment of the Irish Environmental Protection Agency in 1990.

[7] Directive 91/692 [1991] OJ L377, 48.

[8] A Kiss, D Shelton, *Manual of European Environmental Law* (Cambridge, Grotius Publications, 1993) 49.

[9] A Conference on the Codification of Environmental Law was held by the University of Ghent in early 1995.

4. Integration into other Policies Affecting the Environment

Article 130r Treaty of Rome

In 1985 the European Commission proposed to the heads of states and government that, as a basis of Community environmental policy, 'Protection of the environment is to be treated as an integral part of economic and social policies both overall (at macroeconomic level) and by individual sector (agricultural policy, industrial policy, energy policy, etc); the point must be made that an active policy for the protection and improvement of the environment can help economic growth and job creation'.[10] This proposal eventually led to the insertion into the Treaty of Rome, following the Single European Act 1987, of the provision that 'Environmental protection requirements shall be a component of the Community's other policies'.[11] The requirement was altered and, I would argue, strengthened under the version of the Treaty as amended by the Maastricht Treaty, and coming into force on 1 January 1993, and now reads, 'Environmental protection requirements must be integrated into the definition and implementation of other Community policies'.[12] Similar integration requirements concerning culture have been introduced under Article 128 of the Treaty which requires that 'The Community shall take cultural aspects into account in its activities under other provisions of this Treaty', and concerning public health where, under Article 129, 'Health protection requirements shall form a constituent part of the Community's other policies'.

This environmental provision under Article 130r clearly represents a far more ambitious notion of integration than either the moves towards the coordination of pollution control or the codification of environmental laws described above. It is a challenging statement of principle and legal obligation which has yet to be replicated in the national legislation of many countries and has been described as perhaps the most important of all the environmental provisions contained in the European Treaty.[13] Yet, as Ludwig Kramer noted in his commentary on the 1987 version, '...the medium- to long-term consequences of this principle for the Community are a matter of speculation for the moment'.[14] Certainly, if one looks at the potential environmental impacts of important aspects of the Community's sectoral policies such as fisheries and transport, it is far from clear that any serious move towards environmental integration has yet been made. The longer-term environmental implications of those policies remain immense.

[10] (1985) No 3 *Bulletin of the European Communities* 101.
[11] European Treaty (pre-Maastricht), Art 130r, para 2.
[12] Treaty Establishing the European Community as amended by the Treaty on European Union, , Art 130r, para 3. The integration principle is now contained in Treaty of the Functioning of the European Union, Art 11: 'Environmental protection requirements must be integrated into the definition and implementation of the Union policies and activities, in particular with a view to promoting sustainable development'. Its positioning at the head of the Treaty under Title II General Provisions should give the principle heightened significance – see Hession and Macrory, 'The Legal Duty of Environmental Integration: Commitment and Obligation or Enforceable Right' (1998), reproduced in Chapter 23 of this volume.
[13] N Haigh, *EEC Environmental Policy and Britain*, 2nd edn (London, Longman, 1987) ll.
[14] L Kramer, *EEC Treaty and Environmental Protection* (London, Sweet & Maxwell, 1990) 65.

Principle of Law or Policy?

To a large extent such a statement of broad principle, even though expressed in legal language, is bound to be more an expression of policy aspiration than a specific legally binding requirement capable of enforcement by conventional legal routes.[15] Provided policy makers take at least some account of potential environmental consequences, courts are unlikely to wish to become overinvolved in determining the extent to which this should take place. Nevertheless, this does not mean that such a principle is devoid of legal consequence.

Legitimising Environmental Integration

An important area of potential legal dispute within the European Community concerns the identification of the correct Treaty legal provision on which to base subsidiary legislation. The choice of the legal basis is especially significant since it will determine the political procedures that must be followed for the adoption of the proposed measure, and different provisions in the Treaty provide quite distinct procedures giving differing voting requirements and differing degrees of influence to the Community institutions, notably the European Parliament.[16] Despite the political implications of the choice of legal basis, the European Court of Justice has consistently held that this choice must be based on objective factors amenable to judicial review rather than consideration of politics.[17] In *Greece v EC Council*,[18] it was argued by the Member State that a Community regulation restricting imports of agricultural products from third countries following the Chernobyl nuclear accident should not have been adopted under Article 113 of the Treaty, dealing with common commercial policies, but should have more appropriately been based on either the express environmental provisions under the Treaty or under the parallel Euratom Treaty dealing with nuclear matters. The European Court upheld Article 113 as a correct legal basis, and rejected the idea that, because there was a clear environmental dimension to the measure, it should have been treated as part of the Community's express environmental programme of action. In so doing, the Court invoked the integration requirement in Article 130r:

> That provision which reflects the principle whereby all Community measures must satisfy the requirements of environmental protection, implies that a Community measure cannot be part of a Community action on environmental matters merely because it takes into account those requirements.

Ensuring Environmental Integration

Such a legal analysis supports the legitimacy of environmental integration where it takes

---

[15] See L Kramer, *EC Treaty and Environmental Law*, 2nd edn (London, Sweet & Maxwell, 1995) 59.
[16] See M Hession and R Macrory, 'Maastricht and the Environmental Policy of the Community: Legal Issues of a New Environmental Policy' in D O'Keefe (ed), *Legal Issues of the Maastricht Treaty* (London, Chancery Publications, 1994).
[17] *Commission v Council* [1987] ECR 1493.
[18] [1990] ECR I-1527.

place. Policy makers who produce legislation in other sectors with strong environmental associations, such as transport or agriculture, will find their action less vulnerable to legal challenge on the grounds that such considerations were not legally relevant. But one task for environmental law in the future is to devise suitable provisions and techniques which will help to ensure that this process continues to take place to a far greater extent than at present, rather than to merely enable it to take place when policy makers so wish.

Implementing Environmental Integration Principles

One approach is to supplement broad general statements of principles with far more express environmental requirements in subsidiary, 'non-environmental' legislation. For example, Article 7 of Regulation 2052/88, governing the distribution of structural funds within the Community, provides that

> measures financed by the Structural Funds or receiving assistance from the European Investment Bank or from another existing financial instrument shall be in keeping with the provisions of the Treaties, with the instruments adopted pursuant thereto and with Community policies, including those concerning the rules on competition, the award of public contracts and environmental protection.

This is clearly an important requirement which attempts to ensure greater consistency between policies on financial aid and the environment although, in reality, it has not proved easy to implement, not least because structural funds are given on the basis of regional programmes prepared by Member States whereas identifiable environmental impacts are often associated with specific projects which emerge from such programmes, probably at a later date.[19]

Nevertheless, the requirement provided the basis for a legal challenge by environmental groups before the European Court of Justice in 1994 – the first time that such a case had been brought. In Case T-461/93 *An Taisce* [the National Trust for Ireland] *and Worldwide Fund for Nature v European Commission*,[20] two associations were concerned about the environmental implications of the proposed construction of an interpretative centre in a National Park which was to be financed under structural funds already approved by the European Commission under a Programme for Tourism submitted by the Irish govern-ment. The groups had alerted the Commission, and challenged what they alleged to be the Commission's decision not to withdraw the structural fund support on the grounds that the proposals were inconsistent with the requirements of the Structural Fund Regulation concerning compliance with Community environmental programmes. In the event, the Court decided that the Commission had not in fact taken any decision not to withdraw funds and that they were entitled to do so at any time, even after completion of the works. Since the case was rejected on its facts, the Court therefore did not have to determine whether the applicants had legal standing before the Court to bring such a case – clearly an extremely significant issue. However, despite the result of the case, it did underline the extent to which the integration requirements within the Structural Fund Regulation potentially have real legal purchase.

---

[19] See Kramer, above n 15, 29.
[20] Judgment of the Court of First Instance, 23 September 1994.

Enriching Procedures

Another legal technique that may be employed to ensure improved integration is the use of procedural requirements in connection with policy and similar proposals in other sectors. The 1985 Community Directive on Environmental Assessment is expressly limited to proposals for projects such as industrial works and road schemes, but there has been considerable discussion concerning the possible extension of such assessment requirements to cover a much broader category of plans, policies and programmes. To date, any further development on such proposals appears to have been resisted within the European Commission, and would almost certainly be opposed by a number of Member States.[21]

However, in dealing with policies at EU level, the parties to the Maastricht Treaty noted in one of its Declarations 'that the Commission undertakes in its proposals, and that the Member-State undertakes in implementing those proposals, to take full account of their environmental impact and the principle of sustainable growth'. In June 1993 the European Commission adopted internal administrative practices which were aimed at assisting the meeting of those goals; the measures included a commitment by the Commission to describe and justify the significant environmental impacts of proposed legislation, and the appointment of officials within each Directorate-General of the Commission with a specific responsibility to ensure that their Directorate takes on board the principle of environmental integration.

This sort of administrative management has been reflected at national level. In 1991 The UK Department of the Environment published a document intended to encourage other government departments to assess the environmental implications of their policies in a more systematic manner than had hitherto been the case,[22] and so-called 'Green Ministers' were nominated in each department. The document was followed up in 1994 with a series of case studies illustrating how such environmental appraisals were being carried out.[23] Yet the reality of the extent to which such a greening of government has genuinely taken place, against the background of such initiatives, has been consistently challenged.[24] To take one example, the 1994 report of the Royal Commission on Environmental Pollution on Transport and the Environment[25] provided a powerful critique of the extent to which UK transport trends were environmentally unsustainable in the longer run, and took to task the Department of Transport for failing 'to provide this country with an effective and environmentally sound transport policy'.[26]

Forming Environmental Integration Principles

Another example of a legal technique designed to ensure greater environmental integration across departmental interests is the imposition of general duties concerning the environ-

---

[21] A Directive on plans and programmes was eventually agreed five years later – Directive 2001/42/EC of the European Parliament and of the Council of 27 June 2001 on the assessment of the effects of certain plans and programmes on the environment.

[22] Department of the Environment, *Policy Appraisal and the Environment* (London, HMSO, 1991).

[23] Department of the Environment, *Environmental Appraisal in Government Departments* (London, HMSO, 1994).

[24] See, eg J Hill and M Jordan, 'The Greening of Government: Lessons from the White Paper Process' (1993) 14(3/4) *ECOS* 3.

[25] Royal Commission on Environmental Pollution, *Transport and the Environment*, 18th Report, Cm 2674 (London, HMSO, 1994).

[26] Ibid, para 13.65.

ment. An early example to be found in British legislation is the provision in section 11 of the Countryside Act 1968 that 'In the exercise of their functions relating to land under any enactment every Minister, government department and public body shall have regard to the desirability of conserving the natural beauty and amenity of the countryside'. Although the parliamentary debates during the discussion of the provision displayed a surprising degree of passion and conflict,[27] the blandness and generality of the duty has meant that it is effectively unenforceable in law, and it is difficult to pinpoint any real effect that it has had on decision making over the years. Nevertheless, such broadly based duties, even if non-enforceable in a conventional sense, may still, as Ross Cranston has noted, give 'legitimacy to aspirations . . . and can provide a backdrop against which specific decisions with legal consequence can be made'.[28]

In the mid-1980s there was an extended period of political controversy in Britain over the environmental implications of modern agricultural practices, criticism being focused on the relevant government department, the Ministry of Agricultural, Fisheries and Food, which was perceived to have sacrificed environmental concerns in favour of agricultural productivity. As one response, the government eventually introduced legislation which imposed a general duty on the minister to endeavour to achieve a reasonable balance between conservation, rural and agricultural interests.[29] Again, such a duty may be perceived as more of a gravitational rule rather than a enforceable legal obligation legitimising internal shifts of resources and priorities within a department. Certainly discussions with officials can frequently reveal the very real significance that such a duty can have on the internal administrative workings of such an organisation. But the difficulty with the implementation of such duties is not to devalue them by overuse, and in their drafting to achieve a sensible balance between being overgeneralised (and thereby ineffective or open to too many differing interpretations) and so specific that they lose the power to inject an environmental dimension across a broad area of activity.

5. Integration into Policies with Remote Environmental Impact

In reality, there is no single or optimum solution that will ensure greater environmental sensitivity across different industrial and economic sectors. A combination of broadly based legal principles, procedural requirements and the types of administrative restructuring described above must all contribute to reinforcing aspirational goals which are easy to state but infinitely less so to achieve.

But the challenge for environment law can go further. The types of measures so far taken to ensure integration tend to focus on the policies and decisions of non-environmental departments (whether at national or Community level) which demonstrably have significant physical impacts on the environment, energy, transport and agriculture being clear examples. Effective integration, however, goes deeper and implies that other areas

---

[27] See R Macrory, *Loaded Guns and Monkeys: Responsible Environmental Law* (London, Imperial College Centre for Environmental Technology, 1994). See also Chapter 8 above.

[28] R Cranston, *Law, Government and Public Policy* (Melbourne, Oxford University Press, 1987).

[29] Agriculture Act 1986, s 13.

of law must now be examined to determine the extent to which they are environmentally neutral or incur actual benefits or dis-benefits.

The potential conflict between free trade and environmental protection is one that is familiar at international level, and within the Community has had to be tackled by the European Court of Justice. In the landmark 1988 case of *Commission v Denmark*,[30] the European Court expressly permitted a Member State to introduce legislation concerning the recycling of drink cans even though it would have had some restrictive impact on the fundamental principle in the European Community Treaty concerning the freedom of movement of goods. A later case upheld the right of a regional authority to restrict the import of wastes from other regions and countries into its area on the grounds that such unrestricted free movement would have severe environmental consequence.[31]

Competition policy must similarly be examined. Article 85 of the European Community Treaty contains a general prohibition of price-fixing and similar agreements between competitive undertakings, but permits certain agreements which contribute 'to improving the production or distribution of goods or to promoting technical or economic progress, while allowing consumers a fair share of the resulting benefit'. The European Commission has now had to consider to what extent these latter conditions were fulfilled where environmental aims were involved, and in at least one case has confirmed this to be the case.[32] Ludwig Kramer[33] has also noted that the application of competition law principles to the types of voluntary environmental agreements and covenants between industry and government bodies, as favoured in some countries such as the Netherlands, is a new area of potential conflict that has yet to be fully explored.

In the search for integration, however, one can take a more profound approach which demands that the underlying rationale for principles that govern a much broader spectrum of law is examined to determine to what extent they are consistent with the contemporary challenge of the environment. Gerd Winter[34] has noted the extent to which modern environmental law takes an interventionist, regulatory form which has been imposed upon, and restrains, 'the inventiveness and energy of the individual'. The encouragement and release of such inventiveness had been one of the driving forces behind many developments of the law, particularly in the nineteenth century in countries such as Germany and the UK, and can be found in such diverse areas as patent legislation, corporation law and the promotion of freedom of trade. He argues that, set against the scale of environmental problems now facing society, the regulatory, interventionist approach cannot wholly succeed, and that it will be necessary to re-examine those underlying and pre-existing areas of law to ensure that they are more environmentally sensitive: 'The emancipatory law must therefore be inoculated with ecological considerations'.[35] This approach to integration has taken us a long way from the tentative moves towards seeking greater consistency between laws regulating discharges into water and air. Yet, ironically perhaps, the argument reflects, at a deeper level, the debate that has already taken place in the much narrower context of pollution control where the heavy reliance on 'end of pipe' solutions as a means of controlling discharges is seen ultimately to have only a limited role, and the fact that it is

---

[30] Case 302/86 [1988] ECR 4607.
[31] Case C-2/90 *Commission v Belgium* [1992] ECR I-4431.
[32] European Commission, 'XXIInd Report on Competition Policy 1992' (1993).
[33] Kramer, above n 15, 30.
[34] See G Winter, 'Perspectives for Environmental Law – Entering the Fourth Phase' (1989) 1 *Journal of Environmental Law* 38.
[35] Ibid, 45.

preferable to examine the total industry process to ensure improved waste minimisation and an eventual reduced burden on the environment. Environmental law, as it is conventionally written about and analysed, may represent a discrete and bounded field of law, but one role of the true environmental lawyer is to be prepared to re-examine all fields of law from an environmental perspective – ultimately, this is implication of the integration principle.

16

Loaded Guns and Monkeys – Responsible Environmental Law[1] (1994)

Responsibility and a Pet Monkey

One hundred and fifty years ago a pet monkey escaped and then attacked and bit a Mrs Sophia May who in the words of the law report consequently became 'sick, sore, lame and disordered'.[2] With her husband she sought compensatory damages from the owner. There was no allegation of actual negligence or fault in the way that he had secured or looked after the animal, but he was nevertheless held liable. For the first time, the Queen's Bench articulated a general principle that if someone keeps an animal known to be potentially dangerous they should be liable for damage caused by it however careful they had been in its control: the gist of liability lay in keeping the potentially dangerous animal in the first place.

Lawyers and non-lawyers will see immediately the potential for extending such a liability principle from a pet monkey to the storage of chemicals or other potential sources of environmental damage. And the 1846 decision of *May v Burdett*[3] re-emerged in argument at the end of last year before the House of Lords in the *Cambridge Water Company* case.[4] That decision has been described by some as the most important environmental case this century and is one to which I return.

At the heart of both the *May v Burdett* and *Cambridge Water Company* cases lie notions of responsibility, and I want to use the theme of responsibility as a basis for considering various strands of contemporary environmental law. It is critical in the development of the more conventional types of legal liability seen in both those cases, but I will also place it in a wider context of what might broadly be described as institutional behaviour. Some of the underlying questions are not, of course, peculiar to environmental law. Jurists have long wrestled with the relationship between moral responsibility and legal liability. In this country the alignment between actual intention and criminal liability has been broken in many areas of social regulation with the introduction of strict liability offences. These are especially prevalent in the environmental field.

---

[1] R Macrory, *Loaded Guns and Monkeys: Responsible Environmental Law* (London, Imperial College Centre for Environmental Technology, 1994) 1–31.

[2] *May v Burdett* (1846) 9 QB 1213, 1214.

[3] Ibid, 1217–18.

[4] *Cambridge Water Co Ltd v Eastern Counties Leather plc* (1994) 1 All ER 53.

In the last century, Oliver Holmes, in his essays on the Common Law, developed the notion of 'objective liability', a theory designed to impute knowledge and hence liability on individuals who did not actually possess it.[5] The doctrine of vicarious responsibility under which employers can be held liable for actions of their employees can, at least in the field of civil liability, be hardly justified other than on grounds of efficient loss apportionment. In criminal law, companies can face what has been described by Glanville Williams as 'the tyrannous combination'[6] of strict and vicarious liability – criminal liability being imposed even where those in charge of company policy knew nothing of the act concerned or even prohibited it. The doctrine, which incidentally is unknown in Germany where only individuals can be convicted of criminal offences, was reconfirmed earlier this year in the Divisional Court in its application to water pollution offences.[7] According to the Court the magnitude of environmental pollution justified the approach.[8] Over thirty years ago, the British jurist Herbert Hart in his exploration of Punishment and Responsibility quoted a character from Dostoevsky's 'Crime and Punishment' concerned at the way in which Western utilitarian concepts were threatening notions of individual responsibility:'... in this age the sentiment of passion is actually prohibited by science, and that is how they order things in England where they have political economy'.[9]

But I would argue that the environmental field introduces a particular sense of urgency and dimension to the universality of these issues. There is an increasing awareness of the scale and dimension of some of the environmental problems that may face us. Environmental science has an apparently limitless capacity to reveal threats to environmental systems and suggest new causative links, while principles of precaution indicate that what may be unpalatable action should sometimes be taken without any real proof of damage.[10] There has been an extraordinary rise in interest in environmental law by academics and practitioners in this country, both for opportunistic as well as idealistic reasons; taking just one marker, membership of the UK Environmental Law Association has risen from about 40 members to over 1200 in the eight years since its formation in 1986. Equally one can point to the sheer number of regulations made in the environmental field over the equivalent period, or the number of European Community laws agreed in recent years. This is set against a backdrop of what are often divergent and powerfully held moral philosophies of right and wrong concerning the environment. The description by the House of Lords in the 1970s of strict liability pollution offences as not being crimes in a true sense[11] is one that would not be shared by many environmentalists. The German philosopher, Niklas Lumann, concludes rather depressingly, 'The scope and opacity of the causal connections imparted by the environment makes every value consensus trivial'.[12]

At the same time there is a crisis of confidence in the ability of conventional environmental regulation to deliver. We look at the worst examples of environmental legalism in

---

[5] OW Holmes, The Common Law (1881) Lecture II, The Criminal Law.

[6] Quoted by Lord Justice Simon Brown in National Rivers Authority v Alfred McAlpine Homes East Ltd, QBD (Divisional Court), 26 January 1994 (copy of case report on file with author).

[7] National Rivers Authority, ibid.

[8] See judgment of Mr Justice Morland, ibid, 22–23.

[9] HLA Hart, Punishment and Responsibility: Essays in the Philosophy of Law (Oxford, Clarendon Press, 1968) 158.

[10] See, eg Art 130r of the European Community Treaty, which, post-Maastricht, now requires that Community environmental policy 'shall be based on the precautionary principle and on the principles that preventive action be taken'.

[11] Per Viscount Dilhorne in Alphacell v Woodward (1972) 2 All ER 475, 483.

[12] N Lumann, Ecological Communication (Cambridge, Polity Press, 1989).

the States and like not what we see. Solutions are offered by the economist rather than the lawyer. Yet legal notions of responsibility both reflect and inject an ethical dimension which is inherent in many environmental perspectives and which is either unattainable or lost in the language of welfare economic analysis. Or to put it another way, legal concepts of responsibility may need to fill the spaces left unoccupied by the economist.

Enforcement and Competing Models of Liability

Even where environmental legislation expresses liabilities in the strictest of terms, socio-legal research has demonstrated the extent to which enforcement authorities resist acting like automatons. In the early 1980s Keith Hawkins, Genevra Richardson and others explored the actual practice of regulation in the field of water pollution and trade effluent control, and revealed how individual enforcement officers' own notions of justice and responsibility influenced their discretion to prosecute, whatever the actual wording of the law.[13]

My own, more modest contribution to this type of research was in the field of hazardous waste law, when in the mid-1980s the European Commission was concerned at apparent wide discrepancies in the level of sentences imposed for waste disposal offences by national courts in different Member States. A systematic comparative evaluation was commissioned, with academic experts in each country being asked to compile reports examining the results of criminal prosecutions. Sonia Withers, then of Loughborough University, and I were assigned the United Kingdom.[14]

Perhaps somewhat naively, Commission officials initially thought that this would be a fairly straightforward exercise on the assumption that detailed records of criminal convictions were compiled at some central location. In the UK this was not the case. National judicial statistics did not have nearly the level of detail needed, while individual courts did not record offences by subject matter. To provide even some basic information, in part we had to look at newspaper cuttings – on the way availing ourselves of the extensive personal collection collated by Richard Hawkins, then company lawyer for one of the main private waste disposal firms. This was followed by interviews with selected waste disposal authorities.

Even this did not always help. Disposal authorities did not necessarily keep accessible records of prosecutions – as one remarked, 'We don't mark up prosecutions'. Waste disposal regulation was then largely the responsibility of County Councils and here our research demonstrated the importance of the institutional location of waste disposal regulators within a Council's organisational structure, a matter which had been left to the discretion of each authority following implementation of the relevant provisions of Part I of the Control of Pollution Act 1974. To take two extreme examples, in one authority they were located within the Highways Department which had little experience of prosecution work

---

[13] K Hawkins, *Environmental and Enforcement Regulation and the Social Definition of Pollution* (Oxford, Clarendon Press, 1984); G Richardson, A Ogus and P Burrows, *Policing Pollution – A Study of Self-Regulation and Enforcement* (Oxford, Clarendon Press, 1982); BM Hutter, *The Reasonable Arm of the Law?: The Law Enforcement Procedures of Environmental Health Officers* (Oxford, Clarendon Press, 1988).

[14] R Macrory and S Withers, 'Application of Administrative and Criminal Punishments Concerning Hazardous Wastes in England' Report for Directorate General XI, European Commission (1985; copy on file with author).

but was operationally geared up for effective practical clean-ups of spilt or dumped loads of waste. In another, they were located within the Trading Standards Department which traditionally adopts a fairly aggressive approach to enforcement. In a third authority, they were essentially self-standing rather than incorporated within an existing administrative unit. Equally revealing was the often poor relationship between the enforcement officers who were technically qualified but had no formal legal training, and local authority legal staff who were frequently located in the County Solicitor's Department many miles away. These institutional factors had a powerful influence on the approach that each body took towards the law and its enforcement.

A policy-maker trying to rationalise the system that then operated would have argued that such flexible arrangements were appropriate given differing characteristics of local waste issues and, in time-honoured British fashion, the heterogeneous nature of the receiving environment. Even accepting the argument for variety as convincing, our research indicated that in reality important institutional differences that occurred were often explained by historical accident or administrative tradition rather than environmental problems at hand. None of these features were apparent or addressed in the black letter of the relevant statutory provisions, and underlined the importance of this form of socio-legal research in illuminating how legal systems work in practice.

While we conducted this research within the United Kingdom, I thought that this lack of hard information on prosecutions was perhaps a peculiarly British weakness. But not so when it came to comparative discussion with our counterparts. The German researcher, for example, found herself in almost exactly the same position as we did, and similarly had to resort to newspaper cuttings and interviews. Counter-intuitively perhaps, it was the Italians who had the most sophisticated database under which the results of every court decision including magistrates' are logged on a central computer for ready access.[15]

More fundamentally, the research revealed the difficulties of comparing performance of the effectiveness of environmental law even within a comparatively small number of countries, all with developed legal systems and operating under a reasonably common framework of policy and law. Certainly, we argued that comparing numbers of prosecutions and levels of fines was but a crude indicator. A nil or small level of prosecutions might indicate an utterly effective law that was being fully complied with, or it might equally suggest exactly the opposite. Furthermore, unless one knew a lot more about the cultural and political context in which fines and criminal convictions are received, comparing levels per se made little sense. More systematic information concerning environmental quality or the ability of the legal system to secure environmental improvement goals was needed but in the waste disposal field at that time no such data was developed, and even now it remains elusive. The example of the Italian computer system confirmed that comprehensive data collection by itself does not guarantee effective implementation, but nevertheless without it one is swimming in the dark, buffeted by anecdotal prejudice concerning foreign practices. In this context the recent establishment of the so-called Chester informal network of European environmental enforcement authorities can only

---

[15] Il Centro Elletronico di Documentazione (CED), Rome. See also Postiglione (ed), 'La Giurisprudenza Ambientale Europea a la Banca Dati enlex della CEE (Milan, Dott A Giuffre, 1987) 137.

be to the good.[16] So too after so much wrangling concerning its location should be the setting-up of the European Environment Agency.[17]

The need to understand the attitude of environmental regulators towards the implementation and enforcement of law is, of course, made all the more important by the large degree of discretion they possess over how they approach prosecution policy. Strict liability offences which permeate much of British environmental legislation clearly heighten the significance of that enforcement discretion, and the extent to which knowledge and legal responsibility, whether in the criminal or civil field, should be linked remains a critical theme in contemporary environmental law.

On the facts of the case Mr Burdett actually knew that his monkey enjoyed biting people. But later case law developed the idea that what were essentially strict liability principles would apply to certain classes of wild animals, whether or not the particular animal was known to be dangerous or not.

As a law student, the first case which really excited my intellectual curiosity and made me realise that no amount of imaginative thinking could compete with what could occur in real life concerned this principle. Johannes and Emmie Behrens were midgets, Mr Behrens claiming at 30 inches to be the smallest man in the world. In 1954, Bertram Mills' Circus held their Christmas season at Olympia, and the Behrens were exhibited in a booth near the circus ring. One of the acts involved six Burmese elephants who were led to the ring for each performance, but one afternoon as the elephants were being led past the midgets' booth, a dog belonging to their manager and tied up began barking. The third elephant in the procession panicked, chased after the dog, knocked down part of the booth and caused serious injuries to Mrs Behrens.

In an action for damages against the circus owners, it was recognised that these particular animals were not in fact wild but highly trained circus elephants. As Mr Justice Devlin put it, 'The elephant Bullu is in fact no more dangerous than a cow; she reacted in the same way as a cow would do to the irritation of a small dog; if perhaps her bulk made her capable of doing more damage, her higher training enabled her to be more swiftly checked'.[18]

Nevertheless, the principles of liability for animals had already classified all elephants, like monkeys, as potentially dangerous, and the owner was consequently held liable whatever the special characteristics of the particular beast. A tough rule of liability, and one which offended against my own adolescent notions of fairness, whatever my sympathies for the plaintiffs.

Last year's *Cambridge Water* case displayed similarly stark competing models of liability. During the 1960s and 1970s, drums of solvents were regularly delivered to the defendants' tanning company and transferred to a large storage tank. According to the findings of fact, spillages occurred during the transfer process, but at the time anyone would have thought that these would have simply evaporated in the air.

---

[16] See 'Institutional Process in EC Developments' (1994) 3(1) *Review of European Community and International Environmental Law* 49.

[17] Council Regulation 1210/90 of 7 May 1990 on the Establishment of the European Environment Agency and the European Environment Information and Observation Network [1990] OJ L120/1. In October 1993 it was agreed that the location of the Agency would be Denmark: Decision taken by Common Agreement between the Representatives of the Governments of the Member States, Meeting at Head of State and Government Level of 29 October 1993 on the location of the seats of certain bodies and departments of the European Communities and of Europol [1993] OJ C323/01, Art 1(a).

[18] *Behrens v Bertram Mills Circus Ltd* [1957] 2 QB 1, 14.

What in fact appears to have occurred was that the spillages seeped through a concrete floor, into the ground below, and eventually entered a chalk aquifer. A groundwater source owned by the Cambridge Water Company over a mile away was found to be contaminated, proved unusable, and the company sued the tanning company for the cost of developing a new source of supply, over £1m.

The distinctive feature of this pollution case was that the trial judge made a clear finding of no negligence in the sense that at the time of the spillages the defendants did not fall below then accepted standards of precaution and care.[19] But the Court of Appeal rediscovered an old Victorian case concerning natural rights and water and decided that despite no negligence the defendants could still be liable for all the damage that naturally flowed from the spillages whether or not it could have been foreseen at the time.[20]

Whatever one thought of the result, I criticised the way in which the Court of Appeal had argued their principle of liability.[21] Last December, the House of Lords reversed the Court of Appeal decision, holding the company not liable.[22] The judgment is intellectually more sustained, elaborating general principles of environmental liability, and, to condense 22 pages in a few lines, in essence their Lordships held that under the so-called rule in *Rylands v Fletcher* there were certain types of industry and activity for which liability would apply even in the absence of negligence. But even then where the pathway of the pollution was not reasonably foreseeable no liability should arise. In this case, at the time of the spillages no-one could have reasonably foreseen that the escape of the solvents would have travelled the route it did, and therefore there was no liability.

The line between negligence-based liability for all the damage that is reasonably foreseeable and strict liability for damage unless the pathway of the pollutant was not reasonably foreseeable is clearly fine. But it is real, and the practical distinctions must now be addressed by professionals. Their Lordships point out, for example, that the taking of reasonable precautions (say, the construction of a protective bund) would generally suggest the absence of negligence but would not be a defence in itself where *Rylands v Fletcher* applied.

Given the findings of fact – though there remain arguments over exactly what did happen – I personally find the decision a fair result. The House of Lords has accepted that mere control of certain activities is sufficient to impose liability but in determining what the controller is liable for, has rejected the notion, pursued by the Court of Appeal, that responsibility and natural causation are equivalent. Responsibility here incorporates an ethical dimension by asking what were the reasonable standards of predictive knowledge at the time. What the decision does mean is that environmental scientists will now play a significant role in defining the legal boundaries of responsibility which will shift with the passage of time. Changing knowledge, advances in research, and publication of results will be of critical importance in determining what pathways of pollution are or are not reasonably foreseeable at any particular time.

But the decision does contain anomalies. The House of Lords held that in general it is better for Parliament and legislation rather than the courts to impose strict liability

---

[19] 'Cambridge Water Co Ltd v Eastern Counties Leather plc, Queen's Bench Division' (1992) 4(1) *Journal of Environmental Law* 81.

[20] *Cambridge Water*, above n 4.

[21] R Macrory, '£1 Million Award in Historic Aquifer Pollution Case' (1992) 214 *ENDS Report* 41; R Macrory, 'European Initiatives in the Field of Pollution Control: Civil Liability for Environmental Damage', Advocates for Change, 1993 Bar Conference (London, 1993).

[22] *Cambridge Water*, above n 4.

on activities of high risk – since this will lead to much clearer definitions and, to quote, 'Those concerned can know where they stand'.[23] Yet the common law principles of strict liability which the case endorsed and revived applies to an ill-defined group of so-called 'non-natural' users of land. The House of Lords indicated that the storage of substantial quantities of chemicals on industrial premises should be regarded as almost a classic case of non-natural use,[24] a clearly more generous approach than applied in previous case law in Britain.[25] In essence, one is revisiting the old *scienter* rule for animals. Or to put it another way, is, say, the disposal of municipal landfill by waste more akin to a familiar grazing cow or a ferocious wild elephant?

A further twist to the *Cambridge Water* case was the fact that initially and certainly at the time of the spillages the amount of contamination was minuscule. It satisfied the then prevailing British legal standards of 'wholesomeness' for drinking water, there was no evidence of human health risk, and the Cambridge Water Company could have carried on using the bore-hole for water supply.

But in 1980 the EC Drinking Water Directive[26] was agreed, containing a large number of standards for various parameters. Britain adopted the strict values in the Directive relating to organochlorines, and it was only then that testing for the particular solvent was carried out, and the supply found to fail in this respect.

Yet the actual spillages from the solvent deliveries had ceased several years before the Directive was agreed. To that extent it is arguable the damage to the plaintiff's resource was as much due to the introduction of new legislative standards as the previous actions of the company. Or using distinctions drawn by the Royal Commission on Environmental Pollution,[27] contamination – that is the introduction of the substance in question – of the water source may have already occurred but there was no pollution – or damage – until the new standards were applied.

This in itself was not sufficient to excuse the defendants on the grounds that *Rylands v Fletcher* is a type of tort which is completed only when damage occurs. It may be that their Lordships' insistence on introducing a foreseeability test for damage was at least influenced by this factor, though it is little explored in an explicit fashion.[28] But the relationship between liability for present actions and environmental standards that may arise in the future is an issue that is likely to assume more significance, especially in areas of gradual as opposed to acute pollution. In *Cambridge Water* neither contamination nor pollution was predictable. But suppose that the manner in which a substance is introduced into part of the receiving environment is reasonably predictable. In the absence of any new legislative

[23] Per Lord Goff, ibid, 76.

[24] Per Lord Goff, ibid, 79.

[25] In the High Court, following the spirit of such earlier cases, Mr Justice Kennedy had rejected liability in *Rylands v Fletcher* on the grounds that in a modern society this sort of activity could not be regarded as 'non-natural' or out of the ordinary (*Cambridge Water*, above n 4, 96).

[26] Council Directive 80/778/EEC relating to the quality of water intended for human consumption [1980] OJ L229/11.

[27] Royal Commission on Environmental Pollution, *Tackling Pollution – Experience and Prospects*, Tenth Report, Cmnd 9149 (London, HMSO, 1984), especially 1.9–1.12. At the time, some, including the Chemical Industries Association, argued that 'contamination' should be used to describe situations where the presence of substances was believed or positively asserted to be harmless, while 'pollution' implied actual damage. The Royal Commission rejected such a clear-cut distinction and preferred to use the term contamination to imply the presence of alien substances or energy in the environment without passing judgment on whether they cause or are liable to cause damage. In that sense, contamination can be seen as a necessary but not a sufficient condition for pollution.

[28] See case note on the *Cambridge Water* case by A Ogus (1994) 6(1) *Journal of Environmental Law* 137.

standards, the environmental scientist would say that contamination was foreseeable, but not pollution. The lawyer might respond that this foreseeability test is not confined to the actual damage that is foreseeable but encompasses the total extent of the kind of damage that is foreseeable.[29] Once the process of contamination is foreseeable, the concept of 'kind of damage' is sufficient to include the effect of future environmental standards, even if it is not possible to predict precisely what these will be.

Science and Law

The complex policy background in the case raises more fundamental questions concerning the overlay between science and legislation. A key feature in the development of British environmental law in the last ten years is the extent to which precise standards of various types have been incorporated in the structure of environmental legislation. This is particularly so in the field of pollution control.[30] As *Cambridge Water* showed, legislative standards such as 'wholesome' water whose practicable meaning used to be largely left to technical administrators to determine have been superseded by elaborate lists of parameters and concentration levels specified in legislation.

The pressures for such changes have been powerful. The style of Community environmental legislation, doctrines developed by the European Court of Justice concerning the transposition of Community obligations into national law,[31] and the institutional distancing of major utilities from government following privatisation all contribute to the process.[32] The introduction of what I have described as specificity[33] into environmental legislation has been encouraged by other factors at play which are sometimes less clearly articulated: a demand for consistency in the interpretation and application of legal controls; administrative simplicity in application; developments in techniques of measurement and recording; a public lack of confidence in over-extensive discretion being given to environmental regulators; and, at least in the field of criminal law, a need for certainty and clarity. In effect, scientific terminology is being employed to define legal levels of responsibility. Examples can be given where the extent of the scientific language employed in legislation renders it unworkable. As my former Ph.D. student Pat Lucas will recall, until recently, the noise standards for motor vehicles in use on the road contained such complex measure-

[29] The approach taken in the remoteness for damage test applied to negligence and nuisance cases in determining what extent of damage a defendant will be liable for: see *The Wagon Mound (No 1)* (1961) AC 388; *The Wagon Mound (No 2)* (1967) 1 AC 617; *Barnett v Chelsea Hospital Management Committee* (1969) 1 QB 478. Their Lordships' judgment in *Cambridge Water* seems to come close to applying a remoteness test but is not expressed in this way.

[30] See, eg Water Supply (Water Quality) Regulations 1989 (SI 1989/1147); Air Quality Standards Regulations 1989; Surface Water (Classification) Regulations 1989 (SI 1989/1148).

[31] Especially the almost wholesale rejection of the use of national administrative methods such as circulars as opposed to legislation to transpose obligations. Case 238/85 *Commission v Netherlands* [1987] ECR 3989; Case C-131/88 *Commission v Germany* [1991] ECR I-825. See also R Macrory, 'Industrial Air Pollution – Implementing the European Framework' in *National Society for Clean Air 55th Annual Conference Proceedings* (Brighton, National Society for Clean Air, 1988).

[32] Government can ensure that its policy goals are carried out by public sector bodies through less formal means such as directions. Once these bodies are in the private sector, legislative standards must be employed. See R Macrory, 'The Privatisation and Regulation of the Water Industry' (1990) 53 *Modern Law Review* 78.

[33] See R Macrory, 'Environmental Law: Shifting Discretions and the New Formalism' in O Lomas (ed), *Frontiers of Environmental Law* (London, Chancery Law Publishing, 1991) ch 2, reproduced in Chapter 17 below.

ment requirements that they were near unusable in practice.[34] No doubt justifiable and correct from the perspective of an acoustic scientist but paying little respect for day-to-day realities. Similarly the choice of language employed in the legislation may itself constrain or provide opportunities for day-to-day technical solutions. Nicola Atkinson in our Environmental Law Group, along with scientific colleagues in the Waste Management Centre, is currently leading a research study on the relationship between law and the choice of remedy selection for dealing with land contamination.[35]

More importantly, the incorporation of a standard expressed in scientific terminology into the body of law provides it with both respectability and a degree of moral imperative. My colleagues here know only too well some of the contradictions at work. For example, the persuasive concept of critical loads has entered into the language of international agreements following the 1988 Sofia Protocol on Transboundary Movements of NOx.[36] Yet Professor Nigel Bell in his own inaugural explained, to a layman at any rate, some of the fundamental scientific uncertainties inherent in the concept.[37] Attempting to move from the effect of one pollutant on a single plant strain under controlled conditions to a cocktail of mixes in real life conditions is riddled with difficulty. Others can tell of the spurious science involved in coming up with some of the figures for the ICRCL (Inter-Departmental Committee on the Redevelopment of Contaminated Land) guidelines for land contamination currently in use, and maybe yet to enter the legal language.

Let me make it clear that I am not calling for the wholesale return to halcyon days of open-textured legal terminology in environmental legislation. As much as anyone I have been an advocate of a more formalised and transparent structure than used to be the norm in this country. But my concern is where the development can send wrong signals of when there are or are not transcientific judgements involved. To take the Drinking Water Directive again,[38] the changing retrospective justification for the infamous standard of 1 microgram per litre of individual pesticides[39] provides a dramatic example. Some years ago this was frequently justified as a scientific decision taken by Member States at the time. It now tends to be characterised as a political judgment made by Ministers in 1980 that drinking water should contain no pesticides. The truth, as one of our M.Sc. students discovered in research, was no-one now seems quite certain of its origin, though the most likely explanation is that the standard was adopted from then World Health Organisation Guidelines.[40] But as with the nitrate standard appearing in the Directive, heavy qualifications appearing in the WHO documentation were consciously or mistakenly lost in the

---

[34] See R Macrory, 'Science, Legislation and the Courts' in GR Conway (ed), *The Assessment of Environmental Problems* (London, Imperial College Centre for Environmental Technology, 1986); P Lucas, 'Science in Legislation and its Enforcement: A Study of Neighbourhood Noise', PhD Thesis, University of London (1989).

[35] The research is concerned with legal process and technical remedies for cleaning up contaminated land as opposed to principles of law for dealing with civil liability for contamination.

[36] 'Protocol to the 1979 Convention on Long-Range Transboundary Air Pollution Concerning the Control of Emissions of Nitrogen Oxides or their Transboundary Fluxes (Sofia, 1988)' (1989) 28 *International Legal Materials* 214.

[37] N Bell, 'Clearing the Air: Revealing the Hidden Effects of Air Pollution on Plants', Inaugural Lecture delivered in October 1990 at Imperial College of Science, Technology and Medicine, London (copy on file with author).

[38] Council Directive 80/778/EEC, above n 26.

[39] Ibid, Art 3 and Annex 1, Table D, para 55.

[40] G Wood, 'A Critical Review of the Drinking Water Directive (870/778/EEC) with respect to Parameter 55 (Pesticides and Related Products)', unpublished MSc Thesis, ICCET, London (1989).

process of translation from a discursive guideline into a legal instrument.[41] And according to one senior Commission official the figure of 5 micrograms per litre for total pesticides was justified by simply pointing the number of fingers on his hand.[42]

Greater understanding of processes at work in the development of such standards, both at national and international level, and their eventual seepage into law is needed. In my own research group, Steve Hollins is exploring the complex and little understood world of chemical regulation. Rosalind Twum-Barima and John Stonehouse are preparing papers for the United Nations Trade and Environment Programme on international trade issues and environmental science concepts.[43]

Location and Participation

This change in legislative style goes on to raise deeper questions concerning the nature and location of decision making. In 1986, Gordon Conway organised a conference here on the assessment of environmental problems, where I contributed a paper on science, legislation and the courts.[44] I touched upon the changing style of UK environmental laws which were beginning to emerge, and suggested that this was throwing into sharp relief differing styles of administrative and regulatory management.

Developing from an approach of Professor Mashaw of Yale University,[45] 1 characterised two competing models of administrative decision-making as a 'determinate' and an 'accommodatory' model. Both are persuasive but are largely incompatible with each other. In the determinate model the goal of the regulator is to implement a programme of which the goals have been previously prescribed in legislation. Value and political judgements inherent in the establishment of such a goal are removed from the regulator charged with implementation, leaving him with the responsibility of devising effective mechanisms to achieve the goals. The success of their activities is measured by the efficiency and accuracy with which such goals are achieved.

The accommodatory model of decision making does not aim to achieve such a clearly predetermined goal. Instead it requires the administrator to achieve as harmonious accommodation as possible of competing interests involved in a particular issue or problem before him. The means and procedures for doing so may or may not be defined by law. The critical distinction from the determinate model is that the legal framework does not attempt to define in advance the programme to be achieved – the process of accommo-

---

[41] The WHO Guidelines, 'European Standards for Drinking-Water', 2nd edn (Geneva, WHO, 1970), proposed that the contamination of water by pesticides 'should be prevented so far as possible', but stated that, 'it should be stressed that the proposals set out in this report are intended to be for guidance only; they are recommendations and in no sense mandatory'.

[42] Wood, above n 40, 135.

[43] R Twum-Barima, 'Protecting the Ozone Layer through Trade Measures: Reconciling the Trade Provisions of the Montreal Protocol and the Rules of the GATT' (Geneva, Environment and Trade, UNEP, 1994); JM Stonehouse and JD Mumford (1994) 'Science, Risk Analysis and Environmental Policy Decisions' (Geneva, Environment and Trade, UNEP, 1994).

[44] See above n 34.

[45] J Mashaw, 'An Overview – Two Models of Regulatory Decision-making' in JD Nyhart and MM Carrow (eds), *Law and Science in Collaboration: Resolving Regulatory Issues of Science and Technology* (Lexington, MA: Lexington Books, 1983).

dation itself is used to identify and determine appropriate values to be assigned during decision making.

Models of this sort are of course heuristic devices used to illuminate characteristics by artificial exaggeration. In reality many aspects of environmental regulation will not fall completely within one or the other model though dominant strands may be apparent. Common law nuisance concepts often fall within the accommodatory model; likewise, perhaps, local public inquiries over controversial planning developments.

British pollution legislation used to provide the barest indication of precise policy goals or standards. Regulators were given extensive discretion to determine the content of individual discharge consents and standards – a structure endorsed, it should be admitted, by British environmental scientists pushing what is now a less convincing case for the local resilience of the natural environment. And it was an approach which was often misunderstood or subject to suspicion by other countries. Patrick Marnham in his travel book *So Far From God* records meeting an Italian girl in South America who considered that 'the English had been driven to reconcile morality and reality. What they called pragmatic others called immoral'.[46]

That sort of structure only reflected an accommodatory style of regulation, even if in the case, say, of the old Alkali Inspectorate there was criticism that the accommodation process was confined to too narrow a band of interests.[47]

These characteristics no longer prevail.[48] Emission standards and various environmental quality objectives expressed in the language of science increasingly enter the body of legislation.[49] Yet there are contradictions at work. At the same time as we have seen a move towards a more determinate model of decision making, we have also seen the introduction of greater rights of public participation and access to information being introduced into many areas of environmental regulation. For example, licence procedures in the field of water pollution discharges,[50] and Integrated Pollution Control under the Environmental Protection Act 1990.[51] Yet if many of the goals and environmental standards which the regulator must achieve have already been largely predetermined at another level, expectations of what can be achieved in a local participation process may well be frustrated or considered nugatory. Indeed, there are signals that it is just some aspects of these procedures which may first be sacrificed on the altar of deregulation.[52] In effect, new provisions concerning access to information, public registers and the like become a means of checking the performance of regulators rather than a mechanism for influencing or participating in the determination of policy.

There is no easy answer. But at the very least one needs to recognise how frustrations may boil to the surface where the procedures are ill-aligned. This situation is all the more challenging with the growing interplay of local, national, and supranational procedures

---

[46] P Marnham, *So Far From God* (London, Jonathan Cape, 1985).

[47] See especially Royal Commission on Environmental Pollution, *Air Pollution Control: An Integrated Approach*, Fifth Report, Cmnd 6371 (London, HMSO, 1976).

[48] See R Macrory, 'Environmental Policy in Britain: Reaffirmation or Reform?', Discussion Paper 86/4 (Berlin, International Institute for Environment and Society, 1986); R Macrory, 'The United Kingdom' in T Smith Jr and P Kromarek (eds), *Understanding US and European Environmental Law* (Amsterdam, Kluwer Academic, 1990).

[49] For some examples see n 30 above.

[50] See Water Resources Act 1991; Control of Pollution (Registers) Regulations 1989 (SI 1989/1160).

[51] See Environmental Protection Act 1990, s 20; Environmental Protection (Applications, Appeals and Registers) Regulations 1991 (SI 1991 No 507).

[52] See Department of the Environment, 'Proposed Amendments to the Water Resources Act 1991 and the Reservoirs Act 1975', Consultation Paper (October 1993).

at work. My own experience two years ago as Specialist Adviser to the House of Commons Select Committee on the Environment provided a particular vivid example. The Committee had long been interested in the subject of waste disposal, and were aware of proposals by the European Commission for a landfill Directive which would clearly be of key policy significance in this area. They wished to make the proposal a subject of an inquiry, and consciously decided to investigate at a stage when draft versions of the Directive were readily accessible but before a final version had been issued by the Commission. Just as any professional non-governmental organisation knows only too well, it is important to make one's mark at an early stage in policy formulation before view-points become too fixed.

The Committee invited two Commission officials behind the draft to provide evidence on their thinking and an explanation of their approach. I went to Brussels to encourage them to appear, even explaining the nature of such a Committee – an emanation of the State maybe but certainly not part of the executive government. They agreed to do so enthusiastically.

Unbeknown to me, what we had done was to set in train a mini-constitutional row. A few days before they were due to appear, the officials were forbidden to do so by the Commissioner on the grounds that the European Parliament had not yet formally commented on the proposal, and that to allow them to appear would not be 'constitutional'. Yet to rub salt in the wounds of the national Members of Parliament, the officials could and did visit Britain at the same time to talk with representatives of the British waste industry, and these same representatives were then able to provide a second-hand account to the Committee of the Commission's current thinking on the proposed Directive.

Beneath the hurt egos and furious letters that were written at the time,[53] the experience raised serious questions concerning the process of policy-making at national and Community levels. In particular, how does the role of a national Parliamentary body such as the Commons Select Committee relate to its equivalent body in the European Parliament? And what, if any, should be the responsibilities of those initiating policy at supra-national level towards members of national legislatures? Are such members excluded from the accommodatory process at that level? The Maastricht Treaty makes explicit new institutional arrangements for involving local authorities and other regional interests in the process of policy influence via the new Committee of the Regions,[54] but new formal mechanisms for involvement by national Parliaments have not been created, other than an acknowledgement of the need to do something in one of the Treaty's Protocols.[55] I could describe that saga as one of institutional accommodation. Let me take now an example of what I would call the problem of conceptual accommodation. The 1992 Community Eco-Labelling Regulation[56] reflected a new trend in European environmental law – what

---

[53] The correspondence between the Environment Commissioner and the Chairman of the Environment Select Committee is published in the Committee's report: House of Commons Environment Committee, *The EC Directive on Landfill Waste*, Eighth Report, vols I & II, HC263-1 and HC263-2 (London, HMSO, 1992). I should stress that I attach no personal blame to the individuals involved, though for a witty but scathing account of the process see the review of the Committee's report by Richard Hawkins in (1992) 4(2) *Journal of Environmental Law* 307.

[54] Art 198(a)–(c).

[55] Protocol on the Economic and Social Committee and the Committee of the Regions.

[56] Council Regulation 880/92/EEC of 23 March 1992 on a Community Eco-Label Award Scheme [1992] OJ L99/1. See also R Macrory, 'Administering the Eco-Label Scheme in Eco-Labelling of Durable Goods', MR Industrial Conferences (1991); R Macrory, 'Eco-Labelling: Some Legal Considerations', Green Consumerism Conference, Lancaster University (1991).

was at heart a voluntary scheme relying upon market and consumer forces but encased in a regulatory framework. In essence, the scheme provides for production of environmental standards for categories of consumer products, aimed at reducing confusion over misleading and unintelligible environmental claims in the market place. Industries whose products meet the approved standards may, if they wish, apply at national level for the award of an eco-label.

The process of devising eco-labelling criteria is one that takes place at Community level, while the awards of labels to individual products take place at national level. The regulation as originally proposed introduced a degree of public consultation but it seemed to me to be utterly ill-aligned to the real questions of interest.

Applications for the awards of individual labels at national level were to be advertised and a period allowed for representation. The development of approved eco-labelling criteria on the other hand were to be in the hands of closed technical committees at Community level. Yet the application stage seemed to fall within the determinate model – products either meet the preset criteria or they did not. But the really crucial questions of value judgement occur at a different level. For example, the decision to choose a particular product category for development of eco-labelling criteria. Would a motor car ever be eligible as a potential product? Equally significant would be the decision as to the boundaries of that particular product category; or in more legal language, products with the same equivalence of utility. If, say, one was developing eco-labelling criteria for nappies, should one be confining the investigation to the relative environmental merits of disposable nappies, or including in the relative analysis non-disposables? Or should criteria for dishwashers include washing by hand?

These questions are not technical issues, but raise significant ethical questions and value judgements. And they of course echo similar questions over the boundaries for analysis of the best practicable environmental option[57] or the treatment of alternatives in environmental impact analysis.[58] Yet the original mechanisms in the draft Eco-Label Regulation provided no legal requirements for genuine external critique or accommodation at this stage, or even an acknowledgement that this was a live issue. The process was to be largely lost in a world of expert committees and consultants.[59]

The experience of the Canadian eco-labelling board which went to extensive efforts to hold consultation exercises, including formal hearings, on just these sorts of questions, provided one possible model. These concerns were raised by the UK Eco-Labelling Advisory Board and to be fair to the UK government were communicated to Commission officials during the process of negotiation, only to be initially met by the response from Commission officials that they could not see how such a procedure could be incorporated at Community level with so many national Member States involved. We do now, however, at least see in the final version of the Regulation as agreed the introduction of a small

---

[57] See Royal Commission on Environmental Pollution, *Best Practicable Environmental Option*, Twelfth Report, Cmnd 310 (London, HMSO, February 1988).

[58] The European Directive on Environmental Assessment Directive 85/337 of 27 June, 1985 on the assessment of the effects of certain public and private projects on the environment [1985] OJ L175/40 is deliberately coy on the question of considering alternatives in contrast to US legislation on environmental impact statements where 'alternatives' must be considered, and where courts have been involved in determining just how far such considerations should go. See the US National Environmental Policy Act 1970, s 102, 42 USC 4341(a).

[59] I expressed some of these concerns in 'Administering the Eco-Labelling Scheme', above n 56, and 'Eco-Labelling: Some Legal Considerations', above n 56. I also served on the UK National Advisory Committee on Eco-Labelling, 1990–91.

Consultation forum where draft criteria are discussed.[60] But even then I am not convinced that the non-technical nature of many of the issues involved has been fully appreciated or the procedures for their effective consideration effectively devised.

It is already apparent how difficult it is to disentangle developments in environmental law at national, Community and international level. Community law in particular as a working laboratory of a unique supra-national legal system provides endless lessons both of what can or cannot be achieved and sometimes how not to go about issues. The status and impact of the Community on the international environmental stage itself raises legal questions of considerable difficulty, and will assume growing importance in future years. It is a subject matter which Martin Hession within our Law Group is exploring both in relation to Climate Change and in the near future sustainable development issues.[61]

The European Dimension

I have already mentioned concerns with the process of Community law policy-making. For the environmental lawyer one of the most distinctive features of the Community is the enforcement mechanism built into the governing Treaty. The responsibility of the European Commission for ensuring that Community obligations are implemented, together with the quasi-legal procedures it may invoke, eventually bringing a Member State before the European Court of Justice, distinguish the system from most other areas of international law. The new powers of the European Court, post-Maastricht, to fine or penalise a Member State which fails to respect its judgment is unparalleled in international law. According to the Commission in its tenth report on Implementation, some 90 judgments, including 27 in the environmental field, have not yet been complied with by Member States.[62] It is perhaps a sad reflection on the moral authority of the law that fiscal sanctions may have to be threatened to ensure governmental compliance.

I have written elsewhere about the Article 169 procedures and the Commission's own development of the complaint procedure as a means of involving the public in the process of law enforcement.[63] I have also suggested both legal and administrative changes to improve the very real concerns about current practice. But in pursuing my theme of responsibility let me take two issues which are beginning to emerge.

The first arose in both the recent environmental cases brought by the Commission against the United Kingdom, the bathing water and drinking water cases. In the drinking water case,[64] the United Kingdom argued strongly that their duty under the Directive was to do the best they could but not to achieve absolute standards. Not surprisingly, the Court rejected that argument on interpretation of the Directive. But a more subtle argument was raised in respect of nitrates. The United Kingdom argued that the government had

---

[60] Council Regulation 880/92/EEC, above n 56, Art 6.

[61] M Hession, 'The Role of the EC in the Implementation of International Environmental Law' (1993) 2(4) *Review of European Community & International Environmental Law* 341.

[62] Tenth Annual Report to the European Parliament, 'Monitoring of the Application of Community Law', 30 August 1993, OJ 93/C233/01.

[63] R Macrory, 'The Enforcement of Community Environmental Law: Some Critical Issues' (1992) 29 *Common Market Law Review* 347. Reproduced in Chapter 28 below.

[64] Case C-337/89 *Commission v United Kingdom* (1992).

done what it could, but in essence any failure to meet the standards was due to matters beyond their control, notably technical limitations of denitrification processes and disparate agricultural practices. In effect, they were questioning to what extent they should be held responsible for breach of the Directive. Again, the Court rejected the argument with little discussion.

It was, perhaps, not the best of cases on which to base such a submission. But it does raise the question as to what we really mean by saying that the Member State has failed to implement Community law. Are we talking of just governments and are there areas genuinely outside their responsibility for which different considerations applied? In the *Bathing Water* case,[65] an analogous argument was raised, and again rejected. But the Court did hint that absolute physical impossibility to comply with obligations (whatever that means) might justify non-compliance but this was not proved here. How far the new power to fine Member States will change the perception of the Court or allow these sorts of issues to be more fully developed as a mitigation rather than an absolute defence remains to be seen.

In practice, it is central government which appears before the Court representing the Member State. Many areas of British environmental law used to be largely the preserve of local or regional bodies. Nigel Haigh of the Institute for European Environmental Policy some years ago first pointed out how in some fields such as air pollution the need to comply with Community law was forcing the Department of the Environment to assume or threaten to exercise more reserve powers over local authorities than had hitherto usually been the practice.[66] In the United Kingdom we of course live in what is constitutionally a highly centralised system. Parliament has given Ministers extensive powers to implement Community obligations by regulations even if these must amend primary legislation to do so.[67] Many other Member States possess more clearly federated structures.

What is the position where a Member State is failing to implement a provision of Community environmental law because of the inaction of a local or regional administration over which the national government has no internal national power? Can the central government claim it has then no responsibility – on the grounds of constitutional rather than physical impossibility? The simplistic approach adopted by the Court is to turn a blind eye to internal problems of administration and say that is not a matter of Community law. The State still fails.[68] More subtly, Art. 5 of the Treaty requires Member States to abstain from any measures which could jeopardise the attainment of the objectives of the Treaty. In a case before the Court in 1988,[69] Belgium was accused of failing to transpose waste directives into national law, and the Belgian government argued that its recent constitutional reforms involving heavy decentralisation made this impossible for them. Advocate General Mancini raised the question whether such constitutional legislation which prevented the central government from implementing Community obligations was not a failure to comply with the general duties of Art. 5. Perhaps wisely, the ECJ did not address this point recognising that it was, in the words of the Advocate General, a 'delicate' question.

Yet it is a question that should be tackled. One response is simply to ensure that a central government possesses necessary powers – yet this flies in the face of concepts

---

[65] Case C-56/90 *Commission v United Kingdom* (1993).
[66] N Haigh, 'Devolved Responsibility on Centralisation: Effects of EEC Environmental Policy' (1986) 64 *Public Administration* 197.
[67] European Communities Act 1972, s 2(2).
[68] See Case 96/81 *Commission v Netherlands* (1982) ECR 1791.
[69] Joined Cases 227–230/85 *Commission v Belgium* (1988) ECR 1.

of federalism that invoke genuine decentralised powers as well as centralising forces. Or invoking the doctrine of subsidiarity,[70] one can suggest that areas where local or regional administrations possess exclusive powers are just those where the Community should not be acting. Yet this assumes that areas of Community interest are to be determined by the internal allocation of powers within Member States. Furthermore, there are likely to be issues where it is arguable that both the Community and local administrations have a real interest. The practice of sustainable development is one such example.

The new Post-Maastricht Committee of the Regions[71] provides some political recognition of these needs. But from a more formalistic perspective, part of the problem again results from exactly what we mean by the Member State. Maybe we need to recognise that the current assumption that it is always central government which is responsible or represents the Member State needs reconsideration. It is derived from customs of international diplomacy and external relationships which may no longer be appropriate for the European Union post-Maastricht. Could we move to a situation where the Commission can bring Art. 169 enforcement proceedings directly against a local administration where it possesses under national laws exclusive competence to implement a Directive? And it would be the local administration which would be responsible for paying any fines if it failed to respect the Court's judgement. Certainly, this might better reflect the realities of responsibility. And if the alternatives are either greater centralisation or a minimal role for the Community it might be preferable.

International environmental agreements still largely lack the formal enforcement mechanism developed with the Community system. Here it is necessary to rely upon elaborate reporting and review mechanisms of the sort seen in the Climate Change Convention, which ultimately rely upon peer pressure and a degree of trust. For some time there used to be a rather sterile debate as to whether this absence of effective enforcement procedures meant that such agreements, though part of international law, were not law in any real sense. Yet even at a national level the role of legally expressed duties which are non-enforceable in a strict legal sense should not be too readily dismissed. As Ross Cranston has noted, legislation can give 'legitimacy to aspirations . . . and can provide a backdrop against which specific decisions with legal consequence can be made'.[72]

Redefining the Boundaries of Responsibility

In 1986, Robin Grove-White was a research fellow at ICCET and leading an ESRC contract with me concerning the integration of an environmental dimension into policy areas hitherto almost unaffected by such considerations. A principle that now finds expression in the European Treaty,[73] but as Robin Grove-White demonstrated, one that is riddled with uncertainties not least because of fundamental differing perspectives of what is meant by the environment. Part of our research concerned the role and significance of general

---

[70] EC Treaty (as amended at Maastricht), Art 3b.
[71] Ibid, Art 198(a)–(c).
[72] R Cranston, *Law Government and Public Policy* (Melbourne, Oxford University Press, 1987).
[73] Art 130R(2), 'Environmental protection requirements must be integrated into the definition and implementation of other Community policies.'

environmental duties expressed in legislation. The most long-standing and general being the familiar s 11 of the Countryside Act 1968:

> In the exercise of their functions relating to land under any enactment every Minister, government department and public body shall have regard to the desirability of conserving the natural beauty and amenity of the countryside.

For such a blandly expressed duty the Parliamentary debates during the passage of the Bill revealed a surprising degree of passion and conflict.[74] One Bishop noted the long gap between the broad generality and any actual legal compulsion while an opposing view described it as the focal point of the whole Bill.[75]

Certainly it provided a symbolic marker of a new acknowledgement. Other such general duties have generated more intense debate. In 1985, I drafted a clause for the Council for the Protection of Rural England (CPRE) which would have imposed a general conservation function on the Minister of Agriculture, Fisheries and Food.[76] This was at a height of concern over the environmental effects of that Ministry's activities at the time. The clause was supported by the National Farmers Union and the Country Landowners Association but lost in Standing Committee by one vote with William Waldegrave for the Government ridiculing the idea of such specific duties laid on specific departments on the grounds of collective responsibility.[77]

Yet a little less than a year later, the Minister for Agriculture, Fisheries and Food with remarkably little shame introduced under the Agriculture Act 1986 a clause imposing upon himself a general duty of balancing conservation and other interests.[78] Measuring in any quantifiable way the effect of such a duty is near impossible. Would MAFF have acted differently in subsequent years in the absence of such a duty? Direct discussions with senior officials suggested the answer were not so straightforward. For the institution, such duties could be seen as providing a set of underlying principles, and their expression in legal forms provides a permanence and detachment from government policy-making it quite distinct from a White Paper. It legitimised internal sources of pressures for changes and affected the securement of priorities within limited resources.

Such duties par excellence attempt to express environmental responsibilities in aspirational tones which are nonetheless important for that. Yet securing the right balance of

---

[74] The origin of the clause can be found from the recommendations of a Legal Study Group adopted at 'The Countryside in 1970', a major conference organised by the Council for Nature, the Royal Society of Arts and the Nature Conservancy and held in London on 10–12 November 1965. Significantly, perhaps, the original proposal was for the amenity clause to be confined to functions under the town and country planning legislation which would have given it considerably more focus.

[75] 2nd Reading, HL Deb 10 November 1967 Vol 53.

[76] 'In the exercise of such of his functions as relate to agriculture and forestry, the Minister of Agriculture, Fisheries and Food shall, in so far as it is consistent with his statutory duties, further the conservation and enhancement of the natural beauty and the conservation of flora, fauna and geological or physiological features of special interest' (proposed clause in Wildlife & Countryside Amendment Bill 1985 drafted by Richard Macrory).

[77] 'We end up with the ridiculous situation that everybody has duties laid upon them that cancel out all the duties laid upon everybody else. It is almost a logical absurdity' (William Waldegrave, House of Commons Standing Committee E, Hansard, 6 March 1985, HMSO, London).

[78] Agriculture Act 1986, s 13: 'In discharging any functions connected with agriculture in relation to any land the minister shall, so far as it is consistent with the proper and efficient dis charge of those functions, have regard to and endeavour to achieve a reasonable balance between the following considerations: (a) the promotion and maintenance of a stable and efficient agricultural industry; (b) the economic and social interests of rural areas; (c) the conservation and enhancement of the natural beauty and amenity of the countryside, including its flora and fauna and geological and physiographical features; and (d) the promotion and the enjoyment of the countryside by the public.'

specificity and generality is a challenge. The Countryside Act duty was probably expressed too broadly and across too many parties to have real purchase. From 1957 until privatisation in 1990, the Central Electricity Generating Board was under a general duty to take into account environmental considerations in formulating or considering any proposals relating to its functions.[79] The Board had tended to interpret that duty as applying to specific projects, but at the Sizewell inquiry the CPRE argued with some success that it applied at higher levels of decision making and in particular to the formation of general strategies.[80] Now since privatisation the so-called amenity duty has been recast in its application to utility companies – on the one hand in more specific and demanding terms, but on the other no longer applicable at a strategic level but confined to proposals for individual power stations and similar projects.[81] In the long run this shift will, I suspect, be detrimental.

I have argued one role of law is to define and redefine boundaries of environmental responsibility. I started with case law concerning the content of responsibility. Let me conclude with examples of two cases where the location of responsibility was pushed to new limits.

First, a statutory noise nuisance in 1985. A Miss Rossall who lived in the basement flat of a Southwark Council block of flats suffered intensely from the noise of the occupants of the flat above her. The main ground of complaint concerned the loud sound of persistent love-making. The relevant legislation states that the person primarily liable for a noise nuisance is the person 'responsible' for the nuisance, and only if they cannot be identified, can the owner of the premises be taken to court.[82] Rather than taking her neighbours to court, Miss Rossall took her landlords, Southwark Council, on the grounds that by failing to provide effective sound insulation they were in fact the party responsible for the nuisance. It appears to have been the first time a landlord in such circumstances had been taken to court, and Miss Rossall won her case, with the Court ordering the installation of effective insulation. A preventative environmental policy could be introduced by reinterpreting and relocating legal responsibility.

My second example was the 1980 lead in petrol case, *Budden v BP Oil and others*,[83] which in retrospect raised a number of legal issues concerning responsibility well ahead of its time. This was at a time when leaded petrol was available and legal, but the first campaigns and concerns about its effects on children were being raised. Three families living near the Westway section of the A40 in London, concerned at possible lead poisoning of their children, decided to avoid standard political campaigning but sued in the civil courts four parties they identified as being responsible for the situation: Associated Octel, Shell

---

[79] 'In formulating or considering any proposals relating to the functions of the Generating Board or of any of the area Boards (including any such general programme as it is mentioned in subsection (4) of section 8 of this Act), the Board in question, the Electricity Council and the Minister, having regard to the desirability of preserving natural beauty, of conserving flora, fauna and geological or physiographical features of special interest, and of protecting buildings and other objects of architectural or historic interests, shall each take into account any effect which the proposals would have on natural beauty of the countryside or on any such flora, fauna, features or objects.'

[80] See Sir F Layfield, *Sizewell B Public Inquiry Report* (London, HMSO, 5 December 1986).

[81] Electricity Act 1989, s 38 and sch 9.

[82] See now Environmental Protection Act 1990, s 80; *Rossall v London Borough of Southwark* (November 1985, unreported); J Bettle, 'Noise: The Problem of Overlapping Controls' (1988) *Journal of Planning Law* 79.

[83] *Albery & Budden v BP Oil Ltd & Shell UK Ltd* [1980] JPL 586. See also R Macrory, 'Lead in Petrol' [1981] *Journal of Planning and Environment Law* 258.

and BP Oil as two major petrol producers, and the Ford Motor Company on the grounds that a large number of the cars passing by were manufactured by them.

The critical causes of action were in nuisance and negligence, but fundamentally much of the argument as the case worked its way up from a Registrar to the Court of Appeal concerned the location of responsibility. The plaintiffs argued that the companies were putting a product on the market which would inevitably cause damage to children near urban motorways. Individual drivers had no option but to use motorcars with leaded petrol. The analogy was a supplier of a gun and bullets which he knew was to be used in a murder – he would be liable and in this case the car manufacturer was equivalent to a gun supplier. Octel, Shell and BP were equivalent to the companies who make the bullets, and provided innocent drivers with loaded guns. Or to use another analogy put forward in oral argument by one of the plaintiffs – it was like someone sending out robots who spray aerosol cans into strapped prams.

The defendants raised counter-views of responsibility. Ford Motor Company dropped out at an early stage after showing that their cars could run on both leaded and lead-free petrol. The others argued that they were not the equivalent of gun manufacturers and in any event you could not make the manufacturer of a dangerous as opposed to a defective product liable for all the consequences. Furthermore, if one accepted that there might be a problem it was confined to heavily trafficked urban roads. If anyone was responsible it was the highway authorities – the alleged harmful effects were equally well known to them and they could have taken steps to do something about the situation.

In the event the plaintiffs' case came unstuck in the Appeal Court. All along the defendants had been complying with the then statutory limits for lead in petrol prescribed by the Secretary of State. This in itself was not a good defence for those were matters of criminal rather than civil law. But the Court of Appeal argued that since one had to assume that the Secretary of State had acted reasonably when he set those limits, any reasonable manufacturer would have come to the same decision. Hence no case in negligence could ever be proved.

That particular logic can be questioned.[84] But the arguments concerning the nature of responsibility raised by the case are still very much with us today. Lead in petrol may now be of marginal significance. But I am acutely conscious during the Royal Commission on Environmental Pollution's present study into transport and the environment of the nature of our own personal responsibilities with respect to motor cars (and I exclude those present who rely solely on bicycles, walking or public transport).

The trail between Mr Burdett's monkey and the loaded gun of contemporary transport issues has been fairly lengthy, but raises a consistent question of the role of law in ensuring that both collective and individual choices are exercised with environmental sensitivity. 5th-century Irish law developed remarkably extended notions of those to whom legal responsibility were owed and who were entitled to compensation in the event of a wrong being committed. Thus, according to the book of Aicill, in the event of a theft from a house eleven persons were affected and entitled to a compensation-fine from the wrongdoer: namely, the owner of the house, the owner of the object stolen, the owner of the bed in which the person slept who suffered the injury, the person who slept in that bed and the seven noblest chiefs who were in the habit of visiting the house.[85] Even coming from

---

[84] See Macrory (1981) above.
[85] Quoted by JA Costello, *Leading Principles of the Brehon Laws* (1913) 415.

someone with a surname such as mine, that may seem like a peculiarly Irish approach to the definition of standing. But perhaps we should now turn this legal notion of extended rights to compensation on its head. We may all be potential noble chiefs, but in relation to the environment, what matters now is extended notions of responsibility rather than entitlement.

17

Environmental Law: Shifting Discretions and the New Formalism[1] (1991)

Introduction

Public concern and governmental interest in environmental issues has reached new peaks in the last few years. Many of the most serious problems have international or trans-boundary implications, and will not necessarily be receptive to conventional legal solutions. My concern here, though, is with the domestic response as it is reflected in the structure and style of new legislation, and the ensuing implications for future regulatory approaches in this country. The sheer volume of legislative material that has been produced in the United Kingdom, particularly in the field of pollution control, in the space of a little over two years is itself quite remarkable – even more so when set against underlying govern-ment policies promoting industrial deregulation. When one comes to examine in more detail the substantive content of this new body of law, it is clear that fundamental shifts of principle have taken place; from a legal perspective, at least, long-standing characteristics of British practice of environmental management no longer hold true.

Pollution and the Legislative Framework

Legislative development often takes place in a rather haphazard and unco-ordinated fashion. Laws concerning pollution control provide a compelling example. We may talk of 'pollution' as a single all-embracing idea but from a legal perspective it is perhaps only the common law concept of 'nuisance' which comes closest to reflecting this generalised notion of environmental damage. The classic general definition of common law nuisance is that provided by the text-book writer Winfield and subsequently adopted with approval by courts: 'an unlawful interference with a person's use or enjoyment of land, or with some right over or in connection with it.' In contrast, statutory controls, since their substantive emergence in the nineteenth century, have sliced up the subject into specialised fields, generally on a basis of the receiving medium, such as air or water or land – even in the

[1] R Macrory, 'Environmental Law: Shifting Discretions and the New Formalism' in O Lomas (ed), *Frontiers of Environmental Law* (London, Chancery Law Publishing, 1991) 8–23.

latter case the emphasis has been on waste disposal rather than the broader approach of land contamination as such. The fields have been treated distinctly, with different laws emerging at different times.[2] Given the often complex technical questions intimately involved in this field of law, the approach is understandable. But it has been at the expense of developing underlying and consistent legal principles. While it is true that some pre-ferred and common regulatory approaches emerge, detailed examination of significant provisions – such as those relating to public registers or statutory defences – indicate just how uncoordinated the design of legislation has been.[3] Even the apparently reassuring title, the Control of Pollution Act 1974, cannot disguise the fact that it contained essen-tially three separate codes of law concerning waste, water, and land, with little overlap or cross-referencing between them.

This predilection for disaggregated treatment in the law is mirrored and in part explained by the structure of the relevant government departments developing and promoting the legislation, and the manner of their internal administrative divisions. It is not of course a phenomenon that has been confined to Britain. The Environmental Protection Agency in the United States has long been heavily split into separate air and water quality divisions with little real overlap between the two;[4] Federal US air and water legislation has been based on fundamentally different approaches, the former heavily dominated by environmental quality objectives concerning the receiving environment, the latter by emission standards based on what is technically feasible – incidentally, almost the exact reverse of key British legislation in this field. The control of air emissions from major industrial premises has been based on general operator duties under section 5 of the Health and Safety at Work etc Act 1974 and annual registration with a central government inspectorate, formerly the Alkali Inspectorate, and now part of Her Majesty's Pollution Inspectorate. Although the legislation did not generally provide for statutory emission limits, the Inspectorate devel-oped emission limits as an administrative tool for enforcement.[5] The control of discharges into waters has largely been based on a statutory consent system administered by specialist public bodies since 1951, and more recently under the Control of Pollution Act 1974. In a mirror image to the air pollution controls, the legislation made no provision for statu-tory water quality objectives or standards, though authorities tended to adopted a quality objective approach as an aid to setting standards. There remains controversy as to whether this approach was always explicit or as conscious as Government would sometimes have it believed.[6] The most recent pollution control provisions under the Water Act 1989 and more particularly Part I Environmental Protection Act 1990 have rendered this long-standing dichotomy almost obsolete, at least in formal legal terms. Even the European Commis-sion with its much smaller Directorate-General for the Environment shows similar signs

[2] Examples include Alkali etc Works Regulation Act 1906, Public Health Act 1936, Rivers (Prevention of Pollution) Acts 1951 and 1961, Clean Air Acts 1956 and 1968, and Deposit of Poisonous Wastes Act 1972.

[3] See R Macrory, 'Legislation, Enforcement, and the Courts' in *National Society for Clean Air 55th Annual Conference Proceedings* (Brighton, National Society for Clean Air, 1988); R Macrory 'UK Pollution Controls' in *Environmental Regulation in the European Community Conference Proceedings* (London, Legal Studies and Services, 1989).

[4] For a recent critique see Davies, 'The United States: Experiment and Fragmentation' in Haigh and Irwin (eds), *Integrated Pollution Control* (Washington, DC, Conservation Foundation, 1990).

[5] See Department of the Environment, 'Best Practicable Means: General Principles and Practice', BPM Notes 1/88 (London, 1988).

[6] Haigh, *EEC Environmental Policy and Britain – An Essay and a Handbook* (London, Environmental Data Services, 1984); Renshaw, 'Water Quality Objectives and Standards' in Gower (ed), *Water Quality in Catchment Ecosystems* (Chichester, John Wiley & Sons, 1980).

of disaggregation in its internal organisation leading to inconsistencies in principle and even differences in fundamental terminology used in Community legislation. Just to take one example, the term 'limit value' has been used in water pollution Directives to imply minimum standards applicable to discharge emissions, and in strong and pointed contrast to the term, 'quality objective', which indicates the standard of the receiving environment.[3] In those Directives relating to air quality, however, the term 'limit value' is also used but in exactly the opposite sense, and is equivalent to a quality objective.[7] Other examples abound, and are again no doubt in part caused by the internal administrative divisions. It is only at the beginning of this year that the Directorate-General has been reorganised to reflect the need for a rather more co-ordinated approach towards industrial emissions. The internal administrative units of DG XI (Environment, Nuclear Safety, and Civil Protection) were reorganised in early 1990 to reflect new priorities. Previous arrangements contained explicit divisions between technical units for water and air pollution; under the new system, one unit is dealing wholly with 'industrial installations'.

The Environmental Protection Act 1990

Despite its title, the Environmental Protection Act 1990 encompasses only a relatively discrete area of the law relating to the environment. Nevertheless, Part I of the Act introduces the concept of integrated pollution control, and for a specified and limited number of industrial processes will provide a common set of legal controls over physical emissions of whatever type, be they to land, air, or water. This itself represents a major legal advance, and a conscious attempt to produce a single, co-ordinated set of regulatory rules, albeit within a limited sector of industry.[8] If one goes on to take a broader view to encompass the most recent legislative items in the field of pollution control generally, certain common policy themes do now emerge. Formerly divergent legal approaches are being brought into line with each other. I am not convinced that, until the most recent provisions concerning integrated pollution control, these developments took place under the direction of clearly articulated and co-ordinated policies. Nevertheless, the results represent, for the first time in this country, the gradual formulation of a number of consistent legal principles in this field. I will argue that these will have profound and often unpredictable implications to those responsible for enforcement of the resulting controls and the public concerned with their implementation.

Much of the focus of pollution control has been on the direct discharges or deposits from industrial sources. A key legal control mechanism has long been the licensing or authorisation of potential sources, coupled with the establishment of specialist regulatory bodies responsible for the setting of licences and their enforcement. This basic approach will continue to underly much of pollution law. But while the licence mechanism is, of course, familiar in many jurisdictions, it is worth emphasising a number of points of

---

[7] See, eg Directive 80/779/EEC on Air Quality Limit Values and Guide Values for Sulphur Dioxide and Suspended Particulates, plus Directives 85/203/EEC for Nitrogen Dioxide and 82/884/EEC for Lead. In these Directives the term 'limit value' is used in contrast with the term 'guide values' to indicate a mandatory as opposed to a discretionary standard.

[8] For background policy discussion, see Department of the Environment/Welsh Office, 'Integrated Pollution Control', Consultation Paper (July 1988).

British practice which have long played a critical role in shaping the context of this type of regulation.

Legal sanctions for non-compliance for licence conditions or the avoidance of a licence has been based on a combination of criminal penalties and administrative sanctions, such as the revocation of a licence. The concept of civil penalties, well developed in United States environmental laws, is not to be found in equivalent British legislation. Indeed, outside the field of taxation, civil penalties have been little favoured by policy makers – though the emergence of automatic customer payments or credits for failure to comply with performance standards under the Water Act 1989 perhaps represent a cautious and modest shift of approach.[9] Administrative procedures and criminal enforcement have to a large extent been intertwined. The same public bodies have tended to be responsible for both licensing and the enforcement of criminal sanctions, and in many instances have an option as to which route to employ – eg whether to threaten a criminal prosecution or to revoke a licence. In practice, local or regional authorities may adopt different approaches, some finding the use or threat of administrative sanctions more effective that criminal proceedings, and vice versa.[10]

The Use of the Criminal Law

The structures of the legal controls similarly overlap criminal and administrative provisions. Typically, one finds a criminal offence concerning pollution coupled with a statutory defence of acting in accordance with a licence.

From a perspective of administrative management, this type of legal structure is efficient. Social-legal studies of pollution control authorities, though, have shown the extent to which the emphasis on smooth environmental administration rather than law enforcement as such has encouraged a non-confrontational relationship between regulators and those they regulate.[11] Reinforcing what has been effectively a large measure of leeway by the enforcement authority to determine what level of emissions or discharge should be licensed or not has been the general principle that gives a discretion to enforcement authorities to decide whether or not to take legal action in respect of suspected or even admitted offences. In other fields of criminal law, this discretion has been held to be one that is essentially a matter of operational judgement by authorities and one that is virtually unreviewable by the courts.[12] Even this picture, though, is not entirely consistent. The provisions of Part III of the Water Act 1989 concerning water pollution contain no

---

[9] See Water Supply and Sewerage Services (Customer Services Standards) Regulations 1989, SI 1989/1147, as amended. Under these regulations, made under Water Act 1989, the failure by an undertaker to conform to certain standards (such as keeping a domestic appointment) can result in a £5 daily payment or credit to the customer affected.

[10] Macrory and Withers, 'Application of Administrative and Criminal Punishments concerning Hazardous Waste in England', report for European Commission (London, Imperial College Centre for Environmental Technology, 1985).

[11] The best recent UK accounts in the environmental field are K Hawkins, *Environment and Enforcement: Regulation and the Social Definition of Pollution* (Oxford, Clarendon Press, 1984); J Richardson et al, *Policing Pollution: A Study of Regulation and Enforcement* (Oxford, Clarendon Press, 1982).

[12] See *R y Metropolitan Police Commissioner ex p Blackburn* (1968) 2 QB 118; *R v Metropolitan Police Commissioner ex p Blackburn (No 3)* (1973) QB 24.

obligations on the National Rivers Authority as to how it should exercise its powers in respect of suspected offences. (The key pollution offence is section 107 of the Water Act 1989. Significantly, there is no restriction on who may bring prosecutions.) Part III of the Control of Pollution Act, though, concerning noise pollution, required local authorities to service a statutory notice once they are satisfied of the existence of a noise nuisance – an obligation clearly more honoured in its breach in practice, as annual statistics reveal.[13] Section 14 of the Environmental Protection Act, relating to integrated pollution control and air pollution, will oblige enforcement authorities to serve a prohibition notice once they are satisfied that a process within their jurisdiction is carried on 'with a severe risk to the environment'. A similar position on enforcement exists in the United States where the Environmental Protection Agency has resisted legal interpretations that would compel its exercise of enforcement powers.[14] The US courts, too, have supported the presumption of discretion in the absence of explicit statutory provisions, and in at least one case have gone as far as to interpret the statutory obligation that the EPA 'shall' take enforcement action in respect of violations still to imply a discretion.[15]

In England and Wales, at least, an authority's discretion is tempered by the general principle that prosecution is not an exclusive function of public agencies – a position that can be contrasted with that in countries such as West Germany or the Netherlands. Subject to express statutory restrictions, any individual, whether or not they have a legal interest in the matter, may initiate private prosecutions – the closest that British law has come to developing the concept of citizen's suits. The power to impose restrictions on the right to prosecute in any particular statute in turn demands a policy response by government on the issue, and the differing positions that have existed in British pollution demonstrate some degree of unease with the subject. Until 1974 restrictions existed in the field of water pollution, but were removed under Part II of the Control of Pollution Act, and were not reintroduced in replacement provisions under the Water Act 1989. Part I of that Act contained no restrictions in the field of waste disposal, but Part II of the Environmental Protection Act, which will replace these provisions, originally provided that proceedings in respect of offences for uncontrolled deposit could not be initiated without the consent of the Director of Public Prosecutions of a waste regulation authority.[16] This restriction no longer appeared in the Bill when it was presented to the House of Lords. Legislation concerning emissions into the air from scheduled processes restricted private prosecution, but these will no longer apply in the new provisions governing integrated pollution control and air pollution under Part I of the Environmental Protection Act. We are therefore reaching a position where the principle of the availability of private prosecution in the field of most areas of pollution control (radioactive waste disposal being the main exception) has been accepted – its use in practice by environmental groups and other members of the public, and the effect of its availability on the behaviour of regulatory agencies will be an increasingly fruitful area for research.

The legal provisions and principles concerning enforcement might be described as the micro-end of the process. At the macro-end, one of the most distinctive characteristics of

---

[13] See s 58 Control of Pollution Act 1974. The provisions have now been replaced by Part III Environmental Protection Act 1990.

[14] See Reich and Shea, 'A Survey of US Environmental Enforcement Authorities, Tools and Remedies' in International Enforcement Workshop Proceedings (the Netherlands Ministry of Housing, Physical Planning and Environment, 1990).

[15] See *State Water Control Board v Train* 559 F 2d 921 (4th Circuit 1977).

[16] Cl 25(10) of Bill as published.

British pollution laws has been the extent to which the legal provisions have been largely absent of statutory policy goals or precise standards, whether they relate to the content of emissions or the quality of the receiving environment. Where standards have appeared, they have classically been expressed in open-textured language, providing general guidance on performance (such as 'best practical means') or the quality of the product released or emitted ('wholesome' water[17]). The tendency has in part been encouraged by prevailing scientific approaches which emphasised the need to examine the particular receiving environment before determining its capacity to handle potential pollution loads, a principle which was considered would be compromised by the setting of statutory standards which by their nature have a generic effect. Foreign observers, particularly from the United States, have emphasised the peculiar constitutional characteristics of law-making in this country which give the Executive near unfettered power to determine the detailed content of both primary and secondary legislation.[18] In the absence of powerful political pressure, whether domestic or international, the inclination of an executive will be to strive for legislative flexibility and at the very least to avoid placing uncomfortable legal obligations on itself.

Policy and Pollution Control

Pollution control authorities have not, of course, denied themselves the use of technical standards nor have they shrunk from formulating explicit policy goals – but from a legal perspective the significant feature is that these developments have taken place administratively. The use of such broad language as 'best practicable means' in legislative provisions, rich as it is in ambiguity, would at first sight – and especially in a common law jurisdiction – have appeared to have offered a significant opportunity for extensive judicial interpretation. But the enforcement discretion available to regulatory authorities and the prevailing administrative culture which resisted making use of the courts as a testing ground has resulted in a remarkably low level of high-level case law in the field. The fact that the key criterion of industrial air pollution legislation for over 100 years, 'the best practical means', has never been the subject of case-law in the higher courts provides the starkest example of this distinctive feature of the law in this field.[19]

Fundamental legal changes concerning this question of policy expression are now taking place. Statutory environmental quality standards have recently made their first appearance. The 1989 Air Quality Standards[20] introduce into British pollution legislation the concept of legal air quality standards and represent a clear reversal of the preferred

---

[17] See s 38 Health and Safety at Work etc Act 1974. See R Macrory, 'Science, Legislation and the Courts' in GR Conway (ed), *The Assessment of Environmental Problems* (London, Imperial College Centre for Environmental Technology, 1986).

[18] For a general comparison see Vogel, *National Styles of Regulation: Environ-mental Policy in Great Britain and the United States* (Ithaca, NY, Cornell University Press, 1986).

[19] For over 100 years, the general legal duty for operators of many industrial premises was 'to use the best practicable means' to prevent or render harmless emissions into the atmosphere: see s 5(1) Health and Safety at Work etc Act 1974. The phrase has been considered in the context of these controls in at least one case, before an Industrial Tribunal, and another before a Crown Court, but there is no reported decision of the higher courts on the points. Nor is there ever likely to be since the controls have now been replaced by new statutory provisions under Part I Environmental Protection Act 1990.

[20] Air Quality Standards Regulations 1989, SI 1989/31 7.

policy approach, established by the Royal Commission on Environmental Pollution in 1976.[21] Statutory water quality-objectives have begun to be introduced under the Water Act 1989,[22] brought about in part by the initial plans for water privatisation where the government accepted the logic that were the whole water industry placed in the private sector only legal standards would ensure that a non-public body pursued public policy aims.[23] The revised plans for creating the National Rivers Authority invalidated that argument from a purely domestic and administrative perspective, but by then the political advantages of such mechanisms, coupled with pressure from the European Community, ensured the policy shift was maintained.[24] These mechanisms provide visible and binding policy goals on government and public authorities, and will provide a new critical base for judging their individual administrative decisions. The change is not confined to environmental quality objectives. The quality standard for drinking water for human consumption under the Water Act 1989 retains the familiar criterion, 'wholesome' but detailed regulations now provided the technical criteria for interpreting the concept of wholesomeness.[25] Standards for emissions from industrial sources such as large combustion plants and municipal incinerators have been agreed at Community law level in recent years, and will undoubtedly be transposed into national law.[26] The Environmental Protection Act 1990 goes much further, and in relation to integrated pollution and air pollution provides the most extensive power to the Secretary of State to set a range of various types of standards by regulation including, in relation to emissions of specified substances limits on 'the concentration, the amount or the amount in any period of that substance which may be so released'[27] and the establishment of quality objectives or standards for any environmental medium.[28] These developments have mainly been in the field of air and water pollution and one can see a distinct convergence of policy approach in these two fields. Statutory standards in relation to waste disposal on land and soil contamination have yet to be seen in this country, though they must be on the horizon. Following a request from the Council of Ministers, the European Commission is in the process of producing a draft Directive on standards for landfill, and its eventual adoption would require national legislation on the subject. As to soil quality, the House of Commons Select Committee in a report on land contamination earlier this year called for the introduction of a range of legally binding soil quality objectives – not as rigid as those implemented in a country such as the Netherlands but legal innovation in this country.[29]

[21] Royal Commission on Environmental Pollution, *Air Pollution Control: An Integrated Approach*, Fifth Report, Cmnd 6371 (London, HMSO, 1976).

[22] See, eg Surface Water (Classification) Regulations 1989, SI 1989/1148, Surface Water (Dangerous Substances) (Classification) Regulations 1989, SI 1989/2286. Statutory classification under s 104 Water Act 1989 is the first step towards the making of statutory water quality objectives under s 105 of the same Act.

[23] Department of the Environment/Welsh Office, 'The Water Environment – the Next Steps', Consultation Paper (April 1986).

[24] See Department of Environment, Ministry of Agriculture Fisheries and Food, and Welsh Office, 'The National Rivers Authority: the Government's Proposals for a Public Regulatory Body in a Privatised Water Industry' (July 1987). For analysis of the Water Act see Macrory R, *The Water Act 1989: Text and Commentary* (London, Sweet & Maxwell, 1990).

[25] Water Supply (Water Quality) Regulations 1989, SI 1989/1147, as amended.

[26] EC Directive 88/609/EEC of 24 November 1988 on the Limitation of Emissions of Certain Pollutants into the Air from Large Combustion Plants; EC Directive 89/369/EEC of 8 June 1989 on the Prevention of Air Pollution from New Municipal Waste Incineration Plants.

[27] Environmental Protection Act 1990, s 3(2)(a).

[28] Ibid, s 3(4).

[29] House of Commons Environment Committee, *Contaminated Land*, First Report, Session 1989–90 (London, HMSO, 1990).

We are therefore entering a new era of legal formalism in relation to pollution standards and objectives. The long-familiar preferred approach of a legal framework concentrating on administrative structure and procedures, leaving policy content to the realm of shadow mechanisms such as circulars or technical notes no longer holds true.

European Community Influences

Doctrines of European law have undoubtedly provided an underlying dynamic for change. Most Community environmental legislation has been made by means of Directives which according to Article 189 of the Treaty are binding on the Member States as to the result to be achieved but leaves a discretion as to the form and methods for implementing those aims. Case law of the European Court of Justice has elaborated on the extent to which this is an open discretion, and a series of decisions has held that, at least where the Directive concerns matters of harmonisation or affects the rights of individuals they must be transposed in a manner that is clear and certain.[30] Administrative practices and circulars which can be changed at the whim of national authorities have therefore been held as insufficient means of transposition. But there remain grey areas in the current state of case law on the subject, and at least one of the leading textbooks on Community law suggests that where a Member State's previous rules had been in the form of circulars, implementation of a subsequent Directive by circular should be sufficient.[31] Nevertheless the Commission has rejected such an interpretation, and pushed hard for implementation by legal means, probably going further than the present state of case law warrants. After initial resistance, the United Kingdom appears to have largely accepted the Commission's approach

Conclusions

Two other policy themes are reflected in the emerging legislation. The 1974 Control of Pollution Act introduced new public rights to information concerning the detailed workings of the licensing system by means of public registers. These were restricted to waste disposal and surface water pollution control, but are now to be extended generally to the field of integrated pollution control and air pollution under the Environmental Protection Act.[32] The Water Act 1989 made the trade effluent consents to sewers available to public scrutiny for the first time.[33] Again here we see the emergence of a general principle which will now make it hard to resist the presumption of open registers. The European Community's Directive on Freedom of Access to Environmental Information goes a good deal

---

[30] Key cases are *EC v Belgium* (1982) 2 CMLR 622; *EC v Netherlands* (1982) ECR 171. For a discussion of the case law see Macrory, 'Industrial Air Pollution Legislation: Implementing the European Framework' in *National Society for Clean Air 55th Annual Conference Proceedings* (Brighton, National Society for Clean Air, 1988).

[31] Kapteyn and van Themaat, *Introduction to the Law of the European Communities*, 2nd edn, ed L Gormley (Deventer, Kluwer, 1989).

[32] Environmental Protection Act 1990, s 20.

[33] Public Health (Drainage of Premises) Act 1937, s 7A, as inserted by Water Act 1989, sch 8.

further than simply making available registers of consents. Under the Directive[34] public authorities would be required to make available any information relating to the environment in their possession. This will include, according to the definitions in the Directive, information on the state of water, air, soil, fauna, land or natural sites and on activities or measures likely to adversely affect them and on measures designed to protect them.[35] Derogations are provided where matters relate to judicial proceedings, for example, or trade and industrial secrecy, and where the request is 'manifestly unreasonable'.[36] Nevertheless, the Directive is likely to major advance in principle in this area.

These provisions concerning registers and associated information can be characterised as passive environmental legal rights. Obligations to involve members of the public in participating in the actual decision making on individual consent applications represent a more active form of right. In the United Kingdom, the town and country planning system has long provided the most extensive possibilities of participation, while pollution control has largely been a closed system. As with registers, Part II of the Control of Pollution Act marked a first shift in principle in this country, by providing for participation and consultation where consents for discharges into waters were concerned.[37] Again, one can now detect an extension of the principle to other areas of pollution control, though perhaps with a greater degree of caution than for registers. The Environmental Protection Act now provides for the possibility of public consultation and public inquiries where applications of licences under the integrated and air pollution provisions are made.[38] Public consultation for waste disposal is still largely subsumed under development control procedures. In this context, it should be stressed that the requirements for environmental assessment for certain types of development, introduced in 1988 as a result of the Community Directive on the subject,[39] ensure that pollution implications and control strategies are intimately linked into the planning procedures.

Public registers, participation procedures, statutory environmental policy goals and standards, together with rights of private prosecution form a potent mixture unfamiliar to British practice. The rapid process of legal change produces its own institutional dynamic evidenced by the sudden increase of major law firms now offering specialist advice on the interpretation and implications of the new law. (One indicator of the growth in interest is the rapid increase of membership of the UK Environmental Law Association, founded in 1986 with an initial membership of around 40. Five years later there were over 1,000 members.) For the public authorities charged with day to day application of the controls, we may not yet have reached what Richard Stewart described as 'transmission belt justice',[40] but undoubtedly they will be operating in a more constrained framework, and will be obliged to develop a more formal and detached relationship with those that they regulate.

To those who argue that legal obligations should be transparent and should be obeyed the developments will be welcome. But some dangers should be noted. Legal standards

---

[34] EC Directive 90/31/EEC of 7 June 1990 on the Freedom of Access to Informatiron on the Environment.

[35] Ibid, Art 2(a).

[36] Ibid, Art 3.3.

[37] Control of Pollution Act 1974, s 41. For a critical analysis of their use in practice see Burton, 'Access to Environmental Information: the UK Experience of Water Registers' (1989) 1(2) *Journal of Environmental Law* 192.

[38] Environmental Protection Act 1990, s 6 and sch 1.

[39] EC Directive 85/337/EEC of 27 June 1985 on the Assessment of the Effects of Certain Public and Private Projects on the Environment.

[40] RB Stewart, 'The Reformation of American Administrative Law' (1975) 88 *Harvard Law Review* 1667.

by their inherent nature lack flexibility and are slow to change, even when transmitted by secondary legislation. Technical standards that are clothed in legal form assume a quasi-moral justification which may obscure scientific unsoundness. At a Community level, where so many standards are now first developed, securing agreement to change is as complex and time-consuming a process as agreeing a Directive in the first place. Even moves towards establishing procedures for rapid adaptation and upgrading by technical committees can be subject to the charge of constitutional impropriety as witnessed by the difficulties in securing unanimous agreement to proposed new powers for technical committees in the field of water pollution.[41]

In some respects, formalised policy goals and standards enshrined in the law simplify the operation of a consent system. But they also add a new form of complexity. The opportunities to raise legal challenges to the validity of an individual licence or consent on the grounds of incompatibility with legal standards or quality objectives are enhanced even taking on board the somewhat cautious language of some of the legal provisions that now make the formal connection between legal policy and operational decisions (for example, under the Air Quality Standards Regulations 1989, the Secretary of State 'shall take any appropriate measures to ensure' that the prescribed air quality standards are not exceeded. If he granted a planning permission that would be likely to result in local breaches, would his decision be challengeable on the basis of this duty?). The possibility of legal challenge has immediate implications for the regulator but it may in the future raise the type of complex jurisprudential questions on the relationship between criminal administrative law already well developed in West German environmental law (the concept of 'Verwaltungsakzessorietat' (roughly, the subordination of criminal law to administrative law) is discussed in Ensenbach (1989) *Die Probleme der Verwaltungsakzessorielat im Umweltstrafrecht,* Frankfurt). Suppose a company raises a statutory defence to a charge of discharging effluent into waters on the grounds that it acted in accordance with consent. The consent is then proved to be invalid on the grounds that the authority was acting contrary to statutory objectives or policies, or even simply Community obligations. No criminal intent is required for this sort of offence, but can the defence be raised? The solution, to avoid the prospect of retrospective liability, may be to find the consent voidable rather than void, but it is no doubt the type of question that will be required to be explored before too long.

Finally it is important to recognise the possible contradiction between policy formalism of the type I have described and participation procedures of the sort being developed. The expectations aroused by increased legal rights concerning public comment and participation in individual consent procedures will be frustrated the more that fundamental policy questions and applicable standards have been predetermined in the applicable legislation. As a matter of law, it may be that public involvement will have to be confined to the application of nationally prescribed policies to particular local situations, areas still untouched by the relevant law, or for a call for stricter environmental standards to the case in hand to the extent that the legal framework allows for this. It remains to be seen whether these opportunities will prove sufficient to satisfied public needs. However, the trend towards policy formalism is now, I believe, a committed policy approach in this field, and one that is now irreversible. As a result, the exercise of discretion in determining contemporary environmental standards has shifted from the immediate regulators to other fora, reducing the significance of local participation procedures. More than ever it therefore becomes

---

[41] See (January 1989) 168 *ENDS Report* 27.

important to examine critically the procedures surrounding policy development both at central government and Community level. These are constitutional questions that go beyond the immediate subject of pollution control or environmental regulation but they are legitimate issues of great importance all the same.

18

Cycle Lore[1]
(1979)

Cyclists and the Law

The past few years has seen a remarkable revival in the use of the bicycle[2] in urban areas. Hoping, no doubt, to cut down on both transport costs and coronaries, many people now cycle to work, and there are even a fair number of bicycles to be seen chained to railings in the Temple. An All-party Parliamentary Cycle Group was established recently in the House of Commons, and staff solely concerned with cycles have been appointed at the Department of Transport. But as politicians and planners begin to examine seriously better ways of protecting and encouraging the cyclist, a number of intriguing problems and uncertainties have been revealed in the present law relating to cycles.

The legal difficulties surrounding the construction of cycle racks is just one example — though happily one that has now been resolved by the Transport Act 1978. Under the Road Traffic Regulation Act 1967, highway authorities possess general powers to provide on-street parking for all types of vehicles, including cycles. But the erection of a cycle-rack on the side of a carriageway or footway (ie the pavement) would create an obstruction of the highway, and a long line of cases has established that public authorities who wish to create such obstructions must have explicit statutory authority to do so. For instance, the statutory power to provide public lavatories in 'proper and convenient' places was held not to be sufficient to authorise their construction on any part of the highway.[3] Public authorities have been given express powers in a number of statutes to erect street furniture such as traffic signs, lamp stands, bus-shelters and even, under the Public Health Act 1925, 'troughs for watering horses and cattle'. Somehow, they were never given similar powers to erect cycle-racks (though it is arguable that section 46 of the Road Traffic Regulation Act 1967 gives parish councils sufficiently explicit powers), and most highway authorities are therefore unwilling to construct cycle-racks on roads or pavements, even when this might be the most convenient position; one London borough council, however, eager to provide for cyclists, was known studiously to ignore the concern of their legal department, should a pedestrian be injured by such an illegal obstruction.

The position over cycle-racks has now at long last been cleared up by the Transport Act 1978, section 12 of which provides, 'The powers of any authority under the Road Traffic

---

[1] R Macrory, 'Cycle Lore', *New Law Journal*, 21 June 1979, 602.

[2] This article is mainly concerned with bicycles, though the term 'cycle' includes tricycles and other pedal-powered vehicles.

[3] *Vernon v St James Westminster Vestry* (1860) 16 Ch 449.

Regulation Act 1967 to provide parking places shall extend to providing, in roads and elsewhere, stands and racks for bicycles'.

'Driving a Carriage' and Other Legal Conundrums

The cyclist who is on the search for newly erected cycle-racks may also experience some legal difficulties. Section 76 of the Highway Act 1835 makes riding a cycle on the footway a criminal offence, and despite the antiquity of the statute, it remains the main control over this activity.[4] Surprisingly, it may also be illegal to wheel or push a cycle along a pavement, since section 76 goes on to make it an offence to 'drive . . . any carriage' on the footway. A cycle is certainly 'a carriage' for the purposes of this section,[5] while the meaning of 'drive', a term which appears in a number of traffic offences, has been considered by the court in several cases, though all concerning motor vehicles. At one time these suggested that a person pushing a vehicle could be said to drive it, provided it was subject to his control and direction – a test that would include someone wheeling a cycle. But in *R v McDonagh* [1974] QB 448, an appeal from a conviction of driving while disqualified, the Divisional Court disapproved of an artificial use of the word. Where

> the defendant was walking beside a vehicle which was being pushed or moving by gravity, we do not think that the mere fact that he had his hand on the steering wheel is enough to say he was driving in any ordinary sense of the word.[6]

The Court went on to say that someone pushing a motorcycle, an example of a vehicle which 'must from [its] nature be manhandled from time to time', could not be said to 'drive' it in the context of licence and insurance offences. Despite this ruling, it could be argued that since the Highway Act 1835 creates an offence specifically designed to protect the rights of the pedestrian to free passage of the footway, the term, 'drive', in section 76 should be given a broader interpretation than in other traffic offences. At least one local authority is reported to be unhappy at exercising their new powers to erect cycle-racks on the pavement, because this would encourage cyclists to commit what, in its opinion, is the illegal act of pushing a cycle across the footway. And, while the writer has yet to hear of someone being successfully prosecuted for this, there was a cyclist in 1973 who was stopped by a policeman when pushing his bicycle along a pavement in Farnborough; he was later sent a letter by the officer-in-charge, advising him that he had committed an offence under the Highway Act 1835, and trusting that, 'in future you will be more careful'.

The cyclist who wheels his machine across a zebra crossing appears to be at a legal disadvantage in comparison to pedestrians. The Pedestrian Crossing Regulations (SI 1971/1524) provide that, 'Every footpassenger on the carriageway within the limits of an uncontrolled pedestrian crossing shall have precedence within those limits over any vehicle and the driver shall accord such precedence to the footpassenger if the footpassenger is on the carriageway'. Failure to give way to a footpassenger in these circumstances is an offence, but there is no statutory definition of the term 'footpassenger' and it is

---

[4] Written Answer, John Horam, Under-Secretary of State for Transport, House of Commons, 11 November 1977.
[5] *Taylor v Goodwin* (1879) 4 QBD 228.
[6] Lord Widgery CJ at 452.

unclear whether it would include someone pushing a cycle. The only reported case of relevance is *McKerril v Robertson* 1956 SLT 290, a Scottish case concerning similarly worded regulations. A driver was charged with failing to give way to a footpassenger on a zebra-crossing, namely a woman who had just pushed a child's go-chair onto the crossing. The court rejected the defence that she was not a footpassenger:

> In my view this is much too strict a construction of the regulations in question and would produce anomalous, if not ridiculous results. In my view it is essential to treat this lady and the go-chair which she was controlling as parts of one entity.

But it is possible to argue that a cycle, essentially treated in law as a vehicle to be ridden on the carriageway, is distinguishable from a go-chair or pram which cannot but be pushed by a pedestrian. *Wilkinson on Road Traffic Offences* (9th edn) supports this view at page 451, and in 1977 Staffordshire magistrates dismissed a charge, where a driver had failed to give way to a woman pushing a cycle across a zebra-crossing, on the grounds that she was not a 'footpassenger' for the purpose of the regulations.

Cyclists are often seen to dismount at traffic lights showing red, and push their machines across the junction. It is uncertain whether they thereby commit an offence, under section 22 of the Road Traffic Act 1972, of failing to comply with prescribed traffic regulation signs. And what of the cyclists who pushes his bicycle in the road – carefully avoiding the pavement and a possible charge under the Highway Act 1835 – the wrong way up a one-way street? A prosecution on these facts has been successful in a magistrates' court.[7]

Constructing a Cycleway

But it is probably the highway authorities, seeking to make positive plans for the cyclist, who suffer most from some of the present uncertainties in the law. The variety of schemes that can help cyclists has recently been outlined by the government,[8] but the legal method of implementing these schemes is by no means clear in all cases.

Section 66 of the Highways Act 1959 gives highway authorities specific power to construct 'cycle-tracks', but only 'in or by the side of' an existing highway. Some authorities are known to have been discouraged from building cycle-tracks which do not follow existing roads because of this apparent limitation in the Highways Act. However, it has been pointed out that authorities possess general powers to construct 'highways' under section 26 of the Act, and since a 'cycle-track' is defined in section 295 as a 'way *constituting* or comprised in a highway', the section 26 powers are available to build cycle-tracks that do not run beside a road.

There is not always the space or finance to build a new cycle-track, and, in some circumstances, it may make planning sense to move the cyclist off the carriageway and onto part of the footway beside the road. This might be appropriate where, say, there is a busy main road with a little-used, but wide pavement. But this cannot be achieved by simply

---

[7] CXI Justice of the Peace and Local Government Review, 22 November 1947, 679.

[8] Department of Transport, 'Ways of Helping Cyclists in Built-up Areas', Local Transport Note 1/78 (November 1978).

painting a white line down the footway and revoking any existing bye-laws which may forbid cycling on the pavement. The 1835 statutory offence still remains, and anyone may bring a prosecution under the Act. Furthermore, it has been held that the fact that no pedestrian was present at the time of the alleged offence, and that the cyclist was exercising all due care is not a good defence.[9]

In these circumstances, it seems that the authority must 'remove' a proportion of the footway, using their powers under section 67(3) of the Highways Act, and then construct a cycle-track under section 66. But the powers under section 66 are limited to 'constructing', and there is no statutory definition of the term. It may be uneconomical to lay a new surface, but 'construct' seems to imply something more than simply painting white lines and erecting appropriate signs. As yet, the point does not appear to have been discussed in English courts, though a New Zealand case, *Kerridge Odeon Corpn Ltd v Auckland City* [1966] NZLR 266, concerned with building regulations, provides some guidance.

> Giving the phrase, 'construction of a building', its ordinary signification and natural meaning, I am of the opinion that it connotes something different from maintenance, repairs or alteration to an existing building or portion thereof.[10]

The division of an existing pavement may not be possible if it is quite narrow. Where the pedestrian flow is extremely small, it may still sometimes be safer to allow cyclists to ride on it, but with an obligation to give way to pedestrians. Present traffic law does not appear to make provision for such a concept, and the closest analogy is that of bridleways, on which cyclists may ride but must give way to persons both on horseback and on foot.[11] But the conversion of such footways into bridleways hardly seems an elegant solution.

A footpath (defined in the Highways Act 1959 as 'a highway over which the public have rights of way on foot only, not being a footway') also presents difficulties to the planner. In contrast to footways, cycling on footpaths is not a criminal offence, though it is probably actionable in nuisance and trespass, and may well be prohibited by local bye-laws. In some cases, it may be sensible to permit the use of cycles on footpaths, but there appears to be no general power in highway law to upgrade a footpath to a bridleway or other form of highway on which cyclists have a right to ride. The solution suggested by the Department of Transport[12] is that the local authority should first obtain planning permission for development entailing a change of use of the footpath into a way usable by vehicles: 'The footpath could then be stopped up by an order under section 209 or section 210 of the Town and Country Planning Act 1971, and a new way provided along the same route but usable by a wider category of traffic'.

Traffic Law Neglects the Bicycle

The law has to try to reflect the sometimes conflicting interests of users of the highway, whether they be on foot, on a cycle or in a motor vehicle. But the cycle possesses some unu-

---

[9] *McKee v McGrath* (1892) 30 LR Ir 41.
[10] Per Greason J at 269.
[11] Countryside Act 1968, s 30(1).
[12] Local Transport Note 1/78, above n 8.

sual characteristics: it is extremely vulnerable to motor traffic, is easily pushed or wheeled, but, when ridden, is potentially dangerous to pedestrians (though studies of foreign mixed cyclist–pedestrian facilities show surprisingly low accident rates). The special needs of the cyclist appear to have been somewhat neglected in traffic law, and for those highway authorities who now wish to initiate cycle schemes, especially in urban areas, some of the present legal difficulties may prove discouraging obstacles. Perhaps the time has come for a revival of the type of delightful but important case which was often brought by (and sometimes against) cyclists towards the turn of the century, at a time when the cycle had yet to feel the squeeze of the motor vehicle. Cases such as *Cannan v Earl of Abingdon* [1900] 2 QB 66, where an imaginative cyclists' club determined to test the applicability of a Local Act authorising the Earl of Abingdon to collect tolls on a bridge over the Thames to a number of different kinds of cycle. The Act provided a toll of 2d for 'carriages with less than four wheels', but no charge for the driver or any person riding in a carriage. The following cycles were solemnly ridden over the bridge: a bicycle carrying the rider alone; a bicycle with a valise fitted to its frame; a tricycle carrying the rider alone; a trademan's tricycle with a box fitted to its frame for carrying goods; and, finally, a bath-chair tricycle with a passenger (as well as the rider) seated in it. Unfortunately for the club's finances, in a special case stated for the opinion of the court, all were held to be 'carriages with less than four wheels' within the meaning of the Act.

Part IV

The Courts and the Environment

Courts play a critical role in interpreting legislation and developing substantive principles of law, and in this country the last 20 years has seen an ever-growing influence of the higher courts in the environmental field. For many years I have reported on significant case law in the monthly environmental intelligence journal *ENDS Report*, and this chapter contains a selection of reports as written at the time but with some additional footnote references. These reports, of course, by no means cover all of the important environmental decisions, but are intended to provide an impression of the range of issues the judiciary are faced with, and how they tackle them. For this second edition I have included mainly more recent cases, but some older ones are included for reasons explained below.

The last 30 years has seen an enormous growth in the scope and important of European Union environmental legislation, and as the final arbiter of the meaning of Community law, decisions of the Court of Justice of the European Union (CJEU), contained in Chapter 19, are critical. The European Court has generally been seen as environmentally progressive, though its reasoning can often be obscure and frustrating – as witnessed by the Court of Appeal's attempts in the 2007 *OSS* case, analysed in Chapter 21, to derive coherence from the CJEU's jurisprudence on when a recycled waste ceased to be waste in law. It has generally, for example, adopted a liberal approach to access to environmental information, as in *Interseroh Scrap* (2012), and was tough in applying the Aarhus provisions to the European Commission in the case brought by *Stichting Natuur en Milieu and Pesticide Action Network Europe* concerning pesticides.

The Court of Justice remains the only supranational court in the world which can directly impose financial penalties on states that fail to comply with its judgments, and the 2012 decision in *Commission v Ireland* shows that it is not afraid to impose large penalties on countries that do not comply with its judgments – here Ireland was fined a lump sum of 2 million euros and a 12,000 euros daily fine as long as its national waste legislation remained defective. The power of the court to impose direct penalties on Member States was introduced under the Lisbon Treaty amendment, and the first case where they were employed involved EU environmental law.[1] At the time of their introduction, I was rather dubious of their worth – it seemed to me that it was a sad state of affairs for the rule of law when governments (as opposed to individuals or companies) had to be threatened with financial penalties to comply with a judgment of the Court – but I have since changed my mind. Evidence suggests that even the threat of the Commission bringing sanction proceedings has concentrated national minds, and these days national finance ministries take a close interest in how their environment counterparts are implementing EU environmental law. Breaches of the application of EU environmental law in practice often

---

[1] *Commission v Greece* C-387/97 [2000] ECR I-5047.

occur at regional or local level, and in England and Wales Parts 2 and 3 of the Localism Act 2011 have introduced innovative new powers where ministers may recover financial penalties imposed by the European Court directly from local authorities and other public bodies whose acts are considered to have caused or contributed to the breach in question. There is, however, a degree of irony in the fact that it was the UK that promoted the Lisbon amendments to give the Court the power to fine: in 2014 the European Commission initiated infringement proceedings against the UK for failure to comply with 2010 EU NOx levels in some 16 air quality zones. The apparently inability of policy makers to deal effectively with traffic growth in urban areas was the main cause, and the national press took pleasure in the prospect of 300 million euros fines from the European Court,[2] though it will be a number before years before we reach that stage. And if there were a fine, possible arguments between central and local government under the Localism Act as to the real responsibility for failure could be both complex and painful.

Three earlier decisions of the Court have been included in Chapter 19. The Court of Justice has proved a powerful advocate of the Habitats Directive, as witnessed in its 2013 *Sweetman* decision. *First Corporate Shipping* (2000) was one of its earlier decisions in similar vein, where the United Kingdom was condemned for bringing in financial considerations into the task of designating protected sites under the Directive. *Re Criminal Proceedings against Bluhme* (1998) concerns the conflicts between trade and the environment, and is a classical analysis by the Court of the provisions in the Treaty which allow Member States some discretion to restrict trade for environmental reasons. These principles apply in the absence of Union legislation on the subject, but even in the case of EU single market legislation the Treaty allows some discretion to Member States to maintain or introduce stricter standards on environmental reasons. The provisions were first introduced in 1987 under the Single European Act, and heavily revised in the 1997 Amsterdam Treaty following pressure from Sweden (about to join the Union), which was concerned that European market harmonisation measures would lead to lower national environmental standards. *Denmark v Commission* (2003) was one of the first decisions of the Court to consider these provisions.

One of the recent high points demonstrating the significance of EU environmental law in a national context was the 2000 House of Lords decision in *Berkeley* dealing with the environmental assessment, analysed in Chapter 20. There had been a failure to apply the requirements of the Directive, and the House of Lords, recognising the public participation rights that were inherent in the European concept of environmental assessment, quashed the decision in question. In doing so, the House of Lords explicitly refused to follow the more traditional approach of British courts in planning judicial reviews when courts frequently refused to quash decisions on the grounds that the result would not have been different had the proper procedures been followed. *Berkeley* remains of importance, but in subsequent case law the Court of Appeal proved wary of allowing such an approach to give a green light to third parties looking for any procedural fault as an excuse to quash a controversial planning or environmental decision. In 2012, in the *Walton* decision, the Supreme Court took the opportunity of revisiting *Berkeley*, and argued that European law gave considerable more discretion to national courts than *Berkeley* indicated when it came to granting remedies – unless a claimant's rights under EU law had been infringed, a

---

[2] 'UK faces £300million fine from EU for failing to meet air pollution targets by 2010 deadline', *Daily Mail*, 21 February 2014, available at www.dailymail.co.uk (accessed on 31 March 2014). *ENDS Report* estimates it could it as much as £1.5 billion: (April 2014) 470 *ENDS Report* 33.

national court was not obliged under EU law to quash the decision in question. In a 2013 case concerning environmental assessment, the approach of the Supreme Court appears now to have been largely endorsed by the Court of Justice of the European Union.[3]

The 2014 decision of the Supreme Court in *Coventry v Lawrence* shows the extent to which common law principles of nuisance largely developed in the nineteenth century continue to engage the highest courts. The private law action remains especially important where regulators appear to be reluctant to exercise statutory controls, and it is this relationship between the modern density of planning and environmental regulations and the private rights of nuisance action that have particularly exercised the courts. In the absence of clear provisions providing statutory immunity, there are, as the judgments in *Coventry* indicate, no simple answers. The most significant long-term implication of *Coventry* is the Supreme Court's willingness to release judges from the shackles of the Court of Appeal's 1895 *Shelfer*[4] decision, where the court held that in nuisance cases involving continuing interference courts should only grant damages in lieu of an injunction in very narrow circumstances and where the nuisance was minor. Following the *Coventry* decision, it will no longer be the case that an injunction follows 'as of right' in a successful nuisance action, and judges will have to engage, as do many US courts, in an exercise of weighing up the public interest of the defendant's activity continuing at a price, as against protecting claimant's private interests. Economists would argue that for the polluter to compensate those suffering for his right to pollute is often the best solution from an economic perspective. The *Coventry* decision, though not without difficulties, is to be welcomed for a fresh approach which implicitly acknowledges that our contemporary system often does not provide sufficient compensation for those who suffer in the wider public interest.

Yet equally, and in contrast to many courts – say, in the United States or in India – the British judiciary are clearly still cautious in trespassing too much on areas where they perceive specialist bodies are best equipped to make the complex technical and economic judgments so often inherent in modern environmental decision making – the 2004 *Marcic* decision of the House of Lords (investment in new sewerage systems) clearly indicates that the regulatory bodies rather than the courts are best equipped to determine investment priorities. Similarly, the 2007 decision of the House of Lords in *R on the application of National Grid Gas plc* shows that the courts are unlikely to go beyond the clear words of the legislation in determining which bodies should be liable for cleaning up; sites contaminated by past industrial activities.

The Human Rights Act 1998, incorporating the European Convention on Human Rights into UK law, has given rise to much litigation, but perhaps has had less impact in the environmental field than some predicted. This may be in part because the Convention contains no express environmental rights, though the European Court of Human Rights has showed itself quite willing to give an environmental dimension to other rights contained in the convention.[5] The 2001 decision of the House of Lords in *Alconbury* is included here as one of the first examples of major litigation where the Human Rights Act could have had significant institutional implications on long-established ways of handling planning appeals. Indeed, if the House of Lords had decided against the government, a

---

[3] CJEU Case C-72/12 *Gemeinde Altrip et al v Land Rheinland-Pfaiz* 7 November 2013).
[4] *Shelfer v City of London Electric Lighting Co* (1895) 1 Ch 287 Court.
[5] For example, *Lopez Ostra v Spain* (1995) 20 EHRR 277; *Hatton v United Kingdom* (2003) 37 EHRR 28; *Oneryildiz v Turkey* (2005) 41 EHRR 20.

planning and environment court might well have been set up to provide an independent judicial body to determine planning appeals.

The 1998 decision of the House of Lords in *Empress Cars* may be over 15 years ago, but it remains as relevant as ever in interpreting core environmental legislation incorporating strict liability offences and the use of the term 'causes'. Lord Hoffman's rejection of restrictions developed in previous complex case law on the meaning of causation, incorporating suspect distinctions between active and passive involvement, is a model of legal acumen.

As the analysis of the 2012 *Barr v Biffa Waste Services* decision in Chapter 21 indicates, the Court of Appeal has also been faced with questions of the relationship between statutory controls and private rights of nuisance, and rejected the notion of a 'permit defence' in civil cases. Although not strictly relevant to that decision, Lord Justice Carnwath (as he then was) indicated that the long-established principles concerning when courts should grant damages in lieu of an injunction should be revisited to see if they were still appropriate for contemporary society. He probably had little idea that less than two years later the Supreme Court would have that opportunity in the *Coventry* case, and that he would by then have been promoted to the Supreme Court and would write one of the lead judgments. The principles of *Rylands v Fletcher* were revisited by the court in *Stannard v Gore* (2012). When modern environmental law was being developed in the 1970s, there were predictions that strict liability under *Rylands v Fletcher* would form the bedrock of a new era of 'toxic torts' – what, in the view of some, could be more 'ultrahazardous' than genetically modified organisms, new chemicals compounds or radioactive waste? Even the old decision of *Musgrove v Pandelis*,[6] holding the storage of a motor car to be a non-natural activity, might be resuscitated in an environmental campaign against traffic.[7] In fact, though the UK courts have to date refused to follow their Australian counterparts in no longer recognising *Rylands v Fletcher* as a separate head of claim, *Stannard v Gore* follows the modern practice of the courts to limit its application considerably. Significant extensions of strict liability are clearly considered by the judiciary to be a matter for government and Parliament rather than the courts.

Two earlier decisions of the Court of Appeal are included in this chapter. The 2004 *Fisher* case was one of the first times that the court had considered the legality of the procedures for designating sites of special scientific interest (SSSIs) against the general principles of the Human Rights Act. The concept of SSSIs was introduced in post-war nature conservation legislation, and for many years designation was considered a purely scientific exercise carried out by specialist nature conservation bodies and against which there was no statutory appeal other that by way of judicial review. The absence of a right of appeal – which contrasts with the position in many other areas of environmental regulation – was probably accepted by landowners because designation itself had little impact, other than providing a possible source of income or holding up damaging activities for a few months. The so-called voluntary approach to the regime for nature conservation adopted in the United Kingdom was memorably criticised by a Law Lord in 1992 as being toothless.[8] Following the Countryside and Rights of Way Act 2000, a tougher set

---

[6] [1919] 2 KB 43.

[7] See further J Spencer, 'Motor-cars and the Rule in *Rylands v Fletcher* – a Chapter of Accidents in the History and Law and Motoring' (1983) 42(1) *Cambridge Law Journal* 65. In fact, in 1980 activists brought a test civil action concerning leaded petrol against producers of petrol, where *Rylands v Fletcher*, as well as nuisance and negligence, was originally cited as a head of claim. See R Macrory, 'Lead in Petrol – No Cause for Action?' [1981] *Journal of Planning and Environment Law* 258.

[8] Lord Mustill: 'It needs only a moment to see that this *regime* is *toothless*, for it demands no more from the

of regulatory controls was introduced with the consequence that initial designation has much more serious implications for the owner of the land affected. As a result, it was not surprising that legal challenges to designation decisions would emerge. The court examined in detail the procedures developed by the regulatory body to meet potential human rights challenges and ultimately deferred to the technical expertise of English Nature (now Natural England) in exercising its decision to designate. The 2007 *OSS* case contains a fascinating judgment by Lord Justice Carnwath, as he then was, in which he tried to unravel the legal principles as to when waste that has been turned into a usable product ceases to be waste in law. Close analysis of the extensive case law of the Court of Justice of the European Union leads to despair, and it appears to be one of those areas where lawyers and judges had developed layer upon layer of finely tuned concepts, but in doing so had forgotten the overall environmental implications of the law that has been created. Here the recycling of waste into a usable fuel product was effectively being stymied by elaborate legal constructions. While the actual decision has now largely been overtaken by new EU waste law that deals explicitly with the issue, it remains a compelling example of an intellectually confident judge injecting some robust common sense into the equation, but without steering clear of the legal complexities involved.

Chapter 22 contains a selection of recent decisions of the High Court, and provides an impression of the range of issues that can emerge in environmental litigation – from the status of enforcement policies, the legal nature of emissions allowances and the environmental assessment of wind farms to the relationship of judicial review and statutory appeals. The 2013 decision in *Thames Water Utilities and Bromley Magistrates Court* looks to be the culmination of a ten-year legal saga following the escape of sewage into residential gardens from a collapsed pipe. It illustrates well just how complex some modern environmental legislation has become. A criminal prosecution by the Environment Agency in 2004 before local magistrates led to a reference to the European Court of Justice by the Divisional Court essentially on whether water or waste law was applicable in the circumstances, a further decision of the High Court applying the principles of the European Court to the facts in hand and a remission back to a magistrates court. The sentence of the district judge was then appealed against to the Crown Court, while the legality of his decision was challenged by way of judicial review – the decision analysed in this chapter.

Two earlier decision of the High Court are included. *Express Ltd v Environment Agency* (2004) concerns classic water pollution offences, and the responsibility of a company where the immediate cause of the incident was the action of a third party. In some ways, the case reflects the approach of the House of Lords in the 1998 *Empress Car* case, but dealing with a different provision. The case emphasises the extent to which the pollution legislation is interpreted to have a deterrent and preventative effect, in this case requiring the operator to carry out a prior risk assessment to avoid liability. The 1994 decision in the *Edwards* case concerns the question of standing to bring judicial review claims. The last 30 years has seen the British courts adopt an ever more liberal approach to standing, and the Edwards decision represents something of high point in the environmental field, suggesting that it will be difficult to refuse standing to local inhabitants at least where environmental decisions of statutory bodies are challenged. In 2014 the government proposed there should be more restrictive rules for standing in judicial review claims, especially in

owner or occupier of an SSSI than a little patience'. *Southern Water v Nature Conservancy Conservation Body* [1992] 3 All ER 481, 484.

land use planning cases, but acknowledged that these could compromise the provisions of the Aarhus Convention in environmental claims. In my submission to the consultation exercise, reproduced in Chapter 9, I argued that in practice many planning judicial reviews would inevitably engage Aarhus, and that in any event it would be preferable to leave it to judicial discretion to discern those claims that were truly an abuse of process. The 2014 response of the government[9] indicated that it was withdrawing its proposals concerning standing: 'The Government is clear that the current approach to judicial review allows for misuse, but is not of the view that amending standing is the best way to limit the potential for mischief'. The analysis in Edwards therefore continues to be of relevance.

Case Analysis

Chapter 19 Court of Justice of the European Union

C-258/11 *Sweetman v An Bord Pleanala* 11 April 2013

C-374/11 *European Commission v Ireland* 19 December 2012

Case T-338/08 *Stichting Natuur en Milieu and Pesticide Action Network Europe v European Commission* 14 June 2012

Case-1/11 *Interseroh Scrap and Metals Trading GmbH v Sonderabfall-Management-Gesellschaft Rheinland-Pfalz mbH (SAM)* 29 March 2012

Case C-597/10 *Inter-Environnement Bruxelles ASBL v Region de Bruxelles-Capitale* [2012] 2 CMLR 3022

Case C-366/10 *Air Transport Association of America and others v Secretary of State for Energy and Climate Change* [2011] ECR I-13755

Case C-67/97 *Re Criminal Proceedings against Bluhme* [1998] ECR I-5121

Case C-371/98 *R v Secretary of State for the Environment Transport and Regions ex parte First Corporate Shipping* [2001] EC I-9235

Case C-3/00 *Denmark v Commission* [2003] EC I-2643

Chapter 20 Supreme Court and House of Lords

Coventry v Lawrence [2014] UKSC 13

Walton v The Scottish Ministers [2012] UKSC 44

Morgan v Hampshire County Council Supreme Court [2011] UKSC 2

R on the application of National Grid Gas PLC (formerly Transco PLC) v Environment Agency [2007] UKHL 30

Marcic v Thames Water Utilities Ltd [2004] 2 AC 42

Berkeley v Secretary of State and Others [2001] 2 AC 603

---

[9] Ministry of Justice, *Judicial Review – Proposals for Further Reform: The Government Response*, Cm 8811 (February 2014).

R (Alconbury) v Secretary of State for the Environment, Transport (House of Lords) [2001] 2 All ER 929

Environment Agency (formerly National Rivers Authority) v Empress Car Company (Abertillery) Ltd [1998] 2 WLR 350

Chapter 21 Court of Appeal

Barr and others v Biffa Waste Services Ltd [2012] EWCA Civ 312

St Regis Paper Company Ltd v The Crown [2011] EWCA Crim 2527

Stannard v Gore [2012] EWCA Civ 1248

London Borough of Islington v Elliot and Morris [2012] EWCA Civ 56

Hirose Electrical UK Ltd v Peak Ingredients Ltd [2011] EWCA Civ 987

R on the application of Fisher v English Nature [2004] EWCA Civ 663

R ex parte OSS Group Ltd v Environment Agency and Department of Environment Food and Rural Affairs [2007] EWCA Civ 611

Chapter 22 High Court

R on the Application of Great Yarmouth Port Company v Marine Management Organisation [2013] EWHC 3052

Thames Water Utilities and Bromley Magistrates Court [2013] EWHC 472

Moss and Sons Ltd v Crown Prosecution Service [2012] EWHC 3658

Armstrong DLW GmbH v Winnington Networks [2012] EWHC 10

Hargreaves v Secretary of State for Communities and Local Government and other [2011] EWHC 1999

Express Ltd v Environment Agency [2004] EWHC 1710

R (on the application of Edwards) v Environment Agency and another [2004] EWHC 736

19

Court of Justice of the European Union

Nature Conservation and Death by a Thousand Cuts

C-258/11 *Sweetman v An Bord Pleanala* 11 April 2013

A recent ruling by the Court of Justice of the European Union (CJEU), which provided interpretations of the 1992 Habitats Directive, will make it much more difficult to permit projects that destroy very small areas of protected habitats – the so-called death by a thousand cuts.

Sweetman v An Bord Pleanala was referred from the Irish Supreme Court in a dispute between the Environment Ministry and the Irish Planning Board over a proposed bypass road for Galway city. The board had granted development consent for the scheme in 2008. The legal issues concerning the Habitats Directive were raised because part of the road scheme would cross Lough Corrib, which had been designated a site of community importance (SCI). At the time of the consent, the site had been notified to the European Commission but had not yet been formally designated.

The local councils promoting the scheme tried to argue that this meant no reference to the CJEU could be made, but the court dismissed this argument. Picking up on its earlier case law on the Habitats Directive, it argued that as soon as a Member State proposes a site to the commission the site must be protected. A key conservation features of the lough was its 270-hectare limestone pavement habitat. It was accepted that the road would destroy 1.47 ha – less than 1 per cent of the site. The Habitats Directive does not provide absolute protection for SCIs, but contains steps and tests that must be taken where damage is threatened. It was how these tests should apply that was the court's key concern.

Article 6(3) of the Directive provides first that any plan or project 'likely to have a significant impact' on the projected site shall be subject to an appropriate assessment. Much of the previous case law at EU level and within the UK has dealt with situations where no assessment had been made. An assessment had been carried out here, though, and British Advocate General Eleanor Sharpston noted that it had been done with great care. It was the conclusions following the assessment that were in question.

The next stage in the test under Article 6 is that the national authority may only agree to the plan or project where in the light of the assessment it decides it will not adversely affect the integrity of the site. The Directive provides that, even then, if there are no alternative solutions, the project may be approved, but only for imperative reasons of national importance and provided compensatory measures are made to ensure the overall

365

coherence of the community protected sites. In this case the procedures never reached this final stage because the Planning Board concluded that the loss of such a small proportion of the site would not affect its overall integrity. For the first time, the CJEU had to consider the meaning of 'integrity'.

The court began by noting that the integrity requirement and provisions in Article 6 had to be interpreted as a coherent whole in the light of the conservation objectives pursued by the directive. This implied, according to the court, that a site needs to be at least preserved at a favourable conservation status for its integrity to be maintained. This meant that the lasting preservation of the constitutive characteristics of the site concerned that are connected with the presence of the natural habitat type whose preservation was the objective justifying the designation of that site.

In her opinion on the case, Advocate General Sharpston gave a temporary pipeline-digging project as an example of a damaging project but one that would not necessarily affect the integrity of a protected site. If the disturbance were made good following such works, the site's integrity would be maintained.

Here, however, there was the permanent destruction of part of the site. As the court noted, if the national authority concludes that the

> plan or project will lead to the lasting and irreparable loss of the whole or part of a priority natural habit type whose conservation was the objective that justified the designation of the site concerned as an SCI, the view should be taken that such a plan or project will adversely affect the integrity of the site.

There was a further question as to the level of scientific certainty of potential loss that was required. The court stated that the authority must be certain the plan or project will not have lasting effects on the site's integrity – that is so where no reasonable scientific doubt remains as to the absence of such effects. In the court's view, this requirement that there is no uncertainty meant the Directive in effect incorporates the precautionary principle.

The implication is that, where there is a risk of destruction of a protected site, even a very small proportion, an authority cannot authorise the plan or project on the grounds that its integrity is preserved. If it wishes to authorise in those circumstances, the authority must invoke the principles of overriding national importance under Article 6(4), which will include ensuring there are no alternatives and that compensatory measures are provided.

Where priority habitats or species are involved, the opinion of the European Commission must be sought, but, as Advocate General Sharpston pointed out:

> Whilst the requirements laid down under article 6(4) are intentionally rigorous, it is important to point out that they are not insuperable obstacles to authorisation. The commission indicated at the hearing that, of the 15–20 requests so far made to it for delivery of an opinion under that provision, only one has received a negative response.

This latest CJEU judgment reinforces the legal interpretation that the Habitats Directive's main purpose is to preserve the overall integrity and coherence of protected sites. The Directive deliberately did not provide for absolute protection of designated sites, and was a political response to the original Birds Directive, where the court had in effect held that designated sites were inviolate. The decision will no doubt be frustrating to those in government who view the EU Directive as a unjustifiable obstacle to development. The legally correct response is not to ignore the decisions of the CJEU on the Directive or to criticise those bodies responsible for its national implementation, but to seek appropriate political support within other Member States to secure amendments.

Financial Penalties for Non-implementation in Practice

C-374/11 *European Commission v Ireland* 19 December 2012

The CJEU imposed a large financial penalty on Ireland at the end of 2012 for its failure to address internal problems concerning its national waste legislation. This decision is likely to have significant ramifications in many Member States. EU environmental legislation may contain many substantive obligations, but historically has tended to leave issues of implementation and enforcement to the discretion of Member States. The CJEU has frequently said penalties in national law must be effective, proportionate, and dissuasive, but little more detail is prescribed either by the Court or in EU environmental legislation.

But there are exceptions. The EU Emissions Trading System Directive contains mandatory financial penalties for companies that fail to surrender the correct amount of allowances. The Environmental Crime Directive agreed in 2008 requires that Member States create criminal liability for a range of activities harmful to the environment where the breach was committed intentionally or with at least serious negligence. It is less clear whether a Member State must always prosecute in such circumstances, or can impose a non-criminal penalty in particular cases.

As to inspection by regulatory authorities, EU laws contain occasional examples, but normally in broad terms. The 1975 Waste Directive, for example, required waste sites to be subject to appropriate periodic inspections by the competent authorities. The 2010 Industrial Emissions Directive has taken the issue the furthest. Member States must establish inspection plans for installations, with routine inspections carried out on the basis of risk assessment. Non-routine, spot inspections must happen in response to incidents or complaints from the public.

The European Commission has an obligation under the Treaty to ensure EU laws are enforced and has well-known powers to bring infringement proceedings against a Member State failing in its obligations. Much of the enforcement activity ensures that the correct national implementing laws are in place. But the CJEU has long held that, even if the national laws fully reflect EU obligations, the failure to apply them in practice is equally a breach of a Member State's general obligation to ensure that EU law is applied. The Commission has not held back from bringing such cases, even though they can often be controversial at local level.

Yet it is severely hampered in doing so. Member States have long resisted giving the Commission any power of inspection in the environmental field, or even the right to work alongside national environment authorities. This is seen as one political intrusion too far, even though in the field of competition law extensive inspection powers exists. Occasionally, Commission officials have visited problem areas, though there is no power of entry onto private property. By and large, the Commission relies on information being sent to it by individuals or non-governmental organisations, which is then followed up by extensive talks with the relevant government.

In an important case against Ireland, heard before the Court in 2005,[1] the Commission was dealing with evidence that many waste disposal sites in Ireland were not being properly licensed or enforced by local authorities. The Commission could have argued that each example of an unlicensed site itself represented a breach of EU waste legislation, but it went much further and made the case that these examples in fact represented a wholesale systemic failure in the administrative structure for enforcing and implementing waste legislation. It was the first time that non-application in practice had been characterised in this way and the CJEU held that such a systemic failure was indeed established and amounted to a failure to implement EU law in practice.

The most recent case concerned proceedings originally brought before the Court against Ireland in 2008. The Commission argued that Irish legislation relating to the disposal of domestic waste waters through septic tanks and other waste water treatment systems did not comply with EU waste legislation. The Court held in Case C-188/08 that Ireland was in breach, but over the subsequent period the Commission remained dissatisfied with the steps being taken by the Irish government.

In 2012 it brought proceedings against Ireland for failure to comply with the Court judgment. Here the stakes are much higher because, since the 1993 Treaty amendments, the CJEU can impose financial penalties on a Member State not complying with a judgment, a provision promoted by the British government to deal with an apparent growing number of ignored Court judgments.

The Irish government argued that it had promoted new legislation under the Water Services (Amendment) Act 2012 dealing with the issue, but the Commission considered that the system still depended on regulations being made and that there were uncertainties about financing the proposed inspection system, and indeed doubts about the number of inspectors being adequate. The Court agreed that Ireland had still not complied with its judgment and rejected the Irish government's argument that 21 months from the original judgment was insufficient to deal with problem.

The Court imposed a lump-sum penalty of €2m plus a daily fine of €12,000 for each day of delay in adopting the measures necessary to comply with original judgment. It showed little sympathy, noting that, 19 years after the relevant obligations under the EU waste legislation came into force, Ireland had still failed to comply. The principal objectives of the waste legislation was the protection of human health and the environment and the Court cannot but confirm the particularly lengthy character of an infringement which, in the light of such objectives, is also a matter of indisputable gravity.

How quickly this continuing daily penalty forces the hand of Irish officials remains to be seen, but Member States will need to consider the implications of the decision carefully. Both the European Commission and the CJEU are clearly showing a concern at the effectiveness of national systems for implementation and enforcement. This comes at a time when public sector cutbacks in many countries are imposing strains on environmental enforcement bodies at national and local level, but governments will now need to be wary of jeopardising inspection and enforcement systems or face potential high penalties at European level.

---

[1] Case C-494/01 *Commission v Ireland* judgment 26 April 2005.

Aarhus, Access to Information and the European Commission

Case T-338/08 *Stichting Natuur en Milieu and Pesticide Action Network Europe v European Commission* 14 June 2012

The Court of Justice has ruled that the European Regulation[2] implementing the Aarhus Convention at union level is defective in dealing with access to justice. The decision opens many European Commission decisions to challenge. Many Western European governments thought that the main impact of the 1998 Aarhus Convention, concerning access to environmental information, public participation and access to justice, would be on the former Eastern bloc countries, where such rights were less developed in the law. That may well still be the case, but the significance of Aarhus continues to be felt throughout the EU. On 21 June, Ireland finally ratified Aarhus, meaning that all EU Member States have now signed up to the convention. Last year, in what is known as the *Slovakian Brown* case, the Court of Justice of the EU boldly stated that the provisions of Aarhus now form an integral part of the legal order of the European Union.[3]

The European Commission has been bringing infringement proceedings against Member States that fail to comply with Aarhus requirements reflected in EU environmental directives. This includes the UK, where the current costs regime for judicial review is argued to be in breach of access to justice principles in Aarhus. But Aarhus does not just bind Member States. Since the environment is an area that neither falls exclusively within the jurisdiction of Member States or that of the EU, the Union also ratified Aarhus in 2005, meaning that European institutions are now bound by the convention.

In its latest decisions on Aarhus, the Court of Justice said the European Regulation that implements Aarhus at Union level is defective in the way it deals with access to justice. *Stichting Natuur en Milieu and Pesticide Action Network Europe v European Commission* concerned a Regulation adopted by the Commission in 1998[4] amending maximum pesticide levels in products covered by a 2005 EC Regulation on the subject. The applicants wished to challenge the decision.

In its implementation of Aarhus as it affected EU institutions, Regulation 1367/2006 introduced a right for NGOs to make a request for an internal review to the community institution or body that has adopted that administrative act under environmental law.[5] The applicants duly made such a request, but the Commission turned it down. The Commission noted that the definition of an administrative act under the Regulation referred only to measures having an individual scope and could not encompass a more general measure such as a pesticide level. The applicants provided some ingenious arguments that the measure in question was in fact an 'individual' act, but the Court rejected these.

---

[2] Regulation (EC) 1367/2006 of the European Parliament and of the Council of 6 September 2006 on the application of the provisions of the Aarhus Convention on Access to Information, Public Participation in Decision-making and Access to Justice in Environmental Matters to Community institutions and bodies.

[3] Case C-240/09 *Lesoochranárske zoskupenie VLK v Ministerstvo životného prostredia Slovenskej republiky* judgment 8 March 2011, para 30.

[4] Regulation (EC) No 149/2008 amending Regulation (EC) No 396/2005 of the European Parliament and of the Council by establishing Annexes II, III and IV setting maximum residue levels for products covered by Annex I thereto [2008] OJ L58/1.

[5] Regulation 1367/2006, Art 10.

But this did not let the Commission off the hook. The Court pointed out that the 2006 Regulation was adopted to meet the EU's international obligations under the access to justice provisions under Aarhus. The Aarhus provisions also refers to the right to challenge acts and omissions of public authorities, but there is no definition of this. The Court then adopted general principles of international law by looking at the object and purpose of the Aarhus Convention to assist in its interpretation.

The Preamble to Aarhus states that its objective is to contribute to everyone's right to live in an environment adequate to their health and wellbeing, and the Court could see no reason to limit any review procedure to measures of individual scope since acts adopted in the field of the environment are mostly acts of general importance. It followed that the restrictive definition in the 2006 Regulation did not properly reflect the Aarhus meaning of an act, and the Commission's decision to reject the request as inadmissible was therefore annulled by the Court.

The Aarhus review obligations, however, do not apply to a body acting in a judicial or legislative capacity, and this exclusion is also reflected in the 2006 Regulation. It seems odd that in this case the Commission, in adopting an amending regulation of general application, was not considered to be acting in a legislative capacity. But the Court dismissed this line of argument in a rather perfunctory way: 'It is clear from the provisions on the basis of which that regulation was adopted that the Commission acted in the exercise of its implementing powers'.

On the same day the Court dealt with a similar case where the Commission also refused an NGO the right of review. Case T-396/09 *Vereniging Mileudefensie v European Commission* concerned a decision of the Commission permitting the extension of time limits for attaining annual limits for nitrogen dioxide in a number of zones in the Netherlands. The Commission has the power to approve – or, strictly, not to block – such applications by Member States under the 2008 Directive on ambient air quality.

One might have thought that such a decision concerning specific locations was an administrative act having individual scope as defined in the Regulation. But perhaps one of the lessons here is that it is never easy to predict how the Court will approach classifications. Here it held that the decision concerning a derogation under legislation, however limited in time or space, was nevertheless one of general application rather than 'individual'. The Court then, as in the pesticide case, had to ask whether the limited definition of acts that could be reviewed reflected the Aarhus obligations. Again it concluded that it did not and the Commission's decision to reject any review was annulled.

The decision of the Court potentially opens many Commission decisions to challenge by way of a review. It was welcomed, amongst others, by Jeremy Wates, who was secretary to the Aarhus Convention for more than 10 years before moving to the European Environmental Bureau in 2011. He noted that the ruling vindicates long-standing concerns in the NGO community that the EU has failed to provide sufficient opportunities for NGOs to hold EU institutions to account.

But the story will not end there. The Commission might still appeal the decision to the full Court of Justice.[6] If it does not, the applicants in the two cases will now be entitled to a review, but there is no guarantee that the Commission will change its view. What then? The Regulation allows the applicants to challenge this decision by way of application to

---

[6] An appeal against the judgment was brought on 27 August 2012 – Case C-405/12P. The Court has yet to determine the appeal – http://curia.europa.eu/juris/liste.jsf?num=T-338/08&language=en accessed 28/2/2014.

the Court of Justice, but they must satisfy the Court's tests on standing. These tests have long been considered highly restrictive, especially for non-governmental organisations. Although the Lisbon Treaty provided a degree of relaxation, it is by no means certain that the applicants in these cases would satisfy the tests. The Court may then have to ask itself whether its own long-standing restrictive interpretation of the Treaty rules of standing truly reflect the letter and spirit of Aarhus. But such self-criticism is likely to prove much more of a challenge.

When Environmental Requirements Trump Commercial Confidentiality

Case-1/11 *Interseroh Scrap and Metals Trading GmbH v Sonderabfall-Management-Gesellschaft Rheinland-Pfalz mbH (SAM)* 29 March 2012

Environmental regulation often has to tread a fine line between the needs of transparency and openness against demands for business confidentiality. Many of the early reports of the Royal Commission on Environmental Pollution in the 1970s and 1980s argued the case for openness, and its seminal 1984 Report *Tackling Pollution – Experience and Prospects*[7] recommended that a guiding principle behind all legislative and administrative environmental controls should be a presumption in favour of unrestricted access to information, with provisions for secrecy only in those circumstances where a genuine case for it can be substantiated.

The Environment Agency in England and Wales holds around 15 public registers, and common to most of the statutory provisions is the provision for exemptions, including one of commercial confidentiality. The Water Act 1991, for example, allows for the exclusion of commercially confidential information, but it is by no means an unrestricted exemption. Such information is defined in the Act as information which would prejudice 'to an unreasonable degree' commercial interests, implying that some prejudice is permissible, and in any event the Secretary of State has power under the Act to direct the Agency to include commercially confidential information on the register where this is required by public interest.

Within the European Union, access to environmental information is now governed by the 2003 Directive on public access environment information, which toughened up the provisions of the original 1990 Directive on the subject. The 2003 Directive also provides for a number of exceptions, including one of the confidentiality of commercial information, though Member States are not obliged to provide for these exceptions in their national law.

Even if they do, the exceptions are subject to important qualifications. Where such an exception is claimed, the relevant authority must weigh up the interests protected against public interest in disclosure. In 2010, in Case C-266/09 *Stichting Natuur en Milieu and Others*, the Court of Justice of the European Union confirmed that this was an exercise that had to be done in every individual case, and could not be satisfied by general rules

---

[7] Royal Commission on Environmental Pollution Tenth Report, Cmnd 9149 (HMSO, 1984).

or policies. The Court has also held, not surprisingly, that exemptions must be interpreted narrowly.

In 2010 the UK Supreme Court also had to consider the question of exemptions in the context of the 2004 Environmental Information Regulations. *Information Commissioner v Office of Communications* [2010] UKSC 3 concerned a request for the disclosure of information on the location of mobile telephone base stations. Ofcom was clearly required to weigh the public interest test against the exceptions claimed (here public safety and intellectual property), but the question was whether it should also aggregate the public interest, combining two distinct exceptions, before applying the test.

The Supreme Court was split, though the majority argued that aggregation was permissible. But the Court also felt that a reference to the Court of Justice of the European Union was required. Last July the European Court agreed with the majority and held that the Directive must be interpreted as meaning that

> where a public authority holds environmental information or such information is held on its behalf, it may, when weighing the public interests served by disclosure against the interests served by refusal to disclose, in order to assess a request for that information to be made available to a natural or legal person, take into account cumulatively a number of the grounds for refusal set out in that proviso.

The Directive also provides that the commercial confidentiality exception (and a number of others) cannot apply where the information relates to information on emissions to the environment. There is unfortunately no definition of precisely what is meant by emissions to the environment, though courts are likely to adopt a generous approach in line with the spirit of the Directive.

The most recent decision of the Court of Justice of the European Union on information and the protection of business interests is unusual in that it is concerned with a particular piece of environmental legislation rather than the general directive on access to environmental information. *Interseroh Scrap and Metals Trading GmbH v Sonderabfall-Management-Gesellschaft Rheinland-Pfalz mbH (SAM)* was a reference from a German court concerning the interpretation of the 2006 Shipments of Waste Regulation. The 2006 Regulation is a complex piece of legislation largely implementing international law on the transfrontier movements of waste. The Regulation provides for information concerning the origin, nature and destination of the waste that must accompany any shipment.

The case concerned a potential conflict with the requirements of the Regulation and German Basic Law concerning the freedom to conduct business. Case law in Germany has held that a business's sources of supply are essentially business secrets which are protected under the Basic Law as a fundamental right. Interseroh was an intermediary providing scrap metal to various industries, and argued that if it was obliged to reveal the sources of the waste on the consignment notes, this would breach its business secrets. Essentially it would be revealing its know-how to customers who in future could bypass Interseroh and purchase scrap metal direct from the suppliers.

The Regulation provides that the information required is to be treated as confidential if this is required by Community or national law, but the Court held that this provision in itself did not entitle Interseroh to exclude information concerning the waste producers.

As to basic rights, the Court noted that the freedom to pursue a trade or business was a general principle of European Union law and was now reflected in the European Charter of Fundamental Rights. But the Court went on to hold that an inevitable consequence of the tracking procedure under the Waste Shipment Regulation was that consignees would be made aware of the names of the waste producers. The Regulation provided for no exceptions, and even if this disclosure breached the protection of business secrets, this did not justify a restrictive interpretation.

But, as so often happens with judgments of the European Court, the story does not end necessarily end here. The Court accepted that a conflict between the Charter and fundamental rights of business might call into question the actual legal validity of the provisions concerning consignment notes in the Regulation. However, that was not a question referred to them by the national court, and the Court felt in any event it did not have the facts necessary to resolve that issue. We must wait and see whether this closing observation acts as an incentive for the parties and the national court to raise this issue and refer the matter once again the Court. But, given that the Regulation implements an international treaty on the subject of transfrontier movements of waste, it is likely to be a tough call.

Strategic Environmental Assessment

Case C-597/10 *Inter-Environnement Bruxelles ASBL v Region de Bruxelles-Capitale* [2012] 2 CMLR 3022

A partial or total repeal of a plan or programme likely to significantly affect the environment should be subject to the Strategic Environmental Assessment Directive, the Court of Justice of the EU has confirmed. Strategic environmental assessment (SEA) is a potential legal minefield for public authorities. Environmental assessment for specific developments, such as road schemes or waste incinerators, has been a familiar part of the UK's legal landscape for almost a quarter of a century, but SEA for plans and programmes is still relatively new.

The past few years have seen an increasing number of legal cases before the British Courts in which SEA requirements have been at issue. But a decision of the Court of Justice of the EU at the end of March contains some highly creative interpretation of key provisions of the SEA Directive and will give authorities an added headache when deciding if an assessment is required.

US legislation on environmental impact statements introduced in 1969 inspired the development of environmental assessment law in Europe. However, the European Community was determined to avoid two perceived pitfalls of the US law. First, there would be far less legal emphasis on a comprehensive written statement in favour of more consultative procedures. Secondly, European policy makers did not want a repeat of the mass of litigation in the US in deciding when environmental assessment was required. Section 102 of the US National Environmental Policy Act 1969, which is still in force, is expressed in open-ended language requiring an environmental impact statement for every recommendation or report on proposals for legislation and other major federal actions significantly affecting the quality of the human environment. It has been left to the Courts to define these highly ambiguous terms.

The original 1985 EC Directive on environmental impact assessment was therefore confined to specific classes of reasonably well-defined development projects. This approach has not stopped litigation, but it has been nowhere near the scale of that in the US. European policy makers recognised that individual project proposals were often set against a backdrop of existing plans or programmes. It was always intended that environmental assessment requirements would eventually apply to plans and programmes.

The SEA Directive was agreed in 2001,[8] but it proved impossible to define plan or programme types as precisely as had been done for projects. One logical approach might have been to require SEA for any plan or programme likely to significantly affect subsequent decisions on individual projects. This approach was rejected. Instead, Article 2 of Directive 2001/42 confined its application to plans and programmes .required by legislative, regulatory or administrative provisions. The clear implication is that, if there is no obligation to produce such a plan, it is not subject to SEA. Commission guidance on the Directive advises that plans and programmes voluntarily produced by authorities are not covered by the Directive, as does UK government guidance issued in 2005.

This guidance will now have to be revised. *Inter-Environnement Bruxelles ASBL v Region de Bruxelles-Capitale* was a referral from a Belgian Court on interpretation of the SEA Directive. The case related to a local land-use plan of a type referred to in the Brussels Town and Country Planning Code. There was some dispute about whether authorities were obliged to produce such plans, but the national court accepted that they could refuse to do so in certain cases. The question was whether the Directive still applied if such plans were not obligatory. The Court of Justice was not deterred by what would appear to be unambiguous language. It argued that such a reading of the Directive would considerably restrict scrutiny of the environmental effects of plans and programmes and compromise protection of the environment.

According to the Court:

> It follows that plans or programmes whose adoption is regulated by national legislative or regulatory provisions, which determine the competent authorities for adopting them and the procedure for preparing them, must be regarded as 'required' within the meaning and for the application of Directive 2001/42.

The key for the Court is not whether an obligation exists to produce such plans or programmes but whether their production is regulated by law. Government and policy makers will now have to consider what sort of plans or programmes the new ruling might encompass.

In England and Wales one obvious candidate is supplementary planning documents. Planning authorities do not have to produce these, but if they do they are subject to statutory preparation procedures in the 2004 regulations.[9] Authorities need to consider whether such documents are likely to have significant environmental effects and are therefore subject to SEA requirements.

The Court of Justice added another interpretation. The Directive applies to the production and modification of plans and programmes. In this case, there was a proposed repeal of a plan, and the Court held that, although repeals were not expressly referred to in the Directive, the Directive should be interpreted broadly. A partial or total repeal of a plan

---

[8] Directive 2001/42/EC of the European Parliament and of the Council of 27 June 2001 on the assessment of the effects of certain plans and programmes on the environment [2001] OJ L197, 30–37.

[9] See now Town and Country Planning (Local Planning) (England) Regulations 2012, SI 2012/767.

or programme was likely to significantly affect the environment, so in principle should be subject to the Directive. The only exception was where the repeal was in the context of an existing hierarchy of plans or programmes which had themselves been subject to SEA and which laid down a sufficiently precise set of rules governing land use.

The High Court had already anticipated this interpretation at the end of 2010 in the long-running legal saga concerning the government's proposal to abolish regional strategies.[10] Mr Justice Sales held that, since such strategies had been subject to SEA, their revocation in principle should also be subject to consideration as to whether assessment was needed. His ruling was not strictly necessary to the decision that was made in the case but is now vindicated by the Court of Justice.

Aviation Emissions and International Law

Case C-366/10 *Air Transport Association of America and others v Secretary of State for Energy and Climate Change* [2011] ECR I-13755

The Court of Justice of the European Union has rejected challenges by US airline companies to the legal validity of the 2008 Directive proposing to include aviation emissions with the European carbon trading scheme. In doing so it has identified the principles of international law which could affect the legality of such a law, but has held that in this case they had not been affected by the Directive.

The decision of the Court in *Air Transport Association of America and others v Secretary of State for Energy Climate Change* largely follows the lengthy Opinion of the Advocate General delivered in October.[11]

The Court rejected arguments based on two key international treaties, the 1944 Chicago Convention on Civil International Aviation and the Kyoto Protocol. The European Union was not as such a party to the Convention and, while the Kyoto Protocol stated that parties should work through the International Civil Aviation Organization, the Court held that this provision was not sufficiently precise and unconditional to allow individuals to rely upon it to challenge the legality of EU law.

The Court accepted that the 2007 Open Skies Agreement between the EU and the United States was binding on the European Union and that provisions of the Agreement could be relevant here, but none appeared to be fatal to the Directive.

It was the general principles of customary international law that received some of the closest analysis. The core principles relevant here and summarised by the Court were: the principle that each state has complete and exclusive sovereignty over its airspace; the principle that no state may validly purport to subject any part of the high seas to its sovereignty; and the principle which guarantees freedom to fly over the high seas. But the Court noted that, when it came to such principles, the Court's approach towards assessing validity of the law concerned would be rather more restrained:

---

[10] *Cala Homes (South) Ltd v Secretary of State for Communities and Local Government* [2010] EWHC 2866.
[11] 441 *ENDS Report* 59.

Since a principle of customary international law does not have the same degree of precision as a provision of an international agreement, judicial review must necessarily be limited to the question whether, in adopting the act in question, the institutions of the European Union made manifest errors of assessment concerning the conditions for applying those principles.

The Court rejected any argument that these principles were jeopardised by the Directive, and held that the Directive did not affect the right to fly over the high seas. It noted that

It is only if the operator of such an aircraft has chosen to operate a commercial air route arriving at or departing from an aerodrome situated in the territory of a Member State that the operator, because its aircraft is in the territory of that Member State, will be subject to the allowance trading scheme.

The Court was unimpressed with arguments concerning the fact that the calculation of emission allowances under the Directive were based on international elements of the flight, though it did not reject them in quite so forceful terms as the Advocate General had done in her Opinion. According to the Court,

It must be pointed out that, as European Union policy on the environment seeks to ensure a high level of protection in accordance with Article 191(2) TFEU, the European Union legislature may in principle choose to permit a commercial activity, in this instance air transport, to be carried out in the territory of the European Union only on condition that operators comply with the criteria that have been established by the European Union and are designed to fulfill the environmental protection objectives which it has set for itself, in particular where those objectives follow on from an international agreement to which the European Union is a signatory, such as the Framework Convention and the Kyoto Protocol.

The legal proceedings are not yet over since this was a referral from the English High Court, where the validity of the UK regulations implementing the Directive had been challenged. But, given such a strong ruling from the European Court, which has exclusive jurisdiction to determine the validity of EU legislation, this particular aspect of the legal challenge must be now be considered complete.[12]

Biodiversity, Bees and Free Trade

Case C-67/97 *Re Criminal Proceedings against Bluhme* [1998] ECR I-5121

The European Court of Justice has made it clear that the maintenance of local biodiversity can justify a Member State restricting imports and movements of animals which might interbreed with local species. The decision applies classically developed principles, but

---

[12] In March 2012 the American airline companies that had initiated the challenge announced that they would withdraw from any further judicial review proceedings in the English High Court. Despite the legal endorsement of the European provisions by the Court of Justice, politics has now taken precedence. In April 2013 the EU temporarily suspended the enforcement of the emission trading requirements for flights operated to and from non-EU countries to allow time for the International Civil Aviation Organization to reach a global agreement on aviation emissions. In October 2013, the ICAO Assembly agreed to develop a global market scheme by 2016, and as a result in March 2014, following a proposal of the European Commission, the EU Council and the European Parliament reached an informal agreement to amend the EU emissions trading scheme to limit it to only those parts of flights taking place in European air-space.

appears to be the first in which the Court has considered in detail the concept of biodiversity in the context of free trade. *Re Criminal Proceedings against Bluhme* arose out of a reference to the European Court by a Danish criminal court. In 1993, the Danish Ministry of Agriculture had issued a regulation banning the keeping of bees other than the Laeso brown bee on the small island of Laeso. The law also provided for the removal of swarms of other bees, together with compensation for any resulting losses. The underlying intention was to conserve local biodiversity by preventing interbreeding with other types of bees.

A local beekeeper was prosecuted for keeping bees other than the Laeso brown bee, but argued in his defence that the Danish law was in breach of Article 30 of the EC Treaty,[13] which prohibits national restrictions on the free movement of goods. Article 36,[14] together with principles developed by the ECJ, permits Member States to invoke national restrictions on certain defined grounds, though before those principles can be applied it must be established that the issue is not in fact governed by existing Community legislation.

The Court initially considered whether a 1991 Directive laying down zootechnical and pedigree requirements for the marketing of pure-bred animals governed the situation. The Directive provides for the adoption of detailed rules for its application, but since no such rules had been made in respect of bees the Court held that the Directive was not applicable. The 1992 Directive on habitats is concerned with the conservation of threatened biodiversity and the island of Laeso is designated under it, but the brown bee is not one of the species specified in the Directive.

The Court therefore had to consider whether the restrictions concerning Laeso bees amounted to a quantitative restriction or measure of equivalent effect prohibited under Article 30 of the Treaty. The Danish Government argued that Article 30 did not apply. The restrictions applied to only a very small part of the national territory, and the ban on imports of bees other than Laeso brown bees did not discriminate in respect of bees coming from other Member States.

Denmark also raised a more subtle point. In the 1970s and 1980s, the ECJ adopted an extensive interpretation of the meaning of a 'measure of equivalent effect' encompassing practically any sort of rule which could directly or indirectly affect trade. However, in an important decision in 1993 – the *Keck* case[15]– the Court, sensitive to the difficulties arising from challenges to national Sunday trading rules, drew back somewhat from its highly interventionist approach and redefined the boundaries by making a distinction between national rules concerning access to markets, which remained subject to Article 30, and those governing arrangements for selling, which were no longer to be subject to Article 30. In the present case, Denmark argued that since the Laeso rules did not prohibit the import of bees into Denmark in general but merely limited their distribution in a small part of the country, this was equivalent to a 'selling arrangement' and therefore fell outside Article 30.

The Court rejected all these initial arguments. The national rules could not be described as concerning selling arrangements but were directly concerned with the intrinsic characteristics of the bees in question. The fact that the restriction affected only part of the national territory did not prevent it being a restriction of intra-Community trade. The key legal question was therefore whether the national measures could be justified under Community law. Article 36 permits national restrictions on certain grounds, including

---

[13] Now Art 34 TFEU.
[14] See now Art 36 TFEU.
[15] Joined Cases C-267/91 and C-268/91 *Keck* [1993] ECR I-6097.

the 'protection of the health and life of animals'. The ECJ has itself established other grounds not expressly contained in the Treaty, including those of general environmental protection. The distinction between the two sets of grounds can be significant. Where an Article 36 ground is invoked, the national measures may discriminate between national and imported goods provided the discrimination is for good reason. But where one of the ECJ's general principles is invoked, no discrimination is generally permitted.

There was considerable argument before the Court whether the maintenance of biodiversity fell within the concept of the protection of the health and life of animals under Article 36. The Advocate General accepted that the threat of an animal population disappearing through slow interbreeding with other species was rather different from the protection of animals from hunting or disease, which has been held to fall within Article 36. In the former case, it was a 'slower, probably painless process' which would not 'necessarily endanger the life of any individual member of the population in question'. Nevertheless, he felt that Article 36 should apply, and the Court agreed:

> Measures to preserve an indigenous animal population with distinct characteristics contribute to the maintenance of biodiversity by ensuring the survival of the population concerned. By so doing, they are aimed at protecting the life of those animals and are capable of being justified under Article 36.

However, simply coming within the terms of Article 36 is not sufficient to justify a national measure. Member States must also satisfy the Court that the measure was proportionate in the sense that it met a genuine need and was restricted to what was actually necessary to secure the public interest goals. Here, again, there was considerable argument, especially over whether the Laeso bee is a distinct subspecies, whether brown bees of the same subspecies exists elsewhere in the world, and whether the population was under immediate threat of extinction.

The Advocate General was prepared to give considerable latitude to the Member State in this context. He noted that the EC is party to the 1992 UN Convention on Biological Diversity which affirms that the conservation of biological diversity is a common concern of mankind, and is not confined in its application to species and subspecies but is more concerned with genetic resources generally. Even if the Laeso bee was not a distinct subspecies, he felt Denmark was entitled to seek to conserve what was a geographically and morphologically distinctive bee population. And even if there was no immediate threat – though Denmark contended that there was – the precautionary principle argued for anticipatory action.

The Court followed this line of argument:

> From the point of view of such conservation of biodiversity it is immaterial whether the object of protection is a separate subspecies, a distinct strain within any given species or merely a local colony, so long as the population in question have characteristics distinguishing them from others and are therefore judged worthy of protection either to shelter them from a risk of extinction that is more or less imminent, or, even in the absence of such risk, on account of scientific or other interest in preserving the pure population at the location concerned.

The ECJ concluded that the threat of the Laeso brown bees disappearing through interbreeding was genuine, and that the Danish national laws were an appropriate response and justified under Community law.

The Laeso decision is significant in the way that it explores the meaning of biodiversity and the latitude available to Member States to conserve what in their opinion are important local pockets of biodiversity. However, it is important to stress that the freedom of a Member State to invoke Article 36 applies only where no Community legislation on the subject exists. As such, the principles are unlikely to be applicable to, say, the current concerns in Britain over the potential local biodiversity impacts of genetically modified crops, to which specific EC legislation applies. Nonetheless, the sensitivities now raised concerning the vulnerability of local biodiversity, coupled with the potential impact of devolution in heightening local or regional concerns, are likely to increase the political and legal significance of the European Court's approach in the Laeso case.

UK Shipping Company Loses Case against Habitat Designation

Case C-371/98 *R v Secretary of State for the Environment Transport and Regions ex parte First Corporate Shipping* 11 November 2000 [2001] All ER (EC) 177

A rearguard action by a UK shipping company to block the designation of wildlife sites under the 1992 EC Directive on habitats has failed before the European Court of Justice. The Court ruled that economic and social interests, including those of industry, are not be taken into account when Member States tackle the task of designation. The decision is in line with Government policy. *R v Secretary of State* for *the Environment Transport and Regions ex parte First Corporate* was a referral to the European Court of Justice from the High Court. The case arose out of the Secretary of State's decision that he was minded to propose to the European Commission that the Severn estuary is eligible for designation as a Special Area of Conservation (SAC) under the Habitats Directive.

The Habitats Directive contains an annex specifying criteria for selecting sites, with preliminary lists to be sent to the Commission, followed by a complex procedure to establish, by agreement with Member States and the Commission, a network of sites of Community importance known as Natura 2000. Sites on the Commission's final list must be designated as SACs by Member States, though UK policy is to treat candidate sites submitted to the Commission as though they have been finally designated. Once a site is designated, Article 6 of the Directive kicks into play, requiring a Member State to avoid deterioration of habitats and disturbance of species. Plans or projects which might significantly affect SACs are subject to environmental assessment.

In 1991, the European Court of Justice held that the provisions in the 1979 Directive on bird conservation concerning Special Protection Areas (SPAs) did not permit any subsequent deterioration or incursion into such areas once they were designated unless human life was threatened.[16]

Although most environmental groups welcomed that decision, there was real concern that such a strict ruling would make Member States less than enthusiastic in initial designation. In drafting the provisions of the Habitats Directive, Member States were clearly anxious to avoid such strictures. Article 6 therefore allows, under qualified con-

---

[16] Case C-57/89 *Commission v Germany* [1991] ECR I-883.

ditions, that damaging plans or projects may be carried out for 'imperative reasons of overriding public interest', including those of a social or economic nature. In such cases 'compensatory measures' must be taken by Member States to ensure coherence of the Natura 2000 network.

In the Severn estuary case, the concern was with the criteria applied to initial designation. First Corporate Shipping is the port authority for Bristol, and had concerns that designation of the estuary could jeopardise future development of the port's facilities. It pointed to Article 2 of the Directive, which provides that 'Measures taken pursuant of this Directive shall take account of economic, social, and cultural requirements and regional and local characteristics'. The company argued that the identification and selection of candidate sites was a 'measure' within the terms of the Directive. In the European Court, it was supported by the Finnish government which argued that, provided the overall objectives of the Directive were not compromised, Member States should be entitled to take into economic, social and cultural requirements in preparing their lists. This might be the case where there was a large number of potential sites within a single territory, and where some pre-selection would not jeopardise the Directive.

Despite the general wording of Article 2, the European Court of Justice rejected the arguments. It noted that the Directive provides detailed and specific criteria for site selection, and that the criteria were defined exclusively in relation to the objective of conserving habitats or fauna and flora. The overall goal of the designation procedures was to establish a coherent European network of SACs.

> To produce a draft list of sites of Community importance, capable of leading to the creation of a coherent European ecological network of SACs, the Commission must have available an exhaustive list of the sites which, at national level, have an ecological interest which is relevant from the point of view of the Habitats Directive's objective of conservation of natural habitats and wild fauna and flora.

The Court held that the Directive required that the conservation status of habitats and species must be assessed with regard to the entire European territory. It followed that when a Member State drew up its initial candidate list it would have no precise knowledge of the situation of habitats in other Member States. To allow Member States to fillet their candidate lists on non-scientific grounds would prevent the Commission having an exhaustive list of potential sites and thereby jeopardise the Directive's goals.

The decision is hardly surprising, especially in the light of the Court's ruling in the 1996 *Lappel Banks* case,[17] which concerned SPAs under the Birds Directive. The Court held that initial designation of such areas could not involve economic and social considerations, and indicated that the same approach should apply to designation under the Habitats Directive though that matter was not directly in issue. Despite its predictability, the ruling is nevertheless valuable in ensuring that the process of initial selection and designation is not over-politicised. But it is equally clear that the resolution of potential conflicts is now likely to be down the line, and indeed the Directive is essentially structured on that basis. There is room for hard negotiation between Member States and the Commission concerning the initial list of European sites, and clearly there will be difficult decisions in the future concerning the extent to which designated sites may subsequently be damaged.

---

[17] ECJ Case C-44/96, 11 July 1996.

Ruling from European Court on 'Green Guarantee'

C 3/00 *Denmark v Commission* [2003] ECR I-2643

The European Court of Justice has given its second important decision this year on provisions in the EU Treaty allowing Member States to maintain or introduce stricter environmental or health requirements than those contained in EU single market Directives. The provisions were substantially revised by the Amsterdam Treaty which came into force in 1999, and in a decision earlier this year the ECJ gave its first ruling[18] on them as they related to new national measures introduced after the adoption of a Directive.

The latest case, *Denmark v Commission*, relates to the Treaty provisions permitting Member States to maintain stricter national measures that were already in force when a Directive is agreed. The case concerned standards for certain preservatives used in foodstuffs, though the principles will apply to equally to environmental measures. Under a 1989 framework Directive concerning additives in food, various daughter Directives established lists of foods and permitted uses of additives such as sweeteners, colouring and preservatives. A 1995 daughter Directive concerned preservatives, and was agreed under the Treaty's single market provisions by majority voting. Denmark voted against the Directive, arguing that it did not satisfactorily meet health requirements, especially as regards sulphites, nitrites and nitrates used as preservatives in certain foods.

Denmark implemented those parts of the Directive concerning additives other than sulphites, nitrites and nitrates, but in 1966 notified the European Commission that it was maintaining its own existing law concerning those additives by way of derogation. Following discussion with the Commission, further information was sent in 1998, and the Commission then sought opinions from other Member States, several of which expressed concern about Denmark's request. In making its notification, Denmark invoked the existing provisions of the Treaty permitting the maintenance of stricter national measures. But by the time it made its decision in October 1999, the new Amsterdam Treaty provisions were in force, and were the subject of the Court's ruling.

Article 95(4)[19] of the Treaty provides that, in relation to single market measures, Member States may maintain an existing stricter national measure on grounds of major needs referred to Article 30, which includes the protection of public health, the environment or the working environment. However, the Commission has to be notified and be satisfied that the conditions are met, and that the measure is not a means of arbitrary discrimination, a disguised restriction on trade, or an obstacle to the functioning of the common market.

These grounds for maintaining a stricter national measure were a repeat of previous Treaty provisions, and it was in relation to new national measures that the Amsterdam Treaty broke fresh ground by introducing specific conditions, including the requirement for new scientific evidence relating to a problem specific to the Member State seeking derogation. However, the Treaty also introduced new procedural requirements common to both existing and new measures, including a strict time limit for Commission decisions. In the case of the Danish notification, the Commission rejected the Danish case in

---

[18] Case C 512/99 *Commission v Germany* [2003] ECR I-845.
[19] See now Art 114(4) and (5) TFEU, which repeats the wording.

October 1999. It accepted that the Danish measures were aimed at protecting public heath, but decided that they were excessive in relation to the aim. It was the legal validity of this decision which Denmark challenged before the Court.

The first main ground of challenge related to the procedure adopted by the Commission. Denmark argued that it should have had a right to be heard before the Commission reached its decision. Article 95 makes no mention of such a right, but in other cases the ECJ has developed the principle of the right to a fair hearing, both for citizens and for Member States. Here, however, the ECJ noted that the procedure under Article 95 was not initiated by the Commission but the Member State, with the decision of the Commission 'being adopted merely in response to that initiative'. In its notification, the Member State has the opportunity to comment on the decisions it asks to be adopted, and the Court noted that the new Amsterdam Treaty provision which introduced faster decision-making would be jeopardised if the Commission was required to offer further hearings to the Member State. The Court concluded that the principle of the right to be heard was therefore not applicable to these procedures.

The second key ground of challenge concerned the conditions of Article 95(4) themselves. One of the Commission's grounds of rejection referred to Denmark's failure to demonstrate a particular health problem for the Danish population in relation to sulphites or the existence of a specific situation in Denmark relation to nitrites and nitrates. Denmark argued that Article 95(4) makes it clear that a reference to particular national problem was legally relevant only where new national measures were being proposed, not when a Member State proposed maintaining existing measures.

The ECJ agreed that there was a logic in the Treaty making the distinction between existing and new national measures. Where national provisions predate an EU measure, they are 'known to the Community legislature but the legislature cannot or does not seek to be guided by them for the purpose of harmonisation'. By contrast, new national measures were by definition unknown at the date of the EU measure, were more likely to jeopardise harmonisation, and stricter conditions were therefore justifiable. A problem specific to the Member State was therefore not a legally required condition for existing measures.

However, the Court went on to state that if there were such a problem, that would be highly relevant to the Commission's assessment, and in examining the Commission's decision letter it concluded that it had regulation, Enforcement and Governance in Environmental Law in fact treated the national situation as a relevant factor and not a precondition. Denmark's arguments on these grounds therefore failed. The Court added that the same approach would be applicable where there was new scientific evidence. However, in the case of an existing measure, a Member State was entitled to argue that its assessment of the risk to public health was simply different from that made by the EU legislature when making a harmonisation measure: 'In the light of uncertainty inherent in assessing the public risks posed by, inter alia, the use of food additives, divergent assessments of those risks can legitimately be made without necessarily being made on new or different scientific evidence'.

The Commission's decision letter also referred to the possibility of the harmonisation measure being amended in future under the 1989 framework Directive. The Court agreed with Denmark that this was not a legally justifiable reason for rejecting the notification of a Member State, but concluded that the reference was in fact superfluous to the Commission's decision and had not affected its conclusions.

Denmark then raised various arguments claiming that the Commission's decision contained errors of law and fact in how it had assessed the risks posed by sulphites and had reached the conclusion that the Danish measures were disproportionate. One argument alleged that the levels of sulphites permitted in the Directive failed to take account of people with allergies to the additive. The ECJ, however, noted that the limit had been based on levels which would not constitute a danger to the health of the majority of consumers, while the issue of allergies was met by labelling requirements. It could find no sufficient errors in the Commission's assessment to warrant holding it invalid.

When it came to nitrates and nitrites, the ECJ noted that the scientific opinions which formed the basis of the Directive had concluded that the substances were potential carcinogens and that it was not possible to set a no-effect level. It was therefore necessary to set limits which were the minimum strictly necessary to meet the technological requirements of the additives as preservatives. In 1995, shortly after adoption of the Directive, the Scientific Committee on Food, the key EU advisory body in this area, had issued an opinion which criticised the levels fixed as being too high, and felt they could be reduced further without jeopardising the substances' technological function. The ECJ concluded that the Commission had failed to take sufficient account of this 1995 opinion, and indeed had not even mentioned in its decision that the levels fixed in the Directive had been called into question by the SCF. As such, its decision that the Danish national provisions were disproportionate were flawed, and this part of the decision was annulled.

Finally, Denmark claimed that the Commission's decision was flawed because it failed to address the question of whether the Danish measures were a means of arbitrary discrimination, a disguised restriction on trade, or an obstacle to the functioning of the common market. These are also conditions in Article 95 common to both existing and new national measures. The ECJ, however, held that once the Commission had decided to reject the national notification on the ground that the measures did not meet a major need to protect public health, it was not obliged to address all or any other of the conditions in Article 95.

The Treaty provisions allowing Member States to maintain stricter existing legislation in spite of subsequent EU harmonisation measure have long proved controversial. Some commentators have argued, for example, that such a measure could never strictly meet the final condition in Article 95, since by definition it must be an obstacle to the functioning of the common market. As such, the wording must be assumed to imply an unreasonable or inappropriate obstacle. In the present case, the ECJ did not have to rule on this point, though the language of proportionality clearly permeates the judgement. The Amsterdam Treaty amendments introduced greater formality into the procedures, and Commission approval or disapproval is now in the form of reasoned decisions, opening them up to the greater scrutiny and more likelihood of legal challenge. The Danish case, however, suggests that the Court is likely to avoid an over-legalistic approach to the text of a Commission decision. Instead, it will look at the underlying reasoning and factors which determined the Commission's approach, and will overturn the decision only if legally unsound.

20

Supreme Court and House of Lords

Nuisance Principles and Damages in Lieu of an Injunction

Coventry v Lawrence [2014] UKSC 13

The Supreme Court has given a highly important judgment concerning common law principles of nuisance. A key feature of the decision is the signal that in future British courts should be far more willing to refuse injunctions where the defendant's activity is in the public interest, and instead require defendants to pay damages to compensate for future disturbances. *Coventry v Lawrence* concerned agricultural land used for motocross and stock-car racing. Planning permission for an initial stadium was granted in 1975 and, with an expansion of activities, further planning permission for a motocross racing track was granted by the local authority in 2002. A detailed range of conditions concerning hours of operation, maximum rider numbers and noise levels was imposed.

In 2006, the claimants bought a house less than 1,000 metres from the stadium and track, apparently unaware of the scale of the activities that took place there. They complained to the council about the noise, but there was no satisfactory resolution, and they therefore brought an action in private nuisance. The High Court found there was a nuisance in law, and was prepared to grant damages and an injunction to limit future activities. This decision was reversed in the Court of Appeal in 2012,[1] which considered that noisy motor racing was now an established feature of the locality.

The principles underlying nuisance actions essentially concern a degree of give and take between neighbours. In actions concerning noise, smells or other forms of non-physical damage, the courts have always taken into account the character of the neighbourhood in judging what type and level of noise should be reasonably permitted. As Lord Neuberger noted in his judgment, 'Whether a particular activity causes a nuisance often depends on an assessment of the locality in which the activity is carried out'.

The Supreme Court then considered two important issues of principle facing a court considered the locality test. First, was a judge entitled to take into consideration the very activity complained of as a nuisance? And, secondly, if planning permission has been granted for the activity, could that in itself change the character of the land?

As to the first question, Lord Carnwath argued that the key question was whether an existing activity could be considered to be 'part of the established pattern of use' in the area concerned. When it came to the relevance of planning controls, Lord Carnwath noted that planning law might require individuals to bear burdens for the benefits of others and

---

[1] [2012] EWCA Civ 26.

the wider public interest, while nuisance law served the function of protecting property owners. It was generally no defence to a nuisance claim to argue the activity was in the public interest.

Lord Carnwath carried out an extensive analysis of previous case law considering the relationship of planning and nuisance law, and noted the wide variety of circumstances in which planning decisions may be made. This argued against laying down oversimplistic principles. Nevertheless, he felt that generally 'there should be a strong presumption against allowing private rights to be overridden by administrative decision without compensation'. He accepted, though, that there might be exceptional cases where a major planning decision might 'lead to a fundamental change in the pattern of uses which cannot be ignored in assessing the character if the area against which the acceptability of the defendant's activity is to be judged'.

Lord Neuberger, who gave the other main judgment, was rather more equivocal about the effect of planning permissions, and clearly felt that trying to distinguish between major and less significant planning decisions would lead to uncertainty. Nevertheless, both judges felt that, where planning controls has laid down carefully constructed conditions relating to matters such as noise, these might well provide valuable benchmarks for courts in deciding what is or is not reasonable in nuisance cases.

It was when it came to the issue of remedies that the Supreme Court showed itself most radical. Claimants in nuisance cases often seek injunctions to prevent the continuation of a nuisance. An injunction is at the discretion of the court, but in nuisance case is nearly always awarded as of right. The courts have the power to require a defendant to pay damages to compensate for future damage in lieu of an injunction,[2] but have long resisted exercising this power too generously. There seems to be a strong aversion to the idea of a defendant being able to buy the right to pollute, and this strict approach has given the nuisance action a particular strength for the determined claimant.

A key decision of the Court of Appeal in 1895, *Shelfer v City of London Electric Lighting*,[3] held that damages in lieu of an injunction should be awarded in only very limited circumstances, essentially where the damage suffered was very small and could be compensated in money terms. The position is in contrast with jurisdictions such as the United States and Canada (but not Australia), where courts are far more ready to grant damages for future harm where the activity complained of has significant public interest (such as giving rise to local employment).

The Supreme Court has now called for a fresh approach. As Lord Sumption bluntly noted, 'The decision in Shelfer is out of date, and it is unfortunate that it has been followed so recently and so slavishly'. The Court accepted that every case will turn on its own facts and was therefore reluctant to lay down binding rules. But Lord Neuberger considered that the fact that a defendant's business might be shut down should be a relevant factor for a court. Equally, high-handed behaviour by a defendant or the fact that a large number of neighbours were also affected by the nuisance would argue in favour of an injunction.

---

[2] Senior Courts Act 1981, s 50 provides that, 'Where the Court of Appeal or the High Court has jurisdiction to entertain an application for an injunction or specific performance, it may award damages in addition to, or in substitution for, an injunction or specific performance'. The power was first introduced under Lord Cairns' Act 1858.

[3] [1895] 1 Ch 287.

In the present case, the defendants had not argued for damages in lieu of an injunction, but the Supreme Court suggested they could request the High Court for such an order should they so wish. The *Coventry* case is undoubtedly one of the most important decisions on common law remedies in recent years, but its real impact on nuisance action – and especially whether it will encourage or inhibit future claims – will not be known for some years.

Discretion, Remedies and Breaches of EU Law

Walton v The Scottish Ministers [2012] UKSC 44

Although the Court of Justice of the European Union is the final authority on the meaning, national courts have more powers in how they handle cases involving EU law than has been assumed. The relationship between national courts and the Court of Justice of the EU does not follow conventional lines and has long been full of subtleties. Under the European Treaty, the Court of Justice is the final authority of the meaning of EU law, but in carrying out this function, it has gone well beyond the interpretation of legislation and developed new legal principles to ensure EU law is applied effectively.

Unlike a final court of appeal, the European Court essentially confines itself to providing authoritative guidance on the meaning of EU law, leaving it to national courts to make decisions in the light of this guidance. Any national court may seek guidance from the Court of Justice in any case – a system designed deliberately to create a sense of a judicial partnership with Europe rather than a formal hierarchy.

In a recent Supreme Court decision, Lord Carnwath, Britain's most senior judge specialising in environmental law, has re-evaluated a number of core principles, suggesting that national courts have considerably more discretion in how they handle cases involving EU law than has been the assumption in recent years.

Walton v The Scottish Ministers was the legal conclusion to the long-standing disputes over the Aberdeen bypass, which had been planned for more than 15 years. The core issue, and the subject of most of the judgments, was heavily factually based, and was concerned with whether changes to the road scheme required fresh environmental assessment under the EU Strategic Environmental Assessment Directive. The Supreme Court decided unanimously that the Directive was not brought into play.

But it was Lord Carnwath's observations about national judicial remedies where EU law is involved that may have the greatest long-term impact. When courts are dealing with challenges to planning permissions and similar public decisions, they must first consider whether the decision is legal according to principles of public law. Where the decision is held to be illegal, the courts have retained the discretion as to whether or not to quash the decision itself.

When environmental impact procedures were introduced to the UK in the late 1980s following agreement to the 1985 EU Environmental Impact Assessment (EIA) Directive, British courts adopted the same approach that they had taken to national planning cases. Even if the decision was found to have contravened the Directive, the courts would consider whether compliance would have made any difference to the final result. If they felt that planning permission would still have been granted, the decision would not be quashed. In 2001, the House of Lords challenged this approach. *Berkeley v Secretary of State*[4] concerned a failure to consider whether environmental assessment procedures should be applied, contrary to the Directive and national implementing regulations. The lower courts applied the conventional approach and refused to quash the planning decision on the grounds that compliance with the environmental assessment requirements would have made no difference.

The House of Lords overruled that approach. It stressed that Member States had a general duty under the treaty to ensure proper application of EU law. This included the courts, so the discretion not to quash the permission where a breach of EU law was involved was extremely narrow. Lord Hoffman noted that a court was not entitled 'to retrospectively dispense with the requirement of an EIA on the ground that the outcome would have been the same'.

The *Berkeley* decision represented a high point in the acceptance by UK national courts that the judiciary was obliged to apply EU law. Many environmental lawyers took the decision to be a green light for checking compliance with EU environmental assessment procedures with a fine-tooth comb in the hope of quashing planning permissions. However, in a number of cases, the Court of Appeal queried an over-legalistic application of the *Berkeley* principle, emphasising that the environmental assessment requirements were designed to aid decision making rather than being a legal obstacle race.

Lord Carnwath has given a strong signal that the courts should now distance themselves from an over-rigorous application of the *Berkeley* principle. He noted that *Berkeley* was an unusual decision and one where the developer was not represented in the House of Lords since the project had been abandoned by the time of the hearing. He then examined a number of key decisions of the European Court of Justice, deciding that it gave more discretion to national courts than some have argued. The Court has long emphasised national procedural autonomy, but at the same time promoted equivalence. This means that if a particular remedy is available under national law, it must be equally available where EU law is relevant. National courts cannot discriminate when it comes to remedies.

But the Court of Justice has also promoted the principles of 'effectiveness'. So, if national principles satisfy the requirements of equivalence, they may still be defective in that they do not ensure that the requirements of EU law are properly applied. This is a less precise concept, but the court has talked of national rules making the exercise of rights provided by European law 'impossible in practice or excessively difficult'. At that point the court will no longer defer to national procedural autonomy.

Lord Carnwath emphasised these principles and considered that cases that might have suggested a broader principle, including *Berkeley*, really turned on their own particular facts. He concluded:

> Where the court is satisfied that the applicant has been able in practice to enjoy the rights conferred by the European legislation, I see nothing in principle or authority to require the courts to adopt a different approach merely because the procedural requirements arise from a European rather than a domestic source.[5]

---

[4] [2001] 2 AC 603 For a contemporary analysis of the decision, see p 394 below.

[5] This approach appears to have been endorsed in the decision of the CJEU in Case C-72/12 CJEU *Gemeinde Altrip et al v Land Rheinland-Pfaiz* 7 November 2013, where the Court accepted that the Directive gave a discretion to national courts to refuse to recognise the impairment of a right under the Directive if it established 'that it is conceivable, having regard to the circumstances of the case, that the contested decision would not have been different without the procedural defect invoked by the applicant'.

The difficulty with the approach is that it is focused on procedural rights granted by EU environmental law. It becomes more questionable where the EU law in question has a clear substantive goal, and where 'effectiveness' may imply, for example, the protection of a habitat. Nevertheless, as Lord Carnwath accepted, his judgment essentially sets down a marker, albeit an important one, 'in the hope of clearing the way to fuller argument in another case'.

Habitat Protection and Disturbance

Morgan v Hampshire County Council Supreme Court [2011] UKSC 2

The Supreme Court has given an important interpretation of the EU Habitats Directive, overruling a decision of the Court of Appeal last year. The decision in *Morgan v Hampshire County Council* will require local authorities and other public bodies to be especially vigilant that plans and proposals do not unduly disturb protected species under EU law.

The case concerned a proposed rapid bus-way between Fareham and Gosport that would run across a stretch of disused railway line. Planning permission was granted by the Council in 2009, but it was a sensitive issue because the County Council had also proposed the scheme, effectively granting permission to themselves. The disused line was not a conservation area as such, but was used for foraging by bats. Because of concerns about the effects of the development on the bats, Natural England originally opposed the application. The planning authority commissioned a new study which found that there were no actual roosts in the area but that the development would have some adverse effects on the local bats for about nine years, with the impact declining thereafter. Following this study, Natural England withdrew its objections.

A local resident challenged the legality of the decision to grant planning permission on the grounds that the authority has failed to interpret the EU Habitats Directive properly. The bats were a protected species under the Directive, and the argument centred on the meaning of the requirement in Article 12(1)(b) of the Directive that Member States must take measures to prohibit the 'deliberate disturbance' of such species. The Court took note of Guidance issued by the European Commission in 2007, which advised that sporadic disturbance without any likely negative impact of the species should not count as disturbance for the purposes of this provision. On the other hand, the Commission noted that another provision of the Directive had used the phrase 'significant disturbance', and in Article 12 no such qualification applied, implying a broader degree of protection.

The Court of Appeal had interpreted the word in the context of the overall goals of the Directive and held that only a disturbance that could threaten the conservation status of the species was encompassed by Article 12. The Supreme Court felt that this went too far, and was a misreading of the Commission's Guidance Document. Although the Guidance stated that authorities should consider the effect of the activity in question on the conservation status of the species, Lord Brown felt that this did not mean that 'only activity which *does* have an effect on the conservation status of the species (ie which imperils its favourable conservation status) is sufficient to constitute 'disturbance'.

In the view of the Court, the Guidance provided a spectrum of activities, from those with no harm to those affecting the conservation status of the species. The Court endorsed the advice in the Guidance that authorities should adopt a case-by-case approach, and 'reflect carefully on the level of disturbance to be considered harmful'. The Court was tempted to refer the issue to the European Court of Justice, but felt that the ECJ was unlikely to provide any greater assistance in the interpretation of the provision.

A second point of law raised in the case concerned the nature of the duty on the planning authority in respect of the Habitats Directive. Lord Brown noted that the regulations implementing the Directive had made it a criminal offence to disturb protected species. Acting in accordance with a planning permission used to be a statutory defence, meaning that the decision of the planning authority was critical in ensuring the protection of the species, but this was no longer the case. The criminal offence remained in place, and it was the primary responsibility of the Natural England to enforce this law.

The Court felt that, while a planning authority should refuse permission where they felt it was likely that the development would offend Article 12 of the Directive, it did not have to go any further. Where, as in this case, Natural England has decided that it is satisfied that the development is compliant with Article 12, the planning authority is entitled to presume that this is the case, and not have to make its own independent assessment. According to Lord Brown,

> It seems to me wrong in principle, when Natural England have the primary responsibility for ensuring compliance with the Directive, also to place a substantial burden on the planning authority, in effect to police the fulfilment of Natural England's own duty.

The only dissenting judgment on this issue was given by Lord Kerr. He accepted that, if Natural England had unambiguously stated that the proposal would not breach the Habitats Directive, the planning authority would not need to question that statement. On the facts, however, he felt this was not actually the case, and that therefore the authority had not properly had regard to the Directive.

Statutory Successor not Liable under Contaminated Land Regime

R on the application of National Grid Gas PLC (formerly Transco PLC) v Environment Agency [2007] UKHL 30

The House of Lords has held that the contaminated land regime does not impose liability on statutory successors to companies whose gasworks have caused contamination. In overruling last year's High Court decision, the Lords resisted allowing the 'polluter pays' principle to give an extended interpretation of the legislative language. The Lords ruling was a U-turn on the High Court decision and indicated that, where retrospective liability is imposed under a statutory regime, it is for Parliament rather than the courts to define who should be liable.

R on the application of National Grid Gas PLC (formerly Transco PLC) v Environment Agency concerned a site in Bawtry, Doncaster, which had been used as a coal gasworks by the Bawtry and District Gas Company and its successor bodies from about 1915. The site ceased operations shortly after nationalisation in 1948 and the land was sold to a private developer for housing by the East Midlands Gas Board in 1965. The gasworks had deposited coal tar residues under the land. Before the land was sold, it appears the residues had been drawn into underground containers – in line with contemporary practice – but these had probably been breached during development. In 2001 a pit filled with coal tar was found in the garden of one of the properties. The Environment Agency declared the whole area, including 11 residential properties, a special site under the contaminated land regime under Part IIA of the Environment Protection Act 1990. Remediation cost about £66,000 per property and the question in law was who should pay for it.

Liability under the regime is in essence imposed on the person or persons who 'caused or knowingly permitted' the presence of the contaminating substances. If such cannot be found, liability for remediation rests on the current owner or occupier, subject to financial hardship provisions. The Environmental Agency had already indicated that it would not impose any liability on the current householders in this case. The Agency determined that the developers and National Grid Gas, as the contemporary statutory successors to the original gas companies, were equally liable as the persons who caused the contamination. The developers were no longer in existence and the Agency carried out remediation works, seeking a 50 per cent contribution from National Grid Gas.

National Grid challenged the Agency's interpretation of the regime and *Bawtry* was seen as a test case for many other sites formerly occupied by previous statutory bodies. National Grid accepted that if it was the current owner of a contaminated site or had actually caused the contamination it might be liable under the regime, but in this case the land had been sold before the company had existed and before the gas industry was privatised.

The Agency's first argument rested on an extended interpretation of the meaning of the person who caused or knowingly permitted the contamination. National Grid was clearly a separate legal entity from its predecessor bodies, but the Agency argued that statutory succession provisions were intended to preserve legal continuity. The polluter pays principle underpinned the contaminated land regime, it said, and therefore it was permissible to give a more purposeful construction to the meaning of 'person' under Part IIA to avoid remediation costs falling on innocent owners or the public purse. This argument had been accepted in the High Court but was firmly rejected by the House of Lords. According to Lord Hoffmann:

> National Grid did not cause or knowingly permit any substances to be in, on or under the land. This was done by East Midlands Gas Board or its predecessors as gas undertakers many years before National Grid came into existence. There is nothing in the Act to say that an appropriate person shall be deemed to be some other person or which defines who that person shall be.

Lord Scott was even more dismissive of the High Court's approach: 'This is, in my opinion, a quite impossible construction to place on the uncomplicated and easily understandable statutory language'. The Agency has stressed that the contaminated land regime was based on the polluter pays principle and that innocent owners or occupiers of contaminated land should not to have to pay. Lord Scott noted:

> I have no doubt that was so and have no quarrel with that principle. But Transco was not a polluter and is no less innocent of having 'caused or knowingly permitted' the pollution than the innocent owner or occupiers of the 11 residencies.

The Agency's second main line of argument related to the various Acts of Parliament that had created successor gas companies, and the provisions concerning the transfer of assets and liabilities. Both the Gas Act 1948 (nationalisation) and the Gas Act 1986 (privatisation) transferred liabilities that existed 'immediately before' the transfer took place. The Agency argued that the contaminated land regime has imposed retrospective liability in the sense that bodies that have caused contamination could now be liable for actions that were legal at the time. Given that approach, it was acceptable to interpret the previous statutory provisions concerning the transfer of liabilities to now include liabilities under the Part IIA of the Environment Act 1995.

Their Lordships dismissed this interpretation. Lord Hoffmann noted that it was true that the contaminated land regime was retrospective by creating a potential present liability for acts done in the past. 'But it is not the same as creating a deemed past liability for those acts. There is nothing in the Act to create retrospectively in this sense,' he said. In this context, Lord Scott was particularly concerned that, upon privatisation in 1986, the public were invited to invest on the basis of liabilities in the new company as being limited to those existing immediately before the Act. He said:

> I find it extraordinary and unacceptable that a public authority, a part of government, should seek to impose a liability on a private company, and thereby reduce the value of the investment held by its shareholders, that falsifies the basis on which the original investors, the subscribers, were invited by government to subscribe for shares.

Lord Neuberger, though, gave a more nuanced view on the issue of shareholder expectations. People who had bought shares before 1995 in a company that had caused contamination might be equally aggrieved that the application of the polluter pays principle had now unpredictably falsified the basis on which the original investors, the subscribers, were invited by the government to subscribe for shares. But he accepted that this might be a consequence of imposing retrospective liability and that, in such circumstances, public and private interest in decontaminating land outweighed shareholder interests. The increasing awareness of the seriousness and extent to which land has been contaminated must inevitably have unexpected physical and economic consequences.

> Where a polluter has ceased to exist and the whole of its business, or at least the whole of its relevant business, has been acquired by another company, it might well appear to many people to be similarly justifiable, at least in some circumstances, if liability for decontamination was extended to apply to that other company.

In Lord Neuberger's view, however, the circumstances where it would be right to extend the polluter pays concept in such a way is a matter of policy for the legislature, not for the courts. 'The role of the courts is to interpret the relevant statutory provisions which the legislature has enacted, in order to determine whether they have that effect,' he said. He agreed it was not possible to interpret the relevant statutory provisions in the way contended for by the Agency.

The decision in *National Grid* does not necessarily imply that all statutory successor bodies, whether in the public or private sector, are relieved from liability under the contaminated land regime; much will depend on the words actually used in the specific transfer schemes. For instance, the legislation which privatised the water industry – the Water Act 1989 – provided that a transfer scheme made by the Secretary of State could provide that a successor body is to be treated as the same person in law as the water authority from which it is transferred. If a transfer scheme contained such a provision, it is likely that the successor body would be liable as an appropriate person where the previous water authority had caused the contamination. Similarly, some liability transfer provisions expressly include liabilities arising under future legislation, and such provisions could also impose liability under the contaminated land regime. The government no doubt will now have to evaluate carefully the implications of the decision against the different regimes governing statutory bodies. It must decide whether in reality it is confined to a narrow set of circumstances or whether it implies such a significant problem for the contaminated land regime as to require new amending legislation. As their Lordships noted, Parliament can impose what liabilities it sees fit on whom it chooses. But Lord Scott warned that 'very careful statutory language would be needed to impose on a company innocent of any polluting activity a liability to pay for works to remedy pollution caused by others to land it had never owned or had any interest in'.

Key Ruling on Liability for Sewage Flooding

Marcic v Thames Water Utilities Ltd [2004] 2 AC 42

In a test case on the liability of sewerage undertakers for damage caused by flooding from overloaded sewers, the House of Lords has held that private remedies under nuisance law or breaches of the Human Rights Act have no part to play. In doing so, it overturned the decision of the Court of Appeal, which held that both contemporary nuisance law and the Human Rights Act could provide a remedy for individuals affected. *Marcic v Thames Water Utilities Ltd* concerned the owner of a house in Stanmore who had suffered repeated and serious flooding from an overloaded public sewerage system since 1992, and had even resorted to constructing his own defence system at a cost of £15,000. The sewers affecting the claimant's property did not qualify for upgrading under the system devised by Thames Water for determining priorities, although by the time the case reached the House of Lords the necessary remedial works had eventually been completed.

The statutory provisions covering the provision of sewers are contained in the Water Industry Act 1991. Under section 94, a sewerage undertaker has a general duty to provide a system of public sewers to ensure that its area is drained effectively. The Act empowers the Secretary of State and the water regulator Ofwat to serve an enforcement order on undertakers who are in breach of their statutory duties, and such an order can be enforced by an injunction if necessary. The legislation, however, expressly excludes an individual seeking damages for breach of a statutory duty. It is only where an enforcement order has been served that an individual may seek damages where breach of the order results in damage, although the undertaker may plead a due diligence defence in such cases. In the present case, no enforcement order had been served on Thames Water and, while the claimant had made complaints to both the company and the local authority, he had not complained directly to Ofwat.

In its 2001 decision, the High Court did not feel that the statutory provisions excluded the application of common law remedies, but held that the existing principles of nuisance law only applied where an undertaker had carried out a positive act which resulted in damages, and were not applicable where, as here, there was failure to do something.

Nevertheless, the court had held that the damage was sufficiently serious to amount to a breach of the Human Rights Act and its provisions concerning respect for privacy and the peaceful enjoyment of possessions. The Court of Appeal reviewed the old case law on nuisance, and held that a contemporary approach should permit a claim in case of failure to act. Much of its judgment was concerned with this aspect of the case, though it also upheld the claim based on the Human Rights Act.

In overturning the Court of Appeal's decision, the House of Lords gave far greater emphasis to the comprehensiveness of the statutory scheme under the Water Industry Act, which now governs both the provision of sewers and their financing through charges. It noted that, in the absence of an enforcement order, an individual could seek no statutory remedy against the undertaker, and that his only remedy was to seek judicial review proceedings against the Secretary of State or Ofwat to force them to make an order against the undertaker. As Lord Nicholls noted, in pursuing his claim under common law and the Human Rights Act, Mr Marcic was effectively seeking 'to sidestep the statutory enforcement code'.

Lord Nicholls considered the old common law cases concerning the liability of local authorities for sewerage overloads. The Court of Appeal had held that these could no longer stand in the light of more recent case law, such as *Leakey v National Trust* ([1980] I All ER 17), which had held that occupiers of land could be liable in nuisance for failing to take steps to prevent potential hazards in their property from causing damage to their neighbours. Lord Nicholls felt that the Court of Appeal had been mistaken in applying principles concerning the duty of occupiers of land to their neighbours to the duties of statutory undertakers, which were now governed by the statutory scheme contained in the 1991 Act. Under the statutory provisions, Ofwat sets limits on the amount that undertakers can charge for their services, and in the process has to balance the need to alleviate flooding with the costs of doing so, as well as other policy priorities, such as those required under EU Directives. According to Lord Nicholls,

> The existence of a parallel common law right, whereby individual householders who suffer sewer flooding may themselves bring court proceedings when no enforcement order has been made, would set at nought the statutory scheme. It would effectively supplant the regulatory role the Director [of Ofwat] was intended to discharge when questions of sewer flooding arise.

In dealing with the claim under the Human Rights Act, their Lordships were clearly strongly influenced by the decision of the Grand Chamber of the European Court of Human Rights earlier this year in the *Hatton* case, concerning night flights at Heathrow.[6] There the Grand Chamber emphasised that the Convention rights did not grant absolute protection of privacy or property, and that in areas involving complex policy issues a large margin of discretion should be granted to governments in determining the appropriate balances that had to be made between private and public interests. As Lord Hoffmann noted, 'National institutions, and particularly the national legislature, are accorded a broad discretion in choosing the solution appropriate to their own society or creating the machinery for doing so'. Although the claimant had clearly suffered, there was nothing so suggest, according to their Lordships, that the statutory scheme as a whole did not comply with the Convention.

---

[6] Application No 36022/97 *Hatton and others v United Kingdom* 8 July 2003.

The decision reflects a general concern of the courts becoming involved in making decisions about the allocation of public resources for which they consider themselves ill-equipped, especially where, in the nature of litigation, they are normally faced with resolving a discrete dispute between an individual and a public authority rather than considering the wider policy context. Nevertheless, although Mr Marcic lost at the last round, the litigation has clearly had some positive impact. In March last year, Ofwat issued a consultation paper which acknowledged the seriousness of the problem of flooding from sewers, and made proposals for undertakers to deal more speedily with severe external flooding cases, which should in future be included in their investment programmes.

Lord Nicholls also noted that existing regulations provided for modest compensation in respect of internal flooding for those who suffered while waiting remediation schemes. But the regulations made no provisions for compensation for the type of external flooding which had occurred in the present case, with some undertakers voluntarily providing compensation, but others not. Lord Nicholls felt this was unacceptable: 'The minority who suffer damage and disturbance as a consequence of the inadequacy of the sewerage system ought not to be required to bear and unreasonable burden'. Such compensation would eventually be funded through increased charges, but it was perfectly fair that the majority who benefited from an adequate system should compensate the minority who did not. He called on Ofwat and others to reconsider the provisions of compensation for external flooding.

Although the general scheme concerning the provision of sewers might be fair, Thames Water did not escape censure for its handling of Mr Marcic's repeated complaints. According to Lord Nicholls,

> It cannot be acceptable that in 2001, several years after Thames Water knew of Mr Marcic's serious problems, there was still no prospect of the necessary work being carried out for the foreseeable future. At times Thames Water handled Mr Marcic's complaints in a tardy and insensitive fashion.

As a result of the House of Lords decision, future complaints concerning the inadequacy of sewers must be directed to OFWAT, and it is equally clear that the robustness with which it deals with the problem will now be under increasing scrutiny.

Breach of EIA Directive Requires Planning Decision to be Quashed

Berkeley v Secretary of State and Others [2001] 2 AC 603

The House of Lords has held that a court has very limited discretion to uphold the validity of a planning decision where there has been a failure to apply the EC Directive on environmental impact assessment. The ruling sends a powerful signal concerning the importance of compliance with EC rules which may well have implications for other areas of Community environmental law.[7]

---

[7] But see the criticisms by the Supreme Court in the 2012 *Walton* case analysed on p 386 above of applying an overly strict approach when it comes to remedies – the approach of the Supreme Court appears to be endorsed by the CJEU in Case C-72/12 CJEU *Gemeinde Altrip et al v Land Rheinland-Pfaiz* 7 November 2013.

Berkeley v Secretary of State and Others concerned the redevelopment of the Fulham Football Club ground. The club applied for planning permission in 1994 to build a new stadium and a block of flats, including a new walkway along the bank of the Thames. The planning authority, the London Borough of Hammersmith, consulted, among others, the London Ecology Unit, which opposed the development because it felt that the walkway would encroach on the river bank and damage the local ecology. A lengthy report on the application was prepared by the planning department summarising the views of those who had been consulted or made representations, and recommended that permission be granted. The Secretary of State, however, called in the application for his own decision in order to assess the implications of the proposed housing density on local car parking and the development's impact on the Thames. An eight-day public inquiry was held, with the inspector eventually recommending that permission be granted subject to conditions. In August 1996, the Secretary of State accepted the recommendation and granted planning permission. At no time, however, did it appear that either the planning authority or the Secretary of State had considered whether the project should be subject to environmental assessment.

Annex II of the 1985 EC Directive on environmental assessment, mirrored in Schedule 2 of the 1988 implementing regulations, contains a large number of project classes which must be subject to assessment where they are likely to have significant environmental impacts, and the Fulham FC development potentially fell within the category of 'urban development projects'. A local resident challenged the validity of the planning permission on the grounds that the Directive had not been followed. Under the 1988 regulations, the Secretary of State is barred from granting planning permission for a Schedule 2 application unless the information obtained during the assessment procedures has been taken into consideration. The regulations go on to provide that a grant of permission in breach of this requirement is taken to be ultra vires, allowing an aggrieved person to apply to the court to quash the decision.

In the High Court, Mr Justice Tucker had doubted whether the project fell within a category requiring assessment, but the Court of Appeal concluded that there had been a failure to comply with the Directive. However, the Court of Appeal noted that, even where a planning permission is held to be illegal, the court has a residual discretion whether or not to actually quash the decision. The Court felt that, given the extensive public inquiry and background documentation, all the information that would have been prepared under the assessment procedures was in fact considered by the Secretary of State, and therefore refused to quash the decision.

The House of Lords doubted whether this was the correct approach. Lord Bingham observed that, if the Secretary of State had in fact considered that the project fell within a class subject to the EIA requirements, he could not have waived the procedures on the grounds that there had been substantive compliance with those requirements unless he had formally exempted the project under Article 2(3) of the Directive – a procedure that requires notification to the European Commission. 'It would, I think, be strange if the Secretary of State could lawfully achieve by inadvertence a result which he could not lawfully achieve if acting deliberately,' Lord Bingham observed.

Counsel for the Secretary of State conceded that the Court of Appeal had been wrong to imply that a court could exercise its discretion not to quash the permission on the grounds that compliance with the EIA requirements would have made no difference to the final result. This was a significant concession, and Lord Hoffmann elaborated why he felt

it was correct in law. He noted that Article 10 of the EC Treaty[8] imposes a general obligation on Member States to 'take all appropriate measures, whether general or particular, to
ensure fulfilment of the obligations arising out of the Treaty'. The 1985 Directive grants a
discretion to Member States concerning its application to Annex II projects, but clearly
implies that they are

> under an obligation to consider whether or not an EIA is required. If it were not so, a Member
> State could in practice restrict the scope of the Directive to Annex I cases simply by failing to
> consider whether in any other case an EIA was required or not.

Lord Hoffmann noted that the Directive 'requires not merely that the planning authority
should have all the necessary information but that it should have been obtained by means
of a particular procedure, namely that of an EIA'. The European Court of Justice had
already held that the Directive gave directly effective rights to individuals, and Lord Hoffmann concluded that

> the directly enforceable right of the citizen which is accorded by the Directive is not merely a
> right to a fully informed decision on the substantive issue. It must have been adopted on an
> appropriate basis and that requires the inclusive and democratic procedure prescribed by the
> Directive in which the public, however misguided or wrongheaded its views may be, is given an
> opportunity to express its opinion on the environmental issues.

He further concluded that a court was not therefore entitled retrospectively to waive the
EIA requirements on the grounds that the decision maker had all the relevant environmental information before him.

The approach of counsel for the Secretary of State was rather more subtle. He argued
that on the facts of the case there had actually been substantive compliance with all the
procedural requirements of the Directive, even if the term 'environmental assessment' had
not been used. There is one decision of the European Court of Justice, in a 1995 case
between the Commission and Germany,[9] which supports this approach. The case involved
a challenge by the Commission concerning an authorisation of a power plant at a time
when Germany had failed to transpose the 1985 Directive into national law. The existing
national procedures, however, already required an assessment, the developer to supply
information and the public to be consulted. The ECJ felt that the Commission had failed
to produce sufficient details as to which provisions of the Directive had not been complied
with, and dismissed its application.

In Lord Hoffmann's view, that decision established that an EIA by any other name 'will
do as well', but he did not feel that the procedures followed in the Fulham FC case fell in
the same league. He noted that there were in fact implementing national regulations in
place which had not been followed, and felt that a court should be reluctant to validate
an act in breach of the regulations on the grounds that different transposing regulations
would have satisfied the Directive. Furthermore, he did not accept

> that this paper chase can be treated as the equivalent of an environmental statement . . . the point
> about environmental statement contemplated by the Directive is that it constitutes a single
> and accessible compilation, produced by the applicant at the very start of the application process,
> of the relevant environmental information and the summary in non-technical language.

---

[8] Now Art 4 TEU.
[9] Case C-431/93 [1995] ECR I-2189.

The House of Lords unanimously agreed that the planning decision should be quashed. Its reasoning marks a reversal of the traditional approach of British courts towards the exercise of their discretion to quash or not quash planning decisions. In cases of truly minor infringements, the House of Lords accepted that a court might uphold the decision. But it clearly expects a much tougher approach from the courts in future, and one more in line with the stance adopted by courts in countries such as the Netherlands. As Lord Bingham summarised the situation:

> In the Community context, unless the violation is so negligible as to be truly de minimis and the prescribed procedure has in all essentials been followed, the discretion (if any exists) is narrower still; the duty laid on Member States by Article 10 of the EC Treaty, the obligation of national courts to ensure that Community rights are fully and effectively enforced, the strict conditions attached by Article 2(3) of the Directive to the exercise of the power to exempt, and the absence of any power by the Secretary of State to waive compliance (otherwise than by way of exemption) with the requirements of the regulations in the case of urban development projects which in his opinion is likely to have significant effects on the environment by virtue of the factors mentioned, all point towards an order to quash as the proper response to a contravention such as admittedly occurred in this case.

More than any other piece of EC environmental legislation, the EIA Directive is rooted in procedural requirements and rights of public consultation. These features clearly weighed strongly in the decision. Yet the signals given by the House of Lords in the *Berkeley* case may well stretch beyond town and country planning procedures, and colour the approach taken by courts when faced with judicial review challenges in other areas of environmental law, such as integrated pollution prevention and control and waste management licensing, where breaches of Community law are alleged. A number of the environmental directives have been held to give individuals legal rights to standards of environmental quality and, while public participation requirements are far less developed than in the EIA Directive, this may not remain the case for long. At a seminar in London in June 2001 organised by the UK Environmental Law Association, a senior Commission official revealed plans for a Directive to introduce public participation rights into a raft of existing environmental Directives as part of the Commission's preparations for ratifying the pan-European Aarhus Convention.[10] In the light of these developments, the Berkeley decision takes on an even wider significance for UK environmental law.

House of Lords Rules on Planning and Human Rights

R (Alconbury) v Secretary of State for the Environment, Transport (House of Lords) [2001] 2 All ER 929

In what some observers have described as the most important planning case for 50 years, the House of Lords has held that the current system under which the Secretary of State is

---

[10] See now Directive 2003/35/EC of the European Parliament and of the Council of 26 May 2003 providing for public participation in respect of the drawing up of certain plans and programmes relating to the environment and amending with regard to public participation and access to justice Council Directives 85/337/EEC and 96/61/EC.

able to decide important planning decisions is not inconsistent with principles of human rights introduced under the Human Rights Act 2000. The result of the *Alconbury* case is a setback for those arguing for an independent planning court or tribunal, but still leaves open important issues concerning the impact of human rights principles on current procedures. The importance of the case was indicated by the unusual decision of five Law Lords to give separate opinions. In doing so, they comprehensively overturned the decision of the High Court last December. The High Court had held that it was inconsistent with the 2000 Act for the Secretary of State to be both a policy maker and a decision maker in planning and related matters. The position was not saved by the right of judicial review before the courts, since their powers of intervention were limited and did not involve a full appeal on merits.

The starting point for the case was Article 6 of the European Convention on Human Rights, which states: 'In the determination of his civil rights and obligations or of any criminal charge against him, everyone is entitled to a fair and public hearing within a reasonable time by an independent and impartial tribunal'. It was accepted that the number of planning cases where the Secretary of State had called in an application for his own decision or recovered the power to do so from the Planning Inspectorate was tiny compared to the total number of planning applications – around 130 call-ins per year out of some 500,000 applications, and around 100 recovered cases out of 13,000 appeals. But the figures are somewhat misleading, since almost by definition these were likely to be the most important or controversial cases.

The House of Lords accepted, following decisions of the European Court on Human Rights, that disputes under planning rules and areas such as compulsory purchase did involve the determination of civil rights within the meaning of the Convention, even though, as Lord Hoffmann observed, this was not what was necessarily what the original drafters of the Convention had in mind. Although there was no suggestion of any bias against individuals, the Secretary of State did not argue that, in dealing with called-in or recovered matters, he was acting as an independent tribunal within the meaning of the Convention. As Lord Slynn observed, 'He accepts that the fact that he makes policy and applies that policy in particular cases is sufficient to prevent him from being an independent tribunal'.

The critical turning point in the analysis was the role of the courts in reviewing decisions of the Secretary of State, and the extent to which this provided sufficient consistency with the Article 6 principles. The House of Lords examined rather closely decisions of the European Court on Human Rights which accepted that many administrative decisions which affect civil rights are taken by ministers answerable to elected bodies. Assuming that this decision-making system did not involve an independent tribunal, compliance with the Convention required that these decisions be subject to control by an independent judicial body 'with full jurisdiction'. The meaning of 'full jurisdiction' was therefore critical. Despite some earlier, more extravagant judgments, the developing case law of the European Court has indicated that in the context of administrative decisions, Article 6 does not provide a right to a full appeal on the merits of every administrative decision. As Lord Hoffmann put it, 'Subsequent European authority shows that 'full jurisdiction' does not mean full decision-making powers. It means full jurisdiction to deal with the case as the nature of the decision requires'. The core conclusion of the House of Lords was that, in the context of planning and similar disputes, it was not essential or even appropriate for a court to have the power to review questions of policy in the sense that it should substitute its own view of what the public interest required. What is required of the courts, according to Lord Slynn, 'is that there should be a sufficient review of the legality of the decision and of the procedures followed'. Their Lordships accepted that the British courts had in recent years extended the ambit of judicial review, and that a mistaken factual basis of a decision could now be a ground for judicial intervention. Lord Slynn went further and argued that the principle of proportionality, long recognised as important in European law, should now be expressly recognised as being applicable to questions of domestic law in place of the more traditional *Wednesbury* test of unreasonableness.

One of the cases before *Alconbury* involved a government department with a direct financial interest in the outcome of the planning application since it owned the land involved. Here, the House of Lords dealt rather more perfunctorily with the issue than some would have expected. They did so on the basis that the Secretary of State did not claim to be independent, and that a court could exercise powers of judicial review if irrelevant considerations, including financial ones, had been brought into play. In one sense this is a correct analysis, but it does not reflect the difficulties for those wishing to challenge such a decision in producing evidence of any such bias – which is certainly unlikely to be provided in express terms in a decision letter or similar documentation.

The House of Lords' decision will come as some relief to the government, but it by no means marks the end of the application of human rights principles to planning procedures. Indeed, by expressly recognising that the determination of planning issues does involve civil rights within the meaning of the Convention, their Lordships have kept open the exploration of other aspects of the Convention. The question of the rights of third parties – particularly those whose property is affected by planning decisions – still remains unresolved, and there will still be strong arguments that some form of third party right of appeal is required. The immediate pressure on the government to introduce a new independent planning or environmental tribunal is relieved, though there may remain strong arguments for doing so, even in the absence of specific human rights principles. Finally, the decision indicates that, in the exercise of judicial review functions, the courts need to scrutinise carefully the way decisions are reached and their factual basis, albeit without interfering with the policy functions of government. Proportionality as a principle of review will be more extensively applied than at present. In these respects it is likely that, far from diminishing the role of the courts, the decision may enhance their influence.

Strict Liability in Water Pollution Offences

Environment Agency (formerly National Rivers Authority) v Empress Car Company (Abertillery) Ltd [1998] 2 WLR 350

An important ruling concerning the meaning of the key water pollution offences under the Water Resources Act 1991 has been given by the House of Lords. The lead judgment of Lord Hoffmann in the *Empress Car* case provides a fresh analysis of what is meant by 'causing' water pollution, and implies that causation can apply even where the polluter takes no active steps. The decision will require industry and sewerage undertakers to pay extra attention to maintaining pollution control equipment and other preventative measures if they are to avoid criminal prosecution.

Under section 85(1) of the 1991 Act, a person commits an offence if he 'causes or knowingly permits any poisonous, noxious or polluting matter or any solid waste matter to enter any controlled waters'. Compliance with a discharge consent is a good defence. The wording repeats the formulation in previous legislation, and the lead 1972 decision of the House of Lords in *Alphacell Ltd v Woodward*[11] held that the drafting implied two distinct heads of liability – causing the entry of polluting matter, and knowingly permitting its entry.

The enforcing authority, now the Environment Agency, must choose the appropriate charge, but the critical legal distinction is that with the permitting offence some proof of knowledge on the defendant's part must be proved. In contrast, the offence of causing the entry is one of strict liability in that lack of awareness is no defence, though it may be reflected in any sentence imposed. As Lord Hoffmann put it in the *Empress Car* case: 'The notion of causing is present in both limbs: under the first limb what the defendant did must have caused the pollution, and under the second limb his omission must have caused it'.

The *Alphacell* decision insisted that the notion of causation in the offence must be given a common sense meaning. But since that case there have been a large number of High Court and Appeal Court decisions exploring what is meant by 'causing the entry' of polluting matter. Some of these appeared to suggest that there must be a 'positive' act on the part of the defendant, and that where the pollution was caused, say, by the failure of control equipment this could not be an offence under the first limb. Similarly, where the actions of a third party such as a trespasser had caused the direct entry of the polluting matter, the defendant could argue that the chain of causation had been broken.

These decisions now have to be re-evaluated in the light of the House of Lords judgment in the *Empress Car* case. The company maintained a diesel storage tank on its premises, which drained directly into a river. Although there was a bund around the tank, the company had overridden this by fixing an extension pipe to the tank outlet which connected to a drum outside the bund. The tank outlet was governed by a tap which had no lock. In 1995, someone opened the tap, allowing the full contents of the tank to run into the drum, which overflowed into the yard and drained into the river. The person who opened the tap was never identified. It could have been an employee or, since there had been local opposition to the company's business, an act of sabotage may have been involved.

Nevertheless, the company was charged with causing the entry of polluting matter into the river. It was convicted by local magistrates and lost an appeal to the Crown Court on the grounds that it had brought the diesel onto the site and had failed to take adequate preventative measures, such as fitting a lock on the tap and ensuring the integrity of the bund. On appeal, the Divisional Court held that, despite the intervening act of a stranger, the Crown Court was still entitled on the facts to find that Empress Car had caused the pollution. But it agreed that the case law was confusing, and certified that there was a point of law of general public importance for the House of Lords to consider.

The House of Lords agreed that the first limb of the section 85 offence required there to be some positive act on the part of the company – but the critical question was what counted as a positive act. Earlier case law, such as that of the Divisional Court in the 1992

---

[11] [1972] AC 824.

case of *Wychavon District Council v National Rivers Authority*,[12] held that the failure to maintain a sewerage system which resulted in sewage overflows into a river could not amount to a positive act. But in Lord Hoffmann's opinion, such decisions

> take far too restrictive a view of the requirement that the defendant must have done something. They seem to require that his positive act should not have been in some sense the immediate cause of the escape. But the Act contains no such requirement. It only requires a finding that something which the defendant did caused the pollution.

Although the House of Lords reaffirmed that common sense notions of causality must apply, Lord Hoffmann emphasised that answers to questions of causation would differ according to the purpose for which the question was asked. Lord Hoffmann drew the analogy of the owner of a car who left his radio in overnight. A thief breaks the window to steal the radio and in law would be considered to have caused the damage to the car, and he could not argue that it was the owner's carelessness that had caused the damage. But if this had been the third such occurrence in a year, a common sense, non-legal approach might suggest that it was the owner's failure to take reasonable care of his possessions that had also caused the damage and the loss of his radio. Both approaches were correct in their own terms. In the case of a prosecution under section 85, it was therefore wrong to ask the question 'What caused the pollution?' and there might be a number of different answers to that question. Instead, one had solely to consider 'Did the defendant cause the pollution?'

When it came to questions of the acts of third parties or the influence of natural forces, there were situations where both as a matter of common sense and the application of legal rules there were duties to take precautions to prevent losses being caused by external events. But before considering questions of causation, it was necessary first to consider the purpose and scope of the rule in question to determine whether it imposed a duty to require one to guard against the deliberate acts of third parties or the operation of natural forces. This question was not one of common sense but one of law, and in the present case one of statutory construction.

It was clear that Parliament had imposed a strict liability for the first limb of the offence 'in the interests of protecting controlled waters from pollution'. Lord Hoffmann agreed with statements in the *Alphacell* judgments that not every act of a third party could be said to interrupt the chain of causation, and to the extent that other cases such as *Impress (Worcester) v Rees*[13] in 1971 suggested that they did they were wrongly decided.

Although liability under the first limb of the section 85 offence was strict,

> it is not an absolute liability in the sense that all that has to be shown is that the polluting matter escaped from the defendant's land, irrespective of how this happened. It must still be possible to say that the defendant caused the pollution.

Some of the subsequent case law dealing with intervening actions of third parties had employed the test of foreseeability, asking whether the defendant could reasonably have foreseen what took place before he could be said to have caused the pollution. But Lord Hoffmann was unhappy with the use of such language: 'Foreseeability is not a criterion for deciding whether a person caused something or not. People often cause things which they could not have foreseen.'

---

[12] [1993] 1 WLR 125.
[13] [1971] 2 All ER 357.

In his view, the true common sense distinction was between acts and events which were generally a normal and familiar fact of life, and those which were abnormal or extraordinary. Acts and events which were familiar in that sense would often be foreseeable, but foreseeability was not strictly a necessary element. In this context, there was nothing extraordinary about leaky pipes, people putting substances unlawfully into the sewerage system, or ordinary vandalism. On the other hand, in the example given by Lord Hoffmann, a terrorist attack which damaged a defendant's works and gave rise to pollution 'would be something so unusual that one would not regard the defendant's conduct as having caused the escape at all'. The same distinction could be applied to natural events. In the *Alphacell* case, falling leaves and vegetation had blocked the defendant's pumps, causing an overflow, but the House of Lords held that they had still caused the pollution in that there had been no abnormal weather conditions but precisely what one would have expected in the autumn. The situation would have been different if there had been some extraordinary natural event or 'Act of God'.

Lord Hoffmann ended his judgement by summarising the key principles to be applied in the case of a charge under section 85. These are now likely to be widely used by magistrates and other courts dealing with water pollution offences.

First, the prosecution must be asked to identify what it says the defendant did to cause the pollution. If he cannot be said to have done anything then the prosecution must fail, although the circumstances might still warrant a charge of knowingly permitting the pollution. But the prosecution need not prove that what the defendant did was the immediate cause of the pollution – maintaining tanks, lagoons or sewerage systems were all doing something, even if the immediate cause was something else. Courts must then consider whether what the prosecution alleged the defendant did could be said to have caused the pollution, and must not be diverted by questions such as: 'What was the cause of the pollution?' or 'Did something else cause the pollution?'

Where the actual escape was also caused by the act of a third party or a natural event, courts must consider whether this should be regarded as a normal fact of life or something extraordinary.

> If it was in the general run of things a matter of ordinary occurrence, it will not negative the causal effect of the defendant's acts even if it was not foreseeable that it would happen to that particular defendant or take that particular form. It if can be regarded as something extraordinary it will be open to justices to hold that the defendant did not cause the pollution.

This distinction between ordinary and extraordinary was one of fact and degree which courts must apply with common sense and knowledge of what happens in the area. On the facts of the *Empress Car* case, the House of Lords felt that there was ample evidence to entitle the courts below to find that the company had caused the pollution.

The decision clearly throws light on what has proved a difficult area of law, and imposes greater duties on industries and sewerage undertakers to take appropriate preventative steps to guard against the actions of third parties, equipment failure, or natural events such as storm damage. Lord Hoffmann's analysis of what is implied by causation may be of relevance to other areas of environmental law, though the decision is strictly confined to section 85 water pollution offences. Many pollution offences are now contained in the Environmental Protection Act 1990, but these are often drafted in differing terms reflecting their distinct historical origins. The key offences concerning waste disposal, for example, use the term 'cause or knowingly permit' but the term 'knowingly' also qualifies the causation limb, making the distinction of less critical importance. However, there appears to be little rational justification for maintaining such a distinction between the water and waste regimes. The offences concerning integrated pollution control, in contrast, do not use the language of causation or permitting, but are directly related to operating without or in breach of an authorisation. The statutory nuisance provisions of Part III of the 1990 Act employ different terminology and place liability on the person 'responsible' for the nuisance or in some cases the owner or occupier of the land in question. The opportunity was taken in the Environment Act 1995 to introduce greater consistency across the enforcement provisions of the different regimes, but it may be that the time has come for a more detailed analysis of the rationale behind the conceptual distinctions that still exist.

21

Court of Appeal

Civil Liability in Nuisance and the Defence of Complying with a Permit

Barr and others v Biffa Waste Services [2012] EWCA Civ 312

This case concerned a licensed waste disposal site in Ware, Hertfordshire, where local residents had complained about smells from the site over a five-year period. One of the conditions of the waste disposal permit related to odours, and the Environment Agency successfully prosecuted Biffa for breaching this condition on a number of days between 2004 and 2005. The problems continued and eventually the residents brought an action in nuisance against Biffa, seeking compensation for the smells they had suffered.

In the High Court, Mr Justice Coulson noted that the claimants did not allege any breach of the permit conditions. After a lengthy analysis of the law, he essentially agreed with Biffa that, because it had complied with all the regulatory requirements, it could not be said to have committed a nuisance. Although Mr Justice Coulson felt that this was in line with modern authorities, the decision was a bold re-evaluation of familiar principles.

Common law clearly does not ignore regulatory controls. Planning permissions, for example, may change a neighbourhood's character, which is the key starting point for judging many nuisance cases.[1] Previous case law has held that, where an Act of Parliament specifically authorised a project, this would provide a good defence to a nuisance action in the absence of negligence. Similarly, compensation may only be awarded for damage considered reasonably foreseeable. One test that may help determine what is reasonably foreseeable is the presence or absence of statutory regulation concerning the pathway of damage at issue.

But in this particular case, the High Court had gone further by holding that compliance with regulatory controls such as a permit essentially provided a good defence. The Court of Appeal overturned the decision and reaffirmed traditional nuisance principles. Lord Justice Carnwath gave the lead judgment and reasserted classic nuisance principles concerning smells: there was no absolute standard, the locality's character was relevant, the public utility of the activity was not a defence and statutory authority could only be a defence if the statute authorises use of land that will inevitably involve a nuisance.

As to the relevance of the statutory controls, he noted that the common law of nuisance had co-existed with statutory controls since the nineteenth century and 'there is no basis,

---

[1] For the relationship between planning controls and nuisance see now the decision of the Supreme Court in *Coventry and others v Lawrence and another* [2014] UKSC 13, analysed on p 394 above.

in principle or authority, for using such a statutory scheme to cut down private law rights'. In this type of nuisance case a court has ultimately to judge what level of smell or noise is reasonable for someone to put up with. The fact that the defendant had not breached the relevant statutory controls might be a relevant consideration, but it is not compelling.

As Lord Justice Carnwath put it:

> An activity which is conducted in contravention of planning or environmental controls is unlikely to be reasonable. But the converse does not follow. Sticking to the rules is an aspect of good neighbourliness but it is far from the whole story – in law as in life.

Biffa clearly saw this as a test case, while industries subject to detailed environmental controls may be disappointed that the Court of Appeal has reasserted conventional principles of nuisance law. However, Lord Justice Carnwath did offer one potential crumb of comfort to industry: where claimants are seeking an injunction to prevent a continuing nuisance, British courts have long taken a strict approach, granting the injunction as of right, whatever the consequences for the industry or community concerned. They will rarely permit a defendant to pay damages in lieu of an injunction, on the grounds that this amounts to buying a right to commit a nuisance, even though overall this may be considered the most efficient economic solution. By contrast, US courts have generally adopted a more rounded approach when it comes to deciding whether or not to grant an injunction, and they consider the social utility of the defendant's activities as an important factor. No injunction was sought in the Biffa case, but Lord Justice Carnwath hinted that British principles concerning injunctions needed re-evaluation. The Biffa case was one of his last judgments before being promoted to the Supreme Court in April, and one day his new position may give him the opportunity to change the common law in this respect.[2]

Companies and Criminal Liability

St Regis Paper Company Ltd v The Crown [2011] EWCA Crim 2527

The criminal division of the Court of Appeal has re-examined the principles determining when a company can be guilty of a criminal offence under environmental law. *St Regis Paper Company Ltd v The Crown* confirms the long-standing approach that, where an offence requires evidence of intention or recklessness, a very senior company officer must be involved before a conviction can be made. The case involved a company which operated five paper mills. The technical manager of one of them had been convicted of falsifying emission records and the Environment Agency wanted to hold the company also liable for the offence.

The underlying conceptual problem for holding companies criminally liable is that they are artificial entities in law and it is difficult to see how such bodies can be said to have criminal intention. Indeed, in some jurisdictions, such as Germany and Austria, the notion of a company, as opposed to an individual, committing a criminal offence is

---

[2] As indeed happened in 2014, when the Supreme Court in *Coventry v Lawrence* overturned the previous strict approach and argued for a more flexible discretion to award damages in lieu of an injunction more akin to the position in the US. Lord Carnwath gave one of the lead judgments. See the analysis on p 384 above.

unknown. One response, which has been developed in the UK since the beginning of the industrial revolution, is to create 'strict liability offences' where proof of intention or recklessness – the necessary ingredient of most criminal offences – is unnecessary.

The courts have to interpret each offence to determine whether it is strict or not. Typically, the use of words such as 'causes' suggests strict liability, while the use of 'knowingly' or 'intentionally' indicates that evidence of a conscious act needs to be shown. Almost all regulatory offences in the environmental field are now strict liability. For a conviction to be made, it is sufficient simply to have caused the offence in question, and in this context the company will be liable for its employees' actions. The degree of culpability is reflected in the sentencing discretion of the court or whether a prosecution is made in the first place.

The second response which the courts have developed, deals with offences where intention or recklessness must be proved. Here, the courts have held that, if a senior company officer, such as a managing director or a person in a similar position, carries out the act in question, then their intention can be said to be attributed to the company itself because they are in effect the 'directing mind and will' of the company. In such circumstances, the company can be convicted of the offence, as well as the individual officer concerned.

The case in question concerned offences under the Pollution Prevention and Control Regulations.[3] It was clear from the wording that some of the offences, such as failure to comply with a permit, were strict liability, but the offence concerning records was different. It is an offence 'intentionally to make a false entry into any record required to be kept under the condition of a permit'. Proof of intention is therefore a necessary element of this offence.

The core principles concerning senior officers in effect being the mind of the company were elaborated in the leading decision of the House of Lords in 1972: *Tesco Supermarkets v Nattrass*.[4] This concerned liability under trade descriptions legislation, but has since been quoted in many other areas of law. The problem here was that, in a case involving corporate liability under financial securities legislation decided in 1995, *Meridian Global Funds Management Asia Limited v The Securities Commission*,[5] the House of Lords suggested that a rather more flexible approach was now needed; the requirement to identify a senior officer who had the necessary intention before the company could be held liable was too restrictive a rule. According to Lord Hoffman, this might remain the general principle, but there may be some cases where the legislative content and policy indicates that the conduct of less senior employees might still attribute criminal intention to the company itself. Otherwise there might be a danger of the enforceability of the law being called into question.

In the present case, this decision appears to have influenced the judge's direction to the jury. It was told that, if it felt that the technical manager in question was in actual control of the operations, that would be sufficient to ensure the company's conviction, even though he could not truly be said to be a directing mind of the company. However, the Court of Appeal felt that this approach was wrong. The structure of the regulations did not indicate that anything other than the traditional approach should be applied.

According to Lord Justice Moses, the regulations clearly distinguished between strict liability offences and those requiring proof of intention. There was no evidence that the

---

[3] Pollution Prevention and Control (England and Wales) Regulations 2000, SI 2000 No 1973.
[4] [1972] AC 153.
[5] [1995] 2 AC 500.

regime as a whole would be undermined if the traditional principles on corporate liability for intentional offences were applied. This was shown by the fact that the company had already been convicted of a number of the strict liability offences. Applying those principles, the court felt that the manager who had been charged and convicted of falsifying entries could not be described as part of the controlling mind of the company. He was the technical and environmental manager of the smallest of the five mills owned by the company, and reported to the operations manager, who in turn reported to the managing director. The managing director then reported to divisional technical managers.

The whole question of criminal liability and regulatory offences is now under review. The Regulatory Enforcement and Sanctions Act 2008 provided a framework giving regulators the power to impose civil sanctions as an alternative to criminal prosecution, even though the structure of the existing offences, whether strict or not, remains unchanged. The Law Commission is undertaking a more fundamental review of criminal liability in regulatory contexts, and plans to publish a report next spring. Its consultation paper[6] indicates unease with pure strict liability offences, especially where no defence of due care is available.

A more radical option would be to get rid of the notion of strict liability in criminal law altogether. Given the new regime of civil sanctions, a system could develop in which an offence involving intention or recklessness could lead to criminal liability, while strict liability offences only give rise to civil penalties. Despite the Court of Appeal's endorsement of the principle of the controlling mind of a company in the *St Regis* case, the Law Commission was far more critical. It felt that the principle contained too many uncertainties, and in practice would favour prosecution of small companies (where managing directors are more likely to be engaged in day-to-day operations) over larger ones. The Law Commission's final report[7] is likely to call for a more fundamental overhaul of traditional principles in this area and, if implemented, could have a profound effect on the direction of environmental regulation and its enforcement.

Fire Damage and Civil Liability

Stannard v Gore [2012] EWCA Civ 1248

Serious pollution incidents often give rise to compensation claims by those who have suffered damage or loss. A major question facing any legal system is whether liability requires some degree of fault or whether just of the fact of carrying out a potentially dangerous operation is sufficient to impose liability.

Over the years, the prevailing trend in British courts has been to require some degree of negligence or reasonable foreseeability, with true strict liability without fault being increasingly confined to a very narrow band of cases. Now the Court of Appeal has carried out an extensive examination of the basis of liability for damage caused by fire spreading from someone's land. This required the Court to consider cases going back for several

---

[6] Law Commission, 'Criminal Liability in Regulatory Contexts' (Law Commission, 2010).

[7] Currently the Commission has suspended further work on this subject and no final report is expected.

hundreds of years, and in an important decision it has decided that liability for the escape of fire without fault should effectively be relegated to history.

Stannard v Gore concerned a tyre-fitting business. Some 3,000 tyres were stored inside and outside the building, and in 2008 a fire broke out caused by an electrical fault. The tyres eventually caught fire, and the fire spread and destroyed the claimant's neighbouring premises.

Critical findings of fact were that there was no evidence that the fire was caused by poor maintenance of the electrical system. Equally, the tyres themselves were not readily combustible, and the claimant could not show that the tyres could have been kept in another way to prevent ignition, though they had been stored in a haphazard manner. The claim based on negligence therefore failed in the county court.

But the claimant had another head of claim, based on the principle in *Rylands v Fletcher*, a leading case from the 1860s. Here fault or negligence as such is not an ingredient of liability – instead, it depends on there being an escape of something brought onto land likely to cause harm and arising from a 'non-natural' use of the land. The county court had held that in this case the conditions of *Rylands v Fletcher* were satisfied – there had been an escape of fire arising from the storage of the tyres, and the storage in such numbers in a random manner piled on top of each other was a 'non-natural' use of the land.

In 55 pages of judgment, the Court of Appeal carried out an extensive analysis of the case law on *Rylands v Fletcher*. The uncertainties of the language of the test has caused much confusion over the years, so much so that in 1994 the High Court in Australia decided it should no longer be treated as a separate head of liability, and that negligence should predominate.

In 2003, in *Transco v Stockport MBC*, the House of Lords was invited to follow the lead of the Australian judiciary but decided that *Rylands v Fletcher* should remain as a principle of liability, though strictly treated as a subset of nuisance law, and heavily confined to cases of exceptional risk.

In the present case, Lord Justice Ward summarised the current principles on *Rylands v Fletcher*: (a) the defendant must be the owner or occupier of the land; (b) he must bring on to his land or keep 'an exceptionally dangerous or mischievous thing'; (c) he must have recognised or ought reasonably to have recognised that there was an exceptional high risk of danger if the thing did escape; (d) the use of the land must be considered extraordinary and unusual; (e) the thing must escape and cause damage to the claimant's land or property; (f) damages for death or personal injury are not recoverable, since this essentially a land-based nuisance claim; and (g) negligence is not an ingredient but an Act of God or an act of a stranger can provide a defence.

These are clearly pretty tough hurdles to pass. But the Court went on to consider whether the spread of fire from someone's property raised particular liability principles, which required the Court to analyse case law starting from the fifteenth century. Originally landowners were liable for any escape of fire started on their property, but since the Fires Prevention (Metropolis) Act 1774 there is no liability where the fire begins accidentally. Here the evidence was that the electrical fault was an accident, and the statutory defence would be applicable.

The question for the Court was whether the principle of liability in *Rylands v Fletcher*, developed after the 1774 legislation, could still be applicable. Some case law had attempted to modify the principle when applying it to an escape of fire, but eventually the Court concluded that there was no longer justification for any special head of liability over and above the modern restatement of *Rylands v Fletcher*. In the absence of negligence, Lord Justice Ward acknowledged that cases of fire damage would be difficult to bring within the rule since it was the fire that had escaped, not the things stored on the land.

Applying these principles to the facts of the case, the court concluded that the tyres that had been brought on to the defendant's land were not 'exceptionally dangerous or mischievous'. There was no evidence that the defendant ought reasonably to have recognised the risk, and the tyres did not escape as such. In any event, keeping a stock of tyres on the premises of a tyre-fitting business was not, for the time and place, an extraordinary or unusual use of the land. No claim could therefore be based on *Rylands v Fletcher*, and indeed it is difficult to see how *Rylands v Fletcher* could ever now apply to a spreading fire, unless it was the fire that was stored in the first place – perhaps if the Olympic Flame had somehow spread from the stadium causing damage, one might argue otherwise.[8]

When the development of modern environmental law was taking place in the early 1970s, there were arguments that *Rylands v Fletcher* would form the bedrock of a strict liability regime for hazardous activities posing environmental risks. But the courts in this country have resisted generating such general theory of liability, and every time *Rylands v Fletcher* has been considered by the higher courts the principles have generally been narrowed. *Stannard v Gore* follows that trend. If such a regime were to develop, it is clearly now the responsibility of Parliament through legislation rather than the courts.

Securing Injunctions before Damage Occurs

London Borough of Islington v Elliot and Morris [2012] EWCA Civ 56

Despite the intensity of modern environmental regulation, the private right of action in nuisance remains a powerful legal tool, especially where the regulator itself is proving dilatory. But courts will normally only consider a nuisance action once at least some damage has occurred – unlike regulation, the primary aim is not to prevent harm, but to compensate for damage suffered and prevent damaging activities continuing.

The one exception to this approach is the power of a court to grant an injunction before damage has taken place, known as a 'quia timet' injunctions. The Court of Appeal has recently reviewed the principles which a court should apply when considering such an injunction.

London Borough of Islington v Elliot and Morris concerned trees roots that were alleged to be encroaching on a neighbour's property with the potential to cause severe damage. Saplings and small ash trees had been allowed to grow unchecked in the garden of a property owned by the London Borough of Islington and let on short-term tenancies. Some of the trees were about two metres from the wall of the neighbouring property, the owner of which contacted the local authority asking them to cut back or remove the trees.

For over three years, despite a great deal of correspondence, nothing was done by the authority to deal with the trees, and in exasperation the owners instructed solicitors to threaten legal proceedings. An expert civil engineer, commissioned by the claimants,

---

[8] At the 2012 Summer Olympics held in London, a cauldron consisting of 204 individual metal petals and designed by Thomas Heatherwick was used for the Olympic flame during the opening and closing ceremonies.

stated that trees such as ash should not be planted within 15–20 metres from a house because of their high water demand. In this case, he felt that the ash saplings had not yet caused damage but that they needed 'to be dealt with as a matter of urgency so as to prevent them from causing inevitable damage in the short to medium term'.

There was then an impasse, with the local authority arguing that they would not remove the trees until it was proved by the claimants they were causing significant damage. The claimants argued that it made obvious sense to remove them now at low cost – one estimate was around £500 – rather than wait for inevitable damage, when the costs involved would be far greater.

The claimants then issued proceedings seeking damages and a quia timet injunction to have the trees removed even though no damage had occurred. Meanwhile, some common sense appeared to have prevailed within the council and a works order was issued to remove the trees, but somehow this information was never communicated to the claimants.

Given that the trees were to be removed, the main dispute concerned who should bear the costs of the legal action to date. The local authority argued that a quia timet injunction would never have been granted in this sort of case and that they therefore should not bear the costs associated with this remedy. The result was that the county court had to take the rather unusual position of considering hypothetically on the evidence whether a court would have been likely to grant the injunction.

The claimant's expert argued that risk of damage was impending and that significant damage to the drainage system was inevitable in around five years' time. The local authority's expert was more circumspect, arguing that it was impossible to predict if and when the nearest trees would cause damage. Despite the uncertainties, the trial judge made an order relating to costs that reflected his view that an injunction would have been granted. In his view, the local authority would not have taken action without such an injunction and, given that there was a likelihood of substantial damage occurring at some point, there was no reason for delaying the work which would have to take place in the future in any event.

The Court of Appeal had to consider whether the trial judge had been correct in his approach. Lord Justice Patten noted that, because quia timet injunctions interfered with the rights of others and might, as in this case, involve the defendant incurring costs, 'the practice of the court has necessarily been to proceed with caution and to require to be satisfied that the risk of actual damaging occurring is both imminent and real'. He accepted that in this case the argument of the claimant's expert that it would sensible to take preventative steps now at low cost rather than wait was something that any prudent landowner would do. But, he noted, this case was not about the reasonableness of the local authority's position at the time but whether the prospect of damage was sufficiently imminent and certain to justify the grant of a quia timet injunction.

The trial judge has estimated that damage would occur within three to five years, and the local authority argued that three years could not be described as 'imminent'. But Lord Justice Patten rejected a test based on a narrow question of precisely when damage would occur. One had also to take into account a broader set of factors, including the likelihood of the council taking action without the need for an injunction:

> The claimant has to show than an injunction is necessary in order to prevent the occurrence of the nuisance . . . it ought therefore in principle to be only cases where the risk of damage is so imminent and the intransigence of the defendant is obvious that the court should ordinarily be prepared to grant an injunction in order to prevent a nuisance which does not yet exist.

Lord Justice Patten concluded that mandatory injunctions of this type are not justified merely on the ground that if nothing is done a tree at some point may cause damage in the future to neighbouring property. In this case, despite a history of delay and misleading information from the local authority, it had eventually resolved itself to remove the trees, implying 'there was therefore no necessity for the grant of quia timet relief'.

The decision of the Court of Appeal in the *Elliot* case refines the test of granting a quia timet injunction by emphasising that the tests to be applied are not simply about timescales but more about the need for an injunction to resolve the issue. But the decision has wider significance beyond problems of neighbouring trees in that it emphasises the reluctance of courts to take action in nuisance cases before damage occurs. During Margaret Thatcher's administration in the 1980s, some ministers pushing for deregulation were supposed to have argued that environmental regulation and regulators could largely be replaced by simply relying upon the common law action of nuisance and the power of individuals to take action before the ordinary courts. The current administration may yet find such arguments attractive again. Yet the *Elliot* case underlines the fact that common law actions are generally ill-suited as a basis for ensuring that preventative steps are taken before damage occurs.

Neighbouring Nuisance Smells

Hirose Electrical UK Ltd v Peak Ingredients Ltd [2011] EWCA Civ 987

It is fairly rare for a neighbour dispute concerning smells to reach the Court of Appeal, still less one involving two companies. *Hirose Electrical UK Ltd v Peak Ingredients Ltd* contains a valuable restatement of contemporary principles of private nuisance law and a warning of the perils of litigation when more practical and less costly solutions might be at hand.

The claimant in the case was a manufacturer of mobile phones using premises on an industrial estate in Milton Keynes. Their immediate neighbour in the same block, separated by a party wall, was Peak Ingredients, which manufactured food additives.

Hirose complained that strong spicy smells emanating from Peak Ingredients had badly affected the use of their premises, even causing ill health to some employees, and after six years the company moved offices. Local environmental health officers decided that the smell was not sufficient to amount to a statutory nuisance and that any legal action was a matter for the parties.

The Court of Appeal accepted that the basic principle of nuisance law was whether the defendants had made a reasonable use of their property and that the legal principles envisaged a strong element of 'give and take' between neighbours. In assessing whether there was a reasonable use of the premises, a court was entitled to consider the general character of the neighbourhood.

The High Court had dismissed the case. Although Hirose had characterised the industrial estate as a 'high class genteel industrial park', the judge, who made a site visit during the trial, did not agree and held it to be a light industrial estate. The Court of Appeal accepted these findings and held that the judge was entitled to attach significance to this. The light industrial character covered the manufacture of food additives, and Peak's activities were, according to Lord Justice Mummery, carried on without objections or intervention on environmental or health and safety grounds by the relevant statutory authorities. While those matters are obviously not conclusive against the existence of a private nuisance, they are relevant indicators of the level of discomfort and inconvenience caused by the smell.

In the High Court, the judge accepted that there was 'sometimes, but by no means daily, or necessarily throughout the day, a fairly strong disagreeable odour in the warehouse section of Hirose's premises and in the back stairs, kitchen and toilet areas'. But he concluded that there was nothing unreasonable in Peak's use of its premises, and held that the occupier of premises on an industrial estate such as here must expect the possibility of disagreeable smells – 'The discomfort caused on an industrial estate where persons concerned work on weekdays in the daytime is not as great as would be caused to residential neighbours'.

As was always likely to be the case, the Court of Appeal felt that the assessment of the strength and effects of the smells was really a matter for the trial judge, and there were no grounds on which the Court of Appeal could second guess the judge's findings. As the Court noted, the 'judgment on a relativistic issue, such as whether a particular activity amounts to a nuisance, is not 'wrong' simply because, if this court had tried the case, it would not have made the same overall assessment'.

Perhaps the most distinctive feature of the case was the legal relevance of the nature of the party wall between the two companies. In the High Court, the judge had concluded that the root cause of the problem was the inadequate protection against smells provided by the party wall, which was porous and had not been adequately sealed. Peak was not responsible for the condition of the party wall, but the question was whether the porous nature of the wall should have been taken into account by Peak in judging whether the company had acted reasonably.

The Court of Appeal agreed with the High Court and rejected this argument. In its view, no blame concerning the nature of the wall could be allocated to either of the parties or indeed the landlord, and the critical question remained whether in all the circumstances the smell amounted to a 'material interference with the material comfort of Hirose and its employees'.

The Court was surprised, though, that little progress had been made on improving the insulation in the wall between the parties. Hirose had considered that this was a matter solely for Peak to deal with, because its activities caused the smell, and as a result there was a lack of co-operation between the parties. As Lord Justice Mummery wryly noted,

> By now the costs of this litigation, which has achieved nothing of use for the parties to it, must be greater than the expense of a constructive solution to the smell permeation problem by insulation works on the party wall.

Nature Conservation and Human Rights

R on the application of Fisher v English Nature [2004] EWCA Civ 663

The legal validity of English Nature's[9] procedures for designating Sites of Special Scientific

---

[9] English Nature was subsumed into a new body, Natural England, established on 1 October 2006 by the Natural Environment and Rural Communities Act 2006.

Interest has been upheld by the Court of Appeal. The decision contains important principles concerning the significance of government policy and confirms that, ultimately, English Nature must exercise its independent judgment according to the criteria laid down in the legislation.

R on the application of Fisher v English Nature arose out of English Nature's decision to designate some 30,000 acres of arable land on the Norfolk/Suffolk border as an SSSI. The site is home to a substantial proportion of the UK's population of stone curlews, a migratory species present between March and October, and protected species under the EU birds Directive. Patrick Fisher, a farmer with land in the SSSI, challenged the designation. It was clear that the site would qualify as a Special Protection Area under the Birds Directive since it supported more than 1 per cent of the country's population of the species in question, and that designation was not questioned.

The applicant had voluntarily been involved in the protection of the stone curlew population, but questioned whether once an area was designated as an SPA it was always appropriate to designate it as an SSSI under national law. This was especially the case as, following amendments to the legislation brought about by the Countryside and Rights of Way Act 2000, SSSI status brought with it a much tougher system of regulatory controls. Between 1994 and 2000, it had indeed been the policy of English Nature not to designate large areas as SSSIs where migratory species, of necessity present only part of the time, were involved. In a letter to the then Department of Environment, Transport and the Regions, English Nature argued that such areas should still be designated as SPAs, but 'the conservation interest and pattern of ownership means that adequate protection and management action can be taken without SSSI designation'. This was essentially the position that the applicant adopted. However, the Department's policy was that any SPA designation must be underpinned by SSSI designation – otherwise a site deemed of international importance would not be considered of national importance. In February 2000, the general committee of English Nature's council approved the designation of three SPAs as SSSIs, marking a departure from its previous policy. A key argument of the applicant was that the change of policy was irrational, and that English Nature had been unduly influenced by the government's preferred policy on the issue.

The Court of Appeal examined the procedures leading up to designation in considerable detail. It was clear from the paperwork that English Nature recognised that voluntary measures for protecting stone curlews on arable land had achieved much, and that formal designation as an SSSI was novel in this context and might jeopardise existing relationships with landowners. Although it was not legally required to do so, English Nature had engaged in considerable consultation prior to notification, recognising the contentious nature of the proposal. The decision to confirm was taken by the council of English Nature itself, and in accordance with its practice it allowed objectors an opportunity to make oral representations. These procedures had been significant in safeguarding English Nature from a human rights challenge based on a lack of an independent court or tribunal.

The court reviewed a transcript of the discussion by council members with a view to determining what factors had influenced their decision. It felt it to be clear that the council did not consider that SSSI designation automatically followed from SPA designation, but that it had considered whether the site in question was of national importance under the terms of the national legislation, section 28 of the Wildlife and Countryside Act of 1981. SPA status was a relevant factor to this question, but not compelling. The applicant's main concern was that it was a flawed analysis to assume that SSSI designation must automatically apply to land with an SPA status. Although the national legislation used the term 'special scientific interest', it was important, he argued, to interpret the term in the context of both the purposes of the legislation in question and the statutory consequences which followed SSSI designation. On that analysis, the fact that it was important under EU or international law did not necessarily mean that it was important under national legislation.

The Court of Appeal was not convinced by these arguments. It was clear that the court was influenced by the fact that this was a decision by a specialist body, which should only be challenged before the courts on limited grounds of judicial review. Second, the court could not see how English Nature could reasonably have not made a designation of national importance when the site was considered to be of European significance, and rejected the applicant's arguments considering the 'purposeful' construction of the 1981 Act. According to Lord Justice Wall,

> English Nature reasonably formed the opinion that the area of land was of special interest by reason of its internationally important population of stone curlew. This led to the duty to notify under section 28(1) of the 1981 Act. There is nothing in the process of consultation, or in English Nature's considerations of the objections, to which objection can be taken.

There was another, rather subtle argument concerning the Human Rights Act which the court was also asked to consider. According to the High Court, once English Nature had decided to notify the potential designation, it had a duty to confirm if it maintained that opinion as to its special status after hearing the objections. The question raised before the court was whether English Nature should also have considered the potential impact of designation on the applicant's rights under Article 1 of the First Protocol of the Human Rights Convention concerning the protection of private property rights. Essentially the applicant argued that SSSI designation was a disproportionate response to the need to protect SPA status, which could achieved by other, less intrusive, means.

Lord Justice Wall argued that the decision to confirm SSII status was clearly not simply a rubber stamp process following notification:

> I would prefer to construe section 28(5) of the 1981 Act as giving rise to the exercise of a power not to confirm, which is to be exercised in accordance with the conclusion reached as a result of the outcome of a genuine, open-minded consultation/investigation process.

As to the human rights points, he did not find any evidence as presented in objections by the applicant as compelling, and indeed English Nature has clearly made efforts to ensure that there is no undue restraint on farming operations. The specific question as to whether English Nature was under a duty to consider the human rights issues in its confirmation decision was not directly addressed by the court, which preferred to state simply that on the facts there was no disproportionate intrusion on the applicant's rights.

The *Fisher* case is one of a series of recent legal challenges against English Nature on designation procedures brought by landowners. This development has probably been an inevitable consequence of the recent shift from the largely voluntary system at the heart of the 1981 legislation to a tougher regulatory regime, largely brought about by the need to implement EU conservation legislation. The current procedures have survived legal challenges, although last July, in the *Bown* case,[10] the Court of Appeal was highly

---

[10] *Bown v Secretary of State for Transport* [2003] EWCA Civ 1170.

critical of complexities and lack of transparency in the UK procedures for designating SPAs. The present case underlines the extent to which the Government has largely used existing nature conservation legislation, strengthened in parts, to implement EU requirements. Although the *Fisher* case did not question the legality of this approach, it may still give policy-makers some pause for thought as to whether certain types of conservation designation under EU law might be more effective with a more dedicated regulatory regime than that provided by SSSIs which was originally developed in a vary different context.

Waste-derived Fuels Are Not Waste

R ex parte OSS Group Ltd v Environment Agency and Department of Environment Food and Rural Affairs [2007] EWCA Civ 611

The Court of Appeal recently wrestled with the question of whether waste-derived fuels can cease to be waste in law before being burnt. The court rejected the Environment Agency's strict interpretation of the law with a decision likely to encourage greater use of fuels derived from waste or recycled products. Some observers hoped that the decisions in the *OSS* case would provide legal certainty regarding when a waste product ceased to be waste. The lead judgment was given by Lord Justice Carnwath, who is well versed in environmental law and provided an extensive review of the European and national case law on the subject. But even he felt that the European law as interpreted by the European Court of Justice made it impossible to provide a definitive ruling, and he urged the Agency and the Environment Department (DEFRA) to co-operate to produce practical guidance on the issue.

The OSS Group was in the business of reprocessing waste oils into fuel products. Its most recent product was known as 'clean fuel oil' which the company argued was materially indistinguishable from a natural fuel – a point which remains in dispute between OSS and the Agency. However, the key question was whether the product remained a waste in law. If it was waste, then any combustion processes would be treated was waste incineration and be subject to the Waste Incineration Directive's strict requirements. This would be likely to jeopardise any economic advantages of the recycled fuel over non-recycled 'natural' alternatives.

Waste legislation both at a national and European level has tended to focus on whether a material is waste in the first place, rather than on the issue – which is at the heart of this case – of when what is admittedly a waste can cease to be waste. The European Court of Justice has considered the issue on several occasions, but as Lord Justice Carnwath noted with a degree of frustration, its judgments often lacked clarity.

The starting point for any analysis is the definition of 'waste' in the Waste Framework Directive which applies to substances or materials 'which the holder discards or intends to discard'. Annexes IIA and IIB of the Directive list operations which amount to 'disposal' and 'recovery of waste' including as recovery its use principally as a fuel and solvent reclamation. But the European Court of Justice has consistently held that 'discard' has an extensive meaning and can encompass the operations listed in Annexes IIA and IIB. But it does not follow that if a substance is subject to one of those operations it is automatically a waste – one has always to ask whether it was 'discarded'.

Lord Justice Carnwath derived several core principles from the case law. The concept of waste should not be interpreted restrictively and 'discard' was to be considered in the context of the Directive's overall aims to protect human health and the environment, and the general principles of the European environmental policy, including the prevention and precautionary principle. In deciding whether burning a substance amounts to discarding it, the European Court has held that it was not relevant that it could be recovered as fuel in an environmentally responsible manner and without substantial treatment. The Agency, relying on its interpretation of the case law of the European Court of Justice, had adopted a tough but clear test: materials contained in lubricating oils that have been discarded and have become waste only cease to be waste when they are finally burnt. The standard of the prior processing was not relevant. The only exception would be waste fuel oil that was recovered for use as fuel oil which was chemically and physically identical to the original product and required no further processing. But here one was dealing with waste lubricating oil turned to a different use, and the limited exception could not apply. DEFRA had a more generous formulation. It accepted that material derived from waste lubricating oil to be used as fuel was not being discarded as waste provided it had 'the same characteristics' as the virgin fuel which it replaced. It was not a question of 'never' but 'if', and this would be a question of fact. For its part, OSS in the Court of Appeal reduced the test to two simple questions: was the material sufficiently analogous to the virgin product or material which it replaced; and was the material analogous in term of environmental risks in use? In its view the product in question met these tests.

Much turned on the key 2002 decision of the European Court of Justice in *ARCO*[11] which was concerned with waste materials transformed for use a fuel. A key question was whether a waste product which had already been subject to recycling operations listed in Annex II to turn into a fuel remained a waste until burnt. The court did not consider the application of the specified operations definitive:

> Whether it is waste must be determined in the light of all the circumstances, by comparison with the definition set out in Article 1(a) of the Directive, that is to say the discarding of the substance in question or the intention or requirement to discard it, regard being had to the aim of the directive and the need to ensure that its effectiveness is not undermined.

Lord Justice Carnwath found the passage unfathomable. The European Court has accepted that the fact that a waste substance had undergone a recovery operation was a factor in determining whether it was still waste. As such it had impliedly accepted that a substance which was waste could cease to be a waste even if it was destined for use as a fuel. But then the European Court had simply said the decision must be taken in light of 'all the circumstances' but without specifying the other factors to be considered, other than saying this must be done against the discarding definition in Article 1A. Lord Justice Carnwath felt that this was meaningless as a response. The product's user wanted to reuse it not discard it and

> no amount of reference to 'all the circumstances' would change that fact. No doubt the material was discarded by the original user: but the issue was not whether it was then waste, but whether it had since ceased to be waste.

---

[11] Joined Cases C-418/97 and C-419/97 *ARCO Chemie Nederland Ltd etc* 15 June 2002.

The European Court in ARCO also noted that even where a waste had been completely recovered resulting in the substance having the same properties as a raw material, it could still be regarded as waste if the holder discards it or intends to discard it. Lord Justice Carnwath found the reasoning 'extremely obscure'. There were clearly objective factors relating to the product's characteristics and environmental impacts, but he could not see why the subjective intentions of the holder should acquire such significance when dealing with the question of whether waste ceased to be waste. Lord Justice Carnwath concluded that 'a search for logical coherence in the Luxembourg case law is probably doomed to failure'. A fundamental problem, he felt, was the European Court's continued adherence to the discarding definitions which had little relevance to the issue where the holder intends to use the material rather than discard it on any ordinary sense. What should be key was whether the material should continue to be treated as waste until acceptable recovery or disposal had taken place, because of the Directive's environmental policy aims. But as he noted, the European Court had consistently declined invitations to provide workable criteria to decide that question.

It followed that it was up to national courts to apply value judgments in the light of the indicators derived from the Directive's policy goals. Lord Justice Carnwath noted with approval a 2003 decision of the Dutch Council of State which held that waste-derived fuel pellets produced with the sole aim of being used as fuel, in the same way as regular fuel, and containing no contaminants should be considered equivalent to regular fuel and no longer a waste. Lord Justice Carnwath felt that such a decision showed a common sense approach, consistent with the aims of the Directive and the case law, and with the aim of encouraging waste recovery and reuse.

> It should be enough that the holder has converted the waste material into a distinct, marketable product, which can be used in exactly the same way as an ordinary fuel, and with no worse environmental effects. It cannot be said that such a material is being 'discarded' in any ordinary sense of the term and there is nothing in the objectives of the Directive which requires any fictitious assumption of that effect.

Turning to the various tests proposed, the court concluded that the Agency's test was too narrow and not consistent with the case law, and overturned the decision of the High Court which had followed the Agency's approach. Similarly, although DEFRA's arguments were found generally more persuasive than the Agency's, the Court felt DEFRA's 'hardly distinguishable' test was equally too narrow. Equivalence in both environmental implications and usage appears to be the preferred approach, though the Court felt that given that the European Court had declined to provide a definitive test, it was not the domestic court's function to fill the gap. It may be that the European Commission's current work on revising the waste framework Directive will provide greater clarity. In the meantime, Lord Justice Carnwath urged the Agency and DEFRA to pool their expertise to give practical guidance to those concerned with waste treatment and handling. In this context, he noted that the difficulties in interpreting the European Court of Justice case law were compounded by DEFRA and the Agency not being able to agree a common approach. He acknowledged the Agency's concerns of applying a more generous test and finding suitable comparators, but felt that the difficulty was not as great as the Agency suggested. It would be rash to assume that the OSS decision will be the last legal ruling on when a waste product ceases to be waste. Nevertheless, the Court of Appeal has indicated that the issue should be determined by the application of technical criteria and expertise rather than rigid application of legal principles.[12] Lawyers may feel frustrated, but many will see this as a welcome signal.

---

[12] The question of when waste ceases to be waste has now in part been dealt with expressly under the Waste Framework Directive 2008/98/EC, endorsing a more technical approach. Art 6 provides that '1. Certain specified waste shall cease to be waste within the meaning of point (1) of Article 3 when it has undergone a recovery, including recycling, operation and complies with specific criteria to be developed in accordance with the following conditions: (a) the substance or object is commonly used for specific purposes; (b) a market or demand exists for such a substance or object; (c) the substance or object fulfils the technical requirements for the specific purposes and meets the existing legislation and standards applicable to products; and (d) the use of the substance or object will not lead to overall adverse environmental or human health impacts'. End-of-waste criteria have been developed for iron, steel and aluminium scrap (Council Reglation 333/2011) and glass cullet (Council Regulation 1179/2012), with work continuing on copper scrap metal, recovered paper, plastics and biodegradable waste/compost. Where Community level criteria have not been set, Art 6(4) provides that 'Member States may decide case by case whether certain waste has ceased to be waste taking into account the applicable case law. They shall notify the Commission of such decisions in accordance with Directive 98/34/EC of the European Parliament and of the Council of 22 June 1998 laying down a procedure for the provision of information in the field of technical standards and regulations and of rules on Information Society services where so required by that Directive'. Presumably, 'Member States' in this context includes the national courts of Member States. In line with the Court of Appeal's advice, the Environment Agency has been producing an increasing number of Quality Protocols providing end-of-waste criteria from specific waste types.

22

High Court

Tribunals and Judicial Review

R on the Application of Great Yarmouth Port Company v Marine Management Organisation [2013] EWHC 3052

The tribunal system in England and Wales is likely to play an increasingly important role in environmental law. More and more statutory appeals under environmental legislation are being heard by the First-tier Tribunal (Environment), set up three years ago.[1] Defra also recently proposed transferring environmental permitting appeals to the tribunal but has not decided whether to pursue it.[2]

Under the reforms to the tribunal system introduced in 2007, appeals on points of law from the First-tier Tribunal now go to the Upper Tribunal which also has the power to determine judicial reviews. Classes of judicial reviews can be transferred to the Upper Tribunal from the Administrative Court. This has recently happened in areas such as immigration, but not yet in the environmental field. In any other judicial review application, the Administrative Court can transfer the application where it is considered just and convenient. Again, this has yet to happen in the field of environmental law.

The spotlight on the tribunal system is likely to continue. The Ministry of Justice has recently proposed transferring planning judicial reviews to the Land Chamber of the Upper Tribunal and has consulted on whether environmental judicial reviews might also be transferred.[3] Perceived advantages are that the tribunal system can operate with more flexible procedural rules and that those deciding cases combine legal and technical expertise appropriate to the case in hand.

A recent decision of the Administrative Court has endorsed the strengths of the tribunal system and held that those who do not take advantage of exercising statutory rights of appeal to a tribunal should normally be disbarred from bringing a judicial review claim on the same issue.

---

[1] The Ministry of Justice provides information on the Tribunal's current jurisdiction at http://www.justice.gov.uk/downloads/tribunals/environment/environment-rules-rights-appeal.pdf (accessed on 10 March 2014).

[2] In the event, Defra decided not to transfer these appeals to the Tribunal, mainly because of the costs involved – see its response to the Consultation Exercise at https://www.gov.uk/government/uploads/system/uploads/attachment_data/file/264375/env-permitting-sum-resp-201311.pdf (accessed on 10 March 2014).

[3] One of the options proposed in Ministry of Justice, *Judicial Review – Proposals for Further Reform*, Cm 8703 (September 2013) para 47. In the event, the government decided not to pursue this option, preferring instead a new special Planning Court within the High Court – see Ministry of Justice, *Judicial Review – Proposals for Further Reform: The Government Response*, Cm 8811 (February 2014) para 18. See also Chapter 9 above.

R on the Application of Great Yarmouth Port Company v Marine Management Organisation concerned the decision of the Marine Management Organisation (MMO) to vary a marine licence relating to the construction of an outer harbour at Great Yarmouth.

A marine licence under the Marine and Coastal Access Act 2009 had been granted and originally extended until the end of 2012. The construction works had basically been completed by then, but in December 2012 the MMO issued a variation notice to extend it for two years to consider the need for a monitoring regime and the imposition of monitoring conditions.

The company challenged the variation notice by way of judicial review. This was mainly on the grounds that there was no power under the relevant legislation to impose such measures after the licensed activities were complete. The harbour had been authorised under a specific Act of Parliament, and the company also argued that the MMO did not have the power to impose monitoring conditions that were different from those in the legislation that authorised the harbour's construction.

The MMO pointed out that, under 2011 regulations,[4] the company had the right of statutory appeal to the First-tier Environment Tribunal but had not exercised it. They should therefore be refused permission to bring a judicial review claim as this should be a matter of last resort.

The harbour company argued that the real test was one of convenience. Since the parties were now all present and prepared to argue the issues of law in front of a competent judge, the judicial review should be permitted. Reverting back to the First-tier Tribunal would inevitably involve delays, and there was in any event likely to be an appeal on the issues of law to the Upper Tribunal.

Mr Justice Hickinbottom was not persuaded: 'My firm view is that it would be wrong to grant permission to proceed in this claim because of the availability of a statutory appeal'. This was based on constitutional principles in the sense that, where parliament had provided a specific appeals route for persons aggrieved by administrative decisions, the courts should be reluctant to go in the face of clear statutory intention by granting collateral remedies of judicial review.

Previous decisions had largely predated the 2007 reforms to the tribunal system and the court went further in emphasising that there was now a 'sophisticated and comprehensive' system of appeals from the First-tier Tribunal leading to the Upper Tribunal and then to the Court of Appeal. It was clearly parliamentary intention under the Tribunal Courts and Enforcement Act 2007 that in those circumstances the appeal route should be to the exclusion of judicial review.

Mr Justice Hickinbottom went on to underline the practical advantages the tribunal system might have over conventional judicial review. Unlike the Administrative Court, a tribunal is able to conduct both a fact finding exercise as well as deal with issues of law. It had more flexibility in its make-up, and the costs regime in tribunals (which normally require each side to pay their own costs whatever the result) may be more appropriate for a proportionate resolution of the issues.

Equally important was that, while the Administrative Court would normally confine itself to striking down a decision as unlawful or sending it back for redetermination by the original decision maker, tribunals are encouraged not to follow this route, but to make the decision the administrative or public body should have done. This is because they have

---

[4] Marine Licensing (Notices Appeals) Regulations 2011 SI 2011/936.

specialist legal and technical experience and expertise. The court noted that 'the tribunal system looked at as a whole is not only able to deliver justice as well as the court system but, for the types of cases assigned to it, sometimes better'.

The test of whether a judicial review might be appropriate, the court held, was not one of convenience but one where there were 'exceptional circumstances' to justify the route. The High Court's endorsement of the strength of the reformed tribunal system for dealing with specialist issues of law should encourage the transfer of more environmental statutory appeals to the First-tier Tribunal.

Third parties, such as environmental NGOs, do not have statutory rights of appeal as such but must rely upon judicial review before the Administrative Court. Appeals on points of law from environmental statutory appeals go to the Upper Tribunal, and the *Great Yarmouth* decision is likely to strengthen the case for environmental judicial reviews covering the same field of law to be transferred and heard by the same judicial body.

Criminal Liability for Sewerage Escapes

Thames Water Utilities and Bromley Magistrates Court [2013] EWHC 472

In 2003 sewage escaped from a collapsed pipe into residential gardens in Bromley, south London. The incident caused almost 10 years' worth of litigation between Thames Water Utilities and the Environment Agency, but with the 2013 decision of the High Court the legal saga appears to be finally drawing to a close.

It was not just the seriousness of the incident that encouraged both sides to invest so much in legal argument, but the fact that the case touched on fundamental issues concerning the application of water or waste law when breakdowns occur. As such, the decision in *Thames Water Utilities and Bromley Magistrates Court* will be of concern to the whole water industry.

The Environment Agency's response to the incident was that Thames Water had not acted quickly enough to remedy the problem or divert the sewage and it initiated a prosecution under section 33(1)(a) of the Environmental Protection Act 1990. This prohibits the deposit of controlled waste unless authorised by licence. Thames Water's initial response was that the charge was misconceived, on the grounds that sewage did not fall within the definition of controlled waste.

The issue was referred to the Court of Justice of the European Union (CJEU), which in 2007[5] noted that the 1975 Waste Framework Directive excluded waste waters such as sewage from the definition of waste, but only 'where they are already covered by other legislation'. The court accepted that this could refer to both European Community and national legislation – the 2008 Waste Framework Directive now in force refers only to Community legislation – but held that, if the exemption was to be brought into play, it must contain precise provisions that ensured a level of protection equivalent to that provided by the waste directive. The court held that the Urban Waste Water Directive did not provide such a level of protection, but that it was up to national courts to examine any relevant national legislation.

---

[5] R *(Thames Water Utilities Ltd) v Bromley Magistrates Court* [2007] I WLR 1945.

In 2008[6] the High Court examined the relevant national water legislation, and in particular the Water Industry Act. It held that this legislation also did not provide the degree of protection for the escape of sewage as required by the CJEU. The exemption under the waste directive therefore was not engaged and the escaped sewage was waste.

In the present case, Thames Water pursued a different legal tack. It argued that there had been no 'deposit' within the meaning of the offence – a deposit required some conscious or deliberate act. There was no statutory definition of the term, so the District Judge in Bromley magistrates court adopted an ordinary dictionary meaning (put, place or set down) and held that there was a deposit involved.

Thames Water challenged this decision before the High Court by way of judicial review and Lord Justice Gross held it was preferable to look at the context of the legislation: 'There is something to be said for the arguments of each party and neither party's case can be disposed of merely on the basis of a dictionary definition.' The court noted that section 33 of the Environmental Protection Act 1990 contained several different offences – to deposit controlled waste or knowingly cause or knowingly permit the deposit of controlled waste. The fact that depositing controlled waste was not qualified by the word 'knowingly' was, in the view of the court, strong evidence that it could cover unintended escapes.

The Environment Agency argued that this interpretation was supported by the fact that the Act also provides a due diligence defence and, as is common with such statutory defences, one that must be raised and proved by the defendant on the balance of probabilities. This showed that the legislation had been constructed on a proportionate basis. Thames countered this by pointing out that the due diligence defence could not be conclusive since it also applied to the knowingly causing or permitting offences under section 33. Lord Justice Gross did not find this compelling and held that the Environment Agency's construction was a better fit.

Thames Water then pointed out that section 34 of the Environmental Protection Act 1990 creates a separate 'duty of care' offence requiring someone in control of waste to take all reasonable measures to prevent its escape from his control. This, it argued, was the appropriate offence for an unintended escape and if section 33 covered unintended escapes as well, there would be an unjustifiable overlap. The legislation cannot have intended to give the agency complete discretion over whether to choose between section 33 and section 34, especially since the section 33 offence had more serious sanctions, requiring the defendant to prove due diligence.

The court agreed with the agency that there is no unjustifiable overlap between the offences. In applying the CJEU's tests, the sewage was not waste as long as it was in the sewerage system. It was only when it escaped that it fell outside the exclusion and became waste in law. But the section 34 duty of care only applies to waste falling within someone's control and therefore could not apply in this case. Quoting from counsel for the agency, the court noted: 'That which was in the pipes was not controlled waste; once it had escaped, it was not in control of Thames'.

The court confirmed the legality of the magistrates court's decision. There the judge had imposed a large fine of more than £300,000. Thames Water has already appealed to the Crown Court to reduce this. Whether the company will try to challenge the present decision in the Court of Appeal and even the Supreme Court remains another matter. If it does, it is likely to face an uphill struggle. The lead judgment in the 2008 decision of the

---

[6] *R (Thames Water Utilities Ltd) v Bromley Magistrates Court* [2008] EWHC 1763.

High Court, holding that the escaped sewage did not fall within the waste exemptions, was given by Lord Justice Carnwath as he then was. He noted that there was nothing unfair about the escapes 'being subject to the criminal sanctions otherwise thought appropriate for deposit of controlled waste'. Lord Carnwath now sits in the Supreme Court and his observations in the 2008 decision are likely to be extremely persuasive.

Assuming that the decision stands, sewage undertakers will now have to take on board that serious criminal waste offences can now apply to leaks. Response times and asset management procedures will need to be re-examined and more attention paid to whether they will satisfy the requirements of the due diligence defence.

Enforcement Policies and the Courts

Moss and Sons Ltd v Crown Prosecution Service [2012] EWHC 3658

A recent High Court decision argues that criminal prosecution and enforcement policy should be taken out of the hands of non-departmental government bodies, raising concerns for regulators such as the Environment Agency and English Nature. Enforcement policies are an important element of modern regulatory enforcement. A body that can bring its own prosecutions has to follow the Code for Crown Prosecutors when deciding whether to prosecute or not. The Environment Agency, an example of one of these bodies, has also long published its own enforcement policy, now termed an enforcement statement.

But this was not a statutory requirement. When the 2005 Cabinet Office review on regulatory sanctions examined the position of 61 national regulators, it found that less than one-third had published such a policy. Indeed, a number had deliberately not done so for fear of 'giving the game away'. The review[7] recommended that, in the interests of transparency and internal consistency, all regulators should have a legal duty to publish an enforcement policy. The Regulatory Enforcement and Sanctions Act 2008 now makes this a statutory requirement for regulators that can impose civil sanctions under the Act.

One consequence of the more extensive use of enforcement policies has been to encourage defendants to challenge decisions to prosecute on the grounds that they are contrary to such policies. Many regulators were alarmed by the 2004 decision in *R v Adaway*,[8] where the Court threw out a trading standards prosecution by a local council for being an abuse of process because it breached the authority's published enforcement policy. But that policy had been expressed in unconditional terms: 'we will only prosecute where . . .'. Most enforcement policies liberally use words such as generally or usually to give some flexibility, and five years later, in the *Rashid* case,[9] the High Court stressed that the decision to prosecute should normally be left to the discretion of the prosecuting body.

A new High Court decision at the end of 2012 throws further light on the legal status of enforcement policies and will provide some relief to regulators. However, the judgment

---

[7] R Macrory, *Regulatory Justice: Making Sanctions Effective* (London, Cabinet Office, 2006), reproduced in Chapter 2 above, p 21.

[8] [2004] EWCH Crim 2831.

[9] *London Borough of Wandsworth* [2009] EWHC 1844.

appears to contain a potential large sting in its tail for regulators such as the Environment Agency or Natural England. *Moss and Sons Ltd v Crown Prosecution Service* concerned a prosecution originally brought by the Gangmasters Licensing Authority (GLA). The GLA had been set up under the Gangmasters (Licensing) Act 2004 to handle the licensing of businesses hiring out temporary workers to farms and other industries.

A dairy farm had been supplied with a worker by an unlicensed agency and the agency was duly prosecuted under the 2004 Act. The case concerned the prosecution of the farm itself, which had paid a monthly fee to the agency. It was accepted that the farm was unaware that the worker was being financially exploited by the agency, but the offence under the 2004 Act of entering into agreement with an unlicensed gangmaster is one of strict liability and, although there is a due diligence defence, this was not raised by the farm. A conviction therefore resulted, though the lack of true culpability was reflected by a sentence of an absolute discharge.

But it was argued that the prosecution was an abuse of process because it was contrary to the GLA's enforcement policy, the GLA Dairy Policy. The GLA developed this in consultation with its executive board and the environment department (Defra) in 2010. It was agreed before the Court that the policy was not particularly well drafted, but the Court concluded that the prosecution against the farm had not been contrary to the policy and the challenge was dismissed. However, the Court went on to consider the position had the policy been breached, and it is this part of the judgment that has wider significance.

The Court quoted with approval a decision of the Court of Appeal last year, *R v A*,[10] where the Lord Chief Justice stated:

> Even if it can be shown that in one respect or another, parts or part of the relevant guidance or policy had not been adhered to, it does not follow there was an abuse of process. Indeed, it remains open to the prosecution in an individual case, for good reason, to disapply its own policy or guidance.[11]

There had to be some form of misconduct or oppression to justify a stay of prosecution and, according to the Court, the large degree of deference shown by courts to prosecutors such as the Crown Prosecution Service was that they were seen as constitutionally independent from the executive branch of government. The width of the discretion given to prosecutors, according to Mr Justice Beatson, 'is premised on the independence of the prosecutor; it is central to the proper functioning of the administration of justice and to the relationship between the Courts and the prosecutor'.

However, according to the Court, the enforcement policy had been drafted by the executive management board 'of an agency of the executive government and not by a prosecutor, independent of it or any other part of the executive government'. The court argued that in such cases there was an argument for a court to apply a 'more stringent standard' when reviewing decisions to prosecute. But it went further, and concluded that 'there should be clear arrangements which ensure that decisions on prosecution policy and the decision to prosecute are made by persons who can only exercise their judgment entirely independently of the executive government or executive agency'. What is odd about the language of the Court's analysis is that the GLA is, in law, clearly a non-departmental public body rather than an executive agency of a government department. The Secretary

---

[10] [2012] EWCA Crim 434.
[11] Ibid, para 84.

of State does have legal powers to give it directions but, like the Environment Agency, it is legally independent from government.

Since 2011 and as part of general Whitehall cost cutting, the Crown Prosecution Service has been taking over many prosecution functions that formerly rested within government departments. If the High Court is arguing that constitutionally criminal prosecution and enforcement policy should be taken out of the hands of all non-departmental public bodies, then this is likely to raise real concerns with bodies such as the Environment Agency. Where that leaves the power of such bodies to impose civil penalties remains as yet unexplored.

The Legal Status of Emission Trading Allowances

Armstrong DLW GmbH v Winnington Networks [2012] EWHC 10

A High Court ruling has held that European Union Emissions Trading Scheme emission allowances (EUAs) are considered property in English law. The decision is the first time a court has given a definitive ruling on the nature of emission allowances. The ruling is in line with what many lawyers had assumed to be the case, but it is the first time the courts have given a definitive answer to the question.

Armstrong DLW GmbH v Winnington Networks concerned the transfer of just over a quarter of a million euros worth of emission allowances from Armstrong, a German PVC manufacturer, to the carbon emissions trading account of Winnington, a British technology company. Winnington then sold on the allowances at a small profit. However, the transfer was in fact the result of an email fraud carried out by an unknown party, claiming to represent Zen Holdings in Dubai. It had obtained Armstrong's passwords by pretending to be the German emissions trading registry. Armstrong claimed Winnington should compensate it for the loss. The claim involved complex legal principles of restitution and constructive trust, and how these were applied in a case such as this. The defences available to Winnington were influenced by the precise legal nature of an EUA under the scheme.

Stephen Morris QC, sitting as a deputy High Court judge, accepted that EUAs were entirely electronic, existing only on national registries. There was no physical evidence of their existence, such as a share certificate, but each EUA had its own number and was readily identifiable. But, as he noted:

> At the heart of the legal difficulties to which this case gives, or may give, rise is the somewhat novel nature of EUAs. This novelty arises from two particular features: the first is that an EUA is a creature of European legislation and the second is that an EUA exists only in electronic form.

The Court then went on to consider the precise nature of an EUA. Morris held that it did not give the holder the right to emit carbon dioxide, but at most represented a permission or exemption from a prohibition to emit. He felt that an EUA was clearly a form of property in English law because it had the classic characteristics of property in being transferable and identifiable, and having a degree of permanence. However, there were various categories and subcategories of property, and the precise categorisation of EUAs could affect the extent to which losses could be recovered from an innocent party.

The Court recognised that EUAs might be considered a form of tangible property, but this was not pursued by the parties, and Morris concluded that 'the current state of the law has not developed to the point where something which exists in electronic form only is to be equated with a physical thing of which actual possession is possible'. The Court's view that EUAs were a form of intangible property drew on analogous case law, notably a High Court decision in the *Celtic Extraction* case in 1999, *Re Celtic Extraction Ltd (in liquidation)* [2001] Ch 475. There, the Court had held that a waste management licence was property in law for the purposes of insolvency legislation.

Going one stage further into subcategorisation, the Court did not feel that an EUA was what is known as a 'chose in action' (being something that is recoverable by an action but cannot actually be physically possessed), but rather fell within the category of 'other intangible property'. For the purpose of this case, however, the judge doubted whether the distinction made much difference to the principles governing recovery.

In terms of the compensation claim, the Court made an important ruling that the EUAs that were transferred to Armstrong's account were the same property as that owned by Winnington, rather than an equivalent in financial worth: 'Given the unique reference number of each EUA and their transferability between accounts, a specific numbered EUA transferred from one registry account to another constitutes the same "asset" or item of property'. This meant that the claim in respect of the actual EUAs could be based on principles concerning the restitution of property, rather than simply unjust enrichment. Winnington argued that such restitution claims did not exist for intangible property, but the Court disagreed:

> In my judgment, as a matter of authority and principle, if and where legal title remains with the claimant, a proprietary restitutionary claim at common law is available in respect of receipt by the defendant of a 'chose in action' or other intangible property.

The Court then examined the defences that might be available to Winnington and in particular, the extent to which it had acted bona fide in buying the EUAs. These had to be set against an examination of the case's facts. The Court concluded, in essence, that Winnington had turned a blind eye to the possibility of the third party selling the EUAs being a fraudster and had taken a high risk in authorising the transaction. Winnington had in fact asked Zen whether it had proper title to the EUAs, but had not waited for an answer before proceeding with the purchase. In those circumstances, Winnington was liable to recompense Armstrong.

Given the growing number of examples of fraudulent trading transactions in the emissions trading scheme, these passages of the judgment are likely to be important for innocent companies caught up in such dealings. The nature of the regime has clearly raised some novel questions. The Court found, for example, that Zen Holdings, or whoever carried out the fraud, did actually possess the EUAs at some point and therefore could be said to hold them as a constructive trustee for Armstrong, though the judge accepted it was not necessarily easy to apply such concepts to modern practice:

> The intangible nature and electronic form of the EUAs coupled with the speed with which it appears that the EUAs were taken out of one account and transferred to another account make it difficult to compare the situation with the thief who steals physical property or a bag of money and passes it on to a third party. Nevertheless, in my judgment the better analysis is that the third-party fraudster did become a constructive trustee of the EUAs.

The decision also comes at a time when the European Commission is trying to improve the integrity of the carbon emissions regime. Proposals were published in October 2011[12] to classify emissions allowances as financial instruments for the purposes of the Financial Instruments Directive. This would increase the supervisory powers available and is designed to assist in preventing abuse in spot trading.

Wind Farms and Mitigation Measures

Hargreaves v Secretary of State for Communities and Local Government and other [2011] EWHC 1999

Modern environmental legal requirements are often triggered by an assessment of whether a proposal is likely to have significant environmental impacts or some similarly worded threshold. A recent decision of the High Court concerning the potential impact of a wind farm on a bird conservation area is important for two reasons. First, it illustrates how reluctant the courts are to interfere with the judgments of experts and other officials on such matters unless clear illegalities are present. Secondly, developers often incorporate mitigation measures into their plans, and the case explores the extent to which the assessment should take on board the implication of the proposed mitigation or whether that is something to be considered after the initial assessment has taken place.

Hargreaves v Secretary of State for Communities and Local Government and other concerned a proposal to build two 2 MW wind turbines some 80 metres high on a hill in Lancashire about five kilometres from a designated Special Protection Area in Morecambe Bay. The area was inhabited by protected birds including pink-footed geese which used nearby fields for feeding, including those around the site of the proposed turbines. It was accepted that there was a risk of up to 50 goose mortalities a year due to collision.

The local authority had refused planning permission in December 2009 on grounds of visual intrusion and the predicted adverse impact on the bird population. The developer appealed to the Secretary of State and a planning inspector granted the permission in August 2010. A local resident challenged the legal validity of this decision.

Critical to the proposal was the proposal by the developers to provide extra feeding areas amounting to just over 12 hectares and the view by Natural England that, provided these measures were properly incorporated into legally binding agreements which would last the lifetime of the project, there was adequate compensation for the geese that might otherwise have been affected.

The first question raised before the court was whether there should have been a formal environmental assessment under the European Directive on the subject[13] and its implementing regulations. The wind farm fell within a discretionary class of projects, meaning that assessment was only required if it was judged that there were likely to be significant environmental effects. The local authority had decided that this threshold had not been

---

[12] 'Proposal for a Directive of the European Parliament and of the Council on market in financial instruments, COM (2011) 656 final.

[13] Directive 2011/92/EU as now amended by Directive 2014/52/EU.

reached and directed that no formal assessment was required, and the Secretary of State had made a similar direction before the appeal was heard.

The claimant argued that the Inspector ought to have reconsidered this question and required a formal environmental assessment. But His Honour Judge Pelling QC, sitting as judge of the High Court, held that once the Secretary of State had made his direction there was no legal duty on the Inspector to address the issue again. A legal challenge would only succeed if there was some fact or change of circumstances that created a 'realistic prospect' of the Secretary of State changing his mind such that any rational inspector would remit the question to the Secretary of State to reconsider. According to the court, 'It goes without saying that these are substantial hurdles for the Claimant and are designed to be so in the interests of avoiding time consuming, cost expending, and ultimately pointless, circularity of decision-making'.

The claimant challenged the way that the decision concerning the environmental assessment had been reached on a number of grounds, but the most significant was the argument that, in deciding whether the project might have significant environmental effects, the decision maker should ignore the impacts of any proposed mitigation measures. Previous case law in the Court of Appeal had indicated that the project as a whole, including any mitigation measures considered to be an integral element part of the project, should be considered when this question was addressed.[14] However, the claimant argued the matter should be referred to the European Court of Justice, and quoted a letter from a European Commission official written to the claimant's solicitor which stated that mitigation measures should be considered only after the requirement for an environmental assessment was established. The Court dismissed the letter – 'At best it reflects the view of the Commission in January 2008. There is no authority cited for the views expressed by the Commission's official'.

The turbines were to be built on a site some five kilometres from a protected conservation area for the geese and under the Habitats Directive a special assessment has to be undertaken where any plan or project is likely to have significant effects on the protected site. The Secretary of State decided that no assessment was required because no significant effects were predicted once the provision of extra feeding grounds was taken into account.

The claimant challenged the way that the Secretary of State had addressed the issues with a similar argument to that raised on the environmental assessment process. He claimed that the proposed extra land for feeding was not an ameliorating feature of the project but in truth a compensatory measure offered for the damage to be done to the protected area. The Habitats Directive requires compensatory measures to be provided to be provided following an assessment and approval of a project – therefore, the claimant argued, compensation measures should not taken on board when the initial question of whether there was likely to be significant effects on the protected site was considered.

The logic of the argument at first appeared strong. The judge acknowledged that the official European Commission document, *Managing Natura 2000 Sites*,[15] drew a distinction between 'mitigation', which aims to minimise or cancel negative impacts of a proposal, and 'compensatory measures', which are independent of the project and designed to compensate for the effects on the habitat affected by the proposal. It was not quite clear whether the extra feeding ground was provided to deflect existing birds from the blades

---

[14] See, eg *Gillespie v First Secretary of State and Bellway Urban Renewal Southern* [2003] EWCA Civ 400; *R (on the application of Catt) v Brighton and Hove City Council* [2006] EWHC 1337.

[15] European Commission, *Managing Natura 2000 Sites* (Brussels, 2000).

(and therefore was really mitigation) or whether it was to provide extra feeding ground to neutralise the effect of the deaths caused by the turbines (in which case it was more in the nature of compensation).

But the judge concluded that this analysis was flawed. The focus of the Habitats Directive was on the protection of the site rather than the species itself:

> Once this is understood it becomes clear in my judgment that whichever way the ameliorating elements of the scheme are understood they are in substance mitigatory in nature applying the Managing Natura 2000 Sites definition because the adverse effect being addressed is the possible reduction of the total number of pink-footed geese over-wintering at the SPA.

However described, the purpose of the proposed extra provision of feeding sites, according to the court, was to neutralise the reduction in the total number of geese overwintering at the site. 'If the proposal is not likely to have an adverse effect on the relevant site because it incorporates appropriate mitigatory measures at the screening stage', then there was no need for a formal assessment under the Habitats Directive.

Once English Nature had withdrawn any objections to the proposal that included the provision of extra feeding grounds, it was always likely to be an uphill task for the claimant to bring a successful legal challenge. The decision has wider importance in exploring how the question of mitigation should be handled under the Habitats Directive, though this may be an issue which can only eventually be determined by the European Court of Justice in subsequent case law.[16]

Liability for Water Pollution Offences

Express Ltd v Environment Agency [2004] EWHC 1710

The High Court has ruled that businesses must carry out adequate risk assessment if they are to escape prosecution of water pollution caused by third parties on their premises. The court also held that substances entering water can still be polluting within the legislation even if no actual harm occurs.

Express Ltd v Environment Agency concerned a pollution incident at a depot belonging to Express Dairies in Redditch in January 2002. The customer, Pardy's Dairies, was transferring cream contained in a 'grundy', described by the court as a 'somewhat unwieldy drum on wheels', by means of a forklift truck into the back of a van. The grundy collided with a milk crate and toppled over, spilling about 10 litres of cream. The area was served by surface water drains leading to a brook. Immediate efforts were made to contain the spillage by covering the drains and using sand to mop up the cream, and the company reported the incident. But some of the cream ran into a road and eventually entered the brook, causing discolouration for 150–200 metres. As a result, Pardy's was charged with an offence under section 85(1) of the Water Resources Act 1991 of causing poisonous, noxious or polluting matter to enter waters, and pleaded guilty.

It was, though, the liability of Express Ltd which was at issue in the case. The company was charged under section 217(3) of the 1991 Act, which provides that where the com-

---

[16] See now *Briels v Minster of Infrastructur en Mileu* C-521/12 15 May 2014.

mission of a water pollution offences is 'due to the act of default of some other person', that person may also be charged with an offence. Express accepted that the core pollution offence with which Pardy's was charged was one of the strict liability, meaning that no evidence of intent or negligence was necessary. But it argued that in relation to an offence under section 217(3) the words 'act or default' did not imply strict liability, and that it was not sufficient simply to show that Express gave the company an opportunity to cause pollution. Counsel for Express acknowledged that a full risk assessment of the cream transfer operation had not been carried out but argued that there was no statutory duty to do so, nor was Express under any duty to prescribe how Pardy's should carry out its work. Surprisingly, this appears to be the first time that a higher court has considered the meaning of section 217(3) or its predecessor in section 121(1) of the Water Act 1989, and the Divisional Court looked to analogous case law for guidance on the meaning of 'act or default'.

A key recent authority was the 1999 decision of the House of Lords in the *Empress Car* case.[17] That case concerned liability under section 85(1) where a third party had opened a tap on the company's premises causing a diesel spillage into a river. The House of Lords held that causation under the offence did not mean a prosecutor had to show that the defendant did something which was the immediate cause of the pollution, nor was there always necessarily one cause of a pollution incident. If the act or event was something that could be described as a normal fact of life – and this might include vandalism by third parties – then a company which maintained tanks full of noxious liquids could be said to have caused the pollution as well as the third party.

In the present case, the High Court held that to establish liability the prosecution had to show that Pardy's contravention of section 85 was due to the act or default of Express Diaries. Lord Justice Kennedy disagreed with the argument of Express that it had no obligation to take action. The source of the obligation was statutory and not to be found from principles relating to civil obligations between parties. 'If a landowner, such as Express, is going to permit and operation on his land which gives rise to a risk of pollution then, as it seems to me, in order not to fall foul of section 85(1) he must carry out a risk assessment and respond to what the assessment reveals. Otherwise if pollution does occur it may be impossible for him to say that the offence committed by those using his land is not due to one or more of his acts of defaults.'

The second main line of argument by Express was that since the magistrates had found as a matter of fact that there was no actual harm caused by the cream entering the brook it could not be said that the substance was polluting within the meaning of the legislation. It was accepted that there had been discolouration, and that analysis of samples revealed increased biochemical oxygen demand, suspended solids and ammoniacal nitrogen, but there had been no fish kill nor any evidence that the cream was toxic. Express argued that there was no statutory definition of 'polluting matter' in the 1991 Act, and pointed to dictionary definitions of 'pollute'. However, its argument was not helped by a 1995 decision of the Court of Appeal in the *Dovermoss* case[18] where it was held that the term 'polluting' was clearly distinguished from 'poisonous' or 'noxious' in the definition of the offence, and did not imply that a harmful effect had to be shown.

---

[17] [1998] 1 All ER 481; see Chapter 20 above, p 399.
[18] [1995] Env LR 258.

The court was prepared to adopt dictionary definitions of pollute such as 'to make physically impure . . . to dirty, stain, taint'. Even the term 'noxious', according to the court, did not imply actual harm – the likelihood or potential of causing harm were sufficient for a substance to be noxious. The court could see no good reason for not following the approach in *Dovermoss*. According to Lord Justice Kennedy, 'section 85(1) is worded in such a way as to make clear that pollution matter need not be either poisonous or noxious. It is sufficient if it, for example, stains or taints as the cream did.'

The *Express* case is consistent with recent authorities on water pollution offences, which emphasise the very strict nature of the offences, and the extent to which extenuating circumstances are relevant to the mitigation of sentencing rather than as a defence to conviction.

Standing Issues in Judicial Review

R (on the application of Edwards) v Environment Agency and another
[2004] EWHC 736

The High Court has given a liberal interpretation of standing rules where an individual seeks to challenge the legality of an environmental permit.[19] A local resident who was apparently homeless at the time of the application and played no significant part in statutory consultation processes was nevertheless held to have sufficient standing to apply for judicial review, and the fact that he was probably chosen as a test applicant who would qualify for legal aid did not amount to an abuse of legal process.

R (on the application of Edwards) v Environment Agency and another concerned Rugby Cement's works in Rugby. Last year, following an extended consultation exercise against a background of considerable local opposition, the Environment Agency granted the company a pollution prevention and control (PPC) permit authorising it to burn waste tyres on a trial basis. The judicial review application raised two key issues concerning the legality of the permit: whether a PPC permit was a 'development consent' within the meaning of the 1985 EC Directive on environmental assessment, implying that the permitting procedure should have been subject to the assessment requirements, and whether the Agency had failed to ensure that the company used the 'best available techniques' (BAT). The present decision, though, was not concerned directly with these issues, but with the initial question of whether the applicant had sufficient standing to bring the case in the first place. The court also had to consider whether, even if he had standing, it was an abuse of process to bring the claim given the circumstances of the case.

The Environment Agency noted that the claim for judicial review had not been brought directly by known opponents of the permitting decision such as the local council or the campaign group, 'Rugby in Plume'. The applicant had made no representations to the Agency during the consultation process, and did not seem to have attended any of the

---

[19] The *Edwards* case is one of the more liberal decisions on standing in environmental law for many years. In 2013, as part of its proposals for reforming judicial review, the government proposed more restrictive standing rules but in 2014 decided not to pursue this, leaving it to tougher leave and financial procedures to 'limit the potential for mischief'. See *Judicial Review –Government Response*, above n 3, para 35. See also Chapter 9 above.

public meetings. The claim form stated that Mr Edwards was a resident of Rugby but no address was given, and according to a local councillor he was currently homeless, though in the past he had lived at a number of addresses in Rugby. However, it did not follow that he was not concerned about the environmental effects of the permit decision. According to the councillor, he had expressed concern to her about the cement works, and in his witness statement said that he had attended meetings, even if he was not an active member of the local campaign.

According to the court, the leading light of 'Rugby in Plume' was Mrs Lillian Pallikaropoulos, who had instructed solicitors now acting for Mr Edwards, had committed substantial funds of her own to the campaign, and was committed to challenging the legality of the Agency's decision. Following advice from leading counsel, Rugby Borough Council had decided not to seek judicial review itself. Mrs Pallikaropoulos was then reported as stating that since she owned her house she would not qualify for legal aid, and the campaign needed someone who could take the case forward on public funds.

Mr Justice Keith acknowledged that Mr Edwards did not say that he had responded to this request for assistance, but nevertheless concluded:

> It is difficult to resist the inference that Mr Edwards has been put up as a claimant in order to secure public funding of the claim by the Legal Services Commission when those who are moving force behind the claim believe that public funding for the claim would not otherwise have be available.

It was against this background that the court considered whether Mr Edwards should be entitled to proceed with the claim. The test for standing in judicial review is that the claimant has 'sufficient interest' in the matter at hand. A generation ago, courts would tend to interpret this phrase to mean that the individual needed to own property that was affected, but they have since adopted an increasingly liberal approach. In the present case, however, the Agency argued that a central plank of the legal challenge was the failure to apply the environmental assessment requirements to the PPC permitting procedure. This in turn affected the nature of the public consultation process and the way that information was available to the public. Mr Edwards appeared to have played no part in the consultation process and therefore, according to the Agency, could not be said to have sufficient interest in the matter.

Mr Justice Keith was quick to dismiss this line of argument. It failed to deal with the second main line of challenge concerning BAT. Furthermore, it did not acknowledge that Mr Edwards was entitled to leave it to others such as the local authority or Rugby in Plume to act on his behalf:

> You do not have to be active in a campaign yourself to have an interest in the outcome . . . You should not be disbarred from subsequently challenging the decision on the grounds of inadequate consultation simply because you choose not to participate in the consultation exercise, provided you are affected by this outcome.

The court was satisfied that Mr Edwards, even if temporarily homeless, was an inhabitant of Rugby and therefore would be affected by any adverse environmental impact which might result from the permitted operations. Accordingly, he had sufficient interest for the purpose of standing.

The court still had to deal with the question of whether bringing the claim in the name of an individual chosen solely for the purpose of qualifying for legal aid was an abuse of process. The Agency referred the court to two recent cases concerning parents challenging decisions of local education authorities, where the actual proceedings had been brought in the name of their children. In one case, it was clear that the child had been chosen to qualify for legal aid and protect the parents against adverse costs orders. The claim had been dismissed as an abuse of the court process. In the second case, the Court of Appeal had allowed the claim to proceed, but accepted that if there were clear evidence that proceedings had been brought in the name of the child in order to obtain public funding, this might amount to an abuse.

However, Mr Justice Keith doubted whether these cases were on all fours with the present application. There, it was in reality the parents' claim rather than the children's interest that was directly at stake. In the present case, in contrast, Mr Edwards himself was affected by the permit decision and there was nothing in addition which prevented him from having a sufficient interest. Moreover, he felt that if there were an abuse it was one that really was a matter for the Legal Services Commission. It was clear that the Commission was fully aware of Mr Edwards's circumstances, since Rugby Cement had written to it to question whether the proceedings were really for his benefit rather than that of other individuals. Mr Justice Keith noted that if the Commission had really felt that the claim was for the benefit of others who could reasonably be expected to contribute to the costs of litigation, they could have been required to contribute as a condition of the grant of funding. In the event, it was clear that the Commission had granted the certificate in the knowledge of all the surrounding circumstances, and must have addressed the question of whether the grant would or would not be an abuse. The court therefore concluded that no abuse of process was involved. The legal issues at the heart of the dispute over the Agency's grant of the permit will now be aired at a full hearing. Although questions of standing and abuse often turn on their own facts, the present decision is a significant development of principles. Certainly, it indicates that in future it will be difficult to refuse standing to local inhabitants where environmental decisions are involved.

Part V

Europe and the Environment

The European Union is a dynamic source of environmental legislation and legal principles, and for many Member States it remains the dominant source of new environmental law. The European Economic Community as it then was began developing policies and law on the environment in the early 1970s. The range of techniques and approaches that have been employed over the years is impressively rich – including more conventional permitting and standard setting, national 'bubbles', emissions trading, producer responsibility and public participation rights. Many initiatives are increasingly being considered as models by jurisdictions outside Europe. But above all, the European Union presents a unique form of supranational legal arrangement that provides both challenges and opportunities for the development of environmental law.

The so-called environmental integration duty has been described as perhaps the most important environmental provision in the EU Treaty, and the EU Treaty was the first, and probably remains the only, constitutional or quasi-constitutional document in the world that has given expression to the concept. *The Legal Duty of Environmental Integration: Commitment and Obligation or Enforceable Obligation?* (1998) is an analysis of the duty very much from a legal perspective, and was written with my then academic colleague Martin Hession, now a distinguished government expert on international climate change. We recognised that environmental integration can imply a raft of new administrative processes, but our focus was that of the lawyer – how would a court interpret such a duty and who could enforce it? The European Court of Justice had already indicated that the duty could empower the Community institutions to introduce environmental dimensions into other policy areas, but more challenging was the question whether the duty might be used to constrain environmentally damaging policies. When we wrote the article, the integration duty appeared in the environmental provisions of the Treaty, but it now finds its expression in Article 11 of the Treaty of the Functioning of the European Union: 'Environmental protection requirements must be integrated into the definition and implementation of the Union policies and activities, in particular with a view to promoting sustainable development'. Nevertheless, over 15 years later, much of the analysis still has relevance, and the challenge of understanding the legal as opposed to the policy significance of the provisions is as pertinent as it always had been.

Since the article was introduced, the integration duty has proved of significance in a number of cases, and while the Court has not yet taken the tough line on process we suggested, there are indications that it does take it seriously – in the *Preussen Elektra* case, for example, Advocate General Jacobs noted that the duty was not simply programmatic but of a binding nature.[1] The narrative of the integration duty is set to continue. The duty had already appeared in slightly different form in the 2000 EU Charter of Human Rights, Article 37 of which declares that 'A high level of environmental protection and the improvement of the quality of the environment must be integrated into the policies of the Union and assured in accordance with the principle of sustainable development'. Environmental integration might be considered a rather bizarre form of human right, but while the Treaty integration duty now appears in Article 11 of the Treaty on the Functioning of the European Union (TFEU), Article 6 of the Treaty on European Union (TEU) recognises the Charter of Human Rights and declares them to have the same values as the Treaties. What this will imply in legal terms for the integration duty remains to be seen, but the arguments concerning enforceability and legal interpretation identified in *The Legal Duty of Integration* are likely to be worth revisiting in the context of environmental integration being characterised as an individual human right.[2]

Environmental Citizenship and the Law – Repairing the European Road (1996) considers the notion of citizenship of the European Union, introduced in 1993, and what it might imply from an environmental perspective. It is clear from the case law of the European Court of Justice that early Community environmental legislation could be interpreted as giving rights to individuals, whether of a procedural nature such as environmental assessment or to substantive environmental quality standards. But it seemed to me to go much deeper than that. From a legal perspective, citizenship also raised important questions such as those concerning access to the courts, an area where the Court of Justice of the European Union continues to demonstrate a restrictive approach to direct access by individuals or non-governmental organisations that wished to challenge the legality of action by such Union institutions as the European Commission, where it is not possible to do so before national courts.[3] Although the Lisbon Treaty purported to relax standing rules for access to the Court of Justice in respect of 'regulatory acts',[4] the reality is that this is a fairly narrow concession,[5] and the lacuna at the heart of a system so explicitly based on the rule of law remains a serious weakness.

The European Union had its origins as a purely functionalist economic institution, with a free market and all it implied designed to bring about closer political cooperation and union between Member States. It is clear that this is no longer the case – successive amendments to the Treaty have indicated a much broader set of tasks and goals including

---

[1] 'As its wording shows, Article 6 is not merely programmatic; it imposes legal obligations': Advocate General Jacobs, Opinion in Case C-379/98 *Preussen Elektra AG v Schleswag AG* [2001] ECR I-2099.

[2] But maybe less relevant to the United Kingdom and Poland, which attempted to opt out of the legally binding nature of the Charter under Protocol I of the Lisbon Treaty, though it is questionable whether that was achieved. Note that the European Court of Justice had since held that Art 1 of the 'opt-out Protocol' explains Art 51 of the Charter with regard to the scope thereof and does not intend to exempt the Republic of Poland or the United Kingdom from the obligation to comply with the provisions of the Charter or to prevent a court of one of those Member States from ensuring compliance with those provisions. Joined Cases C-411/10 and C-493/10, *NS v Home Secretary and ME v Refugee Applications Commissioner* 21 December 2011.

[3] See, eg CJEU Case T-585/93 *Stichting Greenpeace Council (Greenpeace Int'l) & Others v Commission* [1995] ECR II-2205; CJEU Case C-321/95 P *Stichting Greenpeace Council (Greenpeace Int'l) & Others v Commission* [1998] ECR I-1651. Case C-355/08 *WWF-UK v Council of the European Union* [2009] ECR I-73.

[4] Art 263 TFEU now requires only 'direct' concern' in respect of regulatory acts which do not entail implementing measures rather than 'direct and individual' concern, the test for challenges to other types of acts.

[5] See the interpretation of the CJEU in Case T-18/10 *Inuit Tapiriit Kanatami and Others v European Parliament and Council of the European Union* [2011] ECR II-05599 and Case T-262/10 *Microban v Commission* [2011] ECR II-07697; see also R Roer-Eide and M Eliantonio, 'The Meaning of Regulatory Act Explained: Are There Any Significant Improvements for the Standing of Non-privileged Applicants in Annulment Actions? '(2013) 14(9) *German Law Journal* 1851.

that of sustainable development and a high level of environmental protection. As the then Advocate General, Francis Jacobs succinctly observed in the mid 1990s, the 'mercantilist approach is simply no longer tenable'.[6] But *Environmental Citizenship and the Law* notes how from a legal perspective the environment still was treated differently from economic rights. The core economic rights in the Treaty such as the free movement of goods have been interpreted by the European Court of Justice as individual legal rights that may be invoked to challenge the legality of national legislation that inhibits them. In contrast, the environmental principles in the Treaty grant no equivalent general individual rights, and any such rights may only be determined from individual pieces of Community environmental legislation. In essence, Europe has granted its citizens individual economic rights but in the absence of Union legislation no equivalent environmental rights.

Balancing Trade Freedom with the Requirements of Sustainable Development (1996) is a more detailed analysis of the balance between trade and sustainability within the European Community, and how legal principles and the courts handle the inevitable conflicts that may occur. The tension continues to this day, and the European approaches are echoed in the decisions of the World Trade Organization at international level.

Both *Environmental Citizenship* and *Balancing Trade Freedom* argue that if we are to truly ensure a greater legal balance between trade and the environment, we should consider redefining in the Treaty more explicitly the purposes of free movement of goods as being the 'rational and prudent use of natural resources', reflecting one of the environmental principles of the Treaty. This would transform the basic legal structure and hierarchy of principles, though as with any significant constitutional change, one that consciously leaves open the precise direction that would be taken in the future in its interpretation. In 2003 the Avosetta Group of European environmental lawyers proposed as an input to the then European Convention an alternative but equally radical legal formulation which was also aimed to redress these fundamental legal imbalances between trade and the environment.[7] This would insert a new general provision in the Treaty that, 'Subject to imperative reasons of overriding public interest, significantly impairing the environment or human health shall be prohibited'. Such a provision would – as are the current free trade provisions – be invocable by individuals and be directly applicable to the activities of all Member State's governments and legislatures, as well as Community institutions. It is perhaps hardly surprising that these sorts of profound structural change are not reflected in the current EU Treaties, yet they raise challenging questions of core principle that still need to be faced.

Another core principle of EU law is the principle of subsidiarity, which is still given high prominence. In July 2012 the UK Foreign and Commonwealth Office launched a comprehensive two-year review of the balance of competences within the EU, with all government departments auditing EU competences within their respective. The subsidiarity principle and how it actually works in practice should form an important element of the reflective analysis, and the final element of the audit to take place in the second half of 2014 will indeed be focused on subsidiarity and proportionality and led by the Foreign and Commonwealth Office. Clearly there is a strong political dimension to the concept, but my concern is more with the legal implications. First written into the Treaty under the 1992 Maastricht amendments, the principle was famously described by a former President of European of the Court of Justice as 'legal gobbledygook' and capable of at

---

[6] Jacobs, *Human Rights and the European Union* (Durham, European Law Institute, 1994).

[7] Resolution of the Avocetta Conference, 11–12 October 2002, in Jans (ed), *The European Convention and the Future of European Environmental Law* (Groningen, Europa Law Publishing, 2003).

least thirty different meanings. *Subsidiarity and European Community Environmental Law* (1999) does not attempt to unravel all those interpretations, but explores the principle in relation to European Union environmental law. The environmental policies of the Union represent a concurrent area of competences between the Union and Member States to which the subsidiarity principle will apply. When the principle was originally introduced some Member States hoped that it would roll back the frontiers of Union legislative intervention and even lead to the repeal of a substantial number of existing Directives. This has not happened in any dramatic fashion, and the Court of Justice of the European Union has recognised that the test requires a considerable degree of political judgment to which the Union institutions are entitled a large margin of discretion.[8] Yet the principle has influenced in more subtle ways the substantive content of more recent Community environmental legislation that is rather less dirigiste in tone than earlier examples, and contain more flexibility for Member States in their interpretation and implementation.

This approach in the design of legislation may more truly reflect the complexity of designing contemporary environmental solutions across some 28 countries, but raises challenges for effective supervision and enforcement at Union level. It is a dilemma facing all environmental lawyers and one I recognise in my own concerns. As Peeters and Uylenburg have noted in a recent study:[9]

> Lawyers studying EU environmental law need to balance between, on the one hand, their wish for clear EU environmental legislation that avoids interpretation problems with preferably, where possible, providing enforceable substantive rights to citizens, with on the other hand the values embedded into the subsidiarity and proportionality principle . . . aimed at finding solutions at national and even sub-national levels where democratic organizations have to play a role in increasing legitimacy and providing fine-tuned and adequate solutions.

The enforcement of supranational obligations is always problematical, not least because one is generally dealing with nation states that may subscribe to the principles of compliance with international obligations but in reality are likely to resist undue interference with national sovereignty. The Achilles heel of many international environmental treaties used to be the lack of attention given their enforcement, though more recent international agreements such as the 1987 Montreal Protocol on Ozone Substances and the 1997 Kyoto Protocol on Climate Change contain more sophisticated supervisory mechanisms designed to bring pressure on non-compliant parties. Nevertheless, they largely work 'through collective decision making and co-operation rather than through formal processes of law enforcement and sanctions'.[10] A power of inspection by international enforcement bodies remains very much the exception rather than the rule. International courts have no direct power to impose sanctions on a non-compliant party.

In this context, the machinery of the European Union designed to ensure compliance by Member States of their obligations under Union law offers an intriguing example of a developed supranational enforcement system and, as so often with Europe, one that charts a distinctive course between international and national ways of doing things. The procedures are common to most areas of Union law, and the actual wording of the core

---

[8] See C-377/98 *Netherlands v European Parliament and Council* [2001] ECR I-7079; C-233/94 *Germany v European Parliament and Council* [1997] ECR I-2405.

[9] M Peeters and R Uylenburg (eds), *EU Environmental Legislation – Legal Perspectives on Regulatory Strategies* (Cheltenham, Edward Elgar, 2014).

[10] Birnie and Boye, *International Law and the Environment*, 2nd edn (Oxford, Oxford University Press, 2001) 220.

provisions concerning the European Commission's powers to bring infringement proceedings against Member States has not changed since they first appeared in Article 169 of the 1957 Treaty of Rome establishing the European Economic Community. Over the last 20 years, however, their use in the environmental field has been particularly striking. Distinctive features of the European Union system include a dedicated legal unit, with the DG Environment concerned with the enforcement of all Community environmental legislation, a far broader remit possessed by any specialised secretariat under particular international environmental treaties;[11] a citizen's complaint system allowing any individual or organisation to notify the Commission of suspected breaches of Union law by their own Member State or indeed by any other Member State; and, not least, the power of the Court of Justice of the European Union to impose financial sanctions on Member States that fail to comply with its judgments concerning non-compliance.

Despite its innovative features, the system is by no means perfect. *The Enforcement of EU Environmental Law: Some Proposals for Reform* (2005) was concerned with ways of improving the procedures, designed to make them less bureaucratic and more strategically focused on environmental outcomes. Many Member States remain uncomfortable with the prospect of enforcement actions by the Commission, especially when they are concerned with particular instances of non-compliance in practice rather than merely ensuring than the national law formally reflects Community obligations. The Commission itself is under pressure, and in 2007 the Secretariat General published a policy paper designed to reorientate its general approach towards enforcement.[12] More explicit prioritisation is the order of the day, and the Secretary general identified three areas for priority: (1) non-communication of national implementing measures; (2) breaches of Union law raising issues of principle or having particularly far-reaching negative impacts, such as breaches involving the application of Treaty provisions and the main elements of framework regulations and directives; and (3) respect for judgments of the Court of Justice of the European Union declaring the existence of infringements. The first and third classes of priority are clear enough, but the middle category is open to interpretation. The aspect of the policy explicitly is stated to include non-conformity cases, implying that the Commission will no longer pursue Member States whose transposition measures are defective but do not raise issues of principle or have far reaching effects. Yet in the application of law the devil is often in the detail, and I have argued that, if anything, the focus should be on ensuring that national measures are in full conformity. Then at least there is an opportunity for national courts to take a full role in their enforcement. It is perhaps too early to judge the longer term significance of these signals, and indeed evaluation is made more difficult because the annual reports on implementation produced by the Commission now contain less detail that in previous years. The system can undoubtedly be improved, but not, I hope, in a way that emasculates its distinctive power to bring home the legally binding implications of Union law.

The Enforcement of Community Environmental Law: Some Critical Issues (1992) derived from my experience in working in the enforcement unit of the DG Environment for a short period and seeing at first hand the sorts of legal challenges involved. It was one of the first detailed articles published that focused on the EU enforcement system in

---

[11] In the most recent internal reorganisation of DG Environment, which suggests a weakening of the specialised legal unit, Directorate D, 'Implementation, Governance and Semester', now contains Unit D3, 'Enforcement, Cohesion Policy, and European Semester, Cluster 3'.

[12] European Commission, 'A Europe of Results – Applying Community Law' Com (2007) 502 final.

the environmental field, and considered the system against underlying legal principles. Despite developments that have taken place in the intervening 20 years or so (including a renumbering of the relevant Treaty provisions), the fundamental structures and problems inherent in the system remain today. In particular, I highlighted the critical importance of the precise wording of the relevant legislation and how drafting affected subsequent enforceability by the Commission. In the light of current trends in the style of legislation and the greater discretion being given to Member States within common legislative frameworks, this now has even more contemporary relevance.

Implementation and enforcement is a key feature of the 7th Action Programme on the Environment agreed in 2013, and *European Moves on Environmental Enforcement* (2014) takes stock on some of the major current developments, the Commission's development of new policies requiring more systematic inspection and surveillance at Member State level, and the use of penalty provisions by the Court of Justice of the European Union, including its 2012 decision against Ireland, discussed in more detail in Chapter 19, above page 367.

These chapters have largely focused on the role of the European Commission in the enforcement process. It is clear that it cannot possibly handle every example of infringement, and the Court of Justice of the European Union has developed a number of doctrines which appear nowhere in the Treaties but are designed to make it easier to invoke EU law before national courts where there is defective transposition. Each has its own strengths and limitations. The direct effect doctrine allows provisions of directives to be invoked before national courts, but may only be used in actions against the state or its emanations, and only in respect of provisions of a directive considered sufficiently unconditional and precise. This latter test is often not easy to apply. To take one example, Article 4 of Waste Framework Directive 75/442[13] requires that Member States 'shall take the necessary measures to ensure that waste is disposed of without endangering human health and without harming the environment'. Some might argue that this is an expression of an unequivocal obligation which should have a direct effect, yet the Court of Justice of the European Union held in 1994 that the provision

> must be regarded as defining the framework for the action to be taken by the Member States regarding the treatment of waste and not as requiring, in itself, the adoption of specific measures or a particular method of waste disposal. It is therefore neither unconditional nor sufficiently precise and thus is not capable of conferring rights on which individuals may rely as against the State.[14]

A second doctrine, based on the so-called *Frankovitch* principle,[15] allows a claim for damages against the state for losses caused by the failure of Member State to implement EU law properly. But the conditions for invoking a claim are tough, especially the requirement to prove a causal connection between the loss suffered and the state's failure to implement EU law. The right to claim damages has been available for over 20 years, but a recent study[16]

---

[13] Now repeated in Art 13 of the Waste Framework Directive 2008/98/EC.

[14] C-236/92 *Comitato di Coordinamento per la Difesa della Cava and others v Regione Lombardia and others* [1994] ECR I-485, para 14.

[15] Joined Cases C-6/90 and C-9/90 *Francovitch and Bonifaci v Italy* [1991] ECR I-5357.

[16] J Jans, R Macrory and A Molina (eds), *National Courts and EU Environmental Law* (Groningen, Europa Law Publishing, 2013).

examining environmental case law in 14 Member States could find only one example of a successful *Frankovitch* claim in the environmental field in that period.[17]

It is the third doctrine, the so-called principle of consistent interpretation, that has the potential for greatest impact. The European Court of Justice began developing the doctrine in 1984,[18] requiring national courts to interpret national law as far as possible in the light of the wording and purpose of relevant directives. The doctrine is logical, in line with the concept of the supremacy of EU and arguably the least disruptive to national systems in that courts are being ask to interpret rather than disapply national provisions. Unlike the direct effect doctrine, it has both horizontal and vertical effects. *Consistent Interpretation of EU Environmental Law* (2013) was written with Varena Madner and Stefan Mayr of the Vienna University of Economics and Business, and arose out of a comparative study conducted by the Avosetta Group.[19] We explore the complexities of the doctrine in some detail, examining both the case law of the Court of Justice and examples in Member States where it has been applied by national courts. Understanding how national courts actually use the doctrine in practice is extremely important if one is to have any appreciation of its real impact. The European Court used the phrase that consistent interpretation must be applied 'as far as possible', but beyond stating that this should not be used to impose criminal liability where none existed at national level, the Court has appeared to deliberately refrain from prescribing in any detail what this really implies. National courts are being given considerable discretion to follow their own interpretative tradition, and one can detect differing trends. The phrase 'as far as possible' could be read to mean that national courts should be as creative and innovative as they can in ensuring that national law is read in the light of EU law or, in direct contrast, it could be read to imply a restrictive limitation. It is clear that there remain uncertainties as to what extent the doctrine can be used to impose obligations on individuals and other third parties. And, even though it has the potential for extremely broad reach, there remain two important limitations. First, where there is simply no national rule or law in place for the doctrine to grasp. Secondly, if national law is explicitly and consciously contrary to EU law, the contra legem principle is likely to persuade national courts to give preference to the national rule. As we conclude in the analysis, 'Perversely, then, the doctrine has little to contribute in the most blatant examples of non-implementation by a Member State'. These doctrines of the European Court cannot ensure that Union law is effectively applied in all cases; consequently, the powers of the European Commission to bring infraction proceedings remain of importance.

It is now over 30 years since European Community environmental legislation was first developed. Ten years after the initiation of the first Community action programme on the environment, I organised a conference at Imperial College to reflect on progress to date from both a policy and legal perspective. *Underlying Themes in the Policy Process* (1983) is an analysis of some of the core themes that emerged from the conference, and written with a colleague, the late John Peachey, a resource analyst who had previously worked in government. The chapter can be read simply as piece of historical interest, reflecting core

---

[17] A decision of a French administrative tribunal concerning a claim by environmental NGOs for moral damage (prejudice moral) arising out of the failure to implement the Nitrates Directive 91/676/EC. The tribunal's decision was confirmed by the Administrative Court of Appeal, Nantes – Decision 07NTO3775, 1 December 2009.

[18] Case 14/83 *Von Colson & Kamann* [1984] ECR 1891.

[19] http://www.avosetta.org/.

issues at a particular moment in the development of the EU environmental acquis and the UK relationship with Europe. At the time, there was unanimous voting at the Council of Ministers for Community environmental measures, and no express environmental provisions in the Treaty, which were not introduced until 1987. Proposed environmental laws were either based on free market provisions or a catch-all clause in the Treaty. The British Law Lord, Lord Diplock, was in the audience and complained that the rule of law was being threatened. The legal basis of some of the EU environmental legislation was suspect,[20] but the system did not allow for any review by the European Court. Since there was unanimous voting at Council level, no Member State needed to use their powers to challenge the legality of measures and third parties had no right of direct access to the European Court – a problem still with us today. Essentially, if a measure was deemed politically acceptable, it would be passed, however doubtful its legal basis – a system that was not, in Lord Diplock's view, compatible with the rule of law.

At the time, the United Kingdom was strongly resisting the proposed Directive on environmental assessment, and we were particularly intrigued with the vigour with which the UK government was protecting and championing the more informal approach to assessment then practised in the United Kingdom to the apparently more formalised requirements being proposed by the European Commission. British practice was by no means perfect, but, as we noted, 'It is hardly surprising that the attitudes encouraged by defensive briefing, and the upheavals caused by aggressive Community intervention, may in turn inhibit the domestic search for improved procedures at a national level'. The Directive, which was agreed two years later, was the first environmental directive almost wholly concerned with prescribing a procedure for decision making rather than substantive outcomes, a feature than has since become more significant in subsequent directives, and this aspect of the proposal appeared to exacerbate potential national and community conflicts. *Underlying Themes* may have been a product of its time, but it still contains insights that resonate in the contemporary negotiation of Union environmental law and policy making, let alone the current political debates on Britain's relationship with Europe. As we concluded,

> In the environmental sector, it is necessary to choose levels, scales, and types of intervention and harmonisation that can accommodate regional environmental objectives, ensure consistency of purpose, and yet preserve the flexibility essential to cope with the varied and local nature of the environment and its management.

---

[20] A number of the first wave of environmental directives were based, at least in part, on Art 235 of the Treaty of Rome, which provides that, 'If action by the Community should prove necessary to attain, in the course of the operation of the common market, one of they objectives of the Community and this Treaty has not provided the necessary powers, the Council shall, acting unanimously on a proposal from the Commission and after consulting the Assembly, take the appropriate measures'. The objective referred to in directives such as bathing water or drinking water was one of those contained in Art 2 of the Treaty, 'an accelerated raising of the standard of living'. The arguments of those alarmed at an apparently legally unchecked expansion of powers was that this was treating the standard of living objective as a stand-alone goal. Yet Art 2 refers expressly to the goal being achieved 'by establishing a common market and progressively approximating the economic policies of Member States'. Simply treating Art 235 as a way of avoiding this limitation as to means was legal obfuscation. The interpretation was never resolved before the European Court of Justice for the reasons given by Lord Diplock.

23

The Legal Duty of Environmental Integration: Commitment and Obligation or Enforceable Right?[1] (1998)

Environmental protection requirements must be integrated into the definition and implementation of other community policies.

Article 130r(2), European Community Treaty[2]

Why A Legal Analysis?

In its 1992 report to UNCED, the European Commission described environmental integration as 'the lynch-pin in the process of establishing sustainable social and economic development patterns'. All Member States may now politically subscribe to the goals of sustainable development, but no national constitution or legal system contains an explicit legal requirement concerning the integration of an environmental dimension into other policy sectors. Only within the European Community Treaty, under Article 130r, has the idea been given such an overt and broadly drawn expression in law. The presidency conclusions from the 1997 Amsterdam Treaty reaffirm the integration duty and expressly relate it to the promotion of sustainable development:[3]

> Environmental protection requirements must be integrated into the definition and implementation of community policies and activities referred to in Article 3, in particular with a view to promoting sustainable development.

---

[1] M Hession and R Macrory, 'The Legal Duty of Environmental Integration: Commitment and Obligation or Enforceable Right?' In T O'Riordan and H Voisey (eds), *The European Union and Sustainable Development* (London, Frank Cass, 1998) 100–12.

[2] Now Art 11 Treaty on the Functioning of the European Union: 'Environmental protection requirements must be integrated into the definition and implementation of the Union policies and activities, in particular with a view to promoting sustainable development'.

[3] Referred to in the rest of this chapter as the Amsterdam Treaty amendments. At the time of writing (August 1997), the Conclusions of the Presidency had still not been formally agreed upon and signed by the parties. Formal amendment of the Treaty (which requires referenda in some countries) is probably still several years away. Under the Amsterdam amendments, the integration duty would be repositioned as a new Art 3d at the head of the Treaty.

Other chapters in this collection consider the policy and political implications of environmental integration, together with the tensions and difficulties apparent at European Community and national level as efforts are made to respect the requirement. The approach here is somewhat different. Given the distinctive legal dimension to the integration duty in the Treaty, we feel it is important to consider the nature of a duty from a legal perspective, bringing to bear principles and conceptual approaches developed in the context of the discipline of law. In particular, we need to ask: to what extent does the provision, as a matter of law, require, provide, and constrain the operational criteria for its implementation?

It is tempting to dismiss a duty which is expressed, in such broad and apparently political terms, as merely 'symbolic reassurance'[4] or one that implies no more than a reflection of existing policy developments. It is true that the community commitment to a policy of environment integration predates its express inclusion in the Treaty in 1987 by some five years.[5] The duty first entered the legal language of the Treaty under the Single European Act 1987 and the wording was strengthened under the Maastricht Treaty in 1992.[6]

These developments, however, do not answer the question of the legal significance attached to the duty. Despite the Single European Act requirement, the European Commission made little progress in strengthening its own policy-making procedures to reflect the obligation. It did publish integrative policy documents in a number of sectoral areas,[7] but it is only fairly recently, as considered by Wilkinson in the next chapter, that more substantial internal administrative changes have been made by the commission in order to pursue the goal of integration. A number of these reflect similar administrative initiatives already introduced by Member State governments at national level. It is fairly fruitless to speculate whether these developments were brought about by the existence of the duty in the Treaty, or whether these provisions simply reflected pressures for policy changes that were occurring in any event. Certainly, the developments that have taken place at community level cannot be said to have been the result of any dramatic, interventionist decision by the Court of Justice. This has happened in some other policy areas, such as the common transport policy.[8] The fact that the legal duty existed for almost ten years without any significant internal administrative change at community level indicates that the motor for change was not sparked by a legal dynamic.

It does not follow, however, that the duty is devoid of legal significance. It has already been referred to by the Court of Justice in a number of cases concerning the appropriate legal basis for community environmental legislation.[9] The thrust of the case law to date has been to interpret the duty in the light of measures based on the Treaty's non-environmental

---

[4] M Edelman, *Symbolic Use of Politics* (University of Illinois Press, 1964).

[5] Council resolution endorsing the Third Action on the Environment (1982–86) established the integration of an environmental dimension into other Community policies as a priority, and in 1985 the European Council 'affirmed its determination' to give Community environmental protection policy 'the dimension of an essential component of the economic, industrial, agricultural and social policies implemented by the community and by its Member States'.

[6] A number of expert commentators soon noted the potential significance of the provision. Ludwig Krämer has said that it 'must be considered the most important provision in the entire section on the environment'; Nigel Haigh (1987) also commented that it is 'potentially the most important new provision'.

[7] D Wilkinson, 'Steps towards Integrating the Environment into Other EU Policy Sectors' in O'Riordan and Voisey (eds), *The Transition to Sustainability* (Earthscan, 1998).

[8] See, in particular, Case C-13/83 *European Parliament v EC Council* [1985] ECR 1513.

[9] For example, Case C-62/88 *Greece v EC Council* [1990] 1 ECR 1527.

provisions even where their substantive content has an environmental dimension.[10] In that sense, the integration duty can be said to have an enabling or legitimising effect on Community action already being proposed. But from a legal perspective, perhaps the more critical question for the future is whether the requirement goes further: does it imply a duty which *constrains* Community activities, and which fails to reflect the integration concept or *requires* positive steps to be taken? In other words, the duty to integrate must fall somewhere in the continuum of an expression of general interest in environmental protection and a general duty to protect the environment.

The bald conclusion of the European Court in the Chernobyl I case, namely that the integration provision under Article 130r in its pre-Maastricht version implies that 'all Community measures must satisfy the requirements of environmental protection', hints at something more than a mere enabling provision.[11] But closer analysis is required to test the validity and practicality of that assertion. Ordinarily, the expression of a legal duty implies a concomitant right, as a consequence of the general need that duties should be enforceable. Therefore, in seeking to define its place on the continuum, it is important to consider how and by whom the duty/right is enforceable. In the absence of any enforcing power a duty risks becoming 'a statement of public policy that is contradicted by practice' and 'is nothing but an empty shell ... It may even be pernicious to the reputation of the constitution as a whole and detract from the credibility of the constitutional system derived from it'.[12]

In pursuing the analysis further we can identify five interrelated but essentially distinct lines of inquiry. These are purposely framed in terms of a legal perspective on the issue.

1. Is the integration duty legally binding or merely exhortatory in character?
2. What does the duty apply to?
3. By whom is the duty owed?
4. What is the substance of the duty: what must be integrated, and when is the duty satisfied? Is it a substantive or procedural requirement?
5. To whom is it owed, and if it is legally binding, by whom is it enforceable?

The Integration Duty in Context

Before considering these questions in more detail, it is important to place the duty in the context of the environmental provisions of the Treaty. Although these represent something of a mishmash from a legal perspective, one can provide an analytical overview of the structure.

---

[10] The rule of law underlies the operation of the Community in that any legal measures taken by the Community (such as legislation) must expressly be founded on a specific provisions of the Treaty (such as those concerning agriculture, transport, the environment, etc). Ultimately the European Court has the power to determine whether a particular measures falls within the remit of the provision claimed. Since different procedural consequences can flow from the choice of Treaty provision, there have been frequent legal disputes between the European Council, the European Commission, the European Parliament and Member States over the correct legal base.

[11] For example, *Greece v EC Council*, above n 9.

[12] This was said of the constitution of the German Democratic Republic, which included a mandate to the legislature and a fundamental duty to protect nature. See E Brandi and H Bungert, 'Constitutional Entrenchment of Environmental Protection: A Comparative Perspective' (1992) 16(1) *Harvard Environmental Law Review* 1.

- Ostensibly the Treaty does not guarantee environmental quality or sustainable development nor does it place a duty on the Community to achieve these goals. To paraphrase Article 2, the Community has as one of its fundamental tasks to promote sustainable growth while respecting the environment, which it will achieve by various measures (establishing a common market and an economic and monetary union and by implementing common policies or activities, including the environmental policy). The Amsterdam amendments would expressly add as one of the tasks 'a high level of protection and improvement of the quality of the environment'.[13]
- The Community does, however, have a recognised *interest* in environmental protection, and has legal authority to adopt measures with reference to a range of policies including those contained in Article 130r of the Treaty relating to community policy on the environment.
- The three key objectives are: preserving, protecting and improving the quality of the environment; protecting human health; and the prudent and rational utilisation of natural resources.[14] These indicate that environmental protection is defined according to a variety of philosophical approaches – ecocentric, anthropocentric and what might be described as economic rationality (the rational use of resources).
- The Community authority for action is confined to the range of Community policies listed in Article 3 and their relevant legal base. For those policies which are not exclusively the preserve of the community but exist concurrently with those of Member States (of which the dedicated environmental policy is one), Community authority is further constrained by the principle of subsidiarity.
- Nevertheless, where the Community does take action, there is an identified standard of protection to be achieved, albeit expressed in qualitative terms. In its proposals concerning the internal market and environmental protection, it *must take as a base* a 'high level' of protection (Article 100a), or alternatively in proposals under the environment policy it must aim at a 'high level' of protection, taking into account the diversity of situations in various regions of the Community.
- According to Article 130r, there are express principles upon which environmental policies must be based, notably: the precautionary principle; the principle that preventative action should be taken; the need to rectify damage at source; and the principle that the polluter should pay. Again under Article 130r, additional factors must be taken into account when preparing environmental policy. These are: available scientific data; environmental conditions in the various regions of the community; the potential costs and benefits of action or lack of action; and the socio-economic development of the community and its regions.
- Finally, there is the integration duty, currently contained in Article 130r and analysed in more detail in the chapter that follows. The positioning of the duty is potentially significant, as are the Amsterdam amendments which place it higher up in the Treaty, in a new Article 3. Currently, it falls within the definition of the Community's competence on environmental matters, and after the stated objectives for environmental

---

[13] Following the 2007 Lisbon Treaty, the Treaty on the European Union now provides in Art 3 that the Union 'shall work for the sustainable development of Europe based on balanced economic growth and price stability, a highly competitive social market economy, aiming at full employment and social progress, and a high level of protection and improvement of the quality of the environment'.

[14] There is an important fourth objective of promoting measures at international level to deal with regional or worldwide environmental problems, but this relates more to geographical competence than to substantive content.

policy and the principles of environmental action. Its position suggests a requirement that is exercisable only in the context of community policy formulation and implementation rather than any absolute duty in respect of existing and presumably superior legal principles. Repositioning the provision is intended to give the principle far greater policy significance. As Hallo (1997) has noted, there may be an analogy with the repositioning and reformulation of the subsidiarity duty as a general principle following Maastricht, which brought in its wake considerable political attention designed to flesh out the implications of the requirement.[15]

Is the Integration Duty Legally Binding or Exhortary?[16]

From a practical point of view, only a self executing [judicially enforceable without the enactment of implementing legislation] constitutional provision seems to be worthy of adoption, since it alone has true constitutional value. Any other type of clause could be easily ignored: it would lack the weight and timeless authority of a constitutional provision. (Brandi and Bungarth, 1992)

Most systems of public law, and especially those that require the interpretation of written constitutional provisions, recognise two categories of legal statement:

- *directory duties* which are essentially exhortatory or policy statements not intended in themselves to be legally enforced, though they may colour the interpretation of other duties; and
- *mandatory requirements* which are self-executory in the sense that they impose duties which are enforceable in themselves, without requiring the implementation of further legislation.

The fact that a directory duty may not be legally enforceable does not necessarily render it mere rhetoric. It may influence the legal interpretation of other provisions, as has already happened with the integration duty.[17] Moreover, the existence of such a duty may elevate the status and influence of those parts of government already convinced of the need for such goals, and in turn affect the approach of others. As Cotterrell put it, 'the behaviour of officials and individuals may change even though the legislation does not create enforceable rights and duties . . . non-justifiable legislation performs important functions'.[18]

There are a number of arguments for considering the duty to be directory in character only. The duty is expressed in positive terms ('environmental protection requirements must be . . .'), and therefore, from a legal perspective is generally less susceptible to enforcement than is a negative requirement ('the Community may not promote policies damaging the environment. . .'). It relates to the exercise of judgment in policy develop-

---

[15] Hallo draws an analogy with the subsidiarity principle which 'underwent a similar migration in the Treaty of Maastricht, moving from the environment article to a new separate article at the beginning of the Treaty'. He notes how, following that move, serious political attention was given to refining and developing the principle into workable criteria. R Hallo, 'Sustainable Development and the Integration of the Environment into Other Policies', Conference Paper: IGC and the Environment, Brussels, 1997.

[16] Following the Lisbon Treaty, the integration duty now appears in Art 11 of the Treaty of the Functioning of the European Union in Title II (General Principles). The Subsidiarity Principle now appears in Art 5 of the Treaty on European Union (Title I General Principles).

[17] See *European Parliament v EC Council*, above n 8.

[18] R Cotterrell, *The Sociology of Law* (Butterworths, 1984).

ment and implementation in which a court would ordinarily allow a greater margin of discretion to the decision-maker. The provision can be said to be ambiguous in that it fails to identify specific environmental protection requirements, an issue considered further below. This is a common response to environmental duties, but not necessarily fatal. Given the unconditional character of the duty, a proactive Court of Justice might insist that it has the authority to seek out the environmental protection requirements of the duty. But some commentators have detected a palpably less activist and more consolidatory phase in the court's current approach – and in any event the court has generally been less inclined to hold the Community's actions as contrary to Community law when compared to its tougher approach to the enforcement of community law against Member States. Finally, as a general comment where duties exist with respect to the environment in national constitutions, experience has revealed considerable reluctance on the part of the courts to implement such environmental duties, in whatever language they are expressed.[19]

These are powerful arguments. But despite the ambiguity of the language, the literal meaning and legislative history of the integration provision tend to suggest that it is more in the nature of mandatory requirement. As Haigh notes[20] at Maastricht the Member States consciously took the opportunity to reinforce the mandatory tone of the provision by strengthening the language of the obligation. Furthermore, in the context of community law, it would be unusual for the court not to ascribe some effect to such a statement pursuant to the principle of *effet utile* – the idea that Treaty provisions must have some useful purpose.

To What Does the Duty Apply?

The duty applies integration to 'other community policies' without defining the meaning of that term. Article 2 of the Treaty sets out a range of European Community activities, but only a limited number of these are referred to explicitly as policies:

- a common commercial policy (external trade to developing countries);
- a common policy in the sphere of agriculture and fisheries;
- a policy in the social sphere comprising a European social fund – a common policy in the sphere of transport;
- a policy in the field of the environment; and
- a policy in the sphere of development cooperation.

A restrictive legal interpretation would suggest that the integration duty is confined to these areas only and does not cover other areas of community activity, such as competition law or free movement of goods, which are not explicitly on that list. The drafters of the integration duty could have used, if they wished, broader language. Our own view is that this is too limiting an approach. If the issue were to come before the European Court of Justice it would adopt a more generous interpretation, and not feel confined by the explicit list of policies in Article 3. For a start, the Treaty itself is not consistent in the use of the

---

[19] See Brandi and Bungert, above n 12.
[20] N Haigh, 'Introducing the Concept of Sustainable Development into the Treaties of the European Union' in O'Riordan and Voisey, above n 7.

term 'policies'.[21] The court would be justified in considering the duty's underlying rationale and subject those policy-making activities of the Community, whether or not they are formally described as policies, to the integration duty.[22] In any event, the Amsterdam amendments will remove the doubt. The new version of the integration duty applies to 'policies and activities' (our emphasis) referred to in Article 3.[23] This extends the scope well beyond narrowly defined policies to encompass, amongst others, free movement of goods, competition, consumer protection, and measures of energy.

So much for the substantive areas encompassed by the duty. But we also need to ask what exactly is meant by policies (and 'activities' if the Dublin proposals are agreed). Does it encompass only binding legal acts such as directives, regulations and decisions? Or would it include formal, but non-binding, acts such as decisions, or go further to include informal documents and statements which do not necessarily have a legal status under Community law? Again, our view is that the court would be tempted to adopt a generous view, looking not so much at the legal form or status of the measure in question, but considering its significance in practice – is it, for example, a formulation of principles intended to guide or influence action within a field of community activity? Again the Amsterdam amendments would strengthen that view.

By Whom is the Duty Owed?

No particular institution or body is identified by Article 130r(2), but it is clear that it applies to those bodies with primary responsibility for defining and implementating the community's other policies. These include all relevant Community institutions and Member States in so far as they are charged with implementing Community policies. The Declaration to the Maastricht Treaty refers to the Commission's undertakings in respect of environmental integration, and most attention to date has been focused on the Commission's internal administrative initiatives. But the above interpretation suggests a broader range of subjects than envisaged in current proposals, and would encompass at the very least all those community bodies involved in defining or implementing community policy, including the Council of Ministers, the European Investment Bank and the European Parliament.[24]

As to Member States, they are clearly bound by the duty when acting within the Council of Ministers.[25] The duty, however, refers to 'implementation' as well as to 'design', and since implementation is often the responsibility of Member States, it is arguable that the integra-

---

[21] Part 3 of the Treaty, for example, is entitled 'Community Policies' and covers competition policy, economic policies and free movement of goods. It includes sections entitled 'economic policy' and 'monetary policy'.

[22] This approach is reinforced by the historical background to the proposal and the declaration at the Maastricht Conference that the commission undertakes to take full account of the environmental impact and the principle of sustainable growth in implementing its proposals – no qualification confining the scope of those proposals is provided in the declaration.

[23] The current version of the integration duty also applies to Union 'policies and activities' (Art 11 TFEU).

[24] Both the Council of Ministers and the committees of the European Parliament have been organised along traditional functional lines (transport, agriculture, environment, etc), which does not necessarily assist the integration process. The Council has occasionally held joint meetings (energy and environment), but the European Parliament has yet to establish any 'cross-cutting' committee structure.

[25] UK case law has held that the precautionary principle as expressed in Art 130r binds Member States only when developing a community policy and does not apply to other fields unencompassed by Community

tion duty must apply here as well. This interpretation has considerable implications for Member States. Much would depend on the level of discretion granted at national level, and the extent to which a failure at national level to integrate an environmental dimension could frustrate the effect of Article 130r. To take one example, a national body such as a transport department might be given the responsibility to define routes for Trans-European networks under Article 129b of the Treaty and would, we suggest, be legally vulnerable if no regard were paid to the duty at the time it exercised its responsibilities. Or a national body might be given responsibilities concerned with implementing community policy, such as the distribution of community funds. Again, we would argue that it would be bound by the integration duty. This would be especially relevant where the body has a margin of discretion and choice – in other words, where regard to the duty could have a real influence on the outcome of its decision.

The Substance of the Duty: Regarding Environmental Protection Requirements

The core of the duty refers to the integration of 'environmental protection requirements' and both phrases require interpretation in order to understand the substance of the requirement. But in the legal analysis of similar duties on governmental bodies, it has usually been difficult to disentangle the nature of the duty from the question: to whom the duty is owed. Each inquiry influences the other. The issue of enforceability is considered in more detail in the next section, but at this stage we can usefully identity three broad possible classifications of the duty.

1. *Internal integration:* this implies that the duty is one owed by Community policy-makers only to other Community policy-makers. The duty could take the form of one that is owed and legally enforceable by each institution, or one that is owed by Community institutions to the others but is implemented only by internal administrative methods.
2. *Weak constitutional integration:* here the duty is treated as one that is owed by Community institutions to Member States as well as to other Community bodies. This would permit Member States to challenge, in law, policies and decisions on the grounds that they were in breach of the integration duty.
3. *Strong constitutional integration:* this classification of the duty treats it as one that is owed by the Community to individual citizens, in effect creating an external individual right. Recent case law of the European Court has already treated the code of conduct on public access to information, developed by the European Council and European Commission and the decisions of those bodies to adopt it, as creating such external rights.[26] Nevertheless, as we discuss below, we see considerable difficulty in treating the integration duty as creating similar rights.

---

legislation: *R v Secretary of State for Trade and Industry ex parte Duddridge* Court of Appeal, 6 October 1995; see the case note by Hughes (1995) 1(2) *Journal of Environmental Law* 224, 226.

[26] See Case T-194/94 *Carvel and Guardian Newspapers v Council* [1995] ECR II-2765 and Case T-105/95 *WWF UK v Commission* 5 March 1977. Here the Court concluded that, although the Commission's decision to adopt the code of practice was 'in effect, a series of obligations which the Commission has voluntarily assumed

When considering the meaning of 'environmental protection requirements', there are several possible interpretations. The first, which we call conservative, is the simplest and most narrow. The word requirement implies a legal obligation and thus encompasses only those obligations concerning the environment contained in Community environmental legislation. This has the advantage of providing a clear benchmark and avoids the difficulties elaborated below when determining other, more elusive reference points. This is the approach that appears to have been adopted by the commission in relation to structural funds, as indicated in the analysis by Clare Coffey.[27]

Whatever its superficial attraction, this narrow approach hardly makes long-term sense. All it contributes to the existing legislative framework is an added mechanism for ensuring compliance with existing community environmental law – that is, a requirement to prevent other community policies from undermining compliance by Member States with their obligations under community law. General principles of Community law already exist to prevent this from happening. The general duty under Article 5 of the Treaty requiring Member States to take all appropriate measures to fulfil Community obligations imposes a reciprocal duty on the Commission to assist Member States, and by implication to refrain from action which inhibits implementation. Furthermore, the conservative approach fails to reflect the aspirations of the integration requirement.

The second approach to interpreting environmental protection requirements looks to objective standards of protection. According to this argument, in order to judge whether or not the integration duty has been followed, it is both legitimate and necessary to determine some standard of environmental protection which is neither contained in the Treaty nor, necessarily, in community secondary legislation. To an extent, the idea that there are objective environmental protection requirements derives from the environmental rights ethos – wherever those rights are placed, it is possible to objectively determine what is necessary to protect the environment.

There are considerable difficulties in endorsing this interpretation. By cutting adrift the definition of environmental protection requirements, a court would potentially be involved in substantive moral and ethical choices with respect to the factors that ought to be integrated and the standard of protection to be adopted. The reference to a 'high level' of environmental protection in Article 130r of the Treaty might act as a useful pointer for a court, but remains an aim rather than an obligatory requirement. In general terms, the essential difficulty with enforcing an objective standard of environmental protection is that the standard is not one amenable to judicial application or confidence.[28] The essence

---

for itself as a measure of internal organisation, it is nevertheless capable of conferring on third parties legal rights which the Commission is obliged to respect'.

[27] C Coffey, 'European Community Funding and the Sustainability Transition' in O'Riordan and Voisey, above n 1. Whether the conservative interpretation was correct was at the heart of the *Mullaghmore* case, Case T-461/93 *An Taisce and WWF (UK) v Commission* [1994] ECR II-733. The applicants challenged the Commission's narrow interpretation of the structural funds regulation that measures financed by such funds must be in keeping with 'Community policy on environmental protection'. Unfortunately, the substance of the argument was not considered since the case was ruled inadmissible on procedural grounds, a decision confirmed on appeal, Case C-325/94 [1996] ECR 1-3727.

[28] In a slightly different context, in the *Danish Bottles* case, *Commission v Denmark* [1989] 1 CMLR 619, the European Court was called upon to define an objective standard of environmental protection which was reasonable for a Member State to pursue, where this would inhibit the free movement of goods. The Court studiously avoided providing an answer, and refused to interfere with the judgment of the Member State on the issue. Posing the question of what is a reasonable degree of environmental protection, Kramer (1993) succinctly replied, 'the answer is relatively simple: we do not know'.

of judicial reluctance to become involved in such issues lies in the difficulty of describing an effective dividing line between the application of a rule based on solid criteria and the substitution of judicial judgment for what should be a matter of political discretion. In contrast, reviewing a decision for its procedural regularity is more easily performed. Here, what is examined is the reasoning process of the decision-maker; the substantive result of the decision is not directly tested for its compatibility with some putative environmental protection requirement. Even this approach does not always let a court completely off the hook. Assessing procedural regularities requires some consideration of the facts leading to the decision, their relevance or irrelevance, and some minimum basis to justify the decision.

The limitations of the conservative interpretation and the conceptual challenges of the objective standards suggest that a third approach is required. The Treaty itself contains certain obligatory policy requirements concerning the environment, which can be summarised as follows:

- a contribution towards the objectives of preserving, protecting and improving the quality of the environment, protecting human health, and the prudent and rational utilisation of natural resources;
- a high level of protection;
- adherence to the four principles of precaution, prevention, rectification at source, and polluter pays; and
- the need to take into account certain additional factors including the diversity of situations within various regions of the community, available scientific and technical data, and the potential costs and benefits of action or inaction.

These principles indicate the basis and direction of policy rather than specify a substantive result. The language used and the gradation of terminology (a 'basis in' to 'taking into account') suggest that they are guidelines – directional rather than prescriptive – and indicate a real difficulty in challenging measures claimed to be in breach of such principles, other than in the most clear-cut case of consciously avoiding their consideration. Nevertheless, if the integration duty is to be given any legal significance, we suggest that it represents a basis for interpretation which is consistent with the Treaty rather than relying on the contents of existing secondary legislation.

The Substance of the Duty: Integration

Article 173 of the Treaty,[29] which provides the means to review the legality of community acts, makes a classic distinction between infringement of a rule of law and infringement of an essential procedural requirement. Generally speaking, the former guarantees a particular substantive result, while a procedural right guarantees some form of participation in the process of determining a result. The distinction is important, though in practice

---

[29] Now Art 263 TFEU.

it can become blurred.[30] As we have indicated, courts are more inclined to recognise a procedural right with respect to the environment rather than a substantive right.[31]

The duty to integrate environmental requirements is suggestive of procedural rather than substantive protection. The dictionary definition supports the idea of a duty with respect to formulating policy rather than identifying a *ne plus ultra* of policy results. At the very least, the duty requires that regard must be given to environmental requirements when developing other community policies. As Kramer[32] points out, in the context of the 1987 version of the duty, all Community measures 'must have one eye on the existing community legislation and the other on the environment, which is now a factor in all action [taken] by the community'.

A familiar requirement often imposed on administrative bodies is to 'take into consideration' certain factors, implying that once taken on board they may be rejected if they conflict with other goals. But the terminology of the integration duty implies more than this; conflict with other areas does not entitle environmental requirements to be dismissed. Courts frequently have to make sense of competing goals which appear on the face of law. The European Court is no stranger to this challenge and could adopt a number of tried and tested approaches. The first would be to apply principles of proportionality already seen in the context of conflicts between free movement of goods and environmental protection. According to this model, transport or competition policy, for example, would have to be the most environmentally compatible with the goals of these policies. This approach is not entirely satisfactory since it gives a predominance to those other policy objectives, whereas the integration duty is designed to redefine and redirect those policies.

Another approach that the Court could adopt would be to accept that determining the balance of competing objectives should remain at the discretion of Community institutions rather than within the Court's domain. This essentially is the stance adopted by the court in the agricultural field where the Treaty objectives are themselves potentially in conflict, and where the Court has been reluctant to interfere with the Commission or Council's determination of the purpose or scope of particular measures – even accepting that at any particular time one objective may legitimately take precedence over another.[33] The third approach is to develop a restrictive attitude towards parties entitled to bring legal challenges before the courts, thus relieving the Court of the difficult choices involved. This demonstrates the clear connection between the nature of the substantive duty and the question of locus standi, considered in the next section.

To Whom is the Integration Duty Owed?

This is perhaps the most difficult of all the questions raised and the most important. It

---

[30] For example, the right to procedural protection can include cases where the only evidence of a breach of procedures is the evidence of an inadequate substantive result which would not have occurred if adequate procedural protection had been given.

[31] In the general scheme of rights, individual substantive rights which are guaranteed exclusively to them, whereas collective rights, such as those relating to the environment, do not. The only sense in which a collective right may be ensured is by way of a guarantee in individual participation.

[32] L Kramer, *EC Law and Environmental Protection* (Sweet & Maxwell, 1990).

[33] See, eg Case 5/73 *Balkan-Import-Export GmbH v Hauptzollamt Berlin-Packhof* [1973] ECR 1091.

determines the true nature of the duty, and whether it gives rise to a responsibility in the sense that somebody has the right to enforce it. As we indicated in the section on environmental protection requirements, three categories of potential beneficiaries can be identified: Community institutions; Member States; and, individual citizens.

With respect to the Community institutions, under Article 173 of the Treaty, they have general rights to challenge the legality of Community acts and could conceivably enforce the integration duty against each other in this way. It must be observed that as the institutions share the responsibility of adopting Community acts in most cases, breach of the duty to integrate during this process might arise in the context of disputes over the legal basis of measures. Here, both the European Parliament and the European Investment Bank may act only in respect of their own prerogatives (to protect their own particular rights), and it seems unlikely that either could hold rights with respect to the integration duty per se.

Similarly, Member States are able to challenge the validity of Community acts. Against a background of increased majority voting at Council level, it is possible to predict that a minority country, concerned with the lack of environmental sensitivity in a proposed Community measure, might take advantage of the remedy. But in areas such as structural funds, there has been a marked reluctance by Member States to initiate any legal challenges – perhaps for the simple but cynical reason that all Member States expect to gain from structural funds at some point and have been unwilling to rock the plentiful boat.[34]

To the extent that the integration duty also applies to Member States when defining or implementing Community policy, the European Commission would have a primary duty to initiate enforcement procedures under Article 169 of the Treaty.[35] The decision whether or not to initiate such action is essentially a matter of discretion for the commission and is not reviewable by the Court.[36]

Individuals bringing action before the national courts may also claim the benefit of Treaty provisions, which are considered sufficiently precise and certain to have 'direct effect'.[37] In one sense, the integration duty is relatively precise and unconditional, but it is most unlikely that it would have such direct effects. There are sufficient ambiguities in the terminology (both of court overload and the substantive judgments demanded of the courts) to allow direct challenges of all Community policies by almost anyone; these weigh heavily against such an interpretation.

The Treaty also permits individuals to challenge the legality of Community action directly before the European Court of Justice, although there are two critical limitations to the remedy. First, the Treaty rules, under Article 173, only permit challenge to regulations or legal decisions. They do not allow individuals to challenge directives, resolutions and other non-binding actions of the community. Secondly, the applicant must show 'direct and individual concern' and the Court of Justice has consistently given a restrictive interpretation of this phrase. Essentially, individuals making the challenge must demonstrate

---

[34] L Kramer, 'Public Interest Litigation in Matters before European Courts' (1994) 1 *Journal of Environmental Law* 1.

[35] Now Art 2568 TFEU.

[36] Member States may also initiate enforcement actions under Art 169 against other Member States but are highly reluctant to do so, again for the fairly cynical reason of mutual reassurance.

[37] See Case 26/62 *Van Gend en Loos* [1963] ECR 1, where the court commenced its extensive jurisprudence on this doctrine.

that they are affected in some way which differentiates them from all others affected,[38] and recent decisions of the Court of Justice which deny standing to environmental groups and individuals demonstrate that the test is almost impossible to satisfy where an issue of general environmental concern is raised.[39] During the build-up to the Intergovernmental Conference, environmental interests made proposals to liberalise the standing rule, and in effect to introduce an *actio popularis*, but the current overload in the European Court and concerns about opening the floodgates makes any radical change unlikely. Nevertheless, for a system that is so fundamentally based on the rule of law, the present procedures represent a worrying lacuna.[40]

Procedure and Substance Revisited

It is clear that to the extent that the integration duty amounts to a procedural requirement for adopting and implementating Community legislation, the Community institutions are at least bound by the obligation, and there is liberal standing for them and Member States to challenge the legality of decisions made in breach of them. Article 190[41] requires that Community regulations, directives and decisions must state the reasons upon which they are based – an important requirement to promote transparency in decision making. It is a broad principle which is deeper in scope than are most equivalent rules under national legal systems.[42] The substantive content of the duty to give reasons has varied according to the nature of the act in question, and although a margin of discretion is afforded to the institutions with respect to the detail of reasoning required, the obligation can act as a significant lever to reinforce the application of the integration duty.[43] Interpreting the duty as a procedural requirement would imply a guarantee of certain procedural minima before a policy is agreed upon and implemented.

We have already identified the difficulty of viewing the duty as substantive and relating to specific results. The problem of determining by legal process (as opposed to political means) an objective environmental standard is one that bedevils the whole field of substantive environmental rights. We suggested, however, that the principles of environmental action contained in the Treaty might serve as a basis for more substantive review. And, indeed, in case law concerning the conflicts between free movement of goods and environmental protection, recent legal developments have hinted that the integration principles have given a higher status to those principles of environmental action than previously.[44]

---

[38] Case 25/62 *Plaumann v Commission* [1963] ECR 95 established the key test and has been consistently applied in subsequent cases.

[39] Case T-585/93 *Stichting Greenpeace Council and others v Commission* 12 February 1994; (1996) 8(1) *Journal of Environmental Law*; Case T-219/95R *Danielsson and others v Commission* [1995] ECR II-3051.

[40] R Macrory, 'Environmental Citizenship and the Law' (1996) 8(2) *Journal of Environmental Law* 219.

[41] Now Art 296(2) TFEU.

[42] In *WWF UK*, above n 22, the court argued that Art 190 served two purposes – first, to permit interested parties to know the justification of a measure in order to enable them to protect their rights; and secondly, to enable the Community courts to exercise their power to review the legality of decisions.

[43] Case 5/67 *Baus* [1968] ECR 83. See also Case C-350/88 *Delacre v Commission* [1990] ECR 1-395.

[44] In the *Wallonia Waste* case, *EC Commission v Belgium* [1992] 1 ECR 4431, the court was prepared to invoke the principle of Community environmental action that damage should be rectified at source to justify a local ban on the import of wastes. Although the reasoning in the decision has been much criticised, the court in essence

If, as we have suggested, the integration duty forms an essential procedural require-ment, one can argue that a precondition of the legality of Community measures should be a demonstrable compliance with an environmental appraisal based on the principles of environmental action contained in the Treaty.[45] Difficult though this sounds, it merely supports the simple notion that policy development leading to European Community acts must display a minimum standard of reasoning. The environmental integration require-ment is now an essential element of that reasoning process. Failure to reflect the broad criteria of the Treaty's environmental principles should open the institution in question to at least a minimum review of the stated reasons. Where no reference is made to the basic environmental criteria, or the reasoning is unsupported by substantial evidence, the decision in question must be open to challenge. Applying legal analysis to the integration duty suggests that, despite the conceptual difficulties involved, it can be considered as something more than a political aspiration. But it will require a degree of bold foresight on the part of lawyers and judges to bring about that change.

recognised that Member States could claim the benefit of the principles of Community environmental policy in the face of preemptive Community rules concerning free movement.

[45] Under the Declaration to the Final Act of the 1997 Amsterdam Conference, the conference noted that 'the Commission undertakes to prepare environmental impact assessment studies when making proposals which may have significant environmental implications'.

24

Environmental Citizenship and the Law: Repairing the European Road[1] (1996)

The English are incurious as to theory, take fundamental principles for granted and are more interested in the state of the roads than their place on the map.

RH Tawney, The Aquisitive Society *(1920)*

The European Council invites the Conference which should finalise its work in about one year, to adopt a general and consistent vision throughout its work: its aim is to meet the needs and expectations of our citizens while advancing the process of Europe's construction and preparing the Union for its future enlargement.

Presidency Conclusions, Turin European Council, 29 March 1996

Introduction

On 1 January 1993, as a result of the Maastricht amendments to the European Treaties, all nationals of Member States acquired under the Treaty something called citizenship of the European Union.[2] This new citizenship may not be uppermost in the civic conscious-ness of many, and my starting point will be to consider to what extent it can be said to incorporate an environmental dimension. The second half of the title is derived from RH Tawney's well-known observation about the English, and to pursue his analogy, there already exist a number of pretty substantial potholes. As someone who in his approach to environmental law has attempted to combine both an academic and a practitioner's perspective I will be suggesting some practical repair jobs. But I will also argue that there

---

[1] R Macrory, 'Environmental Citizenship and the Law – Repairing the European Road' (1996) 8(2) *Journal of Environmental Law* 219. This article is a revised text of the inaugural Nathan Environment Lecture, sponsored by Denton Hall, Solicitors, and delivered by the author at the Royal Society of Arts on 25 April 1996.

[2] Treaty Establishing the European Community, Art 8: '(I) Citizenship of the Union is hereby established. Every person holding the nationality of a Member State shall be a citizen of the Union. (2) Citizens of the Union shall enjoy the rights conferred by this Treaty and shall be subject to the duties imposed thereby.' The Maastricht Treaty established both a European Union and a European Community. The Union is essentially a forum for political co-operation, and only the Community possesses legal entity, and it is within the Community structure that legislation is made. My paper will, therefore, for the most part refer to the European Community.

are some deeper issues concerning the way that the Treaty is currently structured and has been characterized in law. However effective the repairs, these also need to be addressed if the route on which we are embarked is to lead to a more environmental sound destination.

Citizenship is of course both a political and legal concept. Yet I will make no excuse for concentrating on legal conception and principle. The law and legal analysis permeates the structure and operation of the European Community. Some years ago, also at the Royal Society of Arts, Lord Dahrendolf observed that, 'In fact almost everything is wrong about the European Community except that it exists as a community of law which united developed democracies in Europe'.[3] Certainly for my part, I subscribe to the immense significance of the unifying and legitimising concept of the rule of law. In taking this argument further, I am not going to describe or analyse in detail the substantive content of European environmental policy since my concern will be more with institutional and legal structure. But as a matter of general background, and whatever the precise content of future environmental policies, I start from the assumption that the European Community and Union will remain a reality. The role of law in that structure will retain its pervasive significance, and the task of reconciling environmental and economic interests, encapsulated in the notion of sustainable development, will continue to provide a major political and intellectual challenge. At the same time, we have nine applicant countries from Central and Eastern Europe together with Malta and Cyprus. We may be many years away from accession but with negotiations due to formally commence after the end of the Intergovernmental Conference, the institutional implications of this prospective enlargement must be addressed.

The concept of citizenship is clearly stated in the Treaty to involve both rights and obligations. The Treaty itself goes on to express a number of individual rights, including the right to move and reside freely,[4] and the right to vote or stand as a candidate in municipal countries in the country in which he or she is residing.[5] Important procedural rights are provided in the rights to petition the European Parliament and to apply to the newly established Ombudsman.[6] The Treaty in its present form does not, however, provide any legally expressed rights to a healthy environment or indeed quality of life.

The Declaration of the first major international conference on the environment, the UN Conference on the Human Environment held in Stockholm in 1972, clearly emphasised a link between human rights and the environment: Principle I declares that, 'Man has a fundamental right to freedom, equality and adequate conditions of life, in an environment of quality that permits a life of dignity and well-being, and he bears a solemn responsibility to protect and improve the environment for present and future generations'. Similarly, the Declaration following the UN Conference on Environment and Development held in Rio de Janeiro in 1992, though giving greater emphasis to the concept sustainable development, made a reference to rights and the environment.[7] Neither Declaration is a legally binding instrument as such, and neither attempt to establish specific environmental rights. Now, however, in the present preparations for the IGC Conference, both the European Commission and a number of Nordic countries are beginning to promote the idea that

---

[3] Lord Dahrendorf, 'Education for a European Britain', Royal Society of Arts, 9 June 1991.
[4] Art 8a.
[5] Art 8b.
[6] Art 8d.
[7] Principle 1 states that 'Human beings are at the centre of concerns for sustainable development. They are entitled to a healthy and productive life in harmony with nature.'

the Treaty should contain an express inclusion of a right to a healthy environment or some similarly worded phraseology.[8]

Many would argue that there are conceptual impossibilities to formulating an individual right to the environment in general terms which has any legally meaningful sense. The experience of those European countries and of certain States in America, whose constitutions do contain some expression of environmental rights, tends to confirm this.[9] They may end up influencing the interpretation and operation of other legal principles and rules, but are near impossible to invoke in themselves.[10] It is an issue to which I will return to later.

Environmental Rights in Community Law

Yet when it comes to specific items of Community environmental legislation concerning environmental quality, the European Court of Justice has been prepared to characterise certain provisions as giving individual environmental rights. Thus in 1991, in a case brought by the Commission against Germany, the Court held that the 1980 Directive prescribing air quality standards for sulphur dioxide and smoke in effect gave individuals the right to air meeting those standards.[11] One characteristic mark of the Directive as a legal instrument is that while Member States are obliged to achieve its goals, it gives Member States a degree of discretion as to how to implement it within their national systems of law and administration.[12] But by characterising the SO_2 Directive as creating individual rights, the Court felt justified in insisting that the Member State no longer had complete discretion as to the means of transposing the obligations within its own legal and administrative system. Instead it held that individuals 'must be in a position to rely upon mandatory rules in order to be able to assert their rights'.

This firm nexus between the concept of a right and its expression in legally binding national law can be traced back to the mid 1980s in case law concerning rights of free movement of professionals within the Community. Here the Court held that the legal position for individuals must be 'sufficiently clear and precise and the persons concerned

---

[8] The 1994 Report of the European Parliament's Committee on Institutional Affairs proposed a model constitution for the European Union which included a Title on Human Rights Guaranteed by the Union. These rights included, inter alia, 'Everyone shall have the right to the protection and preservation of his natural environment'. Doc EN/RR/244/244403 (27 January 1994).

[9] Art 66 of the Portuguese Constitution contains the most explicit expression of environmental right in European Constitutions by providing that everyone shall have 'the right to a healthy and ecologically balanced environment and a duty to defend it'. Nevertheless, only where the state has determined what makes up such an environment are these rights enforceable. For a valuable comparative study which demonstrates the problem of constructing enforceable environmental rights see E Brandi and H Bungert, 'Constitutional Entrenchment of Environmental Protection: A Comparative Analysis of Experiences Abroad' (1992) 16(1) *Harvard Environmental Law Review* 1.

[10] Nevertheless, the UN Sub-Commission on Prevention of Discrimination and Protection of Minorities recently produced an elaborate Draft Declaration of Principles on Human Rights and the Environment: see (1994) No 2 *Environmental Law Network International Newsletter* 120; (1994) 3(5) *RECIEL* 261. See also Aguilar and Popovic 'Law-Making in the United Nations: The UN Study on Human Rights and the Environment' (1994) 3(5) *RECIEL* 197.

[11] *EC Commission v Germany* [1991] 1 ECR 2567.

[12] Art 189 EC Treaty. 'A directive shall be binding as to the result to be achieved, upon each Member State to which it is addressed but shall leave to the national authorities the choice of form and methods'.

are made fully aware of their rights and where appropriate afforded an opportunity of relying upon them before the national courts'.[13]

Yet it is significant that the SO_2 Directive was to a large degree concerned with the protection of human health.[14] Other environmental Directives have granted what might be termed procedural rights, such as those concerning Access to Information[15] or rights to be consulted during Environmental Assessment procedures.[16] Again, the same justification for insisting that such rights appear in formal national law must apply. But many Directives are concerned purely with the protection of the environment per se rather than the direct protection of individuals. Here, the position in Community law remains less clear, and exposes one of the constant dilemmas of the use of the language of rights in relation to the environment – to what extent can they only be conceived of only in anthropogenic terms and thus largely confined to human health and welfare contexts, or can they extend to all areas of the environment whether or not individuals are affected – in which case who should entitled to ensure their protection?

Yet the case law of the European Court remains rather ambiguous. Another case brought by the Commission against Germany in 1991 concerned the Groundwater Directive.[17] This Directive is clearly aimed at the protection of the environment rather than human health as such, yet the Court stated that the Directive, in order to guarantee effective protection of groundwater, laid down precise and detailed rules which are intended to create rights and obligations for individuals. Having so characterised the Directive, it justified the Court in again insisting that it had to be incorporated into national law with the precision and clarity necessary to fully satisfy the requirements of legal certainty. Unfortunately the Court did not spell out precisely the rights and obligations it found in the Directive, but it appeared to have been referring to the various prohibitions and requirements for authorisations under the Directive. Industry and other consumers of the environment who may have obligations imposed upon them under Community law are entitled to know precisely what these entail.[18] But we are still left with some degree of uncertainty over the question of rights where provisions are solely aimed at environmental protection.[19]

Despite the ambiguities, these principles concerning the transposition of Community obligations into formal national law have had immense significance not least for the structure of UK environmental law. They are entirely the creation of the Court and if anything

---

[13] *European Commission v Germany* [1986] 3 GMLR 579. There is another line of authority within the European Court of Justice where the Court has required the formal transposition of Directives into national law but concerned with Directives based on Art 100 or 100A (harmonisation in relation to functioning of the common market). Here the justification for formal transposition is distinct and based on the concept of harmonisation rather than individual rights. See RB Macrory, 'EC Directives and UK Control Policy and Practice' in *National Society for Clean Air 55th Annual Conference Proceedings* (Brighton, National Society for Clean Air, 1988).

[14] Art 2 of the Directive provides that the specified limit values must not be exceeded 'in order to protect human health in particular'.

[15] Directive 90/313 on Freedom of Access to Information on the Environment [1990] OJ L158/56.

[16] Directive 85/337 on the Assessment of the Effects of Certain Public and Private Projects on the Environment [1985] OJ L175/40.

[17] *EC Commission v Germany* [1991] 1 ECR 825.

[18] A similar argument is found in Case C-13/90 *Commission v France* [1991] ECR I-4327, which again concerned the air quality Directives. In insisting upon formal transposition into national law, the Court in part justified their argument by suggesting that these Directives imposed obligations on potential polluters.

[19] It has been suggested that the Court will in practice be liberal in interpreting that Environment Directives create or imply rights, as the case law quoted above suggest: I Pernice, 'Kriterien der normativen Umsetzung von Umweltrichtlinien der EG Lichte der Rechtsprechung des EuGH' [1994] *Europareckt* 325. For a lengthier discussion on various forms of transposition see J Jans, *European Environmental Law* (London, Kluwer, 1995) 119.

goes against the apparent wording of the Treaty. And they form what could be described as a family of doctrines developed by the court designed to ensure that Community law has genuine bite within national systems. They include the direct effect doctrine,[20] the doctrine of sympathetic interpretation,[21] and the more recent emergence of principles concerning the right to damages where a Member State has failed in its Community obligations,[22] Each of these doctrines raise difficult issues, but at their root, they can be seen as attempts by the Court to ensure that Community law is fully applied. And they are in effect an implied criticism of the institutional mechanisms already built into the Treaty and specifically designed to ensure compliance with Community obligations. If they were working fully and effectively, the Court would not have had to develop these doctrines in the way they have.

Improving Community Enforcement Mechanisms

Persuading countries to comply with supranational obligations is not, of course, a problem confined to Community law. The last 25 years has seen a rapid expansion and growth of international environmental treaties between sovereign states, but ensuring implementation of international treaties has long been the familiar Achilles heel of public international law. Earlier environmental treaties made little or no reference to the question of implementation but left it entirely to the goodwill of the parties concerned.[23] Modern practice is commendably different. In many of the more recent environmental treaties, far more attention has been paid to the issue of implementation and enforcement, and treaties such as the Ozone Convention and the Climate Change Convention provide for the establishment of implementation committees composed on signatory states with the express task of reviewing the effectiveness of implementation.[24] Ultimately, however, the pressure that can be brought to bear on recalcitrant states is largely one of peer or political pressure,

---

[20] Under this doctrine, even where a Member State has not implemented a Directive properly into national law, certain provisions of Directives provided they are precise and certain may be invoked before national courts but only against government or other 'emanations of the State' and not other individuals; see Case-91/92 *Don v Recreb Srl* [1994] ECR I-3325, which confirmed that the doctrine could not be invoked against private parties. See generally S Prechal, *Directives in European Community Law* (Oxford, Oxford University Press, 1995). In the environmental field, see especially L Kramer, 'The Implementation of Community Environmental Directives: Some Implications of the Direct Effect Doctrine' (1991) 3(1) *Journal of Environmental Law* 39. In practice, both in the United Kingdom and before the European Court of Justice (but not in countries such as the Netherlands), it has proved difficult to date to convince the courts that environmental directives have direct effect: see J Holder, 'A Dead-End for Direct Effect?' (1996) 8(2) *Journal of Environmental Law* 313.

[21] Case C-106/89 *Marleasing SA v La Commercial International de Alimantiacion SA* [1990] ECR I-4135, where the European Court of Justice held that national law whether or not introduced to implement Community obligations must be interpreted in such a way as to ensure conformity with Community Directives 'in so far as possible'. The limits of the doctrine are still being worked out. See Chapter 26 of this volume.

[22] Cases C-6/90 and C-9/90 *Frankovitch v Italian State* [1991] ECR-I 5357. For the most recent judgment concerning the principles see Cases C-46/93 and C 48/93 *Brasserie du Pêcheur SA v Germany; R v Secretary of State for Transport ex parte Factortame and others (Factortame III)* [1996] 75 CMLR 889.

[23] See generally P Birnie and A Boyle, *International Law and the Environment* (Oxford, Oxford University Press, 1993) esp 160 *et seq*; P Sand, *The Effectiveness of International Environmental Agreements* (Cambridge, Grotius, 1992); D Freestone, The Road from Rio: International Law after the Earth Summit' (1994) 6(2) *Journal of Environmental Law* 193.

[24] Annex IV, Montreal Prototcol on Substances that Deplete the Ozone Layer, 1987; Art 10, Framework Convention on Climate Change, 1992.

though the Montreal Protocol has taken steps somewhat further by providing an elaborate procedure for allegations of non-compliance and an express list of measures that might be brought on respect of non-compliance, including both inducements in the form of financial and technical assistance, and sanctions in the form of the suspension of rights and privileges under the Protocol.[25]

Yet in its formal institutional mechanisms for ensuring the Member States implement their obligations under Community law, the European Community has clearly established a far deeper and potentially more effective structure than anything yet devised under other international arrangements. And I would argue that one mark of citizenship within the Community and Union should be an effective legal structure which can guarantee that both national governments and Community institutions will bona fide implement those Community obligations to which they are a party. The Treaty imposes an obligation on the European Commission to ensure that Member States fulfil their duties under Community law,[26] and quasi-legal procedures are provided allowing eventually the Commission to take Member States before the European Court for failure to implement.[27] And since Maastricht, the Court now has power to fine Member States that do not comply with its judgments – amendments to the Treaty that were promoted by the UK government, and giving the Court a direct sanction power that is unique among international courts.[28]

Much could be done to improve the effectiveness of current procedures, especially in the light of prospective enlargement of the Community. This is not to belittle efforts that have been made in recent years: greater consistency in the reporting requirements by Member States concerning various aspects of environmental quality;[29] improved mechanisms for contact between those working within national regulatory bodies though at present this is largely confined to pollution control bodies,[30] and does not involve, for example, those in nature conservation; the acknowledgement by the Council of Ministers of the importance of implementation; and the establishment of the new Environment Agency[31] which may bring a more rigorous approach towards the comparative analysis of the state of environmental quality within different Member States.

It could be argued that many of these developments were in a sense making up for lost time. One of my main concerns is to improve the procedures for ensuring the national transposition of Community obligations. If Community obligations were faithfully reflected in national law, both in substance and within the time limits specified, we would be a long way down the path of more effective implementation. Not the whole way by any means, since much would then depend on the effectiveness of national procedures, including such questions as ease of access to the courts or other administrative bodies, but at least there

[25] Annex V, Montreal Protocol. Freestone, ibid, describes the enforcement regime as 'one of the strictest devised for a global treaty of this kind'.

[26] One of the four defined functions of the Commission under the Treaty is to 'ensure that the provisions of this Treaty and the measures taken by the institutions pursuant thereto are applied'. The existing case law on standing, however, means that it is not a duty which could be enforced in law by third parties.

[27] In the environmental field see R Macrory, 'The Enforcement of Community Environmental Laws: Some Critical Issues' [1992] *Common Market Law Review* 347. See Chapter 26 below.

[28] Art 171.

[29] Council Directive 91/692/EEC, Standardising and Rationalising Reports on the Implemention of certain Directives relating to the Environment.

[30] Originally known as the 'Chester Network' after the place of its first meeting and established in 1992, now called IMPEL.

[31] Established under EC Regulation 1210/90. Despite pressure from the European Parliament, the powers and duties of the Agency were at the time deliberately restricted to avoid it becoming directly involved in issues of implementation and enforcement, but its terms of reference are to be reviewed.

would be a common starting position. The current practice is that the Community obligation under Directives requires the Member State to send texts of their national measures to the Commission within the time limit specified in each Directive, normally two years, of its being agreed.[32] In practice, this often happens at the last moment, and generally no guidance is given by the Member State to the Commission to relate the national measures to the provisions of the Directive. Indeed, some Member States seem to take an almost perverse pleasure in leaving it to Commission officials to puzzle out the intricacies of what are often complex national laws themselves and relate them to the Directive in question.

For a start, then, I would like to see a requirement for Member States to provide the Commission with a systematic explanation of the relationship between the national measures and the provisions of the Directive – an article by article guide if you like. And, as a acknowledgement of citizen interest in this issues, these should be documents that are publicly available.[33]

Secondly, it needs to be recognised that the reluctance to lose face is a general feature of institutional behaviour. Once national laws have been made, whether in primary legislation or regulations, Member States are likely to resist change or at least will give an exaggerated defence of them against differing interpretations. So I would like to see a general requirement that *draft* legislation proposed to implement a Directive is sent to the Commission at least six months before the date for compliance. This may require longer time limits for compliance – perhaps a general move from two years to three – but is, I believe a price worth paying if the result is a greater opportunity to ensure a truer reflection in national law of Community obligations. The 1994 Packaging Directive does provide something of a model in this respect in that it contains a provisions concerning the requirement of Member States to notify draft measures, though no time limits are provided.[34] Of course, the Commission cannot give a final legal interpretation of Community law which remains the responsibility of the European Court of Justice, and there will remain instances where both Member States and the Commission refuse to compromise on their respective interpretations—but at least there will be greater advance notice of trouble ahead. In practice, discussions are sometimes held between Member States and the Commission over draft legislation,[35] but it appears to be done in an ad hoc manner. I accept that these discussions will not always be plain sailing or conducted in the spirit of perfect rationality, but my complaint is that there is little consistency in the current approach nor is there apparent acknowledgment by Member States that it is important.

The drafting of Community legislation still often leads to ambiguities and inconsistencies, though the blame cannot always be laid at the Commission; late night negotiations at the Council of Ministers can lead to oddly drafted provisions. But certainly there seems to me to be the need for greater attention to drafting, including the use of interpretation sections, together with the greater use of advisory material, akin to circulars, issued by the

---

[32] Sometimes three years as in the Environmental Assessment Directive.

[33] It may be that under the Access to Environment Information Directive there would be a legal right to obtain such documentation. In recent years the European Commission has consistently included an obligation in new proposals for Member States to produce Correlation Tables – see European Commission, 'A Europe of Results – Applying Community Law', COM (2007) 502 final, para 1.2 – but they do not normally survive the legislative process. The United Kingdom often does now publish transposition tables for individual Directives but the practice is not universal, and equally inconsistent among other Member States.

[34] European Parliament and Council Directive 94/62/EG on Packaging and Packaging Waste, Art 16. Reproduced in *JEL* Vol 7 No 2.

[35] Considerable discussions were held between the UK government and the European Commission over the enforcement provisions in the Water Bill 1989 leading to amendments to the text of the Bill.

Commission and explaining their understanding of the new Community legislation and containing, for instance, worked examples of its application. And there are times when the Commission could play a more proactive role in assisting national institutions. Article 5 of the Treaty imposes a general duty on Member States to facilitate the achievement of the Community's tasks. Although the provision refers only to Member States, the duty has been interpreted by the European Court to impose a reciprocal duty upon the Commission to cooperate with national authorities.[36] In the field of competition policy and state aid, the Commission in 1993 and 1995 respectively, issued Notices of Cooperation providing guidance on when it would provide assistance to national courts in the provision of relevant information, including information on points of law.[37] I recognise that developing a more proactive approach is not without difficulties. One reason for the Commission's reluctance to over-commit itself in advance of its view of the law is a fear that this will inhibit it from bringing enforcement procedures against a Member State should its opinion later change, akin to a principle of estoppel. My own view is that it should not.[38] But if a Member State were sued for damages under the *Frankovitch* principles in respect of non-implementation under the principles now being developed by the ECJ, reliance on prior legal interpretation and advice given by the Commission could well provide a justifiable defence. This is acknowledged by the European Court in the latest decision on this issue, *Factortame III*.[39]

In accordance with one of the Declarations attached to the Maastricht Treaty, one of the tasks during the forthcoming intergovernmental conference will be to reconsider the whole question of the hierarchy of Community legislation.[40] As happened before Maastricht, no doubt it may again be argued that Community Directives, one of the major forms of Community legislation which have existed since the foundation of the Community and are really quite distinct to the Community, are now an outmoded legal instrument. By leaving so much room for manoeuvre for Member States, their form has given rise to the sorts of implementation problem I have already outlined. We do of course have another key form of Community instrument, the Regulation, which generally requires no national implementation measures but has immediate effect within national legal systems. Directives have dominated the environmental field, but there are examples of Regulations being used. But it surprised both Lord Nathan and his colleagues when he chaired a House of Lords subcommittee investigating the implementation of Community environmental law[41] to hear how little in the way of principle has been developed by either the Council

---

[36] Case G-2/88 *Zwartweld* [1990] ECR I-3365.

[37] Notice of Cooperation between National Courts and the Commission in Applying Articles 85 and 86 of the Treaty [1993] OJ C39/6; Notice of Cooperation between National Courts and the Commission in the State Aid Field [1995] OJ C312/8.

[38] Once enforcement proceedings are commenced, however, the Commission may find itself inhibited from redefining issues or raising new points as stated in the Reasoned Opinion.

[39] *Factortame III*, above n 22. According to the Court of Justice, one of the factors to be taken in account when determining whether a Member State should be liable was 'the fact that the position taken by a Community institution may have contributed towards the omission' (para 56).

[40] 'The Conference agrees that the Intergovernmental Conference to be convened in 1996 will examine to what extent it might be possible to review the classification of Community Acts with a view to establishing an appropriate hierarchy between the differing categories of Act.' This Declaration followed unsuccessful proposals made at the time, notably by the European Parliament to reclassify Community acts, which included the abolition of Directives and the creation of a new form of general legal instrument, a 'Loi': see Resolution of the European Parliament on the Nature of Community Acts [1991] OJ C/129/136.

[41] House of Lords, 9th Report Session, *The Implementation and Enforcement of Environmental Legislation* (London, HMSO, 1991–92).

of Ministers, or the European Commission, in determining in what circumstances one or other of the instruments is most appropriate. Nor is it an issue that the European Court of Justice has yet been called upon to consider. In 1992 the Sutherland Report called for the transformation of all Directives into Regulations after a period for harmonisation, but my own view is that Directives should continue to play a significant role.[42] They acknowledge and attempt to accommodate the diverse legal and administrative cultures which exist within Member States, and may be all the more appropriate should further expansion of the Community take place. But as I have indicated they place considerable demands on the institutional machinery if effective and consistent implementation is to be achieved.

Applying the Rule of Law to the Commission

The Community system is as the Court of Justice has consistently argued based upon the rule of law. The procedures I have just mentioned concern Member States' obligations. Yet there remain serious problems when it comes to ensure that the Commission itself complies with the rule of law. A central problem is the question of standing before the courts. All jurisdictions develop rules concerning who may or may not bring cases before the courts, especially where issues of public law are concerned. Standing, especially in the field of the environment where private interests in the conventional sense may not be at risk, has long proved a problem. For the most part in the field of public law the UK courts have shown an increasingly liberal approach in their interpretation of the basic test that the person or organisation bringing the case must have 'sufficient interest' in the matter concerned[43] and I do not believe it now presents a major inhibition.

The Treaty provides for challenges of the legality of acts by the Commission directly before the European Court. Member States and the Council of Ministers basically have unrestricted access, and the European Parliament may bring action to protect their own prerogatives. Individual applicants may take action in respect of decisions actually addressed to them personally, but this will be unusual in the environmental field. In those cases where the decision is directed to another person (say the grant of financial assistance to a member state) a third parties may still bring action but must, according to Article 173 of the Treaty, show that the decision or regulation[44] is 'of direct and individual concern' to them. Early case law of the European Court, going back over thirty years, has held that this phrase, 'direct and individual concern', implies that the individual is affected by reason of certain attributes which are peculiar to them or by reason of circumstances in which they are differentiated from all other persons, and the European Court has consistently adopted that interpretation in subsequent case law.[45] The result of this restrictive approach

---

[42] See also G Winter, 'The Directive: Problems of Construction and Directions for Reform' in G Winter (ed), *Sources and Categories of European Union Law* (Baden-Baden, Nomos Verlagsgesellschaft, 1996).

[43] For a recent and firmly argued liberal approach see the judgment of Otton J in *R v Her Majesty's Inspectorate of Pollution and the Minister of Agriculture Fisheries and Food ex parte Greenpeace Ltd* (1994) 6(2) *Journal of Environmental Law* 297; see also the case analysis by Purdue in the same issue at 312.

[44] The Court has also recently confirmed that there is no provision in the Treaty for third parties to challenge the legality of Directives, as opposed to Regulations or Decisions: Case T-99/94 *Asocarne v Council*.

[45] Case 25/62 *Plaumann v Commission* [1963] ECR 95. It would seem that the Court would prefer such issues to be brought to its attention by a reference from the national courts under Art 177, but this will not necessarily deal with the legal control of the Commission's activities.

was confirmed last year in the environmental field where environmental groups and local residents attempted to challenge the legality of the Commission grant of structural funds in respect of the construction of power stations in the Canary Islands.[46] The complaint was essentially that the award of the aid had not been in compliance with environmental requirements contained in the relevant structural fund regulations especially those concerning environmental assessment. But whatever the merits of the case, the Court never considered these issues, ruling that the applicants had no standing. It could find no evidence that the applicants, or the members of the association, were affected in some way different from other residents in the area.[47] A similar approach was adopted in the case concerning the challenge to the legality of the Commission not intervening in the French nuclear testing in the Pacific.[48]

Of course, it could be argued that another Member State could have made the challenge and would not have be inhibited by the standing rules. But the political reality is that this is most unlikely, especially in the case of structural funds, if only because most Member States benefit from such funds to a degree.[49] The result seems to be a lacuna in ensuring compliance with law. And I am reminded of the position some years ago when there was no express legal base for Community environment legislation under the Treaty. Other legal bases under the Treaty were sought to justify the legislation, and in certain cases, they were extremely dubious had they been subject to proper legal scrutiny. But, as I remember the late Lord Diplock eloquently espoused at a conference at Imperial College, the problem then was that all Member States had agreed to the legislation in question, with the result that effectively there was no one with standing who could or would challenge the legality of the laws in question.[50] Political expedience and priorities in effect subsumed the rule of law.

It should also be said that the Court of Justice itself has not been consistent in its approach towards standing, at least, in the non-environmental field. A slightly less restrictive approach is apparent in the fields of competition law and anti-dumping. And a rather more liberal approach appears to have been adopted in a decision in 1994 falling within the sphere of the Common Agricultural Policy.[51] In that case, a sparkling wine producer in Spain challenged a regulation stipulating that a particular term concerning sparking wine could only be used in respect of wines from France or Luxembourg. Although there were other sparkling wine producers in Spain in the same position, the European Court was prepared to accept that the Regulation in question was of individual and direct concern to the complainant producers, and that they had standing.[52] They had a protected economic interest at stake, a registered trade-mark, and were by far the largest producer of the wine

---

[46] Case T-585/93 *Stichting Greenpeace Council and others v EC Commission* 12 February 1994; (1996) 8(1) *Journal of Environmental Law* 39.

[47] For a similar result see Case T-117/94 *Associazione agricoltori della provinca di Rivigo et all v EC Commission* [1995] ECR II-455, concerning a challenge to a decision of the Commission to grant financial assistance for conservation measures under the LIFE fund.

[48] Case T-219/95R *Danielsson and others v Commission of the European Communities* [1995] ECR II-3051.

[49] See L Kramer, 'Public Interest Litigation in Environmental Matters before the European Courts' (1996) 8(1) *Journal of Environmental Law*.

[50] R Macrory (ed), *Britain, Europe and the Environment* (London, Imperial College Centre for Environmental Technology, 1982).

[51] Case G-309/89 *Cordorniu v EC Council* [1995] CMLR 561.

[52] In other cases, the Court appears to have adopted the view that if the challenged act was truly a Regulation which by its nature had general application, third parties would not have the right to challenge it: see T-472/93 *Campo Ebro v EU Council* [1996] CMLR 1038. In *Cordorniu* the Court appeared to have accepted that an act could both be a true Regulation and of individual and direct concern at the same time.

in question, and these factors were sufficient to give them a position distinguished from other producers.

The economic factors clearly in play may permit the Court to develop a rather more liberal test of standing in these sorts of cases as opposed to those concerned with the environment, and maybe we will just have to wait for developing jurisprudence. But the present position is hardly satisfactory, and does not meet my test of citizenship. One political response, at least over the question of structural funds, has been the recent flexing of muscle by the European Parliament using its budgetary powers to impose a greater commitment on the Commission to ensure that the environmental implications of the use of structural funds are more effectively considered. This in fact may have the effect desired in that field,[53] but in many ways represents a failure of the legal system to come to grips with the issue.

Although the Court does not say so explicitly, its restrictive approach towards the definition of standing must to a large degree be due to the familiar floodgates arguments. Time delays before the Court at present are sufficient to raise alarms at the prospect of a whole new tranche of litigation. There will be arguments for amending the provisions of the Treaty to provide for a total liberalisation to allow any individual or organisation to have standing,[54] but I am not convinced that this would be practicable or necessarily the correct response. One approach might be to relax the standing rules, and develop a more vigorous filtering process for applications, akin to the procedure for leave of application to judicial review in this country – this would help to ensure that cases with little merit would not reach the court. Or perhaps, rather than broadening the standing tests, we need a new independent body with power to bring such cases in the public interest against the Commission and other Community institutions. The Maastricht Treaty did establish a new Community post, the Ombudsman, with the duties to investigate complaints concerning maladministration within Community institutions.[55] The Ombudsman, however, is very much the creature of the European Parliament reporting to the European Parliament. As yet the jury is still out on the effectiveness of this new position, and it is very unlikely that the Ombudsman would have independent standing before the Court.[56] Nor am I satisfied that a body concerned with maladministration can be an effective substitute for one responsible for ensuring legality.

Environmental and Economic Rights: The Uneven Hierarchy

It is perhaps no coincidence that the Court's rather more liberal approach towards standing has appeared in more purely economic areas of the Community interest rather than the environment. And similarly, it is telling that in relation to enforcement some of

---

[53] See in particular European Parliament Committee on Budgets, Report on the 1996 Draft Budget as modified by the Council A4-0305/95, 11 December 1995; Final Adoption of the General Budget of the European Union for the financial year [1996] OJ L22 29 January 1996. I am grateful to David Wilkinson of the Institute for European Environmental Policy for information on these political developments.

[54] See, eg 'Greening the Treaty II: Sustainable Development in a Democratic Union' (Climate Action Network et al, 1995).

[55] EC Treaty, Art 138e.

[56] Other than to protect the interests of the position.

the Commission's more recent procedural initiatives concerning enforcement appeared in economic fields. In my final theme, then, I want to consider some deeper structural features of the Community as a legal system in its treatment of economic and environmental interests. Whatever precisely the meaning of sustainable development, it clearly implies a far deeper integration of economic, social and environmental concerns that has hitherto been the case. Sustainable development, albeit in rather garbled form, was inserted at Maastricht as one of the tasks of the Community.[57] The Treaty also contains an obligation to integrate environmental protection requirements into other areas of Community policy,[58] again one of the necessary implications of sustainable development.

The Community may have had its origins as a functionalist economic institution, but clearly has developed beyond those boundaries. The acknowledgment by the Court of Justice of the significance of human rights as an element of the Community legal order which is now reflected in the Maastricht Treaty,[59] and even the change of name of the European Economic Community to the European Community and Union under the Maastricht Treaty underlines those developments. As Advocate General, Francis Jacobs put it in a recent lecture,[60] 'This has among other things put an end to the idea that the Community is a purely economic entity and that it is only as a factor of production that an individual has to be considered under Community. That mercantalist approach is simply no longer tenable'.

But when one looks closer at the current legal structures there is still a long way to go. All systems of law and legal principle are ultimately based on a hierarchical structure – some principles overriding or qualifying others, some mandatory, others merely giving power, some enforceable before the courts, others existing merely as what might be described as gravitational rules. The European Treaty contains no explicit hierarchy as such – indeed the fundamental principle that in case of conflict with national law Community law is supreme is not expressed as such in the Treaty but is entirely a creation of the judiciary. Nor within its own confines does the Treaty explicitly create a structured hierarchy. Yet when one examines its format and the way that it has been interpreted and approached by legal practitioners and the Court of Justice, one can construct a set of interlocking principles and rules, some of which clearly take precedence over others. Understanding the nature and rationale for this approach is of key importance if we are to ever to see a more balanced integration of economic and environmental interests.[61]

At the pinnacle of this pyramid are statements of what can be described as preemptive norms given the highest value by the Court. These are binding, have direct effect, and are invocable against Member States, Community institutions, and in many instances by

[57] Among the general tasks of the Community defined in Art 2 of the Treaty as amended are the promotion of 'sustainable and non-inflationary growth respecting the environment. See generally R Macrory and M Hession 'Maastricht and the Environmental Policy of the Community: Legal Issues of a New Environment Policy' in O'Keefe and Twomey (eds), *Legal Issues of the Masstricht Treaty* (London, Chancery Publications, 1993).

[58] EC Treaty, Art 13: 'Environmental protection requirements must be integrated into the definition and implementation of other Community policies'. Although the sentiment is clear, the precise legal meaning of this requirement, let alone its institutional implementation, remain unclear.

[59] Art F₂: 'The Union shall respect fundamental rights as guaranteed by the European Convention for the Protection of Human Rights and Fundamental Freedoms signed in Rome on 4 November 1950 and as they result from the constitutional traditions common to the Member States as general principles of Community law'. But under Art L this provision is excluded from the jurisdiction of the European Court of Justice.

[60] F Jacobs, 'Human Rights in the European Union' (Durham, European Law Institute, 1994).

[61] See generally R Macrory and M Hession, 'Balancing Trade Freedom with the Requirements of Sustainable Development' in N Emilou and D O'Keefe (eds), *The European Union and World Trade Law: After the GATT Uruguay Round* (Chichester, Wiley, 1996), reproduced in Chapter 25 of this volume.

and in some cases against individuals before their national courts. The most obvious are the provisions in Article 30[62] guaranteeing free movement of goods, and those principles in Articles 85 and 86[63] relating to competition. We can identify further categories of principles, including a duty on the Community to act in favour of particular goals which may include the environmental integration requirement,[64] down to what may described as statements of interests which provide a legal justification for action by the Community or Member States but do not require any such action to be taken.

If we just contrast two sets of important provisions the dilemma is clear. The Treaty now contains a set of environmental principles, but these do not have any pre-emptive effect; rather, they guide and influence Community action where it is taken. Similarly, the environmental integration requirement is a principle that binds the Community where it takes action, but as the cases on standing illustrate is unlikely to be enforceable other than by another Member State or perhaps the European Parliament. In contrast, Article 30, concerning the free movement of goods, has been held to have direct effect, and in essence can be described as a constitutional right. Indeed the freedom of trade has been described by the European Court as a fundamental right of those living within the Community.[65] It can be invoked by individuals and companies before the national courts. It exists quite independently from any measures or policies initiated by the Community or Member States. Any national legislation and any other equivalent measures taken by national governments, whether concerned with Community policy or not, which conflict with the principle can be challenged as illegal.[66] Even Community legislation is in theory subject to the principle.[67] It is true that under both express provisions of the Treaty[68] and principles developed by the European Court[69] Member States in certain circumstances and for certain reasons are permitted to retain measures which conflict with the general principle in Article 30, and environmental protection is one such ground.[70] But the burden is very much on the Member State to justify an incursion into the general principle, and does not detract from its general pre-emptive quality.

The whole issue of trade and environment is, of course, high on the international agenda, in the context of General Agreement on Trade and Tariffs and the World Trade Organization and the forthcoming Singapore meeting.[71] Much of the language in the Treaty concerning free movement and the exemptions that are permissible is very similar to GATT. Yet in terms of their internal legal significance, and one might describe as the

---

[62] Now Art 43 TFEU.

[63] Now Art 101 TFEU *et seq.*

[64] Art 130r.

[65] *ADBHU* [1985] ECR 531. The principle of free movement of goods and freedom of competition, together with freedom of trade as a fundamental right, are general principles of law which the Court ensures are observed.

[66] Since 1969 the Court of Justice has recognised that Community Institutions must comply with basic human rights, and that these doctrines may also apply to Member States when applying Community law. But under Community law they do not apply to national legislation per se, and in this respect can be contrasted with the economic rights granted under the Treaty; see Jacobs, above n 60.

[67] Confirmed in *ADBHU*, above n 65, though in practice the Court is more likely to find other Community policy objectives justify action despite its conflict with Art 30.

[68] Art 36.

[69] The sole called 'rule of reason'.

[70] In Case 302/86 *Commission v Denmark* [1988] ECR 4607 (*Danish Bottles*), the European Court explicitly recognised that environmental protection, though not mentioned as such in Art 36, was such a ground.

[71] For the conclusions of that meeting relating to trade and the environment see Singapore WTO Ministerial 1996: Ministerial Declaration, WT/MIN(96)/DEC, 18 December 1996, para 16.

constitutionalisation of economic rights, it is clear that the Treaty has gone further than anything yet attempted internationally.

The rationale for the priority given to these principles and others such as competition law principles is not hard to find. In part it lies in the historical origins of the Community, where following the failure of the proposed European Political Community in 1954, the central thrust was given to the establishment of economic integration, based on a liberal economic order, as a prelude to further political integration.[72] But there are further reasons why from a legal perspective economic rights are likely to be conceptualised and invocable as legally protected interests more readily than environmental concerns. Lawyers traditionally characterise trade freedom as a classical individual right, which should be equivalent to familiar rights of property, and capable of legal protection as such. In contrast, environmental concerns are viewed in law not so much as an aspect of individual freedom or entitlement but rather as an interest which restricts the freedom of what people may or may not do. As such it is an area appropriate for intervention by government but cannot readily be conceived of as a right directly enforceable before the courts in the same way as the freedom to trade.

There are further important underlying differences in the way that trade and environment interests are conceived which inevitably compound the difficulties of giving them equal or equivalent legal status. The economic market in which the freedom to trade or to enjoy other economic rights is a purely human construction, and demands a certain unity of conditions for its effective operation; this reinforces the attraction of a legally and universally applicable right. In contrast, the environment is not of course an artificial concept, but a physical and heterogeneous reality. Effective and efficient environmental management frequently has to be sensitive to very differing natural conditions in the receiving environment, demanding different responses and hardly consistent with the legal concept of universally invocable rights. Furthermore, the apparent absence of any truly objective standard of environmental protection means that it is all the more difficult to construct an enforceable right. It may be within the capacity of the judiciary to judge what is or is not trade restrictive since this can be legally viewed as an objective test, but the courts should not be burdened with the more political task of determining what level of environmental protection is appropriate,[73] especially when in many areas the nature of environmental science cannot provide hard and fast answers. The dilemma for the courts can already be seen in case law of the European Court of Justice concerning the legality of measures taken by Member States which infringe the right of free movement of goods. As I have already mentioned, Member States may invoke environmental reasons for so doing but do they have right to determine the level of environmental protection desired, or should the Court's apply some objective test? In the *Danish Bottles* case[74] Advocate General Slynn, as he then was, did indeed call for an objective test – 'The level of protection sought must be a reasonable one' – but despite requests from the Court, the European Commission refused to provide guidance on what that reasonable level might be in that case, and the Court decided that it would not interfere or question the Danish government's determination

---

[72] See the Spaak Report (Brussels, 1956).

[73] The contrast between the objective examination of trade restrictive measures and the more political evaluation of environmental appears plausible. But it has to be said that when one examines the cases concerning alleged trade restrictive measures, it is clear the court is often equally faced with many ambiguities, and is often engaged in complex social and political choices.

[74] Above n 70.

of the standard of environmental protection they desired to be achieved by the proposed measures.[75] *Danish Bottles* concerned economic rights of free movement of goods being pitched against government action on the environment, and since such an action implies that a choice as to an appropriate level of environment protection has already been made by a government, it is hardly surprising that the Court felt it did not need to reconsider the question. But if an environmental right was to be invocable to the same extent as an economic right, we would be faced with situations where, unlike *Danish Bottles*, there was no necessary explicit decision taken by a government on the environmental issue at hand. Courts would be constantly faced with determining the standards themselves. The reluctance to develop environmental rights is understandable.

My argument then is that despite the views of Advocate General Jacobs, the Treaty and its legal interpretation has granted us as citizens general individual economic rights but, in the absence of Community legislation no equivalent environmental rights. Giving greater predominance to the notion of sustainable development within the overall aims of the Treaty, or increasing qualified majority voting for Community environmental measures may be the preoccupation of many environmental interests at present during the Inter-Governmental Conference. But these changes will not in themselves alter that fundamental legal construction and bias contained in the current structure.

A New Goal for the Market?

There are no easy solutions, but it is an intellectual challenge that needs to be faced if we are serious about the greater integration of economic and environmental interests implied by sustainable development. One way forward might be to include within the Treaty an individual right to environmental quality, as already been proposed by some quarters.[76] But, as I have indicated, there are very real difficulties whether such a right could be expressed in genuinely enforceable or legally meaningful terms, certainly where it concerned environmental quality. This is not to argue that the incorporation of such an statement of rights would be without any legal or political effect, and certainly the more that such rights are concerned with procedural requirements (such as the right to information) rather than rights to a particular quality of the environment, the more are they likely to be genuinely enforceable before the Courts. Even statements expressed in general terms may guide the legal interpretation of other rules and principles in a more environmentally sensitive manner. But it needs to be appreciated why such rights are unlikely ever to achieve equal legal status with economic rights. Certainly, the juxtaposition of such an environmental right within the Treaty alongside the existing norms and principles of necessity would create difficult and continuing tensions.

Another response – and in essence what has been taking place for the last twenty years – is to simply carry on with the development of explicit Community environmental legislation as a sort of counterbalance where existing fundamental principles are considered

---

[75] An alternative approach might be that the role of the Court should be determine whether an activity harmed the environment but to leave it to the national authority to determine what level of harm should be permitted, subject to proportionality.

[76] See above n 8. Some Nordic countries are thought to support the inclusion of such a right during the current Inter-Governmental Conference. Such a general right has not be included in the current Treaties.

to run counter to environmental interests. This is likely to happen in certain fields, but, although it is too early to determine a definite trend, the pace of Community environmental legislation appears to have slowed down, reflecting in part a greater sensitivity to the subsidiarity principle that now appears in the Treaty. In 1993 and 1994, for example, nearly 50 items of environmental legislation were adopted, dropping to 19 in 1995.[77] Even if qualified majority voting in the Council of Ministers were extended to all environmental matters, the accession of new member states could be expected to make the agreement of new environmental legislation more rather than less difficult.

In any event, such an approach is perhaps over dirigist. Another method, which is more fundamental and long lasting, is to reconsider the purposes of the market whose goals are not defined with precision in the Treaty. Under this model, which I and a colleague have recently suggested,[78] one would take as a starting point the concept of the 'rational and prudent use of natural resources', which is now one of the express principles of Community environmental policy, and could be said to be one of the underpinning goals of sustainable development. It is also a goal with which one would hope an economist would have little to disagree with as a general preferred outcome of market principles. If this were expressed explicitly in the Treaty as one of the goals of the market, the basic legal structure and hierarchy of principles would be transformed. Legislation and policies both at national and Community level which conflicted with these goals would in accordance with the existing principles be susceptible to legal review. Policy makers at both national and Community level would develop an increased sensitivity in the design and development of measures which might conflict with those principles, as they do at present in respect of free movement of goods.[79] Activities of the State which caused or permitted environmental damage would prima facie be contrary to the Treaty as are activities that distort free trade.[80] A true legal integration between market and environmental concerns would lie at the heart of the legal structure, and in essence one would be bringing to bear the full weight of the power of market law and principles developed within the Community behind at least some of the goals of sustainable development.

It takes some imagination to consider the likely outcome of such a change. Indeed far from being a top-down prescriptive solution, it deliberately leaves open the detailed future development of policy and law but against a new, and more balanced legal framework which might be more appropriate for the next century. But in suggesting such a proposal, it will be argued that far from carrying out repairs, I am now pulling up the whole road. My response would be – perhaps echoing the 18th Report of the Royal Commission on Environmental Pollution[81] – that over-obsession with one form of propulsion may end up eventually restricting rather than increasing freedom of choice. Or, in the words of Father Brown 'It isn't that they can't see the solution. It is that they can't see the problem?[82]

---

[77] N Haigh, *Manual of Environmental Policy: the EC and Britain* (London, Longmans, 1998).

[78] Above n 61.

[79] N Neuwahl, 'Individuals and Gatt: Direct Effect and Indirect Effects of the General Agreement on Tariffs and Trade in The European Union and World Trade Law' in N Emison and D O'Keefe (eds), *The European Union and World Trade Law* (Wiley, 1996) 313–28.

[80] No doubt the courts would have to develop thresholds since so many activities are environmentally damaging but the same developments and drawing back can be seen in the case law on restrictions of trade and measures of equivalent effect. But the purpose of the proposal is to permit the development of principle rather than lay down over-prescriptive rules in advance.

[81] *Transport and the Environment* (London, HMSO, 1994).

[82] GK Chesterton, 'Point of the Pin' in *The Scandal of Father Brown* (1935).

25

Balancing Trade Freedom with the Requirements of Sustainable Development[1] (1996)

Introduction

The integration of social, environmental, and economic concerns lies at the heart of the commitment to sustainable development to which the European Community, the Member States and many members of GATT are at least formally dedicated.[2] In purely legal terms the principle of sustainable development, while much talked about, defies precise definition and risks dismissal as a political aspiration rather than a legal concept. Nevertheless, inspirational provisions lie at the heart of many constitutional legal systems, motivating the interpretation of substantive and procedural rules and establishing general principles of law which have a substantial influence in practice. Integration forms the formal kingpin of the Community's sustainability strategy – the legal integration of the principles of free

---

[1] R Macrory and M Hession, 'Balancing Trade Freedom with the Requirements of Sustainable Development' in N Emilou and D O'Keefe (eds), *The European Union and World Trade Law: After the GATT Uruguay Round* (Chichester, Wiley, 1996) 181–216. This article is derived from work undertaken for a research project funded by the European Commission (DG XII) entitled 'Institutional Adjustment to Sustainable Development" coordinated by CSERGE at the University of East Anglia.

[2] While the fundamental task of the Community has always centred on free trade it has also always incorporated other social and political objectives. The question whether free trade is an objective in itself or the means of attaining a broader range of objectives is answered in Art 2, which makes clear that the market is a means to an end rather than an end in itself. Art 2 was amended to reflect the Community's interest in environment protection: 'Article 2 The Community shall have as its task by establishing a common market and an economic and monetary union and by implementing the common policies or activities, to promote throughout the Community a harmonious and balanced development of economic activities, sustainable and non-inflationary growth respecting the environment, a high degree of economic convergence of economic performance, a high level of employment and of social protection, the raising of the standard of living and quality of life, and economic an social cohesion and solidarity among the member states'. The recently adopted WTO contains similar language: Preamble to the WTO 'Recognising that their relations in the field of trade and economic endeavour should be conducted with a view to the raising of standards of living, ensuring full employment, and a large and steadily growing volume of real income and effective demand, and expanding the production and trade in goods and services, while allowing for the optimal use of the worlds' resource in accordance with the objective of sustainable development, seeking both to protect and preserve the environment and enhance the means of doing so.'

trade with those of environmental protection perhaps its most difficult task.[3] In the process of fulfilling the obligation to integrate it will be demonstrated whether the interests of trade and the environment are ultimately reconcilable and by what institutional framework this may be achieved – if at all. The balance achieved at a community level displays some of the difficulties of integration adopted and implemented at a supranational level. Though reinforced by recent amendments to the Treaty, the process towards sustainability might be described as in its early stages, and there is already ample evidence in the eyes of some that the process cannot be completed while leaving protection afforded to both interests undiminished.

Historically, the Legal Order of the European Community has provided a framework within which provisions relating to the free market have been developed and applied in a manner unique between states.[4] Though in many instances the legal language is the same, the essential provisions of the Treaty relating to goods, services and capital go far beyond anything suggested by the Uruguay round of GATT. In particular the existence of an independent enforcement agency and the principles of superiority and direct effect of Community law provide for a particular style and level of enforcement within the EC to which GATT may only distantly aspire. The recognition that individual provisions of the Treaty relating to free trade can have the effect of invalidating national law and that these provisions can be invoked even by individuals has had a profound effect on Member States, ability to regulate the national public interest in matters affecting trade.

Article 30[5] in particular has been broadly interpreted to invalidate measures which potentially indirectly hinder interstate trade – a test very little legislation appears to pass. Adopted by the Court in the interests of establishing an integrated market, this broad interpretation of Article 30 of the EC Treaty[6] has, in the absence of a formal division of powers between the Member States and the Community or an express bill of rights respecting individuals,[7] lead to a commensurate expansion in recognised socially motivated justifications from the general prohibition. These justifications in the form of general principles and interests commonly recognised in the European legal system are interpreted by the European Court of Justice which therefore has a broad power to review national legislation adopted under them. In a similar manner, where the Community has regulated, the Court has allowed an extensive interpretation of the Treaty and Community tasks to justify Community legislation in respect of these concerns. In both cases the principles of legality and certainty have been undermined.

Essential competences relating to the harmonisation of domestic standards and the Common Commercial Policy, both ostensibly directed at the establishment of a single

---

[3] Art 130r(2) reinforced at Maastricht requires that environmental protection requirements be integrated in the definition and implementation of other policy. Integration has been adopted as a formal policy objective in the 5th Action Programme 'Towards Sustainability' 1993.

[4] See Petersmann, 'The EC and GATT on the Economic Functions of GATT Rules' [1984] *Legal Issues of European Integration* 37, who characterises the Community and GATT as incorporating the liberal market idea in legal constitutional form. See also Petersmann, 'Limited Government and Unlimited Trade Powers. Why Effective Judicial Review of Foreign Trade Restrictions Depends on Individual Rights' in Hilf and Petersmann *National Constitutions and International Economic Law* (Dordrecht, Kluwer 1993). But see Staker, 'Free Movement of Goods in the EEC and Australia: A Comparative Study' [1990] *Yearbook of European Law* 10, on Art 92 of the Australian Constitution, for a description of a similar federal provision guaranteeing free trade

[5] Now Art 34 TFEU.

[6] Prohibiting quantitative restrictions and measures having equivalent effect which have been interpreted in the light of the objective of attaining a single market.

[7] 291/69 *Stander v Ulm* [1969] ECR 419; 11/70 *International Handelsgesellschaft* [1970] ECR 1125; 4/73 *Nold II* [1974] ECR 491; 44/79 *Liselotte Hauer v Rheinlandpfalz* [1979] ECR 3752–65.

market within the Community, have always necessarily encompassed other considerations for which trade is commonly regulated. But, ever broader interpretation of the legal bases for market action is, ultimately, an unsatisfactory legal foundation for Community measures which have had only a tenuous connection to the objectives. Even so, the express recognition provided by recent Treaty amendments of separate bases defined according to independent objectives demonstrates the limitations of a system of separate legal bases operated according to a teleological approach, where legitimate objectives and measures adopted to satisfy them increasingly overlap. Resulting tensions within the definition of each basis are reinforced both by the division between broadly unitary trade policy and concurrent policies representing other aspects of the public interest and the proliferation of legislative procedures required for their adoption.

At an international level the increased interrelationship between trade and other issues has caused the Court of Justice to hesitate between an inclusive interpretation of Article 113[8] and the recognition of competence in the Member States.[9] Similarly within the Community while the concept of the market effect was used to justify particular environmental measures under Articles 100 and 235 in the absence of an alternative specific competence, the adoption of a separate legal basis (Article 130r-t),[10] for the environment has outlined a conflict between the interests of competitive equality and market unity and the legally reinforced recognition of a decentralised pursuit of environmental protection.

Developing a Community Framework

To date, a holistic approach to the Treaty and judicial testing of legislative discretion according to developed principles of non-discrimination, necessity and proportionality,[11] as well as the objective factors for review of legal bases, have formed the geography of the Trade and Environment Division in Community law. The place and influence of the newer principles of integration and subsidiarity in the review of action pursued in the general interest remain to be determined according to a defined framework of Community constitutional law itself as yet in its early stages.[12]

The following is suggested as a possible framework within which the principles of free trade and environment might be reconciled or integrated at Community level. While nowhere defined in the Treaty, a broad outline can be gauged in the application of particular community rules.

---

[8] See now Art 207 TFEU.

[9] Most recently the balance has come down in favour of a less monolithic Common Commercial policy than some have argued for, Opinion 1/94 *Re the Uruguay Round Treaties Commission v Council* [1995] Common Market Law Reports 205. For critique see Bourgeois, 'The EC in the WTO and Advisory Opinion 1/94: An Echternach Procession' (1995) 32(3) *Common Market Law Review* 736.

[10] See now Art 191 TFEU.

[11] See 138/79 *Isoglucose* [1980] ECR 333, 114/76 *Bela-Muhle Josef Bergmann KG v Grows Farm GmbH* [1977] ECR 1211 and 122/78 *Buitoni* [1979] ECR 677–86 for examples in practice. See generally De Búrca, 'The Principle of Proportionality and its Application in EC Law' [1993] *Yearbook of European Law* 105.

[12] For the constitutional character of the Community Parti Ecologiste see *Les Verts v European Parliament* [1986] ECR 1339. See generally Lenearts, 'Fundamental Rights to be Included in a Community Catalogue' [1991] *European Law Review* 367.

Statements of Pre-emptive Norms

These are Treaty provisions and General Principles of Law given highest value by the Court, of a binding character invocable against and by the Community institutions, or the Member States, but also in some circumstances are also invocable by and against individuals (in that sense giving rise to what might be termed personal constitutional rights). Article 30 of the Treaty guaranteeing free trade, and fundamental rights recognised as general principles of law fall into this category.[13]

A Duty to Act or to Respect Particular Interests

An obligation on the part of the Community to act in favour of a particular interest. Such a statement is suggestive of a pre-emptive norm, but may perhaps be distinguishable in that it is invocable only by the Community institutions and the Member States between each other. Such obligations may be found in many of the early Treaty articles establishing the common external tariff and the common market and have formed the basis for the courts' jurisprudence on exclusivity.[14] A duty on the Community to respect a particular interest forms a limitation on the exercise of power in judicial review but may not amount to the grant of a right. The integration requirement may fall into this category.[15] And perhaps even the duty to fulfil elements of the general action plan in Article 130s(3) falls into this category.[16]

General Principles of Law

General duties operate in the sphere of Community discretion. These principles are binding but operate in respect of the application of other interests and norms: their effect is therefore dependent on the operation of a norm or interest: Article 5 Duty of Solidarity,[17] Article 7 Nondiscrimination or Equality are examples.[18] Necessity, Proportionality and Subsidiarity (Article 3b)[19] and perhaps at least some of the Principles of Environmental

---

[13] Confirmed in *ADBHU* [1985] ECR 531 at 549 See also Quinn and MacGowan, 'Could Article 30 impose obligations on individuals' 12 *European Law Review* 163. It should be remembered that, whereas the right to trade across frontiers recognised in *ADBHU* applies to Community and national legislation alike, the court recognises the application of other 'human' rights to Community provisions only: see J Temple Lang, 'The Sphere in which Member States are Obliged to Comply with General principles of Law and Community Fundamental Rights Principles' [1991] No 1 *Legal Issues of European Integration* 23.

[14] In particular duties to adopt particular measures by particular dates appear to have this effect. See particularly *Commission v United Kingdom* [1980] ECR 1045.

[15] It appears that, whether by sympathetic interpretation or by formal recognition of the duty to integrate contained in Art 130r(2), the proximity principle has been allowed to modify the application of a Community law rule (derogations to Art 30) in the *Wallonia Waste* case, Case 2/90 *Commission v Belgium* [1993] CMLR 365 (see below).

[16] Hession and Macrory, 'Legal Issues of a New Environment Policy' in O'Keeffe and Twomey (eds), *Legal Issues of the Maastricht Treaty* (Chichester, Wiley, 1994) 163–64.

[17] Giving rise to ERTA implied powers and pre-emption which derives ultimately from Art 5 but gives rise to other duties: *Fisheries Commission v UK* [1980] ECR 1045; Opinion ILO Convention No 170 [1993] Common Market Law Reports 800; Opinion 1/94 Uruguay Round Agreements [1995] CMLR 205.

[18] See now Art 4(3) TEU. See the discussion on non-discrimination below and for relevance of environmental principles on the *Wallonia Waste* case (above n 15) also see below.

[19] See now Art 5 TEU.

Action detailed in Article 130r(2), in particular proximity (see below) are similar principles though perhaps lower-order principles regulating the application of pre-emptive norms, duties and basic principles on recognised interests.[20]

Statement of Community Interest

The Community's interest in a particular objective authorising the adoption of particular measures pursuant to the appropriate legal basis and forming the legal boundaries of a Community power: Article 130r (Environment) and Article 43 (Agriculture). These interests justify an intrusion upon pre-emptive norms subject to the basic principles of nondiscrimination, necessity and proportionality.[21]

Statement of Member States' Interest

The Treaty also recognises Member States' interests which also justify limited exceptions to the pre-emptive norms of Community law subject to the principles of necessity, proportionality and equality: (Article 36, and the Mandatory requirements under *Cassis di Dijon*).[22]

Statements of Interpretative Value

Principles which are suggestive but have no autonomous effect (but nonetheless are likely to have some interpretative value in a legal framework): Subsidiarity may fall into this category.

Pre-emptive Trade Norms and the Environmental Interest

A fundamental assumption is made as to the effects of trade and environment provisions, the reasons for which are rooted in politics and the nature of the interests themselves. Whereas Article 30 of the Treaty presents a pre-emptive and directly effective provision establishing an area of individual protection equivalent to that of an individual right, environmental protection provisions are defined as legislative interests in language which denies the possibility of such effects.[23] The traditional justification for this lies with the dif-

[20] *Wallonia Waste*, above n 15.

[21] The existence of such an interest is a matter of interpretation and not limited to express policy statements, as the *ADBHU* case, above n 10, concerning the environment demonstrated prior to the adoption of an express legal basis.

[22] While the Member States may be said to retain all powers not ceded to the Community the interpretation of the extent of Community power is difficult. Art 36 is one of the few places in the Treaty where state interests are indirectly recognised and listed. Until the formal identification of concurrent policies permanently preserving state rights to legislate under the subsidiarity principle (Art 3b) and more stringent measures powers provisions (Art 130t), these 'police powers' remained subject to the possibility of permanent and absolute harmonisation in so far as this was possible through Art 100.

[23] The Constitutions of Portugal and Greece recognise a right which while not self-executory for these reasons has a certain legal/discretionary value in review. The Court's recognition of a constitutional right to be found in national constitutions would be one alternative approach to founding an environmental norm at Community level.

ficulty in determining the limits and standard of protection required by the latter. And yet the limits of what represents the common market are no more certain than those of environment. Both definitions incorporate questions of scale and degree linked to social and political choices. Indeed the Community definition of the market (single, common and internal) is uncertain and finds an unsteady application in the substantive rules governing its establishment.[24] Nonetheless the current broad hierarchy of principles reflect a legal presumption in favour of trade freedom and economic growth over scientific uncertainty as to the environmental consequences of these choices. This presumption lies at the heart of a liberal economic and social order based on competition and risk.

One element of the distinction is traditional in that trade freedom reflects a classical individual right, falling within traditional notions of property, capable of objective legal protection to the holder of such rights.[25] As a result, Free Movement of Goods in particular[26] has been interpreted to include a sufficiently substantive set of criteria to provide an adequate standard for the judicial review of Community and Member State legislation.[27] This character – one of individual right – derives from the special nature of the Community Treaty which acts increasingly as a constitutional charter. Member States are policed not only by themselves but by the Commission under Article 169 and by individuals in accordance with the doctrine of direct effect.[28] The Community itself is policed under the provisions of Article 173 by the Member States and its own institutions and individuals insofar as a Community decision is of 'direct and individual concern'.[29]

In contrast, environmental protection rather than embodying a freedom more commonly implies a restriction on individual activity mediated through the legislative activities of a state which is either duty bound to protect the environment or is recognised to have a discretionary interest in doing so.[30] As such a right to the environment is not easily associ-

---

[24] The single market is implemented or enforced through several substantive rules. Arts 85 and 86 on Competition (Fair and Perfect Competition between undertakings); Art 12 (prohibiting the introduction of new duties on imports and charges of equivalent effect while further articles provide for the abolition of existing standards now achieved (Art 16); the central Art 30 prohibiting quantitative restrictions on imports and measures having equivalent effect interpreted to establish the principle of mutual recognition of product- related standards throughout the Community. This mutual recognition principle is applied to a lesser but increasing extent in other areas notably Arts 52–62: Services prohibition on the introduction of new Arts 71 and 73b Capital (weaker provisions). Art 48: Free Movement of Workers (standstill plus): Arts 52–53: (standstill plus) Right of Establishment, (standstill plus) and Art 72 on Transport.

[25] R Barents, 'The Community and the Unity of the Common Market: Some Reflections on the Economic Constitution of the Community' (1990) 33 German Yearbook of International Law 9.

[26] Art 8a provides that the internal market is based on four freedoms – free movement of goods, workers, services and capital – which are elaborated in individual provisions of several articles of the Treaty: Arts 12, 30, 59, etc.

[27] Nonetheless the concept of a 'common market' is nowhere defined though it is mentioned in several provisions: Arts 9–102 assist in its definition through detailing aspects of public and private activity which is incompatible with the establishment and functioning of the market though these provisions. The Court has attempted to define the essential character of the market in several cases: 270/80 Polydor v Harlequin [1982] ECR 329: 'The Treaty seeks to create a single market reproducing as closely as possible the conditions of a domestic market'; 15/81 Schul [1982] ECR 1409: 'the elimination of all obstacles to intra-Community trade in order to merge the national markets to those of a genuine internal market'. These cases themselves contain some margin for interpretation – see above n 25, 10.

[28] Directly effective are Art 12 (Customs Duties and Charges having equivalent effect): 26/62 Van Gend en Loos [1963] ECR 1; and Art 30 (Quantitative Restrictions and measures having equivalent effect): 13/68 [1968] Salgoil ECR 453; 74/76 Ianelli [1977] ECR 557; Pigs Marketing Board v Redmond [1978] ECR 2347.

[29] As to the desirability of a trade norm and individual access to it see Petersmann, 'Limited Government', above n 4.

[30] The extension of the state's interest in the environment to include precautionary as well as preventive or protective measures implies an extension of public power without an appropriate mechanism for rational

ated with an individual for enforcement save in so far as some element of the environment amounts to an asset falling within traditional notions of private property or another more traditional right and is protected in this way.

One suggested method of achieving an individualisation of rights and responsibility over the environment is the internalisation or monetisation of environmental costs.[31] Even if distribution of rights according to a market were desirable and could negate all the disadvantages of a more inflexible approach through central regulation it must be doubted whether all environmental problems can be given a value. Reference to such an approach demonstrates nonetheless that the extent to which a market incorporates environmental assets and liabilities may vary in different Member States and this is one way the application of trade rules to environmental problems is delimited.[32]

The central objection to the recognition of an environmental right remains the absence of an objective standard of protection and the judgment than any standard must be set through the legislative rather than the judicial method. The Treaty of Rome has endorsed though not defined a high level of protection but 'normativity' of this statement is doubted or at least limited.[33] The objection is not consistently applied however as while it is used to deny the possibility of a norm against which legislation may be measured in terms of its environmental component, judicial testing of measures against an objectively determinable standard of protection has been suggested where it has been alleged it is trade restrictive. Inherent scientific uncertainty as to the effects of particular actions operating through a complex system of possible processes, interactions and cumulative effects makes an excessive reliance on science to determine an objective assessment of risk or harm of human activity.[34] This is not to deny that the conditions for a trade restriction nor indeed a test insuring protection is not judicially determinable even in conditions of uncertainty, but merely to state that science on its own cannot be relied upon to establish an objective standard against which particular measures may be judged in all cases.

In addition the philosophy of both interests is different. Whereas the single market is a human construction and of its nature requires a certain unity of conditions, the environment is not, and must be regulated according to a hierarchy of provision with regard to the global, regional and local levels according to different conditions and circumstances.[35] In contrast, non-discrimination and universally applicable uniform standards are the founda-

---

review of such policies against objectively determinable facts or reasons (see discussion on precaution and proportionality below). For a US discussion of the problem see McGarity, *Reinventing Rationality: The Role of Regulatory Analysis in the Federal Bureaucracy* (Cambridge, Cambridge University Press, 1991), particularly ch 9. This difficulty has led to warnings of a danger of an authoritarian ecological state: see M Kloepfer, 'An Authoritarian Ecological State?' [1994] *European Environmental Law Review* 112.

[31] Nonetheless, in conditions of uncertainty environmental risks themselves unquantifiable are still less capable of market valuation. The process of cost benefit analysis of environmental messages displays some of the problems of such an apples and oranges approach. See McGarity, ibid.

[32] See the discussion about whether waste is a good in *Wallonia Waste*, above n 15. The issues of patenting living organisms in the area of biotechnology and discussions on civil liability for environmental harm also come to mind.

[33] Lenaerts, 'Fundamental Rights to be Included in a Community Catalogue' [1991] *European Law Review* 367.

[34] J Stonehouse, 'Science Risk Analysis and Environmental Decisions', UNEP Trade and the Environment Series No 5 (ISSN 1020-1610).

[35] A rather crude attempt to define what is appropriate can be made with reference to physical or trans-boundary nature of particular environmental problems: global environmental problems: climate, stratospheric ozone, highly migratory species, the high seas; regional environmental problems: more limited trans-boundary problems, sulphur dioxide, nitrogen dioxide, migratory species, rivers, regional seas; and local environmental problems: suspended particulates, waste disposal, other localised pollution.

tion of Community trade policy, while Subsidiarity[36] and Minimum Standards[37] provision reinforce the non-unitary nature of the environment policy.

Different physical and social conditions logically suggest local regulation. Hence restrictions on trade in environmentally hazardous material are justifiable to protect the local environment (though perhaps invidious to the market). Regulation in the interest of the environment, at a Community level must be justified as being more effective than that at local level suggesting some trans-boundary element. This is supported by criterion of effectiveness – the use of national trade instruments to protect the local environment from external sources of pollution is indirect enforcement of local standards at the best of times. It is also apparently unjustified on environmental grounds given that the definition of environmental interest seems to be restricted to state boundaries.[38] Regulation to achieve conditions of competitive equality or the application of Article 30 to achieve this have no such limitation however and the consequent harmonisation need not reflect local conditions allowing an equalisation of standards.[39]

Article 30 and the Extent of the Free Market in Goods[40]

The Common Market created by the European Community is far more ambitious than anything attempted in the GATT Agreements. The substantive elements of the market defined by the Treaty are a free trade area established in accordance with Articles 12-17 which provide that all customs duties and charges of equivalent effect be progressively abolished between the Member States and a customs union established under Articles 18-28a providing for a common tariff to apply with respect to third states. Much of the effective bite of the internal market in goods has been established by Article 30 which provides that quantitative restrictions and measures having equivalent effect are prohibited.[41] The Treaty as amended provides that the Community may adopt measures to harmonise provisions which directly affect the establishment or functioning of the Common

---

[36] Community action is permissible only if and only in so far as the objectives of the proposed action cannot be sufficiently achieved by the Member States and can therefore by reason of the scale and effects of the proposed action be better achieved by the Community (Art 3b).

[37] Art 130t authorising the introduction of more stringent protective measures compatible with the treaty and Art 100a(4) authorising the maintenance of more stringent environmental protective measure in limited circumstances.

[38] The argument whether an interest in environmental protection justifies unilateral regulation of trade in respect of the external environment (process standards) for Member States or the Community remains untested. The *Dassonville* case (8/74 *Procureur du Roi v Dassonville* [1974] ECR 837) suggests (at 840) that Art 36 justifies measures for the protection a state's own interests and not for the protection of interests of other states. The *Scottish Grouse* case (169/89 *Goumeterrie van den burg* [1990] ECR 2143) suggests a similar analysis. See also Krämer, 'Environmental Protection and Article 30 of EEC Treaty' (1990) 30 *Common Market Law Review* 111, 119–20, for a contrary view.

[39] For discussion of unilateral trade restrictions at an international level see Schoenbaum, 'Trade Sanctions Domestic, Enforcement of Agreement, Anti-Competitive Factors' (1992) 86 *American Journal of International Law* 701. Principle 12 of the Rio Declaration differentiates between direct and indirect regulation.

[40] A subject on which much has been written: see above n 22; Wils, 'The Search for a Rule in Article 30. Much Ado about Nothing' 18(6) *European Law Review* 475; J Steiner, 'Drawing the Line: Uses and Abuses of Article 30 EEC' (1992) 29 *Common Market Law Review* 754; Mortelmans, 'Article 30 of EEC Treaty and Legislation Relating to Market Circumstances: Time to Consider a New Definition' (1991) 28 *Common Market Law Review*; White, 'In Search of the Limits of Article 30 of the EEC Treaty' (1989) 26 *Common Market Law Review* 235.

[41] One of the shorter Treaty articles: Art 30: Quantitative Restrictions on Imports and on all measures having equivalent effect shall without prejudice to the following provisions be prohibited between the Member States.

Market,[42] or measures which have as their object or effect the establishment of the internal market[43] – the latter defined as an area without internal frontiers in which free movement of goods, persons, services and capital is ensured.[44] Both the concept of Common Market and Internal Market are difficult to define further. Even so, on the basis of these provisions and particularly Article 30 the Court has confirmed that 'the principle of Free Movement of Goods and Freedom of Competition, together with freedom of trade as a fundamental right are general principles of law of which the Court ensures observance'.[45] These fundamental principles define a pre-emptive norm of free trade applicable to the Community[46] and the Member States alike, and are invocable as individual rights in the national legal systems, rendering contrary measures inapplicable.[47]

Defining the extent of this putative human right has proved fraught and while it is clear that the prohibition incorporates elements of nondiscrimination and distortion of intra-community trade the latter element in particular has caused some difficulty in application leaving the law in a state of confusion.[48]

Non-discrimination or Equality[49]

The presence or absence of discrimination cannot be established in the absence of other substantive criteria applicable in one situation and not in another in which it is claimed there is discrimination. Here we are concerned with a general freedom to trade across frontiers attaching to goods. Equality of treatment, according to an Aristotelian conception requires consistency in some circumstances and differentiation in others.[50] Discrimination therefore consists in treating either similar situations differently or different situations identically.[51] The basic requirement in Community law is that there be no discrimination on grounds of origin.[52] This requirement is essentially a negative and rather limited requirement which states grounds which are insufficient to justify different treatment but fails to address justifiable grounds upon which products may be differentiated.

---

[42] The formula of Art 100.

[43] The formula of Art 100a.

[44] Art 7a.

[45] *ADBHU*, above n 10.

[46] 80 & 81/77 *Société les Reunis Sarl et al v Receveur des Douanes* [1978] ECR 927, 946–47 (provision authorising charge having equivalent effect to custom duty in Art 31 (2) of Reg 816/70); 61/86 *United Kingdom v Commission* [1988] ECR 431; 37/83 *Rewe Zentral* [1984] ECR 1229; 15/83 *Denkavit* [1984] ECR 2171 (disparities ruled justifiable or inevitable).

[47] *Salgoil, Ianelli* and *Pigs Marketing Board*, all above n 28 (direct effect of Art 30).

[48] To quote Advocate General Jacobs, 'The European Court of Justice: Some Thoughts on its Past and its Future' (Winter 1994–95) *The European Advocate*.

[49] Art 6: 'Within the scope of application of this Treaty . . . any discrimination on grounds of nationality shall be prohibited' – non-discrimination is a general principle not limited to free movement of goods but can mean different things in different places (see standstill prohibition on discriminatory treatment under the transport title Case 195/90 *Commission v Germany* [1990] ECR I-3351 and the case confirms that pre-existing inequality forms no justification for the adoption of more discriminatory measures with respect to charges for heavy goods vehicles).

[50] Aristotle, *Nicomedean Ethics*.

[51] Art 36, 13/63 ECR *Italy v Commission* [1963] ECR 165: 'The different treatment of non-comparable situations does not lead automatically to the conclusion that there is discrimination. An appearance of discrimination in form may therefore in fact correspond to an absence of discrimination in substance. Discrimination in substance would consist in treating either similar situations differently or different situations identically.'

[52] Art 6 above and the final sentence of Art 36: 'such prohibitions shall not constitute a means of arbitrary discrimination'.

The distinction between similar and dissimilar situations can be presented in two ways. The first involves searching for a physical difference inherent in the object of the freedom (in the case of goods, a like products approach). The second alternative involves searching for an objective justification for the distinction made between products (which may be broader than differences in the physical nature of the goods themselves).[53] It is suggested that elements of the general interests recognised by Community law are grounds which justify distinction and render it non-discriminatory.[54] The second alternative allows a greater range of distinguishing features than the former including distinctions justified according to environmental effects of production as well as those inherent in the goods themselves or indeed the objective general principles of environmental policy.[55]

In addition the Court recognises that there may be natural advantages and disadvantages which do not amount to discrimination and are allowed to lie where they fall. These might be said to form the basis of the comparative advantage the internal market is intended to exploit.[56]

Distortion or Restriction of Intra-Community Trade

National treatment of imported goods regulated by a provision on non-discrimination may still have the effect of partitioning the Single Market as goods marketable in one state may not be marketable in another state because of different applicable standards. It is clear that what is prohibited by Article 30 goes beyond simply discriminatory measures as the limited exceptions to the rule provided for are still stated to be the subject of a requirement of non-discrimination. It is equally clear that Article 30 could not have been envisaged to invalidate all measures adversely affecting the operation of the market as the Treaty affords a legal basis for the harmonisation of national measures which do so.

The central problem is determining what is restrictive of *intra-Community trade* without some even indirect discriminatory element. Indistinctly applicable measures may have discriminatory effects when applied to products from different countries.[57] Here the question becomes one of assessing the probity of the distinction adopted: essentially whether

---

[53] In this sense discrimination is not 'arbitrary discrimination' (final sentence of para 36). See also *Italy v Commission*, above n 51.

[54] See *Semide* [1984] ECR 4209, para 28: difference in treatment is objectively justified inter alia in the light of particular provisions of Community law. The question whether the process by which a good is produced is a valid ground for distinction is obviously related to the question whether the decision to restrict access of goods on this ground is justifiable on criteria of effectiveness (it is necessarily indirect regulation after the event). If discrimination on the only criterion upon which a measure might be found trade restrictive the question whether Art 36 applies with respect to the external environment becomes irrelevant. As this is patently not the case, the legitimacy of a process standard must be related to on this question. See above n 38.

[55] Such as precaution, prevention at source and polluter pays. See *Wallonia Waste*, above n 15. The discrimination must necessarily be proportionate to the legitimate differences recognised by the Treaty – which in the case of environment can be difficult to assess and enforce. The principle that damage ought as a priority be prevented at source for instance might work both ways, to encourage process standards dealing with pollution arising at source, or to preclude them, if use of such indirect sanctions rather than direct regulation of the source were considered to breach the principle.

[56] The burdens of natural differences such as physical location and transport costs are allowed to rest where they lie: Case 52/79 *Procureur du roi v Marc JVC Debarre & Others* [1980] ECR 833; Cases 63–69/72 *Wilhelm Werhahn Hansmulne & Oth v Council* [1973] ECR 1229. Art 130r(3) itself seems to confirm this as a general principle in environmental legislation requiring that differences in physical factors be taken into account in Community legislation.

[57] Amount to 'disguised restrictions on trade' (final sentence of Art 36).

the justification provided is objectively justified when compared with its discriminatory effects.[58]

The Court in the *Dassonville* case has drawn a very wide circle about Article 30 ruling that 'all trading rules which are capable of hindering directly or indirectly, actually or potentially, intra-Community trade must be considered measures having an effect equivalent to quantitative restrictions'. Such measures may even include measures which show no discrimination on their face and even measures which do not have a heavier impact on foreign goods per se.[59] In essence indistinctly applicable measures which have a general restrictive effect on trade are technically within the ambit of Article 30. For a time it appeared that there were few areas of market regulation where Article 30 would not apply.[60]

It has been suggested that there has been an attempt by the Court to make the trade rules applicable to states coextensive with those applicable to undertakings under the competition policy.[61] The result has been that the broad *Dassonville* definition 'of measures having equivalent effect' means that Article 30 operates as a quasi-presumption against rules regulating trade rather than a substantive rule invalidating measures restrictive of intra-Community trade.[62] In the absence of a clear standard of competition and trade freedom applicable to trade in a single market[63] the formula is ultimately unsatisfactory.

This test is therefore very broad indeed as the *Cassis de Dijon* case confirmed. Here the Court found that any product legally marketable in the country of origin (and by analogy in free circulation within the Community) must be admitted to the national market in the absence of justification provided for by the Treaty. The presumption becomes one that products legally on the market in one Member State must be admitted without restriction to the domestic market.[64]

Under this test it is difficult to overcome the presumption that any legislation with only a potential and indirect effect on trade is not prohibited. Measures found to fall within the prohibition have included such diverse regulation as limits on production,[65] checks and inspections on goods,[66] packaging requirements,[67] national goods buy-only policies[68] or even restriction on video rentals.[69]

In recent years the full consequences of *Dassonville* and *Cassis de Dijon* has led the Court into difficulties and the Court has found certain restrictions (on working hours or

---

[58] In this way the question whether indistinctly applicable measures are trade retraction and whether they may be justified are intimately interlinked, though the Treaty itself requires these questions are treated separately (Arts 30 and 36).

[59] Interestingly a recurring argument is that not all measures impinging on trade may be considered restrictive – the Advocate General even suggested that veterinary inspection in the general Community interest assisted rather than interfered with trade: 46/76 *Bauhuis* [1977] ECR 5 Opinion of Advocate General, para 7.

[60] This is particularly important in environmental terms as regulation of use and disposal of goods even, if indistinctly applicable and factually non-discriminatory, are still plainly capable of causing an indirect trade restriction – as *Danish Bottles* demonstrates.

[61] This consequence is made explicit in *Cassis de Dijon Rewe-Zentrale AG v Bundesmonopobver-waltung fur Branntwein* [1979] ECR 649.

[62] Kapteyn and van Themaat, *Introduction to the Law of the European Community*, 2nd edn (Kluwer, 1992) 380–81.

[63] See three connotations in Kapteyn and van Themaat, ibid, 356.

[64] *Cassis di Dijon: Rewe-Zentrale AG v Bundesmonopoloverwaltung fur Branntwein* [1979] ECR 649.

[65] Quotas on milling wheat: 190/73 *Van Haaster* [1974] ECR 1123.

[66] 251/78 *Denkavit Futtermittell* [1979] ECR 3369.

[67] *Prantl* [1984] ECR 1299; *Ran v Smedt* [1982] ECR 3901.

[68] 249/81 *Commission v Ireland* [1982] ECR 4005.

[69] Ban on release within one year to protect cinema viewing *Cinetheque v FNCF* [1985] ECR 2605.

sales outlets for spirits and limitations on Sunday trading[70] etc) to fall outside the scope of Article 30. The ground upon which certain indistinctly applicable measures have been found to fall outside the prohibition remain confused despite an attempt to clarify the Court's policy in the recent *Keck and Mithouard* case.[71] Here the Court expressly recognised that its policy of regulating all potentially restrictive legislation through granting exceptions has its limits and that there are indeed areas of legislative policy the effect of which on intra-Community trade is not sufficient to bring them within the ambit of Article 30.[72]

The Recognition of General Interests of the Community and the Member States

A narrow interpretation of Article 30 which is applicable to the Community and the Member States alike would create a Single Market based on competition of regulatory orders in which Member States wishing to preserve higher standards would be in the position of having to pay for them through a commensurate loss in comparative advantage.[73] Alternatively a broad interpretation brings into question the need for a legislative basis for harmonisation of standards where Article 30 appears to achieve a dismantling of trade barriers in the absence of formal harmonisation. The former has the disadvantage of leading to a downward pressure on standards in a race to match the lowest common denominator as to cost, and the latter to a great deal of legal uncertainty.

The broad interpretation favoured in the *Cassis* formula has enabled the review of national regulation of markets and ultimately derives from the Courts dissatisfaction with the pace of harmonisation through legislation. Judicial harmonisation of national standards is effected through the application of Community principles through an extended list of justifications-mandatory requirements. *Keck and Mithouard* notwithstanding, the basic formula of broad prohibition and regulated exception continues. The process initiated by *Dassonville* by which a greater number of trading rules have been caught by an extensive definition of the pre-emptive norm but have been saved by an ever-growing legion of mandatory requirements may be criticised if only because legal certainty has been compromised.

---

[70] 155/80 *Oebel* [1981] ECR 3147; 75/81 *Blesgen* [1982] ECR 11211; 69/93 and C-258/93 *Punto Cas Spa* [1994] ECR I-2355; C-23/89 *Quietlynn v Southend Borough Council* [1990] ECR 3059.

[71] C-267/91 and C-268/91 *Keck and Mithouard* [1993] ECR 1-6097, in particular paras 16 and 17. See also the comment by Roth (1995) 31 *Common Market Law Review* 845.

[72] See also Chalmers, 'Repackaging the Internal Market – Ramifications of the *Keck* Judgment' (1994) 19 *European Law Review* 385. This is again important in environmental terms as common use restrictions based on planning or licensing of activities are just the sort of measures the *Keck* case appears to exempt from the full rigours of the *Dassonville* formula. Measures restricting traffic or the local use of non-biodegradable materials appear to have escaped application of the principle in two cases: *R v London Boroughs Transport Committee ex P Freight Association Ltd* [1992] 63 CMLR 5 and *Enichem Base spa and others v Comune di Cinisello Balsamo* [1989] ECR 2491.

[73] N Reich, 'Competition between Legal Orders: a New Paradigm for Community Law' (1992) 29 *Common Market Law Review* 861.

The Community Interests: Objectives in the General Interest

In the *ADBHU* case[74] the Court confirmed that Article 30 is generally binding on the Community as well as the Member States, but recognised that the Community may adopt measures in pursuit of objects in the general interest which include environment protection: 'the principle of freedom of trade is subject to certain limits justified by the objectives of general interest pursued by the Community provided the rights in question are not substantially impaired'. Here certain provisions of a Community Directive derogating from absolute free movement with respect to waste oil were confirmed by the Court.[75] Judicial review of Community legislation is difficult to effect and the Community has a broad discretion to regulate trade in accordance with the provisions of the legal powers it is granted in pursuit of Community objectives.[76] Nonetheless restrictions on trade adopted by the Community are clearly subject to the requirement that they be non-discriminatory and that they are necessary and proportionate to the end in view, as well as a general obligation not to infringe individual human rights.[77] The discretion afforded to the Community is clearly broad: the Court in *ADBHU* stated that Community measures were reviewable only if they were manifestly inappropriate having regard to the objective being pursued.[78]

The Member States' Interests: Article 36 and Mandatory Requirements

Similarly Member State restrictions can be justified according to a list of interests exhaustively listed in Article 36.[79] The extension of Article 30 implied in *Dassonville* lead the Court to establish a further non-exhaustive list of mandatory requirements which might also justify unilateral action.[80] The *Danish Bottles* case[81] has confirmed that the protection of the environment is a mandatory requirement. It is clear that measures taken in pursuit of Article 36 or the mandatory requirements may not be discriminatory.[82] Nonetheless in certain circumstances different treatment of imported products may be justified according to objective criteria provided equivalent measures are taken with respect to domestically produced products.[83]

---

[74] *ADBHU*, above n 10, 549.

[75] Directive 75/439 on Waste Oils; see the *ADBHU* judgment, ibid, 549.

[76] Above n 25.

[77] This is confirmed by Art 3b of the Treaty: 'Any action by the Community shall not go beyond what is necessary to achieve the objectives of this Treaty'.

[78] 331/88 *The Queen v Ministry of Agriculture ex P FEDESA & Others* [1990] ECR 4032.

[79] Art 36: 'The provisions of Arts 30–34 shall not preclude prohibitions or restrictions on imports, exports or goods in transit justified on grounds of public morality, public policy or public security, the protection of health and the life of humans, animals or plants; the protection of national treasures possessing artistic, historic or archaeological value; or the protection of industrial or commercial property. Such prohibitions shall not however constitute a means of arbitrary discrimination or a disguised restriction on trade between Member States.'

[80] In *Cassis di Dijon*, above n 64. But the interests listed are justifications not reserved powers and are therefore amenable to review by the Court: 35/76 *Simmenthal* [1976] ECR 1871.

[81] 302/86 *Commission v Denmark* [1986] ECR 4607.

[82] The second sentence of Art 36 and, for example, *Gilli and Andres* [1980] ECR 2071 confirm the same limitation on action taken in pursuance of a mandatory requirement: 'it is only where rules which apply without discrimination to both domestic and imported products may be justified as necessary in order to satisfy imperative requirements that they may constitute an exception to the requirements arising under Article 30'.

[83] 4/75 *Rewe-Zentralfinanz eGmbH v Landwirtschaftskammer* [1975] ECR 843: 'different treatment of imported and domestic products based on the need to prevent the spread of harmful organisms could not be regarded as arbitrary discrimination if effective measures are taken in order to prevent the distribution of contaminated

In contrast with the position internally, in the external sphere the right of Member States to take independent protective action is uncertain. The Treaty appears to provide that the Member States are at once required not to agree external trade measures outside the Community framework, but may introduce independent trade restrictions in respect of internal trade. In practice power is delegated to the states acting as trustees of the Community interest; Regulation 288/82[84] provides that Member States may introduce restrictions on grounds similar to those listed in Article 36 but nonetheless there is some uncertainty as to whether this includes environment protection.[85]

Community harmonisation retains as a purpose the harmonisation of national stand-ards justified by Article 36 and mandatory requirements at a Community level, and once this legislation has been adopted it appears to restrict or extinguish recourse to Article 36 in so far as it is exhaustive.[86] The adoption of general provisions authorising the retention or adoption of more stringent measures apparently precludes this restriction in certain circumstances but the Community cannot add to the discretion afforded to the Member States under Article 36 or the Mandatory Requirements.[87]

Discrimination and the Principles of Environmental Action

It has been assumed that the principles of environmental action detailed in Article 130r(2) had a limited, if any, legal effect. The *Wallonia* case[88] provides an interesting precedent for the use of one of these principles to modify the operation of the general non-discrimina-tion requirement relating to measures restrictive of trade.[89] Though no express reference is made to the integration requirement the case appears to mark the first positive integration of environmental protection requirements into the definition and implementation of the Community's other policies.

In the *Wallonia* case a blanket ban on import of non-hazardous waste into the province of Wallonia was upheld by the Court. Much of the judgment was concerned with whether waste amounted to a 'good' subject to the provisions of Article 30. The Court determined that it was and gave little consideration to necessity and proportionally, merely noting that the influx of waste into Wallonia was a serious problem. Most controversially, the non-discrimination requirement was held inapplicable on the grounds that waste originating

---

domestic products and if there is reason to believe in particular on the basis of previous experience that there is a risk of the harmful organism spreading if no inspection is held on importation'.

[84] See the replacement of national with Community quotas see Kapteyn and van Themaat, above n 62, 803. Regulations 288/82, 1765/82 and 2603/69 include national safeguard clauses similar to Art 36.

[85] Demeret, 'Environmental Policy and Commercial Policy: The Emergence of Trade Related Environmental Measures (TREMS) in the External Relations of the European Community' in Maresceu (ed), *The European Community's Commercial Policy after 1992: The Legal Dimension* (Martinus Nijhoff, 1993) 315–19 and 346–47.

[86] 29/87 *Denkavit v Danish Minister for Agriculture* [1988] ECR 2965; 169/89 *Gourmeterne van den Burg BV* [1990] ECR 2143, para 8; 2/90 *Wallonia* [1993] CMLR 365 (see the rather restrictive interpretation of Art 14 of the Birds Directive in the *Scottish Grouse* case, above n 38), as the ability to adopt more stringent standards is confirmed in the Treaty text which is superior to secondary legislation adopted under it (Art 130t). More stringent standards are still required to be consistent with the treaty (Arts 130t and 100a(4)).

[87] *De Peijper* [1976] ECR 613–40, para 31.

[88] *(Wallonia Waste) Commission v Belgium* [1993] Common Market Law Reports 365.

[89] For a comparable case in the United States where a waste import ban was ruled discriminatory see *Philadelphia v New Jersey* 437 US 617 (1978).

outside Wallonia was legally distinguishable from waste originating within Wallonia by reference to the proximity principle recognised in Article 130r(2) of the Treaty.

The Court failed to deal with Advocate-General Jacob's observation that proximity had not been expressly incorporated in the Wallonian legislation giving grounds to his opinion that the regional ban was not sufficient to claim the benefit of the principle.[90] The argument appears to be that either proximity was not the interest actually pursued by the legislation or, alternatively, that the regional ban was not proximate enough to satisfy such a justification. It appears to be conceded that if proximity is relevant to justification for a restriction of trade it would be difficult to rule a measure unjustified simply because it is not sufficiently restrictive of trade.[91] A rule as to the appropriate geographic scope of a waste transport ban might ultimately encourage greater environmental protection but imply a harmonisation of the size and authority of local and regional authorities dealing with waste and invalidate many imperfect measures along the way.

In the same judgment the Court ruled that national legislation might not be applied against provisions of a directive which provided an exhaustive regime for inter-state trade in hazardous waste. A breach *by the Community* of the proximity principle in this case was neither argued nor considered. As a result, and a matter of some criticism, the more hazardous waste remained subject to a more liberal trade regime.

Necessity and Proportionality: Relating the Restriction to the Interest

Two principles directed towards the relationship between the objective authorising a restriction and the means adopted to do so and a test comparing objectives are often rolled into one.[92] In fact proportionality encompasses at least three separate tests factors.[93]

- *Effectiveness*: that the measure is sufficient to achieve the stated objective (and in that sense is necessary to achieve it).[94]
- *Minimum restrictiveness*: requires that the least restrictive effective option is adopted to achieve the stated objective.
- *Proportionality in the strict sense*: which balances not the means to the ends but two ends, where the means adopted to enforce one objective are considered against the seriousness of the infringement of an alternative objective of equal or other value.

It is apparent that measures must show a reasoned relationship to the interest pursued.

---

[90] Citing perhaps the requirement that there should be equivalent treatment of domestic products having the same harmful effects: *Rewe-Zentralfinanz v Landwirtschaftskammer*, above n 83, 843–63. The important point was proximity allowed discrimination on grounds of origin and not the environmentally deleterious character of the waste per se.

[91] It might be argued that a ban at city level would affect intra-Community trade less directly than one effected at state or regional borders and it is not clear whether a ban at national level say in Luxembourg could be supported by the principle expounded in the judgment.

[92] *Buitoni*, above n 11, defines a proportionate measure as 'what is appropriate and necessary to attain the objective sought'.

[93] Schwarz, *European Administrative Law* (Sweet & Maxwell, 1992).

[94] *Cassis de Dijon*, above n 61, 'Obstacles to movement within the Community must be accepted insofar as those provisions may be recognised as necessary in order to satisfy mandatory requirements'.

Establishing this is a matter of some complexity. Both an objective test, based on the actual effects of a supposed restriction, and a subjective test, which looks only to the interest pursued by the legislator, have their attractions.[95] However, the Court is extremely restricted in its capacity to examine factual evidence and relies for the most part on the formal reasoning for a particular measure supplied by the Community or the Member State.[96] The objective test is theoretically the more verifiable but requires the greatest factual input. The subjective test requires that the Court look into the 'mind' of the legislature but even where there is a duty to give reasons for a measure these may be disguised. The real motivation behind the subjective approach is the detection of some failure underlying the reasoning supplied. It is suggested that the terms arbitrary and disguised restriction ought to be interpreted in this light.

The difficulties encountered in establishing an objective standard of environmental protection recur in this context, as assessing the formal necessity of a particular action to achieve the interest requires some appraisal of the standard implied by the interest itself. As already commented upon, an objective standard is difficult to come by. It is submitted that whether a particular standard is justified or not in the interests of environmental protection ultimately must be within the discretion of the legislator to determine. If it is inappropriate to substitute the judgment of the Court for that of the political authorities in one context it must be so in another.[97] If not, environmental protection is as capable of becoming a pre-emptive and directly effective norm as any other.

Nevertheless statements in *ADBHU* that the Community 'cannot go beyond the inevitable restrictions which are justified by the pursuit of an objective standard of protection'[98] seem to suggest that an objective standard is available. Subsequently the Court has managed to avoid the problem directly and has given contradictory signals. The judgment in *Danish Bottles* seems to suggest that there is a reasonable standard of protection to which the Member States will be held. In the *Wallonia* case[99] the objective justification of a trade ban and its relative justification when compared with possible less restrictive measures was accepted by the Court without discussion.[100]

Generally speaking, Community law recognises some discretion whereby Member States may choose to apply standards in pursuit of recognised interests. However as 'such standards cannot be determined unilaterally by the Member States',[101] this discretion is reviewable according to Community law. The level of discretion appears to vary according to the interest pursued.[102]

For example, with regard to human health (an objective of environmental protection) Member States have a wide margin of discretion. In particular the health and the life of

---

[95] In 40/82 *Commission v UK Poultry* [1982] ECR 2793 the real purpose was not to protect health but to protect domestic production.

[96] Art 190 requires that Community measures be reasoned.

[97] Kramer, 'Environmental Protection and Article 30' (1993) 30 CMLR 111, 123 is of the opinion that Member States are free to choose the level of protection.

[98] Para 15 of the judgment.

[99] *Re Imports of Waste EC Commission v Belgium* (1993) 66(8) CMLR 365. See Hancier and Sevenster (1993) 30 *Common Market Law Review* 351.

[100] Such as a licensing system as applied in the case of hazardous waste.

[101] 41/74 *Van Duyn v Home Office* [1974] ECR 1337.

[102] De Búrca above n 11; Sedemund, 'Statement on the Concept of Free Movement of Goods and the respect for National Action under Article 36 of the EEC Treaty' in Schwarze, *Discretionary Powers of the Member States in the Field of Economic Policies* (Baden-Baden, 1988); see 121/85 *Conegate* [1986] ECR 1007; 34/79 *Henn and Darby* [1979] ECR 3795.

humans rank first among their property or interests protected by Article 36 and it is for the Member States within the limits imposed by the Treaty – to decide on the degree of protection they intend to pursue and in particular how strict the checks to be carried out are[103] but even here the Court has suggested the discretion is limited according to objective factors by the requirement that measures may be adopted only in so far as necessary for the effective protection of health and life of humans.[104]

If the guarantee of free movement afforded by the Treaty is viewed as a presumption rather than an absolute standard of protection the problem can be approached as one relating to the onus and standard of proof necessary to rebut this presumption. It is clear in this sense that while the Community must raise evidence establishing the presumption, the onus of justifying trade restrictive measures lies with the Member States.[105]

It is clear that scientific evidence alone may not be sufficient to discharge the standard required. While a measure may be shown to be discriminatory if scientific evidence clearly establishes that there is no difference between products justifying discrimination on health grounds[106] establishing the positive and objective necessity of particular restrictions through scientific evidence can be extremely difficult in many cases.[107] Innumerable factors militate against complete reliance on scientific evidence for environmental protection. The development of new processes and substances far outpaces adequate testing, even where testing the results cannot be reliably extrapolated to conditions in the field etc. The precautionary principle designed to meet these limitations seems to demand at least a certain discretion for Member States where a scientific assessment of effects and risks result in uncertainty. In consequence the application of precaution to the necessity test would provide that uncertainty is in itself a justification for action in restraint of trade.

Several cases in the area of product standards appear to confirm this approach – a recognition of uncertainty as a factor in establishing the Member State discretion to apply trade restrictive measures Indeed the application of proportionality to test measures adopted on this justification risks becoming meaningless.[108] Nevertheless other cases imply that states must at least take steps to establish the uncertainty upon which they rely before a precautionary approach may be relied upon.[109] The adoption of a duty on individuals to establish that there are no harmful effects prior to release of a new substance into the environment is therefore precluded.[110]

---

[103] Case 174/82 *Sandoz BV* [1983] ECR 2445, para 19.

[104] Sedemund, above n 102, 31–32; 104/75 *De Peijper* [1976] ECR 613 showed liberal interpretation of risk which was ruled genuine if claimed one life over 20 years.

[105] The onus is on the Member State to prove justification of necessity: 227/83 *Van Bennekom* [1983] ECR 3883, para 40: 'It is for the national authorities to demonstrate in each case that the marketing of the product in question creates a serious risk to health'.

[106] 124/81 *Commission v UK* [1983] ECR 205. Retreatment of UHT milk was not justified as the technical data showed that it made no difference to the milk.

[107] Sedemund, above n 102.

[108] See generally Sedemund, ibid; see particularly Case 53/80 *Kaasfabriek Eyssen* [1981] ECR 409, paras 13 and 14; 94/83 *Heijn* [1984] ECR 3280; 97/83 *Melkunte* [1984] ECR 2367, 2385.

[109] 178/84 *Van Bennekom* (1988) 35 CMLR 1; 304/84 *Muller* [1980] ECR 1511; 178/84 *German Beer* [1987] ECR 1227: 'it is for the national authorities to demonstrate in each case that the marketing of the product in question creates a serious risk to public health'.

[110] *Sandoz*, above n 103: 'in so far as there are uncertainties at the present state of scientific research it is for the Member States in the absence of harmonisation to decide what degree of protection of the health and life of humans they intend to assure having regard however to the requirements of the free movement of goods within the Community and their limits under the EEC Treaty: here a requirement that manufacturers supply proof that a particular additive was safe was found unlawful' (para 24). However, in *Denkavit Futtermittell*, above n 66, the

The concept of technical need for a particular additive in a foodstuff may reduce still further the importing state's discretion.[111] In *German Beer* Advocate General Slynn adopted a broad interpretation of this concept.[112] The test in *German Beer* points to a case-by-case assessment of particular substances to establish the legality of a ban or restriction in use. Sedemund points out that, contrary to a common understanding of precaution, the solution adopted in a case-by-case assessment of risk still ignores the possible cumulative effects of chemicals and disallows a policy based on reducing an overall risk to the public by a limitation on the amount of chemicals in the food supply.[113]

Given the reality of these factors a full integration of the precautionary principle suggests less reliance on a scientific assessment of risk to justify restrictive measures in the absence of evidence establishing that no harm may result not only from the substance in question but a clearer recognition that the presence or absence of a scientific assessments of risk cannot on its own be relied upon to establish the legality or otherwise of Member State action.[114] The development of a comprehensive framework through which the law may deal with scientific uncertainty and avoid an over-reliance on mechanistic quantitative assessments of risks remains a matter of some controversy world-wide.

Acting in the Community Interest and Finding an Appropriate Legal Basis[115]

In contrast with the GATT system the pre-emptive provisions of the Treaty concerning the customs union and the internal market are supplemented by provisions creating an interest in measures which supplement and support the basic scheme. The Community is expressly provided with the power to adopt measures for the establishment and functioning of the Market and the regulation of international trade. The interaction between

---

Court failed to decide whether a blanket assumption that additives were harmful unless the contrary was proved amounted to a unjustified restriction on trade.

[111] *Sandoz*, ibid, para 19.

[112] *German Beer*, above n 109. The case involved additives in beer. Where the chemical was authorised in another state for use in imported products, the importing state must authorise the chemical in question: (1) provided international scientific data shows it to be harmless to individuals with dietary habits of its population, or (2) if it meets a genuine technical need and there is a procedure for authorisation, the state has taken steps to establish whether it is harmful and action is available for refusal of authorisation. Technical need is to be determined with reference to the imported product.

[113] Sedemund, above n 102, 30.

[114] In the context of Art 100a(4) and the Court's approval of national standards under that provision. The recent *Pentachlorophenol* case, Case 41/93 *French Republic v Commission of the European Communities* [1994] ECR 1829, appears to confirm the requirement that measures must be legally if not scientifically justified or reasoned. As the reasons given by the Commission for confirmation in this case were ruled insufficient, the judgment does not in itself rule out a precautionary approach.

[115] Bradley, 'The European Court and the Legal Basis of Community Legislation' (1988) 13 *Common Market Law Review* 379. Barents, 'The Internal Market and some Observations on the Legal Basis of Community Legislation' (1993) 30 *Common Market Law Review* 85; Geradin, 'Trade and Environment: The Community Framework and National Environmental Standards' [1993] *Yearbook of European Law* 151; Lenearts, 'Some Reflections on the Separation of Powers in the European Community' (1991) 28 *Common Market Law Review* 11; N Emiliou, 'Opening Pandora's Box: The Legal Basis of Community Measures before the Court of Justice' (1994) 19 *European Law Review* 488.

trade provisions and environmental principles is therefore not limited merely to that of pre-emptive norms and public interest (at whatever level) described above.

The definition of the Community task detailed in Article 2 of the Treaty is supplemented by particular provisions which confirm the Community's powers to adopt measures which will ultimately contribute to its attainment.[116] The interpretative value of Article 2 may modify or reinforce these provisions in the ultimate attempt to ensure a holistic interpretation of the whole Treaty, but the difficulty in reconciling individual policies suggests that the final balance of measures adopted in fulfilment of Article 2 remain political choices open to the Community institutions to investigate.[117] Nonetheless the Court maintains a policing role even in the balance of legislative choice through its insistence that an express choice of legal basis is necessary and that this choice must be exercised according to objective factors amenable to judicial review.

The diversification of legal bases for Community action with the adoption of the Single European Act and reinforced at Maastricht has presented the Court with a clear choice between legislative models and little guidance on the factors relevant to their respective application. Initially at least the Court has hesitated in response to the increased complexity of the system and encountered considerable difficulty in the identification and application of objective factors for the review of the selection of particular bases. Case law suggests that the addition of new legal bases to the Treaty have initiated a process of adaptation by the Court.

As already mentioned, in addition to the interposition of additional legal bases, the Community's task has recently been recast by Maastricht to reflect a more equal balancing of economic and environmental considerations.[118] The approach taken is closely mirrored in the preamble to the agreement establishing the World Trade Organization.[119] The Treaty is therefore ambiguous as to the model whereby a sustainable balance of interests may be achieved. It recognises both a system of separate bases dedicated to ostensibly distinct interests and the necessity of integration through the obligation to integrate environmental protection requirements into all policies. The following sections are intended to show both the inherent complexity of operating a series of distinct bases and the particular difficulties arising from the interposition of an obligation to integrate on an already difficult system.

Procedural and Substantive Consequences of the Choice of Legal Basis

The question of choice of legal basis for Community measures is fundamental for two basic reasons concerned with preserving the legitimacy and coherence of Community action, each elements of the rule of law.

---

[116] In addition, (III) Art 43 (Agriculture) and (IV) Art 76 (Transport) may be mentioned as regulatory bases designed to promote integration in particular sectors. (V) Art 130s in common with (VI) Art 118 and others are bases which are dedicated towards social, political or perhaps ethical interests and do not directly promote integration.

[117] See Art 3 listing the Community policies 'for the purposes set out in Article 2 the Community's activities shall include . . .'.

[118] Art 2.

[119] Preamble to WTO Agreement; see above.

First, the requirement of legitimacy and rationality, derived from Article 3b[120] and Article 190[121] of the Treaty, relies on establishing the appropriate Treaty basis which both delimits Community competence (at least theoretically) and determines the division of powers through the procedures according to which measures designed for particular ends may be adopted – unanimously or by qualified majority vote, with parliamentary consultation, co-operation[122] or co-decision.[123] The exercise of a choice between bases is therefore politically charged and constitutionally important, and the courts review the principle method of policing the Communities division of powers.

Secondly, the choice of legal basis has substantive consequences with relation to the nature of the legal order thereby created and affects the coherence of Community law. There are several modes of policy: according to one framework there are those which are exclusive and unitary per se, such force being derived from the Treaty itself,[124] and those which are concurrent allowing Member State action, in accordance with the doctrine of pre-emption, only in so far as Community measures have not yet been adopted.[125] Recent amendments to the Treaty system have added another suggesting that the old assumption that many areas of concurrent policy would ultimately become exclusive by reason of legislative pre-emption has been abandoned.

First, several of the newer areas of policy expressly preserve the ability of Member States to adopt more stringent measures, a factor which the Court has ruled has a fundamental effect on the pre-emptive effect of measures adopted by the Community within the context of these policies.[126] Secondly, Article 3b provides that in non-exclusive areas the principle of subsidiarity applies, which would tend to entrench the concurrent nature of policies deemed not exclusive (though what exclusive means in this sense has yet to be interpreted).

Balancing Pre-emptive Norms Interests and the Trade Environment Relationship

In the ebb and flow of interpretative relationships between various elements of the Treaty system three principle tensions may be described.

Pre-emptive Norm and Interest

First, a tension between 'negative harmonisation', through the disapplication of national rules, and positive harmonisation, through the adoption of Community measures, rests in the relative interpretation of Article 30, and the pre-emptive norm of free trade it contains, and, the Community power to establish the market through legislation detailed in Arti-

---

[120] 'The Community shall act within the limits of the powers conferred upon it by this treaty and of the objectives assigned to it therein.'

[121] '[Measures] adopted . . . shall state the reasons on which they are based . . .'

[122] A procedure detailed in Art 189c.

[123] Detailed in Art 189b. Under TFEU the legislative procedures for approximation measures (Art 114) and most environmental measures (Art 192) are now the same. But the choice of legal base remains important since there are significant legal differences as to the extent to which Member States can adopt stricter national measures.

[124] Eg the common commercial policy or aspects of marine fisheries conservation.

[125] Such as the Environment Policy.

[126] Opinion 2/91 ILO No 170 [1993] Common Market Law Reports 800.

cles 100 and 100a.[127] There is a direct relationship between the extent to which national measures are rendered inapplicable by Article 30 and saved by Article 36 or mandatory requirements and the extent to which measures may be adopted which have as their object the establishment of the internal market. Articles 100 and 100a must be necessary only to the extent that the measures it is proposed to harmonise are not already invalidated automatically. Thus the legislative space for the Community and the Member States in environmental matters is as has been described in the first section limited by the extent of Article 30 and recognised interests justifying departure from this rule.[128]

Exclusive and Concurrent Policies

Secondly, there is a tension between two models of harmonisation within the Community system. The first is a system of progressive adaptation of national rules to conditions of absolute uniformity necessary to ensure non-discrimination and competitive equality between states in a single market upon which the trade policy is based. The second is a system of minimum standards with a concurrent freedom on the part of Member States to adopt more stringent standards with regard to a particular interest where diverse situations are recognised to require a diversity of solutions.

Regulatory and Deregulatory Interests

The third tension lies in implicit regulatory and deregulatory elements of the Treaty system: Harmonisation of Law on whatever basis necessarily includes both deregulatory and regulatory elements. Nonetheless the Court has attempted to draw a distinction between harmonisation pursuing the establishment and functioning of the market which is deregulatory, and harmonisation directed at environmental protection which is necessarily regulatory or restrictive of trade.[129] Whether this can be properly justified given that the trade basis (Article 100a) expressly recognised that harmonisation may have regulatory effects, and more generally it is submitted that even liberalising measures leave intact a degree of market restriction justified in terms of some public interest.

These modes of legal order attributed to the interests represented in the several Community policies reflect not only the division of powers between the Community institutions and between the Community and the Member States, but also fundamental conceptions as to the nature of the policies themselves which repeat and reflect the interaction of the trade norm and the environmental interest discussed above. Of course each individual policy is subject to general requirements as to necessity and proportionality as well as the operation of general principles of law recognised by the Community as embodying fundamental rights, but in addition, the interaction and formal integration of principles governing these policies also present possible limitations on their scope and effect. The Court of Justice in refining its approach to Article 30 and establishing a case law on the choice of legal basis has fluctuated in its approach to all of these relationships.[130]

---

[127] See the extension implied by *Cassis de Dijon*, above n 61.
[128] Remembering always that Art 30 is pre-eminent but still only one of the Market rules which might invalidate state or individual action with an environmental motivation. See particularly R Jacobs, 'EC Competition Policy and the Protection of the Environment' [1993] *Legal Issues of European Integration* 37.
[129] Case 155/91 *Commission v Council* [1991] ECR 2867.
[130] H Somsen on C155/91 [1993] *Common Market Law Review* 121 and 29 (1992) 140–51, *Titanium Dioxide Commission v Council* [1991] ECR 2867. Barents, above n 115, 92, shows problems of delimitation.

The Legal Bases Available

The key legal bases relevant to environmental policy can, in summary, be seen to fall into three groups:

The Trade Bases

These are divided into two bases of general application dedicated to external and internal trade respectively and several internal bases covering sectoral markets.

- Article 113: the Common Commercial Policy dedicated to measures regulating the Community's external trade. Member States are precluded from adopting such measures unilateraterally (it is formally exclusive) and must rely on the Community to adopt measures falling within the scope of this policy. The Community may adopt these by qualified majority voting in the Council and there is only limited parliamentary involvement.
- Articles 100–100c: in effect several bases dedicated to the establishment and continued functioning of the common or internal market. The Community may adopt harmonisation measures affecting the market by co-decision of parliament and the council (the later acting by qualified majority voting)

Already the system provides scope for difficulty in determining the basis applicable to measures which affect external and internal trade simultaneously.

Sectoral Markets

The market is recognised to have several components, some of which serve certain social or economic ends requiring a separate definition and set of objectives principles. Among these are Agriculture (Article 43), Transport (Article 78) and Taxation (Article 99). These sectoral bases are recognised to be *lex specialis* to Articles 100–100c, incorporating measures which though dedicated to establishing a functioning market, affect or are directed at objectives prescribed in these policies. Here again there is potential ground for dispute as each basis is subject to a different procedural regime.[131]

General Non-market Bases

Including Harmonisation of Social Policy (Article 118) and Fiscal Measures (Article 99).

---

[131] Community rules on competition, state aids and free movement of services, capital and persons should not be forgotten, each of which prescribe a particular freedom or substantive rule and recognise the possibility of derogation to various extents.

The Environmental Basis

Article 130r provides an alternative focus for regulation and formally encompasses measures directed at four objectives. The distinction between the basis and some but not all of the market-oriented bases is that measures adopted under the policy are formally, as a requirement of the Treaty, minimum stringency measures and cannot pre-empt more stringent measures consistent with the Treaty. The policy is also subject to a subsidiarity requirement (indeed between the SEA and Maastricht it was the only policy subject to this requirement). Environmental policy specifies no less than four possible procedures for the adoption of measures. Unanimity is preserved for some ill-defined policy areas, though the Council may agree to ordinary qualified majority voting for these, co-decision is prescribed for the adoption of action programmes, co-operation for all other measures.

Finding Objective Factors for Review

The central difficulty with a system of functionally defined legal bases that are procedurally distinct is that many measures formally dedicated to one function in fact effect several. The statement that the choice of legal basis must be made according to objective factors amenable to judicial review,[132] while an essential element of the rule of law, results in considerable difficulty given the way in which the scope of individual bases is defined. An approach based on ascertaining legislative intention or determining the primary objective according to the content or effects of particular provisions will only rarely provide objective factors upon which the choice of legal basis can be exercised or reviewed. A centre of gravity or primary purpose test has been applied under the fiction that in most cases a most important objective may be identified. Even if this were true, this rule remains open to legislative manipulation as legislation might be drafted not according to the needs of different situations but according to which mix of provisions might reasonably be adopted pursuant to a favourable legal basis. As a result, the Commission, the Council, the Member States, and latterly the Parliament have been provided with ample room for argument before the Court. The Court's search for a definition has resulted in controversy and uncertainty. Arguably the Court has not yet managed to define these factors with sufficient certainty, leading in particular to a rather confused division between the different environmental and unitary trade modes of regulation.

The Effect of the Integration Principle

Attempts by the Treaty draftsmen to rationalise the system have perhaps ultimately served only to muddy the waters. The integration principle,[133] the legal effects of which have yet to be examined by the Court, at once promotes environment protection and yet has undermined at least initially the separate legal basis for environment of which it forms a

---

[132] *Re Generalised Tariff Preferences EC Commission v Council* [1987] ECR 1483.

[133] Art 130r(2) states that environmental protection requirements must be integrated into the definition and implementation of other policies.

part.[134] The general requirement that environmental protection requirements be integrated into the definition and implementation of other policies has allowed other bases to be used for this purpose. Article 100a (the basis for internal market harmonisation) expressly refers to environmental objectives and preserves the ability of Member States to maintain more stringent measures even after harmonisation.[135] On the other hand the environment policy is not entirely removed from taking economic factors into account. General integration can work both ways, as Article 130r(3) suggests[136] and the broad freedom granted to Member States to adopt more stringent measures under Article 130 t is more specifically limited by the words 'not incompatible with this Treaty', generally accepted to refer to trade requirements.

The Meandering Balance of Interpretations

Three distinct phases or approaches can be discerned in the Court's approach to striking the balance between legal bases, each of which displays not only the difficulties arising from an attempt to impose rational grounds for review on a system of functional bases but a degree of political activism on the part of the Court in the Community's interest.

An Expansive Interpretation of Trade Objectives

There are two factors driving an inclusive interpretation of the legal basis governing trade. First the Court has always been reluctant to find particular measures ultra vires the Community and has consequently adopted a broad interpretation of Community powers generally. Secondly, the imperative to preserve a unity of conditions in the market and particularly external trade relations has supported an expansive interpretation of the scope of the trade bases in particular, the consequences of which have been to preclude unilateral action by the Member States externally.

Article 113 and the Inclusive Interpretation[137]

There are several statements by the Court that the legal basis for international commercial policy incorporates the power to adopt measures regulating international trade in other interests.[138] The definition of the common commercial policy established to regulate external trade expressly includes the qualification that it should be 'harmoniously achieved'. One might ask harmonious with what? Though the phrase may be adequately

---

[134] *Titanium Dioxide*, above n 130.

[135] Art 100a(4) and Case 41/93 *French Republic v Commission* 17 May 1994 Commission decision confirming provisions annulled. See H Somsen, 'Applying More National Environmental Laws after Harmonisation' [August/September 1994] *European Environmental Law Review* 238.

[136] In preparing its policy on the environment, the Community shall take account of 'environmental conditions in the various regions of the Community; the economic and social development of the Community as a whole and the balanced development of its regions'.

[137] See generally Bourgeois, above n 9.

[138] Demeret, above n 85, 355 and the instrumental character of Art 113.

explained in terms of preserving some internal harmony in the move towards a liberalisation of external trade, the fact that the conditions of trade are to be regulated expressly recognises that the external trade policy at least has a regulatory as well as a deregulatory focus.[139]

In any event the Court of Justice has ruled that while pursuing the objectives of external trade the Community might also pursue objectives not simply promoting the deregulation of world trade. The *International Rubber* opinion confirmed that the establishment of a regulatory system for commodities trading under UNCTAD fell within the Community's Common Commercial Policy even though the instruments adopted did not form part of the traditional armoury of trade instruments.[140] In effect the instrumental theory of legal basis was displaced in favour of a teleological theory of legal basis.[141]

In the Generalised Tariff Preferences (Preferential Treatment itself is not GATT compatible but nonetheless agreed to by the parties) the Court confirmed that development objectives might indeed fall within the CCP. In this case the Council argued that the aims of the measure were developmental and as such went beyond the aims of the Commercial Policy.[142] The Court, expressly noting that the Community's aims included the harmonious development of world trade[143] and developments in international law,[144] suggested that such objectives must be incorporated into trade objectives. If this were not the case the CCP would become nugatory over time as trade instruments developed.[145] It must be noted that development co-operation has since achieved an independent status with the adoption of further provisions in 1992 at Maastricht.[146]

Even after the adoption of a separate environmental basis including the competence to conclude international agreements the Court continued the trend by confirming that measures touching on aspects of environment protection may also be adopted on the

---

[139] Art 110: by establishing a customs union between themselves. Member States aim to contribute, in the common interest, to the harmonious development of world trade, the progressive abolition of restrictions on international trade and the lowering of customs barriers.

[140] Opinion 1/78 *International Rubber*, [45]: 'Art 113 empowers the Community to formulate a commercial policy based on uniform principles, thus showing that the question of external trade must be governed from a wide point of view and not only having regard to the administration of precise systems such as customs and quantitative restrictions. The same conclusion may be deduced from the fact that the enumeration in Art 113 of the subjects covered by commercial policy . . . is conceived as a non-exhaustive enumeration which must not, as such, close the door to the application in the Community context of any other process intended to regulate external trade.' And at p 2917 a measure . . . 'Must be assessed having regard to its essential objective rather than in terms of individual clauses of an altogether subsidiary or ancillary nature'.

[141] See Advocate General Lenz [1987] ECR 1493, paras 57 and 58, objective and subjective tests: is it a measure which aims to influence and at the same time alter the form of world trade? Is trade objectively influenced?

[142] Generalised Tariff Preferences 45/86 *Commission v Council* [1987] ECR 1493 'reflects a new concept of international trade relations in which development aims to play a major role' [18].

[143] Para 17.

[144] Para 17. The link between trade and development has become progressively stronger in modern international relations. It has been recognised in the context of the United Nations, notably by UNCTAD, and in the context of GATT in particular through the incorporation in the GATT of PArt IV entitled trade and development.

[145] Para 20.

[146] Art 130u. The Community policy in the sphere of development co-operation which shall be complementary to the policies pursued by the Member States, shall foster the sustainable economic and social development of developing countries, and more particularly the most disadvantaged of them; the smooth and gradual integration of developing countries into the world economy; the Community and the Member States shall comply with the Commitments and take account of the objectives they have approved in the context of the United Nations and other competent international organisations. Art 130v. The Community shall take into account the objectives referred to in 130u in the policies that it implements which are likely to affect developing countries.

basis of Article 113.[147] In the *Chernobyl* case[148] the Greek government (in a minority on a vote to adopt restrictions on the import of certain agricultural products) challenged the ability of the Community to adopt such a measure on the basis of Article 113. As the matter concerned the protection of public health (an objective of the environment policy) the Greek government argued that such a measure should have been on the basis of 130s (which incidentally required a unanimous decision). Nonetheless the Court found the measure rightly adopted on the basis that (1) the measure was intended to regulate trade between the EC and not member countries (2) the regulation established uniform import rules (3) Article 130r(2) established that environment protection might be part of other policies; (4) and Article 130r-t left intact existing powers to adopt under other bases including this one.

In the environmental sphere there has been a marked reluctance to accept that environmentally related trade measures fall within the Common Commercial Policy. Member States have feared recognition that essential elements of an environmental policy should fall within the ambit of an exclusive policy precluding Member State action. Equally trade policy specialists within the Commission have feared that in recognising an exception the unity of the trade policy has been undermined. Though there have been no cases expressly covering the point, all international environmental agreements have been adopted on a basis other than Article 113.[149]

In addition the Community has adopted unilateral trade restrictions despite concerns as to the legality of some provisions under GATT. Trade measures unilaterally adopted by the Community include; measures to protect whale and cetacean products,[150] seal pups,[151] animals trapped by inhumane methods.[152] In each case there was some argument over the appropriate legal basis and in each, save the last, it was concluded that Article 113 was inappropriate. The Whales and Cetacean Products Directive was proposed using 113 as a basis, but German and Danish arguments that the restrictions were moral rather than environmental prevailed.[153] The Directive was adopted under Article 235 in the days before Article 130s.[154] Britain had pressed for the introduction of the ban partly on the ground of the uncertain legality of its earlier unilateral ban. The Seals Directive was also proposed using Article 113 as a basis but eventually was adopted on the basis of Article 235. The Leghold Trap Directive is the latest in this series of measures and was again

---

[147] 62/88 *Chernobyl* [1990] ECR I-3743.

[148] Ibid.

[149] International Agreements with a trade character adopted under Art 130s: – 88/540 [1988] OJ L297 Vienna Convention for the Protection of the Ozone Layer and the Montreal Protocol Adopted under Art 130s – 81/69 [1981] OJ L252 Washington Convention on International Trade in Endangered Species (note the preamble) Art 235 – 82/461 EEC [1982] OJ L210 Convention on the Conservation of Migratory Species of Wild animals: with Art 235 as a basis – 93/98/EEC [1993] OJ L39 Basle Convention on Transboundary Movements of Waste, with Art 130s as a basis – only one has been adopted on the basis of Art 113 – International Tropical Timber Agreement [1985] OJ L313, 9; 85/424 [1985] OJ L236, 8.

[150] 348/81 [1981] OJ L39 Council regulations on common rules for imports of whales or other cetacean products; 3786/81 [1981] OJ 1377 Commission regulation laying down provisions for the implementation of common rules. These rules were subsumed in CITES Regulation 3626/82.

[151] Directives 83/129, 85/444 and 89/370 concerning the importation into Member States of skins of certain seal pups and products derived therefrom.

[152] Leghold Traps 3254/91 [1991] OJ L308 adopted on a dual basis Art 113 and 130s.

[153] See Haigh, *Manual of European Environmental Policy* (Longman/IEEP, 1992) 9.3–3.

[154] See Haigh, ibid, 9.4–3.

proposed on the basis of 113 but interestingly was finally adopted on a dual legal basis thus preserving a non-exclusive element.[155]

Articles 100 and 100a – An Inclusive Interpretation of the Market

Internally, in the absence of an express power to regulate for environmental protection, those provisions designed to authorise harmonisation regulations affecting trade in the Member States became the subject of an expansive interpretation so as to include the power to regulate trade in pursuit of a rather broader range of objectives. In a sense the shift in emphasis (or more properly definition) was inevitable as the process of replacing national measures with Community harmonisation measures inevitably involved the implicit adoption by the Community through its harmonisation measures of the policy underlying the national regulations it sought to replace. Arguably it was legally justifiable in the treaty's requirement that the essentially economic objectives of the Treaty be harmoniously achieved.[156]

Of particular relevance to the current discussion, in the absence of an express basis for environmental measures, such measures were adopted under Articles 100 and 235. Arguably certain environmental measures 'directly affect the establishment or functioning of the common market' therefore satisfying the objectives prescribed in the former, and in so far as this was not so they were 'measures necessary to attain one of the objectives' where a power did not already exist. This latter proposition is based on a development of language in Article 2 defining the core task of the Community to include the promotion of a 'harmonious development of economic activities' and to achieve 'a better standard of living'.

In a sense the recognition of the environmental interest as one of the elements required in such a harmonious development was also reflected in the recognition of additional mandatory requirements authorising trade restrictive measures following a broader interpretation of Article 30. The objective of the general interest authorising a modification to the operation of Article 30 in ABHU both legitimised Community environmental policy and led inevitably to recognition of the interest at national level through a mandatory requirement.

Again by analogy with external trade, even after the adoption of an express basis for environmental regulation, the Court took the view that environmental measures adopted at least partially with the aim of harmonising competitive distinctions in the Member States, ought in preference to be adopted under Article 100a.[157] In *Titanium Dioxide*[158] the Commission argued that the Directive concerned was more properly adopted under Article 130s than under 100a. The Court, while it agreed that the Directive pursued two interests

---

[155] 3254/91 [1991] OJ L308, 1.

[156] Art 2 before Maastricht amendments 'the harmonious development of economic activities throughout the Community, a continuous and balanced expansion, an increase in stability, an accelerated raising of the standard of living, and closer relations between the states belonging to the Community'.

[157] A burden on undertakings justifies harmonisation of national provisions – 9/79 *Re Detergents: EC Commission v Italy* [1980] ECR 1089; 92/79 *Re Fuel Directive: EC Commission v Italy* [1980] ECR 1115.

[158] *Commission v Council (Titanium Dioxide)* (1993) 68 CMLR 359.

simultaneously decided that where two relevant bases were available, though a measure ordinarily should be adopted pursuant to all relevant bases,[159] where the procedures were different and mutually incompatible, one basis had to be chosen. The Court settled on Article 100a and the co-operation procedure, as to adopt the measure under 130s alone would undermine the very substance of the guarantees afforded to Parliament in Article 100a under 100a. The Court took express comfort in the integration requirement which recognised that measures with an environmental component might be adopted pursuant to other bases.[160] The decision was much criticised as it appears to undermine the operation of 130s.

Recognising the Place of a Separate Basis

Nonetheless, in *Commission v Council*[161] the Waste Framework Directive was confirmed to fall under Article 130s rather than 100a and the internal market. The Court based its finding on the reasoning that the Directive restricted rather than promoted free movement and while it affected the operation of the market, these effects were ancillary to the main objective.

In common with the recent tendency to recognise that trade restrictive measures may be adopted under Article 130s where environmental protection is the primary purpose of the measure it appears to be accepted that 130s is also the basis for external environmentally motivated trade restrictions In *European Parliament v Council*.[162] While Parliament's right to challenge a waste regulation was denied on procedural grounds the Court confirmed the regulatory/facilitatory approach.

The Place of the Sectoral Markets and the Relationship between Internal and External Regulation

The recognition of particular interests or objectives pertaining to particular sectoral markets has also raised questions as to legal basis. The scope of operation of these policies has been determined on the basis that they form exceptions to the generality of the trade provisions. In the *Hormones* Case[163] a prohibition on growth promoters for fattening purposes was ruled to fall within Article 43, which could be interpreted to include aspects of the public interest as *lex specialis* to Article 100.[164] If a measure contributes to the objectives of Article 43 then this basis is sufficient.

As a result, so an argument goes, not only do these bases form a derogation to Article 100-100c (the general provisions) but also to Article 113. This is controversial not least because an assumption had arisen that the Common Commercial Policy represented the external face of all the community's economic competences at least. The ERTA confirmed

---

[159] Paras [17]–[18].

[160] At para 22.

[161] Case 155/91 *Commission v Council* (Waste Framework) [1993] ECR 939; noted by Nicolas de Sadeleer in (1993) 5 *Journal of Environmental Law* 295.

[162] Case 187/93 *EP v Council* Regulation of Waste Shipments [1994] ECR 2857.

[163] 68/86 *United Kingdom v Council* [1988] ECR 855; see also R Barents, 'Some Reflections on the Hormones Judgement' [1988] *Legal Issues of European Integration* 1–19.

[164] Völker, *Barriers to External and Internal Community Trade* (Europa Institute, 1993) 855–96.

that implied external competence was available with respect to all internal competences where this was necessary to fulfil the objectives of individual policies. In the *Veterinary Inspection* Case[165] the question whether Article 43, Article 100 or Article 113 was the appropriate basis was resolved in favour of Article 43.[166] It appears that Article 43 can be used for external trade rules as well as harmonisation of production and marketing agricultural products. In essence these measures served a dual purpose both the removal of distortions and public health.[167]

Trade-related Environmental Measures and the Uruguay Round Opinion

Demeret has argued that in consequence of *Chernobyl* and the *Titanium Dioxide* judgments. Trade Related Environmental Measures (TREMS) ought to be adopted on the basis of 113.[168] On the other hand, Volker[169] suggests that *Chernobyl was* a special case. Here the fact that there are two bases for the adoption of trade measures – one dealing with the internal the other with its external face – created a particular problem. He argues that in *Chernobyl* internal measures had been adopted under Article 31 of the Euratom Treaty which had no external equivalent requiring that Article 113 be chosen as a basis. Otherwise where measures govern internal and external trade simultaneously these are not matters falling within the ambit of Article 113 but fall to be adopted according to the internal basis.

However the recent Opinion 1/94 concerning the Uruguay Round of GATT seems to contradict even this. Here the EEC Court rejected Article 43 as the appropriate bass for provisions on phytosanitary measures. It ruled that such measures should be adopted under Article 113 on the grounds that in the case of this particular agreement the objectives it fulfilled were not of the Community's agriculture policy but that of the trade policy, namely a liberalisation in trade in Agricultural products.

Despite this, the general approach of adopting an inclusive interpretation to Article 113 suffers a general reverse, if not in principle then in practice.[170] Given the concentration on a teleological rather than an instrumental method of ascertaining the legal basis the classic problem looks set to continue. The practise of adopting trade measures with an environmental object pursuant to an environmental basis seems to remain legitimate, as does the adoption of measures intended to liberalise trade which have environmental consequences on the basis of Article 113. While the integration requirement formally requires that environmental protection requirements be incorporated into Article 113 as much as any other basis, the practical effect of the requirement to date must be doubted.

---

[165] 131/87 *Untied Kingdom v Quinal Health and Veterinary Inspections* [1989] ECR 3743.
[166] See also 11/88 *Commission v Council* [1989] ECR 3799.
[167] Ibid, paras 26, 27 and 28 of the judgment.
[168] Demeret, above n 85, 356–57. Nevertheless he does recognise that the direct regulation of trade was not an element of *Titanium Dioxide* which reduces its significance for the trade policy.
[169] Völker, above n 164, 187–89.
[170] Eg paras 40 and 41 concerning GATS and para 54 *et seq* on TRIPs; see generally Bourgeois, above n 9.

Conclusion

The growing jurisprudence of the Court of Justice concerning the choice of legal basis for environmentally related instruments can hardly be said to have brought clarity to the analysis, and, as we have argued, is unlikely to do so in that it is rooted in a classical functional model of separate policies in competition which fails to reflect current and future environmental reality. The concept of sustainable development, if it is to move beyond a mere political commitment, implies in the longer term a far more fundamental integration of an environmental perspective into economic and resource policies than has hitherto been proposed or imagined. We question whether the current constitutional and legal structure of the Treaty adequately reflects these challenges.

It might be argued – and no doubt will be at the forthcoming Inter-Governmental Conference – that if the procedures for adopting Community legislation were harmonised,[171] the political arguments concerning the correct legal basis of instruments would be largely removed. Yet, as we have tried to demonstrate, this in itself will not provide the answer. There remain substantive distinctions between exclusive and non-exclusive policies, which reflect differing principles and hierarchies of norms, and which will continue to give rise to tension. Nor does the mere expression of an overall goal of sustainable development (as already appears in the Treaty since Maastricht, albeit in rather garbled form) or the legal requirement to integrate environmental dimensions into other policy areas (as appears in Article 130R) satisfactorily deal with the problem, but glosses over underlying and more insidious distinctions in philosophy.

We have shown how certain aspects of trade-related principles within the Treaty, and especially Article 30, have been given pre-emptive legal status. One way forward would be to attribute to environmental protection requirements an enhanced status quite independent of specific Community environmental legislation and based on the development of principles of environmental protection and sustainable development.

Ultimately, these principles would provide a basis for the legal review of Community action, but also support the legal justification of national measures where these fall within the scope of Article 30. This process is not perhaps as controversial as might first appear, and can be said to have already begun in the recognition of the proximity and precautionary principles in recent case law on trade-restrictive measures.

This sort of development, however, still implies tensions and balancing acts. A more fundamental restructuring would recognise that the 'rational and prudent use of natural resources', one of the principles of Community environmental policy and inherent in the concept of sustainable development, is also or should be one of the aims of the market system which an economist would support. If such a principle were fully locked into the goals of the market one could envisage a situation where, say, both Community and national restrictions or measures which interfere with the attainment by the market of these objectives, could be legally challenged, both by individuals and governments. The true power of the Community legal structure would then be harnessed towards sustainable development. Such a vision may be too much to stomach for many involved in the process of Treaty development and change. Yet the fundamental philosophical differences

---

[171] Under TFEU the legislative procedures for approximation measures (Art 114) and most environmental measures (Art 192) are now the same. But the choice of legal base remains important since there are significant legal differences as to the extent to which Member States can adopt stricter national measures.

between those promoting free trade and those promoting political union (who at the 1992 Intergovernmental Conference operated as separate committees) cannot be disguised by the fact that their handiwork appears in a single document. The compromise between the philosophy of market freedom and that of sustainable development fails to disguise a fault line in the Community structure between the centralist and the federalist, free marketeers and environmentalists, exclusive and non-exclusive competences, absolute and minimum standards, majority and unanimous decision making. Ultimately, tinkering at the edges may produce only confusion and a misplaced reassurance.

26

Subsidiarity and European Community Environmental Law[1] (1999)

Development of the Concept

The notion of subsidiarity produces conflicting resonances in different audiences. It has yet to touch the political nerves to the degree that federalism can in some European countries, although the two are clearly connected concepts, and in many ways mutually reinforcing ideas. Some writers have gone so far as to describe subsidiarity as one of the basic conditions of federalism.[2] When the principle was formally inserted into the European Treaty following Maastricht, many in the environmental field observed that this was no more an expression of what had been a long standing and express principle of Community environmental policy which can be traced back to the First Action Programme on the Environment in 1973.[3] Among the eleven principles of Community activity, it was stated that in each different category of pollution, it is necessary to establish the level of action (local, regional, national, Community, international) that befits the type of pollution and the geographical zone to be protected. Actions which are likely to be the most effective at Community level should be concentrated at that level. Given this background the new Article 3b suggested it was business as usual in the environmental field. In contrast, more Euro-sceptic policy makers appeared to hope that the new Article 3b would force a reigning back of Community environmental law – no more conservation based legislation, no more Commission interference with national projects,[4] and a retreat to purely trade-related measures.[5] Some lawyers predicted that the expression of the principle in law would give rise to a new era of judicial review and intervention – and at the very least a great deal of work trying to interpret the precise meaning of the words. Lord MacKenzie-

---

[1] R Macrory, 'Subsidiarity and European Community Environmental Law' [1999] *Revues des Affaires Européennes* 363.

[2] Brugmans and Duclos, *Le fédéralisme contemporain. Critères, institutions, perspectives* (Leyden, AW Sythoff, 1963), quoted in N Emiliou, 'Subsidiarity: Paneacea or Fig Leaf' in O'Keefe and Twomey (eds), *Legal Issues of the Maastricht Treaty* (London, Wiley Chancery, 1994).

[3] [1973] OJ C112/7.

[4] In the United Kingdom the threat of Commission Article 169 proceedings in the late 1980s in connection with a major motorway project causing environmental damage (Twyford Down) gave rise to great political concern in governmental circles, reaching the Prime Minister.

[5] According to *The Times* (7 August 1992) the then British Foreign Secretary instructed Cabinet colleagues to draw up a list of Community laws that 'interfere unnecessarily with British sovereignty' which would include laws concerning the environment, workers' protection, food hygiene, and animal welfare.

Stuart, former president of the European Court of Justice, regarded the clause as 'legal gobbledegook' and observed that it was capable of no less than 30 different meanings.[6] Whether the principle is truly justiciable is again a matter of conflicting views. In the same legal volume concerning Maastricht, one writer concludes that it is inevitable that the European Court will be asked to interpret the principle, and that the Court is the institution best placed to undertake that task.[7] Another distinguished writer in the same volume concludes that while the existence of the Article in the Treaty makes legal action based on it possible, the European Court will not, and cannot, become the ultimate arbiter as to whether the principle of subsidiarity has been properly applied in a particular case.[8] Yet a third writer in the same volume urges the Court to restrict itself to what is described as a marginal review of subsidiarity questions, yet concludes that the authoritative interpretation and application of the principles of subsidiarity by the Court will further enhance its function as the Community's constitutional tribunal.[9]

The subsidiarity principle of course since Maastricht applies to all areas of Community policy, but this analysis is confined to the environmental context. What I first want to do is to consider what effect if any the principle has had in the development of environmental policy. Then I will consider some of the more significant legal issues that arise though without trying to unscramble Lord Mackenzie-Stewart's thirty different meanings. Finally, I want to inject some perspectives on the importance of the principle in the area of enforcement of legislation.

Subsidiarity as both a concept of both political philosophy and administrative theory predates the existence of the Community by many years. Its philosophical origins are generally ascribed to the enclyclical letter of Pope Pius XI in 1931: 'It is an injustice, a grave evil, and disturbance of right order for a larger and higher association to arrogate to itself functions which can be performed efficiently by smaller and local societies'.[10] Yet this expression was hardly new. A British Royal Commission in 1869 noted that the theory of the division of powers between local and central government was that, 'all that can be done by local authorities should be done by them . . . whatever concerns the whole nation should be dealt with nationally, while whatever concerns the district must be dealt with by the district'.[11] This statement, in common with the principle stated in the Community's First Action Programme, begs the critical questions of what does concern the various levels, and both are essentially neutral as to division of powers. De Tocqueville, however, in his study on Democracy in America emphasises the benefits of decentralisation by noting that administrative centralisation brings triumph on the day of battle but in the long run diminishes a nation's power.[12]

So these are not new ideas, nor peculiar to the European Community. Even before its current widespread use in discussion of European political circles, the concept of subsidiarity, in that it recognises the strength of employing differing levels of government and administration, permeated many of the fundamental legal structures of the European Community. The lack of a clear divisions of competencies between the Community and Member States, the mark of traditional federal structures, means that the Community has

---

[6] Subsidiarity and the Challenge of Change, Proceedings of the Jaques Delors Colloquium, 1991.
[7] J Steiner, 'Subsidiarity under the Maastricht Treaty' in O'Keefe and Twomey, above n 2.
[8] AG Toth, 'A legal Analysis of Subsidiarity' in O'Keefe and Twomey, ibid.
[9] Emiliou, above n 2.
[10] Encyclical Letter, Quadragesimo Anno 1931.
[11] Royal Commission on Local Government 1869.
[12] A De Tocqueville, Democracy in America (1848).

developed other, more subtle mechanisms for sharing responsibilities. For example, the large measure of discretion given to Member States in the choice of national instruments and mechanisms implementing Community policy objectives as defined in Directives, that legal instrument peculiar to the Community and described by the Commission as an 'instrument hybride et de statut ambigu'.[13] As Prêchai notes, the particular characteristics of the instruments means that the directive seems to go hand-in-glove with the principle of subsidiarity.[14] Despite the more recent jurisprudence of the European Court of Justice constraining a Member State's choice of methods of transposition[15] a large measure of discretion remains. Similarly, the fundamental relationship between national courts and the European Court of Justice under Article 177 References where there is a firm division of responsibilities, where the European Court does not act as a final court of appeal but confines itself to providing authoritative guidance to national courts on the interpretation and application of Community law. As the European Court itself described the system, it establishes a special field of judicial cooperation which requires the national court and the Court of Justice, both keeping within their respective jurisdiction and with the aim of ensuring that Community law is applied in a unified manner, to make direct and complementary contributions to the working out of a decision.[16] These are examples where the structure of the Community recognises the value of decentralised powers albeit within constrained boundaries.

The environmental sector provides a good laboratory for understanding the operation and effect of the subsidiarity principle, not least because it has been operating there longer than any other sector of Community policy. The principle contained in the First Action Programme and quoted above is, perhaps, more a statement of common sense rather than a formal principle as such, and is neutral as to the allocation of responsibilities. But it pre-dated by some two years the first explicit Community reference to subsidiarity, contained in the Commission's submission to the Tindeman's Report on European Union in 1975. There the Commission stated that the European Union is not to give way to a centralising superstate: 'consequently and in accordance with the principle *de subsidiarité* the Union will be given responsibility only for those matters which the Member States are no longer capable of dealing with efficiently'.[17] The amendments to the Treaty of Rome in 1987 which first expressly introduced a legal basis for environmental policy also first introduced a legal principle of subsidiarity. This was confined to the environmental field though based on earlier draft versions of the Treaty which would have contained a general provision concerning the division of competencies between the Community and Member States.[18] The wording was rather simpler than Article 3b:

---

[13] Quoted in F Snyder, 'Effectiveness of European Community Law: Institutions, Processes' [1993] *Tools and Techniques Modern Law Review* 19.

[14] S Prechal, *Directives in European Community Law* (Oxford, Oxford University Press, 1995) 5.

[15] Decisions requiring the use of legal as opposed to administrative measures include *Commission v Netherlands* [1987] ECR 3483; *Commission v Germany* [1991] ECR I-2567.

[16] Case 16/65 *Schwarze v Einfuhr- und Vorratsstelle fur Getreide und Futtermittel* [1965] ECR 877.

[17] European Commission, Report on European Union Bull EC Supp 5/75 (1975).

[18] See the Spinelli draft Treaty: 'The Union shall only act to carry out those tasks which may be undertaken more effectively in common than by the Member States acting separately, in particular those whose execution requires action by the Union because their dimension or effects extend beyond national frontiers' (European Parliament [1984] OJ C77/33).

The Community shall take action relating to the environment to the extent to which the objectives [referred to in paragraph 1] can be attained better at Community level than at the level of the individual Member States.

The new Article uses both the terms 'better' and 'sufficiently achieved' as key criteria. But I tend to agree with Dr Kramer who in considering the 1987 amendments noted that 'better implies a value judgment which is unquantifiable and defines legal definition.' In other words not even the most penetrating interpretation can extract from the term any abstract guidelines in the division of competencies.[19]

Subsidiarity and Justiciability

Nevertheless, the procedural changes that have taken place over the last 25 years in relation to Community environmental legislation have clearly raised the possibility of Member States invoking the doctrine of subsidiarity to challenge the validity of laws. In the early years of the development of Community environmental policy, all legislation was agreed by unanimity at Council level. Concerns over the scope and content of proposed legislation could be expressed through the ability and political nerve of individual countries to block agreement. Since 1987 and subsequent amendments to the Treaty we have seen the growing extension of qualified majority voting in the environmental field. Minority countries, no longer able to secure compromise or the blocking of unpalatable measures by their power of veto may therefore be tempted to secure their policy goals by legal rather than political challenge.

A legal challenge concerning the competence of the Community on grounds of subsidiarity has not yet, to my knowledge, happened in the environmental field. But an example of a similar process was the United Kingdom's challenge to the Working Time Directive (Case C-84/94) decided by the European Court of Justice in 1996.[20] The United Kingdom, which had of course opted out of the Social Chapter, argued that the Directive had wrongly been based on Article 118a dealing with the safety and health of workers, and that this article should be restrictively interpreted. Furthermore the proposed provisions were disproportionate in that they went beyond what was necessary to achieve the objectives pursued. During the written procedure, the United Kingdom did not expressly argue that disregard of the subsidiarity principle was grounds for annulment, but according to Advocate General Leger created some confusion by regularly invoking the principle of subsidiarity in the course of the proceedings.[21]

The Advocate General noted that Article 3b contains both a principle of subsidiarity and a principle of proportionality but criticised the United Kingdom for equating the two. He was clear that the two principles operate in turn at two different levels. The principle of subsidiarity determines whether Community action should be set in motion at all, while proportionality defines the scope of action that can be taken. Reliance on subsidiarity implies that as a matter of principle one is contesting the possibility of the Community taking action in the area covered by the proposed measure. Article 118a of the Treaty

---

[19] L Kramer, *EEC Treaty and Environmental Protection* (London, Sweet & Maxwell, 1990).
[20] *United Kingdom v EU Council* [1996] CMLR 671.
[21] Para 124 of his Opinion.

expressly gave power to the Community to adopt legislation laying down minimum requirements in order to achieve harmonisation of working conditions. According to Advocate General Leger, in so far as harmonisation is an objective, it is difficult to criticise the measures adopted by the Council on the ground that they are in breach of the principle of subsidiarity. It would be illusory to expect the Member States alone to achieve the harmonisation envisaged since it necessarily involves supranational action.[22]

The Court itself was equally dismissive of the subsidiarity argument, and equated the arguments as formulated with questioning the need for Community action. Invoking the wording of Article 118a, it held that once the Council had decided it was necessary to improve the existing levels of worker protection and to harmonise conditions, achievement of that objective necessarily presupposes Community-wide action. The Court went on to note that the concept of minimum requirements in Article 113 did not, as the UK had argued, limit Community action to the lowest common denominator. Member States were free to provide a level of protection more stringent than that resulting from Community law, high as that may be. The principle of the capacity to adopt more stringent environmental measures, subject to some procedural limitations, is now expressly contained in both Article 100a(4) and Article 130t.

Furthermore, the Court showed itself reluctant to provide a hard look at that question. The Council must be allowed a wide discretion in an area which as here involves the legislature in making social policy choices and requires it to carry out complex assessments.[23] Judicial review must be limited to questions of manifest error or misuse of powers, or manifest exceedance of powers.

Although it is unlikely that we have seen the last of legal challenges based on the subsidiarity principle, the approach of the Court in the Working Time Directive case suggests it will be a tough hurdle to mount. The structure of the Treaty has never been based on a clear division of competencies between the Community and Member States, and in the environmental field the system has been described as following the idea of a shared competence or as Laurence Brinkhorst has put it, not so much a separation of powers but rather an intermingling of powers.[24] My own view is that the subsidiarity principle reflects what can be described as a gravitational rule rather than strict rule of competence, but this does not mean that it is deprived of influence.

The Maastricht Treaty moved the principle from one tucked away in the environment section to a general rule at the head of the Treaty, and this action in itself caused considerable political attention. Four months after the signing of the Maastricht Treaty, the Lisbon Summit meeting of the European Council called upon the principle to be expressly considered for all proposed Community legislation and for a reexamination of existing legislation. The 1992 Edinburgh Summit approved a Commission paper considering operational principles of subsidiarity.[25] Reflecting the criticisms of the British arguments in the Workers' Directive, some scholars have accused the Commission of confusing subsidiarity with proportionality in this document.[26] The paper contained three general principles which should be applied to proposed action:

---

[22] Ibid, para 129.

[23] Judgment of the European Court, para 58.

[24] L Brinkhorst, 'Subsidiarity and European Community Environmental Policy – A Pandora's Box?' [1991] *European Environmental Law Review* 16, 20.

[25] Conclusions of the Presidency Bull EC 12-1992, 12.

[26] See, eg Toth, above n 8, 44.

- Did the matter raise cross-border problems which could not be dealt with satisfactorily at Member State level?
- Would existing actions or initiatives by Member State or inaction by the Community infringe other provisions of the Treaty such as competition, trade restrictions or the need to strengthen cohesion?
- Would action by the Community rather than national action produce clear benefits by reason of scale or effects?

These are pretty generous guidelines and, as Jan Jans concluded, if all the existing environmental legislation of the Community were reviewed against those guidelines, it seems highly unlikely whether a single environmental Directive would fail to pass the test.[27] Despite the initial political excitement in some Member States (with talk of the repeal of the Environmental Assessment Directive amongst others) this essentially is what has happened. In 1993 the Commission submitted a report on the adaptation of existing Community laws to the subsidiarity principle which made clear that while it sought reform of a raft of water and air pollution Directives, none would be repealed as such until replaced by others. No formal proposals appear to have been withdrawn on the basis of subsidiarity, though within the Commission early policy sparks may have been extinguished as potentially breaching subsidiarity, and Kramer has noted in 1997 that the most striking feature of EC environmental legislation over the last five years is the significant decrease of the legislative activity at EC level.[28] Even within proposed legislation, it seems clear that substantive principles within proposed areas of action have shown a greater sensitivity to the need for shared action by the Community and Member States, with a shift in favour of Member States. Under the proposed Directive to replace the existing Drinking Water Directive,[29] certain standards such as those related to colour and taste are clearly left for determination by Member States. Greater derogations are provided. The proposed amendments to the Bathing Water Directive[30] amends technical aspects of the Directive but there has been no question raised about repealing the Directive. The proposed directive on the Ecological Quality of Water gave a far greater degree of discretion to Member States than would have been seen under earlier Directives.[31] And the recently agreed Directive on Integrated Pollution Prevention and Control[32] contains more than a nod towards subsidiarity. Article 9, for example, requires that permits are based on best available techniques but taking into account the installations, geographical location and the local environmental conditions. This last provision caused considerable unease with the German government but was very much promoted by the British, and the final drafting of the provisions suggests that the principle of subsidiarity was in the minds of negotiators. In this sense we are seeing the influence of subsidiarity as determining not so much legal competence as administrative responsibility.[33]

It is clear from the wording of the principle in Article 3b that it does not apply to areas of so-called exclusive competence of the Community. Determining what is or is not

---

[27] J Jans, *European Environmental Law* (London, Kluwer, 1995).
[28] L Kramer, *Focus of European Environment Law*, 2nd edn (London, Sweet & Maxwell, 1997).
[29] [1995] OJ C131/95.
[30] [1994] OJ C112/3.
[31] [1991] OJ C222/6.
[32] Directive 96/61 [1996] OJ L257/26.
[33] The notion of 'administrative subsidiarity' has been promoted by the Commission – see SEC 92 (1990). See also M Hession and R Macrory, 'Maastricht and the Environmental Policy of the Community – Legal Issues of a New Environmental Policy' in D O'Keefe and P Twomey, above n 2.

exclusive raises difficult conceptual questions, but a number of areas of policy with environmental significance are encompassed by exclusivity. The narrowest view of exclusive competence confines it to those areas based on the interpretation of the Treaty where the Community is the only authority with competence to act. According the European Court of Justice marine fisheries conservation[34] and the Common Commercial Policy[35] fall within the exclusive competence of the Community and the subsidiarity test cannot apply there. A more generous view would go onto to encompass areas which are not declared exclusive on the basis of Treaty interpretation, but where the Community has potential power, and has exercised to the extent that it preempts actions by Member States. Agricultural policies would be such an example. Toth goes further to argue that exclusivity covers any matter governed by the original EEC Treaty, and that therefore subsidiarity cannot apply to those areas.[36]

Pure environmental policies represent a concurrent area of power where the subsidiarity test applies. As I have already indicated the actual wording of the test involves the application of value judgments which suggests it is unlikely to be wholly justiciable. This seems particularly so in the environmental field which contain a complex web of local, regional, and global problems – and one where the sum of apparently local degradation can have significant regional or global impact.[37] The British Royal Commission on Environmental Pollution recently conducted a major study of soil quality in the United Kingdom which demonstrated the extent to which a different analytical perspective on what had previously be regarded as largely an issue of local significance could raise the level of appropriate policy response – the report concluded that by and large soil quality in the country was in good state but, set against global trends, emphasises the national and international significance of the resource.[38] With that in mind, it is possible to identify three broad types of environmental problem which may be said to pass the subsidiarity test.[39]

1. Global or regional issues which have transboundary affects with respect to other countries or the global commons.
2. Apparently localised problems whose accumulative sum or future trends imply regional or global environmental effects. In effect this amounts to a redrawing of the boundaries of (1) in the light of developing environmental scientific knowledge.
3. Problems which affect what might be described the common heritage of Europe or mankind, a far more subjective though still very real concept.[40]

Even with those areas that may be described as truly of international importance, it may be argued that the Community per se is not necessarily the most appropriate level at which to deal with them – sometimes called the supersidiarity test. Member States may argue that they rather then the Community may still be the most effective players on the international stage. There must be some real doubt whether this is the case given the combined economic and political muscle of the Community.

---

[34] Cases 3, 4, 6/76 *Kramer et al* [1976] ECR 1279.

[35] Case 41/76 *Donckerwolcke v Procureur de la Republique et al* [1976] ECR 1921.

[36] Toth, above n 8. The analysis, in my view, takes far too generous a view of exclusivity.

[37] Hession and Macrory, above n 33.

[38] Royal Commission on Environmental Pollution, *Sustainable Use of Soil*, 19th Report, Cm 3165 (London, HMSO, 1996).

[39] Hession and Macrory, above n 33.

[40] See, in particular, W Wils, 'Subsidiarity and EC Environmental: Taking People's Concerns Seriously' [1994] *Journal of Environmental Law* 85.

The Maastricht Treaty contained an explicit reference to an objective of Community environmental policy being the promotion of international measures to deal with regional or worldwide environmental problems. This did not expressly make such areas the exclusive competence of the Community, but certainly tempers the effect of the subsidiarity doctrine in those areas.

Subsidiarity and Enforcement

Finally, the possible effect of the subsidiarity principle to the question of the enforcement and implementation of Community environmental law should be addressed. The procedures contained in the Treaty, the role of the Commission, the citizens' complaint procedure and the ultimate powers of the European Court represent a developed and unique form of supranational supervision.[41] In the Commission's 1996 communication on implementation and enforcement,[42] what might be described as the administrative form of subsidiarity is strongly reflected. The Communication emphasises the role of national courts and national procedures in ensuring that Member States comply with their Community obligations. There is a distinct shift away from Community involvement in individual cases of poor implementation in practice. I have some sympathy with the approach outlined, but also recognise the dangers involved: it requires that Member States consider carefully the effectiveness and availability of national legal and administrative remedies, many of which are woefully inadequate in many countries. Similarly it has to be recognised that the more that Community legislation contains provisions that give discretion to Member States and their national authorities the less will conventional legal enforcement at Community level prove effective. Far greater open monitoring, harmonisation and consistency between national environmental indicators, and systematic exchange of information will be needed if the protection of the environment is to be maintained.

The original Commission Action Programme on the environment, produced almost 25 years ago, explicitly mentioned local and regional action as well as national and Community. It is perhaps unfortunate that the subsidiarity principle now contained in the Treaty contains no mention of levels of action 'below' the Member State, although the Preamble to the Maastricht Treaty talks of the need to create an ever closer union among the peoples of Europe in which decisions are taken as closely as possible to the citizen. To date, the subsidiarity concept as developed in the Treaty has been largely considered, at least from the Anglo-Saxon perspective, in the context of the relationship between the powers of the Community and those of Member States. But in future it may be more pertinent to consider its application to the notion of regional or devolved responsibility at the expense of central government. This reflects a broader concept of federalism which moves away from the notion of a contractual arrangements between nation states and in which subsidiarity establishes a presumption that the primary responsibility and decision-making competence should rest with the lowest possible level of authority of the political

---

[41] R Macrory, 'Enforcement of Community Environmental Laws: Some Critical issues' [1992] *Common Market Law Review* 347. See also Chapter 28 below.
[42] Com (96) 500 final.

hierarchy.[43] More fluid relationships between the Community and levels of government beyond the nation state would result, and the subsidiarity approach, therefore, may allow the Community to deal directly with subnational governments, interest groups, and citizens without too much concern for the rights and views of the Member States.[44] Yet when it comes to enforcement actions under Article 169 we still retain a model of the central government being held responsible for ensuring the implementation of Community obligations, even where internally those powers have been devolved to sub-regional levels of government. The conventional response is to ensure that where European Community obligations are involved, central government always possesses powers to implement and if necessary to direct local and sub-regional governments to conform.[45] The more imaginative solution – though one that may be resisted by many national governments – would be to embrace the more fluid concept of federalism and allow Article 169 proceedings to be brought directly against regional or sub-regional governments where the relevant powers were clearly within their devolved competence. We are some way from such a model, but at least can note that the legal conceptions and structures in this area are not yet in tune with more flexible visions promoted in political circles. What is, however, increasingly clear is that the concept of subsidiarity in the environmental context, far from representing a lessening of the burden on Member States, in fact strengthens the needs and obligations of each country to look critically at the adequacy of its own systems in delivering effective environmental policies.

---

[43] Emiliou, above n 2, 66.

[44] Ibid, 67; Biancarelli, 'La Communauté et les collectives locales' (1988) 48 *Revu Française d'Administration Publique* 41.

[45] Essentially the model adopted in the United Kingdom. Even under Scottish devolution arrangements, which adopt the principle that all matters are devolved unless reserved by national government, European Community matters are to be reserved.

27

The Enforcement of EU
Environmental Law – Some
Proposals for Reform[1]
(2005)

The Context

My concern is mainly with the procedures available to the European Commission to ensure that Member States fully comply with their obligations under EC environmental laws. As is well known, the Commission has a duty under the Treaty to ensure that Community measures 'are applied', but in the environmental field it was a duty that was largely ignored until the mid-1980s. So while the overall title of this collection is *Reflections on 30 Years of EU Environmental Law*, in reality we are talking of 20 years of Community enforcement of environmental law. Indeed, it was during the period of Ludwig Kramer's headship of the legal unit within DG Environment that the enforcement procedures, available in all sectors of Community law, were significantly reinvigorated and applied in the field of the environment. Currently roughly a third of all complaints and infringements procedures fall within the environment sector.

Effective enforcement of national environmental laws is fraught with difficulties. Bodies responsible for detection and enforcement may be insufficiently resourced, and national courts often lack the specialised knowledge to handle the complexities of contemporary environmental law. The enforcement of many international environmental treaties is even more a challenge, largely due to sensitivities concerning national sovereignty. It is true that in recent years much greater efforts have been made in recent environmental treaties such as the Montreal Protocol to move away from a system that largely relied upon conventional and often ineffective methods of international dispute resolution towards what has been described as a more 'managerial approach' involving more sophisticated methods to encourage compliance including greater transparency, improved reporting procedures, and dedicated secretariats.[2] In the context of supranational obligations, though, the powers and procedures available under the Treaty, including the possibility of the imposition of financial penalties by the European Court of Justice and the encouragement of citizens and

---

[1] R Macrory, 'The Enforcement of EU Environmental Law: Some Proposals for Reform' in R Macrory (ed), *Reflections on 30 Years of EU Environmental Law – A High Level of Protection?* (Groningen, Europa Law Publishing, 2005) 385–95.

[2] M Faure and J Lefevere, 'Compliance with International Environmental Agreements' in N Vig and R Axelrod (eds), *The Global Environment – Institutions, Law and Policy* (Washington, DC, CQ Press, 1999) 138.

non-governmental organisations to lodge formal complaints concerning instances of non-compliance, remain unrivalled in contemporary supranational arrangements. Whatever the shortcomings of the systems – and there are many – this fact should not be forgotten. This does not necessarily mean that the European Union offers an ideal model for other regional systems of environmental law to follow, though there are certainly important lessons to be learnt.[3] The key question for those working in Europe today is the extent to which, particularly in the context of the enlarged Union, we can continue rely upon the existing system, and what improvements might be sought in the light of future challenges.

The Present Picture

The most recent report of the Commission on the implementation of EU environmental law, published in 2004, hardly paints a reassuring picture.[4] In 2003, the Commission brought 58 cases against Member States before the ECJ, with a further 112 reasoned opinions issued. Given the very strict case law of the ECJ concerning the failure of Member States to even communicate national legislation within time limits, it remains surprising that failures still occur. As Somsen has noted, 'The European Court of Justice has always remained unpersuaded by the range of often imaginative justifications that have been forward'.[5] Yet the position at the end of 2003 indicates 88 outstanding cases for non-communication, spread (with the exception of Denmark and Sweden) almost equally among the Member States. Over 50 per cent of these fell with the field of air pollution, probably reflecting a large number of Directives in this field that had been agreed in previous years. In the area of perhaps the most pressing contemporary environmental issue, climate change, only one country had submitted a greenhouse gas emissions trading scheme within the deadline required.[6] Chemicals and Waste form the next highest sectors for non-communication.

There are 118 cases concerning non-conformity of national legislation, clearly a more complex and contestable area of legal interpretation. Cases are open against all Member States, though France and Italy stand out as the current worst offenders. Waste, Water and Nature Protection form the key sectors, accounting for nearly 70 per cent of all cases. As to bad application in practice,[7] there were 93 outstanding cases at the end of 2003, with around a third in the water sector, followed by waste, nature, and air. Surprisingly, perhaps, given the large amount of case law that has been generated by the legislation, there was only one case concerning environmental impact assessment. There are cases

---

[3] See L Krämer, 'Dispute Resolution in Environmental Law – Can the European Union be a Model?' in A Kiss, D Shelton and K Ishibashi (eds), *Economic Globalization and Compliance with International Environmental Agreements* (The Hague, Kluwer Law International, 2003) 271.

[4] European Commission, '5th Annual Survey on the Implementation and Enforcement of Community Environmental Law 2003', SEC (2004) 1025.

[5] H Somsen, 'Discretion in European Community Environmental Law – an Analysis of ECJ Case Law' (2003) 40 *Common Market Law Review* 1413.

[6] The position had improved by mid-2004, though proceedings have been started against Greece and Italy for non-transposition, and further written warnings have been given to 11 Member States for failing to fully transpose Directive 2003/87 on emission trading.

[7] This is now defined in the Commission report as to encompass the 'failure to implement certain derived or secondary obligation contained in Community acts, such as setting out plans, classifying sites and designating areas, adopting programmes, submitting monitoring data, reporting, etc'. It is not clear, whether this implies that the failure, say, to reach a required environmental standard in a particular case is excluded.

against all Member States, though spread unevenly, with the Scandinavian countries and Germany at the lower end, and Ireland, Italy and France into double figures.

It is, of course, not easy to tell whether this represents in any way an objective picture of compliance, though one can be pretty confident that, if anything, it will underestimate what goes on in practice. Differences across individual Member States may well reflect the experience and confidence of individual case-officers within the Commission, as well as the availability of national remedies. In terms of non-application in practice, the Commission is still heavily reliant on complaints being made,[8] and the numbers received from Member States reflect the campaigning tactics of national environmental organisations, national views of the environmental credentials of the Commission and a host of other factors as well as any comparative objective picture of compliance. Nevertheless, in the straightforward words of the then Commissioner Wallstrom, 'Implementation of EU environmental law is bad'.[9]

It is not the purpose of this contribution to review the history of enforcement by the Commission, or to consider in any detail the underlying legal and administrative procedures. There are other sources for this type of analysis.[10] A radical approach for reform would argue for wholesale reliance on the national authorities and national courts to ensure effective enforcement of Community obligations. Even where there have been inadequate or a lack of national implementing measures, it is arguable that the combined effect of doctrines developed by the European Court of Justice such as those concerning sympathetic interpretation, direct effect, *Francovich* damage claims, and duties of national courts to ensure implementation,[11] is now sufficiently powerful to avoid the need for a supranational enforcement mechanism. That might be true in an ideal world. But there remain significant disparities within Member States as to the powers and effectiveness of national enforcement bodies. Equally there remain major differences in the costs of litigation by third parties, and the remedies available to them to prevent abuse or lacklustre performance by local enforcement agencies. The Aarhus Convention, if and when fully implemented throughout the Community, may go some way to meet these concerns.[12] Nevertheless, I start from the proposition that in the foreseeable future there remains an important role for the Commission in the supervision and enforcement of Community environmental law. What follows are a number of suggestions for change which are intended to improve its effectiveness and focus.

---

[8] The total number received during 2003 in the environmental sector was 505, representing a slight decrease from the previous two years. The report does not contain figures for individual countries.

[9] Commission Press Release of 19 August 2004.

[10] See, eg R Macrory and R Purdy, 'The Enforcement of EC Environmental Law' in J Holder (ed), *The Impact of EC Environmental Law in the United Kingdom* (Chichester: Wiley & Sons, 1997) 9; L Krämer, *EC Environmental Law* 5th edn (London, Sweet & Maxwell, 2003) esp ch 12; R Macrory, 'Community Supervision in the Field of the Environment' in H Somsen (ed), *Protecting the European Environment* (London, Blackstone Press, 1996) 27.

[11] As developed in Case C-72/95 *Kraaijeveld* [1996] ECR I-5403.

[12] The Convention was ratified by the European Union on 17 February 2005. All Member States have ratified the Convention, the most recent being Ireland on 20 June 2012.

Suggestions for Improvement

Conformity of National Transposition Measures

Any enforcement body is likely to have limited resources, and the Commission is no exception. Certainly there is a strong argument that the focus of the Commission should be to ensure that national legislation fully reflects obligations under Community law. Of course, perfect transposition does not guarantee effective enforcement at national level, for some of the reasons indicated above, but it is good starting place. The Commission's 1996 paper on implementation[13] indeed indicated that this would be its priority area in future, though the subsequent figures on types of enforcement action do not bear out this policy. But there are real problems with current procedures, and useful changes could be made.

There should be a general legal requirement that Member States supply annotated versions of national transposition measures, clearly indicating which provisions of their national legislation are meant to reflect which provisions of the Directive in question. Some Member States appear to do this as a matter of practice, and recently the United Kingdom has begun to adopt this as a policy, but there seems no good reason where the provision of a compliance table should not be a general Community legal requirement.[14] Equally such tables should be made available publicly. This will assist national courts and enforcement bodies, as well as the general public, to understand the connection between the Community law and its national implementing measures. In recent years, the Commission has (rightly, in my view) made greater use of independent national legal experts to carry out initial compliance reports, but from personal experience, without a systematic annotation table provided by the Member State, it is often extraordinarily difficult to analyse the detailed rationale for all of the transposition measures taken. Directives are intended to allow a degree of latitude in how they are transposed within a national system, and simple 'copy out' of Directives word for word into national law does not necessarily meet the challenge that is required, or the spirit of legislative mechanism. Nevertheless, it is important that Member States resist producing bland annotation tables. Where, for example, there are significant changes in the words used between a Directive and national measures, the table should explain the rationale for doing so. Presumably a national draftsperson has made a conscious decision in interpreting the Directive and formulating a national provision, and there is no good reason where the explanation should not be given.

Once a Member State has enacted legislation, whether in the form of primary national laws or secondary regulations, it is inherently likely to be defensive as to its validity in terms of transposition. Being required to amend legislation once passed at national level at a later date is both time-consuming and represents a certain loss of face for national administrations. Although the Commission has in recent years made greater use of anticipatory meetings and discussions with Member States in some sectors, a far more systematic approach could be adopted. Draft legislation should be regularly provided by Member States, providing a more realistic opportunity for changes where differences of view arise. If this cannot be achieved by agreement, I would prefer to extend the time

---

[13] European Commission, 'Implementing Community Environment Law', COM (96) 500 (22 October 1996).

[14] Since 1991, the Commission has required Member States to identify the provisions of national legislation which correspond with the provisions of the Directive concerned: see [1991] OJ C338, 1, Annex C, s 8. But this is not a legal requirement, and practice by Member States as to the detail provided appears to vary.

limit for implementation, with Directives in future including a requirement that *draft* implementation measures are provided to the Commission within, say, two years of agreement of the Directive, with a further six months or twelve months for provision of final measures.[15] Similarly, the Commission should be prepared to give greater advance guidance as to its own view on the meaning of Directives, thus anticipating possible conflict areas. Such guidance cannot be taken as legally binding, since at the end of the day only the European Court can give a definitive ruling as to the legal meaning of Community legislation, but it would surely assist Member States in considering the design of their own transposition measures. Similarly, the introduction of the submission of draft national legislation for consideration by the Commission cannot inhibit the Commission from taking enforcement action at a later date, should it come to change its view on the meaning of the Directive. And this sort of procedure will not necessarily resolve all conflicts between the Commission and Member States. At the end of the day, there may still be legitimate differences of opinion as to the meaning of a Directive and the adequacy of the national measure concerned, which may eventually only be resolved by enforcement proceedings before the European Court of Justice. My concern is that current practice does not assist in identifying the real areas of dispute, and often allows for defective implementation and the need for subsequent infringement proceedings by default.

Transposition issues are mainly associated with the implementation of Directives,[16] and it is arguable that the more wholesale use of Regulations would remove the problem of transposition. There has been very little detailed analysis on the underlying principles that should determine the use of Directives or Regulations, nor is it an issue yet subject of judicial intervention by the ECJ. Despite the superficial attraction of greater use of Regulations, I suspect that, especially in the context of enlargement and an even greater range of administrative and legal traditions across the Union, the Directive, or its equivalent under the proposed Constitution, will remain a preferred choice of instrument for many areas of environmental policy.

Non-application in Practice

As mentioned above, the ECJ has developed a range of what I have described as 'internalising' doctrines which are designed to ensure that non-transposed provisions of Directives nevertheless still have legal impact within national systems. Nevertheless, each doctrine has limitations, and, even if effectively applied by national courts, cannot provide a comprehensive solution to 'gap-filling'. More liberal national standing rules, less deterrent costs rules, greater use of specialist national environmental tribunals and similar measures may all assist to ensure better enforcement at national level, thereby reducing the burden on the Commission. Nevertheless, realistically there is always likely to be areas where the enforcement of non-application in practice is best suited for the Commission.

This is clearly the most controversial area for involvement by the Commission, since it can threaten real-life projects involving national pride and serious economic commitment.

[15] Interestingly, Art 33 Euratom Treaty requires Member States to provide drafts of national implementing legislation, regulations or administrative action, and gives the Commission a three month period for making recommendations.

[16] I deliberately use the terminology of legislative acts under the existing Treaty rather than the proposed Constitution.

Within my own country, for example, news of the Commission's decision in the early 1990s to consider infringement proceedings concerning environmental impact assessment and a controversial national motorway scheme (Twyford Down) was known to have reached the Prime Minister personally.[17] The decision to initiate enforcement proceedings remains one of discretion by the Commission, and Williams, amongst others, has presented a fairly jaundiced view of the political pressures that can brought to bear on the Commission to refrain from proceedings, particularly those involving non-application in practice,[18] and an equally scathing account of the lack of legal accountability of the Commission.[19]

Nevertheless, it is clear from case-law of the European Court that the failure to implement in practice is as much of a breach of obligations by Member States as is the failure to transpose provisions of Directives into national law.[20] There seems little doubt that well-chosen, high-profile cases can bring home to Member States the reality of the commitments made in Community environmental legislation, and are consistent with contemporary policy approaches that emphasise the need to focus on environmental outcomes rather than simply the formality of legislation. But equally there are significant improvements in current procedures could be developed.

The current mechanisms for the Commission to investigate allegations of non-application in practice are often extraordinary cumbersome, and usually very reactive. Officers in Brussels learn of allegations of non-compliance mainly through complaints sent by individuals or non-governmental organisations, or through Members of the European Parliament. Lengthy correspondence is conducted with the Member State to try to establish further facts, normally working through the national representation office in Brussels, who in turn must liaise with national government departments, who often themselves have to established facts from local authorities or other bodies. Ideally, one might seek equivalent powers of direct inspection by the Commission equivalent to those in the competition field, and fisheries field, but this seems politically unlikely. A more modest reform would be to ensure that initial fact finding and dossier preparation were undertaken by Commission officials based in the Commission offices of Member States rather than conducted at long distance from Brussels. Rather more radical would be to draw from the major reforms introduced to the enforcement of competition law and policy introduced in 2003.[21] These give much greater responsibility to national bodies and courts for the direct enforcement of Community competition, while both strengthening the Commission's own powers of inspection, and establishing a European Competition Network of competition authorities to ensure exchange of experience and a consistent approach. The analogy may not be perfect, since the scope of environmental law is much broader than competition law, and the national bodies responsible for its enforcement are generally far more diffuse

---

[17] According to the *Independent* (22 October 1991), Prime Minister John Major was so incensed that he threatened to block the signing of the Maastricht Treaty, quoted in P Lowe and S Ward, *British Environmental Policy and Europe* (London, Routledge, 1998). Tromans and Fuller note that intervention by the Commission in the early 1990s concerning EIA on a number of major UK projects 'became tied up with general popular anti-EC sentiment and the perception of undue interference by Brussels in domestic decision-making': S Tromans and K Fuller, *Environmental Impact Assessment – Law and Practice* (London, Butterworths, 2003) ch 2.15.

[18] R Williams, 'The European Commission and the Enforcement of Environmental Law: an Invidious Position' (1994) 14 *Yearbook of European Law* 351.

[19] R Williams, 'Enforcing European Environmental Law: Can the European Commission be Held to Account?' (2002) 2 *Yearbook of European Environmental Law* 271.

[20] ECJ Cases C-431/92 *Commission v Germany* [1995] ECR I-7657; C-365/97 *Commission v Italy* [1999] ECR I-7773.

[21] Regulation 1/2003 [2003] OJ L1, 1.

that those concerned with competition law. Nevertheless, one could envisage, as Krämer has argued,[22] the establishment of national centres charged not with direct enforcement, but with monitoring the application of Community environmental law within the country concerned. Such centres would prepare dossiers, and make recommendations to the Commission concerning infringement proceedings.

The Commission should be more systematic in choosing priorities for investigation. This means making judgments (in conjunction, perhaps, with the European Environment Agency) on what areas are posing the greatest risks to the environment at any particular time. The complaint system has provided the Commission with significant information on failures in practice – as well as being an important political tool for connecting the Commission with citizens throughout the Community. Nevertheless, it can lead to a highly reactive rather than proactive system, and one that may often reflect the campaigning priorities of national environmental organisations rather than a considered assessment by the Commission of the threats posed to the environment from a European perspective. All enforcement authorities have limited resources, and many national authorities are now developing risk-based approaches to regulation – a policy that concentrates effort on those areas presenting the most significant problems, and adopting a lighter touch in others where appropriate. I accept that deciding, say, whether chronic air pollution in Athens is a greater priority than the immediate destruction of a habitat in Portugal places the Commission in an invidious position, but the reality for any enforcement body is that difficult choices often have to be made. Criteria could be developed to help identify priorities – Is the likely damage irreversible? Could a complainant make use of national legal remedies? Is the situation one replicated in other countries, meaning that an infringement action that will resonate more widely? Does the infringement reflect a hierarchy of priority environmental risks identified by the European Environment Agency? The reality is that these sorts of questions are probably in the mind of Commission officials, even if only sub-consciously, when they decide on pursuing particular cases. But in a contemporary system we should expect to see a more transparent and developed set of principles which underpin the exercise of administrative discretion in such an important area.

IMPEL (European Union Network for the Implementation and Enforcement of Environment Law) has, since 1992, provided an important focal point for national regulatory bodies to exchange information on actual enforcement in practice, and feedback to the better design of legislation from lessons learnt. But although it has expanded its scope of concerns, it remains largely pollution and waste orientated.[23] We have yet to see equivalent development of the intensity of effort in, say, nature conservation or environmental assessment.[24] Again, the number and range of national bodies involved in enforcement in these

[22] L Krämer: 'The Future Role of the ECJ in the Development of European Environmental Law' in J Jans (ed), *The European Convention and the Future of European Environmental Law* (Groningen, Europa Law Publishing, 2003) 85.

[23] This can be illustrated by looking at its 2004 work programme which covers: 1. IMPEL Review Working Group (IRI); 2. Electronic reporting in IPPC implementation; 3. Waste-related conditions in environmental permits; 4. EMAS project; 5. Transfrontier shipment of waste – threat assessment; 6. TFS network in the accession countries; 7. Consideration of human health through the IPPC Directive; 8. Identification of good practice in the implementation of the EU emissions trading scheme; 9. Implementation and use of BREFs; 10. Informal resolution of environmental conflicts by dialogue; 11. IMPEL Review Initiative (IRI) Sweden; 12. Inspection – environmental inspection guidelines for the tanning industry; 13. TFS seaport project; 14. TFS project – verification of the destination of notified waste.

[24] However, in 2007 a new nature conservation network was established, The Heads of European Nature Conservation Agencies, with the primary aim of 'strengthen[ing] nature conservation in Europe through

areas pose a particular challenge, but it remains a significant lacuna in present network arrangements. Clearly, if one were to see the development of the type of national centres for monitoring the enforcement of Community environmental law advocated by Krämer, they would form the natural basis for an exchange network.

The Commission has often commissioned reports from independent national experts on the state of actual application of environmental legislation, mirroring those concerning formal transposition measures. They can provide valuable independent critiques on the state of compliance in practice within a Member State, but too often, in my view, there have been insufficient procedures for effectively evaluating such reports. All too often, in common with other research reports, they can enter a 'black hole' on completion.

The European Court of Justice

The power of the European Court of Justice to fine Member State for failure to comply with its judgments is unique amongst international courts, and the first two such actions took place in the environmental field. According to the Commission, in 2003, 17 letters of formal notice and 11 reasoned opinions were issued in the environmental field against Member States under Article 228 EC Treaty.[25] My personal view at the time these powers were being proposed, was that they were undesirable – resorting to having to threaten a Member State with a financial payment to ensure compliance with a judgment of the European Court appeared to devalue the notion of the rule of law. But I have changed my view. In practice, even the threat of the powers appear to have had considerable effect in focusing the attention of Member States on resolving issues which hitherto had been presented as largely insurmountable. At national level it has meant that Finance or Treasury Departments now have a direct interest in ensuring that EU environmental legislation is effectively implemented, a positive development that heightens the internal status given to environmental protection.[26]

Although any resort to Court action implies a failure in the regulatory system whether at national or European level, the European Court of Justice will clearly continue to play a significant role in this area. But the current lengthy time in procedures is reaching unacceptable levels. Ludwig Krämer has recently carried out a systematic analysis of periods involved that makes for uncomfortable reading.[27] The average length of proceedings

enhanced cooperation between its Members'. The European Union Forum of Judges for the Environment was formed in 2004 to 'promote the enforcement of national, European and international environmental law by contributing to a better knowledge by judges of environmental law, by exchanging judicial decisions and by sharing experience in the area of training in environmental law'.

[25] Now Art 260 TFEU. Under Art 260(3) TFEU the Commission can now seek a financial penalty for late transposition without having to first wait for a judgment. In 2012, the Commission referred 35 such cases concerning late transposition with a request for financial sanctions: European Commission, '30th Annual Report on Monitoring the Application of EU Law', COM (2013) 726 final.

[26] Part 2 of the Localism Act 2011, applying to England, Wales and Scotland, contains provisions giving power to the government to recover payments in respect of such CJEU fines or penalties from public authorities, including local authorities, where the acts of such authorities 'may have caused or contributed to the infraction of EU law for which the EU financial sanction was imposed' (s 54(2)). These provisions are likely to increase pressure on local authorities and other public bodies to ensure compliance with EU law.

[27] L Krämer, 'Data on Environmental Judgments by the EC Court of Justice' (2004) 2 *Journal of European Environmental and Planning Law* 127.

from the initial issue of a formal notice by the Commission to judgment was 45 months, rising to 52 months (over 4 years) in the case of non-application in practice. Seven cases during 2002/3 took more than 80 months. As he rightly notes, the blame does not wholly rest on the Court, and much of the delay occurs during pre-litigation stages. Certainly, the large variation in periods suggests, there is room for substantial improvements that could be made. The system of environmental enforcement developed within the European Union may be distinctive, but this scale of delay in bringing cases before a court would be unacceptable in most European national systems. It needs to be addressed with urgency, if confidence is to be retained in a legal system, let alone the environment effectively protected. Infringement proceedings could, for example, be assigned to the Court of First Instance, unless raising significant issues of principle. In preparation for the Nice Treaty amendments, the Ole Due Working Group on the Community Court System recommended that the Commission's claim of infringement by a Member State should be binding on the State concerned unless challenged within a specified time limit, a proposal that would also have speeded up the system.[28] The recommendation was never pursued.[29]

Conclusions

The system of supranational enforcement within the European Union remains unique amongst contemporary systems of governance, and European environmental lawyers need not be unduly defensive for what has been developed. It is almost trite to repeat that the environment does not respect national boundaries, but this will remain the reality, and we should be looking to ways of developing and strengthening rather than weakening the current system. My contribution has deliberately avoided examining the actual substance of Community environmental law but focussed on the process of enforcement. Legal substance, of course, vitally influences enforceability, and poorly drafted legislation makes enforcement nearly impossible. The central responsibility of the European Commission in supervising implementation of Community obligations by Member States remains unchallenged in the foreseeable future. The core procedures concerning infringement actions and the powers of the European Court of Justice have remained intact and unchanged in the proposed European Constitution. This may have been something of a lost opportunity, and should not be taken to imply that all is well with the current system. Many of my proposals for reform, though, require no Treaty change, but a recognition that much could be done to improve current procedures, with an approach that is both more systematic and transparent. Member States as well as the Commission need to recognise that effective and consistent enforcement of Community environmental legislation throughout the Union, though uncomfortable at times, is in their long-term interests. In this context, it is salutary to note that the Council of Ministers has never regularly reviewed on a systematic basis the actual implementation of existing Community environmental laws. It should do so. But the first responsibility lies with the Commission. The Commission's last major communication of the implementation of Community environmental law was published

---

[28] Quoted in Dryberg, 'What Should the Court of Justice be Doing?' [2001] *European Law Review* 291, 299.
[29] But Art 260(3) TFEU now gives the power to the Commission to seek a fine or penalty payment from the European Court of Justice for non-transposition without first having to secure a judgment from the Court.

in 1996. Against the background of the expanded Union and the proposed Constitution, it should, for a start, mark the tenth anniversary in 2006 with a fresh examination, and the publication of a new paper that grapples effectively with the contemporary challenges of environmental enforcement.[30]

---

[30] See now 'Communication from the Commission on Implementing European Community Environmental Law', COM (2008) 773 (11 November 2008).

28

The Enforcement of Community Environmental Laws: Some Critical Issues[1] (1992)

Introduction

> Community environmental legislation will only be effective if it is fully implemented and enforced by Member State.[2]

In recent years both the European Parliament[3] and the Council of Ministers have stressed the importance of ensuring that Community law is fully implemented within Member States.[4] New mechanisms and procedures are under discussion at a political level, while traditional tools are employed in the meantime. Yet it is a sensitive area. Member States may subscribe to the concept of the supremacy of Community law and the need for better implementation, but are reluctant to accept interference with national administrative arrangements for enforcement.

The field of environmental policy is particularly striking in this context. Since the Community began development of Community environmental policies in 1972, a large body of directives, regulations, and decisions has been agreed, and in terms of the sheer amount of legislation that now exists the programme must be considered one of the success stories of the Community.[5] The aim of this article is to consider the mechanisms associated with the implementation and enforcement of Community environmental legislation, with 'implementation' denoting the process by which legal obligations under Community law are fulfilled, while 'enforcement' implies the methods available to ensure that implementation takes place. The vast majority of Community environmental laws have been in the form of directives, with the consequence that attention to date has been largely with ensuring that

---

[1] R Macrory, 'The Enforcement of Community Environmental Law: Some Critical Issues' (1992) 29 *Common Market Law Review* 347.

[2] Statement of European Council, Bull EC 6-1990, 18–21, note 4.

[3] See European Parliament Resolutions of 11 April 1984 [1984] OJ C127/67; of 19 March 1990 [1990] OJ C68/172.

[4] At an informal meeting of the Council of Ministers on 11–13 October 1991 it was agreed that there is a need both for the 'further development and enforcement of environmental legislation' within the Community and to 'improve the compliance and enforcement structures concerning environmental legislation and the implementation within the Member States'.

[5] Around 200 regulations, directives and decisions have been agreed in the environmental field.

Member States rather than private interests comply with their obligations under these laws. In that context, my particular concern will be with the use of the Article 169[6] enforcement procedures by the European Commission. I make no excuse for this focus. Although the process has been subject to criticism for reasons that will become apparent, and while new methods of ensuring improved compliance are being considered,[7] the Article 169 procedure will remain a central and critical legal tool for enforcement at Community level, whatever the nature of other initiatives agreed upon.

One of the underlying difficulties associated with the implementation and enforcement of Community environmental law is the differing structural character of the legislation that has been agreed. Some directives prescribe explicit and precise goals that must be achieved in a given sector which in theory should be reasonably straightforward to monitor and enforce.[8] Another class contains similarly precise goals within specified sectors or areas but leaves a large element of discretion to Member States in determining where they are to apply.[9] Examples of more recent legislation cut across conventional administrative boundaries and sectors, and impose obligations that reach deep into national decision making at many levels. This type of 'horizontal' directive, exemplified by the 1985 Environmental Assessment Directive,[10] raises acute difficulties for both Member States and the Community institutions when it comes to ensuring full implementation.

The Role of the Commission

A key function of the European Commission under the Treaty of Rome is to ensure the effective application of Community law.[11] The Commission's role in enforcement is therefore one of its institutional duties, yet it was not until the early 1980s, a decade after the initiation of explicit Community environmental policies, that it began to take its role seriously in this field. The European Parliament played an important part in the process of galvanising concern. The disappearance of toxic waste being transported from Seveso in 1983 revealed the extent of defective implementation of existing environmental direc-

---

[6] Now Art 258 Treaty on the Functioning of the European Union. The core provisions have not changed, but the Court of Justice of the European Union has, since the Maastricht Treaty 1993, the power to impose penalties on Member States that do not comply with its judgments (Art 260). Furthermore, under Art 260(3) the Commission may seek a penalty payment from the Court immediately where the infringement is based on non-communication – there is no longer any need to first secure a Court judgment.

[7] For example, at an informal meeting of the Council of Ministers in October 1991 it was agreed that Member States should establish an informal network of national enforcement officers concerned with environmental law. The European Union Network for the Implementation and Enforcement of Environmental Law (IMPEL), set up in 1992. Other networking bodies concerning with enforcement have since been set up – see Chapter 30 of this volume, p 544.

[8] Eg Directive 80/779 on air quality limit values and guide values for sulphur dioxide and suspended particulates [1980] OJ L229/30; Directive 80/778 relating to the quality of water intended for human consumption [1980] OJ L229/11.

[9] Eg Directive 78/659 on the quality of fresh waters needing protection or improvement in order to support fish life [1978] OJ L229/11; Directive 76/160 concerning the quality of bathing water [1976] OJ L229/11; Directive 79/409 on the conservation of wild birds [1979] OJ L79/409.

[10] Directive 85/337 on the assessment of the effects of certain public and private projects on the environment [1985] OJ L175/40. Another notable example of such a horizontal directive is Directive 90/313 on access to environmental information [1990] OJ L158/56.

[11] Art 155 EEC provides that the Commission shall 'ensure that the provisions of this Treaty and the measures taken by the institutions pursuant thereof are applied'.

tives governing toxic and dangerous wastes, and the Parliament's subsequent inquiry and Resolution criticised both the Commission and Member States over their failure to ensure effective implementation of Community environmental legislation.[12] Since that date, the Commission, largely through its legal unit within Directorate-General XI, has concentrated on improving its enforcement efforts, using both conventional legal processes available under Community law, and less formal methods. Before examining the machinery that is employed, it is worth asking whether there are particular features of the Community's programme of environmental legislation which have fostered problems of poor implementation by Member States.

Dr Ludwig Krämer, head of the legal unit within DG XI, has argued that a fundamental characteristic of environmental law, both at Community and national level, is the lack of readily identifiable vested interests willing and able to secure enforcement.[13] The same is not true of, say, Competition, Employment or Agricultural Law where the failure by Member States to implement Community law can directly affect economic interests. There is undoubtedly considerable truth in this assertion. Many aspects of the environment are not susceptible to conventional concepts of legal property rights which are capable of enforcement by private interests. Amenity and environmental groups who would lay claim to having an interest in general environmental protection may lack the necessary locus to commence legal proceedings, or prefer to devote limited resources to creating political rather than legal pressure on defaulting administrations.

There are other aspects, though, of the Community's environmental policies which have contributed to the problems of implementation. The programme is comparatively young, and before the passing of the Single European Act 1987 lacked explicit legal basis under the Treaty.[14] In that climate, the attraction for policy makers initiating Community activity in this field to concentrate on the creation of an ambitious body of environmental laws, even if this implied legislation at the expense of implementation, would have been understandable. Directorate-General XI still remains comparatively small in staff numbers compared to the rest of the Commission, but its purchase power and influence is considerable given the scope of the legislation now in place.

A further reason relates to the form of legislation adopted. The vast majority of Community laws have taken the form of directives, and many of those now giving rise to serious tensions over interpretation and implementation were passed during the 1970s and early 1980s. The drafting and precise meaning of many of the requirements are open to differing interpretations, and were agreed by Member States at a time when they probably failed to appreciate the extent to which the directives represented more than a commitment of policy intention but a genuine legal obligation. Since that period, the developing jurisprudence of the European Court of Justice, both in relation to the direct effect doctrine[15] the so-called doctrine of sympathetic interpretation,[16] and its strict approach towards the

---

[12] European Parliament Resolution of 11 April 1984 [1984] OJ C127/67.

[13] Krämer, *EEC Treaty and Environmental Protection* (PUB?1990) 26.

[14] See Arts 130r-t and 100a EEC. Before the amendments to the Treaty, environmental legislation was generally based on either Art 100 or Art 235, or both.

[15] See, eg Case 41/74 *van Duyn v Home Office* [1974] ECR 1337; Case 8/81 *Becker v Finanzamt Munster-Innenstadt* [1982] ECR 53; Case 148/78 *Pubblico Ministero v Tullio Ratti* [1979] ECR 1629. There is as yet no decision of the Court of Justice dealing with the direct effect of environmental directives as such, although the *Ratti* case was concerned with the packaging and labelling of solvents and toxic substances.

[16] Case 14/83 *von Colson and Kamann v Land Nordrhein-Westfalen* [1984] ECR 1891. Again, there is no decision of the Court of Justice applying this doctrine to environmental Directives.

transposition of directives into national laws and procedures, has transformed the legal nature of directives.[17] One can only speculate whether Member States would have readily agreed the terms of some the earlier environmental directives had they appreciated their full legal significance, or had the development in the European Court's jurisprudence occurred at earlier date. Certainly, it might have been predicted that these legal developments, coupled with the Commission's own more intensive efforts at enforcement, would have made Member States more reluctant to agree new directives in the environmental field.[18] This does not appear to have happened – or if it did, has been more than counterbalanced by a growing political imperative given to environmental issues within Europe. Environmental directives with significant resource, legal, and administrative implications have continued to be proposed and agreed.

Formal Enforcement Procedures

The formal legal procedures available to the Commission in persuading a Member State to comply with Community obligations, derive from Article 169 EEC, and as such are common to all areas of Community policy. The terms of Article 169 are interpreted to divide into three separate stages: (i) the sending of a formal Article 169 letter to the Member State; (ii) the sending of a reasoned opinion; and finally (iii) referral to the European Court. The first two stages may, and often do, end in a settlement in that either the Member State complies with the Commission's requirements, or a mutually acceptable agreement is reached without the need for intervention by the Court. As might be expected of any complex process of legal enforcement, these formal stages, and particularly the service of an Article 169 letter are not normally initiated without some considerable forewarning and correspondence between the Member State and the Commission.

The Commission's concern is with a Member State's failure to implement Community agreed obligations, but what is actually implied by the concept of 'implementation' is by no means cut and dried. For administrative purposes, the Commission itself has broken down the subject into three main areas: (i) a failure by a Member State to communicate to the Commission national laws and other national measures implementing the Community instruments in question; (ii) incomplete or incorrect transposition of Community obligations into national law; and (iii) the failure to apply the Community obligations in practice, whatever the state of the national law.

Black Letter Implementation

The first two categories are, by their nature, confined to the implementation of directives, and are concerned with what might be described as the formal aspect of implementation,

---

[17] See, eg Case 300/81 *Commission v Italy* [1983] ECR 449; Case 102/79 *Commission v Belgium* [1980] ECR 1473; Cases 361/88 and 59/89 *Commission v Germany* [1991] ECR I-2607.

[18] Rehbinder and Stewart, *Integration through Law: Environmental Protection Policy* (De Gruyter, 1985) argue to this effect at 316 *et seq*.

ensuring at the very least that the 'black letter' national law is in place. Monitoring the failure to communicate national measures within the timescale specified in the directive is a reasonably straightforward and quasi-mechanical process; either communication has been made by the specified date or it has not.

In the early 1980s, the Commission standardised the enforcement machinery relating to non-communication across all sectors of Community law.[19] Member States are notified, within two months of the directive being adopted, that they are required to notify the Commission of the texts of national implementing measures, with a further reminder letter generally sent six months before the deadline specified in the directive. If no notification has been made by the date required, the Commission will generally move straight into Article 169 proceedings without further warning, starting with a formal letter and moving to a reasoned opinion without referring back to Commissioners for approval.

The rise in the volume of legal proceedings for non-communication has been dramatic, with just 15 proceedings begun in 1982 for non-communication in the environmental sector, rising to 131 in 1990 (see Table 1). Indeed, in 1990, proceedings for non-commu-

Table 1 Article 169 Infringement Proceedings, 1982–90

	Non-communication	Non-conformity	Poor application
Environment			
1982	15	1	–
1983	23	10	2
1984	48	15	2
1985	58	10	1
1986	84	32	9
1987	68	30	58
1988	36	24	30
1989	46	17	37
1990	131	24	62
All sectors			
1982	206	10	37
1983	140	19	27
1984	222	46	17
1985	257	30	14
1986	268	51	54
1987	260	42	125
1988	282	33	117
1989	327	25	169
1990	616	37	162

Source: 8th Report of the Commission to the European Parliament on the enforcement of Community law, 1991.

[19] See, eg European Commission, 'Manual of Procedures', 5th update (March 1982).

nication represented almost 60% of the total commenced in the environmental sector, a figure matched on the overall picture. This represents a higher proportion of the three classes of actions than for the previous three years, and could in part simply be attributable to a higher volume of legislation agreed in previous years. At the same time, the Commission has become more confident on legal grounds that the transposition of directives in most cases is required to be in the form of national legislation rather than administrative means, and in this respect has been bolstered by recent decisions of the European Court of Justice.[20] More disturbingly, though, it could suggest that Member States are more complacent on the issue, especially as they must be aware that the European Court of Justice has in its decisions on non-communication showed little sympathy for any excuses made by Member States on internal political or constitutional grounds.[21] In this respect, the Commission's policy of a more aggressive and regularised approach in respect of non-communication may have diluted the shock value of Article 169 proceedings, though in the absence of more effective legal sanctions their tactics are understandable if only to bring to the light the current state of noncompliance with the most basic of obligations.

Determining an infringement of the second type, incomplete or incorrect transposition, is a task that is intellectually much more demanding. Communication of national laws has taken place with the required time limits but it is argued that they fail to reflect the obligations under the directive in question. This requires both an understanding of the legal meaning of the provisions of the directive, itself not always an easy matter, together with the ability to interpret the meaning of national legislation in the light of the Member State's own legal and administrative practice. The position is made more complex because Member States may have relied upon pre-existing legislation to meet the aims of the directive, in which case its detailed terminology is unlikely to be closely aligned with that of the directive.[22]

Furthermore, some of the more recent environmental directives, which cut across conventionally drawn boundaries of administrative and legal responsibility, may as a result prevent the Member State from relying upon a single item of legislation as its means of implementation. The Environmental Assessment Directive[23] offers the prime example, with some countries needing to pass twenty or so individual laws in different sectoral and jurisdictional areas;[24] in communicating the text of these measures to the Commission, only the most selfless of Member States is likely to draw attention to detailed deficiencies that may exist.

Examples have existed where Member States have discussed the draft text of environmental legislation with the Commission well before the implementation date, and common sense suggests that at this stage a Member State faced with criticism may be more ready to

---

[20] See especially Cases 361/88 and 59/89, above n 17, concerning implementation of Directive 80/779 on air quality limits values and guide values for sulphur dioxide and suspended particulates [1980] OJ L222/30 and Directive 82/884 on limit values for lead in air [1982] OJ L378/15.

[21] Eg Case 77/69 *Commission v Belgium* [1970] ECR 237; Case 79/72 *Commission v Italy* [1973] ECR 667; Case 52/75 *Commission v Italy* [1986] ECR 1359.

[22] For recent examples where a Member State relied upon pre-existing national law to implement environmental Directives see Case 360/87 *Commission v Italy* judgment of the Court of Justice [1991] ECR I-791; Case 131/88 *Commission v Germany* judgment [1991] ECR I-825. Both cases involved Directive 80/68 on the protection of groundwater against pollution by certain dangerous substances [1980] OJ L103/1, and in both the Commission was successful in claiming that the Member State had failed to transpose adequately the Directive into national law.

[23] Above n 10.

[24] This has been the case for the United Kingdom and for Germany.

modify the final version. In contrast, once national law has been passed, whether by way of primary or secondary legislation, there must be an understandable tendency on the part of the Member State to defend the status quo. Despite this, there appears to be no regular procedure, either as a legal requirement or as a matter of administrative practice, by which Member States and the Commission discuss draft texts of national laws during the period following agreement of a directive and the state for its implementation.[25]

Implementation in Practice – Conceptual and Practical Difficulties

The third category, non-implementation in practice, is perhaps the most difficult area of enforcement for the Commission, and certainly one that can touch a raw nerve of the sensibilities of Member States. Examples of this category include the failure of local drinking water supplies or particular stretches of bathing waters to meet prescribed Community standards, the failure of a waste disposal licence to meet the prohibitions contained in the Groundwater Directive, failure to carry out an environmental assessment for a project falling within mandatory classes of the Environmental Assessment, and, in the future, no doubt the failure by public authorities to provide members of the public with information as required under the Access to Environmental Information Directive.[26]

The need to ensure effective implementation in practice has been endorsed by Member States, yet clearly there exist tensions and controversy when the Commission takes steps to pursue this task. To start with, it is not always clear whether a particular example of apparent breaches of Community law should be classified as incomplete or incorrect transposition of the directive or a failure to implement in practice. One can again take the case of the Environmental Assessment Directive, where a Member State has failed to introduce the necessary implementing legislation covering all the project classes specified in the Directive. A particular project in that Member State is proposed and no environmental assessment is undertaken. Is that a failure to implement the Directive in practice, or simply an example of the results of failing to correctly transpose the Directive into national law?

At first sight, the distinction seems unimportant. The Article 169 legal procedures are the same whatever category of breach is alleged by the Commission. Yet compared with more general proceedings taken against a Member State for incomplete transposition, action initiated in respect of a particular project may have considerable local political impact, possibly even bringing pressure to suspend or bring to the halt construction of the project in question.[27] Furthermore, injunctive remedies from the European Court may be

---

[25] During oral proceedings in Case 252/89 *Commission v Luxembourg* and Case 330/89 *Commission v Belgium* on 7 November 1990, both concerning the failure to implement the Environmental Assessment Directive, the Court expressed concern that the Commission had failed to give any response when Luxembourg had sent to the Commission the text of a proposed new law implementing the Directive.

[26] Directive 90/313 [1990] OJ L158/56.

[27] It is interesting to note the application of the Environmental Assessment Directive in a procedure in the Netherlands, *Texaco v Minister van Economische Zaken*, where the president of the Court suspended, in summary proceedings, the approval of a plan involving construction of a conventional power station. See the annotation by H Sevenster [1991] *Utilities Law Review* 65.

available to stop continuing work on an individual project, though the Commission's only experience to date with such proceedings in the environmental sector was unsuccessful.[28] Yet in reality in such cases it is the underlying failure of the Member State to introduce appropriate legislation which has given rise to the problem – indeed the national authorities dealing with such a project may themselves possess no power to require environmental assessment procedures.

The above illustrates a further difficulty with this type of infringement proceedings. Assuming that the national legislation is in place, failure to implement in practice may well be due to the action or inaction of a local or regional public authority, or even a local court. All such bodies fall within the overarching concept of the 'Member State', yet in practice it is the central governments of Member State who assume the responsibility for being at the receiving end of infringement proceedings. It is they who will be expected to take appropriate remedial steps against internal authorities who fail to implement Community obligations, be it by the use of default powers or the promotion of new legislation. In an era of greater regionalisation and where federalism is explained by its proponents to imply a real devolvement of powers as much as their centralisation, it must be questioned whether the current focus of infringement proceedings against Member States through the medium of central governments is still appropriate. There may well be a case for adopting a practice of permitting proceedings to be taken directly against the particular authority responsible for the failure in practice, at whatever level of government it is placed. Where a local authority makes an illegal planning decision in the United Kingdom, we expect to see judicial review proceedings taken against that body, not against the Secretary of State for the Environment even though he may have overall political responsibility for the planning system. The same should be true of infringement procedures if one is to view Community environmental law as a mature legal system integral to the national systems within Member States, and a stage removed from more straight-forward international agreements between individual States represented by their central governments.

We can identify further areas of tension that arise from dealing with the failure to apply directives in practice. The economic cost of complying with the requirements of directives may often be the root cause of the failure to implement, and while some environmental directives expressly incorporate an economic criterion such as 'best available technology not entailing excessive costs',[29] others do not.

An important case before the European Court of Justice in 1990 concerned the failure to implement the standards contained in the Drinking Water Directive[30] in local supplies, and suggests that in such cases the Court will take a strict attitude. Although the directive contained provisions allowing Member States to obtain derogations in exceptional cases, mainly due to particular geographical problems, financial and technical difficulties were not expressly mentioned. The Belgian Government had argued that the costs and complexities of constructing suitable treatment works in the localities specified had caused the delay in compliance. The Court rejected this as an excuse:

---

[28] Case 57/89 *Commission v Germany* [1989] ECR 2849.
[29] See Directive 84/360 on the combating of air pollution from large industrial plants [1984] OJ L336/1.
[30] Directive 80/778 relating to the quality of water intended for human consumption.

il y a lieu de rappeler que, selon la jurisprudence de la Cour, un État membre ne saurait exciper des difficultés pratiques ou administratives pour justifier le non-respect des obligations et délais prescrits par les directives communautaires. *Il en va de même pour les difficultés financiéres qu'il appartient aux États membres de surmonter en prenant les mesures appropriées.*[31]

Many provisions in environmental directives involve various types of discretionary powers to be exercised by Member States or competent bodies, and the issue here concerns the principles on which the exercise of such discretionary powers should amount to a failure to implement a directive in practice, giving rise to infringement proceedings. There is some emerging case law, though little in the way of developed principle.

A common provision of a number of environmental directives, particularly those concerning water pollution, is a power given to Member State to designate areas falling within the requirements of the directive. In the Bathing Water Directive, for example, Member States must designate areas of water to be subject to the standards contained in the directive, but the definition of bathing water is expressed in quasi-objective terms: all fresh water or sea water in which 'bathing is either explicitly authorised by the Member States, or is not prohibited and is traditionally practised by a large number of bathers' (Article 1.2). This has given the Commission clear leverage to question the determinations made by a Member State on the basis that water falling outside the definition had not been designated. Other directives, though, contain no such objective definitions, but are expressed in a way that appears to given a clear discretion to Member States. But the failure by a Member State even to address the question of designation may render the aims of the directive ineffective, and here the European Court has held that in such cases there may be an infringement by the Member State.[32]

A similar issue has arisen in the case of the Environmental Assessment Directive which requires assessment procedures to be carried out in respect of proposals for projects falling within classes specified in the directive. For those falling within Annex I, assessment is mandatory, while for those falling within the much larger list in Annex II, assessment is required only where such projects may give rise to significant environmental effects; Member States are given discretion to determine appropriate criteria and thresholds to decide which particular projects falling within Annex II should be subject to assessment. Some Member States, initially at any rate, considered that this was an unfettered discretion giving them the right to exclude totally whole classes of projects from their national provisions on assessment. It is an interpretation that the Commission has firmly resisted; in order to achieve the aims of the directive, Member States are obliged to address the problem of criteria and thresholds for *all* classes of projects specified within the directive.

The European Court is likely to support this approach.[33] That the failure by a Member State to address the exercise of a discretionary power may amount to an infringement of the

---

[31] Author's emphasis. Case 42/89 *Commission v Belgium* judgment of the Court of Justice [1990] ECR I-2821, para 24: 'according to the Court's case law, a Member State may not rely on practical or administrative difficulties for the justification of failure to respect the obligations and time limits laid down by Community Directives. The same holds for financial difficulties, which it is for Member States to overcome by taking appropriate measures' (editors' translation).

[32] Case 322/86 *Commission v Italy* [1988] ECR 3995 concerning the failure by Italy to designate waters under Directive 78/659 on the quality of fresh waters needing protection or improvement in order to support fish life [1978] OJ L222/1 and under Directive 79/923 on the quality required for shellfish waters [1979] OJ L281/47.

[33] The prediction was correct. See C-133/90 *Commission v Belgium* [1996] ECR I-2323: 'Article 4(2) does not empower the Member States to exclude generally and definitively from possible assessment one or more classes mentioned in Annex II' (para 43); see also Case C-301/95 *Commission v Germany* [1998] ECR I-6135.

directive is hardly contentious. A more difficult question, though, arises when it is sought to question the actual judgments made by Member States in the exercise of such powers. On what principles should both the Commission and the European Court approach to the issue? The Environmental Assessment Directive again provides good examples of the type of issue that increasingly is likely to arise. To what extent is the determination of specific thresholds for Annex II projects by a Member State a reviewable decision? Is the actual scope and content of assessment information provided in a particular case grounds for infringement proceedings? Should the decision by a local authority to grant permission for the proposed project to proceed, in the face of overwhelming evidence of adverse environmental effects, be questionable as a matter of Community law?

Leaving aside the particular wording of provisions of the directive in question, one can assume that the exercise of discretionary power would be subject to such general principles as proportionally and non-discrimination. Thresholds for Annex II classes of projects, for example, which made a distinction between projects involving national interests and those of other Member States would therefore be contrary to Community law. Beyond that, principles of review are underdeveloped. But some suggestion of an appropriate approach is found in the 1990 decision of the European Court in *Commission v France*[34] concerning Council Regulation 3626/82 of 3 December 1982 on the implementation in the Community of the Convention on international trade in endangered species (the CITES convention). Under the Regulation, Member States are required to issue permits for the importation from third countries of certain specified animals or plants, and Article 10(b) provides that the import permit may only be issued where, inter alia,

> it is clear or where the applicant presents trustworthy evidence, that the capture or collection of the specimen in the wild will not have a harmful effect on the conservation of species or on the extent of the territory occupied by the population in question of the species.

The proceedings arose out of the decision by the French authorities in 1986 to grant permits for the importation of some 6,000 wild cat skins from Bolivia. It was this decision that the Commission questioned. The decision of the French authorities had been taken against a background of international concern over illicit trade in wild animals from Bolivia, with a meeting of the contracting parties to the CITES Convention calling for a suspension of imports from the country until the Bolivian Government had demonstrated that it had adopted all practical measures to implement the Convention. The Commission had notified Member States of the terms of this Resolution, and in effect argued that in the light of these concerns, the French decision to grant import permits must have been contrary to the terms of Article 10(b) of the Council Regulation. The French argued that the CITES Resolution had no legal effect, and that the decision whether or not to grant import permits was one for national authorities; indeed, Article 9 specifically states that Member States shall recognise the decisions of competent authorities of other Member States, and that import permits granted by one country should be valid throughout the Community. The European Court held that there had been a breach of the directive. In the light of the factual background and the terms of Article 10(b) the French authorities, according to AG Mischo, 'n'ont pas raisonnablement pu aboutir a la constatation qu'il etait evident que la capture des chats sauvages en question n'aurait pas d'influence notive sur leur conservation ni sur l'entension de l'aire de leur distribution'.[35]

---

[34] Case 182/89, judgment of the Court of Justice [1990] ECR I-4337.
[35] Opinion, 18 October 1990, para 13: 'could not reasonably have come to the conclusion that it was obvious

This appears to be very close to *Wednesbury* principles of judicial review of administrative decisions, familiar to British courts.[36] Certainly the very particular nature of the decisions that were the subject of the proceedings illustrates just how deep into the decision making of national authorities the process of enforcement of Community environmental law has reached. British courts have long subscribed to the principle that it is not for them to substitute their own judgment for those in administration entrusted with the task of decision-making. Yet the Bolivian import case comes perilously close to just that. How far the European Court and the Commission will elaborate principles of review which forbear from second judging administrative decisions is likely to prove a challenging area of law over the next decade, especially when set against the political pressures that emphasise the importance of ensuring implementation of Community law in practice.

Information Gaps and the Complaint Procedure

In the environmental sector, the Commission has no express powers to assist its investigations of the kind it has been granted in the competition field.[37] There are as yet no Community environmental inspectors, working alongside national enforcement officers, although the idea has been mooted in the past, and may yet surface again.[38] In 1990, the Council of Ministers adopted a Regulation establishing a European Environmental Agency, though as yet no location for the Agency has been agreed.[39] In any event, the title of the body is rather misleading, since its terms of reference are clearly restricted to data collection and analysis, largely in cooperation with national authorities. During discussions of the draft proposal, the European Parliament pressed hard for the Agency to have more explicit enforcement functions, but in the event managed only to secure a

---

that the capture of the wild cats in question would not have a harmful effect on their conservation or on the extent of the territory occupied by their population' (editors' translation).

[36] *Wednesbury Corporation v Ministry of Housing and Local Government* [1965] 1 WLR 261. In Case 42/84 *Remia BV v Commission* [1985] ECR 2545 the Court of Justice reviewed the discretion of the Commission to determine the permitted duration of a non-competition clause under Art 85(3) of the EEC Treaty. The Court recognised that the Commission's decision was based on a complex economic appraisal, and that its grounds for review should be limited 'to verifying whether the relevant procedural rules had been complied with, whether the statement of the reasons for the decision is adequate, whether the facts have been accurately stated, and whether there had been any manifest error of appraisal or misuse of powers'. These principles were concerned with the Commission's decision-making functions, but it is suggested they might be use fully adapted to those of national authorities in the sorts of examples given in the text.

[37] See Council Regulation No 17 of 6 February 1962, OJ Special Edition 1959–62, 87.

[38] In November 1991 the UK government called for the creation of a small Community 'Audit Inspectorate' to work alongside national enforcement bodies to monitor and report on compliance with EEC environmental legislation. Department of the Environment Press Release, 25 November 1991.

[39] Regulation 1210/90 [1990] OJ L120/1. Despite pressure from the European Parliament to give the agency a more explicit inspection and enforcement function, the Regulation restricts its activities broadly to the gathering and assessment of environmental data, though even this limited role is likely to assist the Commission in its enforcement activities. Art 20, however, provides that two years after the entry into force of the Regulation (which takes place when its location has been agreed) the Council, having consulted the Parliament and on the basis of a report from the Commission, must decide on further tasks for the Agency, including 'associating in the monitoring of the implementation of Community environmental legislation, in cooperation with the Commission and existing competent bodies in the Member States'. It was subsequently agreed that the Agency should be based in Copenhagen, and it became operational in 1994.

commitment in the Regulation to review the role of the Agency in this respect two years after it comes into existence.

Against this background, the Commission has been peculiarly dependent on its own complaint system to enable it to be alerted to possible infringements in practice. The procedures, governed by the Commission's internal rules of administration,[40] permit any member of the public, including environmental groups and industries, to notify the Commission of alleged infringements. The system is common to all areas of Community law, and was first developed in the 1960s in the context of the internal market. But it is environmental issues that have given rise to a spectacular growth in the numbers of complaints received, and they now represent almost half of all total number received annually by the Commission (Table 2).

Table 2 Complaints Registered by Commission, 1982–90

	Environment	All sectors
1982	10	352
1983	8	399
1984	9	476
1985	37	585
1986	165	791
1987	150	850
1988	216	1,137
1989	465	1,195
1990	480	1,252

Source: as Table 1 above.

A number of criticisms can be made about the current system. It means that the Commission is, initially at any rate, playing a largely reactive role to the type of issues and subject matter raised; its stated commitment to investigate every complaint received, while a laudable goal of an administration exercising enforcement powers, leaves little room for strategic decision making, especially given the current limited man-power involved.[41] When the numbers of complaints are broken down on a country by country basis, it is clear that there are considerable disparities, which reveal as much about a country's tradition of environmental activism and political protest as they do about the state of implementation of Community law (see Table 3).

In the Commission's favour, it should be stressed that these realities are recognised, and in the end there is a more balanced approach towards Member States than might be apparent at first glance. Complaints on a particular issue from one Member State may sometimes lead to an investigation of the state of compliance within all Member States, and the figures on the number of reasoned opinions and referrals to the Court indicate

---

[40] See above n 19.
[41] According to Dr Ludwig Krämer, the unit in October 1991 had a staff of 10 lawyers, six of whom were on secondment; evidence taken before House of Lords Select Committee on the European Communities (Sub-Committee F), 13 October 1991.

Table 3 Complaints Registered in Environmental Sector, 1990

Belgium	17
Denmark	3
France	47
Germany	56
Greece	40
Ireland	19
Italy	33
Luxembourg	3
Netherlands	7
Portugal	19
Spain	111
United Kingdom	125

Source: Commission.

Table 4 Reasoned Opinions and Referrals to Court of Justice in Environmental Sector, 1989

	Reasoned opinion	Referral to ECJ
Belgium	8	11
Denmark	0	0
France	6	7
Germany	8	8
Greece	5	3
Ireland	5	0
Italy	16	7
Luxembourg	2	1
Netherlands	5	2
Portugal	4	0
Spain	9	3
United Kingdom	8	5

Source: Commission Report on Enforcement of Community Environmental Law 8/2/1990.

that action against Member States is not eventually dictated by the number of complaints received from each (Table 4).

In 1990, the Commission took the bold step of releasing publicly figures on a country by country basis of the numbers of Article 169 letters that had been issued in the environmental sector, a deliberate political move to highlight the issue of implementation and one that caused considerable disquiet among some Member States at the time. One of the benefits of this unprecedented exercise in public administration was that, as with the reasoned opinions and Court referrals, it confirmed that enforcement action against Member States was not driven by complaint numbers, but probably reflected a reasonable approximation of the relative levels of compliance (Table 5). Nevertheless, when broken down on a sector by sector basis, the figures suggest that the current procedures are vulnerable to the focus

Table 5 Article 169 Formal Letters in Environmental Sector, 1989

Belgium	27
Denmark	5
France	28
Germany	13
Greece	37
Ireland	16
Italy	17
Luxembourg	9
Netherlands	18
Portugal	10
Spain	45
United Kingdom	18

Source: Commission Report on Enforcement of Community Environmental Law, 21 August 1990.
Note: a number of Member States disputed the accuracy of these figures when they were released, though any errors appeared to have been marginal.

Table 6 Infringement Proceedings Sector by Sector as at 31 December 1989

	Water	Air	Waste	Chemicals	Noise	Nature*
Belgium	11	3	18	5	2	7
Denmark	2	–	–	–	1	–
France	15	3	2	1	–	20
Germany	9	4	2	3	–	11
Greece	10	4	6	2	3	20
Ireland	7	2	3	2	–	7
Italy	9	4	10	2	3	12
Luxembourg	5	2	2	–	1	2
Netherlands	6	2	2	3	3	8
Portugal	2	1	4	–	–	7
Spain	12	2	10	4	–	29
UK	16	5	3	3	–	4

Source: As Table 5 above.
*Includes environmental assessment.

of attention of national environmental interests (Table 6). The high number of infringements in the field of water pollution in the United Kingdom, for example, has been largely driven by highly directed campaigns by amenity bodies, while equivalent groups in France appear to have paid particular attention to hunting activities and the protection of wild animals.

A further concern of present procedures is the extent to which the Commission may be dependent on a Member State's co-operation in complying with the Commission's initial requests for information following the lodging of a complaint. An absolute refusal to respond may result in the Member State being threatened with infringement proceedings for failure to comply with its duty to assist the Commission in its tasks under Article 5 of the EEC Treaty.[42] But the provision of poor or incomplete information by Member States poses peculiar difficulties for the Commission, and while in some cases site visits have been undertaken or consultants' reports commissioned, the current system is hardly geared to this type of intensive investigatory work, although it may be required.

Defective implementation in practice is likely to be a continuing focus of attention, and while in formal terms the dispute is between the Member State and the Commission it is clear that in practice private parties may find themselves heavily involved in the process. The complainant himself may dispute a decision of the Commission not to initiate infringement proceedings, particularly where his own private interests are being threatened by alleged illegal action, and given the limitations of the direct effect doctrine it may not be possible to raise such issues before national courts. But parties, other than the complainant, may also find their interests at stake. For example, the legality of an authorisation given under national law to a private project may be thrown into doubt should the Commission decided to commence proceedings against the Member State for failure to apply the Environmental Assessment Directive; similarly, a permit given to a private operator of a waste disposal facility may be questioned because of its incompatibility with the Groundwater Directive.

Current principles of Community law need development to recognise the reality of these relationships. Private interests which are indirectly involved in this way currently have no rights vis-à-vis the Commission to ensure that their point of view is heard during the investigatory procedures. The Court of Justice has continued to confirm that the decision to commence Article 169 procedures is a matter of discretion for the Commission, and that a third party, whether a complainant or, one must presume, another party directly effected by this decision, has no locus before the Court in such cases to question the legality of its action.[43]

The initiation of infringement proceedings concerning failure to implement in practice, is subject to no period of limitation of the type familiar to national systems of administrative law, and designed to provide legal certainty to private and public interests. The extent to which these types of issues are currently addressed is largely left to the discretion and sense of propriety of the Commission; if the enforcement process is to be strengthened and extended in future, the time may now have come to develop more considered legal principles governing the procedures.

Some Concluding Remarks

The Commission's own achievements to date in revealing the extent to which deficiencies of implementation exist within most Member States underlines the continuing importance of the issue. New institutional arrangements such as the European Environment

---

[42] 'Member States shall take all appropriate measures, whether general or particular, to ensure fulfilment of the obligations arising out of the Treaty or resulting from action taken by the institutions of the Community. They shall facilitate the achievement of the Community's tasks.'

[43] Case 246/81 *Bethell v Commission* [1982] ECR 2277; Case 87/89 *Societe National Interprofessionelle de la Tomate (SONITO) v Commission* [1991] 3 CMLR 439.

Agency,[44] the proposed network of national environmental bodies,[45] and the proposed environmental audit inspectorate[46] should all assist in improving the information flow on implementation gaps. But for the foreseeable future the Commission's enforcement role as legal guardian of the Treaty is likely to remain of central importance, and this article has identified a number of areas where current procedures and principles appear to require reassessment to improve both their efficacy and their acceptability. Full implementation of Community law, though, may always be an impossible goal, and in any event is unlikely ever to be achieved solely by the 'top-down' mechanisms implicit in the Article 169 procedure.[47] In the long run, it requires a genuine internal political will by Member States of the need to implement Community environmental policies, and this in turn demands both the dynamic participation of citizens and amenity groups, and an active recognition by national courts and authorities of their own role in giving effect to Community obligations. Until this occurs, the gap between the law in theory and in practice can be expected to remain intact.

---

[44] See above n 39.

[45] See above n 7.

[46] See above n 38. No further development of the prosed audit inspectorate appears to have taken place. But see the recent proposals of the European Commission to improve the standard of inspections and auditing at national level: DG Environment, 'Study on Possible Options for Strengthening the EU Level Role in Environmental Inspections and Strengthening the Commission's Capacity to Undertake Effective Investigations of Alleged Breaches in EU Environment Law', Final report European Commission DG ENV (14 January 2013); see also Chapter 30 of this volume.

[47] Notwithstanding the proposed provisions giving power to the European Court to impose financial penalties on Member States which failed to comply with its judgments; see new Art 171(2) of Draft Treaty on European Union, following the 1991 Maastricht Summit. See now Art 260(2) TFEU.

29

European Moves on Environmental Enforcement[1]
(2014)

The 7th Action Environment Programme[2] was agreed by a decision of the European Council and Parliament in November 2013. It sets the framework for the development of European environmental policies until 2020. Action Programmes have existed since the first European Community environmental policies were initiated in the early 1970s, but under the Lisbon Treaty they now have heightened legal status – indeed, Article 172 of the Treaty of the Function of the European Union provides that 'the measures necessary for the adoption of these Programmes shall be adopted', which could be implied to read that a failure by the Commission and the other Union institutions to turn the policies into reality would open them up to legal action.

The Programme starts with an inspiring vision of Europe in 2050:

> In 2050, we live well, within the planet's ecological limits. Our prosperity and healthy environment stem from an innovative, circular economy where nothing is wasted and where natural resources are managed sustainably, and biodiversity is protected, valued and restored in ways that enhance our society's resilience. Our low-carbon growth has long been decoupled from resource use, setting the pace for a safe and sustainable global society.

However, the Programme can be criticised as being strong on aspirational goals but lacking hard initiatives in the form of new European environmental legislation.

This in part reflects a lack of political appetite for more legislation in the current economic climate, and a concern at the ability of the law itself to achieve some of the profound changes in industrial and consumer behaviour implied by the vision. Nevertheless, the Programme is adamant that the implementation and enforcement of existing EU environmental law must be improved and argues that, in addition to environmental and health benefits, this will have economic advantages in that it will help to create a level playing field within Europe, stimulate innovation and promote first-mover advantage for European companies – 'Improving the implementation of the Union environment *acquis* at Member State level will therefore be given top priority in the coming years'.

The Programme acknowledges that there are enormous differences within Europe on how environmental law is actually implemented and enforced, and, despite the political

---

[1] R Macrory, 'European Union Moves on Environmental Enforcement' in *International Comparative Guide to Environment Law 2014* (London, Global Legal Group, 2014).

[2] Decision No 1386/2013/EU of the European Parliament and of the Council of 20 November 2013 on a General Union Environment Action Programme to 2020 'Living well, within the limits of our planet' Text with EEA relevance [2013] OJ L354, 171–200.

sensitivities sometimes involved, all the signs are that this is an area which will receive increasing attention over the next decade. There have already been signals from other quarters. At the end of 2012, the Court of Justice of the European Union (CJEU) imposed a large fine on Ireland for failing to comply with its judgment three years earlier that Ireland was in breach of its obligations under EU waste legislation.[3] The Court's powers to impose financial penalties on countries were introduced under Treaty amendments in 1993 to tackle the problem of an increasing number of Member States that appeared not to respect its judgments, and is unique in the international field.[4] What is distinctive about the Irish case is that it largely concerned systemic weaknesses in a country's administrative structure for implementing and enforcing environmental law, and signals a more robust approach at a European level to issues of implementation and enforcement.

Effective Penalties under EU Law

European Union environmental legislation now represents a substantive body of law, but has largely tended to be rather cautious when it comes to enforcement and sanctions, leaving this to the discretion of Member States. The CJEU has often held that, when it comes to implementing European Union law, Member States have an obligation to ensure that penalties are effective, proportionate and dissuasive. This mantra sometimes appears in some specific EU environmental laws, but, as with the European Court, these rarely specify the type of sanction – criminal, civil or administrative – that must be employed at national level, still less the size. Very little is ever specified in EU environmental law about the type and level of administrative structures needed at national level to ensure that laws are effectively enforced. For example, the Directive on Industrial Emissions, in dealing with integrated licensing for pollution controls, simply requires that

> Member States shall take the measures necessary to ensure that the conditions of, and the procedures for the granting of, the permit are fully coordinated where more than one competent authority or more than one operator is involved or more than one permit is granted, in order to guarantee an effective integrated approach by all authorities competent for this procedure.[5]

There is no requirement for there to be a single regulatory body granting permits, or for it to be at either the regional or local level. Many Member States deeply resent what is seen as undue intrusion into national ways of doing things, and law enforcement is seen by many to fall squarely within a no-go area.

The European Commission has powers to bring infringement proceedings against Member States who fail to comply with obligations under European Union law, but, despite calls from the European Parliament to give the Commission greater powers of national inspection in the environmental field, Member States have long resisted giving it any such formal powers – a striking contrast to the position in competition law. The Commission is able to examine the text of national laws and policies for compliance, but, when it comes to actual practice on the ground, it must largely rely upon information provided

---

[3] C-374/11 *European Commission v Ireland* 19 December 2012.
[4] See now Treaty on the Functioning of the European Union, Art 260(2).
[5] Directive 2010/75/EU of the European Parliament and of the Council of 24 November 2010 on industrial emissions (integrated pollution prevention and control), Art 5.

by non-governmental organisations and concerned citizens. The new Action Programme notes that 'the way in which complaints about implementation of Union environment law are handled and remedied at national level will be improved where necessary',[6] though it contains no more specific proposals. It is likely that there will be increased efforts to encourage Member States to resolve issues before formal infringement proceedings are commenced. Complaints often require the Commission to obtain more information from Member States before deciding how to proceed, and doing so is currently a pretty cumbersome process, involving communications to the Permanent Representative Offices in Brussels, which then have to contact relevant national ministries, which in turn may need to communicate with local authorities or other agencies, depending on the nature of the complaint. It would seem preferable if the national offices of the European Commission could first be tasked with preparing a factual dossier on complaints, before sending this to Brussels to decide how to respond.

There are other changes taking place. Following disputes about its legal basis under the Treaty, Directive 2008/99 on the protection of the environment through criminal law requires Member States to ensure that they create criminal offences for a whole range of environmentally harmful activity when committed 'intentionally or with at least serious negligence'.[7] The Directive does not specify the actual size of criminal sanctions, using only the familiar formula that they must be 'effective, proportionate and dissuasive'.[8] For companies, the sanctions may be administrative, reflecting legal theory in some EU Member States that artificial bodies do not have the capacity to commit crime. It was the Court of Justice, in its 2007 decision on the Directive,[9] which prevented any detailed specification of penalties in the Directive. It accepted that, where the application of criminal national penalties is an essential measure for combating serious environmental offences, the Community legislature might require Member States to introduce such rules. But it then held that 'the determination of the type and level of the criminal penalties to be applied does not fall within the Community's sphere of competence'.[10] No fuller explanation is given to justify this division of competences, and it is arguable that this had the effect of neutering the true potential impact of the Directive. The Directive should have been transposed in all Member States by the end of 2010, and the European Commission is now completing an implementation review with a view to initiating infringement proceedings where they consider proper transposition has not taken place.

Tough Administrative Penalties under EU Emissions Trading Regime

Directive 2003/87,[11] introducing the greenhouse emissions trading scheme into the

---

[6] 7th Action Programme, para 61.
[7] Directive 2008/99, Art 3.
[8] Ibid, Art 5.
[9] C-440/05 *Commission v European Parliament and Council* [2007] ECR I-9097.
[10] Ibid, para 70.
[11] Directive 2003/87/EC of the European Parliament and of the Council of 13 October 2003 establishing a scheme for greenhouse gas emission allowance trading within the Community and amending Council Directive 96/61/EC (Text with EEA relevance) [2003] OJ L275, 32–46.

European Union, has, perhaps because of its grounding in economic theory, gone the furthest of any European environmental legislation in specifying, in quantitative terms, penalties for the failure to surrender sufficient allowances at the end of each year. In addition to the requirement to make up the shortfall in allowances, a penalty of €100 must be imposed for every tonne of carbon dioxide emitted for which no allowances are provided. This formula can rapidly reach very high figures, and there is apparently no discretion on Member States to reduce the penalty because of mitigating or other circumstances.

The strict nature of the rule was in fact challenged before the European Court last year. In *Billerud Karlsborg v Naturvardsverket*,[12] two Swedish companies had failed to surrender allowances equivalent to their emissions in 2006, and the regulatory authority applying the formula in the Directive had imposed penalties of over €1 million. The companies argued that they in fact had sufficient emissions allowances to cover the shortfall in April 2007, which showed they had no intention to circumvent the obligations, and that the error had been due to internal administrative breakdowns. The European Court refused to allow any mitigation of the provisions on the basis of the general principle of proportionality. The Directive provided a four-month period to prepare to surrender allowances for the previous year, and Member States could provide warnings and other advice to give companies time to get their houses into order. As the Court noted,

> the relatively high level of the penalty is justified by the need to have infringements of the obligation to surrender a sufficient number of allowances treated in a stringent and consistent manner throughout the European Union. That need was, moreover, particularly acute during the phase in which an entirely new EU-wide scheme was being launched.[13]

The decision can be contrasted with a decision of the European Court a few years earlier, which concerned the level of administrative penalties contained in Hungarian legislation implementing European Union tachograph requirements.[14] The system of penalties under the national law contained flat-rate fines and did not appear to allow for adjustment of the penalty in the light of the gravity of the offence, and the European Court held that such a system was inconsistent with the basic principle of proportionality. It is not easy to reconcile this ruling with the approach taken by the Court in the emissions trading case, other than to recognise that the Court can often be tougher in considering the legality of Member States' initiatives than it is with those of the European Union.

As for inspection and enforcement regimes in the environmental field, it is unlikely that the Commission will be given the power to carry out its own inspections or even work alongside national enforcement bodies in the foreseeable future. But the focus of efforts is likely to be concerned with improving the national inspection systems. Over 10 years ago the European Council and Parliament recognised that a consistent and rigorous inspection system at a national level was a key element of effective enforcement of environmental law. A recommendation was passed[15] stating that

---

[12] C-203/12 Court of Justice of the European Union 17 October 2013.

[13] Ibid, para 39.

[14] C-210/10 *Márton Urbán v Vám- és Pénzügyőrség Észak-alföldi Regionális Parancsnoksága*, Court of Justice of the European Union 9 February 2012. I am grateful to Professor Jan Jans for bringing this case to my attention.

[15] Recommendation 2001/331/EC of the European Parliament and of the Council of 4 April 2001 providing for minimum criteria for environmental inspections in the Member States.

environmental inspection tasks should be carried out in the Member States, according to minimum criteria to be applied in the organising, carrying out, following up and publicising of the results of such tasks, thereby strengthening compliance with, and contributing to a more consistent implementation and enforcement of Community environmental law in all Member States.[16]

The recommendation went on to elaborate the core elements of an effective inspection regime, but a recommendation in EU law is just that – essentially it has no binding legal force. However, recent EU environmental legislation is now beginning to refer to explicit obligations relating to inspections by Member States. In the past, occasional directives have referred to inspection – for instance, the 1975 Directive on the use of waste oils as fuels refers to the requirement that undertakings falling within the scope of the directive are 'inspected periodically' by the competent authorities of Member States, 'particularly as regards their compliance with the conditions of their permits'.[17] In 2003 the European Court of Justice held, in a case concerning Portugal, that general legal provisions establishing the competence and powers of administrative authorities were not sufficient to reflect the precise inspection obligations in that directive.[18] Similarly, the 1975 Directive on Waste as amended in 1991 contains a duty on Member States to carry out 'appropriate periodic inspections' of waste management sites.[19]

The Industrial Emissions Directive,[20] which is gradually replacing the Directive on Integrated Pollution and Prevention Control and applies to a large number of industrial installations, has taken the requirements of inspection and enforcement much further. It translates many of the elements of the 1991 Recommendation into obligations. Member States are required to set up a system of inspections and to ensure that all installations are covered by an environmental inspection plan. Routine inspections must be carried out with intervals based on risk assessment, while non-routine inspections are to be conducted in response to incidents or complaints. The intention is to ensure a rational system is in place: Art 23(2) requires that 'Member States shall ensure that all installations are covered by an environmental inspection plan at national, regional or local level and shall ensure that this plan is regularly reviewed and, where appropriate, updated'. The Industrial Emissions Directive attempts to avoid a bureaucratic nightmare of inspecting for its own sake, by insisting that, in the contemporary language of regulatory enforcement, the inspection regime must be risk based:

> Based on the inspection plans, the competent authority shall regularly draw up programmes for routine environmental inspections, including the frequency of site visits for different types of installations. The period between two site visits shall be based on a systematic appraisal of the environmental risks of the installations concerned and shall not exceed 1 year for installations posing the highest risks and 3 years for installations posing the lowest risks.[21]

The Industrial Emissions Directive is confined to specific classes of industrial process – around 45,000 installations across the European Union. But the requirements of the inspection regime are likely to be broadened much further if the European Commission

---

[16] Ibid, para 1.

[17] Council Directive 75/439/EEC of 16 June 1975 on the disposal of waste oils, Art 12.

[18] C-392/99 *Commission v Portugal* [2003] ECR I-3373, paras 163–73.

[19] Council Directive 75/442/EEC of 15 July 1975 on waste (as amended), para 13.

[20] Directive 2010/75/EU of the European Parliament and of the Council of 24 November 2010 on industrial emissions (integrated pollution prevention and control).

[21] Ibid, Art 23(4).

is successful in its current policy development. In discussing the 7th Environment Action Programme, the Council of Ministers in 2012 endorsed the proposals in the Programme to improve implementation and enforcement of EU environmental law, and encouraged the Commission and Member States to improve 'inspections and surveillance regimes where necessary inter alia through guidance for Member States, on the basis of experience with existing provisions and avoiding unnecessary administrative burdens'.[22]

Largely as a result of that lead, in 2013 the Commission published a study[23] commissioned from an external consultancy on possible options for strengthening the EU-level role in environmental inspections. This has been followed by workshops and wider consultation during the past year. Consultation responses[24] suggest the need for strengthening inspection systems across Europe, and the most likely response from the Commission will be a proposal for a directive that will extend the core provisions and requirements of the Industrial Emissions Directive to other areas of environmental law, such as water and nature conservation. Nevertheless, political agreement is not guaranteed, and the Council Conclusions in 2012 perhaps pointedly referred to improving inspections 'inter alia through guidance' – with no mention of binding EU legal requirements on Member States.

Overall, then, the signs are strong that over the next decade more attention than ever will be paid at the European level to the nature and effectiveness of national enforcement systems. It will not simply be the focus of initiatives from the European Commission. There are already various European networks of bodies responsible for various aspects of enforcement, which at least provide a forum for the exchange of information on best practice. The longest and most well known is the European Union Network for the Implementation and Enforcement of Environmental Law (IMPEL), set up in 1992 and largely focused on industrial pollution control. In 2007, a parallel network of agencies involved in nature conservation, the European Network of Heads of Nature Conservation Agencies, was established. Three years earlier, the European Union Forum for Judges for the Environment was set up on the initiative of a number of national judges concerned with environmental law, with a core aim of promoting the enforcement of national, European and international environmental law by exchanging information on decisions and generally raising awareness amongst national judges. A more recent development has been the establishment of a network of environmental prosecutors, an initiative promoted during the Belgian Presidency of the Council in 2010 and formally established in 2012. The European Network of Prosecutors for the Environment, together with Eurojust, held its first meeting in The Hague in 2013, bringing together for the first time prosecutors specialising in environmental crime from all over Europe, as well as representatives from IMPEL, Interpol and Europol. As the chair of the meeting concluded, 'We all agree on the threats, and we also agree on the obvious need to share experience and knowledge; this is exactly why Eurojust bringing together senior environmental prosecutors is so important and highly relevant'.[25]

---

[22] Council of Ministers, 'Conclusions on Setting the Framework for a Seventh EU Environment Action Programme', 3173rd Environment Council meeting, Luxembourg, 11 June 2012, para 6.

[23] DG Environment, 'Study on Possible Options for Strengthening the EU Level Role in Environmental Inspections and Strengthening the Commission's Capacity to Undertake Effective Investigations of Alleged Breaches in EU Environment Law', Final report European Commission DG ENV (14 January 2013).

[24] See http://ec.europa.eu/environment/legal/law/inspections.htm (accessed on 26 February 2014).

[25] See http://eurojust.europa.eu/press/News/News/Pages/Eurojust-and-ENPE-host-environmental-crime-meeting-.aspx (accessed on 26 February 2014).

Integrating Criminal and Administrative Enforcement

It was noticeable at the meeting that in most European countries the prosecution of criminal offences is conducted by specialised public prosecutors, the police or similar bodies, while the licensing and inspection of facilities is the responsibility of central or local government agencies. Many of these agencies will have the power to impose various sorts of administrative penalties for breaches of regulatory requirements but not the power of prosecution, which must be referred to another body. England & Wales is unusual in that regulatory bodies – mainly the Environment Agency –not only license and inspect, but also have the power of initiating a criminal prosecution for breach of regulations. Since 2010, the Agency has acquired an increasing range of powers to impose administrative penalties as an alternative to criminal prosecution, and the institutional structure has allowed the Agency to develop an integrated enforcement system which adopts the most appropriate sanction – criminal or administrative – in the light of the circumstances of the offences and the overall environmental policy objectives.

Such a truly integrated approach is rare in other parts of Europe, though there are exceptions. The Flemish Environmental Enforcement Act 2007, for example, has provided the basis for a far more coordinated enforcement response involving both criminal law and a new system of administrative penalties, though different bodies are still involved and require a good deal of coordination if the system is to work effectively. Nevertheless, a new body, the Flemish High Council of Environmental Enforcement, was established by decree in 2009 to provide greater coordination and consistency, and it has published a detailed Environmental Enforcement Report every year.[26] In many other countries, it is clear that contact and coordination between bodies responsible for criminal prosecution and administrative enforcement remain at a fairly ad hoc level.

It remains to be seen how far the European Commission, building upon its initiatives in inspection, will feel it can trespass on the types of penalties imposed by Member States and their systems for coordinating enforcement responses. The decision of the European Court on the Environmental Crime Directive suggests that, if the European Commission makes a convincing case that a more integrated response is necessary for improved implementation and enforcement of EU environmental law, then the Commission has the competence to embark in this area, provided it does not try to specify actual amounts of fines or penalties. Having the legal competence to act, though, is but one factor, and by no means ensures that the politics are secured.

---

[26] Under Art 16.2.4 of the 1995 Decree, as supplemented in 2007, 'The Flemish High Council for Environmental Enforcement draws up an annual environmental enforcement report. All authorities, who are part of the Flemish Region and are entrusted with the enforcement of the environmental law, provide the Flemish High Council for Environmental Enforcement, either at the simple request of the Flemish High Council for Environmental Enforcement or on their own initiative, all the information which they have at their disposal and which may be useful for drawing up the environmental enforcement report.' Translation available at http://navigator.emis.vito.be/milnavconsult/plainWettekstServlet?wettekstId=22361&lang=en (accessed on 26 February 2014). See Decree of 21 December 2007 to complement the Decreee of 5 April 1995 concerning general provisions on environmental policy with title XVI 'Toezicht, handhaving en veiligheidsmaatregelen', Bel Off Journal 29 February 2008.

EU Court Imposes Penalty for Weak National Enforcement System

It is in this context that the Irish waste case is particularly significant. Many infringement proceedings brought by the European Commission against Member States are concerned with the formal state of the national law – either that the Member State has failed to notify any national implementing laws within the timescale specified in a directive (normally two or three years) or that the laws that have been notified failed on examination to properly reflect the obligations contained in the directive in question. However, the European Court has long held that, even if the national law is formally in compliance with a directive, the failure to apply it in practice is equally a failure by the Member State to comply with its obligations under European Union law. An inadequate environmental assessment procedure, for example, for an individual new power station can be the subject of infringement proceedings, and, despite the evidential challenges, the Commission has been prepared to bring a large number of such cases.

The proceedings originally initiated against Ireland concerned a large number of inadequately licensed waste disposal sites. Each site itself could have amounted to a failure to implement EU waste law, but for the first time the Commission argued that these were examples that reflected a wider systemic failure in the administrative system for enforcement, and that these systemic weaknesses represented the breach. In 2005 the European Court agreed with this analysis and held that, by having an inadequate structure for enforcement and implementation, Ireland was in breach of its EU obligations. The Court did not define in any detail what steps were needed to rectify the situation, and in the subsequent years the Commission had to consider the adequacy of measures proposed by the Irish government, including a timetable for new legislation.

The Commission then brought proceedings claiming that Ireland had failed to comply with the 2009 judgment of the European Court concerning waste water treatment[27] and seeking financial penalties. In its judgment of 19 December 2012 (C-374/11), the Court agreed with the Commission that, whatever the state of the new primary legislation passed in Ireland, regulations were still required for its effective implementation and that no national inspection plan had yet been developed. Since Ireland has still not complied with its obligations some 19 years after the original EU obligations under the waste legislation came into force, it was a particularly serious breach. The Court imposed a lump sum penalty payment of €2 million, plus a daily penalty of €12,000 for each day of delay in adopting the measures necessary to comply with the original judgment. The daily continuing fine is likely to concentrate the minds of civil servants and politicians, and other Member States will be watching with interest and concern. In a period of growing pressure for public sector cut-backs, governments will need to be wary of reducing the effectiveness of their environmental enforcement bodies.

---

[27] Case C-188/08 *Commission v Ireland* [2009] ECR I-172.

30

Consistent Interpretation of EU Environmental Law[1] (2013)

Context

The obligation of consistent interpretation[2] is one of the key methods of ensuring that EU environmental obligations are enforced within Member States where directives have not been properly transposed into national law.[3] The national reports contained in this book indicate that in nearly every jurisdiction the general principle of the doctrine is accepted by the courts and has been applied in practice in individual cases, though in some countries there still remain few examples in the environmental field. The concept of consistent interpretation is not peculiar to EU law as such, but is a principle found in many domestic legal orders, requiring, for example, the interpretation of national law in conformity with the national constitution or with international law. But the techniques of interpretation vary from one domestic legal order to another. The Court of Justice of the European Union (CJEU) is well aware of these differences, and in tying the limits of the obligation to the national rules of construction the Court tries to fit consistent interpretation into the various legal backgrounds. Consistent interpretation is most importantly applied 'where a provision of a directive lacks direct effect, be it that the relevant provision is not sufficiently clear, precise and unconditional to produce direct effect or that the dispute is exclusively between individuals'.[4]

---

[1] R Macrory, V Madner and S Mayr 'Consistent Interpretation of EU Environmental Law' in J Jans, R Macrory and A-M Molina (eds), *National Courts and EU Environmental Law* (Groningen, Europa Law Publishing, 2014).

[2] The obligation to interpret national law in conformity with EU law bears many different labels in the literature (S Prechal, *Directives in EC Law* (Oxford University Press, 2005) 181). For example, 'indirect effect' is frequently used in leading UK literature (D Chalmers, G Davies and G Monti, *European Union Law* (Cambridge University Press, 2010) 294–300), but this seems to be too uncertain a term and even misleading. See the issues with delineating the concepts of 'Geltung', 'Wirkung' and 'Anwendbarkeit' in German and Austrian EU law doctrine, which partly disappear in other languages; then again, some authors in German doctrine differentiate between 'Vorrang *im engeren Sinn*' and 'Vorrang *im weiteren Sinn*' (supremacy in the narrow or wider sense), the latter comprising the concepts of consistent interpretation and state liability: D Jarass and S Beljin, 'Die Bedeutung von Vorrang und Durchführung des EG-Rechts für die nationale Rechtsetzung und Rechtsanwendung' [2004] *Neue Zeitschrift für Verwaltungsrecht* 1; S Beljin, 'die Zusammenhänge zwischen dem Vorrang, den Instituten der innerstaatlichen Beachtlichkeit und der Durchführung des Gemeinschaftsrechts' [2002] *EuR* 351. In this chapter we have used the term 'consistent interpretation'.

[3] It is in the context of directives that the doctrine has most impact, although the CJEU has held that national courts must also interpret national law to be consistent with the aims of the Treaty: Case C-397/01 *Van Munster* [2004] ECR I-8835.

[4] Case C-212/04 *Adeneler* [2006] ECR I-6057, para 113.

It has been argued that consistent interpretation should be the first approach taken by national courts to resolve conflicts in that it is 'less invasive, more finely tuned, and more consistent with the idea of subsidiarity,'[5] and there is evidently support for the idea of a preference of the CJEU, as the court holds that 'it must first be borne in mind that the question whether a national provision must be disapplied in as much as it conflicts with European Union law arises only if no compatible interpretation of that provision proves possible'.[6]

Compared to the direct effect doctrine, consistent interpretation prima facie seems to interfere less intensively with the Member States' sovereignty, as national provisions are being applied instead of being set aside. However, the consequences in the national legal order can be quite far-reaching. National courts sometimes view consistent interpretation simply as an alternative to direct effect where the latter cannot be used. See, for example, the decision of the French Cour de Cassation of 2011 in the context of EU waste legislation, holding that, even where provisions of a directive are not directly applicable, consistent interpretation would require national law to be interpreted so as to be compatible with the objectives of the EU law.[7] Other examples, such as a recent judgment of the Court of Appeal in the United Kingdom on access to justice,[8] show courts applying both doctrines as simple alternatives for reaching the same solution. It appears, though, that only the Dutch courts have explicitly held that courts should first attempt to apply the doctrine of consistent interpretation before considering the issue of direct effect.[9]

Despite the prevalence of the doctrine, a closer look at this interpretative technique raises a variety of complex issues. Some have been resolved, whereas others are yet to be explored in detail. The difficulties arise in part from the way the doctrine has been expressed and developed by the CJEU, but equally from the challenges national judges are facing in its application to individual cases in practice.

Development in the Case Law of the CJEU

Shifting Justifications

Even though the principle of consistent interpretation has primarily been developed and applied in connection with the implementation of EU directives, the concept as such is considerably wider. It establishes a general duty to interpret the national law as a whole

---

[5] J Jans, R de Lange and S Prechal, *Europeanization of Public Law* (Europa Law Publishing, 2006) 106.

[6] Case C-97/11 *Amia* judgment of 24 May 2012, paras 27–28, where the court held with reference to Case C-282/10 *Dominguez* [2012] ECR I-0000, para 23 that 'Consequently before disapplying national provisions, the national court must establish whether, in taking not only those provisions but also the whole body of domestic law into consideration and applying the interpretative methods recognised by that law, it can arrive at an interpretation of that national law which is consistent with the wording and purpose of the Directive at issue'. *Cf* also Case C-208/05 *ITC Innovative Technology Center GmbH v Bundesagentur für Arbeit* [2007] ECR I-181. The court reaffirmed the doctrine of consistent interpretation and held that, only where it was not possible to apply, 'the national court must apply Community law in its entirety and protect rights which the latter confers on individuals, disapplying, if necessary, any contrary provision of domestic law' (para 69).

[7] *Cf* the French national report at www.avosetta.org.

[8] *R (on the application of Garner) v Elmbridge Borough Council* [2010] EWCA Civ 1006. See further at p 551.

[9] *Buitengebied Texel* AB 2000, 303 (Raad van State).

in conformity with the entire body of EU law.[10] Most frequently, however, contentious issues arise in situations of 'remedial interpretation',[11] ie when a directive has not been transposed or implemented properly, and hence it is hardly surprising that most of the literature deals with this specific application of the doctrine.

As Krämer notes,[12] the CJEU has based the obligation of consistent interpretation on various grounds over the years. With regard to directives the Court deduces the obligation from what is now Article 288 TFEU (definition of directive) and Article 4(3) TEU (principle of co-operation). However, as pointed out above, the Court has subsequently stretched the concept beyond directives and, in the absence of a Treaty provision explicitly prescribing consistent interpretation, it therefore required a new basis. In *Pfeiffer*, the Court therefore introduced another legal basis for indirect effect,[13] when it held that '[t]he requirement for national law to be interpreted in conformity with [Union] law is *inherent in the system of the Treaty*'.[14] Only in this way can the full effectiveness of EU law be ensured in national proceedings. In *Pupino*, which concerned the interpretation in conformity with framework decisions under the (former) third pillar, the Court relied on the general objective of an ever closer union (Article 1(2) TEU).[15] Whereas the pillar structure has been dissolved, what remains of this decision after Lisbon is the reasoning of the Court, which establishes an alternative grounding for the obligation to consistent interpretation in EU law.

Milestones in the Development of Consistent Interpretation

In *von Colson & Kamann*,[16] the Court established a duty for all the authorities of Member States including, for matters within their jurisdiction, the courts to interpret national law in conformity with EU law. In the beginning, consistent interpretation was regarded as being applicable only in rather limited circumstances, ie restricted to more or less ambiguous provisions transposing or implementing a certain directive.[17] Subsequently, however, the Court constantly widened the scope of the duty to interpret national law in conformity with EU law. In the landmark decision *Marleasing*,[18] the Court decided:

> It follows that, in applying national law, whether the provisions in question were adopted before or after the Directive, the national court called upon to interpret it is required to do so, *as far as possible*, in the light of the wording and the purpose of the Directive in order to achieve the result pursued by the latter and thereby comply with the third paragraph of Article [288 TFEU].[19]

The Court made it clear in *Marleasing* that provisions of national law – no matter if adopted before or after the directive – fell within the scope of consistent interpretation,

---

[10] Cf Joined Cases C-397/01 to C-403/01 *Pfeiffer et al* [2004] ECR I-8878, para 114, where the Court for the first time explicitly stretched the duty to Community law as a whole.

[11] Prechal, above n 2, 190.

[12] L Kramer 'Direct Effect and Consistent Interpretation " Strengths and Weaknesses of the Concepts" in Jans et al, above n 1.

[13] M Klamert, 'Judicial Implementation of Directives and Anticipatory Direct Effect' [2006] *CMLR* 1251.

[14] *Pfeiffer et al*, above n 10 (emphasis added).

[15] Case C-105/03 *Pupino* [2005] ECR I-5285, para 36.

[16] Case 14/83 *von Colson & Kamann* [1984] ECR 1891.

[17] Chalmers, Davis and Monti, above n 2, 295.

[18] Case C-106/89 *Marleasing* [1990] ECR I-4135.

[19] Ibid, para 8 (emphasis added).

and in *Pfeiffer* the ECJ finally extended the scope of consistent interpretation to national law as a whole.[20] Although the Court also emphasises that national courts are obliged to interpret national law in conformity with EU law 'as far as possible', a concept explored further below, the doctrine of consistent interpretation clearly now goes beyond simply applying an EU-friendly interpretation of evidently ambiguous provisions. It requires more than picking an EU law-compliant solution from the various possible interpretations – the national court has to interpret its national law in the light of the wording and purpose of the respective directive.

The Application of the Duty

Who Is Obliged by the Duty?

Who is obliged to interpret national law in conformity with EU law? Does the duty stretch to administrative authorities or are just national courts covered by this obligation? The CJEU seems to be quite clear about who is obliged to interpret national law in conformity with EU law: all national authorities are bound by the obligation to ensure the achievement of the aims set out in a particular directive. The duty of consistent interpretation clearly binds – though not exclusively so – the national courts, but administrative authorities are under the same obligation. Indeed, it would appear somewhat arbitrary if courts and administrative bodies had to apply different interpretive standards – as a consequence, administrative bodies would have to knowingly decide (or interpret) not in accordance with EU law, and courts would subsequently have to correct these decisions.[21] There seem to be few examples in national environmental case law where this requirement on administrative bodies has been expressed. However, in a 2005 decision concerning the destruction of wolves, the French State Council observed that:

> It is a duty of the national administrative authorities under the supervision of the judge to exercise the powers conferred on them by law by giving them in all cases where it is in the scope of the European Community rule, an interpretation which is consistent with Community law.[22]

What Does the Duty Apply to?

The duty to consistently interpret includes any kind of EU law, even legally non-binding recommendations,[23] but which national norms constitute the object of the obligation? It would appear that it should apply to any form of national rules which have a legal impact

---

[20] *Pfeiffer et al*, above n 10, para 115; *cf* Case C-131/97 *Carbonari* [1999] ECR I-1119, paras 49–50.

[21] *Cf* O Gänswein, *Der Grundsatz unionrechtskonformer Auslegung nationalen Rechts* (Frankfurt am Main, 2009) 38. However, it has to be borne in mind that only courts have the opportunity to make references for preliminary rulings, and in this context it does not seem so far-fetched that 'wrong' administrative decisions are to some extent regarded acceptable within the EU law logic.

[22] Council of State, 20 April 2005, Association for the Protection of Wildlife, No 271216. *Cf* the French national report at www.avosetta.org.

[23] Case 322/88 *Grimaldi* [1989] ECR 4407; formerly (pre-Lisbon) it also comprised legal instruments of the third pillar, such as council framework decisions: *Pupino*, above n 15.

on the decision in question. This would include, for example, ministerial policy rules which authorities are obliged to follow. It should equally apply, say, to previous decisions of the courts where these may legally constrain subsequent decision making in some way. This is especially important for common law countries such as the United Kingdom and Ireland, where doctrines of court precedent are strict and require lower courts to follow previous decisions of higher courts which cannot be readily distinguished. A recent UK decision concerned access to justice and costs principles which were largely determined by judge-made principles developed in court decisions. The Court of Appeal was prepared to reinterpret a previous decision of the Court of Appeal (which under UK precedent principles would otherwise have been binding on it) in a way to ensure consistency with the access to justice provisions of the Environmental Assessment Directive as amended in the light of Aarhus: 'those judge-made rules . . . must be interpreted and applied in such a way as to secure conformity with the Directive'.[24]

When Does the Duty Apply?

But when does the duty of the national courts to interpret national law in conformity with EU law begin? With regard to directives, there are three events which could potentially trigger the obligation: the entry into force of the directive (upon its publication in the Official Journal and after a given time limit); the expiration of the period for transposition; or the entry into force of the national provisions implementing the directive.

Generally, it can be said that if the obligation of the national court depended on the entry into force of the national implementing measures, the Member States could easily 'jeopardise the full effectiveness of Community law and its uniform application'.[25] Hence, in case of belated implementation, the date on which these national measures actually enter into force has no relevance for the obligation to consistent interpretation. However, there is one exception to this rule: if a Member State transposes a directive before the given period expires, its authorities are under the obligation to consistent interpretation as of this earlier point in time.

Still, Member States are not obliged to adopt implementing measures before the period for transposition of a directive has expired. Consequently, the courts are normally (*cf* above) not under an obligation to interpret domestic law in conformity with the directive in question before that point in time.[26] However, as of their entry into force, directives produce legal effects for their addressees (ie Member States). Therefore the national authorities of these Member States, including the courts, 'must refrain from taking any measures liable seriously to compromise the attainment of the result prescribed by [the directive]'.[27] This is even more so if a Member State exceptionally is granted an extended period for transposition.[28]

---

[24] *R (on the application of Garner) v Elmbridge Borough Council* [2010] EWCA Civ 1006. Interestingly, the court also held that the relevant provisions of the directive had direct effect but expressed no preference for which doctrine (direct effect or consistent interpretation) justified the result.

[25] *Adeneler*, above n 4, para 116.

[26] Ibid, para 115.

[27] Ibid, para 121; *cf* Case C-144/04 *Mangold* [2005] ECR I-9981, para 67; Case C-129/96 *Inter-Environnement Wallonie* [1997] ECR I-7411, para 45.

[28] *Cf Mangold*, ibid, para 72.

Moreover, in *Mangold*, the Court found that the directive in question merely elaborated on the (pre-existing) fundamental principle of non-discrimination, which forms part of the EU legal order. Therefore the observance of this principle must be seen independently from the expiring of the period for transposition.[29] In a nutshell, after the deadline to transpose a directive has expired, the national courts are at the latest under a full obligation to interpret national law in conformity with that particular directive; however, even prior to that point in time (subsequent to entry into force of the directive but before its transposition), courts are obliged not to interpret domestic law in a way compromising the realisation of a particular directive's objectives.

The Scope of the Duty

'As Far As Possible' – Opportunity or Constraint?

Where are the limits to the obligation with a view to separation of powers as well as the judicial function as such? There are two diametrical yet interrelated, multifaceted elements which basically determine the scope of consistent interpretation. On the one hand, the Court appears to open the scope widely when it holds that 'When national courts apply domestic law, they are bound to interpret it, so far as possible, in the light of the wording and the purpose of the Directive concerned in order to achieve the result sought by the Directive'.[30]

But some authors consider the formulation 'as far as possible' not so much as an opening but more as a more limiting one, emphasising the importance of the interpretability of the national provision in question.[31] In effect, the phrase is read to imply 'only as far as possible'. This can be contrasted with a more expansive interpretation, as summarised in the Netherlands national report: 'Courts are required to be active, innovative, and if necessary break new ground',[32] and the case law of the CJEU supports this approach – insinuating the principle to imply 'only as far as possible' falls short of the more dynamic understanding of the CJEU based on the full effectiveness of EU law.

Arguably, the effort that the CJEU demands of national courts has changed quite significantly over the time. In its early decisions, the Court had held that:

> It is for the national court to interpret and apply the legislation adopted for the implementation of the Directive in conformity with the requirements of Community law, in so far as it is given discretion to do so under national law.[33]

In more recent decisions, consistent interpretation requires 'national courts to do whatever lies within their jurisdiction, taking the whole body of domestic law into consideration and applying the interpretative methods recognised by domestic law'.[34]

---

[29] *Mangold*, ibid, paras 74–76.
[30] Eg *Adeneler*, above n 4, para 108.
[31] Eg K Sawyer, 'The Principle of Interprétation Conformé' [2007] *Statute Law Review* 165. Gänswein, above n 21, talks explicitly of 'Einschränkung', hence limitation of the obligation to consistent interpretation, at 70 *et seq.*
[32] J Jans, 'Netherlands National Report' in Jans et al, above n 1.
[33] Eg *von Colson & Kamann*, above n 16, para 28.
[34] Joined Cases C-378/07 to C-380/07 *Angelidaki and Others* [2009] ECR I-3071, para 200; *Adeneler*, above n 4, para 111; Case C-97/11 *Amia* judgment of 24 May 2012, paras 29–31.

The emphasis on the increased effort demanded of the national courts indicates that the ECJ has established a rule of interpretative supremacy. This means that a national rule of construction which effectuates a better attainment of the objectives of a directive precedes any other such rule leading to a less favourable realisation of the goal.

The phrase 'as far as possible' was used in the judgment in *Marleasing*, and the formula has been repeated many times in the subsequent case law of the CJEU. But only on rare occasions has the Court specified its demands in any detail and, given the many opportunities for greater analysis, the Court's restraint on this issue must be deliberate.[35] The Court is clearly showing a degree of sensitivity to different national legal traditions in the judicial interpretation of national legislation.[36] The principle of consistent interpretation does not require national courts to interpret national law *contra legem*, but it nonetheless requires a substantial effort from the national courts to do 'whatever lies within their jurisdiction' to ensure the full effectiveness of the directive in question. Mainly this ties the limits of consistent interpretation to the national rules of construction, but these should be applied with a view to the goals of European law: for example, in *Mono Car Styling* the ECJ held that:

> If the application of interpretive methods recognised by national law enables, in certain circumstances, a provision of domestic law to be construed in such a way as to avoid conflict with another rule of domestic law or the scope of that provision to be restricted to that end by applying it only in so far as it is compatible with the rule concerned, the national court is bound to use those methods in order to achieve the result sought by the Directive at issue.[37]

It also lies intrinsically in the nature of the preliminary reference proceedings that the Court does not answer questions of national law. It is equally important to bear in mind that different legal systems tend to draw the line between interpretation and the creation of new legal norms quite differently. German doctrine in particular puts a lot of emphasis on the strict division of the two instruments.[38]

It follows that how far 'as far as possible' really goes can neither be answered abstractly for all Member States nor for a particular Member State without taking into account the national proceedings leading to the preliminary reference as well as the national follow-up.

Criminal Liability

According to the CJEU, a national court's obligation to interpret national law in conformity with, for example, a directive

---

[35] Manthey and Unseld are critical of the Court's reluctance to prescribe in more detail the limits of consistent interpretation with regard to the *contra legem* principle. L Manthey and C Unseld, 'Der Mythos vom contra-legem-Verbot: Vom Umgang des EuGH mit einem Verfassungsprinzip' [2011] *Die öffentliche Verwaltung* 921.

[36] For a good example of the fine balance the CJEU is drawing see Case C-268/06 *Impact* [2008] ECR I-2483, paras 93 *et seq*, where the Court emphasised the obligations of consistent interpretation yet held that, when it came to national construction rules concerning retrospectivity, it was up to the national courts to determine whether they applied. Nonetheless, the Court clearly indicated that it expected the referring court to undertake considerable effort to ascertain whether national legislation contains an indication capable of giving retrospective effect to the applicable national law.

[37] Case C-12/08 *Mono Car Styling* [2009] ECR I-6653, para 63. See also the almost identical formulation in *Pfeiffer et al*, above n 10, para 116.

[38] *Cf* W-H Roth, '§ 14 Die richtlinienkonforme Auslegung' in K Riesenhuber (ed), *Europäische Methodenlehre Handbuch für Ausbildung und Praxis* (Berlin, 2010) 393 at 402.

reaches a limit where such an interpretation leads to the imposition on an individual of an obligation laid down by a directive which has not been transposed or, more especially, where it has the effect of determining or aggravating, on the basis of the Directive and in the absence of a law enacted for its implementation, the liability in criminal law of persons who act in contravention of that directive's provisions.[39]

Quite clearly, general principles of law, like legal certainty and non-retroactivity, by and large prevent national courts from using consistent interpretation as a means of determining or aggravating criminal liability.[40] This restriction of the doctrine appears to be one that is widely accepted throughout the Union. Italian courts, for example, have consistently avoided interpretations which would create criminal offences not foreseen by the national environmental law.[41]

Legal Certainty

The need to avoid the doctrine of consistent interpretation interfering with principles of legal certainty was recognised by the Court of Justice in *Kolpinghuis*.[42] This provides an important limitation to the effectiveness of the doctrine in dealing with explicit contradictions of national law with European Union law. For example, in one of the first judgments concerning EU environmental law, the Austrian Administrative Court held that national environmental impact assessment legislation which disapplied the EU directive in certain cases may have violated EU law but could not be interpreted to provide for the directive's application.[43] In 2008 the French Appeal Court of Orleans in a case concerning the intentional destruction of GMO crops refused to accept the defendant's arguments that the French criminal law be reinterpreted in the light of Directive 2001/18/EC on the Deliberate Release of GMOs. The provisions in questions were not sufficiently precise or unconditional to have direct effect, and the judge noted 'that the respective domains of the Directive and French criminal law applied in the case'.[44] Another illustration of a conflict between consistent interpretation and the need for national certainty is found in the 2011 decision of the Irish High Court in *Environmental Protection Agency v Nephin*.[45] It had been argued that, in line with the EU's 'polluter pays' principle, directors of a company convicted of waste offences should be personally liable, but the court held that such an interpretation went beyond the clear words of the relevant national legislation, and could not be read into the national law.

In the Netherlands, the Council of State has ruled that consistent interpretation is only possible 'within the framework of the regulation', possibly a rather narrower formulation than that provided the CJEU.[46] A number of environmental cases in the Netherlands illustrate the limitations of the consistent interpretation doctrine. For example, in a case concerning the location of GMO testings, national legislation requiring the information to be kept secret could not be reinterpreted to mean 'made available' in line with relevant

---

[39] Case C-168/95 *Arcaro* [1996] ECR I-4705, para 42.
[40] Case 80/86 *Kolpinghuis Nijmegen* [1987] ECR 3969, paras 13–14.
[41] Italian Court of Cassation, Sec III (criminal section) 30 September 2008, No 41839.
[42] *Kolpinghuis Nijmegen*, above n 40, para 13.
[43] Austrian VwGH 23 October 1995, 95/10/0081.
[44] French Appeal Court of Orleans 26 February 2008, No-role 07/00472.
[45] [2011] IEHC 67 Irish National Report.
[46] Council of State 29 May 2001 AB 2001/349, RAwb 2001, 98.

EU law.[47] Limited grounds for reinterpreted to provide authorities with more discretion in line with the IPPC Directive.[48]

Imposing Obligations on Individuals – the Horizontal Impact of the Doctrine

As is well known, in *Marshall*,[49] the ECJ basically ruled out inverse vertical as well as horizontal direct effect. Both concepts refer to situations where a Member State has failed to fulfil its duty of timely transposition; the former means that the Member State itself cannot rely on the directive vis-à-vis (and to the detriment of) an individual, while the latter prevents an individual from relying on the direct effect of such a provision against another individual. At first glance, the rule that directives cannot as such impose obligations upon individuals appears both clear and easily manageable. However, in the light of the subsequent case law, this assumption has not proven tenable. Detrimental effects on private parties regularly occur in triangular relations, where asserting one individual's rights vis-à-vis the state frequently has negative effects on a third party involved. The Court's decision in *Wells* is instructive – as long as only these effects occur[50] individuals can invoke their rights stemming directly from the directive in question. On the other hand, 'an individual may not rely on a directive against a Member State where it is a matter of a State obligation directly linked to the performance of another obligation falling, pursuant to that directive, on a third party'.[51] In *Wells*, the Court therefore tried to systematise its differentiation between negative side effects and obligations imposed on the third party. Obviously the line still has to be drawn in each individual case, and this will often depend on the formulation of the specific provision.

According to the Court's holding in *Arcaro*, consistent interpretation 'reaches a limit where such an interpretation leads to the imposition on an individual of an obligation laid down by a directive which has not been transposed'.[52] The Court seems to be taking a rather restrictive stance, but the decision must not be overestimated due to its specific context of criminal liability. In other decisions, the Court has often taken a less restrictive approach. Recalling that the initial dispute which had lead to the preliminary ruling had arisen between two private parties, the decision in *Marleasing* reveals an important aspect of consistent interpretation which distinguishes it from the direct effect doctrine.

Unlike direct effect, consistent interpretation applies in horizontal relations between individuals (and hence inevitably to the detriment of one private party). Indeed, the CJEU has regarded consistent interpretation applicable in horizontal constellations from the very beginning. This follows from the judgment in *Harz*,[53] which was delivered on the same day as *von Colson & Kamann*.

---

[47] Council of State 25 November 2009, *M en R* 2010, nr 43.

[48] Council of State 13 November 2002, *M en R* 2003, nr 39.

[49] Leading case 152/84 *Marshall* [1984] ECR 737, confirmed in Case C-91/92 *Faccini Dori* [1994] ECR I-3325.

[50] Case C-201/02 *Wells* [2004] ECR I-723, para 57.

[51] Ibid, para 56.

[52] *Arcaro*, above n 39, para 42.

[53] Case 79/83 *Harz* [1984] ECR 1922, in which the Court had to deal with a situation quite similar to *von Colson & Kamann*, above n 16, with the decisive difference that the discrimination had occurred between a private company as the potential employer and a female job applicant.

What remains unclear is the extent to which consistent interpretation may serve as a means to circumvent the restrictions on horizontal direct effect and make them either superfluous or reduce them to absurdity. How far can national law, interpreted in conformity with EU law, therefore impose obligations on individuals? The crucial difference between direct effect and consistent interpretation is that in the latter case a potential obligation derives from the interpretation of valid national law,[54] albeit an interpretation shaped by European Union obligations. Within the boundaries set by the national law, the imposition of obligations for individuals should therefore not be ruled out categorically.

Whereas negative side effects of the direct effect doctrine have been accepted in certain constellations – as outlined above – by the CJEU, the inverse vertical direct effect appears to be prohibited in the light of the estoppel principle. Similarly, for a long time 'inverse vertical indirect effect' seemed to be categorically ruled out by estoppel considerations – at least in situations of incomplete or non-implementation.[55] But if the application of national law underlines the application of the consistent interpretation doctrine, then an interpretation to the benefit of the administration and to the detriment of an individual cannot be ruled out on principle. Decisions of the Council of State in the Netherlands support this approach – see, for example, the 2004 Decision of the Council of State on the deliberate release of GMOs, where the Court was prepared to read into the national legislation grounds for refusing consents that were derived from the relevant EU directive.[56]

In its 2011 *Mücksch* decision,[57] the CJEU appears now to have expressly acknowledged the possibility of the consistent interpretation doctrine being used to allow Member States to impose obligations on third parties directly. The Court had to deal with the question whether the obligation of Member States to ensure that account is being taken of the need, in the long term, to maintain appropriate distances between establishments covered by the Seveso II Directive 96/82 and buildings of public use applied to a public authority that was responsible for issuing building permissions but had no discretionary power. The court pointed out that, 'although the main proceedings are between a public authority and an individual, it is important to bear in mind that . . . a Member State may, in principle, impose on individuals an interpretation of national law in keeping with the Directive'.[58]

But one must take into account that the relevant German legislation included limited grounds for refusing a building permit and thus national law already imposed obligations on individuals applying for a building permit.

---

[54] Prechal, above n 2, 213.

[55] Ibid, 215.

[56] Dutch Council of State 28 June 2004, *M en R* 2004/10, nr 104.

[57] Case C-53/10 *Mücksch* judgment of 15 September 2011, paras 32 *et seq.*

[58] Ibid, para 34, referring to *Kolpinghuis Nijmegen*, above n 40, paras 12-14, and Case C-321/05 *Kofoed* [2007] ECR I-5795, para 45.

Conclusions

As Krämer notes, the consistent interpretation doctrine is logical and in line with the general concept of the supremacy of European Union law.[59] It is a doctrine widely accepted within Member States, and it is arguable that it should be the doctrine of first application in that its application is less disruptive to a national legal system. Yet the application of the doctrine in practice is less easy to judge. The CJEU has held that the duty must be applied with the formula 'as far as possible', yet it has been remarkably restrained in prescribing in any detail what this really means, beyond stating that it should not impose criminal liability on individuals or offend principles of legal certainty. Is it a constraint on the national courts or an opportunity for creative judicial approaches? It is clear that the actual implementation of the doctrine depends much on the discretion of national courts and their own interpretive traditions, and hence the continuing importance of comparative studies of national practice. In the environmental field, we can see extremes in national approaches. On the one hand, there is a limited application, as in Denmark, where authorities are reluctant to acknowledge any gap between national and EU law, a gap which the application of the doctrine necessarily implies.[60] On the other hand, there are countries such as Croatia, where the doctrine is similarly rarely applied not because of a belief that the national law is bound to be consistent with EU law but because the fact that 'a long tradition of strict formalism and positivism in Central and Eastern Europe leaves judges unprepared for their role in the European legal order'.[61] In this context, oversensitivity to national interpretative traditions may hinder the effective application of European law. Many other countries operate at various points within that spectrum.

There remain uncertainties as to the precise extent to which the consistent interpretation doctrine can be used to impose obligations (other than criminal) on individuals, especially by the state. One argument suggests that, since, at its fundamentals, we are dealing with the interpretation of national law, the sensitivities raised in the direct effect doctrine about allowing the state to impose direct obligations on individuals are not relevant. On the other hand, since the doctrine is only raised because, deliberately or otherwise, the Member State has failed to fully transpose the EU legislation in question, it is questionable as to how far it should be permitted to take advantage – or, rather, not be restrained – by its own failings to transpose. Two restraints can, however, inhibit the Member State from an undue use of the doctrine, constraints that are not apparent in the direct effect doctrine. First, if there is no relevant national legislation or rule in place at all, then there is nothing for the doctrine to grasp, and it simply cannot be employed. Secondly, if the national legislation is explicitly contrary to the EU law, then the *contra legem* principle is likely to constrain a national court from applying the doctrine, and there are some striking examples in the environmental field at national level where national courts have felt that no amount of creative interpretation can remedy the explicit language of national law. Perversely, then, the doctrine has little to contribute in the most blatant examples of non-implementation by a Member State – no national legislation or legislation explicitly contrary to the directive in question. There is no guarantee that in those cases the doctrine of direct effect will be applicable since the conditions for its application

---

[59] Kramer, above n 12.
[60] P Pagh, 'Denmark: National Report' in Jans et al, above n 1.
[61] L Ofak, 'Croatia: National Report' in Jans et al, ibid.

– and especially the requirement of precise and unconditional language – may simply not be present. The same is true for the conditions to be fulfilled for a state to be liable in damages for breaching EU law. It follows that, whatever the significance of the doctrine, the supervisory role of the European Commission in ensuring that national legislation fully reflects European Union obligations remains of central importance. It would be rash of citizens, industry, NGOs and – most of all – Member States to assume that the doctrine can always be relied upon to fill the gaps between European commitment and national implementation.

31

Underlying Themes in the Policy Process[1]
(1983)

Policy makers and analysts know only too well the breadth and complexities of the issues involved in the development of environmental policy, whether at national or Community level. The previous contributions in this collection give some striking illustrations of the distinctive strands of scientific, administrative and legal thinking involved.

In his Opening Address to the Conference, Lord Flowers indicated that a rigorous and dispassionate handling and integration of these various approaches is a task of no mean difficulty. Any such analysis of environmental policy must be handled with sensitivity so as to identify and integrate the contributions made by each distinctive approach, without loss of authenticity to the various disciplines and interests involved.

Our attention is drawn more to the process of policy making rather than to the substance of policy development. By 'process' we mean the constitutional style, administrative traditions, and national dispositions which shape, accommodate or even reject the content of policy proposals. The strong reliance on procedure and cross-sectoral cooperation in the environmental field lends a further dimension to this study of process.

In analytical terms, the European Community can be seen either as a simple set of intergovernmental institutions, or as the same plus the sum of the Member States, or as a transcending dimension of European governance. All three pictures are no doubt useful. The wider impact of Community powers has already been discussed in previous contributions. But in the practical handling of specific issues, Member States may see the Community in more straightforward intergovernmental terms, and strive to confine attention by the Community to those issues and initiatives which by their nature, scale, and timing are the most suitable for Community action. It is natural for such matters to be treated on a 'them' and 'us' basis, and to this extent – and notwithstanding the wider and longer-term vision – the Community and Member States can be regarded as things apart. This should help focus analysis on the ensuing boundaries and interfaces as these take the strain of the new requirements.

We belong to a research team which looks for stabilising influences in the processes encountered in resource systems under heavy and conflicting demands – the notion of stability in this context includes both sustainability and adaptability, as well as the more usual preoccupations of productivity and equitability.

---

[1] R Macrory and J Peachey, 'Underlying Themes in the Policy Process' in R Macrory (ed), *Britain, Europe and the Environment* (London, Imperial College Centre for Technology, 1983) Conference Proceedings.

We are seeking a methodology for the review of policy process and of its influence on substantive policy development. The ultimate aim is to produce criteria to help develop the review of existing policy instruments, choose the style and manner of newly proposed policy intervention, improve the administrative design in draft policy proposals, and increase the understanding of the dynamics and functions of procedural style.

In the remainder of this paper, and as an initial step in this analytical direction, we trace certain themes which, in this country, seem to underly much of the discussion and analysis of national and Community environmental policy. These themes may only rarely be mentioned explicitly. But it is clear that they each raise a number of central questions relating to the functioning of policy process and the design, installation, and operation of new Community-based procedures. We describe these themes under the following headings:

- Handling the status quo;
- International ramifications;
- Intergovernmental effectiveness;
- Priorities and feasibility;
- Alignment and harmonisation;
- Member States as neighbours.

Handling the Status Quo

Negotiations within the Community have to reckon with widely differing circumstances, attitudes and practices as between Member States. Community Institutions also have their own distinctive style and approach. Sometimes these differences can be seen in largely technical terms where (as in the present context) varying environmental situations, development pressures, conservation needs, and technical capabilities may clearly indicate differing professional treatment. But the position is often further complicated because some differences are more telling of the national approach to getting things done than of the particular problems at issue.

All too often, the seemingly intractable nature of these differences and difficulties puts governments more firmly on the defensive than is usual for the protection of the national interest. The ensuing inhibition of response to Community initiatives can spread through the inevitable 'linkage' of one policy issue with another.

This hardening of attitude and freezing of policy advance has two effects of central importance to our analysis. Firstly, there is a somewhat exaggerated support for the status quo, and, secondly, there is the inevitable slowing and narrowing of procedural development. These difficulties have to be resolved one way or another. There may be a need to return to the design stage so as to produce more measured intervention. But it is often too late to do more than try to soften the proposals already on the table, sometimes by recourse to an uneasy plurality of approach.

It is hardly surprising that the attitudes encouraged by defensive briefing, and the upheavals caused by aggressive Community intervention, may in turn inhibit the domestic search for improved procedures at a national level. This inhibition may continue longer than would often be the case, in order not to risk disturbing the validity of past compromises or attracting fresh attention from 'the Community.

Community environmental policy provides some good examples of these difficulties – not least insofar as the United Kingdom is concerned. The Community's advocacy of fixed pollution standards in certain areas (as discussed elsewhere in this collection) is somewhat at odds with the UK preference for achieving similar levels of pollution control through the deployment, in each particular case, of the 'best practicable means' available. The technical arguments have included considerations as to how far the absorptive capacity of the receiving environment should influence the suitability and extent of the operationally feasible controls required.

In the Directive of 4 May 1976, concerning dangerous substances discharged into the aquatic environment, the UK was, in essence, allowed to retain its emphasis on pollution concentrations in the receiving environment. This is an example of where the uneasy plurality of approach to which we have already referred was chosen as the way forward.

The draft Directive concerning the environmental assessment of certain projects (COM (80) 313 final) has already run into difficulties reminiscent of those experienced with pollution standards. The UK has again sought to defend traditionally informal, and flexible procedures for planning assessment against more formalised approaches to the identification and assessment of environmental factors in development.

These kinds of differences in approach can indeed be often explained and treated as fundamental differences of administrative style and procedural approach, peculiar to their respective constitutional settings. These 'processes' are evolutionary in nature and, paradoxically, delicate but hard to change. It is common for joint policy agreements to paper over such differences, and the Community has no such monopoly of this device. This means, however, that even the initial and purely technical discussions of new policy proposals, at Community level, must bear the full weight of procedural dissent to be found within the Community and Member States.

The handling of the draft Directive concerning environmental assessment illustrates the kinds of administrative and policy losses that may now have to be endured. The Community is deprived of the signal contribution which the UK could bring to the design of assessment procedures through its own particular experience of adaptive planning. Britain itself loses because the argument has all but stopped a fundamental debate on national requirements for strengthening the domestic assessment of environmental factors in strategic and land-use planning. Moreover, the apparent clumsiness of the proposed intervention has further alienated industrial developers who might otherwise have accepted more rigorous forms of environmental assessment.

It is clear that reckoning with the status quo must figure large in the design of Community intervention. One step forward would be to see how the apparently contradictory procedures and practice in Member States stand up to careful monitoring and analysis, in comparative terms and as part of the working compromises of the Community. Mere assertions that one practice or procedure is better than another will not do, given the complexity of the policy issues and the scale and magnitude of the judgement involved.

International Ramifications

In the inevitable calculations as to the benefits, disbenefits and untapped opportunities in Community action, it is important to consider the extent to which such action can complement other environmental programmes such as those of the Organization for Economic Cooperation and Development, the United Nations Environment Programme, the Economic Commission for Europe, and other more specialised and regional bodies.

It is also necessary to consider the implications of Community concepts of self-sufficiency and external responsibility in terms of regional environmental strategy and global resource management. These international implications of Community action raise a number of questions: can the Community act more powerfully than individual Member States to revitalise international environmental programmes? Can the Community's own resource management strategies be presented and adjusted so as to hinder the collapse of other environmentally-dependent resource systems, especially in the developing world? Can the Community do more than any other state to mobilise the protection of precious environmental treasures? Given the Community's economic power and influence in world markets, what kinds of issues would be best suited to adoption as global cause celebres?

The dovetailing of wider Community action to wider international initiatives repeats in essence – though perforce not so much in requisite sensitivity – the same process as the Member States experience in dealing with the Community. But in addition, Community states in the international scene are freer to act independently, being less limited in the exercise of their sovereignty. The challenge is to steer a middle way between the potentially unbalancing effect of a single Community input to international programmes, and the unnecessarily complicated consequence of uncoordinated responses to such programmes from separate Community states. There are a number of arrangements on the environmental side which fall between these extremes, such as those concerning the development of environmental monitoring and data systems.

Intergovernmental Effectiveness

Mention has been made of the need to look at the Community in intergovernmental terms; this may be extended to see how well its institutions compare with other intergovernmental agencies. All these bodies should attract as much critical review and independent evaluation as that taken for granted in their national equivalents.

Apart from the more specific concerns of institutional and programmatic efficiency, there is also the question of those who have fundamental doubts about the value of the Community in any case. Because of the dominance and exclusivity of the Community ideal, such doubts can only presently be entertained in terms of conventional political alignment – at least in the UK. This is not satisfactory. A way forward, in the analysis of such doubts, would be to see how well the Community stands in comparison with other kinds of intergovernmental environmental action, in terms of design, implementation, and appropriateness. A considerable injection of policy analysis skills would be needed in such studies, if the geopolitical significance of the Community is to be properly assessed. These comparisons would have to include analysis of underlying attributes which govern Community arrangements and their nearest non-Community equivalents. For instance, the absence of the rules and discipline of a common market in non-Community arrangements may weaken the individual and collective governmental will to shoulder consistent levels of responsibility. The economic intimacy implicit in the common market, let alone its wider social and political implications, can be expected to permit a greater degree of mutualism by Member States than may be available in other frameworks for intergovernmental action.

The economic emphasis in the Community concept allows environmental resources to be treated as economic resources, as a basis for mutual action, even though such considerations may not yet have fully reached the market place. This readiness to see environmental issues in economic terms enables common action to be considered for a range of environmental protection measures, which might not otherwise have a basis for consensus. The way in which the Community finally deals with the acid rain issue will be exceptionally interesting in this respect.

The Community cannot rest content in the expectation that regionalism will provide a ready answer. We have already alluded to some of the external factors, in terms of relationships with international environmental programmes. But internally, within the Community, there are huge variations in regional environment and development, conflicting policies for natural resources and agriculture, and the unevenness of the environment – economic connection.

The Sixth Amendment of the Directive of 27 June 1967 concerning dangerous substances provides a new example of a procedure which, if carried out in one Member State, is automatically valid, for the case in question, throughout the Community. It would help the intergovernmental understanding of the impact of Community policy process in national affairs to know the detailed effects that the implementation of this policy is having on the relevant administrative procedures of Member States throughout for the environmental, industrial, health and safety, and trade sectors.

Priorities and Feasibility

However ambitious Community policy making, there is no doubt that attention must be given to the extent to which proposed actions can be implemented, given present professional and administrative capabilities and intervention techniques. The style of the policy maker and the nature of his or her policy planning machine affect the content and scope of any proposal, and it can be argued that environmental policies are best advanced by bold initiatives. But policy gains are all too quickly lost if policy concept and policy device are not rigorously defined. This is where priority gives way to feasibility, and principle to practice

The more distant nature of Community intervention and the sheer comprehensiveness of Community actions impose extra burdens in this reckoning with feasibility. This is because these actions are often dismissed as inflexible or profligate at national or local level. The fact that intervention may be legal will not in itself remove the difficulties of its enforcement or the antagonism it may provoke. It is not fair, however, to blame the Community for those disturbances and adjustments which any Western state has to face in pursuit of acceptable environmental policies, and in the making of a responsible contribution to the integrated management of its own region. But whatever the volume of Community legislation, it is unsafe and unsound to plead the urgency and priority of the cause – or indeed the novelty of the problem – as a licence for taking liberties with administrative process.

Some recognition of these considerations is to be found in the present climate of Community thinking. More generally, in the developed world, there has been a movement away from the 'grand design' in the emphasis of national and international policy. In the UK, in particular, there has been a shift towards a more opportunistic and even minimalist approach to public sector intervention and resource allocation. The Community's Third Action Programme on the environment is indeed more strategic in emphasis than its predecessors. It might even be argued that constancy of national purposes and congruency of national style, especially within an enlarged Community, could prove insufficient to support fundamental harmonisation of the kind once assumed essential for Community intervention and development.

These changes of policy appreciation will have profound effects for the design of policy proposals and for the conduct of negotiations. Priorities may depend far more on a real but highly selective meeting of minds; feasibility will figure larger in the determination of priorities. More limited initiatives may be the order of the day. Or, perhaps, greater emphasis on policy components other than the harmonisation of procedure would form a more effective basis for Community action. There may be, for example, potential for advance in the design and setting of criteria and guidelines, in which emphasis centres on strategic policy frameworks rather than on the detail of executive action.

Alignment and Harmonisation

In order to appraise, design and measure performance, it is important to be clear as to the particular objectives on which specific proposals for harmonisation are based. One purpose may be to bring recalcitrant Member States into line with a prevailing status quo. But more positively, harmonisation may be seen as a precondition for reaching new levels of policy coordination or for installing new policies or practices on a Community-wide basis. The most familiar justification for harmonisation, whether in the general or the particular, rests on the need to avoid direct or indirect distortion of the common market.

Although the economic dimension dominates the present remit of Community action, the limitations that would follow from this economic preoccupation are not accepted by all of those involved in the development of Community policy. Some would claim that the Treaty of Rome provides a mandate to explore every policy opportunity for extending the harmonising and uniting influence of the Community. The environmental sector, however, raises formidable challenges to this approach, because of its peculiar heterogeneity and uncertainty. The emphasis in environmental management on designing for adaptability rails against the more singular approach. These contrasts have already been seen as they affect such issues as pollution control, conservation priorities, and environmental assessment. However, the more intensively developed the environmental setting, the easier it may be to take a simpler line and see the extension of the concept of the common market as a means of meeting the required common standards throughout the Community but with an equality of the burdens thus inflicted. The need to avoid pollution havens would be the simplest example of how the equality of the environmental burden on industries is required directly in order to help sustain the common market in which those industries may compete on a Community-wide basis. This approach poses a fundamental question – how 'natural' or underdeveloped does an environment have to be before it gains legitimate administrative exemption from the harmonising influence of the Treaty of Rome?

In lowlier vein, opportunities for harmonisation of technical or management procedures are often seen as providing new areas of agreement which would not be possible at higher policy levels. The commitment is thought to be comparatively modest, and such exercises may even be seen as paving the way to a longer-term meeting of minds. Indeed, some adaptive convergence of approach is a common feature of the influence of the Community in all walks of life, even when brought about by seemingly nebulous compromise or quite low levels of harmonisation. In the environmental sector, the British attitude to pollution control has moved sufficiently for environmental quality objectives to be regarded at least in terms of some fixed target for pollution levels. Conversely, the continental view has taken in a greater awareness of considerations of resilience in the receiving environment.

There are a number of valuable lessons to be learnt from carefully measuring the performance of Directives that have been in operation for some time. For example, are there unintended industrial havens in one part of the Community and unnecessary environmental burdens elsewhere, as a result of Community action? Have steps been taken in consequence – and within the spirit of the various compromises – to adjust the emphasis in both the Member States and in the Community in favour of the superior approach? What conclusions may be drawn for the future as to required levels and styles of harmonisation?

It would not, however, be wise to assume that harmonisation automatically becomes easier at lower levels of policy. What is gained by avoiding the irreconcilable is to some extent lost to the irreducible. As we have noted with environmental Directives, some of the difficulties are also in part due to subtle but fundamental differences of administrative or technical detail. This illustrates how important it is for the analyst and designer to achieve the finest and earliest possible calibration of similar practices in Member States – before, any attempt is made to adjust such practices for the purposes of Community harmonisation or intervention.

The importance of detail in the design of harmonisation and intervention suggests that it may not always be prudent to set aside procedural and methodological objections even though these delay major policy advances. The detail cannot always be easily disposed of after the broader agreement especially when inevitably lower levels of decision may prove too limited to cope with the design challenges of the technical, administrative, let alone constitutional, factors involved.

Member States as Neighbours

The interrelationships inherent in the concept of a European Community and fundamental to the operation of a common market require a high degree of mutual interest between Member States. There are a number of obstacles to be faced. Member States fear that other Community partners may be less observant of Community requirements, or that these requirements may favour one part of the Community rather than another. There is resistance from Member States to upheaval of their own national procedures, especially when these are seen domestically to be working well, or where intervention has been largely dictated by the needs of less advanced neighbours.

All of these factors, in one way or another, may be seen to have contributed to the frosty reception given in the UK to the current proposals for environmental assessment procedures. But, as argued earlier, defensive briefing, often sound enough in purpose, should not obscure the obligation to question and study, even in purely domestic terms, the appropriateness of national procedures. The changing needs in environmental assessment arising from the new technology industries, energy supply, agricultural expansion, and shared land-use provide good examples of where much procedural work has now to be concentrated

The treatment of the Community as a single planning unit or resource conservation region, which inevitably transcends national boundaries and priorities, introduces a new order of sensitivity into the relationships of the Member States as neighbours. The consequences may be seen in terms of planning zones and locational incentives. These last devices may affect the extent to which the importance of a particular set of national environments assets might be downgraded as a result of a Community-wide strategy under which similar assets are more conveniently conserved or protected in some other part of the Community. It would be good to be able to predict at what stages in the development of the Community Member States might be prepared to sacrifice certain national environmental assets, resting content in the knowledge of their protection elsewhere in the Community.

Conclusions

We have sought to draw some critical attention to the procedural themes and administrative issues that have surfaced in the first 10 years of Community action on the environment. This means dwelling more on the conflicts as between the new, Community ways and the older, national approaches, rather than concentrating on the considerable advances that have been made in terms of policy content. A concern for the process rather than the substance of policy is sometimes seen to be fastidious, 'legalistic' or possibly obstructive of change. But we have seen that the more subtle aspects of administrative process cannot be neglected or ignored simply because they cannot compete with the excitement and speed with which the substantive aspects of policy are generally handled and analysed.

Policy gains, however good the substance, can all too readily be lost if their operational demands are even just subtly and perhaps unwittingly discordant with administrative process. This is not to suggest that the underlying policy process may not, in turn, have to adapt and change as new policy arrangements come into force. But the essentially more evolutionary and stabilising nature of such processes may require a more delicate adjustment than the sudden shifts which may be taken for granted in substantive policy.

The experience with environmental policy suggests that quite modest Community initiatives have become key issues – not so much because of their policy substance but because of the procedural and administrative implications of the measures in question for Member States. Indeed, some of the subsequent adaptations in national administrative process have been quite startling.

We conclude that a number of important analytical opportunities are to be found in the environmental sector of the Community, for the design and definition of policy concepts, assessment procedures, control functions, intervention strategies, and administrative mechanisms, on which the substantive aims of the Community and its Member States all have to depend. Many policy concepts do not always do full justice to the wealth of experience on which they are based. Their meaning should be more precise so as to remove some of the familiar ambiguities and looseness which hinders the design and discussion of environmental policy. Environmental assessment procedure requires considerable methodological development and administrative testing. Control functions need to be seen as designed components of the administrative, environmental, and economic systems which they serve. In the environmental sector, it is necessary to choose levels, scales, and types of intervention and harmonisation that can accommodate regional environmental objectives, ensure consistency of purpose, and yet preserve the flexibility essential to cope with the varied and local nature of the environment and its management.

Administrative mechanisms, as we have indicated, are the key to all these other components and activities. They need a sympathetic but rigorous analytical perception, if they are to be fully harnessed and carefully adapted in the interests of Member States, through the development of the Community and the protection of the European environment.

Index